D0768682

Public Administration
in American Society

AMERICAN GOVERNMENT AND HISTORY INFORMATION GUIDE SERIES

Series Editor: Harold Shill, Chief Circulation Librarian, Adjunct Assistant Professor of Political Science, West Virginia University, Morgantown

Also in this series:

AMERICAN EDUCATIONAL HISTORY—*Edited by Michael W. Sedlak and Timothy Walch*

AMERICA'S MILITARY PAST—*Edited by Jack C. Lane*

IMMIGRATION AND ETHNICITY—*Edited by John D. Buenker and Nicholas C. Burckel*

PROGRESSIVE REFORM—*Edited by John D. Buenker and Nicholas C. Burckel*

PUBLIC POLICY—*Edited by William J. Murin, Gerald Michael Greenfield, and John D. Buenker**

SOCIAL HISTORY OF THE UNITED STATES—*Edited by Donald F. Tingley*

U.S. CONSTITUTION—*Edited by Earlean McCarrick*

U.S. CULTURAL HISTORY—*Edited by Philip I. Mitterling*

U.S. FOREIGN RELATIONS—*Edited by Elmer Plischke*

U.S. POLITICS AND ELECTIONS—*Edited by David J. Maurer*

URBAN HISTORY—*Edited by John D. Buenker, Gerald Michael Greenfield, and William J. Murin**

WOMEN AND FEMINISM IN AMERICAN HISTORY—*Edited by Donald F. Tingley and Elizabeth Tingley**

*in preparation

The above series is part of the
GALE INFORMATION GUIDE LIBRARY

The Library consists of a number of separate series of guides covering major areas in the social sciences, humanities, and current affairs.

General Editor: Paul Wasserman, Professor and former Dean, School of Library and Information Services, University of Maryland

Managing Editor: Denise Allard Adzigian, Gale Research Company

Public Administration in American Society

A GUIDE TO INFORMATION SOURCES

Volume 11 in the American Government and History Information Guide Series

John E. Rouse, Jr.

Assistant Professor
Department of Political Science
Ball State University
Muncie, Indiana

Gale Research Company
Book Tower, Detroit, Michigan 48226

Library of Congress Cataloging in Publication Data

Rouse, John Edward, 1942-
    Public administration in American society.

    (American Government and history information guide
series ; v. 11) (Gale information guide library)
    Includes indexes.
    1. United States—Politics and government.
2. Administrative agencies—United States. 3. Public
administration—United States. I. Title. II. Series.
JK421.R63   353   80-24633
ISBN 0-8103-1424-X

VITA

John E. Rouse, Jr. received his Ph.D. in government and politics from the University of Maryland, College Park. He has written extensively on the re-organization and decentralization of the U.S. Department of Housing and Urban Development. His publications include URBAN HOUSING: PUBLIC AND PRIVATE (Detroit: Gale Research Co., 1978) as well as published articles in the MIDWEST REVIEW OF PUBLIC ADMINISTRATION, JOURNAL OF RELI-GIOUS THOUGHT, and POTOMAC REVIEW. He is the Indiana correspondent for the MIDWEST REVIEW OF PUBLIC ADMINISTRATION. He served as a mem-ber of the councils of the Maryland (1971-74) and Indiana (1978-80) chapters of the American Society for Public Administration and currently is editor of INDI-ANA PUBLIC ADMINISTRATOR, the Indiana Society for Public Administration chapter newsletter.

Rouse is moderator and producer of "Public Affairs Roundtable," a weekly radio program concerning national and international political and economic issues, broadcast and syndicated by WBST radio, Muncie, Indiana. He is a student of religion and politics. His current research includes examining the impacts of Jimmy Carter's presidency upon Southern Baptists.

He was a member of the faculties of the University of Maryland, College Park, and the George Washington University, Washington, D.C., before becoming assistant professor in the department of political science at Ball State Univer-sity, Muncie, Indiana, in 1976. He taught for Ball State University's Euro-pean Program in Frankfurt and Kaiserslautern, West Germany. Rouse is listed in the current (1980) edition of Marquis's WHO'S WHO IN THE MIDWEST.

CONTENTS

Preface ix
Acknowledgments xi
Introduction xiii

Chapter 1. Federalism and Administrative Structure 1
    A. Intergovernmental Relations 1
    B. The New Federalism and Governmental Subsidy 15
    C. Urban and Suburban Administration 25

Chapter 2. Governmental Divisions and the Administrative Process 37
    A. Theories of Democratic Government 37
    B. Bureaucracy 48
    C. The Chief Executive as Administrator 59
    D. Public Administration and the Legislative Process 70
    E. Government Reorganization 79
    F. Government Departments and Agencies 87

Chapter 3. The Discipline of Public Administration 101
    A. History and Ideology 101
    B. Textbooks and Readings 121
    C. Education and Research 129
    D. Internships 140

Chapter 4. The Practice of Public Administration 147
    A. Evaluation of Administrative Process 147
    B. Policy Making and Analysis 159
    C. Accountability 168

Chapter 5. The Administrative Revolution 173
    A. General Selections 173
    B. Organizational Behavior and Theory................. 183
    C. Administrative Structure, Control, and Conflict 194
    D. Organization Development and the Individual 201
    E. Management 212
    F. Future Organization Changes 219

Chapter 6. Public Personnel Administration 229
    A. General Selections 229

Contents

B. Professionalism in Public Service 244
C. Labor-Management Relations 257

Chapter 7. Governmental Discrimination and Equal Employment 271
A. General Selections 271
B. Minorities 280
C. Sexual Discrimination 287

Chapter 8. Productivity 295
A. General Selections 295
B. Productivity Measurement 309
C. Effectiveness and Efficiency...................... 314
D. Motivation 319
E. State and Local Government Productivity 323

Chapter 9. Political Economy and Finance 329
A. Budgeting 329
B. Organizational Decision Making..................... 344
C. Planning, Programming, and Budgeting Systems (PPBS) 353
D. Management by Objectives (MBO) 359
E. Zero-Base Budgeting (ZBB) 364
F. Political Economy and Finance 371

Chapter 10. Centralization and Decentralization 379
A. Citizen Participation 379
B. Ethics and Power 389
C. Administrative Centralization and Decentralization 399
D. Administrative Leadership and Communication 409

Chapter 11. Comparative and Developmental Administration 421

Addendum 445

Appendix A. ASPA--American Society for Public Administration 465
Appendix B. ASPA Nationwide Chapter Directory and 1980 Chapter
Presidents 469
Appendix C. NASPAA--National Association of Schools of
Public Affairs and Administration...................... 481
Appendix D. NASPAA 1980 National Representatives 483
Appendix E. Associate Members 499

Author Index 501
Title Index 517
Subject Index...................................... 525

PREFACE

One can safely write that no comprehensive annotated bibliography on the literature of public administration has been published. Therefore, this volume is most likely the first.

Public administration is not a discipline. Neither are we sure that it is even a field. It is neither a field nor a discipline because it draws from other disciplines and fields. The literature of public administration originates from political science, history, psychology, business, management, sociology, social work, and economics.

Undergraduate students arrive in public administration classes with little concept of what they will be studying. The subject has a somewhat bland title. Public administration. Administration of the public. The subject title is more appealing when the words "public affairs" are added. Public administration and public affairs sound more interesting.

Because public administration is neither a discipline nor a field, for certain, why would anyone attempt to assemble the vast, widely scattered literature of this subject matter? Gale Research Company offered me the opportunity to do something in public administration that had not been attempted previously on a comprehensive basis.

Chapter 1 considers administrative structure. Selections include federalism, intergovernmental relations, including the New Federalism, revenue sharing, block grants, grants-in-aid, municipal, metropolitan, suburban, and urban administration. Chapter 2 covers bureaucracies and government, politics, and institutions. Entries originate from sources on society, democracy, the administrative presidency, the role of the legislature in administration, government reorganization, and government agencies. Chapter 3 examines the discipline, history, texts, education, and internships in public administration. Selections on paradigms, values, and profession are included. Chapter 4 includes program evaluation, policy analysis, administrative accountability and responsibility. Chapter 5 includes readings on organizations, administrative behavior, authority and conflict, organization development, government executives, and organizations in the future. Public personnel administration selections constitute chapter ter 6. Readings concerning civil service, merit, labor-management relations, collective bargaining, and unions in the public service dominate the literature of this section. Chapter 7 concerns discrimination and equal employment in government administration, including selections on minorities and sexual discrimination. Productivity, effectiveness, efficiency, and motivation literature comprise the readings in chapter 8. Chapter 9 revolves around budgeting, rationality and decision making, and political economy. Topics include readings on Planning, Programming, and Budgeting Systems (PPBS), zero base budgeting (ZBB), and Management by Objectives (MBO). Chapter 10's entries come from readings on citizen participation, administrative ethics and power, centralization and decentralization, and administrative leadership and communication.

Chapter 11 covers comparative and developmental administration. This subject, in fact, may become one of the new exports of the United States over the next generation! It may very well be that we can export our knowledge of bureaucracy and public administration to the developing countries of the world. In those nations, bureaucracy is where most of the skills exist. The political systems are not yet fully developed as they are in the United States, Western Europe, and Japan. The knowledge of the organization of public bureaucracy in this nation will be very useful to the development of less industrialized societies.

Appendixes include descriptions of the professional activities of the American Society for Public Administration (ASPA), the objectives of the National Association of Schools of Public Affairs and Administration (NASPAA), and names, addresses, and telephone numbers of chapter presidents of ASPA, and the national representatives of NASPAA.

It is my hope that this book will prove useful as a reference work in academic, county, municipal, and state and federal government libraries in the United States and elsewhere. The selections (approximately 1,700) should aid the college and university student and the bureaucrat in his or her government office. The book approaches the study of American society and culture from the political, organizational, bureaucratic, economic, psychological, business, sociological, administrative, and management viewpoints. In essence, these adjectives describe the literature of public administration.

ACKNOWLEDGMENTS

At the end of the 1960s, Dr. Conley H. Dillon, now professor emeritus in the
department of government and politics at the University of Maryland, introduced
me to the field of public administration. In the fall of 1969, Professor Dillon
had a way of persuading his students to join and to participate in the American
Society for Public Administration (ASPA). Join I did, and I subscribed to the
PUBLIC ADMINISTRATION REVIEW. For the first, I was introduced to the
literature of public administration in American society. This annotated book on
American public administration has its beginnings with Professor Dillon's graduate
seminar in 1969.

Dr. Franklin L. Burdette and Professor Dillon were "great friends" as Franklin
used to say, but they were "public administrators of a different kind." Dr.
Burdette, late professor of government and politics, and director, Bureau of
Governmental Research, University of Maryland, was a biographer of directories
for the American Political Science Association and editor of textbooks on government and politics. He was a great influence on my concern for the exactness
of the written word, the significance of accuracy in biographies and edited
volumes, and of academic excellence. While working for Dr. Burdette as a
faculty research assistant, I gained much appreciation for writing, editing,
selecting, and examining biographical information.

Several years ago Dr. Thomas P. Murphy, currently Deputy Assistant Secretary
for Personnel at the Department of Health and Human Services, Washington,
D.C., and at that time, director of the Institute for Urban Studies, and professor of government and politics at the University of Maryland, offered me the
opportunity to edit my first annotated book, URBAN HOUSING: PUBLIC AND
PRIVATE (Detroit: Gale Research Co., 1978). As general editor of his series
on urban studies, I learned from Dr. Murphy that productivity and determination are crucial elements in editing annotated volumes. I am thankful to him
for the opportunity and his direction.

I received both time and encouragement for editing PUBLIC ADMINISTRATION
IN AMERICAN SOCIETY from the Department of Political Science, Ball State
University. In teaching classes in public administration and administrative

Acknowledgments

management in government, I have the opportunity to review the literature constantly and extensively. I am thankful to the leadership of my professional colleagues in politics and government, Dr. Thomas A. Sargent and Dr. Robert T. (Tad) Perry, chairmen of the department for the duration of this volume, for their emphasis on scholarship and research.

Mrs. Elsa S. Freeman, director, Library Division, Assistant Secretary for Administration, Department of Housing and Urban Development, Washington, D.C., and her staff were very helpful to me in compiling this volume and my previous one, URBAN HOUSING: PUBLIC AND PRIVATE. The HUD Library is a magnificent administrative operation, and I am appreciative to the HUD library staff for suggestions on methodology for both annotated volumes.

Dr. Harold B. Shill, series editor of the American Government and History Information Guide Series, and chief circulation librarian, and adjunct assistant professor of political science, West Virginia University, Morgantown, edited, corrected, proofed, and offered much needed constructive criticism on the development of this manuscript. Dr. Shill spent many hours encouraging rewrites of entries and analyzing the intent of each annotation. If this volume is accepted as one of excellence, Dr. Shill will share in the satisfaction of that kind of professional criteria.

Denise Allard Adzigian, managing editor of the Gale Information Guide Library, Gale Research Company, Detroit, has been a valuable editor and reviewer of both annotated volumes. The Gale Research Company is fortunate to have a person of her skills to manage the compilation and review of such texts. To Denise, I am especially grateful for her understanding in missed deadlines.

Barbara Maves is the "significant other person" in my life and is director of the Planned Parenthood of East Central Indiana, Muncie, Indiana. It is from Barbara that I get some current understanding of what bureaucracy in the public service is like. For Barbara, I have promised never to get involved with a book of annotations again!

These persons have been very supportive in my efforts to edit and to write this annotated bibliography of the literature of public administration, a professional discipline with no fixed principles, ideology, or methodology.

Although the literature of this volume covers the past fifty years of administrative life in the United States, it is most reflective of the growing impacts of public bureaucracy in the 1970s. PUBLIC ADMINISTRATION IN AMERICAN SOCIETY is a very pertinent and timely editing of a most important aspect of American society. Bureaucracy, bureaus, bureaucrats, budgets, and bureaucratic procedures tell us much about life in American society in the early 1980s.

John E. Rouse, Jr.
Muncie, Indiana

INTRODUCTION

In order to conceptualize more clearly the place of PUBLIC ADMINISTRATION IN AMERICAN SOCIETY, the setting of life in the United States is divided into fourteen clusters. These clusters are presented to aid the reader in better understanding the role of public administration, or public bureaucracy, in American society. The following clusters are not intended to be all inclusive or mutually exclusive. This clustering of American society is intended to provoke different perspectives in viewing life in the United States.

ADMINISTRATION

Bureaucrats
Civil Service
CODE OF FEDERAL REGULATIONS
Evaluation of Programs
Executive Departments and Agencies
THE FEDERAL REGISTER
General Accounting Office
Implementation of Services, or welfare state
Legislative Oversight
Max Weber
Merit Systems Protection Board
Office of Personnel Management

BUSINESS SECTOR

Capitalism
Entrepreneurs
Flea Market
Individualism
Lowi's Interest Group Liberalism
Marketplace
Partnerships

* The editor expresses his appreciation to Mr. Gary L. Crawley, Assistant Professor of Political Science, Ball State University, Muncie, Indiana, for his commentary and discussion on these clusters.

BUSINESS SECTOR (Cont.)

Private Corporations
Profits and profit maximization
Shopping Center

EDUCATION AND RESEARCH

American Association of University Professors
American Federation of Teachers
Colleges and Universities
Head Start Program
Innovation
Local School Boards
National Education Association
Professions
Public Broadcasting System
Secondary, Elementary Education
Technology

ENGLISH HERITAGE

Bill of Rights
Common law
Constitutional Convention 1787
Declaration of Independence 1776
John Locke, John Milton, Thomas Hooker, Roger Williams,
   Tom Paine, Sir Edward Coke
Joint-stock (merchant-adventurers), government compact, and
   proprietary colonies
Lawyers, or managers of conflict
Legal system
Magna Carta
Majority Rule
Mayflower Compact 1620
Minority rights
Rule by law, not men (persons)
Sovereignty
State and Federal Court Systems

ENTERTAINMENT

Actor's guild
Frank Sinatra
Fred Waring's Pennsylvanians
Hard Rock
Hollywood and Vine
Home Box Office
Motown Sound
Movies
Nashville Sound
Norman Lear Productions
Prime Time Television
Show Business

FISCAL AND MONETARY POLICIES

Alfred Kahn
Banking
Bert Lance
Chase Manhattan Bank
Council of Economic Advisers
Council on Wage and Price Stability
David Rockefeller
Federal Deposit Insurance Corporation
Federal Home Loan Bank Board
Federal Reserve System
Grants-in-Aid, Revenue Sharing
Inflation
Mortgage Bankers Association of America
Office of Management and Budget
Paul Volcker
Regressive and Progressive
Secretary of the Treasury

INDEPENDENT REGULATORY AGENCIES

Civil Aeronautics Board
Federal Communications Commission
Federal Maritime Commission
Federal Reserve System
Federal Trade Commission
Interstate Commerce Commission
Securities and Exchange Commission

INTEREST GROUPS

Apportionment
Chamber of Commerce
Common Cause
Consumers/self-interest
Good government/profits
Labor Unions
    AFL-CIO
    Teamsters
Lowi's Interest Group Liberalism
National Association for the Advancement of Colored People
National Association of Manufactures, or NAM
National Rifle Association
Public/private lobbies
Ralph Nader's Raiders
Representation
Responsiveness

Introduction

MEDIA

Barbara Walters
CBS "60 Minutes"
First Amendment to United States Constitution
Freedom of religion, speech, press, and assembly
James Reston
NEW YORK TIMES
News Magazines
Newspapers
Radio
Television
Walter Cronkite
WASHINGTON POST

MILITARY-INDUSTRIAL COMPLEX

Barter
Coinciding Interests
Defense Budget
Demand for Natural Resources
Dwight Eisenhower
Economic Capitalism
F15
Image of Power
International relations
Joint Chiefs of Staff
Military-technology complex
Multinational corporations
Nation-state decline
National Security Council
North Atlantic Treaty Organization
Political Capitalism
Trade and Empire
Transnational organizations
War Department
Western economic community

POLITICS

Commonwealth, or state, concept
Compromise
Facts and Values
Federalism
Federal, state, and local executives
Federal, state, and local legislatures
Fourteenth Amendment to the United States Constitution Equal
  Protection of the Laws Due Process Concept
Gallup Poll
Norms and Opinions
Political parties (Republicans, Democrats, and Independents)
Politics, or who gets what, where, when, and how

POLITICS (Cont.)

Public Opinion
Socialism, or state capitalism
Universal suffrage

RELIGION AND MORALS

Agnosticism
Alternatives
Catholic/Protestant/Jew/Moslem
Choice
700 Club
Correct/Incorrect
Culture
Evangelical Christianity
Freedom from religion
Freedom of religion
Fundamentalism
Old Time Gospel Hour, Moral Majority
Religious television networks
Religious Toleration

SOCIAL REGULATORY AGENCIES

Consumer Product Safety Commission
Department of Agriculture
Environmental Protection Agency
Federal Aviation Administration
Federal Railroad Administration
Food and Drug Administration
Mine Safety and Health Administration
National Highway Traffic Safety Administration
National Transportation Safety Board
Nuclear Regulatory Commission
Occupational Safety and Health Administration
Occupational Safety and Health Review Commission

SPORTS AND RECREATION

Amateur Athletic Union
Babe Ruth
Boating races
Boston Celtics
Bowling leagues
College Football
Dallas Cowboys
Forest Hills
Joe Namath
Major Leagues
Masters Tournament
National Basketball Association

Introduction

SPORTS AND RECREATION (Cont.)
National Collegiate Athletic Association
National Football League
National and State Parks
Professional
Swimming regulations

Politics and administration, including regulatory activities, impact all clusters or categories of American society. Under the cluster of administration, the CODE OF FEDERAL REGULATIONS and the FEDERAL REGISTER impact other clusters. Max Weber, the German sociologist, was the most significant influence upon administration and bureaucracy literature in the United States.

Regarding the business sector or cluster, public administration in the United States exists in the economic setting of capitalism. Profits and profit maximization are legislated to some degree by government laws and administrative regulations. The American marketplace is regulated by the public bureaucracy, especially the independent and social regulatory agencies.

American colleges and universities are bureaucracies which often depend on the appropriation of federal dollars. Innovation is an American product which originates in education and research centers throughout the nation. Government bureaucracies have no little amount of influence upon education, technological development, and innovative research in the United States.

The rule of law, majority rule and minority rights are ideological elements of our English heritage of which every bureaucrat or public administrator must be aware. Administrative law takes its origins from the American political system. Lawyers are managers of conflict. The American legal system is based upon the philosophical groundings of common law. Our English heritage is important and often overlooked. What would have been the impact of a French or a Spanish heritage in the United States?

The field of entertainment may escape some of the administrative rules and regulations that other clusters experience. However, entertainers must be conscious of government laws and their impact on the entertainment profession. Entertainers are impacted by the Internal Revenue Service (as is everyone), and entertainers' performances are taxed by federal, state, and local governments. Concerts by entertainers are held in public-financed stadiums and arenas, subject to local government regulations with regard to crowd control, safety, and fire hazards.

Fiscal and monetary policies illustrate a direct impact of government laws, regulations, and administrative rules upon this cluster of American society. The Council of Economic Advisers (CEA), the Federal Deposit Insurance Corporation (FDIC), the Federal Home Loan Bank Board (FHLBB), and the Federal Reserve Board (FED) are government institutions which have tremendous impact upon the activities of this cluster and other categories. Government fiscal and monetary policies directly impact the dynamics of inflation and unemployment in the United States.

The independent regulatory agencies have a long history of impacting the activities of American society. For example, the Federal Communications Commission (FCC) regulates the broadcast media (radio and television in particular). The Federal Trade Commission (FTC) monitors consumer activities. The Securities and Exchange Commission (SEC) examines the activities of stocks and bond markets. The oldest independent regulatory agency is the Interstate Commerce Commission (ICC), established in 1887, to regulate railroads, pipelines, motorcoach lines, and intercoastal waterways.

Interest groups seek to have legislators enact their views into laws. After an interest group's proposed legislation becomes law, all members of American society must obey those laws. "Common Cause" and Ralph Nader's "Raiders" are illustrations of public interest groups. The Chamber of Commerce represents business interests in the United States. The National Association of Manufacturers (NAM) and the National Rifle Association (NRA) are examples of private, self-directed interest groups with particular aims they would like for the federal, state, or local bureaucracies to regulate or to avoid. Government laws and the public administrators who implement those laws impact all of these interest groups and their activities.

The relationship between the media and government is always tenuous. The media often investigate activities of government departments and agencies. The "60 Minutes" program of the Columbia Broadcasting Company (CBS) exercises the power of investigation over government activities. The Federal Communications Commission exercises enormous control or power over the activities of radio and television media in the United States. The First Amendment of the United States Constitution is perhaps the most difficult aspect of our constitutional guarantees that the president must implement. Barbara Walters and Walter Cronkite represent television media as sources of investigation and credibility in American society. Public administration in American society impacts them and vice versa.

The military-industrial complex is impacted by government decisions. The decision by the Carter administration not to build the B-1 Bomber had a serious impact upon employment in the aviation industry. Should Chrysler build cars or tanks? This dilemma is a decision often made in the Pentagon. The military is a prototype for bureaucracy in the United States. The impact of the bureaucracy on the military is beyond calculation.

The impact of the cluster of politics is the most obvious influence on public administrators and what they do. The political cluster is at the root of public administration in American society. For decades practitioners of bureaucracy or public administration and academics in political science and public administration have argued about the separation or continuum of politics and administration. Does the commonwealth, or state actions, have more impact upon American society than the marketplace, or the business sector? Norms and opinions are constantly changing with regard to the answer to this important question.

Bureaucracy and administrative laws and rules impact religious institutions and their activities in American society. The distinctions illustrated in freedom of religion and freedom from religion are subtle. When former President Richard Nixon was queried regarding his responsibility in the Watergate scandal, there was some concern in the public's mind concerning Nixon's interpretation of moral quality of government decision making. Was it a mistake (correct or incorrect) for Nixon and his close associates to be involved in Watergate? Or was it a moral (right or wrong) issue? Government decisions as illustrated in the moral issues of the 1980s (abortion, for example) impact directly the concerns of religion and morals in American society.

During the 1970s, the social regulatory agencies had perhaps the greatest impact of all these clusters upon American society. Food, drugs, highway safety, nuclear power, occupational safety, air and water pollution, and product safety became concerns of several government departments and agencies. The social regulations and rules of these government decision making entities caused no little amount of concern from the American society, and many of their actions were quite unpopular with the American people.

The Civil Rights Act of 1964 and the Equal Employment Opportunity Act of 1972 impact sports and recreation activities of colleges and universities throughout the nation. Government legislation similar to the above laws affect directly sports and recreation activities in the United States. The differences between professional and amateur status is one of degree, in some cases, and government laws and regulations reflect contrasting applications. College football is a nonprofit operation in the United States as recreation activities are not taxed at all or pays less tax. Government regulations give less consideration to professional sports as professional sport and professional athletes are considered like business enterprise or business persons.

The logical deduction of this clustering of American society is that public administration (or public bureaucracies, bureaucrats, public administrators, government regulations, legalisms, etc.) impacts every aspect of life in the United States.

Chapter 1

FEDERALISM AND ADMINISTRATIVE STRUCTURE

A. INTERGOVERNMENTAL RELATIONS

1   Bahl, Roy W.; Greytak, David; Campbell, Alan K.; and Wasylenko,
     Michael J. "Intergovernmental and Functional Aspects of Public Em-
     ployment Trends in the United States." PUBLIC ADMINISTRATION
     REVIEW 32 (November-December 1972): 815-32. Tables.

     This article undertakes two tasks: a description of trends
     in public employment and an assessment of the value and
     comparability of available data. It examines public em-
     ployment in terms of budgetary implications, rather than
     efficiency, management, or political implications.

2   Bell, Michael, and Gabler, L. Richard. "Government Growth: An
     Intergovernmental Concern." INTERGOVERNMENTAL PERSPECTIVE
     2 (Fall 1976): 8-14.

     Bell and Gabler reveal that there are centralization ten-
     dencies at both the federal and state levels as the federal
     proportion of aggregate domestic spending has increased.
     They point out that total public expenditures, public ex-
     penditures as a percent of the gross national product,
     public expenditures adjusted for price changes, number of
     public employees, number of public employees per 1,000
     population, and tax burden for the middle income family
     are indicative of growth of the public sector in the United
     States.

3   Berkley, George E., and Fox, Douglas M. 80,000 GOVERNMENTS:
     THE POLITICS OF SUBNATIONAL AMERICA. Boston: Allyn and
     Bacon, 1978. xi, 403 p.

     This textbook centers on the basic theme that the state
     and local system consists of nearly 80,000 governments,
     most of which display a great deal of independence and
     individuality. The authors discuss the implications and

problems of this fragmentation. Sections include state government, local government, economics, social welfare, criminal justice, and the federalist future of subnational governments. It is useful for comprehending the roles of subnational governments in the federal system.

4   Bradford, James C. "Thomas Jefferson and Federalism." In THE AD-MINISTRATION OF THE NEW FEDERALISM: OBJECTIVES AND ISSUES, edited by Leigh E. Grosenick, pp. 112-14. Washington, D.C.: American Society for Public Administration, 1973.

The author notes that Jefferson was a firm believer in federalism. He concludes that the goal of revenue sharing is to revitalize federalism, or to revitalize the partnership between local and national governments in serving most effectively, efficiently, and economically the needs and desires of the people.

5   Brown, F. Gerald, and Saunders, Robert J. "Suburban Intergovern-mental Network for Management Development." PUBLIC MANAGE-MENT 56 (April 1974): 12-14.

The Suburban Intergovernmental Network for Management Development, a consortium of five Missouri cities, and the Center for Management Development of the University of Missouri at Kansas City, provide cross-organizational training and a program of organization development for each city. The authors maintain that the major objec-tive was to increase organizational capability to identi-fy, define, and work through administrative and policy issues important to the organizations' effectiveness.

6   Brownlow, Louis. "Reconversion of the Federal Administrative Ma-chinery from War to Peace." PUBLIC ADMINISTRATION REVIEW 4 (Autumn 1944): 309-26.

Brownlow recommended that the administrative machinery be organized to facilitate the achievement of at least five principal purposes or goals as the nation turned to peace after World War II. His list includes the durability of the peace and the prevention of war, in which the United States must act in concert with other united na-tions, maintenance of prosperity in a system of free en-terprise, maintenance of a high level of employment, the extension of the social security system, and the extension and enrichment of opportunities for individual cultural advancement.

7   Campbell, Jack M. "Are the States Here to Stay?" PUBLIC AD-MINISTRATION REVIEW 28 (January-February 1968): 26-29.

The author believes that the states are the logical fulcrum for balancing the system. He discusses problem areas and potential regional approaches for interstate arrangements. At no point in this brief essay does Campbell reassure the reader that the states are here to stay.

8   Critchfield, Brevard, and Reeves, H. Clyde. "Intergovernmental Relations: A View from the States." ANNALS OF THE AMERICAN ACADEMY OF POLITICAL AND SOCIAL SCIENCE 416 (November 1974): 99-107.

The authors contend that the utilization and viability of cooperative devices formally recognized by the Constitution of the United States, such as interstate compacts and agreements, are measurably offset by preemptive actions of the central government. The article suggests that an emergent trend may be seen toward reversal of the theory that power is best exercised in the nation's capital. The authors conclude by advising that the states lead the way by working together to increase their individual and collective capacities.

9   Etheredge, Lloyd S. "Optimal Federalism: A Model of Psychological Dependence." POLICY SCIENCES 8 (June 1977): 161-71.

Etheredge postulates that increased size, scope, and visibility of government may strengthen psychological dependence as an unintended aggregate effect of liberal programs. Such an effect depends upon citizens' experiences with government and bureaucrats. The article maintains that trends in American politics suggest the possibility of a growing substructure dependent on government programs. If dependency increases, political and administrative problems can be expected to increase.

10   Feld, Richard D., and Grafton, Carl, eds. THE UNEASY PARTNERSHIP: THE DYNAMICS OF FEDERAL, STATE, AND URBAN RELATIONS. Palo Alto, Calif.: National Press, 1973. 322 p.

This book of readings includes chapters on federalism in transition, fiscal federalism, role of the states, federalism and the urban scene, the welfare debate, higher education, technology and federalism, and the future of federalism. An authoritative group of authors penned these twenty-seven essays.

11   Finney, David R. "Federal-Interstate Compact: An International Economic Approach to the Border Problem." STATE GOVERNMENT 48 (Summer 1975): 164-69.

Finney notes that the mass migration of Mexican aliens

3

into the southwestern United States has become an international crisis and maintains that the appropriate solution
to this problem is not policing of the border but economic
development of this depressed region. He believes a
regional plan is needed in order to ensure that no one
state assumes an excessive responsibility. Finney suggests
that a federal-interstate compact be established and that
the main concerns of the compact should be the establishment of social services for migrant workers and the building
of an industrial base along the border. According to
Finney, Mexico is willing to cooperate.

12   Freeman, Sidney C. "A Rational Federal Structure." MIDWEST RE-
      VIEW OF PUBLIC ADMINISTRATION 3 (August 1969): 137-40.

      The author posits that government must coordinate its
      efforts from the federal level to the local implementing
      agency in order to insure effective, consistent program
      execution. He lauds President Richard M. Nixon's de-
      centralization plans and the creation of a uniform pattern
      of regional offices for the Departments of Housing and
      Urban Development; Health, Education, and Welfare;
      Labor; Office of Economic Opportunity; and Small Business
      Administration. He concludes that much of the decision
      making has been placed on state and local governments,
      where the effects and impacts are most direct.

13   Gamm, Larry. "Planning in Administration of Intergovernmental Programs."
      In PUBLIC ADMINISTRATION AND PUBLIC POLICY, edited by H.
      George Frederickson and Charles R. Wise, pp. 135-46. Lexington,
      Mass.: D.C. Heath and Co., 1977.

      The author discusses conceptions of planning in admini-
      stration, planning as control in intergovernmental admini-
      stration, and the evidence of planning in selected inter-
      governmental programs. He predicts the recent legislation
      requiring intergovernmental coordination in planning and
      administration promises to create substantial conflict among
      organizations at the state and substate levels.

14   Gibson, Kenneth. "A Case for Equity in Federal-Local Relations."
      ANNALS OF THE AMERICAN ACADEMY OF POLITICAL AND SOCIAL
      SCIENCE 439 (September 1978): 135-46.

      A historical review of federal-local relations reveals that
      shared responsibility between the varying levels of govern-
      ment has been basic to the American way of government.
      This case maintains that building up this partnership should
      be a principal objective of the Carter administration as it
      strives to revamp the government and create an effective
      policy for the nation's third century.

4

Federalism and Administrative Structure

15   Gilmer, Jay; Guest, James W.; and Kirchner, Charles. "The Impact
        of Federal Programs and Policies on State-Local Relations." PUBLIC
        ADMINISTRATION REVIEW 35 (December 1975): 774-79.

> This article attempts to demonstrate that certain key factors
> are present or may need to be present where one finds
> sound state-local relationships and a workable policy
> management framework. The authors examine the impacts
> of the Safe Streets Act (law enforcement), the Compre-
> hensive Employment and Training Act of 1973 (manpower),
> the Housing and Community Development Act of 1974
> (community development), and the Allied Services Act
> (human resources) in analyzing the force of federal pro-
> grams and policies on state-local relations.

16   Glendening, Parris N., and Reeves, Mavis Mann. PRAGMATIC FED-
        ERALISM: AN INTERGOVERNMENTAL VIEW OF AMERICAN GOV-
        ERNMENT. Pacific Palisades, Calif.: Palisades Publishers, 1977.
        334 p.

> The authors maintain that American government can no
> longer be understood from the singular perspective of the
> national, state, or local levels. They write from the
> viewpoint that American federalism is pragmatic. Glen-
> dening and Reeves point out the dynamics of intergovern-
> mental accommodation in American federalism, probe the
> role of people in intergovernmental relations, explain the
> evolutionary character of American federalism in national-
> state relations, cite the change and accommodation in
> national-state relations, note trends in the fiscal federal
> system, and discuss interactions among equals in interstate
> relations, the strong interdependence in state-local rela-
> tions, the dynamics of national-local relations, and the
> fragmented federalism of interlocal relations. The ex-
> perience of the authors on all governmental levels, in
> party politics, and in teaching and research convinced
> them that knowledge of how governments in America in-
> terrelate is necessary to a meaningful understanding of
> governmental systems.

17   Grodzins, Morton. THE AMERICAN SYSTEM. Edited by Daniel J.
        Elazar. Chicago: Rand McNally and Co., 1966. xviii, 404 p.

> The author explored the idea of "creative federalism" in
> American public administration in the 40s and 50s, before
> the arrival of the "Great Society." He perceived in
> federalism not the hypothetical separation of governments,
> but a "marble cake" of shared operations with citizen
> access through many cracks fortified by loose political
> parties. He described the system as decentralized, mildly
> chaotic, responsive, and democratic. Containing sixteen

5

chapters, this book examines the "marble cake," the past development of federalism, the influence of civilian projects looked at locally, the American party system, several policy issues, and rigorous censorship of efforts to decentralize power through central control.

18   Grosenick, Leigh E. "Institutional Change to Improve State and Local Competencies." In his THE ADMINISTRATION OF THE NEW FEDERALISM: OBJECTIVES AND ISSUES, pp. 91-110. Washington, D.C.: American Society for Public Administration, 1973.

The author discusses institution building versus institutional change, grants-in-aid as institution builders, the reform of federal management as the first step in institutional change, the role of federal assistance for improving central management in states and localities, and the role of revenue sharing in this process. Grosenick provides an insightful analysis of the structural arrangements of American administrative federalism.

19   Grupp, Fred W., and Richards, Alan R. "Variations in Elite Perceptions of American States as Referents for Public Policy-Making." AMERICAN POLITICAL SCIENCE REVIEW 49 (September 1975): 850-58.

The authors reveal that executives in large complex organizations often make decisions by emulation and analysis, that administrators in the fifty states are linked by both formal and informal communication networks, and that they are increasingly cognizant of both programs and policies in other states. Grupp and Richards maintain that the evidence from the literature and the data provides support for the hypothesis that the state executive is likely to assume policy cues from state agencies known to administer effective programs.

20   Jones, Charles O. "Federal-State-Local Sharing in Air Pollution Control." PUBLIUS 4 (Winter 1974): 69-85.

Jones states that the federal authority has increased markedly in response to public demand due to the lack of information exchange at state-local levels. He asserts that federal legislation has promoted development of state and local air pollution programs where none existed and that federal legislation has increasingly centered responsibility for meeting federally established air quality standards in the states. Jones concludes that a period of adjustment will permit continued information gathering and exchange, development of support for design and engineering, and the stabilization of governmental organizational relationships.

21   Kennedy, David J. "The Law of Appropriateness: An Approach to a
        General Theory of Intergovernmental Relations." PUBLIC ADMINI-
        STRATION REVIEW 32 (March-April 1972): 135-43. Figures.

        The system of American intergovernmental relations is
        traditionally approached by observing how it operates
        rather than analyzing why it works as it does. The au-
        thor attempts to develop general principles about the
        federal system cast in terms the practitioner of public
        administration can understand. The concept of "appro-
        priateness" in intergovernmental relations, though simple,
        is not simple-minded, and perhaps is closer to true prin-
        ciples than more complex analyses of the subject.

22   Levitan, Sar A., and Zickler, Joyce K. THE QUEST FOR A FEDERAL
        MANPOWER PARTNERSHIP. Cambridge, Mass.: Harvard University
        Press, 1974. 131 p.

        The authors suggest that the passage of the 1973 Compre-
        hensive Employment and Training Act (CETA) may seem in
        many ways to be a climax in the history of manpower
        organization and planning since it suggests workable solu-
        tions to the difficulties of intergovernmental relations and
        accommodations between public and private sponsors. The
        reader learns that CETA legislation provides a blueprint
        for integrating manpower planning and operations.

23   Light, Alfred R. "Intergovernmental Sources of Innovation in State
        Administration." AMERICAN POLITICS QUARTERLY 6 (April 1978):
        147-66.

        Light surveys American state administrators and examines
        a variety of sources of novel ideas and program innova-
        tions in the states. The reader learns that administrators'
        understandings of state innovation processes seem to be
        linked to cultural environments.

24   Lovell, Catherine. "Where We Are in IGR and Some of the Impli-
        cations." SOUTHERN REVIEW OF PUBLIC ADMINISTRATION 3
        (June 1979): 6-20.

        Lovell discusses the complexity of intergovernmental re-
        lations in the United States, the concerns of centralization
        and decentralization, implications of changes, instrumen-
        talities for coordination, role prescriptions, theories of
        accountability, and transformations in theory of the in-
        tergovernmental processes. She believes that "the single
        most important conclusion is that the quantitative change
        in numbers and modes of intergovernmental relationships
        over the last twenty years has led to important qualitative
        changes in our governmental operations."

25   MacDougall, William. "The Current Status of Our Intergovernmental
      Relations." In THE ADMINISTRATION OF THE NEW FEDERALISM:
      OBJECTIVES AND ISSUES, edited by Leigh E. Grosenick, pp. 34-39.
      Washington, D.C.: American Society for Public Administration, 1973.

           Crucial in the author's perspective on intergovernmental
           relations is the need to overcome common myths, namely
           "the doctrine of inevitable federal superiority," "the home
           rule myth," "biggest is best," "local governments are more
           responsible and responsive," "whatever is municipal is
           crucial," "the local government challenge is an urban
           challenge," "counties are the wave of the future," and
           "all we need is more discretionary money." This essay
           is an insightful analysis by the former executive director
           of the Advisory Commission on Intergovernmental Relations
           (ACIR).

26   Mathewson, Kent. "Councils of Government: The Potential and the
      Problems." In EMERGING PATTERNS IN URBAN ADMINISTRATION,
      edited by F. Gerald Brown and Thomas P. Murphy, pp. 195-220.
      Lexington, Mass.: Heath Lexington Books, 1970.

           The author traces the development of the Councils of
           Governments (COG) movement and highlights the strengths
           and problems associated with councils. He notes three
           problems which are sometimes present and have proved
           significant in impeding the growth and effectiveness of
           COG: 1) unwillingness or fear to move ahead, 2) in-
           adequate citizen involvement, and 3) the tendency to
           restrict the business of a council of governments to physical
           development.

27   Newton, Robert D. "Administrative Federalism." PUBLIC ADMINI-
      STRATION REVIEW 38 (May-June 1978): 252-55. Table.

           "If our federal system, which is a parceling out of roles
           and responsibilities, is to function better, we need in-
           stitutional means to illuminate and reorder the networks
           of relationships in which we find ourselves. We need to
           know who does what and why in federal/non-federal re-
           lationships. We need a system which can rationally
           accommodate both the shifting of maximum responsibility
           to non-federal parties and the significant amount of federal
           intervention that became necessary in the 1960s. We
           need to provide program managers with realistic and
           effective project and activity implementing alternatives
           or means to realize national objectives."

28   Ostrom, Elinor. "Size and Performance in a Federal System." PUBLIUS
      6 (Spring 1976): 33-74.

Recognizing that there is little empirical evidence concerning the effects of jurisdictional reform in metropolitan government, Ostrom simulates models for testing the hypothesis that consolidation of a metropolitan region's police force results in the improvement of service. The author examines police services in the city and county of St. Louis for determining relationships between the size of the police department and citizen concerns, citizen evaluations, and costs per capita for providing such services.

29   Ostrom, Vincent. "The Study of Federalism at Work." PUBLIUS 4 (Fall 1974): 1-17.

Ostrom maintains that the choice of strategy is a move in a series of simultaneous games in a federal system. The article observes that it is impossible to study federalism as a whole but that problems associated with federal systems provide some examples of the tasks that confront its students. The article concludes, "A lack of consciousness of citizens, Congressmen, Senators, Presidents, university professors, and others could mean an end to federalism and the end to American democracy as well."

30   Passel, Peter, and Ross, Leonard. STATE POLICIES AND FEDERAL PROGRAMS: PRIORITIES AND CONSTRAINTS. New York: Praeger, 1978. 168 p.

This book focuses on the debate on federal decentralization and centers on two questions: whether states and localities are capable of running effective programs and whether they are politically sensitive to the same political values as the federal government. The book alludes that even without detailed federal legislation, the power of the state to accomplish its objectives is limited by the nature of the federal system.

31   Porter, David O.; Warner, David C.; and Porter, Teadie W. THE POLITICS OF BUDGETING FEDERAL AID: RESOURCE MOBILIZATION BY LOCAL SCHOOL DISTRICTS. Beverly Hills, Calif.: Sage Publications, 1973. 93 p.

The authors find that components other than the objective requirements of legislation and guidelines of the executive branch are decisive in the mobilization and utilization of federal funds in local school districts. The article reviews two patterns of budgeting behavior: 1) multipocket budgeting obligates the resources of an organization so as to place its own priorities ahead of those of its donors, and 2) marginal mobilizing centers on those income sources which return the greatest amount of revenue for the time and effort used.

32   Remy, Ray. "The Professional Administrator in Regional Councils."
PUBLIC MANAGEMENT 56 (January 1974): 11-13.

> Remy states that employees within the Council of Govern-
> ments program are not only new to the difficulties of
> coping with regional problems, but lack firsthand ex-
> perience with sensitive political relationships. The role
> of the COG director consists of salesmanship, suggestion,
> persuasion, and planning. There are increasing require-
> ments for traditional management systems in the areas of
> finance, personnel, purchasing, and employee affairs.

33   Ricketts, Edmond F., and Waltzer, Herbert. "American Federalism:
Creative or Stifling?" MIDWEST REVIEW OF PUBLIC ADMINISTRA-
TION 4 (August 1970): 81-86.

> The authors posit ten assumptions that underlie the down-
> ward relations of the federal government. They develop
> the idea that our present federalism does not and cannot
> have the creativity which some of its molders and chroni-
> clers would have the American people think. The authors
> urge more vigorous action by state and local governments
> to promote creativity and initiative in confronting state
> and local difficulties.

34   Schechter, Stephen L. "Federalism and Community in Historical Perspective." PUBLIUS 5 (Spring 1975): 1-14.

> Schechter discusses the Temple University graduate program
> called "Urbanization in Federal Systems" which encourages
> the comparative study of federal principles and institutional
> arrangements and their applications to urban problems and
> policies. The article reports that one product of this
> project is the publication of a group of essays, "Federalism
> and Community," which provides a theoretical view,
> valuable local insights into the workings of intergovern-
> mental relations in Western European federal systems, and
> a shift in focus from the workings of federal systems per
> se to the nature and relative strength of the constituent
> states they contain.

35   Seidman, Harold. POLITICS, POSITION, AND POWER: THE DYNAMICS
OF FEDERAL ORGANIZATION. New York: Oxford University Press,
1975. 354 p.

> More than any writer or practitioner in the field of public
> administration, Seidman describes with expertise the politics
> of government organization. He gives the views of ex-
> ecutive branch organization from the White House and
> Congress. The author's text on politics, position, and
> power tells us a great deal about the dynamics of

federal organization. This book is highly recommended
to both students and practitioners interested in the federal
government.

36   Seligman, Lee, and Karnig, Albert K. "Black Representation in the
American States: A Comparison of Bureaucracies and Legislatures."
AMERICAN POLITICS QUARTERLY 4 (April 1976): 237-45.

Civil service data for the years 1970-72 indicates that
the black population is underrepresented in thirty-eight
state bureaucracies and legislatures. This study confirms
that blacks were underrepresented in both areas in most
states and that there is little tendency for blacks to be
more represented in state bureaucracies than in state
legislatures. In the federal system, there is little difference in the ratio of black representation between the
legislative and bureaucratic areas, as blacks are underrepresented at both levels.

37   Sigelman, Lee. "The Quality of Administration: An Exploration in
the American States." ADMINISTRATION AND SOCIETY 8 (May
1976): 107-44.

In this article the reader is told that the quality of administration is in fact higher in more affluent, industrialized,
urban settings; but contrary to expectation, administrative
quality is not closely related to centralization of the
decision-making process. Sigelman asserts that it is very
hard to sort out the relative impact of socioeconomic and
political factors on the quality of administration.

38   Singer, Neil M. "Federal Aid to Minority Business: Survey and
Critique." SOCIAL SCIENCE QUARTERLY 54 (September 1973):
292-305.

Minority-owned businesses account for less than 1 percent
of total sales and are concentrated in low-productivity
industries, chiefly personal services, and retail trade.
Singer suggests that small businessmen generally and
minority businessmen in particular are usually thought to
be deficient in the areas of access to capital and to
managerial skill. The article suggests that the Small
Business Administration's Equal Opportunity Loan program
should be enlarged, the ceiling on the maximum loan
raised, and the agency encouraged to increase its loan
guarantees. The author believes that management help
to minority firms should continue to be made available
through local business groups.

39   Stone, Donald C. "Achieving a Capable and Manageable Federal
        System." PUBLIC ADMINISTRATION REVIEW 35 (December 1975):
        728-37.

        Stone believes that the challenge is to weave the insti-
        tutional and program elements of 78,000 governmental
        jurisdictions, districts, and authorities into a strong enough
        fabric to serve the nation in its third century. The author
        emphasizes strengthening management processes and de-
        veloping administrative personnel, knowledge, and tech-
        nology to increase performance and effectiveness through-
        out the entire federal system.

40   Sundquist, James L., in collaboration with David W. Davis. MAKING
        FEDERALISM WORK: A STUDY OF PROGRAM COORDINATION AT
        THE COMMUNITY LEVEL. Washington, D.C.: Brookings Institution,
        1969. viii, 293 p.

        This is a tabulation of the administrative shortcomings of
        President Johnson's domestic policies and an excellent
        summary of federal administration during the current pro-
        gram period. The author centers on the effort toward
        program coordination necessitated by the commitment to
        "creative federalism." The adventure with community
        action programs, Model Cities, and a number of programs
        planned for agrarian America is presented. Discussion is
        undertaken of conditions determining the need for program
        coordination and the administrative components which must
        be developed in order to make federalism work.

41   U.S. Advisory Commission on Intergovernmental Relations. AMERICAN
        FEDERALISM: INTO THE THIRD CENTURY, ITS AGENDA. Washington,
        D.C.: 1974. 39 p.

        This text recommends that third century American federalism
        reorganize and simplify local government, that city areas
        become governable and their internal socioeconomic dis-
        parities be lessened, that equality of educational oppor-
        tunity become a living reality instead of a meaningless
        phrase, that growth policies be structured and reconciled
        among localities, states, and nations and among economic,
        environmental and social values, that the property tax
        be made equitable and effective, that state governments
        perform imaginatively for both their urban and rural con-
        stituencies, that the federal grant system be made man-
        ageable and "grantsmanship" dethroned, and that the re-
        form of the welfare and criminal justice systems continue.
        Ways should be found to insure that the diversity in the
        federal system continues to operate as a strength, not a
        weakness.

How You Can Avoid Eternal Torment In Hell And Get To Heaven

1. Admit that you have sinned.

2. Be willing to turn from sin.

3. Through prayer ASK JESUS CHRIST (GOD) TO COME IN AND CONTROL YOUR LIFE.

(Receive JESUS as your Lord and Savior.)

JESUS CHRIST, GOD IN HUMAN FORM, PAID THE PRICE FOR YOUR SINS.

For God so loved the world, that he gave his only begotten Son, that whosoever believeth in him should not perish (IN THE LAKE OF FIRE), but have everlasting life (IN HEAVEN).

John 3:16

AND WHOSOEVER WAS NOT FOUND WRITTEN IN THE BOOK OF LIFE WAS CAST INTO THE LAKE OF FIRE. *REVELATION 20:15*

HE DIED, SHED HIS PRECIOUS BLOOD TO WASH AWAY YOUR SINS.* HE WAS BURIED, ROSE FROM THE DEAD,** AND WENT BACK TO HEAVEN.‡ THAT WAS HIS FIRST MISSION TO THIS PLANET EARTH. THE BIBLE SAYS HE'S COMING AGAIN.‡

*Heb. 9:12   **1 Cor. 15:3-4   ‡Acts 1:11

42   _____. THE INTER-GOVERNMENTAL GRANT SYSTEM AS SEEN BY
LOCAL, STATE, AND FEDERAL OFFICIALS. Washington, D.C.: 1977.
287 p.

> This text includes surveys of local, state, and federal
> officials on the effects of grant-in-aid systems. This
> work points out that from the local perspective, cate-
> gorical grants have a pervasive, stimulating and lasting
> effect on local decision making and that the most pressing
> problems are those of administrative implementation rather
> than congressional design of the categorical aids. State
> administrators favored greater decentralization from the
> national level to the states and agreed that national-
> local contacts should be channeled through the states.
> From the federal side, only 18 percent of the respondents
> felt that special revenue sharing or block grants would
> help states and localities meet their program needs better
> than categorical grants.

43   _____. THE STATES AND INTERGOVERNMENTAL AIDS. Washington,
D.C.: 1977. 83 p.

> The changes and growth that have marked the state aid
> system is evaluated and attention is given to the states'
> direct servicing role. Chief findings include the growth
> in state aid during the twentieth century, which has been
> virtually uninterrupted in both money and real terms, and
> the direct servicing role, which showed a general expan-
> sion for the 1957 to 1972 period. This report asserts that
> the two most serious problem areas were inequitable dis-
> tribution formulas and uncertainty of state funding.

44   U.S. General Accounting Office. ASSESSMENT OF FEDERAL RE-
GIONAL COUNCILS. B-178319. Washington, D.C.: Government
Printing Office, 31 January 1974. 49 p.

> This report recommends that federal regional councils
> should increase their efforts in disseminating information
> and providing technical assistance by fully acquainting
> officials of the councils' role and responsibilities and the
> means by which their assistance can be secured. This
> document states that the councils can more effectively
> accomplish their purposes with stronger management direc-
> tions by the Under Secretaries Group. This GAO analysis
> also reviews federal regional council's activities and
> effectiveness and factors preventing the councils from
> achieving their potential effectiveness. This is an ex-
> cellent primer on standard federal regions.

45   _____. IMPROVED COOPERATION AND COORDINATION NEEDED
AMONG ALL LEVELS OF GOVERNMENT. Office of Management

and Budget Circular A-95. GGD-75-52. Washington, D.C.: Government Printing Office, 11 February 1975. 102 p.

> This report assesses the performance of the Office of
> Management and Budget and other federal agencies in
> implementing title IV of the Intergovernmental Cooperation
> Act of 1968 and section 204 of the Demonstration Cities
> and Metropolitan Development Act of 1966 through Office
> of Management and Budget Circular A-95. GAO evaluates
> 1) the legislative history of these two acts and the suc-
> cession of OMB circulars preceding the current version of
> Circular A-95, and 2) evaluation reports prepared by
> OMB, federal agencies, and private consultants.

46   Walker, David B. "The Changing Pattern of Federal Assistance to
State and Local Governments." In PUBLIC ADMINISTRATION AND
PUBLIC POLICY, edited by H. George Frederickson and Charles R.
Wise, pp. 81-97. Lexington, Mass.: D.C. Heath and Co., 1977.
Tables.

> Walker indicates that the program emphasis of federal aid
> has shifted somewhat in recent years away from specialized
> functions toward block grants and general revenue sharing.
> He states that federal aid, in the aggregate, is mildly
> equalizing and emphasizes that the programs direct rela-
> tively larger sums of federal money to low per capita
> income states than to high per capita income states.

47   _____. "How Fares Federalism in the Mid-Seventies?" ANNALS OF
THE AMERICAN ACADEMY OF POLITICAL AND SOCIAL SCIENCE
416 (November 1974): 52-66.

> Walker maintains that conflicts over concepts, finances
> in flux, and muddled intergovernmental management are
> themes that have dominated the politics of contemporary
> American federalism. He predicts that the system of the
> late 1970s will be considerably different from the one we
> have known, but the essence of its basic intergovernmental
> relations will depend on how these issues and conflicts
> are resolved.

48   _____. "The Intergovernmental Personnel Act: Manpower, the Quiet
Crisis in Federalism." In GOVERNMENT MANAGEMENT INTERN-
SHIPS AND EXECUTIVE DEVELOPMENT: EDUCATION FOR CHANGE,
edited by Thomas P. Murphy, pp. 245-54. Lexington, Mass.: D.C.
Heath and Co., 1973.

> Walker states that manpower (i.e., personpower) has been
> one of the most critical dimensions of the crisis in con-
> temporary federal-state-local relations. He states that the
> enactment of the Intergovernmental Personnel Act of 1970
> made governmental personpower a focal point of national
> concern and action.

49 _____. "The New System of Intergovernmental Assistance: Some Initial Notes." PUBLIUS 5 (Summer 1975): 131-45.

> Walker states that over the past ten years the mode of federal assistance to states and localities experienced a dramatic modification, changing from a categorical approach to a combination of categorical and block grants and to a tripartite system which included general revenue sharing. Each plan has its own separate systematic goals, distinctive administrative approach, and program effects. Walker believes that the failure to appreciate these differences could curb the benefits of this diversified package.

50 Wright, Deil S. "The Advisory Commission on Intergovernmental Relations: Unique Features and Policy Orientation." PUBLIC ADMINISTRATION REVIEW 25 (September 1965): 193-202.

> The author outlines several unique structural characteristics of the ACIR and examines the general policy orientation developed by the commission. Wright notes that ACIR, created in 1959, was a congressional rather than executive initiative. He concludes that ACIR's influence will have an increasing impact on efforts to perfect the federal system.

51 _____. "Intergovernmental Relations: An Analytical Overview." ANNALS OF THE AMERICAN ACADEMY OF POLITICAL AND SOCIAL SCIENCE 416 (November 1974): 1-16.

> Wright states that the five distinctive features of intergovernmental relations are that it occurs within the federal system; that there are no intergovernmental relations but only relations among officials in different governing units; that IGR is the continuous, day-to-day pattern of contacts, knowledge, and evaluations of government officials; that IGR concepts reflect an awareness of the role played by all public officials; and that IGR was recognized from its origins in the 1930s as anchored in politics and in policy. Wright stresses that complexity is an inherent and persistent characteristic of IGR and that accomplishments in the intergovernmental arena depend on the successful management of complexity.

B. THE NEW FEDERALISM AND GOVERNMENTAL SUBSIDY

52 Anderson, William. "The Myths of Tax Sharing." PUBLIC ADMINISTRATION REVIEW 28 (January-February 1968): 10-14.

> The author, a late professor of political science at the University of Minnesota, offers a concise essay with arguments against revenue sharing. Anderson's myths include

the notions that the national government is "rolling in unneeded wealth," that tax sharing is going to pump new public funds into the states and into the national economy, and that all the states have reached the absolute limit of their ability to find and to raise additional revenues for support of their own public services.

53   Barth, James R.; Bennett, James T.; and Kraft, John. "An Econometric Analysis of a Federal Revenue-Sharing Allocation Formula." PUBLIC FINANCE QUARTERLY 4 (January 1976): 17-32.

The proposed allocation of the 1973 Better Communities Act is studied as an example of the allocation process in federal revenue sharing legislation. The object is to determine the degree to which funds are allocated according to the specific formulas in the legislation. The article suggests that the allocation criteria are relatively unimportant and that there exist other variables which should be included in the model.

54   Browne, Edmond, Jr., and Rehfuss, John. "Policy Evaluation, Citizen Participation, and Revenue Sharing in Aurora, Illinois." PUBLIC ADMINISTRATION REVIEW 35 (March-April 1975): 150-57. Tables.

The revenue sharing committee in Aurora, Illinois, receives high marks for both citizen participation and policy evaluation responsibilities.

55   Caputo, David A. "General Revenue Sharing and American Federalism: Towards the Year 2000." ANNALS OF THE AMERICAN ACADEMY OF POLITICAL AND SOCIAL SCIENCE 419 (May 1975): 130-42.

Caputo stresses that general revenue sharing will be a significant contributor to the future of American federalism only if it is in fact a proclaimer of other federal programs which make available substantial amounts of unrestricted federal funds to be employed in discretionary fashion by state and local governments. The article notes that general revenue sharing does not constitute a large enough percentage of federal revenues to be the prime determinant of future intergovernmental relations in America. Caputo believes that general revenue sharing's most profound contribution may be its role as a catalyst for increased citizen impact on state and local governmental decisions.

56   Caputo, David A., and Cole, Richard L. "General Revenue Sharing Expenditure Decisions in Cities over 50,000." PUBLIC ADMINISTRATION REVIEW 35 (March-April 1975): 136-42. Tables.

The authors conclude 1) that general revenue sharing expenditures continue to be concentrated in a very few categories; 2) that health and social service programs normally associated with low-income or socially disadvantaged groups have not received a large proportion of general revenue sharing funds; 3) that general revenue sharing funds have gone, to the largest extent, to support already existing programs and have not been widely used to develop new and innovative programs; 4) that general revenue sharing has not drastically affected the tax rates prevalent in American cities over 50,000, but the funds have helped to stabilize the rates; 5) that probably the most important impact of general revenue sharing funds is the general satisfaction of city officials with the program and the apparent increase in that satisfaction as the program continues; and 6) that the debate over the renewal of general revenue sharing will deal with specific changes and recommendations in the program rather than deciding to leave it intact or eliminate it.

57   Carlson, William A. "New Federalism and a New Program--The Rural Development Act of 1972." In THE ADMINISTRATION OF THE NEW FEDERALISM: OBJECTIVES AND ISSUES, edited by Leigh E. Grosenick, pp. 65-76. Washington, D.C.: American Society for Public Administration, 1973. Table.

"The federal role under the Rural Development Act and the New Federalism is not one of providing the main source of development assistance or energies. Rather, the federal government has peripheral responsibilities and only marginal leverage through five major functions: 1) technical assistance, both in terms of transmitting information on technical subjects like soil surveys; 2) shared revenues and block grants; 3) guarantees for commercial credit at market rates; 4) research; and 5) evaluation."

58   Carroll, Michael A. "The Impact of General Revenue Sharing on the Urban Planning Process--An Initial Assessment." PUBLIC ADMINISTRATION REVIEW 35 (March-April 1975): 143-50. Table.

This article attempts to assess the impact of general revenue sharing, a major element of the New Federalism, on the urban planning process as a function of local government. The author surmises that the impact of general revenue sharing on urban planning has been substantial and penetrating.

59   Chauhan, D.S. "Impact of Revenue Sharing on Local Government: Psychological and Temporal Dimensions." MIDWEST REVIEW OF PUBLIC ADMINISTRATION 8 (April 1974): 142-51. Tables.

Chauhan illustrates the distribution of revenue sharing funds and highlights the original revenue sharing concept

(State and Local Fiscal Assistance Act of 1972) as it applies to local government. The author concludes that it is too early to judge whether the revenue sharing program will fail or succeed. An excellent article for understanding some of the original emphases of the 1972 law.

60   Dwight, James S. "The Four D's of the New Federalism." In THE ADMINISTRATION OF THE NEW FEDERALISM: OBJECTIVES AND ISSUES, edited by Leigh E. Grosenick, pp. 17-28. Washington, D.C.: American Society for Public Administration, 1973.

The four D's of the New Federalism are dollars, discretion, decentralization, and delivery.

61   Elazar, Daniel J. "Fiscal Questions and Political Answers in Intergovernmental Relations." PUBLIC ADMINISTRATION REVIEW 32 (September–October 1972): 471-78.

This article is devoted to the political analysis of certain fiscal questions affecting federal-state-local relations in the United States. The author examines the consequences of federal aid and offers explanations for contradictory trends in federal-local relations, including the federal government as servant, national uniformity, and local right-national interest theories.

62   GENERAL REVENUE SHARING: INFLUENCING LOCAL BUDGETS. Washington, D.C.: Center for Community Change, 1978. 23 p.

This guide defines how citizen groups can play a major part in the budget process and the ways in which general revenue sharing funds are utilized under 1976 legislation. This text gives the background of revenue sharing and provides detailed explanation of those sections of the 1976 law which have particular significance for citizen action.

63   Goetz, Charles J. WHAT IS REVENUE SHARING? Washington, D.C.: The Urban Institute, 1972. 78 p.

Goetz warns about the potential trouble areas in revenue sharing and denotes the confusion over goals deriving from the legislative process. He offers a pessimistic evaluation of prospects of revenue sharing in its present form (ca. 1972). He also notes some problems with the arguments used to promote passage of revenue sharing legislation.

64   Grosenick, Leigh E. "The Learning Agenda of the New Federalism: An Analysis of Questions Raised by Governmental Executives." In his THE ADMINISTRATION OF THE NEW FEDERALISM: OBJECTIVES

AND ISSUES, pp. 116-36. Washington, D.C.: American Society for Public Administration, 1973. Tables.

> Grosenick probes what state, local, and federal executives want to know about the New Federalism. He includes 136 questions about the intergovernmental system, general policy issues, the New Federalism, federal regional agencies, federal regional councils, the role of the states, state and local planning, federalism and citizen participation, state and local structures, processes, and competencies, Office of Management and Budget Circular A-95 and planning requirements, substate regionalism, and general and special revenue sharing. Grosenick concludes that there is a desperate need to develop new and comprehensive channels to communicate information and ideas concerning the New Federalism.

65   Ingram, Helen. "Policy Implementation Through Bargaining: The Case of Federal Grants-in-Aid." PUBLIC POLICY 25 (Fall 1977): 499-526.

> This essay questions the basic assumption which underlies the utilization of federal grants-in-aid as an instrument for implementing federal policy, in which states can be enticed by financial reward to pursue whatever objectives the federal government has projected. This article states that while a federal agency has money, expertise, and other resources with which to bargain, states have counteracting powers of numbers, important information, and access to Congress. The reader is informed that Congress often undercuts the first bargaining position of a federal agency in the legislative process by which it authorizes a grant. The result is that some of the federal organizational and management objectives may be realized, but it is difficult for the federal government to encourage states to alter substantive policy unless federal goals are shared.

66   Ink, Dwight A. "The Origin and Thrusts of the New Federalism." In THE ADMINISTRATION OF THE NEW FEDERALISM: OBJECTIVES AND ISSUES, edited by Leigh E. Grosenick, pp. 29-33. Washington, D.C.: American Society for Public Administration, 1973.

> The author discusses the background of the federal system, defines the concept of creative federalism, and explains in detail the Federal Assistance Review (FAR) program, which attempted to redesign the federal part of the system through the establishment of standard federal regions and regional councils, to decentralize programs, simplify federal grant processes, standardize administrative requirements, integrate grants administration, and place more reliance on state and local governments, and the A-95 process.

67   Kolberg, William H. "The New Federalism: Regional Councils and
          Program Coordination Efforts." In THE ADMINISTRATION OF THE
          NEW FEDERALISM: OBJECTIVES AND ISSUES, edited by Leigh E.
          Grosenick, pp. 51-64. Washington, D.C.: American Society for
          Public Administration, 1973.

              The author discusses the role of federal regional councils,
              the development of the FRC system, the importance of the
              decentralization concept in this structural arrangement,
              the career-political interface of regional directors, the
              introduction of the Integrated Grant Administration (IGA)
              concept, the contribution of President Nixon to federal
              regional councils via Executive Order 11647, communica-
              tions with state and local governments, and problems and
              possible new directions for the FRCs.

68   Lehne, Richard P. "Employment Effects of Grant-in-Aid Effects."
          PUBLIUS 5 (Summer 1975): 101-9.

              By enabling the federal or state governments to seek one
              form of goals while still recognizing diversified local
              preferences and experiences, grants-in-aid have become
              a chief organ of intergovernmental correspondence in the
              United States. Lehne examines modifications in municipal
              government employment trends and local grant-in-aid
              receipts between 1957 and 1972 in five-year periods. He
              reviews the utilization of an empirical prototype collective
              model on earnings and employment for all local govern-
              ments within each state.

69   _____. "Revenue Sources and Local Government Employment." PUBLIC
          FINANCE QUARTERLY 3 (October 1975): 400-410.

              Lehne examines the relationship between variations in
              local government employment patterns and grant-in-aid
              receipts for three time periods--1957-62, 1962-67, and
              1967-72. The author studies three facets of local govern-
              ment employment patterns--per capita payroll costs, average
              monthly wage per employee, the number of public employees
              per capita--and concludes that in the past revenue sources
              were significantly related to municipal budgeting decisions.

70   Lucey, Patrick J. "State Payments for Municipal Services." STATE
          GOVERNMENT 48 (Autumn 1975): 220-25.

              Lucey maintains that state facilities and institutions are a
              burden to municipal governments and taxpayers because
              they require police, fire, and other service needs which
              increase local property taxes. He states that Wisconsin
              began a program--Payments for Municipal Services (PMS)--
              to provide state payments to local communities affected

by state facilities. Lucey contends that local property
taxes should only support government services that relate
to property ownership.

71   Margolis, Larry. "Issues of Fiscal Federalism Are Too Important to Be
      Decided by the National Government Alone." PUBLIUS 6 (Fall 1976):
      161-67.

      The author suggests that the federal system has become
      imbalanced because Congress has become the legislature
      of the national government, contrary to the intentions of
      the Founding Fathers. Margolis believes that those in
      Congress who defend the existing grant system and who
      oppose general revenue sharing have lost sight of the fact
      that the money belongs to the American public and have
      failed to perceive the varying capabilities of state govern-
      ments. He asserts that the states should retrieve part of
      their relinquished power.

72   Murphy, John C. "General Revenue Sharing's Impact on County Government."
      PUBLIC ADMINISTRATION REVIEW 35 (March-April 1975): 131-35.

      Murphy maintains that general revenue sharing is a sound
      program and is absolutely essential to the financial survival
      of county government. He contends that general revenue
      sharing is allowing counties to at least maintain and, in
      some instances, increase the level of public services and,
      at the same time, relieve pressures on local revenue
      sources, particularly the property tax.

73   Mushkin, Selma J. "Fiscal Outlook in the States." STATE GOVERN-
      MENT 48 (Spring 1975): 116-21.

      Despite increases in tax rates and inflation, Mushkin
      reveals that the fiscal outlook for the states is dismal and
      declares that the economic slowdown of the past five years
      has caused a drop in the rate of increase of state taxes.
      The author asserts that federal revenue sharing and direct
      federal takeover of some categories of public assistance
      have lessened the burden, but federal aid is essential to
      make up for the effects of economic recession on state
      revenue. Mushkin posits that the rate of population growth
      is declining, that federal appropriations may replace state
      funding, and that there may be an increasing federal
      takeover of welfare.

74   Mushkin, Selma J., and Cotton, John F. FUNCTIONAL FEDERALISM:
      GRANTS-IN-AID AND PPB SYSTEMS. Washington, D.C.: State-Local
      Finances Project of The George Washington University, 1968. 208 p.

      Chapters in this report concern intergovernmental fiscal

trends and prospects, the federal view of grants, grant-in-aid design, the structure of HEW grants, the measurement of need and fiscal capacity, national-state-local priorities, grant packaging, consolidated and target grants, general support or overhead grants, and strengthening state and local taxes. The focus of this text is economic, not political or administrative. The emphasis is on the design, structure, priorities, impact, and reforms related to federal grants-in-aid.

75   Nathan, Richard P. "Federalism and the Shifting Nature of Fiscal Relations." ANNALS OF THE AMERICAN ACADEMY OF POLITICAL AND SOCIAL SCIENCE 419 (May 1975): 120-29.

This article suggests that the New Federalism is divided into four major budget categories: human resources, community development, income security, and natural resources. Nathan notes that human resource and community development programs are appropriate programs for decentralization. The implementation of many income security and natural resource proposals have resulted in increased central government responsibilities. The reader learns that the Brookings Institution studied distributional, fiscal, and political effects of revenue sharing during a five-year period.

76   _____. "The New Federalism Versus the New Structuralism." PUBLIUS 5 (Summer 1975): 111-29.

The New Structuralism calls for action by the federal government to reform the structure of state and local governments in order to improve their capacity to take advantage of revenue sharing funds and other federal grants-in-aid. If the real aim of the New Structuralists is to aid poverty-impacted central cities more adequately, Nathan believes that the way to achieve this purpose may well be through changes in the distribution of fiscal assistance and transfer payments.

77   _____. "The Roots and Sprouts of Revenue Sharing." PUBLIUS 6 (Fall 1976): 169-75.

Nathan stresses that revenue sharing was chiefly a political reform, a technique for decentralization to give power to the people and to revitalize state and local government. He believes the distributional effects depend upon whether large cities and poor states receive relatively more generous treatment than they do under the current formula grants. Comparisons on a county-area basis show that the most populous and highly urbanized counties receive much less shared revenue than others in relation to their nonschool tax revenue.

78   Rondinelli, Dennis A. "Revenue Sharing and American Cities: Analysis of the Federal Experiment in Local Assistance." JOURNAL OF THE AMERICAN INSTITUTE OF PLANNERS 41 (September 1975): 319-33.

> General revenue sharing payments have been allocated primarily for the operation and maintenance of existing programs, services, and facilities in larger cities and for backlogged capital investments in smaller cities. The author relates that revenue sharing operates most effectively as a federal income supplement to local taxing powers and as a redistributive device for assisting central cities and smaller towns to expand limited revenue bases.

79   Ross, John P., and Gustely, Richard D. "Changing the Intrastate General Revenue Sharing Formula: A Discussion of the Issues." PUBLIC ADMINISTRATION REVIEW 36 (November-December 1976): 655-60.

> The purpose of this essay is to examine the major issues surrounding the intrastate component of the general revenue sharing formula and to present empirical findings regarding these issues. Based on the authors' empirical work, Ross and Gustely suggest potential ways of resolving the issues of need, bounds, and tiering.

80   Rouse, John E., Jr. "The New Federalism at the Department of Housing and Urban Development." In MAKING GOVERNMENT WORK: ESSAYS IN HONOR OF CONLEY H. DILLON, edited by Richard P. Claude and James C. Strouse, pp. 216-25. College Park: University of Maryland, 1977.

> The author discusses the 1971 devolution of decision-making authority within the Department of Housing and Urban Development to its field offices. Rouse points out that there was a vertical decentralization to the area and insuring offices within HUD, that the burden for implementation of decentralization was placed upon the career bureaucrats, that decentralization failed, in part, because the area and insuring offices lacked well-trained staff, and that the most outstanding aspect of the area office concept was its administrative, not programmatic, features. HUD was the only federal government department or agency to undergo decentralization during Nixon's New Federalism administrative decentralization.

81   Stenberg, Carl W. "Block Grants: The Middlemen of the Federal Aid System." INTERGOVERNMENTAL PERSPECTIVES 3 (Spring 1977): 8-13.

> Stenberg maintains that block grants give generalists the opportunity to become involved in decision making, but are less well suited to achieving targeting, innovation,

and program enlargement. He insists that if block grants
are to realize their potential as change agents, sufficient
funds need to be made available to provide a catalyst
effect.

82   Stenberg, Carl W., and Walker, David B. "The Block Grant: Lessons
      from Two Early Experiments." PUBLIUS 7 (Spring 1977): 31-60.

      The authors project that, because of its decentralization
      thrust and its relationship to economy and efficiency, the
      block grant will have considerable appeal to those seeking
      to restructure and to rationalize the federal aid system.

83   Terrell, Paul. "Competing for Revenue Sharing: The Roles of Local
      Human Service Agencies." URBAN AFFAIRS QUARTERLY 12 (December
      1976): 171-96.

      Terrell indicates that whereas county health and welfare
      agencies generally view revenue sharing as an extension
      of regular budgetary proceedings, community action pro-
      grams and model cities agencies seek funds as vital pro-
      tection against cutbacks in an era of lessened national
      commitment to social programs. The reader learns that
      revenue sharing increased the visibility of social efforts
      in local government and underscored the need for equitable
      and systematic arrangements for funding, operating, and
      evaluating social programs.

84   Tomer, John F. "Revenue Sharing and the Intrastate Fiscal Mismatch:
      A Critical View." PUBLIC FINANCE QUARTERLY 5 (October 1977):
      445-70.

      Tomer asserts that an important declared goal of the general
      revenue sharing (GRS) program is to reduce the fiscal
      mismatch among local governments, especially between
      the problem-ridden center cities and the wealthier suburbs.
      The article mentions that the GRS intrastate allocation
      formula was designed to allocate funds among localities
      inversely with per capita income.

85   Wright, Deil S. FEDERAL GRANTS-IN-AID: PERSPECTIVES AND
      ALTERNATIVES. Washington, D.C.: American Enterprise Institute,
      1968. 158 p.

      This is an excellent overview of the alternatives facing
      federal grants-in-aid at the end of the 1960s. Wright
      defines and provides the legal basis for grants, notes
      historical development and causal factors, cites aims,
      advantages and disadvantages, of grants, explores pro-
      gram scope and financial significance, examines participants'

perspectives of national, state and local government expenditure levels, analyzes the strengths and weaknesses of state government, and probes various grant alternatives.

86 _____. "Revenue Sharing and Structural Features of American Federalism." ANNALS OF THE AMERICAN ACADEMY OF POLITICAL AND SOCIAL SCIENCE 419 (May 1975): 100-119.

Wright suggests that general revenue sharing may have an impact on three structural features of American federalism-- governmental entities, institutional and actor roles, and behavioral perspectives--while the short- and long-term effects of general revenue sharing on the number of governmental units will probably be modest and marginal. The article reveals that perhaps the most abstract and unappreciated effect of general revenue sharing has been some reduction in the tension, competition, and rivalry pervading the relationships among intergovernmental actors.

C. URBAN AND SUBURBAN ADMINISTRATION

87 Bish, Robert L., and Ostrom, Vincent. UNDERSTANDING URBAN GOVERNMENT: METROPOLITAN REFORM RECONSIDERED. Washington, D.C.: American Enterprise Institute, 1973. 111 p.

The authors state that the customary wisdom utilized to reform metropolitan government presumes that fragmentation of authority and overlapping jurisdictions are the primary causes of urban ills. Bish and Ostrom inform their readers that a new reform movement, demanding community control and neighborhood government within large central cities, challenges traditional prescriptions of a single unit of government controlled by a few policy officials. They reveal that some political economists offer a public choice approach which says that different public goods and services are most efficiently provided under different organizational arrangements.

88 Black, Guy. "The Decentralization of Urban Government: A Systems Approach." In EMERGING PATTERNS IN URBAN ADMINISTRATION, edited by F. Gerald Brown and Thomas P. Murphy, pp. 222-47. Lexington, Mass.: Heath Lexington Books, 1970.

The author is concerned with ways in which urban management might be substantially reorganized with available technologies of analysis and decision making and the increasingly articulated need for greater participation by people in the programs that directly affect them within metropolitan areas. Black develops a very creative application of systems concepts. The methodology developed

by the author makes possible pragmatic, informed judgments about which functions can be decentralized with
efficiency while other key social values are protected.

89 Committee for Economic Development. RESHAPING GOVERNMENT
IN METROPOLITAN AREAS. New York: Research and Policy Committee of the Committee for Economic Development, 1970. 83 p.

  CED advocates the two-tier system of metropolitan government, calls for the use of the reconstituted county
where that unit includes the entire urban area, and
stresses community level responsibility for various functions.
This report also recognizes the problems and obstacles
to government reform in metropolitan areas.

90 Costello, Timothy. "The Change Process in Municipal Government."
In EMERGING PATTERNS IN URBAN ADMINISTRATION, edited by
F. Gerald Brown and Thomas P. Murphy, pp. 13-32. Lexington,
Mass.: Heath Lexington Books, 1970.

  The author focuses upon a variety of ways in which change
occurs in urban public agencies. He emphasizes change
processes rather than prescriptions for preferred outcomes.
Costello provides an overview of the parameters within
which the urban administrator must function and develops
a typology of five major ways in which change in urban
government can come about, giving examples of each way
and discussing ways in which persons close to or involved
in the administrative process can effectively utilize each
type of process.

91 Florestano, Patricia S. "The Municipal Connection: Contracting for
Public Services with the Private Sector." MUNICIPAL MANAGEMENT
1 (Fall 1978): 61-71.

  Florestano's research considers the nature and extent of
contracting with private enterprise in small communities in
Maryland and across the country. The article offers further
input on the safeguards and methods utilized in contracting
and on administrators' views about this practice. The
author reports that less than one-third of twenty-six common
governmental services are being contracted out to the
private sector. The most often contracted services are
those which are interest oriented or depend heavily on
unskilled labor.

92 Gabris, Gerald T., and Reed, B.J. "Responses of Cities to Federal
Aid Decentralization: Community Development." SOUTHERN REVIEW
OF PUBLIC ADMINISTRATION 2 (December 1978): 301-24. Tables.

  This article analyzes how eight small Missouri cities, with

different forms of municipal government, utilized their Community Development Block Grants (CDBG). The authors' findings tend to conform with those studies which indicate that decentralized forms of federal aid are becoming subsidies for local public works projects.

93   Grant, Daniel R. "Political Stability in Metro Government." In EMERGING PATTERNS IN URBAN ADMINISTRATION, edited by F. Gerald Brown and Thomas P. Murphy, pp. 34-63. Lexington, Mass.: Heath Lexington Books, 1970.

The author is concerned with the over-all structuring of a large unit of government encompassing the total metropolitan areas, a unit sometimes called metro government. His essay is a case study of three governments which have adopted metropolitan forms. He reports particularly on the political stability of these forms of government and the factors which have affected that stability.

94   Grubb, W. Norton, and Osman, Jack W. "The Causes of School Finance Inequalities: Serrano and the Case of California." PUBLIC FINANCE QUARTERLY 5 (July 1977): 373-91.

This essay examines the determinants of school revenue and expenditure variation, based on a model of school district behavior, by utilizing data for California unified school districts. The authors review the effects of stratifying the statewide California unified school districts by district size and by wealth. The article declares that the hypotheses of the model prove useful in explaining otherwise puzzling results and presents implications for the Serrano case and legislative reforms.

95   Grundstein, Nathan D. "Future Manpower for Urban Management." In EMERGING PATTERNS IN URBAN ADMINISTRATION, edited by F. Gerald Brown and Thomas P. Murphy, pp. 140-70. Lexington, Mass.: Heath Lexington Books, 1970.

The author believes that the interlocking of three things-- the general design of the organization itself, the technology for managing this structure, and the management competence to realize the potentials of the technology and the organizational design--has never been resolved for the public sector. This essay is on the applicability of these three concepts to the city and metropolitan area.

96   Hawkins, Robert B. "Administration Must Not Supplant Politics in Neighborhood Government." PUBLIUS 6 (Fall 1976): 145-47.

Hawkins asserts that the most rational course of action for New York City advocates of neighborhood government was to abandon efforts to achieve locally governed units and to work within the existing political structure. The idea of centralization of authority and responsibility as a prerequisite for decentralization differs considerably from the conventional idea of centralization.

97   Howitt, Arnold M. "Improving Public Management in Small Communities." SOUTHERN REVIEW OF PUBLIC ADMINISTRATION 2 (December 1978): 325-44.

The author analyzes institutional weaknesses in small communities and spells out options for improving public management in them. These options include increasing the employment of management personnel, improving technical assistance, and improving state-local liaison.

98   Jones, Bryan D. "The Distribution of Urban Public Services: A Preliminary Model." ADMINISTRATION AND SOCIETY 6 (November 1974): 337-60.

Jones states that a general prototype of the local public services distribution process has been developed in that service delivery systems can either discriminate in the distribution of services to city neighborhoods or respond to the needs and demands of citizens. He suggests that the distribution of services may still be cumulative to certain segments of the population and that more theoretical work is necessary in developing a model of service distribution.

99   Kaufman, Herbert. "Robert Moses: Charismatic Bureaucrat." POLITICAL SCIENCE QUARTERLY 90 (Fall 1975): 521-38.

Robert Moses is portrayed as motivated by a desire for power in a recent biography, THE POWER BROKER by Robert Caro (1974). The reader is told that Moses's impact affected not only New York City, but also every city in the country. Kaufman maintains that Moses's methods were grouped into six categories: move quickly and vigorously, supervise personally, discover provisions that add to one's power, affect an imperial style of public life and administration, use public relations methods, and share in patronage. Kaufman states that the Caro book is not a balanced appraisal, that it is an indictment and a prosecutor's brief which is lighted by hindsight and the author's values.

100   Keller, Lawrence F., and Wamsley, Gary L. "Small Government As an Interorganizational Governance Network." SOUTHERN REVIEW OF PUBLIC ADMINISTRATION 2 (December 1978): 277-300.

The authors review several parallel conceptual developments which converge in interorganizational network
analysis. They suggest that a political economy framework can be used to make such analysis more powerful,
generate better behaviorally based hypotheses, and accelerate theory development. Keller and Wamsley delineate the major characteristics of small government and
conclude that the political economy approach confronts
small governments, processes raw materials, and operates
in a political setting which is fundamentally and orga-
nizationally political in nature.

101   Labovitz, I.M. "Federal Expenditures and Revenues in Regions and
       States." INTERGOVERNMENTAL PERSPECTIVE 4 (Fall 1978): 16-23.

       Labovitz asserts that federal revenues and expenditures
       have changed drastically over the last quarter century
       while the yearly volume of federal revenues and expendi-
       tures is now about five times the level of 1952. This
       article reports that payroll taxes and social insurance
       contributions are now a chief source, increasing from less
       than 7 percent of the total in 1952 to 30 percent in
       1974-76.

102   Lakshmanan, T.R. "The New Technical Competence for Urban Man-
       agement." In EMERGING PATTERNS IN URBAN ADMINISTRATION,
       edited by F. Gerald Brown and Thomas P. Murphy, pp. 172-92.
       Lexington, Mass.: Heath Lexington Books, 1970.

       The author discusses applying refined planning technology
       to some urban public policy problems. Lakshmanan pre-
       sents a model for ordering the use of analytic technologies
       in a community.

103   Liebert, Roland J. "The Partial Eclipse of Community Government:
       The Trend toward Functional Specialization." SOCIAL SCIENCE
       QUARTERLY 56 (September 1975): 210-24.

       Liebert states that the increase in the populations of com-
       munities was, in part, dependent on the number of func-
       tions performed. Suburbs came about as municipal illus-
       trations of specialized government with narrow workable
       charters and little likelihood to expand beyond those
       mandates. He indicates that some functions respond
       better to specialization than others.

104   Long, Norton E. "Federalism and Perverse Incentives: What is Needed
       for a Workable Theory of Reorganization for Cities?" PUBLIUS 8
       (Spring 1978): 77-97.

       Long asserts that the city is currently perceived almost

entirely as an institution involved with the consumption
rather than the production of wealth. This article alludes
that it is the unemployment or underemployment of the
city's populace that is the main source of its poverty,
while the municipal leaders must be taught to promote a
full employment program for the community's material and
human resources.

105   _____. "A Marshall Plan for Cities?" PUBLIC INTEREST 46 (Winter
        1977): 48-58.

The possibility of reformed governance in metropolitan

Long notes that the concept of a Marshall Plan for cities
has often been recommended, since the federal government
must help cities develop adequate plans for improving
local economies and should assist in the training and
supply of competent staffs. The article contends that
addressing the difficulties of the cities requires a politics
of civic and moral reconstruction that far transcends
central business district renewal, mass transit, low-interest
loans, or the shifting of the burden of welfare to the
shoulders of the national government.

106   Mogulof, Melvin B. "A Modest Proposal for the Governance of
        America's Metropolitan Areas." JOURNAL OF THE AMERICAN IN-
        STITUTE OF PLANNERS 41 (July 1975): 250-57.

The possibility of reformed governance in metropolitan
areas remains an interesting choice on the American urban
setting. Multifunctional capacity, a geographic scope
approximating the urban area, broader taxing potential,
and authority are the necessary four components. To a
certain extent, these are available in a number of re-
vamped areas like the Toronto area and Dade County,
Florida. The experience of these areas is viewed as a
prototype for city legislation which would consist of 1)
local components of government able to facilitate decisions
about the make-up and responsiveness of public services;
2) regional unique purpose districts; 3) metropolitan gov-
erning councils possessing power to restrain local governments and special districts; and 4) state government capable
of serving as a mediator between local and regional governments.

107   Morgan, David R. MANAGING URBAN AMERICA: THE POLITICS
        AND ADMINISTRATION OF AMERICA'S CITIES. North Scituate, Mass.:
        Duxbury Press, 1979. xii, 333 p.

Morgan's approach in this textbook is essentially descriptive
and "frankly academic." He attempts to present "the best
current information on how cities are administered," emphasizing that "this is not a nuts-and-bolts handbook or

a collection of how-to admonitions." His basic purpose is to combine the best available academic information on the subject and to illustrate how the world of urban managers really works. Sections include the environment of urban management, making and implementing urban policy, internal management processes, and planning and the urban future.

108   Moynihan, Daniel P. MAXIMUM FEASIBLE MISUNDERSTANDING: COMMUNITY ACTION IN THE WAR ON POVERTY. New York: The Free Press, 1969. xxi, 218 p.

Moynihan outlines the background for the poverty program with reference to the necessity for the greatest possible involvement of the poor. Social scientists are reprimanded for inadequate preparation before postulating the policy that destitution was a consequence of "powerlessness." The author maintains that the only confirmed relationship was that such a policy would produce friction in community action programs. The key thrust of the book is a historical treatment of the poverty program from idea to utilization, while also exploring the desire for community in America, the professionalization of reform, and the position of social science in social policy.

109   Mudd, John. "Beyond Community Control: A Neighborhood Strategy for City Government." PUBLIUS 6 (Fall 1976): 113-35.

Mudd states that the thrust of the decentralization movement of the past ten years has been almost exclusively directed toward increased citizen participation, or political decentralization, and that this focus has led to the demand for local control of the public schools and ultimately to various proposals for full-scale neighborhood government. Beginning in 1970, the Office of Neighborhood Government in New York City has struggled with the problem of administrative decentralization as a technique to increase the effectiveness of municipal service delivery in neighborhoods and to establish a foundation for possible political decentralization in the future.

110   Murphy, Thomas P. "Ethical Dilemmas for Urban Administrators." URBANISM PAST AND PRESENT 4 (Summer 1977): 33-40.

Murphy asserts that administrative responsibility is a complex issue and that public employees must share in establishing standards for their own professions. The article maintains that responsibility extends beyond usual operating methods that ethical predicaments can be avoided if public officials would disqualify themselves from situations in which personal interests are included.

111   _____. "Intergovernmental Management of Urban Problems in the
Kansas City Metropolitan Area." In EMERGING PATTERNS IN URBAN
ADMINISTRATION, edited by F. Gerald Brown and Thomas P. Murphy,
pp. 248-75. Lexington, Mass.: Heath Lexington Books, 1970.

> The author develops a detailed metropolitan study covering
> the governmental institutions and public policy issues in
> the Kansas City metropolitan area. He reviews the state
> of development of metropolitan institutions and the expan-
> sion of intergovernmental cooperation.

112   Murphy, Thomas P., and Florestano, Patricia. "Allocation of Urban
Governmental Functions." In ORGANIZING PUBLIC SERVICES IN
METROPOLITAN AMERICA, edited by Thomas P. Murphy and Charles
R. Warren, pp. 85-105. Lexington, Mass.: Lexington Books, 1974.
Table.

> According to the authors, general criteria for allocation
> of functions include the nature of the activity, the scope
> of the problem, the costs, the cost basis, and govern-
> mental environment. They review rationales for allocation
> of functions in transportation, water supply and sewerage,
> welfare, police departments, hospitals, fire protection,
> housing and urban renewal, recreation, sanitation, libraries,
> and planning.

113   Murphy, Thomas P., and Zarnowiecki, James. "The Urban Observatory:
A University-City Research Venture." In UNIVERSITIES IN THE URBAN
CRISIS, edited by Thomas P. Murphy, pp. 15-47. New York: Dunellen
Publishing Co., 1975.

> The authors cite the need for systematic urban data, give
> details of the Urban Observatory proposal, posit operational
> objectives and criteria for selecting cities, offer ways of
> organizing local programs and comprehensive research
> efforts, review local agenda items, profile Urban Observa-
> tory cities, and describe the role of the National Academy
> of Public Administration.

114   Muskie, Edmund S. "Urban Administration and Creative Federalism."
In EMERGING PATTERNS IN URBAN ADMINISTRATION, edited by
F. Gerald Brown and Thomas P. Murphy, pp. 83-98. Lexington,
Mass.: Heath Lexington Books, 1970.

> The author discusses the evolutionary process whereby in-
> struments have been and are being designed to deal re-
> sponsibly with urban problems through governmental struc-
> tures. He notes the importance of new regional institu-
> tions emanating from the Water Quality Act and the Clean
> Air Act, realistically discusses the added value that states
> can provide in the formation of urban policies and inter-

governmental grant programs, and elaborates on the kind of federal machinery that might effectively provide the most creative role for the federal government in the urban problem-solving process.

115   Nigro, Lloyd G., and DeMarco, John J. "Training in Local Governments: Attitudes and Practices." SOUTHERN REVIEW OF PUBLIC ADMINISTRATION 2 (March 1979): 475-87. Tables.

The authors point out that public personnel administration has not addressed, in any serious or systematic way, the problems and possibilities of the smaller jurisdictions.

116   Rapp, Brian, and Patitucci, Frank. "Improving the Performance of City Government: A Third Alternative." PUBLIUS 6 (Fall 1976): 63-91.

The authors declare that a third alternative available to local government officials confronted with soaring costs and increased demands for more and better services, aside from raising taxes or cutting back services, is that of increasing the capacity of local officials to use available resources more efficiently and effectively. The article suggests that strengthening the management process can improve the performance of any institution, public or private.

117   Reeves, Mavis Mann. "Change and Fluidity: Intergovernmental Relations in Low Cost Housing--Montgomery County, Maryland." PUBLIUS 4 (Winter 1974): 5-44.

The author states that the agencies involved in Montgomery County housing are constantly changing organization, structures, and personnel. He maintains that until functional consolidation takes place, an interpersonal, fluid, dynamic relationship is all that can be expected by agencies providing low cost housing.

118   Rogers, Theresa F., and Friedman, Nathalie. "Decentralizing City Government: The Citizen Survey as a Guide for Planning and Implementing Institutional Change." ADMINISTRATION AND SOCIETY 10 (August 1978): 177-202.

The authors analyze citizen evaluations of two alternative forms of decentralizing city government--administrative and political--from the perspective of the respondents' ethnicity, the socioeconomic composition of their neighborhoods, and their appraisal of the delivery of essential city services. Rogers and Friedman collect data from a sample of 1,288 residents in selected Community Planning Districts in New York City. They point out that the strongest commitment to decentralization comes from residents most dissatisfied with current service delivery and from a small but politically active segment of the public.

119   Roos, Lawrence K., and Kelly, Thomas C. "Executive Leadership in the Urban County." In EMERGING PATTERNS IN URBAN ADMINISTRATION, edited by F. Gerald Brown and Thomas P. Murphy, pp. 112-23. Lexington, Mass.: Heath Lexington Books, 1970.

The authors contribute a lively exchange on the management of urban counties. This essay deals with application of urban management competencies in two very different urban areas under different forms of government--St. Louis County, Missouri, and Prince George's County, Maryland. The number of parallels is striking as both county administrators agree on the pivotal role of urban counties in metropolitan areas and on the value of councils of governments.

120   Rowe, Lloyd A. "The Coming Crisis of the Urban Administrator." MIDWEST REVIEW OF PUBLIC ADMINISTRATION 5 (August 1971): 105-9.

The author illustrates trends that appear certain to create crisis situations for the urban administrator due to the conflicting values implicit in existing governmental and social systems. Rowe concludes that the administrator has at least two points of attack, both of which require cooperative efforts of a participatory nature and reevaluating the role of the professional administrator.

121   Shapek, Raymond A. "Federal Influences in State and Local Personnel Management: The System in Transition." PUBLIC PERSONNEL MANAGEMENT 5 (January-February 1976): 41-52.

This article discusses three factors which have caused human resource management to become an important issue for local and state governments in the 1970s: the quickly growing state and local government employment and payroll costs, making human resources the most expensive part of government; new national laws which have made the roles of public managers more complex; and new and wider management responsibilities caused by complex rules and regulations in federal grants-in-aid.

122   Snyder, James C. "Financial Management and Planning in Local Government." ATLANTA ECONOMIC REVIEW 23 (November-December 1973): 43-47.

Snyder states 1) that the method of planning deals with the procedure rather than the end result, 2) that it involves

a change from the customary line item to grouping which
reflects efforts aimed at particular public objectives, 3)
that it involves scientific methodology, and 4) that it
introduces an extended time horizon into the customary
annual budgeting technique. The reader is given three
interrelated responses to the problems: extend the goals
and objectives formulation function from land use to incorporate all major public services, institute a current
issues analysis capability, and formulate ten- to twenty-
year estimates of revenues and expenditures.

123   Stone, Clarence N.; Whelan, Robert K.; and Murin, William J.
      URBAN POLICY AND POLITICS IN A BUREAUCRATIC AGE. Engle-
      wood Cliffs, N.J.: Prentice-Hall, 1979. xiv, 399 p.

      The authors cover a wide variety of topics including
      leadership, political organization, major policy questions,
      and the bureaucracy problem. This text is an overview
      of urban policy, politics, and administration that shows
      the need for understanding the micropolitics of organiza-
      tions as well as the macropolitics of the larger community.
      The book examines the changing urban political scene
      and describes the still emerging prereform style of politics.

124   "Team Management in Local Government." MANAGEMENT INFOR-
      MATION SERVICE REPORT 5 (July 1973): 1-12.

      Team management involves people in a mode of decision
      formation and mutual work. Group dynamics, problem
      resolution, and organizational development are approaches
      and principles contained within the concept. The approach
      is organized around four premises: 1) group decision making
      is more effective than individual decision making; 2) co-
      operation is superior to competition; 3) awareness is better
      than no knowledge; and 4) agreement is better than discord.
      Four requirements for team management to be efficient
      are: 1) the team laboring together; 2) personal and group
      skill development; 3) technical support employing the
      tools of management technology and information programs;
      and 4) the task initiation of the team.

125   Unruh, Jesse M.   "State Government and the Urban Crisis." In
      EMERGING PATTERNS IN URBAN ADMINISTRATION, edited by F.
      Gerald Brown and Thomas P. Murphy, pp. 100-111. Lexington, Mass.:
      Heath Lexington Books, 1970.

      The author, a former Speaker of the General Assembly of
      California, discusses viable means for strengthening the
      institutions of state government suitable to the problems
      of the 1970s. He finds the success of federal programs
      for the poor questionable and urges states to take the initiative

and formulate rules of the urban game with which citizens
can better identify.

126   West, Jonathan P., and Davis, Charles. "Images of Public Admini-
       stration: A Study of Supervisors in a Metropolitan Bureaucracy."
       PUBLIC PERSONNEL MANAGEMENT 7 (September-October 1978):
       316-22.

           The authors examine models of public administration main-
           tained by local government administrators in the city of
           Tucson, Arizona. They reveal the impacts of sex, parti-
           sanship, ethnicity, political jurisdiction, education, and
           job satisfaction on perceptions of government administra-
           tion and length of tenure. The article suggests that dis-
           satisfied supervisors tend to project their negative attitudes
           onto the employing organization. It concludes by requesting
           more research on the elements affecting supervisors' and
           employees' views of public administration and consequences
           for government functions.

127   Williams, Robert L. "The Planning Role in Urban Decision-Making."
       In EMERGING PATTERNS IN URBAN ADMINISTRATION, edited by
       F. Gerald Brown and Thomas P. Murphy, pp. 127-39. Lexington,
       Mass.: Heath Lexington Books, 1970.

           Williams discusses the role of urban planning and planners
           in the urban administrative process. He places the plan-
           ning movement in historical context and outlines the prag-
           matic contribution of the planning profession. He intro-
           duces some of the tools of planning and decision making
           that are now being put to urban use.

128   Wood, Robert C. "Federal Role in the Urban Environment." PUBLIC
       ADMINISTRATION REVIEW 28 (July-August 1968): 341-47.

           How do we provide a decent living environment--housing,
           schools, public facilities, recreational areas--for the 20
           million Americans presently living in slum areas? How
           do we overcome generations of inability to feel a sense
           of belonging to a community? How do we offer free
           accessibility to decent housing in all parts of the urban
           area? How do we build housing in sufficient volume to
           meet our national goal of a decent house for every American
           family? The author, a former under secretary of the De-
           partment of Housing and Urban Development, discusses
           the role of HUD in meeting needs raised in the questions
           above.

Chapter 2
GOVERNMENTAL DIVISIONS
AND THE ADMINISTRATIVE PROCESS

A. THEORIES OF DEMOCRATIC GOVERNMENT

129   Appleby, Paul H. BIG DEMOCRACY. New York: Alfred A. Knopf,
        1945. viii, 197 p.

        Appleby makes suggestions for enhancing the utility of
        public programs based upon twelve years of involvement
        with the federal government. He criticizes the limitations
        of the administrative science movement and advocates the
        creation of politically determined programs through the
        coordination process. Appleby sees democratic values
        protected through the elimination of the willful use of
        bureaucratic power. His solution is the correct organiza-
        tion of government positions. This book foretells the
        demise of the policy-administration dichotomy and an-
        ticipates the future stress upon the coordinated public
        programs of the 1960s.

130   Bennett, George. "The Public Interest and Public Unions." PUBLIC
        PERSONNEL MANAGEMENT 3 (November-December 1974): 545-50.

        Bennett suggests that management's continuing responsibility
        is to be accountable in decision making while enhancing
        public authority's capability to deliver and improve the
        quality of service, at a cost that can be met within an
        available budget. He believes that public unions cannot
        assume that management will make the right decisions
        about cost, efficiency, productivity, and the scope of
        service and that the union must be involved in these
        decisions.

131   Browne, William P. "Organizational Maintenance: The Internal
        Operation of Interest Groups." PUBLIC ADMINISTRATION REVIEW
        37 (January-February 1977): 48-57.

        The author focuses on urban interest groups as bureaucratic

organizations. He examines staff attitudes and behavior
and finds that a great deal of attention must be directed
toward the nonlobbying wants and needs of the members.

132   Deutsch, Karl. THE NERVES OF GOVERNMENT. New York: Free
       Press, 1963. 316 p.

       This book presents the most important cybernetics model
       in the policy sciences, discussing a theoretical analysis
       of communications, political control, and social and po-
       litical development. Government is depicted as less a
       problem of power than a problem of "steering," which is
       primarily a situation of communication. The author re-
       views the capability of a political organization to re-
       arrange the learning of information and how the ideas of
       "will" and power may be used to close off systems from
       information incompatible with preordained goals. A re-
       view of existing theories and models in political science,
       concepts in cybernetics applied to political and social
       behavior, and the presentation of his political decision-
       making model based on communications theory comprise
       the three sections of the book.

133   Downs, Anthony. AN ECONOMIC THEORY OF DEMOCRACY. New
       York: Harper, 1957. 310 p.

       This is an exploratory study in political science and
       public policy analysis. The author puts forth an example
       of democratic elections and coalition-building formed upon
       welfare economics, which posits a logical voter with a
       sample of ordered preferences and political parties whose
       sole purpose is to win elections. Downs discusses the
       problems of information and uncertainty in this theoretical
       parliamentary democracy and discovers a recurring conflict
       between individual utility and sane social policy. The
       concluding chapter offers a description of party-motivation
       and citizen rationality and compares this to the existing
       democracies as a test of the applicability of this "economic"
       prototype.

134   Eimicke, William B. PUBLIC ADMINISTRATION IN A DEMOCRATIC
       CONTEXT: THEORY AND PRACTICE. Beverly Hills, Calif.: Sage,
       1974. 62 p.

       Eimicke identifies many concrete problems connected with
       operationalizing democracy in modern America: gerry-
       mandering and partisan reapportionments, the seniority
       system in Congress, increasing complexity and specializa-
       tion in government. He concludes that the preeminent
       danger is a growing bureaucracy increasingly dominated
       by professional experts who are unresponsive to the public

interest. The American answer to the size and scope of
modern democracy has been pluralism.

135   Etzioni, Amitai. THE ACTIVE SOCIETY: A THEORY OF SOCIETAL
AND POLITICAL PROCESS. New York: Free Press, 1968. xxv,
698 p.

Etzioni progresses into the arena of value-laden, relevant
research in exploring the situations under which societies
attain various degrees of self-control, such as capacity
for alteration and sensitivity to fluctuating memberships.
The author's goal is to diminish estrangement resulting
from alterations in the technology of production or human
values. The book covers a theory of the active society,
knowledge and cybernetics, power, the consensus-building
process in society, and international societies. The author reviews and rearranges existing theories and thought
trends and concludes that project-oriented societal structures best satisfy human needs.

136   Gawthrop, Louis C., ed. THE ADMINISTRATIVE PROCESS AND
DEMOCRATIC THEORY. Boston: Houghton Mifflin Co., 1970. vii,
446 p.

Gawthrop states that "the purpose of this volume is to
trace the development of certain basic concepts and
premises of the public administration process in the U.S.
and to relate these concepts and premises to various
principles of democratic theory." In this book of readings,
the editor includes selections on the normative pendulum
of public administration, historical antecedents, administration as management science, administration as politics,
administration as interpersonal behavior, administration
and incrementalism, administration and analytic methods,
the politics of analysis, and administration as turbulence.

137   Goodnow, Frank J. POLITICS AND ADMINISTRATION: A STUDY
IN GOVERNMENT. New York: Russell and Russell, 1900. Reprint.
New York: Atheneum, 1967. xiii, 270 p.

This text sets forth the role of public sector administration
in American society at the beginning of the twentieth
century. Goodnow discusses the primary functions of the
state, the function of politics, the functions of central
and local politics, the function of administration, the
effects of the administrative system on the relations of
politics and administration, the political party boss, and
the responsibility of political parties in a public administration classic.

138   Gross, Bertram M. "An Organized Society." PUBLIC ADMINISTRA-
       TION REVIEW 33 (July-August 1973): 323-27.

       The author discusses the difficulties in recognizing the
       'organized society' and posits these proverbs for the era
       of the emerging Organized Society: 1) never talk principles
       in public; 2) strengthen that elite structure; 3) advance
       the opportunities for a careerist meritocracy; 4) recognize
       the power realities of other countries; 5) provide more
       participation at the local level; 6) encourage more posi-
       tivistic social science.

139   Gulick, Peter R. "Governance Arrangements and Governmental Per-
       formance." MIDWEST REVIEW OF PUBLIC ADMINISTRATION 9
       (October 1975): 173-86.

       The author describes proposals for governance reform, in-
       cluding the "good government" movement by advocates of
       city manager government, consolidation of governments in
       metropolitan areas, and decentralization of governmental
       organizations. He reviews the accomplishments of gov-
       ernmental reform approaches and suggests alternatives to
       governance reform.

140   Herring, E. Pendleton. PUBLIC ADMINISTRATION AND THE PUBLIC
       INTEREST. New York: McGraw-Hill, 1936. xii, 416 p.

       This book covers the economic and political view of
       public administration. The author looks at the control of
       economic life by governmental bureaucracy and the results
       for the democratic way of life. Herring cautions against
       the control of administration by structured minorities,
       encouraging the government to maintain a federal planning
       commission which is beyond the competition of special
       interest groups. Case studies set forth the problems of
       defending public administrators against the propaganda of
       politicians and lobbyists. The Federal Trade Commission,
       Interstate Commerce Commission, the Internal Revenue
       Service, the Departments of Labor, Commerce, State,
       and Agriculture are reviewed in this book.

141   Hyneman, Charles S. BUREAUCRACY IN A DEMOCRACY. New York:
       Harper and Brothers, 1950. Reprint. New York: AMS Press, 1978.
       xv, 586 p.

       This public administration classic stresses the importance
       of bureaucracy in the structure of democratic government.
       Hyneman asks: "What can we do to increase our assurance
       that the officials and employees who do the day to day
       work of government will actually provide the kind of
       government the American people want?" Sections of this

volume include the reality and ideal of bureaucracy and democracy, direction and control by Congress, direction and control by the President, the central staff agencies, direction and control within the administrative organization, and unification of political direction and control. Hyneman advocates the creation of a Central Council which would be composed of leaders of that party which has been given the responsibility for running the government.

142   Kaufman, Herbert. ARE GOVERNMENT ORGANIZATIONS IMMORTAL? Washington, D.C.: Brookings Institution, 1976. 79 p.

This book is an exploratory effort to get facts about the birth, longevity, and death of government organizations. Kaufman examines the major components of seven executive departments of the federal government in 1923 and compares that group with their counterparts in 1973. He inquires into some of the factors that produce and destroy government organizations and into some of the proposals for limiting their numbers. The author's findings lend weight to the belief in the hardiness of government organizations.

143   Levitan, Sar A., and Taggart, Robert. "The Great Society Did Succeed." POLITICAL SCIENCE QUARTERLY 91 (Winter 1977): 601-18.

Levitan and Taggart assert that a careful reexamination of the evidence for the complete spectrum of the 1960s social welfare initiatives suggests that the conventional wisdom of the Great Society's failure is wrong. They analyze a vast array of program data, evaluations, and related statistics and challenge the widespread negativism toward governmental social welfare efforts. They conclude that the goals of the Great Society were realistic, if steadily moving, targets for the improvement of the nation, that the social welfare efforts initiated and accelerated in the 1960s moved the nation toward a more just and equitable society, that the Great Society's social welfare programs were reasonably efficient, and that there was frequently no alternative to active intervention, that the negative spillovers of social welfare efforts were often overstated and were usually the unavoidable concomitants of the desired changes, that the benefits of the Great Society programs were more than the sum of their parts, and more than the impact on immediate participants and beneficiaries, and that there is no reason to fear the modest steps which are positive and constructive in alleviating age-old problems.

144   Lewis, Eugene. AMERICAN POLITICS IN A BUREAUCRATIC AGE:
       CITIZENS, CONSTITUENTS, CLIENTS AND VICTIMS. Cambridge,
       Mass.: Winthrop Publishers, 1977. ix, 182 p. Paper.

> This textbook integrates a series of participation concepts
> with a notion of public bureaucracy somewhat different
> from those typically found in the public administration
> literature. Lewis presents a theoretical structure which
> deals with bureaucratic elaboration in terms of identified
> historical changes in political values. The focus of this
> text is generally directed at those points at which public
> bureaucracies interact with their environments. The au-
> thor construes organizations as actors and places emphasis
> on internal characteristics significant to policy-making
> processes. Chapters include public bureaucracy in every-
> day life, a conceptual framework, and analyses of political
> economy, of social welfare and control, of national defense,
> and of the evolving bureaucratic state.

145   Lindblom, Charles E. THE INTELLIGENCE OF DEMOCRACY: DE-
       CISION MAKING THROUGH MUTUAL ADJUSTMENT. New York:
       Free Press, 1965. viii, 352 p.

> Lindblom applies the concept of mutual adjustment through
> markets to political negotiating in government. He con-
> tends that people can adapt to each other without being
> dominated by a mutual purpose or listed rules. He pro-
> jects an advanced concept of pluralism that involves
> methods of party adaptability, dual prototypes of govern-
> ment (centralist and pluralist), the employment of common
> adjustment for logical decision making, the failings of
> designated central coordination, and the way be which
> mutual adjustment sets forth a balance of values in the
> political arena. Lindblom cites cases from American
> government.

146   Long, Norton E. THE POLITY. Edited with introduction by Charles
       Press. Chicago: Rand McNally and Co., 1962. xiv, 247 p.

> This book contains a selection from the articles written
> by Professor Long from the mid-1930s until the early
> 1960s. Long's essays cover rationality and responsibility
> in policy making, politics and the economy, the politics
> of the metropolis, and the study of local government.
> This book includes the significant works of one of the
> discipline's most original thinkers with regard to politics
> and administration, covering issues from the Great De-
> pression to the Kennedy administration.

147   Lowi, Theodore J. THE END OF LIBERALISM: THE SECOND RE-
       PUBLIC OF THE UNITED STATES. 1969. 2d ed. New York: W.W.
       Norton and Co., 1979. 331 p.

Lowi's main argument is that the liberal state grew to its
immense size and presence without self-examination and
without recognizing that its pattern of growth has prob-
lematic consequences. He concludes that the government
expanded by responding to the demands of all major organized interests, by assuming responsibility for programs
sought by those interests, and by assigning that responsibility to administrative agencies. Lowi states that the
agencies became captives of the interest groups via cli-
entelism and through a process of accommodation. This
is a highly recommended book for both students and practitioners of public administration.

148   Martin, Roscoe C., ed. PUBLIC ADMINISTRATION AND DEMOCRACY:
ESSAYS IN HONOR OF PAUL H. APPLEBY. Syracuse, N.Y.: Syracuse
University Press, 1965. vii, 355 p.

Fifteen major scholars in public administration offer articles
stressing the value-laden technique which Paul H. Appleby
brought to the scrutiny of the public sector of administration. These essays treat the study of public administration, basic processes of administration, public administration and people, comparative public administration, and
morality in administration.

149   Meltzer, Alan H., and Richard, Scott F. "Why Government Grows
(and Grows) in a Democracy." PUBLIC INTEREST 52 (Summer 1978):
111-18.

In this article, the authors review varying reasons for the
rapid government growth in a democratic milieu and posit
that government continues to accelerate because there is
a considerable difference between political and market
processes. The article relates that politicians have a
tendency to attract voters with incomes near the median
by offering benefits that impose a net cost on those with
incomes above the median and that the redistributive programs change from place to place and time to time as the
makeup of the electorate fluctuates.

150   Mitnick, Barry M. "A Typology of Conceptions of the Public Interest."
ADMINISTRATION AND SOCIETY 8 (May 1976): 5-28.

The author classifies public interest conceptions. The
conceptions include public interest preferences and agreement among them, appearance and intensity of the persons'
preferences, participation of public interest units in certain actions, and rules or nonrules in public interest determination. Mitnick argues that the construction of
typologies aids the development of a general theory of
public interest conceptions.

151   Mosher, Frederick C. DEMOCRACY AND THE PUBLIC SERVICE.
        New York: Oxford University Press, 1968. xii, 219 p.

        Mosher's premises are that "governmental decisions and
        behavior have tremendous influence upon the nature and
        development of our society, our economy, and our policy;
        the great bulk of decisions and actions taken by govern-
        ments are determined or heavily influenced by administrative
        officials, most of whom are appointed, not elected; the
        kinds of decisions and actions these officials take depend
        upon their capabilities, their orientations, and their
        values; and these attributes depend heavily upon their
        backgrounds, their training and education, and their
        current associations." The focus of this volume, a classic
        in public personnel administration, is upon the public
        service and its relation to democracy as an idea and a
        manner of governing. Chapter discussions include educa-
        tion and public service, the evolution of American
        civil service concepts, the professional state, three systems
        of merit, the collective services, and merit, morality,
        and democracy.

152   Murray, Michael A. "Comparing Public and Private Management:
        An Exploratory Essay." PUBLIC ADMINISTRATION REVIEW 35 (July-
        August 1975): 364-71.

        The author reviews substantive issues (fact vs. value,
        measurable objectives, government vs. business attitudes)
        and procedural issues (accountability factor, evaluation
        techniques, rational man vs. political man, personnel
        systems, planning, efficiency), and concludes that there
        is more blurring than bifurcation on substantive issues and
        distinctions but not differences on procedural issues.

153   Nurick, Lloyd. "Access to Public Records: Strengthening Democracy."
        BUREAUCRAT 4 (April 1975): 34-44.

        Nurick relates that until passage of the Freedom of Infor-
        mation Law in 1974, New York's laws on public access
        to records were vague and often necessitated court inter-
        pretation. The New York law is significantly different
        from the federal law as New York's basic approach is
        that not all records are available but only those covered
        by this legislation.

154   Peters, B. Guy. "Insiders and Outsiders: The Politics of Pressure
        Group Influence on Bureaucracy." ADMINISTRATION AND SOCIETY
        9 (August 1977): 191-218.

        This article declares that interest groups and public ad-
        ministration are both universal components of political

life and that their interaction is crucial for an understanding of the formation of public policy. Peters discusses four categories of interaction between pressure groups and bureaucracy--legitimate, clientele, parantela, and illegitimate.

155   Presthus, Robert V. THE ORGANIZATIONAL SOCIETY: AN ANALYSIS AND A THEORY. New York: Alfred A. Knopf, 1962. 323 p.

This general composition on big bureaucracies draws upon the concepts of C. Wright Mills and psychological studies of neurosis and anxiety. The text pessimistically conveys the Marxian opinion that bureaucratic structures juggle and dehumanize their members. Mobile ascendancy, ambivalence, and indifference are described as three overall systems by which people accommodate themselves to organizational pressures. The nonproductive effect organizational demands have upon personal initiative, the bureaucratic prototype, the development of the corporate society, and the sociology-psychology of structured societies are covered in this book.

156   Redford, Emmette S. DEMOCRACY IN THE ADMINISTRATIVE STATE. New York: Oxford University Press, 1969. x, 211 p.

The purpose of this book is to reconcile the practice of effective democracy with the positive and energetic public administration required by the modern state. Redford examines the potentialities for democracy in the places where decisions are made and carried out via administrative institutions. Chapters include discussions of democratic morality, public policy and the political system, reflections on the administrative state, interaction in the national administrative system, micropolitics and subsystem politics, the macropolitical system, man as subject of administration, man as worker in organization, and the administrative state in perspective.

157   Ricks, Artel. "Managing Government Paperwork." BUREAUCRAT 4 (October 1975): 268-85.

Records management was formalized in the federal government with the Federal Records Act of 1950, which required every agency to possess an active and continuing program to handle its records. Ricks believes that if pending legislation becomes law, the ultimate effect will be to increase the quality and quantity of attention given paperwork by agencies and to produce substantial benefits to the taxpayers. The author concludes that records management is a still emerging and ever-changing process and that it will change as modifications in the means and forms

of communication take place and as new technologies for
recording information evolve.

158   Schubert, Glendon A. THE PUBLIC INTEREST. New York: Free
Press, 1960. 244 p.

> The focus of responsibility for political decision making
> is the theme of this book. The author defines three ap-
> proaches to an interpretation of the public interest: ra-
> tionalists see a political system in which rules are given
> and government officers incorporate them into public
> works; perfectionists believe in a corporate public whose
> interests must be found through authoritative social plan-
> ning; realists consider the part of public officers as the
> negotiators of arguments developing from spoken interests.
> Within this structure, he considers what twentieth-century
> scholars say about Congress, the presidency, administra-
> tion, the judiciary, and the public with its parties and
> interest groups.

159   Shariff, Zahid. "How Big is Big Government?" SOCIAL POLICY 8
(March-April 1978): 22-27.

> Whether revealed as opposition to taxes or fear of tyranny,
> the author asserts that antigovernment sentiment often
> stands for opposition to programs and policies of the federal
> government that strive to minimize inequalities or increase
> human freedoms. Shariff compares ten indicators of the
> size of the federal government for the years 1947-77.
> The indicators span from gross national product to the per
> capita federal outlays for a given year.

160   Sorauf, Frank J. "The Silent Revolution in Patronage." PUBLIC AD-
MINISTRATION REVIEW 20 (Winter 1960): 28-34.

> Sorauf argues that the trend of declining patronage will
> affect not only local politics but the national party system
> and the entire political process. He concludes that pa-
> tronage does not meet the needs of present day party
> operations, that patronage is no longer the potent in-
> ducement to party activity that it once was, and that
> incentives once provided by patronage are being replaced
> in the political system. He believes that the case against
> patronage, based largely on the need for administrative
> expertise and professionalism, is overwhelming.

161   Thompson, James D. "Social Interdependence, the Polity, and Public
Administration." ADMINISTRATION AND SOCIETY 6 (May 1974):
3-20.

The author states that when the society attains the degree of interdependence sufficient to warrant full-fledged bureaucracy, it is bordering on specialized interdependence. He believes that where action is taken through pluralistic decision processes, the polity must create more sophisticated infrastructures.

162   _____. "Society's Frontiers for Organizing Activities." PUBLIC ADMINISTRATION REVIEW 33 (July-August 1973): 327-35.

Two fundamental assumptions underpin the author's discussion: " 1) Complex organizations were invented, have existed, and will continue to exist because they are tools for doing what must be done or what most of us want done, and we judge them to be doing more good than harm; 2) Human desires will not be fundamentally different in 2000 than they have been through the 20th century."

163   Truman, David B. THE GOVERNMENTAL PROCESS: POLITICAL INTERESTS AND PUBLIC OPINION. Rev. ed. New York: Alfred A. Knopf, 1971. xlviii, 544, xv p.

The revision of this classic text, one of the most influential in political science, is a systematic study of interest groups and their function in the governmental process. Truman analyzes the whole range of American politics through an examination of politically relevant groups. His introduction discusses events in the governmental process since publication of his earlier edition in 1951. Sections of this text include groups in the political process, group organization and problems of leadership, and the tactics of influence. A central purpose of this volume, besides that of analyzing the role of interest groups in American politics, is to account for and to indicate the necessary conditions for the long-term survival of the system in the context of interest-group conflict.

164   U.S. General Services Administration. National Archives and Records Service. Office of the Federal Registrar. UNITED STATES GOVERNMENT MANUAL. Washington, D.C.: Government Printing Office, 1935-- . Annual.

This manual is the official handbook of the federal government. It describes the purposes and programs of most government departments and agencies and lists key officials. Briefer statements are included for the quasi-official agencies and certain international organizations. Department and agency descriptions emphasize programs and activities rather than internal agency structure. This document is very useful for understanding the institutional and programmatic arrangements of the federal government.

It is recommended to all students and practitioners of public administration.

165   Wynia, Bob L. "Federal Bureaucrats' Attitudes Toward a Democratic Ideology." PUBLIC ADMINISTRATION REVIEW 34 (March-April 1974): 156-62.

From questionnaires sent to 405 federal executives representing 52 different federal agencies and all geographic areas of the country, Wynia reveals that the attitude scale items included "rules of the game," "support for general statements of free speech and opinion," "belief in equality," "political cynicism," and "sense of political futility," and that the findings indicate that democratic principles and beliefs seem to be learned over time. He maintains that the data supports the need to have a system for moving federal executives regularly across agency lines, making for a variety of experiences and environments and allowing for the development of a more balanced set of attitudes.

B. BUREAUCRACY

166   Bendix, Reinhard. "Bureaucracy." In INTERNATIONAL ENCYCLO-PEDIA OF THE SOCIAL SCIENCES, edited by David L. Sills, pp. 206-19. New York: Macmillan Co. and Free Press, 1968.

This essay deals with the historical development of bureaucracy as a mode of government. The author discusses the modern type of bureaucracy, the development of European bureaucracies, administrative reform in England, developing areas of bureaucracy, bureaucracy in Communist countries, problems of modern bureaucracy, political control of public officials, bureaucratic culture patterns, bureaucracy and accountability, legislative and executive supervision, the influence of interest groups, and the study of bureaucracy in an excellent review of the literature. This essay is especially useful for the beginning student in public administration.

167   Benveniste, Guy. BUREAUCRACY. San Francisco: Boyd and Fraser Publishing Co., 1977. 247 p.

Written for practitioners, for those who aspire to become planners, for those who hire planners and for those who distrust them, the author attempts to blend political insights with first-hand knowledge of planning in government and industry. Benveniste assumes that there is a universal culture of organizations that transcends political or economic ideologies of the Left or of the Right. He assumes that control, rewards, punishment, careers, promotions, corruption, errors, and fear exist anywhere modern bureaucratic structures are established. The author addresses the current bureaucratic crisis, reviews current remedies, and presents new approaches about thinking about the future of bureaucracy.

168   Blau, Peter M. THE DYNAMICS OF BUREAUCRACY. Chicago: University of Chicago Press, 1955. 322 p.

This is a noteworthy study dealing with the sociology of bureaucracy. The author reviews the activities of low-level officers in two bureaucratic settings. He examines the adjustment of behavior following the introduction of statistical performance records in a subunit of a state employment agency and relaxed work assignments among twenty subunit members of a district office in a federal law enforcement agency. The informal, work-enhancing conduct of the federal bureaucrats produces thoroughness, but violates departmental rules. The final assertion is that bureaucracy does not naturally resist alteration, unless status security is threatened.

169   Blau, Peter M., and Meyer, Marshall W. BUREAUCRACY IN MODERN SOCIETY. Rev. ed. New York: Random House, 1971. viii, 180 p.

This revision of the 1956 edition by Blau conveys important lessons about the apparently paradoxical role of bureaucracy in contemporary society. Blau and Meyer explore reasons for studying bureaucracy, examine the theory and development of bureaucracy, review bureaucracy in process, analyze bureaucratic authority, explore the comparative study of organizations, probe bureaucracy and social change, observe the transformation of bureaucracy, and relate bureaucracy and democracy.

170   Dimock, Marshall E. "Bureaucracy Self-Examined." PUBLIC ADMINISTRATION REVIEW 4 (Summer 1944): 197-207.

Dimock examines complexity, size, organization, specialization, rules and regulations, character of executive direction, improper staff activity, central staff controls, group introversion, lack of sales motive, security, seniority, age, and tradition as institutional and administrative factors characterizing bureaucracy. He defines bureaucracy "as the composite institutional manifestations which tend toward inflexibility and depersonalization."

171   Downs, Anthony. INSIDE BUREAUCRACY. Boston: Little, Brown and Co., 1967. xv, 292 p.

This is a comprehensive treatment of American bureaucracy which attempts to create laws and proposals that can aid analysts in predicting the decisions of bureaucrats. The author maintains that bureaucrats try to achieve their goals rationally, that personal aggrandizement is substantially realized among those goals, and that the social actions of an organization are closely attached to its inner structure. Bureaucrats are stereotyped as climbers, conservers, advocates, zealots, and statesmen. Downs asserts that personal choice is greater in bureaucratic societies. Subjects include bureaucratic inflexibility and change, control problems in bureaus, goal consensus and bureaucratic ideology, and individual behavior of bureaucrats.

172   Eisenstadt, S.N. "Bureaucracy, Bureaucratization, and Debureaucratization." ADMINISTRATIVE SCIENCE QUARTERLY 4 (December 1959): 302-20.

The author suggests some ways to analyze the conditions which give rise to the development of bureaucratic organization, analyze such organizations as composite social systems that are in continuous interaction with their environment, and analyze the forces in this environment that impinge on these organizations. He proposes some preliminary hypotheses about conditions of development of processes of bureaucratization and their relation to the internal structure of bureaucratic organizations.

173   Ermer, Virginia B. "Strategies for Increasing Bureaucratic Responsiveness: Internal Monitoring or an Executive-Clientele 'Alliance.'" MIDWEST REVIEW OF PUBLIC ADMINISTRATION 9 (April-July 1975): 121-32.

This article is based on extensive interviews of housing inspectors and administrative officials and on insights gained from the author's participation in numerous inspections conducted by the Department of Housing and Community Development in Baltimore, Maryland. Ermer states that an executive-clientele alliance may bring significant payoffs to a chief executive and his or her department, noting that a department whose executive enjoys the widespread public support which such a reform image brings is more likely to ward off political attacks and to secure financial support.

174   Gulick, Luther, and Urwick, L., eds. PAPERS ON THE SCIENCE OF ADMINISTRATION. New York: Institute of Public Administration, 1937. 195 p.

Essays in this public administration classic include notes on the theory of organization (Gulick), organization as

a technical problem (Urwick), the principles of organization (James D. Mooney), the administrative theory in the
state (Henri Fayol), the function of administration (Urwick),
the need for the development of political science engineering (Henry S. Dennison), the effects of social environment (L.J. Henderson, T.N. Whitehead, and Elton
Mayo), the process of control (Mary Parker Follett), the
pros and cons of functionalization (John Lee), relationship in organization (V.A. Graicunas), and science,
values, and public administration (Gulick). The authors
of these essays were instrumental in shaping American
public administration during the FDR years.

175   Heclo, Hugh. "Political Executives and the Washington Bureaucracy."
        POLITICAL SCIENCE QUARTERLY 92 (Fall 1977): 395-424.

        Heclo contends that the main component of political
        statecraft in a bureaucracy is strategy and that political
        appointees usually do not have massive political or public
        backing and must work at procedures for building support.
        The reader is informed that appointees who have access
        to higher political levels can gain support in the bureau-
        cracy by acting as an agency's advocate. Heclo suggests
        that the process of goal-setting can be an important source
        of strength in dealing with the bureaucracy and that com-
        munication and consultation with existing bureaucratic
        personnel can be an important way to build support.

176   Hummel, Ralph P. THE BUREAUCRATIC EXPERIENCE. New York:
        St. Martin's Press, 1977. xiii, 238 p.

        Hummel describes bureaucracy as an entirely new way of
        organizing social life, stating that bureaucracy succeeds
        society, just as society succeeded community. Chapters
        include bureaucracy as the new society, as the new
        culture, as polity, the psychology and the language of
        bureaucracy, and the terminal world of bureaucracy. The
        author assumes that we will be better able to live and work
        with, in, or against bureaucracy if we view it as an entirely
        new world, become aware of the practical impact of its
        differences from the world with which we are familiar, and
        understand how that impact will vary for each of us depend-
        ing on the form of our involvement with bureaucratic life.

177   Hyneman, Charles S. BUREAUCRACY IN A DEMOCRACY. New York:
        Harper, 1950. xiv, 586 p.

        This is a personal observation on the problems of admini-
        strating the national bureaucracy through the domination
        of elected officers. A "Central Council" is advocated
        to bring together the political party in power and impede

_unruly bureaucratic conduct. The reader benefits from
the author's insightful views into administration and democracy and draws from Hyneman's activities as a civil servant
and a political scientist. Subjects covered in the six sections
of the book are: presidential direction and control, the central staff agencies, administrative divisions and delegations,
and presidential advocation for a Central Council. Hyneman
also takes a look at bureaucracy and democracy and congressional control of administration.

178   Jacoby, Henry. THE BUREAUCRATIZATION OF THE WORLD. Trans-
        lated by Eveline Kanes. Berkeley and Los Angeles: University of
        California Press, 1973. 241 p.

        Jacoby provides an interdisciplinary perspective in a
        broad analysis of the growth of bureaucracy throughout
        the world. The author's primary concern is the impact
        of bureaucracy upon the individual. He believes that
        the growth of bureaucracy has had both positive and
        negative influence upon individual development.

179   Kahn, Robert L., et al. "Americans Love Their Bureaucrats." PSY-
        CHOLOGY TODAY 9 (June 1975): 66-71.

        The author surveys 1,431 American adults concerning their
        experience with problems that government bureaucracies
        service: employment, job training, compensation for
        accidents and injuries at work, unemployment compen-
        sation, medical and hospital care, public assistance, and
        retirement benefits. The article establishes that the ma-
        jority of the sample thought that agency people made
        the right amount of effort to help them and 16 percent
        thought they helped more than they had to, but 21 per-
        cent thought they expended less effort than they should
        have. This research suggests that there are administrative
        solutions to most problems encountered.

180   Kaufman, Herbert. RED TAPE: ITS ORIGINS, USES, AND ABUSES.
        Washington, D.C.: Brookings Institution, 1977. 100 p.

        Most people talk about red tape as though it were some
        kind of loathsome disease, the deliberate product of a
        group of evil conspirators, or the result of bureaucratic
        stupidity and inertia. It is rarely discussed rationally,
        dispassionately, and analytically; most of us rage about
        it when it comes up. In this book, Kaufman attempts
        a detached examination of the subject to find out why
        something so universally detested flourishes so widely and
        enjoys such powers of endurance.

181   Krislov, Samuel. REPRESENTATIVE BUREAUCRACY. Englewood Cliffs, N.J.: Prentice-Hall, 1974. ix, 149 p.

Krislov discusses the emergence of the representative concept and its dilemmas, bureaucracy and representation, why bureaucracies can never be fully representative, how bureaucracies can and should be representative, some patterns of bureaucratic representatives and misrepresentatives, and the American bureaucracy as a representational service. He evaluates and mediates claims regarding the public service, not in the popular terms of discourse, but in the light of the application of a quite different principle, that of representative bureaucracy.

182   Kroeger, Naomi. "Bureaucracy, Social Exchange, and Benefits Received in a Public Assistance Agency." SOCIAL PROBLEMS 23 (December 1975): 182-97.

This article deals with a client-official interaction study in two district offices of a large metropolitan public assistance agency in which a random sample of women who had been receiving AFDC (Aid To Families With Dependent Children) grants for at least six months was drawn for each of 111 caseworkers. The author reveals that demographic and personality characteristics of clients had little effect on the number and amounts of grants received.

183   Levine, Charles H. "Unrepresentative Bureaucracy: Or Knowing What You Look Like Tells You Who You Are (And Maybe What to Do About It)." BUREAUCRAT 4 (April 1975): 90-98.

This essay presents a classification of bureaucratic types based on the predominant pattern of differential incorporation found in an organization. In addition to constructing a typology of bureaucratic unrepresentativeness, the author offers some suggestions for formulating affirmative action strategies in three types of unrepresentative organizations--consociational, stratified, and apartheid bureaucracies. Levine points out that two dimensions of social structure--the degree of organizational stratification and the degree of organizational segmentation--underlie the affirmative action problems.

184   Mainzer, Lewis C. POLITICAL BUREAUCRACY. Glenview, Ill.: Scott, Foresman and Co., 1973. 187 p.

Mainzer discusses political bureaucracy in four chapters, including three faces of governmental bureaucracy, public administration under law, public administration under politics, and beyond political bureaucracy. He seeks to convey a sense of change, problems, proposals, and potentialities for political bureaucracies.

185   Mathews, David. "The War on Bureaucracy." SOUTHERN REVIEW
       OF PUBLIC ADMINISTRATION 1 (September 1977): 247-53.

       The author, former Secretary of Health, Education, and
       Welfare in the Ford administration, believes that the
       most common complaint about bureaucracy from an in-
       creasing number of Americans is that it is inefficient,
       bumbling, ill-mannered, uncontrolled, and uncontrollable.
       Mathews offers interesting insights on the potential and
       problems of bureaucracy in the United States.

186   Merton, Robert K., et al., eds. READER IN BUREAUCRACY. New
       York: Free Press, 1952. 464 p.

       In a comprehensive collection of readings on bureaucracy,
       the editors include selections on theoretical conceptions,
       bases for the growth of bureaucracy, bureaucracy and
       power relations, the structure of bureaucracy, recruitment
       and advancement, social pathologies of bureaucracy, the
       bureaucrat, and field methods for the study of bureaucracy.
       The editors emphasize the sociological study of bureau-
       cracy, American and West European bureaucracies, and
       various institutional sectors of society.

187   Meyer, Marshall W., and Brown, M. Craig. "The Process of Bureau-
       cratization." In ENVIRONMENTS AND ORGANIZATIONS, edited
       by Marshall W. Meyer and Associates, pp. 51-77. San Francisco:
       Jossey-Bass, 1978.

       This study makes clear that the process of bureaucratiza-
       tion commences with environmental pressures and proceeds
       by developing rules to accommodate these pressures. The
       centrality of the environment as a determining component
       of bureaucratization and the dependence of organizational
       structure on sanctions encompassing external demands are
       stressed.

188   Niskanen, William A., Jr. BUREAUCRACY AND REPRESENTATIVE
       GOVERNMENT. Chicago: Aldine Publishing Co., 1971. 241 p.

       Niskanen applies economic analysis to the problem of
       design and operation of a bureaucracy and provides a
       prescription for some radical changes. The author em-
       phasizes how to insure that the bureaucracy provides optimal
       service. His conclusions are data-based to a significant
       degree, with supply and demand curves and appropriate
       equations.

189   Rosenbloom, David H., and Kinnard, Douglas. "Bureaucratic Repre-
       sentation and Bureaucrats' Behavior." MIDWEST REVIEW OF PUBLIC
       ADMINISTRATION 11 (March 1977): 35-42.

This analysis strongly suggests that the social representation of members of minority groups in upper level positions in the federal service can be an important means of assuring representation, in a substantive sense, of minorities in the American society as a whole. The authors conclude that the relationship between social representation and policy outputs is a complex one, and it is conditioned by such factors as age, seniority, the nature and place of education, the type of position, frequency of requests to further minority interests, the attitudes of one's colleagues toward one's activities, and the extent to which one received preferential treatment in the past.

190   Rossel, Robert D. "Autonomy in Bureaucracies." ADMINISTRATIVE SCIENCE QUARTERLY 16 (September 1971): 308-20. Tables.

Rossel presents data comparing managerial and supervisory orientations to bureaucratic procedures in nine bureaucratic organizations. He finds that a negative orientation to bureaucracy, called autonomy, typifies middle managers more than other positions. The author argues that desire for autonomy expresses frustrated mobility needs of those unlikely to advance within their organization.

191   Rourke, Francis E. BUREAUCRACY, POLITICS, AND PUBLIC POLICY. Boston: Little, Brown and Co., 1968. ix, 173 p.

This text is a discussion of the part that bureaucrats play in the public policy-making process. Rourke suggests that assigned officials use their power more thoroughly than elected politicians. He attributes their thoroughness to specialized skills and the capacity to advance outside constituencies, and explores recent trends to professionalize and rationalize executive policy making.

192   Seitz, Steven Thomas. BUREAUCRACY, POLICY, AND THE PUBLIC. St. Louis: C.V. Mosby Co., 1978. x, 216 p. Paper.

This textbook draws heavily from political science, sociology, anthropology, business administration, psychology, and history, synthesizing materials from these disciplines. The author believes too often "research on bureaucracies focuses on the static structural dimension of bureaucracy to the exclusion of regard for its macro- or micro-dynamic functions." This volume is both theoretical and empirical as its theory provides a structural functional framework that integrates middle range theory, previous research, and new data analyses into a comprehensive overview of bureaucracy, policy, and the public.

193   Smith, Michael P.   "Alienation and Bureaucracy: The Role of Par-
       ticipatory Administration."   PUBLIC ADMINISTRATION REVIEW   31
       (November–December 1971):   658–64.

              This essay explores the paradoxical factors which contribute
              to the public's growing sense of bureaucratic alienation
              within the context of the massive urban public service
              bureaucracies.   The author illustrates the roots of the
              modern person's sense of estrangement from bureaucratic
              life.

194   Taylor, Frederick Winslow.   SCIENTIFIC MANAGEMENT: COMPRISING
       SHOP MANAGEMENT, THE PRINCIPLES OF SCIENTIFIC MANAGE-
       MENT, TESTIMONY BEFORE THE SPECIAL HOUSE COMMITTEE.
       New York: Harper and Brothers, 1911.

              This text consists of three subtitles, SHOP MANAGE-
              MENT, THE PRINCIPLES OF SCIENTIFIC MANAGEMENT,
              and TAYLOR'S TESTIMONY BEFORE THE SPECIAL HOUSE
              COMMITTEE.   The initial subtitle, SHOP MANAGEMENT,
              is a handbook for those interested in the management of
              industrial enterprises and in the production of goods; it
              was first published in 1903.   In the second subtitle, THE
              PRINCIPLES OF SCIENTIFIC MANAGEMENT, Taylor
              points out the great loss which the entire country is suf-
              fering through inefficiency, tries to convince the reader
              that the remedy for this inefficiency lies in systematic
              management instead of searching for some unusual or ex-
              traordinary person, and attempts to prove that the best
              management is a true science, resting upon clearly de-
              fined laws, rules, and principles as a foundation.   In the
              final subtitle, TAYLOR'S TESTIMONY BEFORE THE SPECIAL
              HOUSE COMMITTEE, Taylor states the essential features
              and development of scientific management philosophies.

195   Thompson, Victor A.   BUREAUCRACY AND THE MODERN WORLD.
       Morristown, N.J.:   General Learning Press, 1976.   141 p.   Paper.

              Thompson believes that this textbook will be useful for
              courses in organization theory, administrative theory,
              management theory, and theory of bureaucracy.   He
              attempts to provide a moral or philosophical basis for or-
              ganization without sacrificing the behavioral understanding
              gained in recent years.   The author makes explicit the
              moral assumptions of modern institutions, with emphasis
              upon those providing goods and services, both public and
              private.   The most unique facet of this text is its fusion
              of the social, the scientific, and the philosophical.
              Chapters include organizations as systems; the development
              of modern bureaucracy, decision theory, pure and applied;
              bureaucracy and innovative action; and bureaucracy and
              compassion.

196   Tullock, Gordon. THE POLITICS OF BUREAUCRACY. Washington,
        D.C.: Public Affairs Press, 1965. 228 p.

> "There are important areas for which the economists's
> assumptions are clearly inapplicable, notably the govern-
> mental bureaucracy. In the monolithic societies that have
> dominated much of the world throughout its history the
> analysis of markets has relatively little application. Here
> the dominant relationship is that between superior and
> inferior. It is this type of social relationship, this type
> of social situation, that this book will discuss."

197   Von Mises, Ludwig. BUREAUCRACY. New Haven, Conn.: Yale
        University Press, 1944. viii, 125 p.

> This is a challenging defense of the free enterprise system
> versus socialism and bureaucratic administration. Von Mises
> refutes the notion that bureaucracy is unavoidable. Em-
> ploying historical knowledge, he connects its ascendancy
> to totalitarianism and governmental attempts to regulate
> trade. He condemns bureaucracy for demolishing personal
> freedom under the premise of traditional legal sanction.
> France, Russia, and Germany, which the author believes
> more departmentalized than America, are the models used.
> Material on the tenets of bureaucracy, its push towards
> departmentalization in private enterprises, and its social
> and psychological results are included.

198   Weber, Max. FROM MAX WEBER: ESSAYS IN SOCIOLOGY.
        Translated, edited, and with an introduction by H.H. Gerth and C.
        Wright Mills. New York: Oxford University Press, 1946. xi, 490 p.

> This includes Weber's essay which notes the chief charac-
> teristics of an ideal-type bureaucracy which contains rules,
> hierarchy, impersonality, specialization, career service,
> and an orientation toward effectiveness. The content
> determines the method of bureaucratic development, with
> Weber advocating components such as the presence of a
> money economy, logical authority, and the ascendancy
> of mass democracy. Other points of discussion are the
> sociology of discipline, religion, the landed aristocracy,
> castes in India, science and politics, imperialism, social
> groups, charismatic authority, rural life in Germany, and
> the Chinese intellectual ruling class.

199   Weinstein, Deena. BUREAUCRATIC OPPOSITION: CHALLENGING
        ABUSES AT THE WORKPLACE. New York: Pergamon Press, 1979.
        145 p.

> The author identifies the phenomenon of bureaucratic
> opposition, its dynamics, and its prospects for success,

and assesses the possibilities for change from employees
at middle and lower levels of the organization. She
provides specific illustrations of employee resistance to
organizational abuse.

200   Wilson, James Q. "The Rise of the Bureaucratic State." PUBLIC
        INTEREST 41 (Fall 1975): 56-76.

        Wilson believes the need for federal economic regulation
        led to the creation of the Interstate Commerce Commission
        in 1887, followed by the Antitrust Division of the Justice
        Department, Federal Trade Commission, Food and Drug
        Administration, Federal Communications Commission, Na-
        tional Labor Relations Board, and Maritime Commission.
        The author sees such agencies as ominous in that they
        broaden their own regulatory reach, respond slowly to
        technical and economic changes, resist deregulation, con-
        tribute to bureaucratization of private agencies, and in-
        crease corruption in that they control entry, fix prices,
        and affect profitability. Wilson concludes that the re-
        sponsibility to alter or abolish bureaucracies whose be-
        havior is not acceptable on an economic or general wel-
        fare basis should be placed with the Congress, which
        creates and finances them.

201   Woll, Peter. AMERICAN BUREAUCRACY: THE EMERGENCE OF THE
        FEDERAL BUREAUCRACY AS A MAJOR FORCE IN AMERICAN GOV-
        ERNMENT AND THE EFFECT OF ITS ROLE ON THE CONSTITUTIONAL
        SYSTEM OF CHECKS AND BALANCES. New York: W.W. Norton
        and Co., 1977. ix, 260 p.

        Woll gives attention to presidential attempts to control
        the bureaucracy that reached their peak during the Nixon
        administration and to the decline in presidential authority
        over the bureaucracy that has occurred as a result of the
        Budget Control and Impoundment Act of 1974. Chapters
        include: the nature of bureaucracy and constitutional
        government, the development and organization of bureau-
        cracy, administrative law and the courts, the bureaucracy
        and Congress, the Presidency and the bureaucracy.

202   Yarwood, Dean, and Nimmo, Dan. "Bureaucratic Roles and Participa-
        tion: Variation on Two Themes." In PUBLIC ADMINISTRATION AND
        PUBLIC POLICY, edited by H. George Frederickson and Charles R.
        Wise, pp. 63-79. Lexington, Mass.: D.C. Heath and Co., 1977.

        This essay elaborates a role theory perspective for political
        science and public administration. The authors review the
        literature about political and administrative roles from the
        perspective of broadened participation, suggest an alter-
        native kind of role analysis that they contend is especially

useful in considering participation, and explore the implications of role theory for administrative and political
structures when applied to the problem of expanded participation.

C. THE CHIEF EXECUTIVE AS ADMINISTRATOR

203 Aberbach, Joel D., and Rockman, Bert A. "Clashing Beliefs Within the
Executive Branch: The Nixon Administration Bureaucracy." AMERICAN
POLITICAL SCIENCE REVIEW 70 (June 1976): 456-68.

> This study, based upon interviews undertaken in 1970 with
> 126 administrators from eighteen federal agencies within the
> Washington, D.C., metropolitan area, finds that agency
> and party affiliation were particularly important variables
> in accounting for differences in administrators' views.
> It concludes that the White House will continue to reflect
> short-term political alternatives and that the Congress and
> bureaucracy will be relatively immune to these dynamics.

204 Barber, James David. THE PRESIDENTIAL CHARACTER: PREDICTING
PERFORMANCE IN THE WHITE HOUSE. 1972. Rev. ed. Englewood
Cliffs, N.J.: Prentice-Hall, 1977. 576 p.

> The author postulates and proves a fascinating theory: if
> we can see the pattern a person has followed in political
> life, we can estimate the pattern that will emerge under
> the pressures and prerogatives of the presidency. Barber
> uses the personal and political histories of former presi-
> dents to categorize them as active-negative, active-
> positive, passive-negative, and passive-positive characters.
> He relates these basic categories to each president's world
> view and style, and to the political situations each president
> confronted. A recommended book for probing the dynamics
> of administrative leadership.

205 Beam, David R. "Public Administration Is Alive and Well--and Living
in the White House." PUBLIC ADMINISTRATION REVIEW 38 (January-
February 1978): 72-77.

> Discusses reorganization of the federal government's de-
> partments and agencies, the application of the zero base
> budgeting concept, and the implementation of civil service
> reform as concrete illustrations that public administration
> is alive and well in the Jimmy Carter White House.

206 Berman, Larry. "The Office of Management and Budget that Almost
Wasn't." POLITICAL SCIENCE QUARTERLY 92 (Summer 1977): 281-
303.

Berman asserts that the Office of Management and Budget
was developed from the reorganization of the Bureau of
the Budget (BOB) in 1970 and that three presidentially
appointed advisory groups recommended reorganizing or
abolishing the BOB so that the management processes in
the executive office could improve. The reader learns
that despite BOB-initiated studies which uncovered serious
problems in the agency's organization, mission, and staffing,
the BOB viewed the recommendations as downgrading the
bureau. The article concludes that a council chaired by
Roy Ash stated that the recommendations would upgrade
the agency's management functions by downgrading its
budget responsibilities.

207   Brown, David S.   "The President and the Bureaus: Time for a Renewal
       of Relationships?" PUBLIC ADMINISTRATION REVIEW 26 (September
       1966): 174-82.

       Brown concludes that there is real merit in restudying and
       rethinking the relationships between the president and the
       approximately 125 bureaus which perform the basic work
       of government. According to the author, presidential in-
       fluence should not be halted at the departmental level;
       what is needed is a means by which presidential leadership
       can reach below the departmental level.

208   Caldwell, L[ynton].K.   "Alexander Hamilton: Advocate of Executive
       Leadership." PUBLIC ADMINISTRATION REVIEW 4 (Spring 1944):
       113-26.

       Caldwell discusses Hamilton's public career (". . . the
       public interest. This in my eyes is sacred."), his theory
       of politics ("The science of policy is the knowledge of
       human nature."), constitutional principles ("Power must
       be granted, or civil society cannot exist."), executive
       responsibility ("The administration of government . . .
       falls peculiarly within the province of the executive de-
       partment."), and Hamilton's program ("The public good
       must be paramount to every private consideration."). The
       author believes that the theory of the national executive
       as leader in the formulation of public policy is the great
       constructive contribution of Hamilton to American govern-
       ment.

209   Cole, Richard L., and Caputo, David A.   "Presidential Control of the
       Senior Civil Service: Assessing the Strategies of the Nixon Years."
       THE AMERICAN POLITICAL SCIENCE REVIEW 73 (June 1979): 399-
       413.

       The authors assess the extent of President Nixon's success
       in gaining some degree of management control over the

bureaucracy through the manipulation of the civil service personnel system. They found that Republicans were more likely to be selected to top career positions during the Nixon years, that career executives calling themselves Independents were more likely to resemble Republican executives in their support of Nixon's policies and goals, and that Independent career executives were likely to provide a president with a considerable reservoir of bureaucratic support.

210   Fisher, Louis. "The Politics of Impounded Funds." ADMINISTRATIVE SCIENCE QUARTERLY 15 (September 1970): 361-77.

This article explores the political factors which give rise to disputes over impounded funds: prevention of budget deficiencies, wartime diversion of human and material resources from domestic public works; presidential restraints on interservice rivalries over procurement; and fiscal measures to reduce inflationary pressures.

211   Flash, Edward S., Jr. ECONOMIC ADVICE AND PRESIDENTIAL LEADERSHIP. New York: Columbia University Press, 1965. x, 382 p.

This is a treatment of the Council of Economic Advisers from 1946 to 1962 highlighting economists and their dealings with politicians and administrators. It describes the "politics of advice." The author credits the accomplishments of the Council to its capacity to balance knowledge, viewed as consistent and objective, with power, which demands utility, flexibility, and a tendency to indoctrinate politicians in respect to their own requirements. This book analyzes the Council's participation in defense readiness during the Korean War, the adaptation to Eisenhower economic opinions, the recession of 1953-54, the acceptance by President Kennedy of Keynesian economics, and tax amendment in a cold war situation, ending with a discussion of the similarity between knowledge and power.

212   Gawthrop, Louis C. BUREAUCRATIC BEHAVIOR IN THE EXECUTIVE BRANCH: AN ANALYSIS OF ORGANIZATIONAL CHANGE. New York: Free Press, 1969. ix, 276 p.

Gawthrop argues that making decisions and resolving conflict, two major functions of every organization, are integrally related to each other and to the concept of organizational loyalty and that both are indirectly related to the problems of organizational change. He examines the manner in which the executive branch of the federal government resolves internal conflict, makes decisions, develops a sense of loyalty within its ranks, and responds to the internal and external forces of change. He compares each concept in the executive bureaucracy with a similar analysis of private, nongovernmental organizations. This text presents a concise analytical model that can be used in explaining the functioning of bureaucratic systems.

213   Gordon, George J. "Office of Management and Budget Circular A-95: Perspectives and Implications." PUBLIUS 4 (Winter 1974): 45-68.

Gordon stresses that two of the basic objectives in President Nixon's "new federalism" concept were better federal program management and blending more productively the programs, ideas, and efforts of states and localities. He reports that the Office of Management and Budget is in the forefront of this undertaking, employing as its principal tool Circular A-95, a coordinative mechanism originally promoted by the Bureau of the Budget in mid-1969. Gordon suggests that although the provisions of A-95 do not by themselves constitute a judicially enforceable obstacle to federal program implementation, they are sufficiently specific to necessitate both additional investments of time and at least somewhat controlled behavior patterns on the part of federal agencies and state, regional, and metropolitan clearinghouses.

214   Haider, Donald. "Presidential Management Initiatives: A Ford Legacy to Executive Management Improvement." PUBLIC ADMINISTRATION REVIEW 39 (May-June 1979): 248-59.

Haider discusses five presidential management initiatives (PMI), which include decision making and departmental organization, evaluation of current programs, reduction in the burden of federal reporting and regulations, contracting out and overhead cost control systems, and personnel management. He reviews the accomplishments and problems confronted by the Ford administration and provides an insightful analysis of administrative continuity during the 1974-77 period.

215   Hart, John. "Executive Reorganization in the USA and the Growth of Presidential Power." PUBLIC ADMINISTRATION 52 (Summer 1974): 179-91.

Hart states that three months after President Nixon came into office he set up an Advisory Council on the Reorganization of the Executive Branch and by December 1970, the Council had presented the president with a 427-page book of recommendations. By executive order, Nixon shifted policy-making responsibilities from the departments to the White House. The author asserts that the Cabinet can no longer be regarded as a policy-making body. He feels that, outside of the Executive Branch, the influence of Nixon reforms will be felt most strongly in the Congress, for there is a potential in the new structure to change the equilibrium in the executive-legislative relationship.

216   Heclo, Hugh. "OMB and the Presidency--the Problem of 'Neutral Competence.'" PUBLIC INTEREST 38 (Winter 1975): 80-98.

The author points out that neutral competence is a relatively recent growth in the Anglo-American democracies and corresponds roughly with the appearance of a higher civil service about a century ago. Heclo maintains that neutral competence envisions a continuous, uncommitted facility at the disposal of, and for the support of, political leadership. He reveals that neutral competence is not a prescription for sainthood and that this idea does not mean the possession of a direct-dial line to some overarching, nonpartisan sense of the public interest. Heclo concludes that neutral competence consists of giving one's cooperation and best independent judgment of the issues to partisan bosses and of being sufficiently committed to be able to do so for a succession of partisan bosses.

217   Henry, Laurin L. "Transferring the Presidency: Variations, Trends, and Patterns." PUBLIC ADMINISTRATION REVIEW 20 (Autumn 1960): 187-95.

Henry writes that the national interest will be endangered at least every eight years hereafter by the possible impotence of a "lame duck" administration, by divided responsibility for national leadership between the election and inauguration, by the administrative confusion of a simultaneous turnover of the top layer of federal officials, and by the possibility of either indecision or uninformed, irresponsible decisions by the new administration. The author concludes that the extent to which the transitions of the future will repeat the patterns of the past remains debatable, and that many problems of transition remain unchanged.

218   Hess, Stephen. ORGANIZING THE PRESIDENCY. Washington, D.C.: Brookings Institution, 1976. 228 p.

The author uses the history of the White House staffs during the administrations of Franklin Roosevelt through Richard Nixon as the background for prescriptive conclusions on how the presidency could be organized to improve policy formulation, delivery of services, and

fidelity to democratic principles. Hess's proposals are
meant to correct what he perceives as serious imbalances
in the presidential system that have developed over past
decades.

219   Ink, Dwight A. "A Management Crisis for the New President: People
       Programs." PUBLIC ADMINISTRATION REVIEW 29 (November-December
       1968): 546-52.

       The author, at the time of this article Assistant Secretary
       for Administration at the Department of Housing and Urban
       Development, offers a presidential plan of action to
       strengthen management, cut red tape, and streamline the
       government's system of response to the urban crisis. Ink's
       eight recommendations include cutting red tape, bringing
       together federal regions, decentralizing administration,
       strengthening agency leadership roles, making effective
       White House and Bureau of the Budget (now Office of
       Management and Budget) monitoring and support, stream-
       lining the federal funding system, making management a
       part of new programs, and hiring managers.

220   _____. "The President as Manager." PUBLIC ADMINISTRATION
       REVIEW 36 (September-October 1976): 508-15.

       Ink, a part president of the American Society for Public
       Administration and high level administrator at the Depart-
       ment of Housing and Urban Development and Office of
       Management and Budget, offers eight proposals for the
       rapid development of a meaningful presidential managerial
       role. He provides an excellent overview of the president's
       managerial responsibilities.

221   Laski, Harold J. "The Parliamentary and Presidential Systems." PUBLIC
       ADMINISTRATION REVIEW 4 (Autumn 1944): 347-59.

       Laski writes: "I should not for one moment claim that one
       system is better than the other, still less that the par-
       liamentary system is more suited to the genius of the
       American people than the presidential system. A system
       of government is very like a pair of shoes; it grows to
       the use of the feet to which it is fitted. But it is well
       to remember of governments what is true, also, of footwear--
       that the shoe must be suited to the journey it is proposed
       to take." The author, professor of political science at
       the London School of Economics and Political Science in
       the 1940s, offers an insightful analysis of the parliamentary
       and presidential systems of democratic government.

222   Moe, Ronald C. "The Domestic Council in Perspective." BUREAU-
        CRAT 5 (October 1976): 251-72.

        Moe traces the genesis, legislative history, institutional
        development, and operating procedures of the Domestic
        Council. He assesses the impact of the late Vice Presi-
        dent Nelson A. Rockefeller's role as working chief of the
        council and implies that the Council's flexibility is the
        key to its durability. Moe concludes that the working
        style of the incumbent president will determine the future
        of the Domestic Council. He points out that as the visi-
        bility of the Office of Management and Budget deceased,
        the role of the Domestic Council was enhanced in the
        Nixon administration.

223   Murphy, Thomas P.; Nuechterlein, Donald E.; and Stupak, Ronald J.,
        eds. THE PRESIDENT'S PROGRAM DIRECTORS: THE ASSISTANT
        SECRETARIES--A SYMPOSIUM. Charlottesville, Va.: U.S. Civil
        Service Commission, 1976. 112 p.

        This symposium was developed as a result of new directions
        undertaken by the Federal Executive Institute. Its objec-
        tive was to more effectively increase and enrich communi-
        cation in the federal bureaucratic environment among po-
        litical and career executives. The program focused on the
        roles of the assistant secretary, the political-career inter-
        face, and the processes of policy formulation and imple-
        mentation. Program objectives included the sharing of
        experiences by assistant secretaries so as to enhance their
        knowledge, pass on what they have learned, and to im-
        prove the capability of the Federal Executive Institute to
        communicate the viewpoints of political executives to
        career executives.

224   Nathan, Richard P. THE PLOT THAT FAILED: NIXON AND THE
        ADMINISTRATIVE PRESIDENCY. New York: John Wiley and Sons,
        1975. 193 p.

        The author, assistant director of the Office of Management
        and Budget from 1969 to 1971, offers an authoritative
        account of how former President Richard M. Nixon and
        Nixon staff persons tried radically to reorganize the ex-
        ecutive arm of government. Nathan reveals that Nixon
        attempted in 1972 and 1973 to achieve his major aims in
        domestic policy by controlling the management of domestic
        government. He writes that a cadre of newly appointed
        Cabinet and sub-Cabinet officials was to take over en-
        trenched bureaucracies and achieve Nixon's goals via
        administrative action. Nathan calls this Nixon strategy
        the "Administrative Presidency."

225   Neustadt, Richard [E.]. PRESIDENTIAL POWER: THE POLITICS OF
       LEADERSHIP. New York: John Wiley and Sons, 1960. 224 p.

              This book was written to inform President Kennedy of the
              hardships of maintaining presidential power. The author
              offers the argument that a president must convince in-
              fluential people that it is in their own best interest to
              implement his policies. Professional renown and public
              reputation are provided through the power to persuade.
              The Truman and Eisenhower administrations provide case
              studies for the author to develop. Initially accepted,
              the book fell from favor when President Johnson demon-
              strated to political scientists how successfully political
              power could be wielded.

226   _____. "Staffing the Presidency: Premature Notes on the New Ad-
       ministration." POLITICAL SCIENCE QUARTERLY 93 (Spring 1978):
       1-9.

              Recognizing that the Carter administration inherited struc-
              tures and procedures from previous administrations, the
              author reveals that some innovations originating in the
              Nixon and Ford administrations operate under President
              Carter. Neustadt indicates that the Office of Manage-
              ment and Budget, Council of Economic Advisers, and
              Domestic Council maintained significant responsibilities
              in all three administrations.

227   Pearson, Norman M. "A General Administrative Staff to Aid the
       President." PUBLIC ADMINISTRATION REVIEW 4 (Spring 1944):
       127-47.

              Pearson probes the principal functions of a Chief Executive;
              reviews the great variety of meanings and concepts of
              staff, and points to the care with which they must be
              used; analyzes the executive functions of the president,
              including planning, organizing, staffing, directing, co-
              ordinating, controlling, budgeting, and presenting and
              reviewing legislation; distinguishes among the basic kinds
              of delegation; and surmises that the "basic functions of
              the general staff agency are all delegable aspects of the
              functions of the chief executive." This article is an
              excellent review of the potential of and problems con-
              fronting the President of the United States in the mid-
              1940s.

228   Polsby, Nelson W. "Presidential Cabinet Making: Lessons for the
       Political System." POLITICAL SCIENCE QUARTERLY 93 (Spring
       1978): 15-25.

              Polsby concludes that no president, in modern times, has

pursued a pure strategy of cabinet building, that the strategies have been mixed. He points out that the character of the mixture at any given time is instructive about the claims to legitimacy made by each incumbent administration. Polsby indicates that Carter's appointments illustrate a combination of specialists, client-oriented selections, and generalists. This article describes three alternative ways to build a cabinet.

229   Rose, Richard. MANAGING PRESIDENTIAL OBJECTIVES. New York: Free Press, 1976. 180 p.

Rose traces the chief executive's concern with organizing the presidency from the 1800s through the Nixon administration, evaluates in detail the background and application of management by objectives (MBO) in the executive branch, and reveals that the Nixon administration's concentration on noncontroversial objectives contributed to MBO's reputation as a technique best suited to the least important political activities in the federal government. The motto "to govern is to choose" is a theme of this text.

230   Silver, Howard J. "Presidential Power and the Post-Watergate Presidency." PRESIDENTIAL STUDIES QUARTERLY 8 (Spring 1978): 199-214.

This essay strives to evaluate the schema of Richard Neustadt, who in 1960 described presidential power as the power to persuade others, in the context of the post-Watergate presidencies of Gerald Ford and Jimmy Carter. Silver asserts that a variety of factors affect the president's ability to guard his power prospects, make the correct choices, and bargain well in order to attain presidential power. Silver discusses alterations from the vantage point of the presidency since Watergate and centers on the presidents' use of power in his relations with the legislative branch.

231   Somers, Herman M. "The President as Administrator." THE ANNALS OF THE AMERICAN ACADEMY OF POLITICAL AND SOCIAL SCIENCE 283 (1952): 104-14.

"The Presidency is today the prime motive force in our Constitutional system. Our political and economic evolution and the nature of our party system have focused upon the President's responsibility for the origin of major policies and programs and for the implementation and effectuation of policies approved by Congress. The American system, in which the Presidency is a representative institution--elected by universal suffrage--emphasizes the fact

that co-ordination of politics and administration is necessary in a democratic nation."

232   Sorensen, Theodore C. DECISION MAKING IN THE WHITE HOUSE:
THE OLIVE BRANCH OR THE ARROWS. New York: Columbia University Press, 1963. xvi, 94 p.

This book is based on the Gino Speranza Lectures for
1963, delivered at Columbia University on April 18, and
May 9, 1963. The author describes the setting for decision making at the White House, the "outer limits" of
decision making, presidential politics, presidential advisers, and the presidential perspective. Sorensen offers
this conclusion: "A great President is not the product of
his staff but the master of his house. He must know when
to reject the advice of his experts and when to back up
a Secretary. He must be able to win a consensus without
waiting for one. He must be attuned to public opinion
but not bound by it. He must know the limitations of
his office as well as its powers. He must reign in Washington, but he must also rule."

233   Sundquist, James [L.]. "Four More Years: Is Deadlock the Only
Prospect?" PUBLIC ADMINISTRATION REVIEW 33 (May–June 1973):
279–84.

This is an excellent article describing the difficulties for
public administration when one political party occupies
the White House and the other party controls the majority
of the American Congress. The author probes the nature
of the party system, the presidency, and the legislature
in the implementation of public policies since 1954.

234   _____. "Jimmy Carter as Public Administrator: An Appraisal at
Mid-Term." PUBLIC ADMINISTRATION REVIEW 39 (January–February
1979): 3–11.

Sundquist states: "In bureaucratic organizations far less
complex than the executive branch of the national government, the responsibilities of management are seen as
too crucial and too difficult to be placed in the hands
of amateurs. But in the United States government there
is no such doctrine. . . . All presidents even those with
long experience in Washington, have surrounded themselves
with home-state personnel to some degree. . . . Yet
Carter seems to have carried home-state cronyism beyond
the point of any other recent president. . . . The critical
period is just ahead . . . the Carter administration needs
to develop a philosophy as to where professional managers
fit within the government, and then proceed to reserve the
appropriate posts for them." This article is highly recom-

mended for better understanding the impact of President
Carter upon the Washington federal bureaucracy, and
vice-versa.

235   Vale, Vivian. "The Obligation to Spend: Presidential Impoundment
of Congressional Appropriations." POLITICAL STUDIES 25 (December
1977): 508-22.

Vale asserts that controversy has arisen over impoundment
of congressional appropriations by the president via the
Office of Management and Budget. He states that impoundment seems to be the way in which President Nixon
substituted his own legislative priorities for those of the
Congress. Vale evaluates recent reform and the balance
of responsibility between the president and Congress in
fiscal matters.

236   Waldmann, Raymond J. "The Domestic Council: Innovation in Presidential Government." PUBLIC ADMINISTRATION REVIEW 36 (May-
June 1976): 260-68.

Waldmann points out that the Domestic Council was an
innovation of President Nixon's first term designed to
assist in managing domestic affairs, providing the president the tools necessary to exercise policy control over
the functions of the executive branch. The author believes that the Domestic Council has proved to be a
useful instrument for planning and managing government
action and should assist future presidents in domestic
policy planning.

237   Wann, A.J. THE PRESIDENT AS CHIEF ADMINISTRATOR: A STUDY
OF FRANKLIN D. ROOSEVELT. Washington, D.C.: Public Affairs
Press, 1968. 219 p.

The author emphasizes that presidential effectiveness
largely depends on an ability to control the vast administrative machinery of government. Roosevelt's reshaping
of the federal bureaucracy through expansion and reorganization and FDR's response to wartime problems are
given attention. Wann's focus is on administrative organization and the executive branch of government, and
on FDR's views about bureaucracy and his impact upon
government.

238   White, Richard W., Jr. "The CAA Transition Task Force: How Bureaucracy Responded to a Change in Presidential Policy." POLICY
ANALYSIS 2 (Fall 1976): 623-34.

White studies the activities of an interagency task force
set up by the Federal Regional Council in 1973 to determine

what might be done about problems resulting from the
discontinuance of federal funding of community action
programs and the Office of Economic Opportunity. He
explores what avenues might be taken as the community
action agencies, which provided a means for participation
by low-income persons, were phased out. White notes
that many of the OEO programs were restored with the
establishment of the Community Services Administration
in 1974.

239   Wildavsky, Aaron. "The Past and Future Presidency." PUBLIC IN-
        TEREST 41 (Fall 1975): 56-76.

        Wildavsky maintains that a possible effect of Watergate
        and of the recent unpopularity of presidents may be the
        flight of the presidency from the people. He does not
        see a weakening of the presidency because: 1) the presi-
        dent is still more powerful than the courts, the Congress,
        and the bureaucracy, 2) he is entrusted with foreign and
        defense policies, and 3) he is the focus of interest groups.
        Wildavsky concludes that a better alternative to "offensive
        retreat" of the president would be the strengthening of
        the political parties in order that they can exercise con-
        trol over what presidents do and bring presidents in line
        with the sentiments of citizens.

D. PUBLIC ADMINISTRATION AND THE LEGISLATIVE PROCESS

240   Aspin, Les. "The Defense Budget and Foreign Policy: The Role of
        Congress." DAEDALUS 104 (Summer 1975): 155-74.

        Aspin relates that the reason Congress does not cut yearly
        appropriations for defense spending is that congressional
        members vote mostly for their constituents, and when con-
        stituencies benefit from defense spending, members con-
        tinue to support large defense budgets. The reader learns
        that Congress presently performs three basic roles well:
        it is a conduit for constituent views; it is a general over-
        seer of government policies and resource allocation; and
        it is a guardian of the process of government procedure.

241   Baaklini, Abdo I. "Public Administration and Legislatures: Caveats
        and Approaches." PUBLIC ADMINISTRATION REVIEW 35 (September-
        October 1975): 504-8.

        Baaklini reviews empirical, normative, and theoretical
        linkages in describing the movement for public admini-
        stration concern in this area. He states that public ad-
        ministration now recognizes the need for involvement with
        legislatures and concludes that the field's embryonic in-

volvement with legislatures should proceed with an awareness that the discipline is far from having answers to controversial issues.

242   Balutis, Alan P., and Heaphey, James J. PUBLIC ADMINISTRATION
        AND THE LEGISLATIVE PROCESS. Beverly Hills, Calif.: Sage
        Publications, 1974. 58 p.

        The authors state that a new approach to the study of
        legislative institutions is needed which will adequately
        relate the individual to his social setting and allow legis-
        lative units to be approached in terms of their systematic
        positions and roles. Balutis and Heaphey project that if
        administration is to be seen as a process as well as an
        academic discipline, it is needed in legislatures as in
        other organizations. The authors stress that legislatures
        could be assisted if they had systematic procedures by
        which to identify and grant careful attention to significant
        proposals.

243   Beckman, Norman. "Policy Analysis for the Congress." PUBLIC AD-
        MINISTRATION REVIEW 37 (May-June 1977): 237-44.

        The purposes of this essay are to examine the main policy
        analysis institutions available to the Congress, to identify
        factors that affect the use of policy analysis by the Con-
        gress, and to describe some current reform proposals aimed
        at strengthening the policy analysis capability of the
        Congress. This article provides useful insights into the
        role of the Congress in public administration and policy.

244   _____. "Use of a Staff Agency by the Congress: The Congressional
        Research Service." BUREAUCRAT 3 (January 1975): 401-15.

        This article states that the role of the Congressional Re-
        search Service is to improve Congress' research base by
        providing factual information, analysis of issues, alter-
        natives to various proposals, and the evaluation of alter-
        natives. It takes assignments from committee staffs, mem-
        bers of Congress, constituents, and as provided by statute.
        Beckman maintains that in growing to fulfill its role, the
        CRS must operate within the objectives of confidentiality,
        nonadvocacy, and nonpartisanship.

245   Bolling, Richard. "The Management of Congress." PUBLIC ADMINI-
        STRATION REVIEW 35 (September-October 1975): 490-94.

        Bolling, a member of the U.S. House of Representatives
        from Missouri, relates the importance of logistical support
        for the organization of Congress, discusses its information
        and analysis system, and emphasizes the need for coherent
        policy formulation and execution.

246   Carron, Andrew S. "Congress and Energy: A Need for Policy Analysis and More." POLICY ANALYSIS 2 (Spring 1976): 283-97.

> Carron says that in energy legislation, Congress is curtailed by a lack of committee focus and hence a lack of leadership. The reader is told that committee jurisdictional disputes, political showmanship, narrow interest, and inconsistent public attitudes are among the political obstacles to congressional action. Carron relates that most of the suggested energy problems have come from the administration, with Congress assuming primarily reactive and passive roles.

247   Crane, Edgar G. "Legislatures as a Force for Government Accountability." In COMPARATIVE LEGISLATIVE REFORMS AND INNOVATIONS, edited by Abdo I. Baaklini and James J. Heaphey, pp. 115-53. Albany: State University of New York, 1977.

> The author asserts that American legislatures are trying to strengthen program control through the utilization of new tools for program analysis and that success depends upon using professional expertise to make political choices. He makes clear that to meet this need, legislatures are initiating various program reviews as a part of their political function. Crane believes that a bureaucracy cannot adequately control and criticize itself, and therefore depends upon the legislature for necessary feedback.

248   Davidson, Roger H. "Congressional Committees: The Toughest Customers." POLICY ANALYSIS 2 (Spring 1976): 299-323.

> Davidson contends that the Congressional Research Service, General Accounting Office, Office of Technology Assessment, and Congressional Budget Office rely heavily on policy analysts, whereas members of Congress do not. The article mentions that the largest potential market for policy analysis is in the committees and subcommittees. Davidson believes that it is crucial for policy analysts to be aware of the complexities of committee structure and operations if they wish to contribute to legislative policy making.

249   Dreyfus, Daniel A. "The Limitations of Policy Research in Congressional Decisionmaking." POLICY STUDIES JOURNAL 4 (Spring 1976): 269-74.

> Dreyfus projects that congressional decision making concerning legislative oversight and policy adjustment is redundant to the overall role which Congress exerts. The author indicates that the executive manages information and data analysis better than the legislature. He stresses that an open legislative process, an inquisitive press, and

lobby groups generate adequate information for debate.
Dreyfus believes that Congress will provide responsive and
responsible decisions if its members are sensitive to the
demands of American society.

250   Eulau, Heinz. "Bases of Authority in Legislative Bodies: A Comparative
        Analysis." ADMINISTRATIVE SCIENCE QUARTERLY 7 (December
        1962): 309-21.

        This essay assumes that the authority of leaders in legis-
        lative bodies must rest on bases other than their formal
        position alone. The author compares legislative leaders
        and rank-and-file members of four American state legis-
        latures in terms of respect, affection, and expertise.
        Heinz notes that expertise in a particular area of spe-
        cialization does not seem to be a highly valued requisite
        of leadership.

251   Fitzgerald, Martin J. "The Expanded Role of the General Accounting
        Office in Support of a Strengthened Congress." BUREAUCRAT 3
        (January 1975): 383-400.

        The author relates that the Congressional Budget and Im-
        poundment Control Act of 1974 was a significant event in
        the restoration of equilibrium between the executive and
        legislative branches of government. The reader is informed
        that Congress has had an effect on government operations
        only through the auditing procedures of the General Ac-
        counting Office (GAO). Fitzgerald indicates that GAO's
        service includes: 1) a review and analysis of existing
        and proposed programs, and 2) the rendering of advice
        and assistance.

252   Frye, Alton. "Congressional Politics and Policy Analysis: Bridging
        the Gap." POLICY ANALYSIS 2 (Spring 1976): 265-81.

        Frye relates that legislators are acknowledging that Congress
        must improve its capacity to define realistic choices among
        competing policy and program proposals and that key par-
        ticipants in the revised congressional budget process un-
        derstand the necessity for budgetary analyses to incorporate
        scientific, engineering, and other noneconomic elements
        of policy planning. The reader is informed that there
        have been promising policy analysis developments in the
        General Accounting Office and Congressional Research
        Service.

253   Harris, Joseph P. CONGRESSIONAL CONTROL OF ADMINISTRATION.
        Washington, D.C.: Brookings Institution, 1964. xi, 306 p.

        The author maintains that control of administration is one

of the most important functions of legislative bodies in modern democracies. In examining congressional control of the bureaucracy, Harris discusses control of executive organization and activities, Congress and the budget, the appropriation process, proposals for budget control reform, control via the audit, Congress and the civil service, the legislative veto, and control by investigation. In this age of the administrative state, when immense power and sums of money are entrusted to public officials who serve, defend, and regulate the American people in innumerable ways, this book remains the most authoritative text on this subject.

254   Haveman, Robert H. "Policy Analysis and the Congress: An Economist's View." POLICY ANALYSIS 2 (Spring 1976): 235-50.

Haveman maintains that Congress is subject to an incentive structure that rewards legislators for responding to organized vested interests and fails to reward them for concentrating analytic resources on programs or issues where serious inefficiency or inequity exists. By ensuring sufficient reporting, the House and Senate Budget Committees and the Congressional Budget Office enhances public understanding of what government does and how it does it. Haveman suggests this is necessary for a more productive national debate on economic priorities and policy directions.

255   Jackson, Henry M. "Environmental Policy and the Congress." PUBLIC ADMINISTRATION REVIEW 28 (July-August 1968): 303-5.

"A new emphasis in national policy is needed to meet the threatening deterioration in the quality of our environment. The time has come to make explicit what had been implicit in our national policy since the early days of the republic. We need to affirm by appropriate policy statement and by institutional means that protection of the life-sustaining elements of our natural environment is a public responsibility."

256   Jones, Charles O. "Why Congress Can't Do Policy Analysis (or Words to that Effect)." POLICY ANALYSIS 2 (Spring 1976): 251-64.

This article notes that Congress has sought to extend its policy analysis capabilities by increasing the responsibilities of the General Accounting Office and the Congressional Research Service and by creating the Office of Technology Assessment. Jones maintains that these agencies and the Congressional Budget Office represent an impressive analytical capability, but they must adapt to the political needs of Congress.

257   Kammerer, Gladys M. "The Administration of Congress." PUBLIC
        ADMINISTRATION REVIEW 9 (Summer 1949): 175-81.

        The author discusses organization for administration of
        congressional housekeeping functions, the selection of
        elective administrative positions and related personnel,
        fiscal management of Congress, and needed changes.
        Kammerer concludes that the present administrative struc-
        ture of Congress probably needs drastic reorganization
        more seriously than does the executive branch.

258   Klay, William Earle. "A Legislative Tool to Encourage Agency Effi-
        ciency." PUBLIC PRODUCTIVITY REVIEW 3 (Spring 1978): 23-31.

        The author outlines a new idea to increase the efficiency
        of government agencies. He bases this concept on the
        assumption that efficiency will be greatest when both the
        agency and its members are rewarded for sincere and
        creative efforts to do things more efficiently. Klay's
        strategy is based upon the frequently overlooked fact that
        the legislature, with its final authority over appropriations,
        is the key institution which encourages or discourages true
        cost consciousness in public agencies. He offers a strategy
        to achieve greater levels of public service per dollar
        appropriated.

259   Laurance, Edward J. "The Changing Role of Congress in Defense
        Policy-Making." JOURNAL OF CONFLICT RESOLUTION 20 (June
        1976): 213-53.

        Laurance asserts that there is important evidence that the
        congressional defense decision-making system significantly
        changed during the period 1968-74. Some of the reasons
        cited for the change were the Vietnam War, decreased
        public perception of an external threat, non-Department
        of Defense policy alternatives, the nonmilitary com-
        mittee role in defense policy making, increased over-
        sight of military procurement, a balanced Senate Armed
        Services Committee, continuing debate on national pri-
        orities, and a legitimate antidefense bloc.

260   Morrow, William L. CONGRESSIONAL COMMITTEES. New York:
        Charles Scribner's Sons, 1969. 272 p.

        Morrow emphasizes that congressional committees perform
        vital roles in resolving conflict for Congress and the
        entire political system, that the committees' importance
        is due to the enhancement of the legislative role in
        solving social problems, and that the behavior of com-
        mittees and committee members should be seen in light
        of their constitutional, organizational, social, and po-
        litical system roles.

261   Patterson, Kenneth D. "Legislative Budget Review: An Economist's
        Viewpoint." PUBLIC ADMINISTRATION REVIEW 24 (March 1964):
        7-13.

        Patterson posits that the review of governmental budgets
        involves questions of economic efficiency which require
        the quantitative expression of the relation between "things,"
        money, and output. He argues that conflict resulting
        from the rational questioning of the executive budget may
        be evidence of the presence of real economic alternatives.
        He includes activities of state legislative budget agencies,
        the economics of budget review, rationality and the legis-
        lative fiscal staff, and post-audits in this analysis.

262   Ripley, Randall B., and Franklin, Grace A. CONGRESS, THE BU-
        REAUCRACY, AND PUBLIC POLICY. Homewood, Ill.: Dorsey Press,
        1976. xii, 193 p. Paper.

        The authors expect students using this textbook to come
        away with an understanding of the critical nature of the
        relationship between Congress and the federal bureaucracy.
        Ripley and Franklin believe that central to the complex
        and important business of public policy making is the in-
        teraction between Congress and the federal bureaucracy.
        Chapters include the nature of policy and policy making in
        the United States; actors in the relationship; congressional-
        bureaucratic interaction; distributive domestic policy;
        regulatory domestic policy; redistributive domestic policy;
        foreign and defense policy; and Congress, the bureaucracy,
        and the nature of American public policy.

263   Roback, Herbert. "The Congress and Super Departments." BUREAU-
        CRAT 1 (Spring 1972): 31-41.

        The author suggests that reorganization will have a long,
        painful, uphill climb, with an uncertain outcome, in the
        Congress. He notes that members of Congress are espe-
        cially skeptical of reforms that come in big packages
        (President Richard Nixon proposed in 1971 that seven
        domestic departments and a number of independent agencies
        be consolidated into four super departments of Community
        Development, Natural Resources, Human Resources, and
        Economic Affairs). The hearing process on Capitol Hill
        is examined in this essay, and a reassessment of reorgani-
        zation is presented.

264   _____. "Program Evaluation by and for the Congress." BUREAUCRAT
        5 (April 1976): 11-36.

        Roback relates that there has been a renewed interest in
        congressional oversight of the executive since the excesses

of the Vietnam War and Watergate. He asserts that the
linkage of oversight and evaluation reflects Congress' concern with mounting governmental costs, but adds that
attempts to deal with the problems have been far from
systematic. This article suggests that although a common
complaint about congressional oversight is that the efforts
are time-consuming and, with relatively few exceptions,
devoid of political profit, the changing constitutional
balance means that far more intervention by the Congress
in executive prerogatives and administrative processes may
be expected under the banner of program evaluation.

265   Robinson, James A. "Decision Making in the House Rules Committee."
        ADMINISTRATIVE SCIENCE QUARTERLY 3 (June 1958): 73-86.

        Robinson analyzes the process by which an important con-
        gressional committee, the House Rules Committee, makes
        its decisions in terms of a series of propositions containing
        the following major variables: spheres of competence,
        communication and information, and motivation. The au-
        thor concludes that the making of decisions in a legis-
        lative committee appears to resemble decision making in
        other organized political institutions.

266   Sapp, Carl. "Executive Assistance in the Legislative Process." PUBLIC
        ADMINISTRATION REVIEW 6 (Winter 1946): 10-19.

        Sapp reviews the responsibilities of the president for as-
        sisting in the legislative process, analyzes the assistance
        of executive departments in reporting on bills before the
        legislature, describes the manner in which reports are
        prepared in the departments, and appraises such depart-
        mental assistance. He also examines assistance by the
        Bureau of the Budget (now Office of Management and
        Budget) in influencing legislation before Congress.

267   Schick, Allen. "Congress and the 'Details' of Administration." PUBLIC
        ADMINISTRATION REVIEW 36 (September-October 1976): 516-28.

        Schick discusses the quiescence of Congress, the resurgence
        of Congress, legislative oversight and evaluation responsi-
        bilities, congressional veto of administrative actions, and
        congressional authorization of legislation in emphasizing
        that the details of administration are important and that
        control over the details is also important. This is an ex-
        cellent essay describing congressional responsibilities in
        public administration.

268   _____. "The Supply and Demand for Analysis on Capitol Hill."
        POLICY ANALYSIS 2 (Spring 1976): 215-34.

Schick asserts that the congressional attitude toward policy analysis is not an all or nothing proposition but depends substantially on the conditions facing Congress. This article suggests that four conditions promote the demand for and supply of analysis on Capitol Hill: congressional independence from the executive branch, abundant and dispersed staff resources within the legislative branch, available analytic resources outside Congress, and a legislative process open to diverse interests and participants.

269   Sigal, Leon V. "Official Secrecy and Informal Communication in Congressional-Bureaucratic Relations." POLITICAL SCIENCE QUARTERLY 90 (Spring 1975): 71-92.

Sigal relates that the three channels in which informal communications in Washington flow are: bootlegging, or hidden dissemination of information; informal briefings of groups of members of Congress, not reported to Congress as a whole; and leaks to the press. The article discusses how the formal provision of information to Congress enables senior officials to monitor and control the activities of bureaucratic subordinates.

270   Silverman, Eli B. "Public Budgeting and Public Administration: Enter the Legislature." PUBLIC FINANCE QUARTERLY 2 (October 1974): 472-84.

Silverman contends that neglect and criticism of the legislature is attributable to public administration's intellectual content and value processes and that reforms designed to increase public administrative input into legislative budgetary formulation have been abandoned. The author informs the reader that alternative strategies for enhanced legislative budgetary power are based on a division of labor rather than centralization, selective retrospective evaluation and oversight rather than comprehensive policy formulation, and economic and political costs and benefits instead of pure economic analysis.

271   Thurber, James A. "Legislative-Administrative Relations." In PUBLIC ADMINISTRATION AND PUBLIC POLICY, edited by H. George Frederickson and Charles R. Wise, pp. 109-18. Lexington, Mass.: D.C. Heath and Co., 1977.

This article is a review of the most important literature and recent reforms that have had an impact on legislative-administrative relations. Thurber focuses primarily upon congressional oversight and recent congressional efforts to increase legislative influence over administration. He probes knowledge of legislative-administrative relationships, policies affecting these relationships, legislative oversight

and control, impact of legislative oversight upon administration, and major recent reforms that have had an impact on legislative-administrative relations.

272   Worthley, John A. "Public Administration and Legislatures: Past
Neglect, Present Probes." PUBLIC ADMINISTRATION REVIEW 35
(September-October 1975): 486-90.

The author focuses on a historical review of public administration literature in examining administration of legislatures. He emphasizes the lack of interest in legislative
organization and describes current developments in this
area. Worthley believes that public administration stands
to benefit in that significant organizational lessons might
be ascertained from the legislative experience.

273   Worthley, John A., and Crane, Edgar G. "Legislative Organization
in the United States: Concepts and Practices." ADMINISTRATION
24 (Summer 1976): 159-74.

Emphasizing that administrative concepts have not been
applied to the management of state legislatures, the authors believe that analyzing the impact of organizational
development on the political functions of the legislature
could provide a more integrated approach to organizations and enhance the application of administrative theory.

E. GOVERNMENT REORGANIZATION

274   Arnold, Peri E. "Reorganization and Politics: A Reflection on the
Adequacy of Administrative Theory." PUBLIC ADMINISTRATION
REVIEW 34 (May-June 1974): 205-11.

Arnold states that public administration theory has always
rejected politics. He indicates that federal executive
reorganization provides an interesting setting for an analysis
of the consequences of this apolitical theory. The author
concludes that orthodoxy remains the preeminent theoretical
element within most recent reorganization plans.

275   Ascher, Charles S. "Trends of a Decade in Administrative Practices."
PUBLIC ADMINISTRATION REVIEW 10 (Autumn 1950): 229-35.

The author reviews administrative practices from the
Brownlow Committee to the Hoover Commission (1939-49),
program planning and the performance budget, fiscal
policy, devolution of authority to line supervisors, administration as a social process, intergovernmental relationships, wider use of the social sciences, broader social involvement, humanization, and coordination in this discussion.

This essay is a good review of the literature of administrative practices at mid-century.

276   Brademas, John. "Federal Reorganization and Its Likely Impacts on
State and Local Government." PUBLIUS 8 (Spring 1978): 25-37.

Brademas, Majority Whip in the 95th Congress and U.S.
Representative from Indiana, believes that reorganization
of the executive branch must be considered in the context of the American constitutional and political system.
He maintains that reorganization influences the distribution
of power and influence over policy. For reorganization
to be beneficial, the place of politics in reorganization
must be recognized.

277   Brown, David S. "'Reforming' the Bureaucracy: Some Suggestions for
the New President." PUBLIC ADMINISTRATION REVIEW 37 (March-
April 1977): 163-70.

The author warns President Carter and his advisers that
bureaucratic reform is not as easy as it sounds and that
reorganization, while necessary and useful, is only part
of the answer. Brown suggests a seven-point approach
to bureaucratic reform, including: 1) understanding the
limitations of the system; 2) involving the bureaucrat;
3) the matter of congressional support; 4) the client, the
citizen, and the bureaucrat; 5) focusing on bureaucratic
specifics; 6) the improvement of governmental productivity;
and 7) systems analysis and bureaucratic deficiencies.

278   Dean, Alan L. "The Goals of Departmental Reorganization." BU-
REAUCRAT 1 (Spring 1972): 23-31.

"The primary emphasis in the development of the detailed
proposals was on increasing the effectiveness of government. Although economies were expected to be realized
through greater administrative efficiency and improvements
in the quality of program decisions, the central objective
was to revitalize the federal executive branch and thereby
to help restore the confidence of the public in their government." This essay was written soon after President
Richard Nixon's proposal (1971) to consolidate seven domestic executive departments and a number of independent
agencies into four new departments of Community Development, Natural Resources, Human Resources, and Economic
Affairs.

279   Dempsey, John R. "Carter Reorganization: A Midterm Appraisal."
PUBLIC ADMINISTRATION REVIEW 39 (January-February 1979): 74-78.

Dempsey considers agency reorganization, conversion of

federal executive budgeting to a zero-base format, and
civil service reform as the major elements of the Carter
reorganization effort. He concludes that the President's
Reorganization Project may be a conscientious, hard-
working group, but its results to date leave a great deal
to be desired.

280   Dimock, Marshall E. "The Objectives of Governmental Reorganization."
PUBLIC ADMINISTRATION REVIEW 11 (Autumn 1951): 233-41.

Dimock states that skillful reorganization is about the
most difficult task in the whole range of human relations.
He concludes: "It takes a statesman of the first order to
relate group goals and individual aspirations to the complexities of administrative structure. Reorganization is a
phase of institutional life; the institution is part of culture;
reorganization should be judged by its effect on the economy
and on the good life. . . . In the last analysis, principles
of organization are principles of cultural growth and of
national aspiration."

281   Divine, William R. "The Second Hoover Commission Reports: An
Analysis." PUBLIC ADMINISTRATION REVIEW 15 (Autumn 1955):
263-69.

Divine finds that the reports of the second Hoover Commission should once and for all time lay the ghost of the
proposition that principles of organization are applicable
without regard to policy and value judgments." In analyzing the prospects for adoption of these reports, the
author believes that the most important factor to consider
is that the major issues of the second Hoover Commission
are controversial questions of public policy. Divine
discusses the organization and composition of the commission, organization and policy, improving departmental
management, the role of the expert, business enterprises,
and expected results in this essay. This is a very useful
document for ascertaining the role of government in
American society in the mid-1950s.

282   Emmerich, Herbert. FEDERAL ORGANIZATION AND ADMINISTRA-
TIVE MANAGEMENT. University: University of Alabama Press, 1971.
304 p.

Emmerich, a participant in the work of the historic
Brownlow Committee under President Franklin D. Roosevelt
and the two Hoover Commissions under Presidents Harry S.
Truman and Dwight D. Eisenhower, offers unique insights
into the continuing process of executive reorganization.
He discusses landmarks of administrative management from
1789 until 1933, describes the activities of the President's

Committee on Administrative Management, or Brownlow
Committee, reviews the administrative legacy of Franklin
D. Roosevelt, discusses the backgrounds, philosophies,
and results of the two Hoover Commissions, and probes
the relationships between the executive branch, government agencies, and Congress.

283   Fain, Tyrus G., ed., in collaboration with Plant, Katharine C., and
Milloy, Ross. FEDERAL REORGANIZATION: THE EXECUTIVE BRANCH.
New York: R.R. Bowker Co., 1977. xxxiii, 671 p.

This valuable documentary collection covers many of the
subjects which the Carter administration and Congress will
have to examine and contains some of the proposals which
President Carter intends to employ. Most of the documents
in this volume have appeared in government publications
and are either out of print or difficult to obtain. The
scope of this book encompasses documents released from
1971-76 and includes a variety of congressional hearings,
reports, and statements. The focus of the text is on the
consolidation of executive departments and agencies (Ash
and Nixon recommendations), regulatory reform (Nixon
and Ralph Nader proposals), and zero base budgeting-
sunset legislation (Carter approach). This is highly recommended to students and practitioners interested in reorganization of the federal government.

284   Fox, Douglas M. "The President's Proposals for Executive Reorganization:
A Critique." PUBLIC ADMINISTRATION REVIEW 33 (September-
October 1973): 401-6.

President Nixon's proposal to reorganize the executive
branch involved transferring the functions of six domestic
cabinet-level departments--Interior, Commerce, Labor,
Housing and Urban Development, Health, Education, and
Welfare, and Transportation--into the Departments of Natural Resources, Human Resources, Economic Affairs, and
Community Development. Nixon argued that the adoption
of this proposal would have resulted in a much more coordinated set of national policies, more amenable to presidential control. Fox concludes that this was not the case
and that the Nixon proposal contained profound policy
implications which the Nixon administration had not acknowledged.

285   _____, et al., eds. "President Nixon's Proposals for Executive Reorganization." PUBLIC ADMINISTRATION REVIEW 34 (September-
October 1974): 487-95.

Fox is editor of remarks offered by Alan L. Dean, Harold
Seidman, Harvey Mansfield, James Fesler, and Robert

Gilmour on President Nixon's proposal to consolidate the
Departments of Interior, Commerce, Labor, Housing and
Urban Development, Health, Education, and Welfare, and
Transportation, plus some functions of Agriculture, into
four new departments: Community Development, Natural
Resources, Human Resources, and Economic Affairs. These
comments offer insightful analysis into the problems and
prospects of government reorganization.

286   Grafton, Carl. "The Reorganization of Federal Agencies." ADMINI-
STRATION AND SOCIETY 10 (February 1979): 437-64.

This study presents a theory of federal agency reorganization covering a large percentage of reorganization cases
occurring from 1934 through 1976. The author views
federal agency reorganization as closely related to de novo
agency creation. Grafton states that agency reorganization and creation are often the last two steps in an esca-
lation process through which society deals with problems
generated by large scale discontinuous socioeconomic-
technological changes. He concludes: "If an agency is
created before conceptualization has ended, it is very
likely that it will be reorganized repeatedly until conceptualization is complete."

287   Hawkins, Robert B., Jr. "Federal Principles for Government Reorganization." PUBLIUS 8 (Spring 1978): 133-40.

The author emphasizes the complexity of government reorganization in the federal system, the lack of consensus
on particular purposes, means of examining information
and interchange in the federal system, federalism as a
set of political arrangements, the institutionalization of
power and interests and the movement toward greater
centralization, and new formulations of federal solutions.
Hawkins portrays the American federal system as solving
conflictual situations through negotiations and compromises.

288   _____. "Government Reorganization: A Federal Interest." PUBLIUS
8 (Spring 1978): 3-12.

Hawkins defines the concepts of government reorganization
and structure. He reviews historical commentary on theories of government reorganization, pointing out the contributions of Alexander Hamilton and Woodrow Wilson.
He notes that the terminology of government reorganization
has changed throughout the history of American federalism,
but that the emphasis upon structure remains crucial to
shaping the federal system. The concern for structural
changes continues.

289   Heady, Ferrel. "The Reorganization Act of 1949." PUBLIC ADMINI-
        STRATION REVIEW 9 (Summer 1949): 165-74.

        In belated response to urgent and repeated requests by the
        Commission on Organization of the Executive Branch and
        by President Harry S. Truman, Congress passed a general
        reorganization act in 1949. The immediate reason for
        this legislation was to make the time-tested presidential
        reorganization plan procedure available as a means for
        putting into effect many of the recommendations of the
        Hoover Commission.

290   Mansfield, Harvey C. "Federal Executive Reorganization: Thirty Years
        of Experience." PUBLIC ADMINISTRATION REVIEW 29 (July-August
        1969): 332-45. Tables.

        "This review of lessons from 30 years' experience with
        efforts at federal reorganization treats three main topics.
        Considering first the range of purposes actually served or
        intended by reorganizations, most of which involve shifts
        in control or status, in contrast with the officially recog-
        nized criteria, it concludes that we are no nearer to
        measurable and mutually compatible standards. Turning
        next to the processes of initiation and approval, it ana-
        lyzes the provisions of the successive Reorganization Acts
        and the disposition of Plans submitted. . . . Dealing
        finally with prospects, it concludes that the doctrines so
        far developed are inadequate to solve the impending
        problems of interdepartmental and intergovernmental co-
        ordination."

291   Marando, Vincent L. "An Overview of the Political Feasibility of
        Local Government Reorganization." In ORGANIZING PUBLIC SERVICES
        IN METROPOLITAN AMERICA, edited by Thomas P. Murphy and
        Charles R. Warren, pp. 17-51. Lexington, Mass.: Lexington Books,
        1974. Tables.

        Marando offers an extensive overview of the reorganization
        scorecard, reform initiation, reorganization campaigns,
        voter response to reorganization referenda, selected voting
        patterns, reorganization in large metropolitan areas, and
        case studies of defeat and success, respectively, in Tampa
        and Jacksonville, Florida. This is a very useful essay on
        the literature of local government reorganization histories.

292   Miles, Rufus E., Jr. "Considerations for a President Bent on Reorgani-
        zation." PUBLIC ADMINISTRATION REVIEW 37 (March-April 1977):
        155-62.

        Offering thirteen criteria for President Carter and his
        advisers to consider when debating major government

reorganization controls, Miles points out that organization is important at the federal level in expressing the nation's priorities, in allocating resources, in attracting competent leader-executives to key positions, and in accomplishing the purposes of the president, the Congress, and the body politic. Miles's thirteen criteria and discussion are valuable teaching tenets for academics and practitioners concerned with government reorganization plans.

293   Murphy, Thomas P., and Florestano, Patricia. "Unimplemented Metropolitan Reorganizations." In ORGANIZING PUBLIC SERVICES IN METROPOLITAN AMERICA, edited by Thomas P. Murphy and Charles R. Warren, pp. 71-81. Lexington, Mass.: Lexington Books, 1974. Table.

Noting that most attempts at metropolitan structural reorganization have been unsuccessful, the authors review some of the city-county consolidation, two-tier, and multipurpose district models and proposals that have been rejected, including efforts in Sacramento-North Sacramento County, California; Atlanta-Fulton County, Georgia; Charlotte-Meckleburg County, North Carolina; Cleveland; St. Louis; and Denver.

294   Musicus, Milton. "Reappraising Reorganization." PUBLIC ADMINISTRATION REVIEW 24 (June 1964): 107-12.

The author concludes that reorganization must be a continuing process and not an act of periodic political change. He examines the growth and proliferation of government, the objectives of reorganization, varying degrees of acceptance and opposition to reorganization, the results of reorganization, judging accomplishments of reorganization, and the impacts of future government reorganizations.

295   Pettigrew, Richard A. "Improving Government Competence." PUBLIUS 8 (Spring 1978): 99-103.

Pettigrew, an Assistant for Reorganization to President Carter discusses the reorganization objectives of the Carter administration, its recommendations to promote these objectives, its priorities in attaining reorganization, and the reasons why the Carter administration will succeed in its reorganization efforts where previous administrations have not.

296   "Reorganization Plan No. 2 of 1970." PUBLIC ADMINISTRATION REVIEW 30 (November-December 1970): 611-19.

This article provides details for the establishment of the

Office of Management and Budget and the Domestic
Council. OMB replaced the Bureau of the Budget, and
the Domestic Council provided a "mission oriented" approach for forming specific project groups to analyze
policy options.

297   Rouse, Andrew M. "Selecting Reorganizers." BUREAUCRAT 1 (Spring
        1972): 11–23. Tables.

"To a greater extent than might seem apparent at first,
the process of a reorganization study succeeds in bringing
about the reorganization that it proposes. . . . The reorganization study process, unlike many of the other
factors which will affect the outcome, is relatively con-
trollable, and, through careful attention to it, an initiator
may increase his chance of success. . . . The form of
the study mechanism as an element of process either dampens
or amplifies the intensity of conflict, and hence, partially
determines if and how divergent aims, values, and interests will be balanced. The selection of a study mechanism is therefore an important issue."

298   Stevenson, Adlai E. "Reorganization from the State Point of View."
        PUBLIC ADMINISTRATION REVIEW 10 (Winter 1950): 1–6.

The former governor of Illinois and Democratic candidate
for president suggests that we must recognize the need
for cooperation rather than hostility or capitulation between
levels of government, that we must remove duplications
in federal, state, and local services, assigning each program to the government most fitted to administer it in the
public interest, that we should encourage further federal
and state studies to reduce the number of governmental
units, that we should expand sound interstate agreements
wherever possible, and that we should press for wise and
efficient administration of the federal grants which are
made for national programs, with only those controls which
the public interest requires.

299   "Summary of Reports of the Hoover Commission." PUBLIC ADMINI-
        STRATION REVIEW 9 (Spring 1949): 73–99.

Included in this summary report are commission conclusions
concerning the general management of the executive branch,
personnel management, budgeting, reorganization of accounting in the government, statistical activities, organization and management of federal supply activities, foreign
affairs, the national security organization, Departments
of Agriculture, Treasury, and Interior, veterans affairs,
federal medical activities, Indian affairs, federal research,
and federal business enterprises.

300   Weinberger, Casper W. "Government Reorganization and Public
       Purpose." PUBLIUS 8 (Spring 1978): 39-48.

       This article reviews problems involved in federal govern-
       ment reorganization and suggests changes that would make
       government more efficient and responsive. The author
       discovers that reorganization is not a party concern, nor
       is it even an ideological or philosophical problem. Wein-
       berger believes it is a matter in which small, narrowly
       based groups who have what they want, and are afraid
       of losing it, invariably have proven stronger than large
       groups with more diverse aims.

F. GOVERNMENT DEPARTMENTS AND AGENCIES

301   Borst, Diane, and Montana, Patrick J., eds. MANAGING NON-
       PROFIT ORGANIZATIONS. New York: American Management As-
       sociation, 1977. 322 p.

       The editors offer a comprehensive source book complete
       with selected articles and speeches by authorities in the
       field on how to apply business management techniques to
       nonprofit organizations in government, education, health,
       religious, and charitable organizations.

302   Breyer, Stephen G., and MacAvoy, Paul. ENERGY REGULATION
       BY THE FEDERAL POWER COMMISSION. Washington, D.C.: Brook-
       ings Institution, 1974. 163 p.

       Breyer and MacAvoy examine the policies of the Federal
       Power Commission in order to demonstrate the problems of
       utility regulation, price control, and industrial planning.
       They ask if the FPC serves the interests of the energy
       consumer and link FPC policies to the gas shortage, lack
       of more rapid growth in pipeline construction, and the
       prevention of hundreds of millions of dollars in savings
       per year for energy consumers.

303   Cramton, Roger C. "Regulatory Structure and Regulatory Performance:
       A Critique of the Ash Council Report." PUBLIC ADMINISTRATION
       REVIEW 32 (July-August 1972): 284-91.

       This article considers the basic premise of the Ash Council
       Report--that the structure of a regulatory agency has a
       profound effect on regulatory performance. The Ash Council
       recommended that the independent regulatory commissions
       in the transportation, power, securities, and consumer
       protection fields be transformed into executive agencies
       headed by single administrators responsible to the president.

The author is critical of the Ash Council proposals, but he does not defend the status quo either.

304 Dunn, James A., Jr. "Public Ownership of U.S. Railroads in Comparative Perspective." POLICY STUDIES JOURNAL 4 (Autumn 1975): 49-53.

Loans and subsidies to the railroad industry have given rise to the perpetual argument over nationalization. The experiences of other countries with publicly owned railroads seems pertinent to both positions of the debate. Nationalization does not protect railroads against contemporary developments in economics and technology. Some approaches include the encouraging of profit, the protecting of rail travel from the problems of economic deficiency, and the alteration of the balance of competitive advantage between rail transport and competing trends.

305 Engman, Lewis A. "How Government Regulation has Become the Curse of Consumerism." BARRISTER 2 (Winter 1975): 58-64.

This article projects that industries subject to direct federal regulation account for 10 percent of everything made and sold in the United States and that they tend to be industries whose costs influence the prices of other products. Engman suggests that the most regulated industries, protected from competition and existing on cost-plus, are federal protectorates. He cites that the Civil Aeronautics Board regulates the entry of the air carriers' market, disapproves or modifies rate-change proposals, and directs the distribution of air carrier routes. The author also cites that the Interstate Commerce Commission controls market entry by trucking firms and fixes the rates. Engman surmises that the ICC investigates rates in fewer than 1 percent of ICC-related cases.

306 Etzioni, Amitai. "The Third Sector and Domestic Missions." PUBLIC ADMINISTRATION REVIEW 33 (July-August 1973): 314-23.

Etzioni examines the role of the third sector in the American political economy. He concludes that the most promising solutions to our domestic problems are among the third sector approaches now evolving. Examples of third sector organizations include the U.S. Postal Service, Amtrak, universities, hospitals, the Federal National Mortgage Association (Fannie Mae), and the Communications Satellite Corporation (Comsat).

307 Grafton, Carl. "The Creation of Federal Agencies." ADMINISTRATION AND SOCIETY 7 (November 1975): 328-65.

Grafton studies federal agencies created between 1933
and 1972 and explains their formation in terms of organization and timing. The reader is informed that only
those agencies existing in 1972 are part of the study and
that SET (socioeconomic or technological) novelty was
supposed to be a chief motivation to agency creation.
The author surmises that twenty-six of fifty-one federal
agencies were formed as a direct result of an objective
SET novelty occurrence and that these twenty-six agencies
account for over 90 percent of the current agency budgets.

308   Gregg, James M.H., and Diegelman, Robert F. "Red Tape on Trial:
       Elements of a Successful Effort to Cut Burdensome Federal Reporting
       Requirements." PUBLIC ADMINISTRATION REVIEW 39 (March-April
       1979): 171-76. Table.

       The authors offer five lessons to be learned from their ex-
       periences at the Law Enforcement Assistance Administration,
       including the realizations that rhetorical commitment to
       cutting red tape is not enough, that a specific target must
       be selected, that game playing tactics should be used,
       that a measurable target should be set, and that top
       officials must participate in this process.

309   Hamilton, Randy H., and Kelsey, Judy. "The Administrative Conference
       of the U.S." PUBLIC ADMINISTRATION REVIEW 29 (May-June 1969):
       286-90.

       The authors outline the organization of the conference,
       including the roles and responsibilities of the chairperson,
       the conference itself, the council, and the assembly. The
       authors conclude: "Nearly a quarter century's effort to
       establish a federal agency with responsibility and power
       for investigating and reforming federal administrative
       practices and procedures has been crowned by the appoint-
       ment of a chairman for the Administrative Conference of
       the United States. . . . Current insistence for finer at-
       tunement of administrative agencies to the needs of their
       clientele lends added interest and importance to this unique
       agency as part of the panoply of the American admini-
       strative state."

310   Hershey, Cary. "Responses of Federal Agencies to Employee Risk-
       Taking." BUREAUCRAT 2 (Fall 1973): 285-93.

       This article outlines some of the important institutional
       characteristics and organizational strategies which discourage
       federal employees from incurring risks by protesting and,
       at the same time, mitigate and contain the impact of
       employee activism. Hershey points out that federal em-
       ployees participation in protest activities directed at

changing the policies and practices of public agencies is highly unconventional behavior. The author adds that the institutional values and norms of federal agencies hold that employees must obey superiors' orders, must operate within their policy guidelines, and must keep their own advocacy discreet and within prescribed channels.

311   Horton, Frank. "The Commission on Federal Paperwork: A Mechanism for Reform." BUREAUCRAT 4 (October 1975): 260-67.

Horton states that the Commission on Federal Paperwork was established to enable significant reductions in federal paperwork and that paperwork comprises the most visible part of government operations. The reader is told that the commission will assure that necessary information is made available to federal officials, minimize the burden imposed by federal reporting requirements on private citizens, guarantee appropriate standards of confidentiality for information held by private citizens or the federal government, and provide that information held by the federal government is processed and disseminated to increase its usefulness to all federal agencies and the public.

312   Huntington, Samuel P. "The Marasmus of the ICC: The Commission, the Railroads, and the Public Interest." YALE LAW JOURNAL 61 (1952): 467-509.

This case study concerns the Interstate Commerce Commission (ICC) and illustrates the way in which regulatory agencies tend to become the captives of the groups that they regulate. This article reviews the history of the ICC, railroad support for the ICC, ICC aid to the railroads, and the pattern of affiliation of the ICC with the railroads.

313   Ink, Dwight A. "Establishing the New Department of Housing and Urban Development." PUBLIC ADMINISTRATION REVIEW 27 (September 1967): 224-28.

Ink, a former Assistant Secretary for Administration at the Department of Housing and Urban Development, describes the organization of HUD as various housing functions and responsibilities of former federal agencies were consolidated under the authority of the HUD secretary. In this essay, Ink discusses the problem-solving basis of the new department, decision making in the field offices, interdepartmental cooperation and intergovernmental relations, and the human factor in the department.

314   Jenkins, John A. "How to End the Endless Delay at the FTC." WASHINGTON MONTHLY 8 (June 1976): 42-50.

Jenkins asserts that the experience of the Federal Trade
Commission suggests that regulatory reform will not work
as long as the agency itself is burdened with administrative rules that govern every action. The reader is informed that when FTC lawyers file charges, the case goes
first to an administrative law judge. If the decision is ap-
pealed, the FTC considers the case anew and this process
can take years.

315   Jones, Charles O.   "The Limits of Public Support: Air Pollution
        Agency Development."   PUBLIC ADMINISTRATION REVIEW   32
        (September-October 1972): 502-8.   Tables.

        The author applies Prof. Francis E. Rourke's maxim--"the
        first and fundamental source of power for administrative
        agencies in American society is their ability to attract
        outside support"--to the National Air Pollution Control
        Administration. He concludes: "The experience of na-
        tional air pollution agency development over the past
        decade provides both modifications and expansions on
        Professor Rourke's analysis of agency power. Massive
        expression of public interest and support for action in an
        issue area does not automatically result in increased
        agency power. A weak agency, by definition, is in-
        capable under normal circumstances of managing that kind
        of support."

316   Kharasch, Robert N.   THE INSTITUTIONAL IMPERATIVE: HOW TO
        UNDERSTAND THE UNITED STATES GOVERNMENT AND OTHER
        BULKY OBJECTS.   New York: Charterhouse Books, 1973. x, 257 p.

        Kharasch describes the method of his book in this manner:
        "What is necessary . . . if the functioning of our insti-
        tutions is to be understood, is a short statement of the
        laws which institutions follow. The method here adopted
        is to begin, without apology, with a few definitions and
        a few axioms that, like all axioms, have to be accepted.
        From these, theorems are deduced as logical consequences.
        These deduced theorems in turn require to be matched to
        occurrences in the real world, to see if they fit and are
        indeed laws of general application." Sections include
        discussions of the laws of institutional behavior, the laws
        of relevance, institutional disasters, and directions for
        assembly and control of institutions.

317   Krasnow, Erwin G., and Longley, Lawrence D.   THE POLITICS OF
        BROADCAST REGULATION.   2d ed. New York: St. Martin's Press,
        1978. 213 p.

        The authors discuss the roles of the Federal Communications

Commission, the communications industry, citizens groups, the courts, the White House, and Congress in determining the regulatory process. They offer case studies on Frequency Modulation (FM) broadcasting, Ultra High Frequency (UHF) television, broadcast commercial time, comparative license renewal policies, and Citizens Band (CB) radio economic, social, cultural, and technological impacts. Krasnow and Longley maintain that the FCC is one of the most important and least understood government agencies.

318   Leone, Robert A. "The Real Costs of Regulation." HARVARD BUSINESS REVIEW 55 (November–December 1977): 57-66.

This article declares that regulation of business activities is dramatically increasing at all government levels and that regulations not only control such variables as labor and safety but also the environment in which business is conducted. Leone believes that this increase is caused by the desire for economic equality, the sophistication of the natural and social sciences, and the convergence of interests.

319   Levy, Sidney J. "The Public Image of Government Agencies." PUBLIC ADMINISTRATION REVIEW 23 (March 1963): 25-29.

Levy believes that government agencies cannot do much to improve public recognition of their accomplishments and that Americans prefer to believe that their government is bureaucratic, lazy, and authoritarian. Being critical of government is part of the American way.

320   Lundberg, Craig C. "Organization Change in the Third Sector." PUBLIC ADMINISTRATION REVIEW 35 (September–October 1975): 472-77.

Lundberg states that organizational change in the modern world is an attempt to link together the demands of the organization with the demands of the individual--within the context of the demands of the organization's domain through integrative strategies of change. He posits that third sector organizations often come about in response to the rapid, often linear change which many organizations experience.

321   McGill, Michael E., and Wooten, Leland M. "Management in the Third Sector." PUBLIC ADMINISTRATION REVIEW 35 (September–October 1975): 444-55. Table.

In this article, the authors attempt to identify some new directions in management theory and practice relating to

the emergence of third sector organizations as important
entities in our post-industrial society. They specify defi-
nitional criteria of the third sector, advance a model of
third sector organizations, and discuss the implications of
this model for management in coming decades.

322   Meier, Kenneth J., and Plumlee, John. "Regulatory Administration
and Organizational Rigidity." WESTERN POLITICAL QUARTERLY 31
(March 1978): 80-95.

This article alleges that government regulation of the
private sector has become a source of considerable controversy in American politics and that the growth of the
consumer movement has created an additional impetus to
examine the effects of regulation. Meier and Plumlee
assert that simplistic solutions to regulatory problems, such
as eliminating regulatory agencies, are not advisable.
They suggest that an examination of the reasons for its
failure is a much better solution if the agency is not
effectively performing its tasks.

323   Miles, Rufus E., Jr. "A Cabinet Department of Education: An Unwise
Campaign Promise or a Sound Idea?" PUBLIC ADMINISTRATION
REVIEW 39 (March-April 1979): 103-10.

Miles concludes that "the creation of a cabinet department
of education makes abundant good sense." He discusses
the roles and priorities of the president, denotes the potential hazards of a strong voice for education at the
federal level, compares the concerns of energy and education as appropriate cabinet functions, examines the role
of education in American society, analyzes the problem
of organized pressure groups, and states that "education
. . . could be the foundation of a revised social ethos.
. . . It could become the most significant avenue toward
a society that is simultaneously more just and more dynamic
and interesting."

324   _____. "The Case for a Federal Department of Education." PUBLIC
ADMINISTRATION REVIEW 27 (March 1967): 1-9.

The author analyzes the following concerns in stating his
case for a separate Department of Education: Would the
creation of a new Department of Education aid or hinder
the president in improving the management of the federal
government? How difficult to manage is the Department
of HEW? What would be the effect of a super Department
of HEW, with three sub-Cabinet Departments? Is a new
Department of Education the most logical split-off, if one
should occur? If a Department of Education is desirable,
what should be the scope of its functions?

325   Mitnick, Barry M. "Deregulation as a Process of Organizational Re-
        duction." PUBLIC ADMINISTRATION REVIEW 38 (July-August 1978):
        350-57.

> Mitnick discusses the concept of deregulation and describes
> four types of formal methods for deregulation: 1) cata-
> strophic ending, 2) guided-unguided wind-down, 3) strip-
> ping, and 4) disintegration with transfer of programs. He
> concludes that "work on understanding the decline or re-
> duction of public organizations, including regulatory agen-
> cies, is in its infancy."

326   Mogulof, Melvin B. "Federal Interagency Action and Inaction: The
        Federal Regional Council Experience." PUBLIC ADMINISTRATION
        REVIEW 32 (May-June 1972): 232-40.

> The Nixon administration's concern for federal administra-
> tive effectiveness was reflected in the growth of federal
> regional councils. These councils, established in ten
> federal regional headquarters cities, include those federal
> agencies primarily concerned with special programs. This
> article focuses on problems in interagency coordination,
> as well as the dilemmas created for the councils by their
> lack of authority to undertake actions which are viewed
> as costly by any of its members. A series of suggestions
> are made to strengthen the councils so that they can play
> a proper role within a national decision system.

327   Moore, John E. "Recycling the Regulatory Agencies." PUBLIC AD-
        MINISTRATION REVIEW 32 (July-August 1972): 291-98.

> The author's definition of recycling implies a deliberate
> provision for invigorating and redefining the goals of the
> regulatory agencies. He notes that the circumstances
> that contribute to an agency's initial effectiveness will
> favor the redirection or invigoration of its activities in
> face of changing conditions and concludes that these
> circumstances are far from uniform. Moore reveals that
> the most encouraging feature of renewed vitality is to be
> found in the additional points of access that are being
> opened to un- or underrepresented interests, making
> systematic what has too often depended on crisis.

328   Morrill, William A. "Services Integration and the Department of
        Health, Education, and Welfare." EVALUATION 3 (1976): 52-57.

> Morrill contends that the fusion of services at HEW has
> become important in the last decade and that the de-
> velopmental and demonstration projects (Allied Services
> Act, the Services Integration Targets of Opportunity
> Grants, and the partnership Grants) assisted state and

local governments to improve their human services. He
notes that in 1975 Secretary Casper Weinberger issued the
Capacity Building Policy Statement in which he committed
HEW to improve planning and management of human service
programs. HEW developed nine principles to improve
evaluation of these services.

329   Murphy, Richard J. "The Difference of a Decade: The Federal Government." PUBLIC ADMINISTRATION REVIEW 32 (March-April 1972):
108-13.

The author, a former assistant postmaster general for personnel, concludes that the changes in federal personnel
administration that were set in motion in the decade of
the 1960s were as profound as any occurring in any single
decade since the passage of the Pendleton Act in 1883.
He notes the historical evolution of changes occurring in
salary, labor relations, equal opportunity, and appeals
reform issues.

330   Murphy, Thomas P.; Nuechterlein, Donald E.; and Stupak, Ronald J.
INSIDE THE BUREAUCRACY: THE VIEW FROM THE ASSISTANT
SECRETARY'S DESK. Boulder, Colo.: Westview Press, 1978. 221 p.

The authors state that in recent years the role of White
House political executives tends to overshadow the contributions of assistant secretaries and other political executives in the Cabinet and other agencies. This work
is the first noteworthy study in more than ten years of
assistant secretaries' roles, relationships, and career patterns, as well as those of presidential appointees. This
book contributes valuable insights into the backgrounds of
political executives who implement the president's programs
and help make his policies.

331   Rycroft, Robert W. "Bureaucratic Performance in Energy Policy Making:
An Evaluation of Output Efficiency and Equity in the Federal Energy
Administration." PUBLIC POLICY 26 (Fall 1978): 599-627.

Rycroft evaluates the performance of the Federal Energy
Administration by submitting agency policy outputs to the
evaluative criteria of equity and efficiency. The reader
is informed that this study centers on the compliance and
enforcement aspects of the FEA's fuel allocation and
pricing programs and that evaluation discovered the FEA
to be both ineffective and inequitable in its implementation of compliance and enforcement rules and regulations.

332   _____. "Energy Policy Feedback: Bureaucratic Responsiveness in the
Federal Energy Administration." POLICY ANALYSIS 5 (Winter 1979):
1-20.

The objective of this essay is to consider the responsiveness of the Federal Energy Administration during the years
of 1973-75. The author reviews the literature and the
methodological and theoretical difficulties in utilizing
responsiveness in an evaluative process. The study concludes with a discussion of the FEA's sensitivity to policy
feedback, analyzing responsiveness "in terms of the cor-
respondence between agency decisions and both public
opinion preferences and interest-group demands."

333   Schultze, Charles. THE PUBLIC USE OF PRIVATE INTEREST. Wash-
      ington, D.C.: Brookings Institution, 1977. 90 p.

      Schultze asserts that government has become too large, is
      inefficient in handling the special problems of an advanced
      industrial society and that shortcomings concerning crucial
      issues are not simply connected to excessive spending.
      He notes that in order to attain national goals, government
      has legislated a series of regulations which alter the de-
      cisions of businessmen and consumers and that these regu-
      latory efforts largely have been ineffective. The author
      believes that the central problem has been that regulatory
      agencies have tried "to force" rather than "to encourage."

334   Seidman, Harold. "The Government Corporation: Organization and
      Controls." PUBLIC ADMINISTRATION REVIEW 14 (Summer 1954):
      183-92.

      Seidman discusses the stages of institutional development
      of public enterprises, probes the organizational relation-
      ships of public enterprises to departments and agencies,
      outlines financial controls and legislative relationships,
      and suggests that the problem of organizational relation-
      ships is greatly complicated when ownership of public
      enterprises is shared with private individuals or groups.

335   Selznick, Philip. TVA AND THE GRASS ROOTS: A STUDY IN THE
      SOCIOLOGY OF FORMAL ORGANIZATION. Berkeley and Los Angeles:
      University of California Press, 1949. viii, 274 p.

      Selznick gives us one the best reviews of political thrust
      in public administration. He makes a case study of the
      developing years of the New Deal's Tennessee Valley
      Authority. He discusses democratic planning, decentrali-
      zation, local administration, and the ideological goals of
      TVA, and then tells how this philosophy becomes a tool
      in the quest for authority. The author discusses coop-
      tation, in which the TVA's commitment to conservation
      and land-use planning was compromised by uses of the
      administrative ideology to gain farm backing for the TVA's
      controversial public electric programs. Some interpret

Selznick's thesis as a negatively moral bureaucratic theory
in the tradition of Michel's "iron law of oligarchy."

336   Speth, Gus.   "Polluters versus Protectors--The Continuing Regulatory
      Conflict." CENTER MAGAZINE 11 (June 1978): 66-69.

Speth labels constraints against further progress toward
eliminating pollution as "institutional" or "technological."
He declares that American society should go beyond environmental concerns and reach out for broader social adjustments if their land, air, and water are to be preserved.

337   Stone, Alan. "Business Regulation: The System is the Problem."
      POLICY STUDIES JOURNAL 4 (Autumn 1975): 58-62.

Stone concludes that only under a democratic system of
public ownership of the means of production, distribution,
and exchange can the vast area of economic policy making
be made responsible to the public. Under democratic socialism, the author maintains, motives to undertake economic acts in conflict with the public interest in order
to improve profits and sales disappear. He believes that
"a more fruitful line of inquiry than better styles of regulation
under capitalism is how can socialism be instituted without the repressive apparatus" with which Socialist regimes
are burdened.

338   U.S. Congress. Joint Economic Committee. Subcommittee on Economic
      Growth and Stabilization. THE COSTS OF GOVERNMENT REGULA-
      TION OF BUSINESS. 95th Cong., 2d sess. Washington, D.C.: Gov-
      ernment Printing Office, 1978. 29 p.

This study discusses capital formation, small business, entrepreneurial functions, federal expenditures, innovation,
and inflation upon which government regulation has an
important impact. It considers budgeting as a management
tool, benefit-cost study, altering attitudes, and alternatives
to regulation as approaches to regulatory reform. An
appendix includes expenditures for numerous areas regulated
by government agencies.

339   Wallerstein, Louis S. "The Role of the Assistant Secretary in Shaping
      the Federal Labor Relations Program." BUREAUCRAT 2 (Spring 1973):
      27-38.

One of the basic ideas comprising the "Labor-Management
Relations in the Federal Service" program is that the well-
being of employees and efficient administration of the
government are promoted by providing employees an opportunity to share in the formulation and implementation
of personnel policies and practices.

340   Walsh, Annmarie Hauck. THE PUBLIC'S BUSINESS: THE POLITICS
       AND PRACTICES OF GOVERNMENT CORPORATIONS. Cambridge:
       MIT Press, 1978. 436 p.

          Walsh maintains that the main purpose of this text is to
          examine the relationships between organizational charac-
          teristics, decision making, and resource allocations in
          government corporations. She concludes that the money
          markets establish a system in which public enterprises
          dependent on such markets react in similar ways.

341   Weidenbaum, Murray L. "Viewpoint: On Estimating Regulatory Costs."
       REGULATION 2 (May-June 1978): 14-18.

          The author asserts that government control of business is
          one of the growth areas of the U.S. economy, that this
          activity projects both benefits and costs, and that the
          growth of costs is an important factor in judging the value
          of the activity. Weidenbaum holds that, because of their
          varied nature, many problems arise in establishing com-
          pliance costs. The reader is informed that the analysis
          strives to explore only the costs of regulation, not to
          determine if they are excessive or not.

342   Weinberger, Casper. "The Federal Perspective on Third Sector Man-
       agement." PUBLIC ADMINISTRATION REVIEW 35 (September-October
       1975): 456-58.

          Weinberger, former secretary of the Department of Health,
          Education, and Welfare, maintains that it is reasonable to
          approach the question of third sector management largely
          as a case-by-case problem in which the particular costs
          and benefits to all parties are considered. He states that
          the third sector, without federal control, is one of the
          brightest possibilities for preventing excessive bureaucrati-
          zation and conformity in our society.

343   Williams, Robert J. "Politics and the Ecology of Regulation." PUBLIC
       ADMINISTRATION 54 (Autumn 1976): 319-31.

          Williams notes that American regulatory agencies exercise
          executive, legislative, and judicial functions and maintain
          a separate identity from other governmental institutions.
          He reports that the hypothesis that the ineffective behavior
          of the regulatory agencies is explained by the "capturing"
          of such agencies by interests they are set up to regulate
          ignores the impact of more powerful and influential con-
          straints.

344   Witte, Edwin E. "Administrative Agencies and Statute Lawmaking."
       PUBLIC ADMINISTRATION REVIEW 2 (Spring 1942): 115-25.

This essay focuses upon the extensive participation by administrative departments in statute lawmaking. The author believes that this lawmaking has become a necessary part of the efficient functioning of democratic government and that the basic problem is how to make administrative participation a more effective instrument for an improved democracy. Witte concludes that the functions of Congress in statute lawmaking have not been rendered any the less important by the increased participation of the administrative departments in this process. Congress, he notes, must examine legislative proposals in much the same way as it does upon those originating with private interests.

Chapter 3

THE DISCIPLINE OF PUBLIC ADMINISTRATION

A. HISTORY AND IDEOLOGY

345   Appleby, Paul H. "Toward Better Public Administration." PUBLIC ADMINISTRATION REVIEW 7 (Spring 1947): 93-99.

> Writing soon after World War II, the author is clear in his appeal: "My plea today is for a broader, more humanitarian, and more deeply democratic approach to public administration, the recognition of its whole content, its finally general nature, its conduct dependent in high degree on generalists. To think thus broadly about public administration, we have constantly to come back to the kind of society with which we are concerned. . . . We must remember that there is nothing so fully democratic as the totality of the political processes in a free society."

346   Bailey, Stephen K. "Objectives of the Theory of Public Administration." In THEORY AND PRACTICE OF PUBLIC ADMINISTRATION: SCOPE, OBJECTIVES, AND METHODS, edited by James C. Charlesworth, pp. 128-40. Philadelphia: American Academy of Political and Social Science, 1968.

> Bailey discusses descriptive-explanatory theory, normative theory, assumptive theory, and instrumental theory in this essay. He states that "the objectives of public administration are to draw together the insights of the humanities and the validated propositions of the social and behavioral sciences and to apply these insights and propositions to the task of improving legitimated goals by constitutionally mandated means."

347   Biller, Robert P. "Some Implications of Adaptation Capacity for Organizational and Political Development." In TOWARD A NEW PUBLIC ADMINISTRATION: THE MINNOWBROOK PERSPECTIVE, edited by Frank Marini, pp. 93-121. Scranton, Pa.: Chandler Publishing Co., 1971.

Biller posits that the U.S. experience with public administration has two themes: 1) domestic theme in which the public's business is conducted with competence, efficiency, and care; and 2) international theme in which there is a responsibility to share our success abroad. He states: "Public Administration in both its professional and disciplinary dimensions must discover a new basis upon which to define itself and guide its central contributions. . . . We are in need of a redefinition that would be geared to uncertainty, based on assumptions of change rather than stability, capable of dealing with situational interdependencies, able to convert complexity into error-correction capacity, and facilitative of those process-discovery procedures which would not block the realization of human values."

348   Brownlow, Louis. "Woodrow Wilson and Public Administration." PUBLIC ADMINISTRATION REVIEW 16 (Spring 1956): 77-81.

The author recalls the "teaching" impacts of Wilson's 1887 essay on "The Study of Administration" and CONGRESSIONAL GOVERNMENT (1884). This brief article is also a personal account of the author's association with the former president.

349   Caldwell, Lynton K. THE ADMINISTRATIVE THEORIES OF HAMILTON AND JEFFERSON. Chicago: University of Chicago Press, 1944. ix, 244 p.

Caldwell maintains that the American administrative system is founded on two differing theories. One such theory is Hamilton's concept of the prevalent administrator ruling by control, centralization, career tenure, and formal responsibility to the public good; the other is Jefferson's dream of agrarian simplicity which stresses pluralism, coordination, temporary administrative arrangements, and decentralization. Caldwell reviews the statements and actions of the two statesmen in terms of their personalities, their politics and their opinions concerning public organization, policy, and the public service. In a concluding part, he delves into the struggle between the two statesmen during their lives and their background in the American administrative system.

350   _____. "Methodology in the Theory of Public Administration." In THEORY AND PRACTICE OF PUBLIC ADMINISTRATION: SCOPE, OBJECTIVES, AND METHODS, edited by James C. Charlesworth, pp. 205-22. Philadelphia: American Academy of Political and Social Science, 1968.

Caldwell's quest for new methodological directions in the
theory of public administration is clearly outlined in forty
sections. The main body of the author's essay is concerned
with the alternatives available for a realistic theory of
public administration and with the methods by which such
theory may most effectively be validated. He considers
why public administration has not heretofore developed a
satisfactory body of theory concerning public administration
and why it is necessary for public administration to do so
now.

351 _____. "Novus Ordo Seclorum: The Heritage of American Public
Administration." PUBLIC ADMINISTRATION REVIEW 36 (September-
October 1976): 476-88.

Caldwell discusses the legacy of English political ideas,
the Americanization of colonial government, and the
ideology of the new order, offering ten principles of political democracy. This article is excellent for understanding the background of American public administration.

352 Campbell, Alan K. "Old and New Public Administration in the 1970s."
PUBLIC ADMINISTRATION REVIEW 32 (July-August 1972): 343-47.

Writing in 1971, the former dean of the Maxwell Graduate
School of Citizenship and Public Affairs of Syracuse University suggests that central to the problems of the 1970s
will be the facts that the nation's affluence is limited
and that "improvement in public sector productivity will
probably become one of the top issues of the 1970s. It
will be difficult to achieve not because of worker attitudes, but rather from lack of management leadership."
This short essay is an insightful review of public administration and its challenges at the beginning of the last
decade.

353 Charlesworth, James C. "A Report, and Also Some Projections, Relating to the Present Dimensions and Directions of the Discipline of
Public Administration." In his THEORY AND PRACTICE OF PUBLIC
ADMINISTRATION: SCOPE, OBJECTIVES, AND METHODS, pp. 322-
36. Philadelphia: American Academy of Political and Social Science,
1968.

Charlesworth states: "We need both professional public
administration and academic public administration. . . .
In academic institutions, public administration should be
separated from political science. . . . The training of
public administration should emphasize administrative
methods rather than public policy. . . . In teaching
public administration, cases should be illustrative and
adjectival, not substantive and basic. . . . The literature

in public administration should be exoteric, not esoteric.
. . . Only small parts of the discipline of public administration can be made scientific. . . . Method in public
administration cannot be standardized and prescribed;
method is man himself. . . . Behavioralism in public
administration gives us the 'what' but not the 'how' and
the 'why.'"

354   Dahl, Robert A. "The Science of Public Administration: Three Problems."
        PUBLIC ADMINISTRATION REVIEW 7 (Winter 1947): 1-11.

        Dahl assumes that normative values, human behavior, and
        social setting pose difficulties for constructing a science
        of public administration. "No science of public admini-
        stration is possible unless: 1) the place of normative values is
        made clear; 2) the nature of man in the area of public
        administration is better understood and his conduct is more
        predictable; and 3) there is a body of comparative studies
        from which it may be possible to discover principles and
        generalities that transcend national boundaries and peculiar
        historical experiences."

355   deGrazia, Alfred. "The Science and Values of Administration--I."
        ADMINISTRATIVE SCIENCE QUARTERLY 5 (December 1960): 362-97.

        In the first of two parts, deGrazia asserts that all action
        has purpose and calls group-performed habitual actions
        "administration." He contends that the task of admini-
        strative science is to generalize about all administrative
        situations, that an administered situation has actors, tar-
        gets, and effects, and that goals are substantive and in-
        strumental and include especially power, wealth, and
        prestige. He describes how science selects and abstracts
        data and chooses and phrases propositions.

356   _____. "The Science and Values of Administration--II." ADMINI-
        STRATIVE SCIENCE QUARTERLY 5 (March 1961): 556-82.

        In this part, the author is concerned with the elements of
        the science of administration, as represented by his original
        definition and conception of administrative action (see
        entry 355), which lend themselves to translation into the
        applied science of administration.

357   Denhardt, Robert B., and Denhardt, Kathryn G. "Public Administration
        and the Critique of Domination." ADMINISTRATION AND SOCIETY
        11 (May 1979): 107-20.

        The Denhardts portray public administration as facing a
        crisis of legitimacy which derives from 1) the field's asso-
        ciation with societal tendencies toward regulation and

control, and 2) the failure of public administration theory to adequately connect with administrative practice. They outline a critical approach to public administration which calls for enlightened action in the public sector.

358   Dillon, Conley H. "How ASPA Takes a Stand: A Case Study of the Process of Developing a Position/Action Proposal on a Public Policy Issue." BUREAUCRAT 4 (October 1975): 316-23.

After making reference to the neutralist domination of the American Society for Public Administration reflecting the historical role of the nonpartisan civil servant, Dillon points out that the civil rights and environmental issues of the 1960s prompted many civil servants to become more activist in those directions. The author discusses a congressional proposal for establishing a Committee on Research in Public Administration. He emphasizes the evolutionary nature for policy development within ASPA.

359   Egger, Rowland. "The Period of Crisis: 1933 to 1945." In AMERICAN PUBLIC ADMINISTRATION: PAST, PRESENT, FUTURE, edited by Frederick C. Mosher, pp. 49-96. University: University of Alabama Press, 1975.

Egger concludes that the people of the United States came to grips with the national purpose in terms that had not been confronted since the Civil War and with their international obligations in terms that had never before been encountered during the 1933-45 period. The author states: "At no time in the history of the country did the professoriate receive more deference or command more attention as its members roamed freely the corridors of power. At no time did graduates specialized in the newly emerging art and science of public administration encounter more interesting job opportunities on the basis of their still-damp diplomas."

360   Emmerich, Herbert. "Scope of the Practice of Public Administration." In THEORY AND PRACTICE OF PUBLIC ADMINISTRATION: SCOPE, OBJECTIVES, AND METHODS, edited by James C. Charlesworth, pp. 92-108. Philadelphia: American Academy of Political and Social Science, 1968.

Emmerich defines the scope of public administration by type of program, including external programs, regulatory programs, directly administered service programs, directly administered development programs, programs administered by grants-in-aid to states, programs administered by grants-in-aid to local authorities, programs administered by voluntary local groups, programs of loans, insurance, and grants to private industries and banks, administration by

states and localities, particularly federally aided programs
and problems of financing, programs of government by contract, and programs of over-all management of the government and the economy.

361   Fesler, James W. "Public Administration and the Social Sciences:
1946 to 1960." In AMERICAN PUBLIC ADMINISTRATION: PAST,
PRESENT, FUTURE, edited by Frederick C. Mosher, pp. 97-141.
University: University of Alabama Press, 1975.

With regard to the 1946 to 1960 period, Fesler states:
"The real world pressed in on us, affecting our university
setting, providing new models of scientific scholarship,
suggesting new agendas for our research, and providing
many of us with sensitizing experiences in the public
service. Of even greater importance, public administration scholars were challenged to absorb the theories,
findings, and methods of the behavioral sciences. The
appropriate response to this challenge was not self-evident,
for the most sympathetic response demanded abandonment
of the field's identity in favor of a generic 'administration'
that had no species labeled 'public.'"

362   Frederickson, H. George. "The Lineage of New Public Administration."
ADMINISTRATION AND SOCIETY 8 (August 1976): 149-74.

In this article five basic prototypes in current public administration are identified and described: classic bureaucratic, neobureaucratic, institutional, human relations,
and public choice. Frederickson insists that elements of
each may be found in the dominant interpretations of the
new public administration, along with maximization of
certain values--responsiveness, worker and citizen participation in decision making, social equity, citizen choice,
and administrative responsibility for program effectiveness.

363   _____. "Toward a New Public Administration." In TOWARD A NEW
PUBLIC ADMINISTRATION: THE MINNOWBROOK PERSPECTIVE,
edited by Frank Marini, pp. 309-31. Scranton, Pa.: Chandler Publishing Co., 1971.

Frederickson interprets and synthesizes the new public administration as it emerged at the Minnowbrook Conference
on New Public Administration, describes how his interpretation and synthesis of the new public administration
relates to the wider world of administrative thought and
practice, and interprets what the new public administration
means for organization theory and vice versa. He concludes that "the search for social equity provides public
administration with a real normative base."

364   Gaus, John M. "Leonard Dupee White 1891-1958." PUBLIC AD-
        MINISTRATION REVIEW 18 (Summer 1958): 231-36.

        Gaus reports on Leonard White's efforts to study and re-
        port on the new field of public administration, reviews
        White's influence on scholarship in public administration,
        and estimates White's significance to the field of public
        administration and the development of the profession.

365   _____. REFLECTIONS ON PUBLIC ADMINISTRATION. University:
        University of Alabama Press, 1947. 153 p.

        The author is concerned with the ecology of government,
        with distinguishing the characteristics of politics and ad-
        ministration, with analyzing the processes of policy and
        administration, with explaining the roles of devolution
        and federation in the government process, with examining
        the purposes and procedures of control, and with the re-
        vision of policy by administrative personnel in working
        relations with citizen groups.

366   _____. "Trends in the Theory of Public Administration." PUBLIC
        ADMINISTRATION REVIEW 10 (Summer 1950): 161-68.

        "A theory of public administration means in our time a
        theory of politics also," writes the author, formerly a
        professor of government at Harvard University. This essay
        serves as an excellent review of the literature of public
        administration at the half-century mark.

367   Gaus, John M.; White, Leonard D.; and Dimock, Marshall E. THE
        FRONTIERS OF PUBLIC ADMINISTRATION. Chicago: University of
        Chicago Press, 1936. ix, 146 p.

        "These essays . . . represent at once the pleasure which
        the authors have taken in discussing among themselves
        problems of mutual interest and also their belief that the
        governmental problems revealed by the depression and the
        efforts to deal with it require for their solution both im-
        provements in administrative techniques and equally more
        accurate ideas concerning the nature of administration."
        Gaus, White, and Dimock, discuss the meaning and scope
        of public administration, the meaning of principles, re-
        sponsibility, role of discretion, theory of organization,
        American society, and the criteria and objectives of public
        administration.

368   Gladden, E.N. A HISTORY OF PUBLIC ADMINISTRATION. 2 vols.
        London: Frank Cass, 1972. 419 p.

        These volumes constitute the first historical survey of public

administration covering the entire period of known history.
Gladden examines those societies and empires which best
illustrate the range of experience on which data is available. Included in these volumes are analyses of ancient
Egypt, Mediterranean city states, Imperial Rome, ancient
India and China, Byzantium, the West (500-1066 A.D.),
medieval Europe, the Middle East, sixteenth-century
Europe, Prediscovery America, Europe to 1786, the West
(1649-1815), and modern public administration. The author's themes are direction and top management, functions
and organization, techniques, biography, and theory.

369   Gulick, Luther. "Next Steps in Public Administration." PUBLIC AD-
MINISTRATION REVIEW 15 (Spring 1955): 73-76.

Gulick offers five steps that need to be taken for the
sake of the future of the art and science of public administration in the mid-1950s. He writes: "1. Public
administration as a field of action needs to be more
closely adapted to changing human requirements, particularly in three areas of spectacular development: the
international, the economic, and the metropolitan. . . .
2. Public administration as a field of analysis and understanding needs to be more closely related to the study
of business and other administration. 3. For the next
decade, at least, public administration needs to bring the
problem of personnel into the center of its attention as
never before. 4. Public administration must accept and
move forward with the new opportunities of automation.
5. Public administration must reexamine and reformulate
its doctrine and practice with reference to the use and
control of the expert in public as well as private management."

370   _____. "The Twenty-Fifth Anniversary of the American Society for
Public Administration." PUBLIC ADMINISTRATION REVIEW 25 (March
1965): 1-4.

Gulick finds the American Society for Public Administration still lacking a synthesis of theory capable of transla-
tion into a new technology. He approaches public administration theory via 1) the function of administration,
2) the policy planning process in administration, and 3)
a more valid concept of the American politico-administrative
system.

371   Hawley, Claude E., and Weintraub, Ruth G., eds. ADMINISTRATIVE
QUESTIONS AND POLITICAL ANSWERS. New York: D. Van Nostrand
Co., 1966. v, 604 p.

The editors conclude "that the volumes of the PUBLIC

ADMINISTRATION REVIEW were comfortably representative of the periodical contributions of the period" between the founding of the profession of public administration in 1939 and the publication of this volume in 1966. They group the contents of the readings into six parts: theory, political setting, administrative practice, personnel, comparative administration, and education and training. These essays serve as an excellent review of important literature from the PUBLIC ADMINISTRATION REVIEW during its first twenty-five years.

372   Henry, Nicholas. "Paradigms of Public Administration." PUBLIC AD-MINISTRATION REVIEW 35 (July-August 1975): 378-86.

The author sketches five paradigms of public administration to indicate that the notion of public administration as a unique, synthesizing field is relatively new. Henry conceives the discipline as an amalgam of organization theory, management science, and the concept of the public interest. He suggests that it is time for public administration to establish itself as an institutionally autonomous enterprise in colleges and universities in order to retain its social relevance and worth.

373   Jreisat, Jamil. "Public Administration and the Theory/Practice Controversy." SOUTHERN REVIEW OF PUBLIC ADMINISTRATION 1 (March 1978): 503-9.

This article deals with the proposition that a growing student dissatisfaction with the teaching of public administration is discernable. Jreisat writes that this dissatisfaction is caused by the heavy accent on theory instead of practice in the design and delivery of university curricula.

374   Kaufman, Herbert. "Emerging Conflicts in the Doctrines of Public Administration." THE AMERICAN POLITICAL SCIENCE REVIEW 50 (December 1956): 1057-73.

The central thesis of this article is that an examination of the administrative institutions of this nation suggests that they are organized and operated in pursuit of the values of representativeness, neutral competence, and executive leadership. In an important essay on the history of public administration, Kaufman states that there are inherent conflicts in these doctrines.

375   Karl, Barry D. "Public Administration and American History: A Century of Professionalism." PUBLIC ADMINISTRATION REVIEW 36 (September-October 1976): 489-503.

Karl writes that "administration became the way of coping

with political problems without actually solving them, a process its defenders labeled pragmatic, or pluralist, but which its critics saw as muddling--and worse." He examines the paradoxes, ironies, puzzles, and dilemmas of public administration in American history. The author recognizes the contributions of the Woodrow Wilson and PODSCORB (Planning, Organizing, Developing, Staffing, Coordinating, Reporting, and Budgeting) eras.

376   Kirkhart, Larry. "Toward a Theory of Public Administration." In TOWARD A NEW PUBLIC ADMINISTRATION: THE MINNOWBROOK PERSPECTIVE, edited by Frank Marini, pp. 127-64. Scranton, Pa.: Chandler Publishing Co., 1971. Tables.

Kirkhart finds that many of the difficulties of defining or building a theory of public administration are related to the history and context of the social sciences. He traces some of the newer trends in philosophy, sociology, and psychology and attempts to discern their implications for a theory of public administration.

377   Kronenberg, Philip S. "The Scientific and Moral Authority of Empirical Theory of Public Administration." In TOWARD A NEW PUBLIC ADMINISTRATION: THE MINNOWBROOK PERSPECTIVE, edited by Frank Marini, pp. 190-225. Scranton, Pa.: Chandler Publishing Co., 1971.

Kronenberg selects two bodies of theoretical literature for special focus: comparative national public administration and organizational behavior. He maintains that comparative public administration and organizational behavior are the main growth points of empirical theory in the new public administration. He concludes that the new public administration must cope with weaknesses in empirical theory and become more innovative.

378   Kurzman, Paul A. "The Impact of Harry Hopkins on Public Administration." SOUTHERN REVIEW OF PUBLIC ADMINISTRATION 1 (December 1977): 350-63.

The author concludes that Hopkins introduced a new era of intergovernmental relations (more realistic, flexible, and modern), and recognized public administration concepts which were dominant during the first two decades of the twentieth century (new directions, procedures and unorthodox style).

379   Marini, Frank, ed. TOWARD A NEW PUBLIC ADMINISTRATION: THE MINNOWBROOK PERSPECTIVE. Scranton, Pa.: Chandler Publishing Co., 1971. 372 p.

Marini edits a controversial, provocative, and rewarding
collection of essays which is a response to the early 1970s
generation of public administrators. The essays of this
text look to the future, offering ideas that are more conservative than radical.

380   Millett, John D. "A Critical Appraisal of the Study of Public Ad-
        ministration." ADMINISTRATIVE SCIENCE QUARTERLY 1 (September
        1956): 171-88.

        Millett claims three primary hypotheses as the basis for
        the study of public administration: 1) that public admini-
        stration must be conducted in such a way as to promote
        rather than impair the essential elements of a free society,
        2) that the legislative, executive, and judicial branches
        exercise continuing oversight of administrative agencies
        in order to ensure a politically responsible bureaucracy,
        and 3) that all fields of governmental endeavor contain
        a common core of similar concern which the author labels
        "management." The author recognizes that underlying
        these hypotheses is the uncertainty about the present con-
        text of public administration as a branch of political
        science.

381   Montmollin, Maurice de. "Taylorism and Anti-Taylorism." INTER-
        NATIONAL STUDIES OF MANAGEMENT AND ORGANIZATION 5
        (Fall 1975): 4-15.

        Montmollin states that anti-Taylorism is really neo-Taylorism.
        He describes the Taylorism ideology as being characterized
        by the division of labor, rationalism, order and harmony,
        individualism, and productivity. Anti-Taylorism differen-
        tiates from Taylorism under the same tenets in its ideology
        only humanism is involved. The author reveals that anti-
        Taylorism evokes ideas and actions under such terms as
        job restructuring, job enrichment, job enlargement, so-
        ciotechnical systems, quality of life in work, new work
        organizations, and problems of unskilled labor.

382   Morrow, William L. PUBLIC ADMINISTRATION: POLITICS AND THE
        POLITICAL SYSTEM. New York: Random House, 1975. xiv, 272 p.
        Paper.

        This textbook attempts to explain the behavior of agencies
        in terms of the pressures and claims placed upon them by
        external institutions and examines and assesses the effects
        of decisions made as a result of these pressures. Morrow
        places heavy emphasis upon institutions and pressures that
        are so often associated with process democracy in the
        United States--political parties, interest groups, legis-
        latures, elected representatives, citizen participants, and

fragmented constitutional power. Chapters include politics
and the enduring traditions of public administration; politics, society, and theories of public administration; institutional inputs and administrative behavior; administrative agencies and the budget; and issues in contemporary public administration.

383   Ostrom, Vincent. THE INTELLECTUAL CRISIS IN AMERICAN PUBLIC
ADMINISTRATION. University: University of Alabama Press, 1974.
179 p.

In one of the most provocative examinations of public
administration literature, Ostrom delineates the crisis of
confidence in the discipline, reviews the intellectual
mainstream in American public administration (Wilson,
Weber, Gulick, Simon), notes the contributions of contemporary political economists, presents theories of bureaucratic and democratic administrations, and probes the choice
of alternative futures.

384   _____. "The Undisciplinary Discipline of Public Administration: A
Response to Stillman's Critique." MIDWEST REVIEW OF PUBLIC AD-
MINISTRATION 11 (December 1977): 304-8.

This is a response to Richard Stillman's critique (vol. 10,
MRPA, December 1976) of THE INTELLECTUAL CRISIS
IN AMERICAN PUBLIC ADMINISTRATION (1974) (see 397)
in which he doubts that he and Stillman agree upon the meaning of the term "paradigm." Ostrom writes: "The INTELLEC-
TUAL CRISIS is concerned with the discipline of reasoned discourse. It is concerned with opening new opportunities
and possibilities in the study of human organization as it
pertains to public administration. I am not so foolish as
to advocate that one way of thinking is the only way of
thinking.

385   Redford, Emmette S. IDEAL AND PRACTICE IN PUBLIC ADMINISTRA-
TION. University: University of Alabama Press, 1958. 155 p.

This book republished by the Press in paperback in 1975, examines the ideals of efficiency, rule of law, performance by
competent and responsible persons, democracy, and public
interest in the consideration of administrative ideal and
practice. In this descriptive and prescriptive analysis,
Redford contrasts the ways in which administrative responsibilities are discharged.

386   Rehfuss, John. PUBLIC ADMINISTRATION AS POLITICAL PROCESS.
New York: Charles Scribner's Sons, 1973. viii, 247 p. Paper.

The primary emphasis of this textbook is to restore politics
to center stage as the main impetus behind most administrative behavior. Rehfuss believes that public administration has placed entirely too much emphasis on organizational structure and on matters such as staff functions
of the executive, budgeting mechanisms, and personnel
issues. He believes that administrative behavior is more
meaningfully understood within a broader political process.
Chapters include discussions of politics, administration,
and bureaucratic policy making at the national, state,
and local levels.

387   Riggs, Fred W. "Professionalism, Political Science, and the Scope
       of Public Administration." In THEORY AND PRACTICE OF PUBLIC
       ADMINISTRATION: SCOPE, OBJECTIVES, AND METHODS, edited
       by James C. Charlesworth, pp. 32-62. Philadelphia: American
       Academy of Political and Social Science, 1968.

       Riggs states that the study of public administration as a
       part of the science of government needs to be carried
       forward within the discipline of political science. He
       suggests that the underlying reason for the difficulties of
       political science and public administration rests on our
       failure to distinguish clearly between structures of gov-
       ernment and government functions. Riggs believes that
       we can study the administrative function or the political
       function only by looking at both political systems and
       bureaucracies.

388   Savage, Peter. "Dismantling the Administrative State: Paradigm Re-
       formulation in Public Administration." POLITICAL STUDIES 22 (June
       1974): 147-57.

       Savage states that the new public administration portrays
       the resolution of administrative difficulties as bringing
       back politics. He believes the commitment is not to re-
       arrange the administrative state, but rather the movement
       assumes the position that administration is the predominant
       mode of social control, that the administrative state should
       be dismantled, and that consideration must be paid to the
       essence and workings of political life.

389   Schick, Allen. "Coming Apart in Public Administration." MAXWELL
       REVIEW 10 (Winter 1973-74): 13-24.

       The discipline of public administration has been in a state
       of flux for a quarter of a century. The now-rejected
       politics-administration dichotomy functioned as a con-
       solidating force by defining the relationship between
       politics and administration and by establishing the domi-
       nance of the administrative over the political. The roles

have been switched and politics is now supreme with its
values penetrating all administrative methods.

390 _____. "The Trauma of Politics: Public Administration in the Sixties."
In AMERICAN PUBLIC ADMINISTRATION: PAST, PRESENT, FUTURE,
edited by Frederick C. Mosher, pp. 142-80. University: University
of Alabama Press, 1975.

Schick summarizes public administration in the 1960s:
"It was the best of times. It was the worst of times.
It was a time of hope. It was a time of despair. It
was a time of bringing together. It was a time of
tearing apart. It was a time of doing. It was a time
of not knowing what to do. Amidst all the contradictions, it was throughout a period of turbulence."

391 Schott, Richard L. "Public Administration as a Profession: Problems
and Prospects." PUBLIC ADMINISTRATION REVIEW 36 (May-June
1976): 253-59.

This article argues that public administration lacks the
hallmarks of a true profession and has little chance of
becoming one despite claims to the contrary. Schott
believes that public service has become professionalized,
not because of the contributions of the field of public administration, but rather because those from science and
the professions have come to dominate its upper levels.
He suggests that this dominance, and the lack of professional stature of public administration, have some important implications for schools of public affairs and administration.

392 Sherman, Harvey. "Methodology in the Practice of Public Administra-
tion." In THEORY AND PRACTICE OF PUBLIC ADMINISTRATION:
SCOPE, OBJECTIVES, AND METHODS, pp. 254-90. Philadelphia:
American Academy of Political and Social Science, 1968.

Sherman reviews what is new and consequential in the
methods used for practicing public administration and discusses current and likely future developments in five principal areas: government-private sector relationships,
government-government relationships, science and technology, government-employee relationships, and government-
citizen relationships.

393 Simon, Herbert A. "A Comment on 'The Science of Public Administration.'" PUBLIC ADMINISTRATION REVIEW 7 (Summer 1947):
200-203.

This brief article is a response to Prof. Robert A. Dahl's
essay (see no. 354) concerning three problems with regard to

the science of public administration. While in fundamental agreement with Dahl, Simon believes there is a need for some qualification and elaboration of Dahl's comments on normative values, human behavior, and social setting in the science of public administration. This exchange of ideas in the late 1940s by Simon and Dahl is most interesting for its original thinking on this dilemma.

394   _____. "The Proverbs of Administration." PUBLIC ADMINISTRATION REVIEW 6 (Winter 1946): 53-67.

The purpose of this essay is to substantiate the criticisms of administrative theory. Simon's ideas for solving the dilemma of administrative theory include reviewing some accepted administrative principles, analyzing administrative characteristics of specialization, understanding unity of command, span of control, and organization by purpose, process, clientele, and place. This article is one of the classics in the literature of administrative theory.

395   Stene, Edwin O. "The Politics-Administration Dichotomy." MIDWEST REVIEW OF PUBLIC ADMINISTRATION 9 (April-July 1975): 83-89.

Stene concludes that either the defense or the denial of a distinction between politics and administration depends upon the definition of politics. He states that using the term politics with government renders the word useless. He encourages political scientists to seek to develop clarified distinctions among such terms as goals, policies, politics, and administration rather than dogmatically pronouncing the death of the dichotomy of the terms politics and administration.

396   Stillman, Richard [J.] II. "Controversy in Public Administration--A Reply to Professor Ostrom." MIDWEST REVIEW OF PUBLIC ADMINISTRATION 12 (March 1978): 41-44.

In a continuing debate between the author and Vincent Ostrom, author of THE INTELLECTUAL CRISIS IN AMERICAN PUBLIC ADMINISTRATION (1974), Stillman responds to Ostrom's defense of the INTELLECTUAL CRISIS (MRPA, vol. 11, December 1977) (see 383, 384). Stillman's critique of Ostrom's book appeared in this journal in December 1976 (see 397). Stillman points out some internal contradictions and puzzling interpretations of theorists cited by Ostrom and concludes that Ostrom, in his response to Stillman's critique, sidestepped or avoided the central issues.

397   _____. "Professor Ostrom's New Paradigm for American Public Administration--Adequate or Antique." MIDWEST REVIEW OF PUBLIC ADMINISTRATION 10 (December 1976): 176-92.

> Stillman offers a comprehensive critique of Vincent Ostrom's THE INTELLECTUAL CRISIS IN AMERICAN PUBLIC ADMINISTRATION (1974) and concludes that Ostrom's book "tells us more about the author and his own generation's 'crisis' in public administration scholarship than it does about the future of the discipline." Stillman writes: "For neat and tidy minds used to clear-cut academic disciplines with an accepted 'core of knowledge' (which for even many traditional fields like history, sociology, and economics is no longer the case), public administration is frequently viewed as most 'undisciplinary.'" This essay, along with later exchanges between Stillman and Ostrom of ideas on the paradigm problem in public administration, is quite valuable for attempting to comprehend "what P.A. is."

398   Storing, Herbert J. "Leonard D. White and the Study of Public Administration." PUBLIC ADMINISTRATION REVIEW 25 (March 1965): 38-51.

> Noting that education in public administration has been strongly influenced by White's text, INTRODUCTION TO THE STUDY OF PUBLIC ADMINISTRATION (1926), the author traces the theoretical issues of public administration through the four editions of the INTRODUCTION into the administrative histories which constitute White's final work. Storing reviews White's literature under the following headings: 1) administration is a single process; 2) administration has its base in management; 3) administration--an art, in transformation to a science; and 4) administration--the central problem of modern government. This is a very useful essay for learning about the writings of one of public administration's most influential thinkers.

399   Turner, Henry A. "Woodrow Wilson as Administrator." PUBLIC ADMINISTRATION REVIEW 16 (Autumn 1956): 249-57.

> "In determining Wilson's place in the historical development of public administration in the United States, one must make a broad interpretation of his influence and contributions. Woodrow Wilson's administrative theory and practice, when viewed in their proper perspective, must be ranked with his social reform program, his wartime leadership, and his advocacy of the League of Nations as foundation for his standing as one of our great Presidents." The author believes Wilson's greatest weakness as an administrator was his inability to manage and manipulate men.

400   Urwick, Lyndall. "Experiences in Public Administration." PUBLIC
        ADMINISTRATION REVIEW 15 (Autumn 1955): 247-50.

>   In an address to the Minnesota chapter of the American
>   Society for Public Administration, the author reflects upon
>   his life in management. Urwick, coauthor with Luther
>   Gulick of the PAPERS ON THE SCIENCE OF ADMINI-
>   STRATION, had a significant impact in shaping the present
>   state of the federal bureaucracy in the United States, and
>   this speech is interesting for its personal view as well as
>   its professional perspective upon the man. One repre-
>   sentative quotation is: "The way to cut your paper down
>   is not to 'damn the office work.' The way to cut your
>   paper down is to do the office work properly, to simplify
>   it to the last possible degree. The more that people in
>   the higher echelons think, 'What can I do to reduce the
>   paper for the fellow down the line?' the more smoothly
>   will administration work. What is more, the paper will
>   be accurate."

401   Wald, Emanuel. "Toward a Paradigm of Future Public Administration."
        PUBLIC ADMINISTRATION REVIEW 33 (July-August 1973): 366-72.
        Tables.

>   Wald channels professional knowledge, intuitive thinking,
>   intentionality, and the subjective values of authorities in
>   public administration and related fields toward the pre-
>   diction of a paradigm of future public administration. The
>   basic elements of this paradigm include: 1) 'a softened' norma-
>   tivism, 2) fluctuating boundaries, 3) movement toward social
>   technology, 4) policy orientation, and 5) synchronization.
>   He elaborates on each element and offers an agenda for
>   future study.

402   Waldo, Dwight [A.]. THE ADMINISTRATIVE STATE: A STUDY OF
        THE POLITICAL THEORY OF AMERICAN PUBLIC ADMINISTRATION.
        New York: Ronald Press Co., 1948. viii, 227 p.

>   This text is a study of the public administration movement
>   from the viewpoint of political theory and the history of
>   ideas. Waldo seeks to review and analyze the theoretical
>   element in administrative writings and to present the de-
>   velopment of the public administration movement as a
>   chapter in the history of American political thought. His
>   objectives are to assist students of administration to view
>   it in terms of historical perspective and to appraise the
>   theoretical content of the literature. Sections include
>   the rise of public administration, problems of political
>   philosophy, and fundamental concepts. This volume is a
>   classic in the field and was written at a crucial time in
>   the history of the profession by the profession's most eminent

philosopher-historian. It is highly recommended to both
students and practitioners.

403 _____. "The Administrative State Revisited." PUBLIC ADMINISTRA-
TION REVIEW 25 (March 1965): 5-30.

The former editor of the PUBLIC ADMINISTRATION RE-
VIEW reflects upon the title of his public administration
classic, THE ADMINISTRATIVE STATE (see 402). This essay
is one of the most important reviews of the origins, ideological background, theory of organization, and scientific
methods in public administration and is an excellent way to
understand where public administration has been, where it
was in the mid-1960s, and where it might be going.

404 _____. "Public Administration." In INTERNATIONAL ENCYCLO-
PEDIA OF THE SOCIAL SCIENCES, edited by David L. Sills, pp.
145-56. New York: Macmillan Co., and Free Press, 1968.

This essay is an excellent review of public administration
and the study of relevant governmental phenomena. Waldo
discusses terminological difficulties, the field in the United
States (origins, the 1920s and 1930s, criticism and transition of the 1940s, main currents of recent years), the
field outside the United States, and trends, problems, and
prospects for public administration in the future. For the
beginning student, this article serves as a very useful review of the literature.

405 _____. "Public Administration in a Time of Revolution." PUBLIC
ADMINISTRATION REVIEW 28 (July-August 1968): 362-68.

The former editor of the PUBLIC ADMINISTRATION RE-
VIEW probes the discipline's responsibility for contemporary
revolutions, inquires how public administration is involved
with contemporary revolutions, questions whether public
administration ought to respond consciously to the revolutions of the day, and denotes problems, opportunities, and
strategies for analyzing these difficult issues. This is an
excellent blend of self-interest and altruism, and of realistic appraisal and idealistic commitment in dealing with
problems of public bureaucracy in the late 1960s.

406 _____. "Scope of the Theory of Public Administration." In THEORY
AND PRACTICE OF PUBLIC ADMINISTRATION: SCOPE, OBJECTIVES,
AND METHODS, edited by James C. Charlesworth, pp. 1-26. Phila-
delphia: American Academy of Political and Social Science, 1968.

Waldo includes problems of personal ethics in and related
to administration; politics and power; of constitutional
status, law, and jurisprudence; of public policy; and of

political theory and philosophy as value problems confronting public administration. His theoretical concerns
include external and internal security, justice, education,
government by osmosis and symbiosis, science, and technology, urbanism, and development. He argues that
public administration's crisis of identity was not and cannot be solved at the level of subdiscipline or discipline
and that the set of concepts and attitudes designated by
the word "profession" will enable public administration
to resolve its crisis of identity at the proper level.

407   Wamsley, Gary L. "On the Problems of Discovering What's Really
New in Public Administration." ADMINISTRATION AND SOCIETY
8 (November 1976): 385-400.

Criticisms of pluralistic democracy and social equity concerns, advocation of citizen participation with emphasis
upon human rights, an emphasis on values or substance
(ideas) as well as process or procedures, enhancement
organizational vitality instead of bureaucratic forms and
procedures, and the managing of knowledge and administrative actions entail elements of the "new" public administration. Wamsley notes that activities and relations
between organizations and bureaucracies as well as developments within organizations concern analysts of the
"new" public administration.

408   White, Leonard D. THE FEDERALISTS: A STUDY IN ADMINISTRATIVE
HISTORY. New York: Macmillan Co., 1948. xii, 538 p.

For annotation see entry 411.

409   _____. THE JACKSONIANS: A STUDY IN ADMINISTRATIVE
HISTORY, 1829-1861. New York: Macmillan Co., 1954. xii,
593 p.

For annotation see entry 411.

410   _____. THE JEFFERSONIANS: A STUDY IN ADMINISTRATIVE
HISTORY, 1801-1829. New York: Macmillan Co., 1951. xiv,
572 p.

For annotation see entry 411.

411   White, Leonard D., with the assistance of Jean Schneider. THE REPUB-
LICAN ERA, 1869-1901: A STUDY IN ADMINISTRATIVE HISTORY.
New York: Macmillan Co., 1958. 406 p.

These are sophisticated histories of the federal government
from 1789 to 1901, provided by private letters, office
memoranda, and public reports. The two central themes

which are highlighted are the continuation of administrative institutions despite political and economic disturbances, and the contention between Federalist and Jacksonian tenets of administration. The Federalists desired a stable, efficient, politically nonpartisan public service within a government functioning as a creative force in society, administrative conditions which the Jeffersonians generally continued. The Jacksonians drastically altered this administrative system with democratic tenets, the rule of rotation, and the mass political party. These were modified with Federalist tenets during the Republican age. Each book contains four divisions dealing with the relationship between the executive and legislative branches in controlling administration, the function of the departments, the employee system, and a review of the chief administrative problems in each era.

412   Willbern, York. "The Advancement of Public Administration." PUBLIC ADMINISTRATION REVIEW 17 (Summer 1957): ii-iii.

Willbern, at the time, editor of this journal, spells out the purposes and goals of the American Society for Public Administration, explains the functions of the PUBLIC ADMINISTRATION REVIEW in seeking those goals, and identifies the clientele of both the society and journal.

413   Wilson, Woodrow. "The Study of Administration." POLITICAL SCIENCE QUARTERLY 56 (June 1887): 481-506.

Wilson's essay is considered one of the classics of the field of public administration. Wilson writes: "The field of administration is a field of business. It is removed from the hurry and strife of politics; it at most points stands apart even from the debatable ground of constitutional study. It is a part of political life only as the methods of the counting-house are a part of the life of society; only as machinery is part of the manufactured product. . . . Most important to be observed is the truth already so much and so fortunately insisted upon by our civil-service reformers; namely, that administration lies outside the proper sphere of politics. Administrative questions are not political questions. Although politics sets the tasks for administration, it should not be suffered to manipulate its offices." Wilson's views provide interesting insights into concepts of public administration in the late nineteenth century.

414   Wise, Charles R., and Frederickson, H. George. "Crosscurrents in Public Administration and Public Policy." In PUBLIC ADMINISTRATION

AND PUBLIC POLICY, edited by H. George Frederickson and Charles R. Wise, pp. 213-23. Lexington, Mass.: D.C. Heath and Co., 1977.

> The authors discuss organization and administration of human resources, among actors in public administration, in public administration decision processes, and in accountability in public administration. They conclude: "Whether they (national policy initiatives) will achieve major societal impacts will in large depend on how the participant navigators (public administrators) are able to steer a course through these crosscurrents of public administration."

B. TEXTBOOKS AND READINGS

415   Altshuler, Alan A., ed. THE POLITICS OF THE FEDERAL BUREAU-CRACY. New York: Dodd, Mead and Co., 1968. xi, 452 p.

> Altshuler's objectives are to introduce beginning students of public administration to the controversies of political bureaucracy, opinions and interests, sources of influence and weakness, to indicate how the American governmental system typically deals with these conflicts, to present a variety of provocative viewpoints on how it ought to deal with them, and to spur students to consider what they ought to know about the federal bureaucracy and its patterns of interaction with the other major forces in American political life. Although this collection was published in 1968, it presents a distinguished group of authors in key substantive areas.

416   Berkley, George E. THE CRAFT OF PUBLIC ADMINISTRATION. 2d ed. Boston: Allyn and Bacon, 1978. x, 555 p.

> This textbook includes both narrative and case studies. Chapters include the administrative craft, the American political system, anatomy of organization, physiology of organization, personnel, unionism, leadership, communication, budgeting, centralization, administrative law, support, change, and the administrative future. Berkley combines the best of descriptive analysis with actual case histories of administrative activities.

417   Caiden, Gerald E. THE DYNAMICS OF PUBLIC ADMINISTRATION: GUIDELINES TO CURRENT TRANSFORMATIONS IN THEORY AND PRACTICE. New York: Holt, Rinehart and Winston, 1971. 341 p.

> Caiden's text is divided into five parts: the study of public administration (meaning); politics, policy, and administration (public-policy, politicization, structures);

function, structure, process, and behavior (expertise, private contractors, finance, service); theory and comparative administration; and administration in the 1970s. It also includes a useful bibliographical guide.

418   Dimock, Marshall Edward, and Dimock, Gladys Ogden. PUBLIC ADMINISTRATION. 4th ed. Hinsdale, Ill.: Dryden Press, 1969. vi, 634 p.

The 1969 edition differs from previous editions in the authors' emphasis that public administration is more comparative, behavioral, economic, and political than it was in the 1950s. The Dimocks illustrate how public policy and public administration join action and that "policy plus management equal politics." In this edition, the authors place emphasis on the human aspects of the field, including analyses of the client-consumer of governmental programs created in response to social need, citizen democratic control, and the vocational appeal of the public service. They stress the substantive, programmatic aspect of government in its relationship to the economy.

419   Golembiewski, Robert T.; Gibson, Frank; and Cornog, Geoffrey Y., eds. PUBLIC ADMINISTRATION: READINGS IN INSTITUTIONS, PROCESSES, BEHAVIOR, AND POLICY. 3d ed. Chicago: Rand McNally College Publishing Co., 1976. xvii, 726 p.

The editors provide a most comprehensive collection of essays on the literature of public administration. This volume proves useful in the teaching of public administration.

420   Gordon, George J. PUBLIC ADMINISTRATION IN AMERICA. New York: St. Martin's Press, 1978. xii, 470 p.

This textbook is both basic and comprehensive; the reader is assumed to have some background knowledge of government and politics in the United States. The text discusses decision making, budgetary processes, organization theory, federalism, intergovernmental relations, government regulation, and administrative leadership. It emphasizes the central importance of public administration in modern government and the role of politics and political influence in shaping public administration. The author also provides a useful glossary of public administration terms.

421   Gortner, Harold F. ADMINISTRATION IN THE PUBLIC SECTOR. New York: John Wiley and Sons, 1977. xv, 343 p.

Gortner writes that many books on public administration describe public policy to the extent that management of

public affairs is overlooked. He attempts to restore a
balanced perspective in the interaction of public policy
and public administration. Chapters include the substance
of public administration, existence, bureaucracy in the
political system, accountability and responsibility, the
administrative machine, decision making, planning, control, communication, bureaucratic conflicts, incentives
for public employees, leadership, public personnel administration, and public financial administration.

422   Henry, Nicholas. PUBLIC ADMINISTRATION AND PUBLIC AFFAIRS.
Englewood Cliffs, N.J.: Prentice-Hall, 1975. xviii, 380 p.

Henry's premises are that the "muddling through" decision
making in government no longer is adequate in a society
characterized by "future shock" and that more rational
policy making is mandatory, that much of public administration consists of learning the symbolic languages of
other people and other professions, and that, academically,
public administration is entering an era of overdue institutional expansionism and intellectual independence.
Sections include the paradigms of public administration,
theories, concepts, people in public organizations, techniques of public administration, and public affairs.

423   Hills, William G., et al., eds. CONDUCTING THE PEOPLE'S
BUSINESS: THE FRAMEWORK AND FUNCTIONS OF PUBLIC AD-
MINISTRATION. Norman: University of Oklahoma Press, 1973.
xiv, 491 p.

This book is designed for the practicing administrator.
It deals with the functions of administration--planning,
organizing, controlling, and developing and directing
human resources. The sixty-two essays from thirty-seven
publications are useful to those seeking to cope with the
complex administration problems of the 1970s and especially
useful to middle- and lower-level administrators.

424   Kramer, Fred A. DYNAMICS OF PUBLIC BUREAUCRACY: AN IN-
TRODUCTION TO PUBLIC ADMINISTRATION. Cambridge, Mass.:
Winthrop Publishers, 1977. xiii, 290 p.

Kramer attempts to deal with political-administrative responses to policy problems in the American governmental
system. His aim is to give the student a greater awareness of the workings of public organizations in relation
to the policy outputs of government. He stresses organization theory and American political practices, with emphasis on interest groups and describes personnel administration, budgeting, administrative law, and administrative
responsibility. The impetus for this textbook was the

author's experience as an ASPA fellow in the Department of Housing and Urban Development and the Bureau of the Budget.

425   Lane, Frederick S., ed. CURRENT ISSUES IN PUBLIC ADMINISTRA-
TION. New York: St. Martin's Press, 1978. xiv, 572 p.

This text provides a comprehensive set of readings that cover, with clarity and depth, all the main topics in public administration. The emphasis is on current issues and problems, and the readings are largely drawn from the recent literature. The selections cover both the po-litical setting of public agencies and the management of large public bureaucracies. State and local as well as federal government issues are given attention.

426   Lorch, Robert S. PUBLIC ADMINISTRATION. St. Paul, Minn.:
West Publishing Co., 1978. xi, 314 p. Paper.

Lorch's textbook is "deliberately informal and argumenta-tive in style." He addresses controversial areas of public administration, but provides no overarching philosophy or theme. He recommends that this text be used in issue-oriented, introductory public administration courses or as supplementary reading. Chapter headings include the managerial revolution; education in the mysterious science; getting it all together; ebb and flow of central power; down with spoils; getting hired; bureaucrats unite; internal communications; the Goebbels touch; how to run things; judgment day; high rollers and moneygrubbers; pink spiders in policy making; and controlling the beast.

427   Lutrin, Carl E., and Settle, Allen K. AMERICAN PUBLIC ADMINI-
STRATION: CONCEPTS AND CASES. Palo Alto, Calif.: Mayfield
Publishing Co., 1976. xiv, 392 p.

This textbook is oriented toward the basic concepts, tools, and issues of public administration. The authors have combined a personal interest in personnel administration, budgeting, decision making, communication, and bureau-cratic power with an interest in comparative administra-tion, administrative organization, bureaucratic behavior, and administrative responsibility. They present admini-strative concepts and related case studies in a single volume.

428   McCurdy, Howard E. PUBLIC ADMINISTRATION: A SYNTHESIS.
Menlo Park, Calif.: Cummings Publishing Co., 1977. ix, 424 p.

This textbook brings together the divergent theories and methods that make up the essential lessons contained in

the books, articles, and management strategies that have
had the greatest impact upon the development of public
administration. McCurdy presents the various approaches
that public administrators should master in order to manage
government programs. Sections include principles, problems, strategies, and contexts of public administration
and is abundantly illustrated with case studies.

429   Meier, Kenneth J. POLITICS AND THE BUREAUCRACY: POLICY-
       MAKING IN THE FOURTH BRANCH OF GOVERNMENT. North
       Scituate, Mass.: Duxbury Press, 1979. xviii, 221 p. Paper.

       This textbook attempts to explain the reasons for the
       growth of bureaucratic power. Meier emphasizes that
       "nearly all public policy . . . has degenerated into in-
       structions to bureaucracy" and claims that "yielding to
       bureaucracy and its influence . . . is not inevitable,"
       as mechanisms and procedures can limit or structure bu-
       reaucratic policy making. The author provides a working
       knowledge of what a bureaucracy is, how it is organized,
       and how it works, primarily at the federal level. He
       seeks to provide a basis for estimating the conditions for
       bureaucratic abuse of authority and reviews the techniques
       for controlling these abuses.

430   Miewald, Robert D. PUBLIC ADMINISTRATION: A CRITICAL PER-
       SPECTIVE. New York: McGraw-Hill Book Co., 1978. xi, 272 p.
       Paper.

       Miewald believes that "this is no time for a dull book in
       public administration. There is rather a need for a rowdy,
       contentious book." He raises a question that he believes
       is often ignored by most writers: What if the knowledge
       of the administrators is defective or at least severely limited?
       Chapters include administration and its limits, politics and
       administration, bureaucratic politics, federalism, the life
       and hard times of bureaucracies, budgets, measurement,
       knowledge and decisions, management, public personnel
       administration, and responsibility.

431   Morstein Marx, Fritz. THE ADMINISTRATIVE STATE: AN INTRO-
       DUCTION TO BUREAUCRACY. Chicago: University of Chicago Press,
       1957. x, 202 p.

       Marx discusses the nature of the "administrative state,"
       aspects of bureaucracy, essentials of public administration,
       types of bureaucracies, safeguards of civil service status,
       the making of career men, the integrity of service, con-
       cepts of service, and the bureaucratic world in examining
       the main forms of bureaucracy in mid-twentieth-century
       America. This text is a good primer for public admini-
       stration study.

432   _____, ed. ELEMENTS OF PUBLIC ADMINISTRATION. New York: Prentice-Hall, 1946. xxiv, 637 p.

> In one of the classics of post-World War II public administration, Morstein Marx includes sections on the role of public administration, organization and management, working methods, and responsibility and accountability. Essay topics include democratic administration, bureaucracy, social functions, planning, the chief executive, regulatory commissions, interest groups, legislative control, field organization, informal organization, supervision, morale, discipline, and fiscal accountability.

433   Nigro, Felix A., and Nigro, Lloyd G. MODERN PUBLIC ADMINISTRATION. 4th ed. New York: Harper and Row, 1977. xiv, 492 p.

> The Nigros include new developments in the field and combine the best elements of both the theory and practice of public administration. New chapters in this latest edition include discussions of policy analysis, administrative ethics, program evaluation, and organization theory. Sections include the nature of the field, administrative organization, basic problems of management, personnel administration, financial administration, administrative responsibility, and international administration. Their work ranks among the best in the discipline.

434   Present, Philip E., ed. PEOPLE AND PUBLIC ADMINISTRATION: CASE STUDIES AND PERSPECTIVES. Pacific Palisades, Calif.: Palisades Publishers, 1979. x, 292 p.

> The theme of this book of readings is the human perspective and influence on public administration. The editor states that the subject introductions and selections should alert readers to the importance of the attitudes, values, and behaviors of individuals in the administration of government and give a clearer picture of what public administrators actually do in their work. The readings are not drawn solely from academic journals, but come from cases written by professional journalists and political writers. Sections or topics include characteristics and challenges of public administration, ethical choices of the individual in administration, the individual and the organization, the individual in the public personnel process, the administrator as decision and policymaker, and budgets and program evaluation.

435   Presthus, Robert. PUBLIC ADMINISTRATION. 6th ed. New York: Ronald Press Co., 1975. ix, 432 p.

> This textbook is recognized as a classic in modern public

administration literature with Leonard D. White's INTRO-
DUCTION TO THE STUDY OF PUBLIC ADMINISTRATION
(see 443) and W.F. Willoughby's PRINCIPLES OF PUBLIC
ADMINISTRATION (see 444). Parts of this edition include
the study and context of public administration, community
participation and organizational theory, personnel, financial
policy and the budget process, and administrative responsibility.

436   Reynolds, Harry W., Jr. "The New Public Administration Texts--Where
Are We Going?" MIDWEST REVIEW OF PUBLIC ADMINISTRATION
11 (March 1977): 21-34.

This article examines fourteen publications in public administration in an attempt to ascertain the discipline's
dimensions and directions. Among the points made by
the author are that policy considerations are of greater
interest than organizational design and theory, that closer
examination of the administrator's role in policy formulation and evaluation is needed, that there is an increasing
recognition of political considerations, that there is a
diminishing emphasis on case studies and comparative administration, and that texts in public administration afford
a wide range of choices in terms of what is presented,
in what depth, and to what end.

437   Richardson, Ivan L., and Baldwin, Sidney. PUBLIC ADMINISTRATION:
GOVERNMENT IN ACTION. Columbus, Ohio: Charles E. Merrill,
1976. x, 342 p.

This textbook "represents an attempt to introduce the subject of public administration to the new student and to
map some of the terrain of public administration in a
more ecumenical spirit. The central organizing principle
underlying this book is that while government is many
things, it is intended to act, and that the pivot on which
government turns is public administration." Parts include
the study of public administration, public administration
in the web of government, the tasks of public administration, administration as management, and the challenge of
change.

438   Shafritz, Jay M., and Hyde, Albert C., eds. CLASSICS OF PUBLIC
ADMINISTRATION. Oak Park, Ill.: Moore Publishing Co., 1978.
x, 446 p.

In perhaps the most comprehensive collection of essays in
the field of public administration, the editors cover the
discipline of public administration, the political context
of public administration, bureaucracy, organization theory,
organizational behavior, organization development, per-

sonnel management, the budgetary process, public policy
and analysis, and planning evaluation. The essays are
also divided chronologically into sections on the World
Wars, the later 1940s, the 1950s, the 1960s, and the
1970s. This is a most useful resource material for both
academics and practitioners in public administration.

439   Simon, Herbert A.; Smithburg, Donald W.; and Thompson, Victor A.
       PUBLIC ADMINISTRATION. New York: Alfred A. Knopf, 1950.
       xv, 582 p., xviii.

       This classic textbook emphasizes the organization of
       federal, state, and local governmental structures, ad-
       ministrative behavior, and relationships between politics
       and administration. Chapters include discussions of what
       is public administration, the origin of government orga-
       nizations, human behavior and organization, formation
       and values of groups, specialization of work, the au-
       thority, status, and communication for securing teamwork
       in organizations, civil service, recruitment and careers
       in government, personnel processes, efficiency, admini-
       strative responsibility, planning, and costs of change.
       This is an excellent resource guide for public admini-
       stration in the United States at mid-century.

440   Stillman, Richard J. II, ed. PUBLIC ADMINISTRATION: CONCEPTS
       AND CASES. Boston: Houghton Mifflin Co., 1976. xii, 372 p.

       In this book of readings, Stillman includes essays con-
       cerning the search for the substance and boundaries of
       public administration, the pattern of public administration
       in America (people, institutions, and environment), the
       functions of public administrators (major activities and
       responsibilities), and enduring and unresolved value ques-
       tions (the relationship between administration and politics,
       the employer and the employee, and the public servant
       and ethics). He seeks to interrelate many of the classic
       conceptual works in the discipline with contemporary ad-
       ministrative case studies.

441   Uveges, Joseph A., Jr., ed. CASES IN PUBLIC ADMINISTRATION:
       NARRATIVES IN ADMINISTRATIVE PROBLEMS. Boston: Holbrook
       Press, 1978. xiii, 394 p.

       Uveges states that "this book reflects the belief that, re-
       gardless of the short-term consequences of the Watergate
       episode and the ensuing 1976 presidential campaign against
       'big government,' the long term march toward greater
       governmental involvement in the administration of eco-
       nomic, social, and political policies continues." He in-
       cludes essays on the interfacing of persons, groups, and

institutions, managing organizations through change and toward administrative effectiveness, responsiveness, collective action, and administrative morality in public personnel management, budgets and fiscal policy as management tools, and the case for administrative regulation and citizen participation.

442   Waldo, Dwight [A.]. PERSPECTIVES ON ADMINISTRATION. University: University of Alabama Press, 1956. 143 p.

The author addresses how administration fits into the entire human enterprise, how it looks to other disciplines, how other disciplines look to the student of administration, and what conceptual lenses or spectacles are available to administrators in scrutinizing the administrative world. In addressing these concerns, Waldo probes models, or analogies or idioms, used in the study of administration and offers perspectives from history, literature, and social science.

443   White, Leonard D. INTRODUCTION TO THE STUDY OF PUBLIC ADMINISTRATION. New York: Macmillan Co., 1926. xiii, 495 p.

White has composed the first public administration textbook. It centers upon the methods of administration used by all levels of government. He presents concepts in the administration-politics division and the organic division of management chores, with chapters on departmentalization, centralization, integration, personnel, recruitment, morale, stipend standardization, promotion, discipline and removal, retirement systems, and administrative rules.

444   Willoughby, W.F. PRINCIPLES OF PUBLIC ADMINISTRATION. Baltimore: Johns Hopkins Press, 1927. xxii, 720 p.

This textbook is considered a classic in the literature of public administration along with Leonard D. White's INTRODUCTION TO THE STUDY OF PUBLIC ADMINISTRATION (see entry 443). The author states that "the present volume has for its purpose to make such a study . . . with special reference to the problem of administration as it confronts the national government and secondarily the state governments." Parts include general administration and organization, personnel, and finance.

C. EDUCATION AND RESEARCH

445   Anderson, William. RESEARCH IN PUBLIC ADMINISTRATION. Part I: REPORT OF THE COMMITTEE ON PUBLIC ADMINISTRATION OF

THE SOCIAL SCIENCE RESEARCH COUNCIL, 1934-1945; part II: RE-SEARCH IN PUBLIC ADMINISTRATION, 1930-1945. Chicago: Public Administration Service, 1945. xiv, 221 p.

> Part I reviews major research projects, case reports in public administration, general planning and promotion of research and makes recommendations for a postwar research program in public administration. Part II reviews changes in the setting of public administration in the United States and sets unfinished business before public administrators after the end of World War II. This text is valuable for its insights into the role of public administration in American society in the late 1940s.

446   Beaumont, Enid. "Distinctive But Not Elitist." JOURNAL OF URBAN ANALYSIS 3 (October 1976): 131-42.

> The Graduate School of Public Administration of New York University, the second largest school of public affairs-public administration in the United States, has since 1971, eliminated many narrow vocational courses and weeded out many students with narrow vocational goals through qualifying and comprehensive examinations. The article notes that the school is oriented toward the application of social science theory to the analysis of public issues and the management of public affairs.

447   Bowman, James S. "Undergraduate Education in Public Administration: A Look at the Core Course." SOUTHERN REVIEW OF PUBLIC AD-MINISTRATION 1 (September 1977): 203-30. Tables.

> Bowman provides a review of literature and methods, de-notes characteristics of the introductory public admini-stration course, distinguishes between form and substance of the course, and offers faculty views on teaching public administration. He concludes that "perhaps the greatest challenge for those interested in public administration is to effectively integrate politics and management, theory and practice, in order to demonstrate to students that it is an important and crucial part of their collegiate studies."

448   Brandl, John E. "Public Service Education in the 1970s." JOURNAL OF URBAN ANALYSIS 3 (October 1976): 105-14.

> Brandl points out the importance of economics, micro-economics, ethics, societal stability, and policy imple-mentation in curriculums of new institutes or schools of public administration or policy.

449   Byrd, Jack, Jr. OPERATIONS RESEARCH MODELS FOR PUBLIC AD-MINISTRATION. Lexington, Mass.: D.C. Heath and Co., 1975. xxi, 276 p.

Byrd examines the role of quantitative analyses in public administration and decision making. He evaluates quantitative analyses in light of the different levels of decisions that public administrators encounter, emphasizes the scientific method of problem solving, analyzes how models of decision making should be developed, and discusses specific public oriented case studies. Chapter discussions include the concepts of operations research as they relate to public administration, the myths and realities of the systems approach, the role of information systems in the development of quantitative models, and the problem of implementation of the quantitative study.

450   Caldwell, Lynton K. "Public Administration and the Universities: A Half-Century of Development." PUBLIC ADMINISTRATION REVIEW 25 (March 1965): 52-60.

From the legacy of Woodrow Wilson and the works of Charles Beard, the author traces the evolution of the study of public administration within the university establishment. Caldwell concludes that the existence of diverse organizational structures for university teaching of public administration results from the lack of compelling logic in our knowledge of administrative behavior.

451   Carroll, James D. "Education for the Public Trust: Learning to Live with the Public and the Absurd." BUREAUCRAT 4 (April 1975): 24-33.

Carroll posits that education for public service has not been widely accepted in the United States as has education for law, medicine, accounting, or architecture. The reader is told that much of the frustration encountered in American public administration is because the constitutional system is based on a distrust of power, a condition which makes it difficult and sometimes impossible to get things done.

452   Cikins, Warren I. "Graduate Education, Public Service, and the Negro." PUBLIC ADMINISTRATION REVIEW 26 (September 1966): 182-91.

The author states that graduate schools, and, to some extent, undergraduate as well, need to devise imaginative programs for accelerated training in order that opportunities in the public service be genuinely available to all Americans with the capability.

453   Collins, Morris W.H., Jr. "MPA Programs Today." PUBLIC MANAGEMENT 57 (May 1975): 4-9.

The reader is told that specialized programs in urban affairs and policy analysis are impressive and that joint business-public administration programs have been the most prominent.

454   Donaldson, William V. "Continuing Education for City Managers." PUBLIC ADMINISTRATION REVIEW 33 (November-December 1973): 504-8.

The author offers a continuing education program for city managers that is useful and relevant to their jobs. He argues that most of the present continuing educational opportunities for managers are based on erroneous understandings of the city manager's job and are at best a waste of time. He attempts to develop a more accurate description of the manager and his job which will provide a framework for a suggested training program that may be more useful to managers.

455   Edmonds, Thom. "Financing Graduate and Graduate Professional School Education." EDUCATION AND URBAN SOCIETY 8 (May 1976): 333-54.

Edmonds maintains that whereas fellowships provide a considerable part of income for graduate school students, no similar financial aid structure has arisen for graduate professional students, such as law students. This, in part, is due to the fact of the "high expected income" for such fields. The reader is informed that pay-as-you-earn plans are in fact designed to benefit the institution, rather than the student.

456   Engelbert, Ernest A. "Standards of Graduate Programs in Public Administration." PUBLIC MANAGEMENT 57 (May 1975): 10-12.

The author maintains that public-sector employers have expressed some dissatisfaction with the uneven quality of graduates produced by various public administration programs.

457   _____. "University Education for Public Policy Analysis." PUBLIC ADMINISTRATION REVIEW 37 (May-June 1977): 228-36.

Engelbert focuses on the origins of this field, the major tracts of study, the approach and content of the subject matter, the developing relationships to the public service, and some unresolved educational issues. This is an excellent essay for reviewing some of the problems and potentialities confronting programs in public administration and policy.

458   Fisher, Frederick E. "Give a Damn about Continuing Adult Education in Public Administration." PUBLIC ADMINISTRATION REVIEW 33 (November-December 1973): 488-98.

Fisher approaches adult education for public administrators from the perspectives of 1) the self, 2) the individual as a member of an organization, and 3) the individual, his or her organization, and the external environment. Concerning self, organization, and environment, the author forms a matrix which includes goals, or where the person wants to go, strategy, or how he or she gets there, and timetable, or costs. Educational objectives are placed in one of three major categories or domains: cognitive, affective, and psychomotor.

459   Fritschler, A. Lee, and Mackelprang, A.J.; with Blaustein, Eric, and Brozen, Richard. "Graduate Education in Public Affairs/Public Administration: Results of the 1975 Survey." PUBLIC ADMINISTRATION REVIEW 37 (September-October 1977): 488-94. Tables.

Data for this article was taken from completed survey questionnaires from the 1975 National Association of Schools of Public Affairs and Administration (NASPAA) survey. The survey covered 138 separate programs of public affairs and administration, a figure representing nearly all of the programs in the United States. In terms of content and focus of public affairs and administration programs, the authors conclude that the discipline appears to be reaching a "fair degree" of consensus on the fundamental aspects of graduate education in public affairs and administration.

460   Gibson, Frank, and Hildreth, William Bartley. "The Challenge of Professional Development: Teaching Public Administrators at the Graduate Level." SOUTHERN REVIEW OF PUBLIC ADMINISTRATION 1 (June 1977): 62-73.

The authors believe "that effective graduate education in public administration must combine the numerous elements that comprise the administrator's world." They maintain that these elements should be present whether the programs be pre-service or in-service and that it is important to recall that public administration programs are offered by universities, not trade or vocational schools.

461   Graham, George A. "Trends in Teaching of Public Administration." PUBLIC ADMINISTRATION REVIEW 10 (Spring 1950): 69-77.

Graham begins his essay: "To avoid any misunderstanding, the reader is put on notice that the remarks which follow are not 'scientific,' and they are not based on a systematic

survey. They are subjective impressions, bulging with
bias--the product of old-fashioned armchair research."
With this warning in mind, the author is concerned with
who teaches public administration, the teachers' philosophy,
the elements of public administration, administrative theory,
how public administration is taught, and a look into the
future.

462   Gregg, Roy G., and Van Maanen, John. "The Realities of Education
as a Prescription for Organizational Change." PUBLIC ADMINISTRA-
TION REVIEW 33 (November-December 1973): 522-32.

The purpose of this essay is to suggest that we are now
at a position, both historically and structurally, where
educational techniques can no longer be expected to
provide the impetus for institutional change. Gregg cites
individual orientation, segmentation of life, rationalization
of existing structures, man as a merchandisable product,
unanticipated consequences of measurement, creation of
false expectations, and solidification of the organization
culture as the illogical basis for continuing education as
a change strategy.

463   Gulick, Luther. "George Maxwell had a Dream." In AMERICAN
PUBLIC ADMINISTRATION: PAST, PRESENT, FUTURE, edited by
Frederick C. Mosher, pp. 253-67. University: University of Alabama
Press, 1975.

The author describes the personality and character of
George Maxwell, founder of the Maxwell School of Citi-
zenship and Public Affairs at Syracuse University, New
York. He writes that five major original streams of
thought and effort were the result of ideas promoted by
Mary Averell Harriman, George Maxwell, Frederick
Davenport, Charles W. Flint, and William E. Mosher.

464   Honey, John C. "Research in Public Administration: A Further Note."
PUBLIC ADMINISTRATION REVIEW 17 (Autumn 1957): 238-43.

The author probes the nature of public administration,
examines the relationship between research and public
administration, expresses the need for utilitarian research,
calls for research on the administrative process, notes the
significance of fundamental research, and explains the relationship of research and the professional society. Honey
struggles with the lack of understanding over what public
administration is and whether it is a separate field or
discipline from the other social sciences.

465   Kirlin, John J. "The School of Public Administration at the University
        of Southern California." JOURNAL OF URBAN ANALYSIS 3 (October
        1976): 179-86.

> The author states that all programs offered by this school
> build from a management-oriented core and that the cur-
> riculum stresses the implementation dimension of the policy
> process as opposed to policy analysis. Kirlin mentions
> that the period of growth and elaboration of new programs
> is terminating and that a number of activities are under-
> way to strengthen the curriculum and develop the faculty.

466   La Porte, Todd. "The Recovery of Relevance in the Study of Public
        Organization." In TOWARD A NEW PUBLIC ADMINISTRATION: THE
        MINNOWBROOK PERSPECTIVE, edited by Frank Marini, pp. 17-48.
        Scranton, Pa.: Chandler Publishing Co., 1971.

> La Porte argues that the public administration discipline
> and profession, its values, and its literature are out of
> touch with the problems American society is encountering
> in the 1970s. He states that the discipline of public
> administration is "under an urgent requirement to recover
> substantive and analytical relevance so that our intellec-
> tual efforts afford insights and understanding about the
> major changes of our culture and clarify our vision of
> what can be the future as well as what is present and
> past."

467   Loveland, John, and Whately, Arthur. "Improving Public Administra-
        tion School Effectiveness Through Upward Performance Evaluation."
        PUBLIC ADMINISTRATION REVIEW 37 (January-February 1977): 77-
        80. Tables.

> The purpose of this essay is to report the results of a
> survey of schools of public administration designed to
> determine the extent of both student evaluation of teach-
> ing effectiveness and faculty evaluation of administrative
> effectiveness.

468   McArthur, Robert E. "The Master of Public Administration Program."
        PUBLIC ADMINISTRATION SURVEY 22 (March 1975): 1-4.

> This article reveals that the University of Mississippi in-
> troduced a Master of Public Administration course to pre-
> pare men and women for managerial positions in public
> organizations and that a full-time internship in a govern-
> mental agency is offered to candidates.

469   Mackelprang, A.J., and Fritschler, A. Lee. "Graduate Education in
        Public Affairs/Public Administration." PUBLIC ADMINISTRATION
        REVIEW 35 (March-April 1975): 182-90. Tables.

This article presents an in-depth analysis of the 1974 graduate program survey of member institutions of the National Association of Schools of Public Affairs and Administration (NASPAA). The results provide a firm empirical base for continued dialogue on the state of professional education in public affairs–public administration.

470   Marini, Frank. "The Minnowbrook Perspective and the Future of Public Administration Education." In his TOWARD A NEW PUBLIC ADMINISTRATION: THE MINNOWBROOK PERSPECTIVE, pp. 346–67. Scranton, Pa.: Chandler Publishing Co., 1971.

Themes and concerns at the Minnowbrook Conference at Syracuse University in September 1968 have come to be known as "the Minnowbrook perspective," "the young Public Administration movement," and "new Public Administration." Concepts which seem important to the author for public administration education include a "relevant" public administration, postpositivism, adapting to turbulence in the environment, new organizational forms, and client-focused organizations. This essay provides useful insight into public administration educational directions in the early 1970s.

471   Medeiros, James A. "The Professional Study of Public Administration." PUBLIC ADMINISTRATION REVIEW 34 (May–June 1974): 254–60.

Medeiros reports that a survey reveals that no agreement is available on common requisites for graduate students in public administration. He notes that a striking characteristic of many of these programs is a limitation on courses that may be taken from other departments and that considerable disparity exists concerning the total number of courses required.

472   Mosher, Frederick C. "Research in Public Administration: Some Notes and Suggestions." PUBLIC ADMINISTRATION REVIEW 16 (Summer 1956): 169–78.

Mosher probes the background of public administration research, denotes postwar developments, cites current needs and problems, acknowledges the rapid development of social science research, examines the problem of interdisciplinary communication, recognizes the potential of the interdisciplinary effort, and makes suggestions for the advancement of knowledge as one of the objectives of the American Society for Public Administration.

473   Murray, Michael A. "Strategies for Placing Public Administration
        Graduates." PUBLIC ADMINISTRATION REVIEW 35 (November-
        December 1975): 629-35.

                Murray contends that job placement is a serious problem
                in public administration programs and that many programs
                do not encourage development of a network of informal
                contacts. He believes that every public administration
                program should assign a placement officer, hold orienta-
                tion programs for students, and encourage students to
                assume the initiative; the faculty should also establish
                an intern program.

474   _____. "Trends in Public Administration Education." BUREAUCRAT
        4 (July 1975): 192-203.

                This article notes that the National Association of Schools
                of Public Affairs and Administration conducted a national
                survey of the programs of its 128 member institutions. The
                data reveal that approximately half of the programs were
                classified as separate units and that most faculty members
                were associated with separate schools and divisions. Murray
                finds that political science theory and methodology con-
                tinue to dominate the design of public administration programs.

475   Nagel, Stuart, and Neef, Marian. "What Is and What Should Be In
        University Policy Studies?" PUBLIC ADMINISTRATION REVIEW 37
        (July-August 1977): 383-90.

                This article describes what is happening in university
                policy studies activities within political science depart-
                ments and within interdisciplinary programs, then analyzes
                a set of prescriptions for improving policy studies activities
                which have been recommended by academics and by gov-
                ernment practitioners. The authors' main conclusion is that
                policy studies are alive and well in political science de-
                partments and interdisciplinary programs across the country.

476   Rose, Gale W. "An Individualized Learning Model of Organizing for
        Graduate Education." EDUCATION AND URBAN SOCIETY 9 (November
        1976): 27-46.

                Rose posits that because learning is directly related to
                learner self-motivation, such learning is likely to be
                meaningful and promote the learner's ability to proceed
                in an independent manner. He discusses the Individualized
                Learning System for Administrators at New York University
                and explains reasons for success of the students and faculty
                using this model. Rose points out that students exemplify
                "success" in professional preparation when faculty indicate
                with clarity performance criteria and standards.

477   Sloan, Royal D., Jr. "The Introductory Public Administration Course:
       Approach for the 1960s and Beyond." PUBLIC ADMINISTRATION
       REVIEW 23 (June 1963): 93-98.

       The author concludes that educators charged with the
       formulation of introductory courses in public administration
       have failed to keep abreast of the changes in public
       policy and administration. He believes that government
       by contract, the role and function of the military, the
       administration of overseas programs, and public admini-
       stration in the developing nations are topics that should
       be covered in the introductory public administration course.

478   Somit, Albert. "Bureaucratic Realpolitik and the Teaching of Admini-
       stration." PUBLIC ADMINISTRATION REVIEW 16 (Autumn 1956):
       292-95.

       The author believes that the public employee who lacks
       at least an elementary comprehension of the major oper-
       ational concepts and objectives of administrative real-
       politik is professionally handicapped despite his/her other
       qualifications. After scanning the literature of American
       public administration, Somit maintains that anyone familiar
       with the realities of bureaucratic existence is confronted
       by the almost total absence of any dispassionate analysis
       of the nature and importance of administrative realpolitik.

479   Stone, Alice B., and Stone, Donald C. "Early Development of Edu-
       cation in Public Administration." In AMERICAN PUBLIC ADMINI-
       STRATION: PAST, PRESENT, FUTURE, edited by Frederick C. Mosher,
       pp. 11-48. University: University of Alabama Press, 1975.

       The authors describe the development of education in
       public administration in response to national and local
       dissatisfaction with the performance of government. They
       state that in order to comprehend the seedbed in which
       public administration education first rooted and developed,
       one must be aware of the condition of government before
       the turn of the century. The Stones claim that not until
       well into the twentieth century was there any serious
       recognition of the function of administration and of the
       idea that professional training was feasible.

480   Strauch, Ralph E. "A Critical Look at Quantitative Methodology."
       POLICY ANALYSIS 2 (Winter 1976): 121-44.

       This article addresses the expansion in the role and in-
       fluence of quantitative methods and techniques in gov-
       ernment decision-making processes. The reader learns
       that quantitative methodology provides valuable insights
       but these evaluations depend on the interpretations of the
       analyst.

481   Useem, Michael. "Government Mobilization of Academic Social Re-
       search." POLICY STUDIES JOURNAL 4 (Spring 1976): 274-80.

       Useem states that the evidence from a survey of social
       scientists indicates that the national government is distrib-
       uting research funds among academic social scientists in a
       fashion likely to produce research of utility to both federal
       agencies and academic disciplines.

482   Waldo, Dwight [A.]. "Education for Public Administration in the
       Seventies." In AMERICAN PUBLIC ADMINISTRATION: PAST, PRESENT,
       FUTURE, edited by Frederick C. Mosher, pp. 181-232. University:
       University of Alabama Press, 1975.

       Waldo divides his essay into three parts: 1) the "ambience,"
       the conditioning environment of ideas, values, perceptions,
       and events; 2) recent and current educational activities,
       responses, and initiatives; and 3) problems and prospects
       of the educational enterprise in and for public administration.

483   Weiss, Carol H. "Policy Research in the University: Practical Aid
       or Academic Exercise?" POLICY STUDIES JOURNAL 4 (Spring 1976):
       224-28.

       This article explores the idea that university social scientists
       have become increasingly engaged in research that tries
       to influence the direction of government decisions, but
       effective application of policy research to policy making
       is constrained by limitations of the research, competing
       factors in the policy system, difficulties in communication
       between researcher and policy maker, and disparities in
       values.

484   Yarwood, Dean L., and Nimmo, Dan D. "Perspectives for Teaching
       Public Administration." MIDWEST REVIEW OF PUBLIC ADMINISTRA-
       TION 9 (January 1975): 28-42. Tables.

       The authors present the findings of research undertaken to
       explore the attitudes and opinions toward bureaucracy of
       persons affected by decision making. They employ factor
       analysis to analyze responses and find four images of bu-
       reaucracy forthcoming, including "the cautious trusting,"
       "distrustful critics," the advocates of broader participation
       and pluralistic responses, and proponents of bureaucracy
       for underdogs.

485   Zauderer, Donald G., and Ross, Bernard H. "Curriculum Reform
       and Organizational Culture: Public Administration at the American
       University." JOURNAL OF URBAN ANALYSIS 3 (October 1976):
       187-96.

This article discusses the curriculum for the masters degree in public administration program at American University. The authors mention that the program stresses problem-solving skills and that professors are expected to produce research and are rewarded for community liaison, administration, and program development.

D. INTERNSHIPS

486   Adams, Thomas W., and Murphy, Thomas P. "NASA's University Research Programs: Dilemmas and Problems on the Government Academic Interface." PUBLIC ADMINISTRATION REVIEW 27 (March 1967): 10-17.

The authors describe how the National Aeronautics and Space Administration attempted to draw the heterogeneous capabilities of universities into the national space effort. They outline a number of government-academic issues and offer some questions and suggestions regarding resolution of these issues.

487   Banovetz, James. "The HUD Urban Fellowship Program: A Partial Response to the Urban Manpower Crisis." In GOVERNMENT MAN-AGEMENT INTERNSHIPS AND EXECUTIVE DEVELOPMENT: EDUCATION FOR CHANGE, edited by Thomas P. Murphy, pp. 79-93. Lexington, Mass.: D.C. Heath and Co., 1973.

Banovetz discusses the role of internships, the concept of internships versus the idea of training, and the acceptance of new ideas by the people involved in examining the impacts of HUD's Urban Fellowship Program. He surmises that the program's principal failing was the miniscule level of support provided by Congress.

488   Campbell, Alan K., and Strakosch, Lynn D. "The Presidential Management Intern Program: A New Approach to Selecting and Developing America's Future Public Managers." PUBLIC ADMINISTRATION REVIEW 39 (May-June 1979): 232-36.

The authors review the various levels that Presidential Management Interns must successfully pass (nomination, eligibility review, regional screening panel, and final selection), provide a profile of the first Presidential Management Intern program class (1978), note the role of affirmative action in this process, and conclude that the success of the PMI program "will be measured by its contribution to improved public management."

489 Dworkis, Martin B.; Thomas, Samuel F.; and Weintraub, Ruth. "Establishing an Administrative Internship Program." PUBLIC ADMINI-STRATION REVIEW 22 (Spring 1962): 75-81.

> This article is based upon the growing need of the federal government for outstanding college graduates. The experimental intern program described herein was designed with the idea that a substantial work experience by college seniors would develop in them a greater awareness and appreciation of the challenge offered in the federal government. The authors cite program results and offer recommendations for similar intern programs with government departments and agencies.

490 Finkle, Arthur L., and Barclay, Warren M. "State Government Internships." PUBLIC ADMINISTRATION REVIEW 39 (May-June 1979): 236-38.

> Finkle and Barclay describe state internship practices, denote general models of state internship programs, and cite common denominators of all state internship programs. They discuss sources of program funding, program responsibility, and means of compensating student interns.

491 Fisher, Frederick E. "Emerging City Internship Patterns." In GOVERNMENT MANAGEMENT INTERNSHIPS AND EXECUTIVE DEVELOPMENT: EDUCATION FOR CHANGE, edited by Thomas P. Murphy, pp. 65-78. Lexington, Mass.: D.C. Heath and Co., 1973.

> Fisher reviews internship patterns of the Urban Corps, the Southern Regional Educational Board's Resource Development Project, the Urban Careers Program administered by American University and the District of Columbia Personnel Office, and the National Urban Fellows program. He concludes that these emerging patterns of urban internships indicate a growing acceptance and spread of service learning as preparation for careers in the public service.

492 Heimovics, Richard D. "An Intern's Perspective." In GOVERNMENT MANAGEMENT INTERNSHIPS AND EXECUTIVE DEVELOPMENT: EDUCATION FOR CHANGE, edited by Thomas P. Murphy, pp. 25-33. Lexington, Mass.: D.C. Heath and Co., 1973.

> The author believes that it is helpful not to think about the internship in the context of task accomplishment but rather how skillful an observer the intern can be. He sees the internship as a maturation process.

493 Henry, Nicholas. "Are Internships Worthwhile?" PUBLIC ADMINI-STRATION REVIEW 39 (May-June 1979): 245-47.

To discern the answer to the above question, the author mailed 1,351 questionnaires to graduates of nine major public administration programs across the country. Henry's research discovered that "former interns felt their internships were useful from a practical, career standpoint" and that "fully three-quarters of them responded that their internships provided valuable contacts for the future."

494   Honan, Joseph C., and Day, H. Talmage. "Linking Public Affairs Internship Experience and Academic Study: A Strategy for Program Design." SOUTHERN REVIEW OF PUBLIC ADMINISTRATION 3 (September 1979): 146-63.

The authors offer suggestions for internship design criteria to be used for evaluating the academic relevance of placements, alternative modalities for organizing concurrent academic instruction, and hypotheses concerning interrelationships of academic topics, placement quality, and instructional modalities.

495   Hughes, Larry, and Murphy, Thomas P. "The Emergence of State Management Internships." In GOVERNMENT MANAGEMENT INTERNSHIPS AND EXECUTIVE DEVELOPMENT: EDUCATION FOR CHANGE, edited by Thomas P. Murphy, pp. 95-107. Lexington, Mass.: D.C. Heath and Co., 1973. Table.

The authors conclude that state management internship and development programs are growing at the same time that the public administration role of the state is expanding at an ever-increasing rate. They review internship programs in California, New York, and Maryland.

496   Jadlos, James P. "The Federal Management Interns." In GOVERNMENT MANAGEMENT INTERNSHIPS AND EXECUTIVE DEVELOPMENT: EDUCATION FOR CHANGE, edited by Thomas P. Murphy, pp. 157-78. Lexington, Mass.: D.C. Heath and Co., 1973.

Jadlos probes the origins of the Management Intern program, discusses the administration of the intern program, reviews the advance development of management interns, denotes intern criticism and suggestions, reviews the wide variety of training opportunities, and recognizes the importance of research in this area. The author states that the Management Intern program is the result of almost forty years of development and changing philosophy about how best to fulfill the government's need for managers.

497   Koehler, Cortus T. "The Responsibilities of Internship Supervisors." SOUTHERN REVIEW OF PUBLIC ADMINISTRATION 3 (September 1979): 137-45.

"Participation in an internship program is not a one way activity, benefiting only the intern. The internship provides agency personnel with an opportunity to keep up with advances and innovations in their professional areas."

498   McCaffery, Jerry L. "Perceptions of Satisfaction-Dissatisfaction in the Internship Experience." PUBLIC ADMINISTRATION REVIEW 39 (May-June 1979): 241-44. Tables.

McCaffery concludes that "if a school's interns do well in the field, then they advertise the strength of the school's program and increase the market value and marketability of its graduates." He notes that public administration has made a major commitment to mid-curriculum internships.

499   McGill, Michael E. "Learning from Administrative Experience." PUBLIC ADMINISTRATION REVIEW 33 (November-December 1973): 498-503.

The author suggests a complement to continuing education for public administrators which he calls "learning from administrative experience." He believes that a move toward helping administrators learn from their administrative experiences requires a slower, more individualized, more theoretical approach than has been the practice in management and organization development programs in public administration.

500   Morgan, Glenn G. "On Being an Intern--and Afterward." PUBLIC ADMINISTRATION REVIEW 16 (Spring 1956): 95-101.

The author provides a diary of his progress during a development program which indicates how he was affected by, and reacted to, training in management.

501   Murphy, Thomas P. "An Academic Perspective on Internships." In his GOVERNMENT MANAGEMENT INTERNSHIPS AND EXECUTIVE DEVELOPMENT: EDUCATION FOR CHANGE, pp. 3-23. Lexington, Mass.: D.C. Heath and Co., 1973.

Murphy writes that the public management internship is an educational innovation that is assuming increasing significance in academic programs designed to train and educate public administrators. He describes the rationale of internships, types of internships, the placement of interns, and the processes of selling an internship program and selecting interns for government service.

502   _____. "Internships in Urban Government." In his UNIVERSITIES
IN THE URBAN CRISIS, pp. 71-92. New York: Dunellen Publishing
Co., 1975.

> In this essay, Murphy concludes that one of the most
> effective options available to universities to help meet
> the administrative, professional, and technical manpower
> needs of cities is the internship. He explores the theory
> of internships, reviews academic questions in this regard,
> discusses the role of faculty internship directors, and
> suggests new directions in city management internships,
> including the National Urban Fellows Program, the Na-
> tional Urban Corps, the Community Service Learning
> Program, the National Center for Public Service Intern-
> ships, and the National Association of Schools of Public
> Affairs and Administration.

503   _____. "Potential Pitfalls of Internships." In his GOVERNMENT
MANAGEMENT INTERNSHIPS AND EXECUTIVE DEVELOPMENT: EDU-
CATION FOR CHANGE, pp. 35-47. Lexington, Mass.: D.C. Heath
and Co., 1973. Table.

> The author reviews participant interrelationships, organiza-
> tional pitfalls, political hazards, and personal pitfalls and
> concludes that pitfalls may be a question of attitude and
> definition. If political, organizational, and personal pit-
> falls did not exist, the intern certainly would not learn
> as much.

504   _____. "State Legislative Internships." In his GOVERNMENT MAN-
AGEMENT INTERNSHIPS AND EXECUTIVE DEVELOPMENT: EDUCA-
TION FOR CHANGE, pp. 109-33. Lexington, Mass.: D.C. Heath
and Co., 1973. Tables.

> Murphy analyzes benefits and objectives of legislative
> internships, selection and placement of interns, program
> control, program variations and evaluations, and internship
> finances. He examines the California and Oklahoma ex-
> periences in some detail, but studies the extent of intern-
> ships in all the American states. He concludes that a
> lesson to be learned from these observations is that new
> internship programs should not attempt to expand too
> rapidly.

505   _____. "State Legislative Internships: The Evolving Reality."
SOUTHERN REVIEW OF PUBLIC ADMINISTRATION 3 (September
1979): 175-88.

> Murphy reveals that most state legislative internship pro-
> grams have been regarded as successful by legislators,
> academic officials, and students. He concludes that both
> legislators and interns benefit from internships.

506   "NASPAA Guidelines for Public Service Internships." SOUTHERN
       REVIEW OF PUBLIC ADMINISTRATION   3 (September 1979): 189-95.

           The National Association of Schools of Public Affairs and
           Public Administration guidelines include purpose, duration
           and timing, academic component, placement, supervisors,
           compensation, and evaluation aspects.

507   Trachtenberg, Stephen J., and Paper, Lewis J.   An Overview of
       Federal Internships."   In GOVERNMENT MANAGEMENT INTERNSHIPS
       AND EXECUTIVE DEVELOPMENT: EDUCATION FOR CHANGE, edited
       by Thomas P. Murphy, pp. 137-55.   Lexington, Mass.:   D.C. Heath
       and Co., 1973.

           The authors review internships for undergraduates and
           high school students (congressional and federal depart-
           ments), internships for graduate students and career pro-
           fessionals, the White House Fellows Program, and the
           politics of selection and retention, including the art of
           being chosen and the art of hanging on.

508   Weaver, Michael.   "The Washington Semester Internship Program: The
       Case of the State University of New York."   In GOVERNMENT MAN-
       AGEMENT INTERNSHIPS AND EXECUTIVE DEVELOPMENT: EDUCA-
       TION FOR CHANGE, edited by Thomas P. Murphy, pp. 209-17.
       Lexington, Mass.:   D.C. Heath and Co., 1973.

           Weaver discusses the initiation of an internship program
           as the State University of New York chose to join a con-
           sortium of colleges to finance its Washington program.
           He states that the underlying assumption of the intern
           program is that cognitive development occurs to a large
           extent in ways that make it nonmeasurable with ordinary
           tools of evaluation (examinations, oral reports, term
           papers, etc.).

509   Wolf, James F.   "The Student Responsibility Model of Public Service
       Internships."   SOUTHERN REVIEW OF PUBLIC ADMINISTRATION   3
       (September 1979):   127-36.

           Wolf discusses the purpose of an internship in professional
           career education, the unique qualities of the public ad-
           ministration environment that place constraints on intern-
           ship programs, and the roles of the major actors in an
           internship program.   He believes that a student responsi-
           bility approach is the model most suitable for public man-
           agement careers.

Chapter 4

THE PRACTICE OF PUBLIC ADMINISTRATION

A. EVALUATION OF ADMINISTRATIVE PROCESS

510   Alwin, Duane F., and Sullivan, Michael J. "Issues of Design and
       Analysis in Evaluation Research." SOCIOLOGICAL METHODS AND
       RESEARCH 4 (August 1975): 77-100.

> This article addresses the question of internal validity in
> quasiexperimental and nonexperimental social policy re-
> search. The authors focus primary attention on problems
> of selection in research designs where assignment to ex-
> perimental conditions occurs on a nonrandom basis. Alwin
> and Sullivan discuss five different solutions to the prob-
> lems of selection--randomization, covariance adjustment,
> gain scores, matching, and explicit selection--and ex-
> amine the conditions under which these solutions are
> useful. They discuss the problem of random measurement
> error within the context of their elaboration of these
> techniques.

511   Anderson, Scarvia B., and Ball, Samuel. THE PROFESSION AND
       PRACTICE OF PROGRAM EVALUATION. San Francisco: Jossey
       Bass, 1978. 252 p.

> The authors provide a guide for the planning and conduct
> of evaluations for dealing with professional issues. They
> discuss the major purposes of evaluating educational and
> social programs, general methods of evaluation best suited
> for each purpose, types and sources of methods of evi-
> dence frequently associated with the general methods of
> investigation, targeted dissemination of evaluation infor-
> mation and results, professional predispositions and pref-
> erences of evaluators thay may influence what they view
> and how they view it, the complex fiscal and administra-
> tive relationships among funding agencies, program directors,
> and evaluators, defining, instilling, and assessing the com-
> petencies of evaluators, and the status and prospects for
> evaluation.

512   Andrieu, M. "Benefit Cost Evaluation." In EVALUATION RESEARCH
        METHODS: A BASIC GUIDE, edited by Leonard Rutman, pp. 217-32.
        Beverly Hills, Calif.: Sage Publications, 1977.

        Andrieu relates that the use of benefit-cost analysis is a
        recent development in public program evaluation, reflec-
        ting government's increasing involvement in such areas as
        education, manpower, health, social services, and income
        maintenance. The reader is informed that benefit-cost
        analysis is particularly useful in the case of social pro-
        grams, where it is difficult to quantify expected benefits.

513   Banner, David K. "Problems in the Evaluation of Social Action Pro-
        grams." ITCC REVIEW 3 (April 1974): 19-31.

        Banner suggests that, despite the methodological and po-
        litical problems associated with evaluation research in a
        social milieu, there is increasing reliance upon scientific
        evaluation data to determine which social action programs
        should be expanded and which should be terminated or
        reoriented. Much evaluation research has been poorly
        designed and poorly implemented. Banner sees a restruc-
        turing of the orientations and expectations of various
        actors within the federal hierarchy as necessary to create
        a positive environment for evaluation.

514   Beigel, Allan, and Levenson, Alan I. "Program Evaluation on a
        Shoestring Budget." In EVALUATION OF HUMAN SERVICE PROGRAMS,
        edited by C. Clifford Attkisson et al., pp. 97-124. New York:
        Academic Press, 1978.

        This study describes some of the principal ideological and
        pragmatic dilemmas faced by the human service program
        administrator who does not have access to evaluation staff
        and adequate budgetary resources. The reader learns
        which evaluation strategies are useful and easily utilized.

515   Blackwell, Barbara L., and Bolman, William M. "The Principles and
        Problems of Evaluation." COMMUNITY MENTAL HEALTH JOURNAL
        13 (Summer 1977): 175-87.

        The authors assert that evaluation can determine the future
        of mental health in the United States as evaluation is
        useful in determining goals. Different goals come from
        different kinds of multilevel evaluation and expansion of
        participation in determining goals and in developing
        methods to achieve objectives increases the numbers of
        persons committed to the task.

516   Bunkder, Douglas R. "Organizing Evaluation to Serve the Needs of
        Program Planners and Managers." EVALUATION AND PROGRAM
        PLANNING 1 (1978): 129-34.

The author distinguishes the conceptual definitions and functional applications of evaluation and of program planning and operations management. He advocates a broad definition of the evaluation task and emphasizes that administrators and evaluators should recognize the interdependence of these concepts and functions. He offers guidelines for enhancing success for utilizing formal evaluation assessments of public social programs.

517   Campbell, Donald T. "Focal Local Indicators for Social Program Evaluation." SOCIAL INDICATORS RESEARCH 3 (September 1976): 237-56.

Campbell relates that one of the most important uses of social indicators is in evaluating the impact of specific social programs. For successful evaluation, statistics must be available for local areas which often do not conform to standard administrative units.

518   Caputo, David A. "Evaluating Urban Public Policy: A Developmental Model and Some Reservations." PUBLIC ADMINISTRATION REVIEW 33 (March-April 1973): 113-19. Tables.

The author considers the need for effective techniques for policy evaluation and develops a model for the evaluation of urban public policy. The model consists of five separate components and includes a time variable. Caputo concludes that subjective considerations may still form the basis for supposed "objective" decisions despite the attempted comprehensiveness of the model.

519   Cary, Charles D. "An Introductory Course in Evaluation Research." POLICY ANALYSIS 3 (Summer 1977): 429-44.

Cary indicates that the curriculum for the Master of Arts in Public Affairs at the University of Iowa includes an introductory course in evaluation research. This course provides an overview of what is involved in program evaluation and examines conception, execution, use of evaluation, and stresses competent management as well as evaluation research.

520   Cox, Gary B. "Managerial Style: Implications for the Utilization of Program Evaluation Information." EVALUATION QUARTERLY 1 (August 1977): 499-508.

Cox declares that a crucial problem with program evaluation is that results are not utilized sufficiently in decision making.

521   Craver, Gary. "Survey of Job Evaluation Practices in State and County
       Governments." PUBLIC PERSONNEL MANAGEMENT 6 (March-April
       1977): 121-31.

              Although in the past the public sector employed non-
              quantitative methods of job evaluation, Craver reveals
              that factor point methods are now employed by 35 percent
              of the states and 16 percent of the counties and that
              about 40 percent of the states and 35 percent of the
              counties plan to use this method in the future. He in-
              dicates that the preference is for rank-in-person methods
              in the professions and for factor point methods in clerical,
              labor, trade, and service occupations.

522   Dror, Yehezkel. PUBLIC POLICYMAKING REEXAMINED. San
       Francisco: Chandler Publishing Co., 1968. xiii, 370 p.

              Dror's objectives are to advance the study of public policy
              making and to contribute to the improvement of public
              policy making. His thesis is that there is a significant
              gap between the ways that individuals and institutions
              make policy and the available knowledge on how policies
              can best be made. He analyzes and evaluates contemporary
              policy making and identifies its main weak spots by com-
              paring it with a proposed optimal model. Dror integrates
              his analysis of actual policy making, his construction of
              normative models, and his suggestions for improving public
              policy making.

523   Floden, Robert E., and Weiner, Stephen S. "Rationality to Ritual:
       The Multiple Roles of Evaluation in Governmental Processes." POLICY
       SCIENCES 9 (February 1978): 9-18.

              Floden and Weiner assert that evaluation works to provide
              information needed by rational decision makers for sub-
              jective decisions and that the evaluation function is a
              means for managing conflict and promoting social change.
              They believe that evaluation can be viewed as a societal
              ritual whose purposes are to placate the citizenry and to
              perpetuate an image of government rationality.

524   Franklin, Jack L., and Thrasher, Jean H. AN INTRODUCTION TO
       PROGRAM EVALUATION. New York: John Wiley and Sons, 1976.
       233 p.

              This book is intended for neophyte evaluators and prac-
              titioners as well as a reference book and source book for
              operating program managers and program evaluators. It
              is also intended to assist the managers and evaluators of
              social programs to understand better the needs of each
              other so that the full promise of program evaluation can

be realized. The authors discuss program evaluation as a process from the organizational, managerial, and research perspectives and indicate areas of difficulty, accomplishment, and promise.

525   Hatry, Harry [P.]; Winnie, Richard E.; and Fish, Donald M. PRACTICAL PROGRAM EVALUATION FOR STATE AND LOCAL GOVERNMENT OFFICIALS. Washington, D.C.: Urban Institute, 1973. 134 p.

The authors describe the basic steps to follow in an evaluation system. They illustrate the identification of objectives associated with criteria and clientele groups. They explain a variety of evaluation designs and techniques that can be applied and provide a case study of one city's solid waste collection cleanup campaign.

526   Hatry, Harry [P.], et al. PROGRAM ANALYSIS FOR STATE AND LOCAL GOVERNMENTS. Washington, D.C.: Urban Institute, 1973. 134 p.

The authors provide a systematic approach for estimating the costs and effectiveness of future public programs. They address the following issues: 1) what program analysis is all about, 2) staffing and institutional setting for successful program analysis, 3) five basic elements of launching program analysis, 4) estimating program costs, and 5) estimating program effectiveness.

527   Havens, Harry S. "Measuring the Unmeasurable: Program Evaluation in an Unquantified World." BUREAUCRAT 5 (April 1976): 53-64.

Havens observes that the process of program evaluation is elusive in areas where questions are nonquantitative and that the bulk of literature on research methodology is addressed to the manipulation of reliable quantitative data. The reader is told that an analyst must be able to do the best with available data and that he must give his client an idea of what can be expected as a product of program analysis.

528   Hawkins, J. David, and Sloma, Donald. "Recognizing the Organizational Context: A Strategy for Evaluation Research." ADMINISTRATION IN SOCIAL WORK 2 (Fall 1978): 283-94.

This article discusses procedures for designing, implementing, and reporting evaluation studies. The procedures consist of identifying evaluation audiences, establishing and negotiating evaluation designs, involving practitioners in operationalizing processes, developing data collection instruments, and providing feedback of results to evaluation clients.

529   Heiss, F. William. "The Politics of Local Government Policy Evalua-
        tion: Some Observations." URBAN ANALYSIS 5 (May 1978): 37-
        45.

                Heiss probes the politics of evaluation at the local gov-
                ernment level. He questions the capability of local gov-
                ernments to implement program evaluation programs, main-
                taining that there are constraints upon program evaluation
                studies in local governments that are not present in other
                government jurisdictions. Heiss also concludes that local
                government leaders would not want to admit program
                failures revealed via evaluation studies.

530   Horst, Pamela; Nay, Joe N.; Scanlon, John W.; and Wholey, Joseph S.
        "Program Management and the Federal Evaluator." PUBLIC ADMINI-
        STRATION REVIEW 34 (July-August 1974): 300-308.

                The authors review the apparent causes of evaluation
                problems and explain why these apparent causes are sus-
                pect. They contend that lack of definition, clear logic,
                and management more properly describe the causes of
                evaluation problems. This article serves as a good in-
                troduction to the concept of program evaluation.

531   Hyde, Albert C., and Shafritz, Jay M., eds. PROGRAM EVALUA-
        TION IN THE PUBLIC SECTOR. New York: Praeger Publishers,
        1979. 325 p.

                This book comprehensively and comparatively examines
                program evaluation in government, from its theory and
                environment to the use of its end product. Contributors
                focus on program evaluation from substantive area, view-
                point of the evaluator, level of government program,
                evaluation methodology, and from its relation to other
                management, administrative, and political processes.
                Sections include essays on the process and methodology
                of evaluation, a comparative perspective of the executive
                practitioner, state legislative evaluation, and the future
                of program evaluation. Essay authors include David M.
                Rosenbloom, Aaron Wildavsky, Frank Thompson, James D.
                Carroll, Harry A. Bailey, Jr., Orville F. Poland, Alice
                Rivlin. The editors provide a useful bibliography of re-
                lated sources and directory of program evaluation prac-
                titioners.

532   Kiresuk, Thomas J., and Lund, Sander H. "Program Evaluation and
        the Management of Organizations." In MANAGING HUMAN SERVICES,
        edited by Wayne F. Anderson, Bernard J. Frieden, and Michael J.
        Murphy, pp. 280-317. Municipal Management Series. Washington,
        D.C.: International City Management Association, 1977.

This article provides a comprehensive overview of the
program evaluation field and outlines the development,
current meaning, and potential human services applications of evaluation. Kiresuk and Lund consider the
problems associated with the implementation of evaluation
systems and the most efficient utilization of evaluation-
generated information.

533   Krause, Merton S., and Howard, Kenneth I. "Program Evaluation in
the Public Interest: A New Research Methodology." COMMUNITY
MENTAL HEALTH JOURNAL 12 (Fall 1976): 291-300.

Krause and Howard indicate that evaluation in the public
interest is unlikely to be decisive in any logical manner.
They maintain that the interests of patients, clients, staff,
management, and sponsors must be considered in evaluating
a service program in the public interest. Modifying and
extending the scientific model is pertinent for evaluating
service programs.

534   Levinson, Harry. "Appraisal of What Performance?" HARVARD
BUSINESS REVIEW 54 (July-August 1976): 30-36+.

The author suggests that the weakness of performance
appraisal and management by objectives concerns the
conception of the items being appraised. Practice dic-
tates that people are actually appraised on how they do
things while performance appraisal usually emphasizes
outcomes of behavior instead of behavior itself. Levinson
indicates that a development process which includes social
and political skills entails a dynamic job description, a
critical incident process, and a psychological support
system.

535   Lewis, Frank L., and Zarb, Frank G. "Federal Program Evaluation
from the OMB Perspective." PUBLIC ADMINISTRATION REVIEW 34
(July-August 1974): 308-17.

The authors describe program evaluation as relatively structured, systematic analyses of operating programs designed
to assess their impact or effectiveness in attaining their
stated objectives, or to assess their efficiency. Some
major evaluation steps which the Office of Management and
Budget initiated include consultation with senior evaluation
officials, inventory of federal evaluation activities, cross-
cutting budget review of evaluation activities, continuing
legislative review, and monitoring individual studies.

536   Marvin, Keith E., and Hedrick, James L. "GAO Helps Congress

Evaluate Programs." PUBLIC ADMINISTRATION REVIEW 34 (July-August 1974): 327-33.

> This article concerns the growing demand of the Congress for information on evaluations of federal programs, the sources of information, and especially the role of the General Accounting Office in helping to meet this demand. Marvin and Hedrick give a factual accounting of actions taken and identify a pattern of GAO involvement in developing aids to the Congress.

537   Milburn, Thomas W.; Negandhi, Anant R.; and Robey, Daniel. "Evaluating Systems Theory Concepts." In GENERAL SYSTEMS AND OR-GANIZATION THEORY, edited by Arlyn J. Melcher, pp. 11-13. Kent, Ohio: Kent State University Press, 1974.

> Chief components of general systems include subsystems or varying units in a given system, open systems, input-transformation-output concepts, system boundaries, cybernetics, multiple goal-seeking, and internal elaboration. The test is to utilize these qualities in comprehending the working of complicated organizations. Theory-building requires a distinct definition of variables, delineation of relationships between two or more variables in the mode of hypotheses or propositions, and confirmation of propositions or hypotheses through empirical testing. The value of general systems theory is not an aesthetic one but is tested in terms of its worth to practicing social scientists.

538   Morehouse, Thomas A. "Program Evaluation: Social Research Versus Public Policy." PUBLIC ADMINISTRATION REVIEW 32 (November-December 1972): 868-74.

> "Program evaluation research has emerged from and contributed to attempts to depoliticize federal domestic policy making and administration, and the failures of evaluation research in recent years can be explained in large part as a consequence of the researchers' attempts to respond to divergent and conflicting political and technical imperatives. The imperatives of experimental social research methodology have been no match for the complex and elusive objectives and processes of the social action and economic development programs to which evaluation requirements have been attached."

539   Morse, Ellsworth H. "Evaluating Results of Government Programs." BUREAUCRAT 2 (Winter 1974): 368-77.

> Morse notes that, in recent years, the General Accounting Office devoted an increasing proportion of its professional staff resources to evaluating the effectiveness of federal

programs and activities. Careful identification of the
objectives of the audited program is essential. He concludes that sometimes a program is created by law to
achieve highly desirable results but that the responsibility
of the agency charged with program implementation is
limited.

540   Nash, Christopher; Pearce, David; and Stanley, John. "Criteria for
        Evaluating Project Evaluation Techniques." JOURNAL OF THE AMERICAN
        INSTITUTE OF PLANNERS 41 (March 1975): 83-89.

        The authors establish that alternative evaluation techniques
        should be compared in terms of their value content and
        the consistency between their execution and their value
        content. The reader is informed that any project selection
        criterion must reflect some value set, and the net social
        worth of a project depends on the criterion. They suggest
        that criteria for choosing an evaluation criterion include
        moral considerations and feasibility.

541   Patton, Michael Quinn. UTILIZATION-FOCUSED EVALUATION.
        Beverly Hills, Calif.: Sage Publications, 1978. 303 p.

        Patton indicates how to conduct evaluations and why,
        reviews the history of evaluation research, and offers a
        new comprehensive prototype for evaluation called the
        utilization-focused approach.

542   Pedersen, Kjeld Moller. "A Proposed Model for Evaluation Studies."
        ADMINISTRATIVE SCIENCE QUARTERLY 22 (June 1977): 306-17.

        This article discusses evaluation classifications and dis-
        tinguishes between evaluation and policy studies and the
        possible uses of evaluation studies as they relate to the kinds
        of decisions and organizational framework in which de-
        cision making takes place. The organizational framework
        of the functional relationships is used in a model which
        shows that the resistance of program managers to using
        evaluation studies is rational and understandable in terms
        of maximizing utility. Terms often encountered in the
        literature, such as outcome, outputs, inputs, efficiency,
        effectiveness, and policy analysis, are tied together in
        a general evaluation model.

543   Pillsbury, Jolie Bain, and Nance, Kathy Newton. "An Evaluation
        Framework for Public Welfare Agencies." PUBLIC WELFARE 3 (Winter
        1976): 7-51.

        This article discusses the establishment of a program
        evaluation division in the Texas Department of Public
        Welfare, emphasizing that the division analyzes policies

and procedures affecting program operations, develops
techniques to determine how programs affect clients, and
realizes programmatic and policy evaluation capabilities.

544   Poland, Orville F. "Program Evaluation and Administrative Theory."
       PUBLIC ADMINISTRATION REVIEW 34 (July–August 1974): 333–38.

       Poland discusses utilization of controlled experiments
       undertaken in the context of research designs of the so-
       cial scientist, placement of evaluation in that context,
       and placement of evaluation in the context of cost-
       effectiveness analysis with a primary concern for program
       objectives and describes the inputs, outputs, and processes
       of programs as themes in program evaluation. He states
       that most evaluations are undertaken in terms of the
       achievement of objectives, yet public administration is
       entering an age in which other values are being emphasized.

545   Quay, Herbert C. "The Three Faces of Evaluation: What Can Be
       Expected to Work?" CRIMINAL JUSTICE AND BEHAVIOR 4 (De-
       cember 1977): 341–54.

       Quay relates that evaluations of criminal justice inter-
       vention programs concentrate on adequacy of research
       design and specification of outcome. While tending to
       ignore the integrity of the evaluated programs, assessment
       of programs provides information on adequacy of treatment
       conceptualization, duration and intensity of the program,
       quality and quantity of personnel, and match of treatment,
       treater, and treated.

546   Reardon, Diane Frances. "A Model for Communicating About Program
       Evaluation." JOURNAL OF COMMUNITY PSYCHOLOGY 5 (October
       1977): 350–58.

       This essay sets forth an overview of evaluation techniques
       with an emphasis on their interrelationships. Reardon
       emphasizes the clarification of terminology and offers a
       prototype for improved communication in decision making.

547   Rivlin, Alice M. SYSTEMATIC THINKING FOR SOCIAL ACTION.
       Washington, D.C.: Brookings Institution, 1971. 150 p.

       This book begins with budgeting and common sense and
       ends with accountability. It is concerned with identifying
       objectives of social programs and with producing effective
       services, systematic experimentation, innovation, decen-
       tralization, and community control. Rivlin focuses on
       evaluating the effectiveness of government programs to
       meet social needs, on estimating the costs and benefits of
       alternative programs, and on identifying social problems and
       estimating who would gain if social programs are successful.

548   Rocheleau, Bruce. "Evaluation, Accountability, and Responsiveness
       in Administration." MIDWEST REVIEW OF PUBLIC ADMINISTRATION
       9 (October 1975): 163-72.

           The purpose of this article is to examine the complex
           relationships which exist among the concepts of evaluation,
           accountability, and responsiveness. The research focuses
           on the elements which determine how much responsiveness
           is or is not achieved through evaluation. The author
           studied the role and impact of evaluation in fourteen
           mental health organizations in Florida. He concludes
           that evaluation and other accountability mechanisms do
           not automatically produce responsiveness.

549   Rossi, Peter H. "Issues in the Evaluation of Human Services Delivery."
       EVALUATION QUARTERLY 2 (November 1978): 573-99.

           Rossi notes the general consensus that human services are
           difficult to evaluate, that the concepts behind delivery
           systems are often deficient, and that delivery of such
           services is highly operator-dependent. He introduces a
           plan for the evaluation of human services delivery in
           which he tests the theory, considers the capability of
           the system to deliver the services, and determines whether
           the delivery system can deliver services effectively.

550   Rossi, Peter H., and Wright, Sonia R. "Evaluation Research: An
       Assessment of Theory, Practice, and Politics." EVALUATION QUARTERLY
       1 (February 1977): 5-52.

           The authors assert that the main difficulties limiting the
           application of social research techniques to policy evalua-
           tion are methodological in character and include the
           problem of designing research capable of answering the
           questions posed by policy makers. The article mentions
           distinctive features of evaluation research, including
           precise definition of the program, goals, and success
           criteria, which can only be supplied by policy makers,
           not by the researcher. Findings must be reported in a
           form and style that policy makers can understand.

551   Rutman, Leonard. "Planning an Evaluation Study." In EVALUATION
       RESEARCH METHODS: A BASIC GUIDE, edited by Leonard Rutman,
       pp. 13-38. Beverly Hills, Calif.: Sage Publications, 1977.

           Rutman's focus is on processes and outcomes without re-
           stricting outcomes to objectives. He states that infor-
           mation needs of decision makers are an important con-
           sideration. He concludes that the evaluation research
           should include a clearly articulated program which specifies
           goals and effects.

552   Staats, Elmer B. "The Challenge of Evaluating Federal Social Pro-
        grams." EVALUATION 1 (1973): 50-54.

            Staats maintains that among the factors utilized in de-
            ciding where to direct its audit resources, the General
            Accounting Office considers statutory requirements, con-
            gressional interest, expenditures, size of assets, amount
            of revenue, and weaknesses in program management or
            perceived program effectiveness. The reader learns that
            the methods used by GAO vary widely.

553   U.S. Congress. Senate. Committee on Governmental Affairs. PRO-
        GRAM EVALUATION ACT OF 1977. 95th Cong., 1st sess. Wash-
        ington, D.C.: Government Printing Office, 1977. 70 p.

            This committee report summarizes this legislation, gives
            its history, details the issues involved, projects cost esti-
            mates, and provides the text of the bill as reported out
            of committee.

554   Weidman, Donald R. "Writing a Better RFP: Ten Hints for Obtaining
        More Successful Evaluation Studies." PUBLIC ADMINISTRATION
        REVIEW 37 (November–December 1977): 714-17.

            Weidman maintains that the success or failure of a con-
            tracted evaluation study is determined, to a great extent,
            by the characteristics of the request for proposal (RFP).
            He summarizes observation and experience into ten hints
            which should prove useful to the government official who
            must prepare or approve an RFP.

555   Wholey, Joseph S. "The Role of Evaluation and the Evaluator in Im-
        proving Public Programs: The Bad News, The Good News, and a
        Bicentennial Challenge." PUBLIC ADMINISTRATION REVIEW 36
        (November–December 1976): 679-83.

            Wholey discusses the roles for evaluation in policy for-
            mulation and communication and in program management
            and suggests how evaluators can play a stronger role in
            government policy and administration.

556   _____, et al. FEDERAL EVALUATION POLICY: ANALYZING THE
        EFFECTS OF PUBLIC PROGRAMS. Washington, D.C.: Urban Institute,
        1970. 134 p.

            The authors discuss federal evaluation, what it is and why
            it is needed, the administration of an evaluation system,
            organizational relationships and responsibilities, evaluation
            resources, and methodology and offer recommendations in
            this regard for the executive, Congress, and federal
            agencies. This text is an excellent review of evaluation

policy and procedures in the federal government. The authors also provide a useful bibliography.

557   Wildavsky, Aaron. "The Self-Evaluating Organization." PUBLIC ADMINISTRATION REVIEW 32 (September-October 1972): 509-20.

The thesis of this article is that evaluation is primarily an organizational problem. The organization's needs and its people conflict with the continuous monitoring of activities and changing of policies. The author considers how an organization totally devoted to evaluation might operate and how people might survive the tension of maintaining resources and objectives. Noting the difficulty of structuring evaluation and organization, the article includes suggestions for bringing together substantive evaluation of policy and the imperatives of organizational life.

B. POLICY MAKING AND ANALYSIS

558   Anderson, James E. PUBLIC POLICY MAKING. 2d ed. New York: Holt, Rinehart and Winston, 1979. viii, 200 p. Paper.

This textbook focuses primarily on the process of policy formation. Anderson sets forth an approach to the analysis of public policy formation which is useful in organizing inquiry and untangling the complexities of American public policy analysis. He considers the roles of institutions, processes, and political elements. Chapters include discussions of the study of public policy, policy makers and their environment, policy formation and adoption, the implementation of policy, public policies, policy impact, evaluation and change, and policy study and the public interest.

559   Appleby, Paul H. POLICY AND ADMINISTRATION. University: University of Alabama Press, 1949. 173 p.

This is one of the foremost arguments against the policy-administration dichotomy from the "politics" period of public administration. Appleby offers a study of the essence of political administration. He maintains that "public administration is policy-making," subject to the same restrictions as other political processes. The eight political processes, as well as administration as the compatibility of politicians and expertise, politics and administrative structure, the controls exacted upon arbitrary administrative action, and the impact of ideology and citizen participation are covered in this work.

560   Bish, Robert L. "The Assumption of Knowledge in Policy Analysis."
        POLICY STUDIES JOURNAL 3 (Spring 1975): 256-62.

        Bish states that knowledge available to the analyst is
        one of the most critical considerations in policy analysis.
        He believes that we can never be as certain of benefits
        from public programs as we are of benefits from private
        products, so knowledge of the value of the service to
        citizen consumers may never be directly revealed. The
        article shows that analysts ultimately must choose the
        epistemological assumption they wish to use for a specific
        policy analysis.

561   Brigham, John, ed. MAKING PUBLIC POLICY: STUDIES IN AMERICAN
        POLITICS. Lexington, Mass.: D.C.Heath and Co., 1977. xxiii,
        424 p. Paper.

        The editor provides a source of documentary materials
        presented in a topical format and examines some of the
        elements of the American governmental process. He raises
        complexities in politics that add depth to an institutional
        focus. Brigham includes a public policy situation in each
        chapter and divides the material into sections that treat
        an aspect of American government or the policy-making
        process. Chapter discussions include the Supreme Court
        and abortion, Congress and military appropriations in the
        budgetary process, the policy agenda, keeping house,
        policy making by the president, the determinants of na-
        tional economic policy, formulating and implementing
        American Indian policy in the bureaucracy, and interest
        groups and the governmental process.

562   Caputo, David A. POLITICS AND PUBLIC POLICY IN AMERICA:
        AN INTRODUCTION. Philadelphia: J.B. Lippincott Co., 1974.
        xvi, 302 p. Paper.

        The main purpose of this textbook is to introduce the
        student to the complexities of American politics without
        overwhelming him with less important information and
        data. Sections include American national political in-
        stitutions, subnational politics, group and party politics
        in America, and public policy. A brief, well-organized,
        but complete introduction for the freshman public policy
        student is provided.

563   Daneke, Gregory A. "Policy Analysis as Bureaucratic Reform."
        SOUTHERN REVIEW OF PUBLIC ADMINISTRATION 1 (June 1977):
        108-28.

        Daneke describes reform from within and reform from
        without and concludes that policy analysis could realize

its potential under the general rubric of bureaucratic reform. He concludes that "the various policy development and assessment techniques being generated within the general framework of systems analysis are merely skeletal processes devoid of content."

564   Donovan, John C. THE POLICY MAKERS. New York: Pegasus, 1970. 255 p.

Donovan examines the increasingly influential role of technicians within the agencies of an institutionalized presidency, the predominant power of congressional barons in the legislative arena, the rise of the military-congressional complex, the professionalization of social reform, the persistence of budgetary politics, and the changing nature of the American polity. He focuses on the issue of policy leadership in the modern technocratic state in an era of affluence marked by the decline of traditional political ideology. This text is a critical reassessment of American policies in the 1960s.

565   Dye, Thomas R. UNDERSTANDING PUBLIC POLICY. 3d ed. Englewood Cliffs, N.J.: Prentice-Hall, 1978. xii, 338 p.

This textbook is concerned with "who gets what" in American politics and "why" and "what difference it makes." Dye is concerned not only with what policies governments pursue but also why, and what the consequences of these policies are. He maintains that political science can be "relevant" to public policy questions without abandoning its commitment to scientific inquiry. Each chapter concludes with a series of propositions, which are derived from one or more analytic models, which attempt to summarize the policies discussed. Chapter topics include policy analysis, models of politics, civil rights, crime, violence and repression, poverty, welfare and health, education, population, energy and the environment, urban affairs, priorities and price tags, budget and taxes, defense policy, inputs, outputs, the policy-making process, and policy impact. If Dye's text is not the best in this field, it is very close.

566   Frohock, Fred M. PUBLIC POLICY: SCOPE AND LOGIC. Englewood Cliffs, N.J.: Prentice-Hall, 1979. xiii, 332 p.

The basic plan of this textbook is to combine theory with practice, to consolidate the best literature of public policy, to communicate the excitement of actual politics, and to treat the normative and empirical issues of public policy. Each chapter includes theoretical analysis and a case study. Frohock places emphasis on treatment of

ethical issues and social justice. Chapter discussions include politics and policy, decision models of policy,
groups and elites, positive and negative participation,
organizational decisions and public planning, public
policy evaluation, ethics, justice and public policy,
and public policy and democracy.

567   Froomkin, Joseph. "Needed: A New Framework for the Analysis of
        Government Programs." POLICY ANALYSIS 2 (Spring 1976): 341-50.

        Froomkin relates that the four types of difficulties faced
        by policy analysts in the evaluation of federal programs
        include the limitations of program objectives, absence of
        an overall model to test the effects of new programs,
        failure to understand the scope of a program, and lack
        of planning. He makes clear that the contribution of
        human resource programs to productivity must be considered.

568   Harmon, Michael Mont. "Administrative Policy Formulation and the
        Public Interest." PUBLIC ADMINISTRATION REVIEW 29 (September-
        October 1969): 483-91.

        The author maintains that the public interest must be
        viewed as individualistic rather than unitary, descriptive
        rather than prescriptive, procedural rather than substantive,
        and dynamic rather than static. He concludes that "the
        public interest is the continually changing outcome of
        political activity among individuals and groups within a
        democratic political system."

569   Haveman, Robert H., and Weisbrod, Burton A. "Defining Benefits of
        Public Programs: Some Guidance for Policy Analysis." POLICY
        ANALYSIS 1 (Winter 1975): 169-96.

        Haveman and Weisbrod contend that a clear understanding
        of the meaning of benefits is the fundamental requirement
        for undertaking any sound cost-benefit study of public
        activities. They emphasize that the accounting framework
        for the analysis must be comprehensive and include adverse
        and beneficial effects of a project. Wiser resource allo-
        cation decisions in the public sector will be made if the
        importance of redistributional considerations is recognized.

570   Kramer, Fred A. "Policy Analysis as Ideology." PUBLIC ADMINI-
        STRATION REVIEW 35 (September-October 1975): 509-17.

        Kramer maintains that policy analysis employs scientific
        techniques and gives the appearance of objectivity in
        implying that the data it generates are value-free. He
        believes that policy analysis is an art in which the cre-
        ativity and skill of the practitioner are of prime importance.

571   Lambright, W. Henry. "The Minnowbrook Perspective and the Future
       of Public Affairs: Public Administration Is Public-Policy Making."
       In TOWARD A NEW PUBLIC ADMINISTRATION: THE MINNOW-
       BROOK PERSPECTIVE, edited by Frank Marini, pp. 332-45. Scranton,
       Pa.: Chandler Publishing Co., 1971.

       Lambright states: "The politics-administration dichotomy
       is dead, but the ghost continues to haunt us, to narrow
       the vision of even those who take Public Administration
       seriously. . . . The administrator is a participant in
       the political process, a politician in that he must engage
       in conflict resolution, exercise discretion, and make de-
       cisions affecting competing claims. . . . A public ad-
       ministrator who is not both manager and politician will
       fail as public-policy maker. He cannot spend all his
       time on the politics of a program or he will neglect to
       manage it effectively. He cannot devote himself only
       to its management . . . or he will soon find he has no
       program to administer."

572   Lindblom, Charles E. THE POLICY-MAKING PROCESS. Englewood
       Cliffs, N.J.: Prentice-Hall, 1968. vi, 122 p.

       This textbook makes some comparisons to Great Britain
       and the Soviet Union in introducing public policy analysis
       to the discussion of American government. The intro-
       ductory material discusses the techniques and shortcomings
       of the concept of policy examination. The middle portion
       of the text treats in a traditional fashion the parties,
       citizens, lobbyists, and government officers who make
       policy decisions. The concluding part takes a look at
       concepts and ways of resolving policy preferences.

573   Majone, Giandomenico. "Pitfalls of Analysis and the Analysis of
       Pitfalls." JOURNAL OF URBAN ANALYSIS 4 (1977): 235-53.

       Majone asserts that analytical pitfalls include problem-
       setting, data, and information; tools and methods; evi-
       dence and argument; and conclusions, communication,
       and implementation. He argues that analytic methods
       and techniques can best be understood in terms of the
       pitfalls that they are designed to prevent.

574   Meltsner, Arnold J. "Bureaucratic Policy Analysis." POLICY ANALYSIS
       1 (Winter 1975): 115-31.

       Meltsner believes that the primary incentive for policy
       analysts to work in government bureaucracy is power and
       relevance. The reader is informed that politics is very
       much a part of analysis. The author concludes that the
       policy analyst is not a policy scientist but is a person
       who is a force for change in bureaucracy.

575 _____. "Political Feasibility and Policy Analysis." PUBLIC ADMINI-
STRATION REVIEW 32 (November-December 1972): 859-67.

"A current deficiency of the analysis of public policy
issues by governmental agencies is the slighting of political implications. Analysis should lead to policies
that can be implemented, and the study of political feasibility is one way of bridging the gap between the desirable and the possible."

576 Mushkin, Selma J. "Policy Analysis in State and Community."
PUBLIC ADMINISTRATION REVIEW 37 (May-June 1977): 245-53.

Mushkin calls for qualified analysts trained to work in
state and local governments, adequate information communicated in usable form, a linking of personnel management and policy decision, innovation and social intervention that can be put before the public, and more resources for building analytic capability in the states and
communities. She also emphasizes that states and communities have been thwarted in their attempts to institutionalize the above changes.

577 Nachmias, David. PUBLIC POLICY EVALUATION: APPROACHES
AND METHODS. New York: St. Martin's Press, 1979. x, 195 p.

Nachmias is concerned with the theory and methodology
of public policy evaluation. He attempts to analyze and
compare various conceptual models on which evaluations
can be based and to explain the statistical techniques
most useful in evaluation research. Chapters include discussions on policy evaluation for particular purposes,
policy experimentation, quasi-experimental evaluations,
measurement and social indicators, regression as a data-
analysis system, and structural equation methods. He includes a very useful bibliography.

578 Neiman, Max. "Policy Analysis: An Alternative Strategy." AMERICAN
POLITICS QUARTERLY 5 (January 1977): 3-26.

Neiman states that urban political systems are looked upon
as communication networks linked to their environments
by communication flows. He views public policy outputs
as the results of political systems adjusting outputs or re-
arranging channels in response to information about the
wants and demands of newly mobilized groups.

579 Ostrom, Vincent. "Language, Theory and Empirical Research in Policy
Analysis." POLICY STUDIES JOURNAL 3 (Spring 1975): 274-82.

Ostrom states that the use of language as a tool for

reasoning is the basic ingredient in policy analysis and,
until we develop and learn to use a language system
where we can make elemental terms and postulated relationships explicit, we shall be unable to use human
reason to derive conclusions, to think through problems,
and to communicate meaningfully with one another. He
argues that policy analysts need to develop a much greater
critical and self-conscious awareness of the language
systems that they use as tools.

580   Owen, Henry, and Schultze, Charles L., eds. SETTING NATIONAL
       PRIORITIES: THE NEXT TEN YEARS. Washington, D.C.: Brookings
       Institution, 1976. xvii, 618 p. Paper.

       A concern with the appropriate role of the nation abroad
       and the government at home is a common theme upon
       which these essays focus. There are five essays on foreign
       and defense policy which deal with the major threats to
       peace and to U.S. interests overseas, national defense
       policy, and organizational changes intended to improve
       the formulation and execution of foreign policy. Six
       chapters deal with domestic problems and include dis-
       cussions on economic stabilization policy, size of the
       federal budget and of state and local budgets, energy
       and the environment, governmental regulation of health
       and safety for workers and consumers, and income security
       policy. This book includes examinations of congressional-
       executive relations and the problems of formulating and
       implementing increasing complex national programs in a
       government of divided powers.

581   Poister, Theodore H. PUBLIC PROGRAM ANALYSIS: APPLIED RE-
       SEARCH METHODS. Baltimore, Md.: University Park Press, 1978.
       616 p.

       Poister integrates quantitative analysis with the more
       qualitative aspects of problem definition, general research
       design, development of measures, and data collection
       procedures. He illustrates applications of quantitative
       analysis to needs assessment, the analysis of internal pro-
       gram operation, and program impact evaluation. The au-
       thor concentrates on the specific skills needed for program
       analysis. Sections include applied program analysis, sta-
       tistics, and general research models.

582   Sharkansky, Ira. PUBLIC ADMINISTRATION: POLICY-MAKING IN
       GOVERNMENT AGENCIES. 4th ed. Chicago: Rand McNally College
       Publishing Co., 1978. xvii, 386 p.

       Sharkansky states that "this book is different from other
       texts in the field of public administration in that it em-

phasizes the political processes within and surrounding administrative agencies more than it stresses the management techniques that a budding administrator should master. It is written for the student who seeks to understand the operations of public administration in its political environment." Sections include the inputs, the conversion process, and the outputs of the administrative system.

583   Stein, Harold, ed. PUBLIC ADMINISTRATION AND POLICY DEVELOPMENT: A CASE BOOK. New York: Harcourt, Brace and Co., 1952. xlv, 860 p.

This book is a collection of case studies which illustrates a multitude of facets of public administration. Sections deal with the general theoretical concepts reflected in the cases, the nature of the case method and its application to the study of public administration, the use of the case method in the study of public administration and to the cases in this volume, teaching via the case method, and the case-writing projects that preceded and led to the preparation and publication of this text. This is especially valuable for its insights and histories of the administrative problems of the early post-World War II era in the United States.

584   Tullock, Gordon, and Wagner, Richard E. "Rational Models, Politics, and Policy Analysis." POLICY STUDIES JOURNAL 4 (Summer 1976): 408-16.

This article asserts that the tools of economics, as they are the most rigorous and reliable models available, are now being widely applied to noneconomic phenomena, particularly to politics and to issues of public policy. The reader learns that while economists are aware that not all political motives are selfish, Tullock and Wagner claim that the models are realistic enough to provide meaningful explanations of political events.

585   Ukeles, Jacob B. "Policy Analysis: Myth or Reality?" PUBLIC ADMINISTRATION REVIEW 37 (May-June 1977): 223-28.

The purpose of this essay is to present an overview of policy analysis that may shed some light on its growth. The article is divided into two parts: 1) current views of policy analysis, including what it is and what its intellectual and pragmatic roots are; and 2) an assessment of the state of policy making and how various policy options might enhance American governance.

586   Van Meter, Donald S., and Van Horn, Carl E. "The Policy Imple-
       mentation Process." ADMINISTRATION AND SOCIETY 6 (February
       1975): 445-88.

       The authors relate a model for the description and analysis
       of the policy implementation process and propose expla-
       nations for program achievements and failures. According
       to Van Meter and Van Horn, a model of the policy de-
       livery system emphasizes policies adopted and services
       actually delivered, directs attention to the determinants
       of public policy, and identifies relationships among the
       diverse concerns of policy analysts. They elaborate on
       the components of this model.

587   Wildavsky, Aaron. SPEAKING TRUTH TO POWER: THE ART AND
       CRAFT OF POLICY ANALYSIS. Boston: Little, Brown and Co.,
       1979. xiv, 431 p.

       This text is a comparative analysis of a wide range of
       American domestic policies. The author states that "policy
       analysis is about the realm of rationality and responsibility
       where resources are related to objectives." Sections in-
       clude discussions of resources and objectives, social in-
       teraction and intellectual cognitation, dogma and skepti-
       cism, and policy analysis.

588   Woll, Peter. PUBLIC POLICY. Cambridge, Mass.: Winthrop Pub-
       lishers, 1974. vii, 264 p. Paper.

       This textbook concentrates upon the policy-making roles
       of major political institutions: interest groups, political
       parties, the presidency, Congress, courts, and the bu-
       reaucracy. Woll covers the formal and informal context
       within which these institutions operate. He assesses the
       capability of each institution to affect public policy and
       seeks to determine where real power to make public policy
       resides in the political system.

589   Yin, Robert K., and Heald, Karen A. "Using the Case Survey Method
       to Analyze Policy Studies." ADMINISTRATIVE SCIENCE QUARTERLY
       20 (September 1975): 371-81.

       The authors recognize that a common feature of most policy
       literatures is that the bulk of the empirical evidence is
       embodied in case studies and that this aspect presents a
       problem for subsequent analysis. Although each case study
       may provide insights into a specific situation, it is diffi-
       cult to generalize about the studies as a whole. Yin and
       Heald describe one means of dealing with the problem:
       analyzing the content of case studies by using a closed-
       ended questionnaire. They indicate that the resulting

case survey method allows an analyst to aggregate the
case study experiences and to assess the quality of each
case study in a reliable and replicable manner.

C. ACCOUNTABILITY

590   Birch, Frank.   "Internal Accountability in Local Authorities." PUBLIC
        ADMINISTRATION BULLETIN 17 (December 1974): 53-61.

> Birch states that the principles of public accountability
> and finance are so fundamental to local government that
> an elaborate system of rules, regulations, and procedures
> has evolved within each local authority. He suggests
> that despite changes in the sizes and functions of local
> authorities, organizations remain highly bureaucratic and
> basically unchanged.

591   Finer, Herbert.   "Administrative Responsibility in Democratic Govern-
        ment." PUBLIC ADMINISTRATION REVIEW 1 (Autumn 1941): 335-50.

> Finer writes: "Administrative responsibility is not less
> important to democratic government than administrative
> efficiency; it is even a contributor to efficiency in the
> long run." What do we mean by responsibility? The
> author defines responsibility as meaning that X is ac-
> countable for Y to Z and as meaning that responsibility
> is an inward personal sense of moral obligation. He con-
> cludes that never was the political responsibility of officials
> so necessary as in modern times.

592   Friedrich, Carl J.   "The Nature of Administrative Responsibility."
        In PUBLIC POLICY, edited by Carl J. Friedrich, pp. 3-24. Cambridge,
        Mass.: Harvard University Press, 1940.

> Friedrich states that as the scope and functions of modern
> administration have widened, the difficulty of securing
> responsibility has greatly increased. He analyzes respon-
> sibility and policy formation, policy making and execution,
> administrative discretion, political responsibility, the role
> of citizen participation, and the imperative for functional
> responsibility. He concludes that there are many ways
> by which a measure of genuine responsibility can be secured
> under modern conditions.

593   Gawthrop, Louis C. "Administrative Responsibility: The Systems State
        and Our Wilsonian Legacy." In PUBLIC ADMINISTRATION AND PUBLIC
        POLICY, edited by H. George Frederickson and Charles R. Wise, pp.
        197-209. Lexington, Mass.: D.C. Heath and Co., 1977.

Gawthrop believes that power becomes increasingly priva-
tized (which is to say that power made private is administration made private) as analytical capacity increases.

594   Harmon, Michael M. "Normative Theory and Public Administration:
       Some Suggestions for a Redefinition of Administrative Responsibility."
       In TOWARD A NEW PUBLIC ADMINISTRATION: THE MINNOW-
       BROOK PERSPECTIVE, edited by Frank Marini, pp. 172-85. Scranton,
       Pa.: Chandler Publishing Co., 1971.

       Harmon approaches the topic of normative theory in public
       administration through the problem of administrative re-
       sponsibility. He finds current ideas of administrative re-
       sponsibility quite inadequate in terms of present social and
       political conditions and believes that some recent thought
       introduces promising ideas which are no more devoid of
       empirical support than traditional notions and suggests
       that these ideas have substantial implications for public
       administration.

595   Johnson, Nevil. "Defining Accountability." PUBLIC ADMINISTRA-
       TION BULLETIN 17 (December 1974): 3-13.

       Johnson indicates that much of the difficulty in defining
       and enforcing accountability in administration is attribut-
       able to the scale and character of public activities and
       services and to the complexity of executive structures.
       These difficulties are compounded by the alleged benefits
       of economies of scale, administrative rationalization, and
       integrated management. The author believes one should
       envisage the administrative world as consisting of com-
       peting and colluding agencies which need to be con-
       trolled and checked in a variety of ways.

596   Kayali, Kaled M. "Public Accountability and the Growth of Science
       in Government." In MAKING GOVERNMENT WORK: ESSAYS IN
       HONOR OF CONLEY H. DILLON, edited by Richard P. Claude and
       James C. Strouse, pp. 117-27. College Park: University of Mary-
       land, 1977.

       Kayali sees a trend toward making scientific activity in
       government more accountable to elected public officials.
       He believes that the huge budget of the science-related
       agencies, the diminishing recollection that science con-
       tributed significantly to the winning of World War II,
       calls by interest groups to examine scientific activities,
       the passage of the Public Information Act, the inclusion
       of nonscientists in science-related agencies, and the dis-
       agreements among scientists over their freedom to make
       decisions without controls by the executive or legislative
       branches of government constitute significant reasons for

the trend toward holding the scientific community more accountable.

597   Kernaghan, Kenneth. "Responsible Public Bureaucracy: A Rationale and a Framework for Analysis." CANADIAN PUBLIC ADMINISTRATION 16 (Winter 1973): 572-603.

Kernaghan suggests that administrative responsibility cannot be divorced from administrative power. The literature abounds with suggestions for new and improved institutional methods by which administrative power and responsibility may be reconciled. The purpose of such proposals is to acquire a larger measure of objective responsibility by holding bureaucrats more accountable for their actions. Greater attention to administrative responsibility is necessary to bring about an environment in which subjective responsibility may be engendered.

598   Kramer, Fred A. "Public Accountability and Organizational Humanism." PUBLIC PERSONNEL MANAGEMENT 3 (September-October 1974): 385-91.

Kramer indicates that there is no serious conflict between organizational humanism and accountability agreements between the federal bureaucracy and Congress. He maintains that both professional, traditional government agencies and those agencies leaning toward humanism will benefit from an emphasis on organizational accountability. He also discusses impediments to humanism in government agencies.

599   Maass, Arthur A., and Radway, Laurence I. "Gauging Administrative Responsibility." PUBLIC ADMINISTRATION REVIEW 9 (Summer 1949): 182-93.

This essay is an effort to establish criteria which will be useful in determining the extent to which any administrative agency conducts itself as a responsible instrument of government. The emphasis is on the development of criteria applicable to particular functioning agencies. The authors' discussion includes a general and historical view of responsibility as well as concepts relating responsibility to the people at large, pressure groups, the legislature, the chief executive, political parties, the profession, and courts.

600   Rycroft, Robert W. "Bureaucratic Responsibility in the Federal Energy Administration." BUREAUCRAT 6 (Fall 1977): 19-33.

Rycroft attempts to determine the level of bureaucratic responsibility shown by the FEA in its implementation of the fuel allocation and pricing programs. The reader is told that bureaucratic responsibility in the FEA seems to have been attained chiefly through congressional statutes, appropriations, and investigations.

601   Spiro, Herbert J. RESPONSIBILITY IN GOVERNMENT: THEORY AND PRACTICE. New York: Van Nostrand Reinhold Co., 1969. 179 p.

This book treats the subject of expanding the individual's responsibility for his own fate and that of the nation and mankind through political participation. Its thesis is that responsibility is the central problem of government and of life, and that most of the revolutionary issues of our time are rooted in a yearning for greater responsibility. Spiro discusses the meaning of responsibility, responsibility as obligation, as accountability, and as cause. He examines the purpose of bureaucratic accountability and contributions in the history of bureaucratic accountability.

602   Staats, Elmer B. "GAO Audit Standards: Development and Implementation." PUBLIC MANAGEMENT 56 (February 1974): 5-7.

Staats reports that General Accounting Office auditors are interested in applicable laws and regulations, whether federal agencies are economical and efficient in their employment of money, materials, and manpower, and whether they are achieving the aims and objectives for which their programs were established. He states that the three types of standards developed by the GAO are general standards, examination and evaluation standards, and reporting standards.

603   _____. "The GAO: Present and Future." PUBLIC ADMINISTRATION REVIEW 28 (September-October 1968): 461-65.

The author, Comptroller General of the United States, spells out the five broad purposes and functions upon which the activities of the General Accounting Office are founded, and reviews the work of the GAO in the Department of Defense, civil agencies, transportation, financial management, and others. This is an excellent article for gaining better appreciation for the role and responsibilities of GAO in American government and society.

604   Stanyer, Jeffrey. "Divided Responsibilities: Accountability in Decentralized Government." PUBLIC ADMINISTRATION BULLETIN 17 (December 1974): 14-30.

There is a conflict between accountability to the central

government and accountability to area, or subnational, governments. Stanyer emphasizes that problems of accountability and decentralization in administrative organizations do not fall into precise categories.

605   Stretch, John J. "Increasing Accountability for Human Services Administrators." SOCIAL CASEWORK 59 (June 1978): 323-29.

Stretch asserts that human services agencies are commencing to address the necessity for sounder management. This article relates that accountability necessitates development, deployment, and delivery of human services to satisfy the criteria that human services be germane, efficient, and effective.

Chapter 5

THE ADMINISTRATIVE REVOLUTION

A. GENERAL SELECTIONS

606   Agranoff, Robert. "Designing Public Organizations." In PUBLIC AD-
MINISTRATION AND PUBLIC POLICY, edited by H. George Frederickson
and Charles R. Wise, pp. 15-28. Lexington, Mass.: D.C. Heath
and Co., 1977.

> Agranoff asserts that the design of public organizations
> has shifted in emphasis toward centralization and jurisdic-
> tional coherence in order to strengthen the ability of
> policy leaders to harness independent power and conflic-
> ting demands and priorities into a functionally organized
> system. He stresses that organization, as well as program
> content, can become an impediment to policy management.

607   Backoff, Robert. "Operationalizing Administrative Reform for Improved
Governmental Performance." ADMINISTRATION AND SOCIETY 6
(May 1974): 73-106.

> Backoff describes characteristics of a bureaucratic reform
> program, which include sufficient support; magnitude of
> change; rate of change; sequence of change; reform pro-
> gram goals' properties; reform instrument; and criteria for
> program evaluation. He stresses the utility of empirical
> research for practitioners of bureaucratic reform. The
> author is concerned with the operationalization of public
> administration theories.

608   Berkley, George E. THE ADMINISTRATIVE REVOLUTION: NOTES
ON THE PASSING OF ORGANIZATION MAN. Englewood Cliffs,
N.J.: Prentice-Hall, 1971. 130 p.

> Berkley's theme is that the capital versus labor conflict
> in society is fading out and that it is being replaced by
> organization versus individual conflict. He examines the
> rise and fall of bureaucracy, the passage of organization

man, the increased linkage between private and public organization, and the growth of employee participation in decision making. The dynamics of the capital-labor and organization-individual ideas constitute Berkley's concept of a new administrative revolution.

609   Caiden, Gerald. ADMINISTRATIVE REFORM. Chicago: Aldine
        Publishing Co., 1969. 239 p.

        Caiden defines administrative reform as "the artificial in-
        ducement of administrative transformation, against resis-
        tance." He considers approaches, processes, and obstacles
        to reform. His focus is upon the achievement of admini-
        strative reform, but his doubts seem realistic: "I realize
        that I have shifted from seeking dramatic and speedy
        remedies for administrative failings to recognizing the many
        obstacles in the path of reformers and the virtue of waiting
        for the opportune time."

610   Denhardt, Robert. "Organizational Citizenship and Personal Freedom."
        PUBLIC ADMINISTRATION REVIEW 28 (January-February 1968): 47-54.

        The author believes that the current institutional approach
        of organizational analysis requires the establishment of a
        set of characteristics or attributes defining organization.
        With reference to the concepts of "citizenship" as per-
        ceived by two major organization theorists, Philip Selznick
        and Herbert Simon, Denhardt concludes that the necessity
        of imputing certain values to the "organizational condition"
        has placed severe restrictions on the ability of theorists
        to respond adequately to the valuational questions raised
        by the organizational world of modern man.

611   Etzioni, Amitai. A COMPARATIVE ANALYSIS OF COMPLEX ORGA-
        NIZATIONS. New York: Free Press, 1975. xxiv, 584 p.

        Etzioni points out that the plan of this book may be vi-
        sualized as a wheel. Compliance--the organizational
        equivalent of social order--is the core variable or center.
        He is concerned primarily with the relationship between
        compliance and each variable introduced, for instance,
        cohesion, leadership. Parts include Etzioni's concepts
        and classification scheme, correlates of compliance (goals,
        effectiveness, and elites), the development of compliance
        structures over time, and suggested lines for the develop-
        ment of the study of compliance. Whereas the first and
        second parts focus on the compliance of lower participants,
        the third part examines compliance of higher participants.
        The major task of this study is to formulate new proposi-
        tions, report existing ones, and relate propositions to each
        other.

612   Golembiewski, Robert T. RENEWING ORGANIZATIONS: THE
        LABORATORY APPROACH TO PLANNED CHANGE. Itasca, Ill.:
        F.E. Peacock Publishers, 1972. 593 p.

        This book deals with how individuals and organizations
        can go about making more effective choices and cope
        better with change. Golembiewski dedicates this effort
        to enlarging the manageable and meaningful choices open
        to individuals and organizations, via emphasis on a tech-
        nology for renewal and change.

613   Gouldner, Helen P. "Dimensions of Organizational Commitment."
        ADMINISTRATIVE SCIENCE QUARTERLY 4 (March 1960): 468-90.

        The author reports on a factor analytic study which dis-
        tinguishes different dimensions of organizational commit-
        ment among the members of a voluntary association. She
        studies forms of organizational commitment: cosmopolitan
        integration (the degree to which the individual is active
        in and feels a part of the varying levels of a particular
        organization and is active in other organizations), and
        organizational introjection (the degree to which the in-
        dividual's "ideal" self-image includes a number of or-
        ganizationally approved qualities and values). Gouldner
        hypothesizes that commitment to specific values of an or-
        ganization is distinct from commitment to the organization
        as a whole.

614   Hart, David K., and Scott, William G. "The Organizational Im-
        perative." ADMINISTRATION AND SOCIETY 7 (November 1975):
        259-85.

        The authors maintain that the needs of organization tend
        to overwhelm other considerations. Three rules for or-
        ganizationally healthy behavior resulting from the organi-
        zational imperative are pragmatism, stewardship, and
        rationality. They state that administration links organi-
        zation with the institutional infrastructure of society and
        indicate that administrators must discipline themselves,
        subordinates, and relevant clients to arrange values, ex-
        pectations, and practical affairs in order that organiza-
        tional imperative is served.

615   Katz, Daniel, and Kahn, Robert L. THE SOCIAL PSYCHOLOGY OF
        ORGANIZATIONS. Rev. ed. New York: John Wiley and Sons,
        1978. vi, 838 p.

        This volume champions the cause of the open systems
        approach to the study of organizations. The authors em-
        phasize that social psychological principles can be ap-
        plied to all forms of collective organized effort. The

text is divided into the theoretical approach, models of organization, and problems and processes. Katz and Kahn analyze the systems concept, organizational structures, environment, organizational roles, organizational effectiveness, power and authority, communication, leadership, conflict, and organizational change. They provide chapter outlines and summaries for the reader and a useful 42-page bibliography.

616   Kaufman, Herbert. "The Natural History of Human Organization." ADMINISTRATION AND SOCIETY 7 (August 1975): 131-49.

An organization is a set of people who, as a group, are distinguishable from all other sets of people and whose relations with each other have the effect of maintaining the identity of the set. The reader is told that the elements for creating an organization include the desire to create one, material resources, and opportunities for fruitful exchanges with the environment. Kaufman concludes that the chief reason for the demise of organizations is change in their internal or external environments that render ineffective their established processes of self-maintenance.

617   Khandwalla, Pradip N. THE DESIGN OF ORGANIZATIONS. New York: Harcourt Brace Jovanovich, 1977. xvii, 713 p.

The author aims to systematize an amorphous and rapidly growing body of knowledge about organizations and to show how this knowledge can be applied to the practical work of designing effectively performing organizations. This text, intended for use in undergraduate and graduate courses on organization theory, is divided into two parts. The first part explores the foundations of organizational analysis and ends with a model of how organizations function. Part 2 draws on a more recent body of research and systematically explores the design implications of the model presented in part 1. Khandwalla takes the position that organization theory can explain the structure and functioning of organizations.

618   Landau, Martin. "On the Concept of a Self-Correcting Organization." PUBLIC ADMINISTRATION REVIEW 33 (November-December 1973): 533-42.

The purpose of this essay is to defend the principle of scientific management. Landau believes that bureaucracies are inflexible and inadequate problem solvers because they are not scientific enough. He posits that the proper application of scientific principles to management reinforces the Weberian concept of bureaucratic administration as the exercise of control on the basis of knowledge and that the cardinal function of bureaucratic administration is to prevent and to correct errors.

619   Leavitt, Harold J., ed. THE SOCIAL SCIENCE OF ORGANIZATIONS: FOUR PERSPECTIVES. Englewood Cliffs, N.J.: Prentice-Hall, 1963. ix, 182 p.

This book consists of four essays which are a product of the 1962 Seminar in the Social Science of Organization, sponsored by the Graduate School of Business of the University of Pittsburgh, and supported by the Ford Foundation. George B. Strother discusses the problems in the development of a social science of organization, George Strauss examines power-equalization, Henry A. Latane reviews the rationality model in organizational decision making, and David Mechanic presents some considerations in the methodology of organizational studies. Leavitt emphasizes that these four views illustrate the extent to which the organization has become a center of multidisciplinary study.

620   Lerner, Allan W. "On Ambiguity and Organizations." ADMINISTRATION AND SOCIETY 10 (May 1978): 3-32.

Lerner maintains that ambiguity is inherent in the authority, reciprocity, and jurisdictional facets of relationships. He reviews the value of ambiguity as a common theme linking rational actor and system level concepts.

621   Levine, Charles H. "More on Cutback Management: Hard Questions for Hard Times." PUBLIC ADMINISTRATION REVIEW 39 (March-April 1979): 179-83.

Levine defines cutback management, why is it different and difficult, what are the unique problems and paradoxes of cutback situations, what strategic choices managers must make in cutting back, and what these questions and problems suggest as directions for future research. The author states: "We are entering a new era of public budgeting, personnel, and program management. It is an era dominated by resource scarcity. It will be a period of hard times for government managers that will require them to manage cutbacks, tradeoffs, reallocations, organizational contractions, program terminations, sacrifice, and the unfreezing and freeing up of grants and privileges that have come to be regarded as unnegotiable rights, entitlements, and contracts."

622   . "Organizational Decline and Cutback Management."   PUBLIC
ADMINISTRATION REVIEW 38 (July–August 1978): 316-25.

Levine asserts that we know very little about the decline
of public organizations and the management of cutbacks.
He notes that "the decline and death of government organizations is a symptom, a problem, and a contingency"
and reports that "we are now reappraising cases of public
organization decline and death as exemplars and fore-
runners in order to provide strategies for the design and
management of mainstream public administration in a
future dominated by resource scarcity." This article
should be consulted by all public sector managers.

623   March, James G., ed. HANDBOOK OF ORGANIZATIONS. Chicago:
Rand McNally and Co., 1965. xvi, 1,247 p.

The editor offers selections which summarize existing
knowledge about human organizations and describe the
present state of organizational research and organization
theory. March states that "the study of organizations
has a history but not a pedigree." Sections include
foundations, methodologies, theoretical-substantive areas,
institutions, and applications. All kinds of human organizations are examined. If there is a classic among books of
readings in public administration, this is that volume.

624   March, James G., and Simon, Herbert A. ORGANIZATIONS. New
York: John Wiley and Sons, 1958. vii, 262 p.

This public administration classic is about the theory of
formal organizations. March and Simon offer propositions
which suggest that organization members are primarily
passive instruments, assume that members bring attitudes,
values, and goals to their organizations, and conclude
that organization members are decision makers and problem
solvers. Chapters include discussions on organizational
behavior, "classical" organization theory, intraorganiza-
tional decisions, the decision to participate, organizational
conflicts, cognitive limits on rationality, and planning
and innovation in organizations. The authors include an
extensive bibliography.

625   Marcus, Philip M., and Cafagna, Dora. "Control in Modern Organizations." PUBLIC ADMINISTRATION REVIEW 25 (June 1965):
121-27. Figure.

Focusing on control because of its central importance in
the operation of large scale enterprises, the authors present insights into the control mechanisms of organizations.
They concentrate on control and individual adjustment,
organizational effectiveness, consensus, and experimental
studies and conclude that both organizational characteristics and humane considerations require that some control
be delegated to the lower echelons of organizations.

626   Pfiffner, John M., and Sherwood, Frank P. ADMINISTRATIVE OR-
       GANIZATION. Englewood Cliffs, N.J.: Prentice-Hall, 1960. xiii,
       481 p.

       "Studies of administrative organization tend to cluster at
       one or the other of two poles. At one end is the tradi-
       tional framework of job content, job structure, and job
       relationships--the mechanistic, engineering approach to
       the problem. At the other end is the human behavioralism
       orientation, in which the sociologists, psychologists, and
       anthropologists have been most prominent. As a result
       there has been a need for introductory materials which
       seek a middle ground between these two contrasting ex-
       tremes. To provide such materials is the essential purpose
       of this book." Sections include organization in society,
       organization structure, modifying systems, two modern
       models of organization, and perspectives. This book re-
       mains an excellent resource for instruction in organization
       theories despite its publication date.

627   Pittsburgh. University. Administrative Science Center. COMPARATIVE
       STUDIES IN ADMINISTRATION. Pittsburgh: University of Pittsburgh
       Press, 1959. xiv, 224 p.

       This volume is intended as a contribution to the study of
       administration instead of a handbook for administrators.
       The contributors consider diversified types of organizations,
       including manufacturing, mining, and shipping industries;
       higher education; hospitals; and military and social welfare
       organs of government. The diversity of authors and range
       of activities results in an inevitable lack of uniformity in
       terminology. Sections include discussions of organizational
       comparisons, environmental comparisons, variations in
       process, and research frontiers.

628   Presthus, Robert. THE ORGANIZATIONAL SOCIETY. Rev. ed.
       New York: St. Martin's Press, 1978. ix, 288 p.

       This book is an interdisciplinary analysis of modern orga-
       nizations and their influence upon the individuals who
       work in them. The author's analysis includes the society
       as a whole, the big, rational organization, and the in-

dividual. The author shows how individuals work out an accommodation in "miniature societies" in which the dominant values of society are inculcated and develops a theory of organizational behavior that posits three ideal types of accommodation to big organizations: upward-mobiles, indifferents, and ambivalents. The analysis and theory of this book draw upon several social sciences.

629   Randall, Ronald. "Influence of Attitudes on Organizational Control." ADMINISTRATION AND SOCIETY 7 (February 1976): 475-96.

Attitudes of middle-level managers in the Wisconsin State Employment Service were examined as an influence on behavior consistent with or contrary to organizational goals and objectives regarding the Human Resource Development (HRD) policy, which was particularly concerned with helping disadvantaged persons. Randall informs the reader that pre-HRD managers reserved employment office resources for the HRD program when the need for such services was high; as that need decreased, more of these resources went to regular activities. Anti-HRD managers made no similar accommodation.

630   Rushing, William A., and Zald, Mayer N., eds. ORGANIZATIONS AND BEYOND: SELECTED ESSAYS OF JAMES D. THOMPSON. Lexington, Mass.: D.C. Heath and Co., 1976. x, 299 p.

The editors include fifteen essays of the late James D. Thompson, one of the foremost sociological thinkers about the dynamics of complex organizations. Parts 1 and 2 of this text present articles on Thompson's major statements on the structure and dynamics of organizations, while part 3 contains essays reflecting his interests in occupations, community, and society. Rushing and Zald believe that these essays, taken as a whole, are a profound statement on organizations and society.

631   Sherman, Harvey. IT ALL DEPENDS: A PRAGMATIC APPROACH TO ORGANIZATION. University: University of Alabama Press, 1966. 218 p.

The author seeks to arouse in practicing managers an interest in the problem of organizing, to make them aware of the importance of this problem, to bring to their attention some of the major current and likely future problems in the field, and to provide a general framework for examining problems of organizing. Sherman mixes his practical experience with a review of the literature and presents some useful insights for a pragmatic approach to organization.

632   Simon, Herbert A. "On the Concept of Organizational Goal." AD-
       MINISTRATIVE SCIENCE QUARTERLY 9 (June 1964): 1-22.

       Simon suggests that "it is doubtful whether decisions are
       generally directed toward achieving a goal. It is easier,
       and clearer, to view decisions as being concerned with
       discovering courses of action that satisfy a whole set of
       constraints. It is this set, and not any one of its members,
       that is most accurately viewed as the goal of the action."

633   Starling, Jay D. "Organization and the Decision to Participate."
       PUBLIC ADMINISTRATION REVIEW 28 (September-October 1968):
       453-60.

       Using the theoretical models suggested by Amitai Etzioni
       and Chris Argyris which address the problem of personnel
       commitment to organization, the author indicates that the
       Department of Defense was encountering considerable diffi-
       culty retaining personnel in the armed services. Starling's
       analysis suggests that functional methods for building a
       more committed military are unrealistically expensive.

634   Thayer, Frederick C. AN END TO HIERARCHY! AN END TO COM-
       PETITION! New York: Franklin Watts, 1973. 232 p.

       Proceeding from both theoretical and illustrative bases,
       Thayer argues that hierarchy and competition are unde-
       sirable. As an advocate for the new public administra-
       tion, the author believes that there is movement toward
       informal intraorganizational groupings which can act via
       consensus.

635   Thompson, James D. ORGANIZATIONS IN ACTION: SOCIAL
       SCIENCE BASES OF ADMINISTRATIVE THEORY. New York: McGraw-
       Hill Book Co., 1967. xi, 192 p.

       Thompson considers behavior within organizations to the
       extent that this focus helps understand organization in a
       general sense. In part 1, the author argues that orga-
       nizations are expected to produce results and their actions
       are expected to be reasonable or rational. He maintains
       that "concepts of rationality . . . establish limits within
       which organizational action must take place." Part 2
       deals with the extent to which organizations gain a mea-
       sure of certainty or predictability with respect to the be-
       havior of their members or of others in the task environ-
       ment and concerns the exercise of discretion by organiza-
       tion members. The author explores who participates in
       the exercise of discretion, relationships among such par-
       ticipants, what discretion is about, and how it is expressed.

This text is a valuable contribution to understanding organizational behavior and theory.

636   Thompson, Victor A. MODERN ORGANIZATION. 2d ed. University: University of Alabama Press, 1977. ix, 197, xi p.

This book is intended as a contribution to the growing understanding of organizations. Thompson focuses on the general aspects of modern organizations with emphasis on their common characteristics instead of their differences. He maintains that studies of the relation between leadership styles and output compare the behavior of superiors toward subordinates and meticulously classify small variations in this behavior, but overlook the fundamental institutional fact that we have superiors and subordinates. Thompson's book is oriented toward the "neglected ninety percent." Chapters include discussions of bureaucracy, specialization, hierarchy, conflict, ideology, dramaturgy, bureaupathology, and cooperation.

637   White, Orion F., Jr. "The Dialectical Organization: An Alternative to Bureaucracy." PUBLIC ADMINISTRATION REVIEW 29 (January-February 1969): 32-42.

The author presents two models of client relations, adults and children. He notes characteristics of bureaucratic clienteles based on the client-as-adult and client-as-child models. He describes client relations and interactions, administrative structure, and organizational ideology and mentality in dialectical analysis of bureaucratic organizational structure.

638   Whyte, William H., Jr. THE ORGANIZATION MAN. New York: Simon and Schuster, 1956. 429 p.

In this classic on the rise of conformity in the life of the organization, Whyte contends that the Protestant ethic has been supplanted by a social ethic idolizing science, collective responsibility, lukewarm cooperation, routine, impersonal communications, and subservience to the organizational cause. He sets forth the education of organization men, their status frustration and their ambition drives, personality testing, the bureaucratization of technological and scholarly life, the social moral in popular fiction, and the domiciles of organization families. Sections include discussions on the ideology of organization man, the training of organization man, the neuroses of organization man, the testing of organization man, the organization scientist, the organization man in fiction, and the organization man at home in the new suburbia.

639   Wilcox, Herbert G. "Hierarchy, Human Nature, and the Participative
       Panacea." PUBLIC ADMINISTRATION REVIEW 29 (January-February
       1969): 53-63.

       The author is concerned with the theological damnation
       of hierarchy, examines concepts of self-actualization,
       participative ideology, and technology, and concludes
       that American society is besieged by conflict generated
       by changes in cultural values and social action. Wilcox
       writes: "The assault upon hierarchical organization in-
       volves fundamental matters. It is proposed that one of
       the most prevalent forms of social action be eliminated
       or restricted to the greatest possible extent."

640   Zald, Mayer N., and Jacobs, David. "Compliance/Incentive Classi-
       fication of Organizations: Underlying Dimensions." ADMINISTRATION
       AND SOCIETY 9 (February 1978): 403-24.

       The authors contend that various incentive-compliance
       classification systems explain differences in the power and
       hold of organizations upon their members and that these
       classification systems partly overlap and utilize terms in
       different ways. They offer power-dependence concepts
       as an explanatory technique.

B. ORGANIZATIONAL BEHAVIOR AND THEORY

641   Argyris, Chris. UNDERSTANDING ORGANIZATIONAL BEHAVIOR.
       Homewood, Ill.: Dorsey Press, 1960. xii, 179 p.

       The author's theme is that organizational mandates are in
       conflict with the individual's psychological needs. Chapters
       include discussions of the focus of the research, the theo-
       retical model, and methodological guideposts supplementing
       the framework; the role of the researcher, the type of
       interview, the research strategy underlying the questions
       used, and the primary and secondary objectives of each
       question; a concrete example (called Plant X) illustrating
       how the theory and the method diagnose a particular or-
       ganization; and some of the positive results of the research.
       In summary, Argyris is concerned with how behavioral
       scientists conduct research in an organization, the require-
       ments of research upon the participants, and the advan-
       tages that might accrue from the research to the organi-
       zation.

642   Becker, Selwyn W., and Gordon, Gerald. "An Entrepreneurial Theory
       of Formal Organizations, Part I: Patterns of Formal Organizations."
       ADMINISTRATIVE SCIENCE QUARTERLY 11 (December 1966): 315-
       44. Tables.

Becker and Gordon argue that all formal organizations
have resources and establish procedures for the use of
those resources. They develop a taxonomy primarily based
on how the procedures are established and how the organization stores its resources. They identify three simple
bureaucratic forms: the Complete, the Enucleated, and the
Truncated Bureaucracies and describe four complex organizational types: internally coupled organizations, ex-
ternally coupled organizations, parallel decentralization,
and functional decentralization.

643   Bennis, Warren G. CHANGING ORGANIZATIONS: ESSAYS ON
THE DEVELOPMENT AND EVOLUTION OF HUMAN ORGANIZATION.
New York: McGraw-Hill Book Co., 1966. xi, 223 p.

The author identifies some important evolutionary trends
in organizational development, focusing on the ways in
which behavioral scientists illuminate and direct processes
of change, discusses developments and tendencies toward
democracy and science, and illustrates how action based
on knowledge and self-determination can change the
nature of organizational life. He approaches the problem
of change from many different angles, all of which focus
on the cause and consequences of change in organizational
behavior. Chapters include discussions of the decline of
bureaucracy and organizations of the future, the inevitability of democracy, scientific management, changing
patterns of leadership, and planned organizational change.

644   Benson, J. Kenneth. "Organizations: A Dialectical View." AD-
MINISTRATIVE SCIENCE QUARTERLY 22 (March 1977): 1-21.

Benson contrasts dialectical and conventional approaches
to the study of organizations. He notes that the dialectical approach includes the basic principles of social construction, totality, contradiction, and praxis. He believes
that the established perspectives of conventional approaches
do not deal satisfactorily with organizational arrangements
and do not analyze accurately theories originating from
such arrangements. He reveals that the dialectical method
analyzes the processes producing organizational arrangements and portrays the multilevel and contradictory phenomena of the organizations' features.

645   Blau, Peter M., and Scott, W. Richard. FORMAL ORGANIZATIONS:
A COMPARATIVE APPROACH. San Francisco: Chandler Publishing
Co., 1962. x, 312 p.

Blau and Scott present a sociological analysis of some of
the main facets of organizational life. They examine the
nature and types of formal organizations, connecting them

with the larger social context. They review peer group and hierarchical relations in organizations, processes of communication, management and impersonal mechanisms of control. Chapter discussions include the nature and types of formal organizations, the organization and its publics, the social structure of work groups, processes of communication, the role of the supervisor, managerial control, the social context of organizational life, and organizational dynamics.

646   Dowling, John, and Pfeffer, Jeffrey. "Organizational Legitimacy: Social Values and Organizational Behavior." PACIFIC SOCIOLOGICAL REVIEW 18 (January 1975): 122-36.

The authors believe that an empirical focus on organizational efforts toward legitimacy can aid in explaining and analyzing many organizational behaviors with respect to the environment. These behaviors in turn can generate hypotheses and a conceptual perspective for additional research upon organizational legitimacy. The article focuses on the problem of legitimacy, the processes of organizational legitimation, and constraints on organizational behavior.

647   Dunn, William N., and Fozouni, Bahman. TOWARD A CRITICAL ADMINISTRATIVE THEORY. Beverly Hills, Calif.: Sage Publications, 1976. 75 p.

The author discusses Scientific Public Administration (SPA), Conventional Public Administration (CPA), and New Public Administration (NPA). CPA follows traditional American norms and values, SPA utilizes a logical empiricist paradigm, and NPA is both incomplete and unskillful in its approach. Dunn and Fozouni maintain that SPA is the dominant paradigm in public administration.

648   Etzioni, Amitai. A COMPARATIVE ANALYSIS OF COMPLEX ORGA-NIZATIONS: ON POWER, INVOLVEMENT, AND THEIR CORRELATES. Rev. ed. New York: Free Press, 1975. xxiv, 584 p.

Etzioni classifies organizations on the basis of organizational properties and systematically examines variations among different types of organization. His approach encompasses a wide variety of organizations, from religious societies to concentration camps. His analysis of charisma, and his critique of Max Weber's well-known discussion of this phenomenon, are among the most insightful analyses in this text. Etzioni makes a significant contribution to the literature of organizations.

649   Golembiewski, Robert T.   BEHAVIOR AND ORGANIZATION: O & M
        AND THE SMALL GROUP.   Chicago: Rand McNally and Co., 1962.
        238 p.

> This book deals with small-group analysis in the context
> of the organization and methods approach, attempts to
> provide an explicit theoretical and methodological base
> for small-group analysis as it applies to problems encoun-
> tered in O & M applications, and contributes to the rec-
> onciliation of the formal and behavioral emphases.

650   Hage, Jerald.   "An Axiomatic Theory of Organizations."   ADMINI-
        STRATIVE SCIENCE QUARTERLY 10 (December 1965): 289-320.

> Hage defines the organizational variables of complexity,
> centralization, formalization, stratification, adaptiveness,
> production, efficiency, and job satisfaction.   The author
> relates these variables in seven basic propositions suggested
> by the theoretical writings of Weber, Barnard, and Thompson.
> He uses the seven propositions to derive twenty-one corol-
> laries and to define two ideal types of organizational
> systems, and then tests the axiomatic theory, consisting
> of twenty-nine hypotheses, against a number of research
> studies.   The axiomatic theory appears useful in analyzing
> organizational problems, including organizational change,
> centralization versus decentralization, and morale.

651   Hall, Richard H.; Haas, J. Eugene; and Johnson, Norman J.   "An
        Examination of the Blau-Scott and Etzioni Typologies."   ADMINISTRA-
        TIVE SCIENCE QUARTERLY 12 (June 1967): 118-39.   Tables.

> The authors use data from seventy-five organizations ana-
> lyzing the utility of the two typologies.   They discover
> that the typologies are related to each other and, to a
> lesser degree, to indicators of goal specificity, power
> structure, relationships between internal segments, and
> relations with the external environment.   They find weak-
> er relationships between the typologies and indicators of
> complexity, formalization, major activities, and changes
> in activities and emphases.

652   Hammer, W. Clay, and Organ, Dennis W.   ORGANIZATIONAL BE-
        HAVIOR: AN APPLIED PSYCHOLOGICAL APPROACH.   Dallas:
        Business Publications, 1978.   xii, 437 p.

> The authors articulate and systematize what they perceive
> as the definitive conceptual core of organizational be-
> havior.   They focus on individual and group behavior in
> organizations, pursue a descriptive as opposed to normative
> approach, emphasize contemporary developments, and con-

centrate on the topics that the authors believe to be
richest in their implications for the management of people
in organizations.

653   Hickson, D.J. "A Convergence in Organization Theory." ADMINI-
        STRATIVE SCIENCE QUARTERLY 11 (September 1966): 224-37.

        Hickson argues that a linear relationship between degree
        of role prescription and other behavior variables in almost
        universally taken for granted, that relatively little work
        is being done to devise measures of role prescription, and
        that the development of new ideas may be limited unless
        organizational scientists are more aware of their preoccu-
        pation with the concept of the degree of specificity, or
        precision, of role prescription.

654   Kurzman, Paul A. "Rules and Regulations in Large-Scale Organiza-
        tions: A Theoretical Approach to the Problem." ADMINISTRATION
        IN SOCIAL WORK 1 (Winter 1977): 421-31.

        Kurzman relates that all employees in large-scale organi-
        zations have resented the rules and regulations that sanc-
        tion their actions and curtail their options. Unpopular
        with worker and client alike, these regulations seem to
        persist, even increase, though they seem to have few
        proponents. The author asserts that the innovative employee
        will consider administrative theory in order to comprehend
        this organizational reality and will strive to work imagi-
        natively within boundaries.

655   Levine, Charles H., et al. "Organizational Design: A Post Minnow-
        brook Perspective for the 'New' Public Administration." PUBLIC AD-
        MINISTRATION REVIEW 35 (July-August 1975): 425-35.

        This article sketches possible elements of a new public
        administration consistent with the field's traditions and
        strengths. The authors conclude that "the basic problem
        of action design as an important element of a "new"
        public administration is the limited amount of determinate
        theory, or knowledge, that can be brought to bear in
        concrete particular efforts."

656   Litchfield, Edward H. "Notes on a General Theory of Administration."
        ADMINISTRATIVE SCIENCE QUARTERLY 1 (June 1956): 1-29.

        Litchfield suggests that a lack of an adequate theory of
        administration has hindered both the integration of knowl-
        edge developing in allied fields and the orientation of
        thought to a larger concept of social action. He states
        that the lack of a generalized theory makes it appear that
        there are no universal aspects of administration, but only

special types of administration. He believes that more is
known about the parts of administration than about the
totality. He offers a number of major and minor propositions, designed to be testable.

657   Mouzelis, Nicos P. ORGANISATION AND BUREAUCRACY: AN
ANALYSIS OF MODERN THEORIES. Chicago: Aldine Publishing
Co., 1967. 230 p.

The author posits a carefully integrated and very straight-
forward guide to the labyrinth of theory on organizational
phenomena and surveys the most important approaches to
the study of organizations and the manner in which these
approaches are interrelated. Mouzelis discusses the writings
of such theorists as Marx, Weber, and Michels who, from
a very broad perspective, tried to assess the impact of
large-scale bureaucracy on the power structure of modern
society. He examines the organizational writings of Taylor
and the movement of scientific management and indicates
a convergence of the bureaucracy and managerial lines
of thought.

658   Natemeyer, Walter E., ed. CLASSICS OF ORGANIZATIONAL BE-
HAVIOR. Oak Park, Ill.: Moore Publishing Co., 1978. x, 362 p.

Natemeyer includes in this book of readings articles on
management and the behavioral sciences, individual behavior and motivation, interpersonal and group behavior,
leadership and power, behavioral dimensions of organizations, and organizational change and development.

659   Parsons, Talcott. "Suggestions for a Sociological Approach to the
Theory of Organizations--I." ADMINISTRATIVE SCIENCE QUARTERLY
1 (June 1956): 63-85.

In the first of two essays, Parsons outlines an approach to
the analysis of formal organizations in terms of the general
theory of social systems. He discusses: 1) procurement
of the necessary resources, financing, personal services,
and the "organization" in the economic sense, 2) the
operative code centering on decisions which are classified
as policy decisions, allocative decisions, and coordinating
decisions, and 3) the institutional structure which integrates the organization with others, centering on contract,
authority, and the institutionalization of universalistic
rules.

660   _____. "Suggestions for a Sociological Approach to the Theory of
Organizations--II." ADMINISTRATIVE SCIENCE QUARTERLY 1
(September 1956): 225-39.

In the second essay of a two-part series (see above), Parsons identifies power as the central phenomenon of organization. He states that the generation of power, both within and outside the organization, depends on four fundamental conditions, which are identified. He outlines a classification of organizational types, based on primacy of different types of organizational goals, and illustrates its utility by analyzing variations among the business firm, the military organization, and the university in this society.

661   Pfeffer, Jeffrey, and Salanick, Gerald R. "Organization Design: The Case for a Coalitional Model of Organizations." ORGANIZATIONAL DYNAMICS 6 (Autumn 1977): 15-29.

This article raises the question of how can structures be designed that incorporate managerial fallibility and provide for the expression of alternative interests, preferences, and ideas while at the same time providing enough order to facilitate action. The authors maintain that because organizations are inherently vulnerable to various pressures from an unstable external environment, they must be designed in ways that increase their responsiveness to these pressures. According to Pfeffer and Salanick, the predicament is to strike a balance between the need for adaptation, which requires less institutionalization, and the need for action, which demands substantial institutionalization.

662   Presthus, Robert [V.]. BEHAVIORAL APPROACHES TO PUBLIC ADMINISTRATION. Rev. ed. University: University of Alabama Press, 1972. 158 p. Tables.

Presthus discusses behavioralism in public administration including behavioralism as mood and method, behavioral research in community power structure, behavioral research in organizational effectiveness, behavioral research on British executives, and the uses of behavioralism.

663   _____. "Toward a Theory of Organizational Behavior." ADMINISTRATIVE SCIENCE QUARTERLY 3 (June 1958): 48-72.

Presthus uses several theoretical formulations from sociology and psychology in an attempt to set down a general theory of organizational behavior. He defines the typical bureaucratic model as a "structured field," in the sense that authority, status, and role are clearly articulated and thus provide behavioral cues that facilitate perception and learning. Since reactions to authority will differ in terms of genetic composition, class, and idiosyncratic experience of a given individual, Presthus posits upward-mobiles, indifferents, and ambivalents as three ideal types of accommodation.

664   Ramos, Alberto Guerreiro. "Models of Man and Administrative Theory."
        PUBLIC ADMINISTRATION REVIEW   32 (May-June 1972):   241-46.

        The author states that administrative theory can no longer
        legitimize the functional rationality of the organization,
        as it largely has done. This article is an attempt to
        reassess the evolution of administrative theory. It takes
        models of man (operational man, reactive man, and paren-
        thetical man) as its point of reference.

665   Schein, Edgar H.   "In Defense of Theory Y."   ORGANIZATIONAL
        DYNAMICS 4 (Summer 1975): 17-30.

        This article discusses Theory Y which states that workers
        are capable of integrating their own needs and goals with
        those of the organization, that they are not inherently
        lazy and indolent, that they are by nature capable of
        exercising self-control and self-direction, and that they
        are capable of directing their efforts toward organizational
        goals. The explanation offered for Theory Y does not
        argue that human needs and organizational goals are always
        congruent and integrative, nor does it imply participative
        management; it is only a statement of what people funda-
        mentally are and what kinds of organizational behavior
        are possible if the conditions within the organization are
        appropriate.

666   Scott, William G.   "Organization Government: The Prospects for a
        Truly Participative System."   PUBLIC ADMINISTRATION REVIEW   29
        (January-February 1969):   43-53.

        Scott discusses the evolution of managerial ideologies,
        gives an interpretation of the present state of management
        ideology, makes a proposal for representative government
        in organizations, and offers a dismal forecast of the chance
        that a representative government would have. The author
        describes contemporary management creeds and the evolu-
        tion of management creeds and states his case for a truly
        participative system of organizational government.

667   Scott, William G., and Mitchell, Terence R.   ORGANIZATION
        THEORY: A STRUCTURAL AND BEHAVIORAL ANALYSIS. Rev. ed.
        Homewood, Ill.:   Richard D. Irwin, and Dorsey Press, 1972.   x,
        409 p.

        This book is a major revision of ORGANIZATION THEORY:
        A BEHAVIORAL ANALYSIS FOR MANAGEMENT (1967).
        Part 1 deals with organizations and rationality, the Euro-
        pean and American perspectives. Part 2 includes chapters
        on formal organization, the systems concept, personality
        dynamics and motivation, attitudes, and group dynamics.

Part 3 includes chapters on communication, decision, balance and conflict, status and role, influence (authority and power), leadership, and technological processes. Parts 4, 5, and 6 focus on organization change, organizational research and methodology, and organizational issues.

668 Shafritz, Jay M., and Whitbeck, Philip H., eds. CLASSICS OF ORGANIZATION THEORY. Oak Park, Ill.: Moore Publishing Co., 1978. xi, 323 p.

Shafritz and Whitbeck offer selections in this book of readings in classical organization theory, neo-classical organization theory, the systems perspective, organizational structure, patterns of organizational adaptation, and contemporary organizational analyses. By "organization," the editors imply "a social unit designed to attain a particular goal."

669 Smith, Michael P. "Barriers to Organizational Democracy in Public Administration." ADMINISTRATION AND SOCIETY 8 (November 1976): 275-317.

Smith maintains that making the job environment in public organizations more democratic will aid in developing members' interpersonal skills, decreasing buck-passing, increasing job satisfaction, productivity, and public-agency contacts, recruiting talented leaders, and bringing more creative solutions to problems faced by public sector organizations. He reveals that prevailing political arrangements, needs, habits, and interests of organizational elites, organizational ideologies, and agency socialization and reward systems are barriers to more democratic work environments.

670 Stene, Edwin O. "Conflict, Compromise, and Cooperation: A Model of Organization Theory." ADMINISTRATIVE CHANGE 1 (December 1973): 1-11.

Stene advocates a conflict model of organization theory. He examines the response of the central authority to dissent and ways in which diverse interests attempt to limit the central authority. The author indicates that alternatives of conflict resolution are total suppression, laissez faire, compromise, and mobilization of support. This model does not seek the elimination of conflict.

671 Stone, Donald, and Stone, Alice. "The Administration of Chairs." PUBLIC ADMINISTRATION REVIEW 34 (January-February 1974): 71-77.

The Stones write a humorous but serious essay on the positioning of chairs and state that "it is now possible for any organization man or woman who participates in meetings to determine their success by applying the principles of a new science: chair administration." The authors employ thirteen figures to illustrate various positioning in the administration of chairs.

672   Stupak, Ronald J. "Organizational Behavior in the 1970s: The Missing Links?" BUREAUCRAT 5 (October 1976): 335-39.

Stupak points out that entries in the junior or middle executive ranks are significantly younger than their counterparts of the 1950s and 1960s, that the young males entering the public service in the 1970s are often without military service experience, and that the college graduates of the 1970s express a "new conservatism" which impacts perspectives and training concepts. He maintains that management practitioners and organizational theorists have not recognized and incorporated these variables into a sound and practical model of organization for the remainder of the 1970s.

673   Tansik, David A., and Radnor, Michael. "An Organization Theory Perspective on the Development of New Organizational Functions." PUBLIC ADMINISTRATION REVIEW 31 (November-December 1971): 644-52.

As organizations become more complex and as pressures on management grow to respond to developments in their organizations' environments, an understanding of the process by which new technological functions are established in organizations becomes crucial. The purpose of this article is to put the evolution of the PPBS concept into an analytical perspective which can be used to understand and explain the events that have occurred.

674   Teasley, C.E. III. "Administrative Behavior: Applications, Research Results, and Prospects." In PUBLIC ADMINISTRATION AND PUBLIC POLICY, edited by H. George Frederickson and Charles R. Wise, pp. 43-52. Lexington, Mass.: D.C. Heath and Co., 1977.

The major conclusion of this article is that organization development and management by objectives management improvement programs enjoy, at best, qualified support in public organizations. Teasley states that these programs and the theories underpinning them have met with mixed results and that they must be considered in the context of many, often unspecified, situational and contingent variables.

675   Thayer, Frederick C. "The President's Management 'Reforms': Theory
       X Triumphant." PUBLIC ADMINISTRATION REVIEW 38 (July–August
       1978): 309-14.

         Thayer writes that "the theory of the President (Carter)
         and his advisors holds that public and business admini-
         stration are different, but the difference lies in the su-
         periority of business administration." He posits that "the
         proposed Office of Personnel Management will no doubt
         develop quantitative standards for the number of employees
         to be fired or denied pay raises each year if the govern-
         ment is to prove its diligence."

676   Vogel, Donald B. "Analysis of Informal Organization Patterns: A
       Training Technique." PUBLIC ADMINISTRATION REVIEW 28 (September–
       October 1968): 431-36. Figures.

         The purpose of this essay is to present a training technique
         designed to provide greater input for management level
         personnel in decisions involving administrative structure
         patterns and their effect on organizational decision making,
         leadership, control, and communications. The author rec-
         ognizes that informal organization patterns and relation-
         ships exist and play an important role in determining the
         functional and/or dysfunctional characteristics of bureau-
         cracies.

677   Waldo, Dwight A. "Organizational Analysis: Some Notes on Methods
       and Criteria." PUBLIC ADMINISTRATION REVIEW 7 (Autumn 1947):
       236-44.

         Writing in the early post–World War II period, the author
         posits eight factors to consider in reaching an organiza-
         tional decision. They include: Is the problem organiza-
         tional or procedural? Will executive control, policy co-
         ordination, and functional coherence be facilitated? Is
         there need for autonomy and will this need be served?
         Will manpower or materials be saved? Will cooperation
         be facilitated? Will clientele, beneficiary, ward, or
         employee convenience, welfare, or satisfaction be served?
         Are personal factors involved that must be considered?
         Should the factor of tradition or esprit de corps be con-
         sidered? Waldo concludes that a decision to make an or-
         ganizational change must be supported by conclusive evi-
         dence demonstrating beyond reasonable doubt that change
         is desirable. This essay is quite useful for understanding
         Waldo's ideas on organizations during the late 1940s.

C. ADMINISTRATIVE STRUCTURE, CONTROL, AND CONFLICT

678   Auerbach, Arnold J. "Confrontation and Administrative Response."
       PUBLIC ADMINISTRATION REVIEW 29 (November-December 1969):
       639-46.

> Confrontation, accompanied by violence and vandalism,
> has interfered with the ability of administrators of public
> institutions to discharge their responsibilities with ratio-
> nalism and efficiency. This article discusses some of the
> sociological and psychological effects of organizational
> conflicts, and suggests some operational principles to guide
> administrators of public institutions in meeting the con-
> frontation tactics of activist groups.

679   Blau, Peter M., and Schoenherr, Richard A. THE STRUCTURE OF
       ORGANIZATION. New York: Basic Books, 1971. 480 p.

> Blau and Schoenherr investigate the interdependence among
> elements in the structure of government bureaus, including
> the dynamics of size, complexity, environment, automa-
> tion, and individual behavior. This text is based on a
> study of state employment security offices in the United
> States. The authors assume that social structures show
> regularities in their own right, independent of the in-
> dividual behavior of their members.

680   Carzo, Rocco, Jr., and Yanouzas, John N. "Effects of Flat and Tall
       Organization Structure." ADMINISTRATIVE SCIENCE QUARTERLY 14
       (June 1969): 178-91. Tables.

> In a laboratory experiment, the authors test tall and flat
> organization structures for their effects on group perfor-
> mance. They conclude that comparisons of performance
> on the time taken to complete decisions showed no sig-
> nificant difference between tall and flat organization
> structures. They reveal that tall organization structures
> were superior on profits and rate of return on revenues.

681   Corwin, Ronald C. "Patterns of Organizational Conflict." ADMINI-
       STRATIVE SCIENCE QUARTERLY 14 (December 1969): 507-20. Table.

> Corwin identifies relationships between indices of organi-
> zational conflict and five organizational variables: struc-
> tural differentiation, participation in the authority system,
> regulating procedures, heterogeneity and stability of per-
> sonnel, and interpersonal structure. He reveals that size,
> specialization, hierarchy, complexity, staff additions and
> heterogeneity were related to organizational conflict; par-
> ticipation in the authority system and cohesiveness of peer
> group relations seemed to facilitate conflict; while experience
> and close supervision seemed to be integrative variables.

682   Derr, C. Brooklyn. "Conflict Resolution in Organizations: Views
       from the Field of Educational Administration." PUBLIC ADMINISTRA-
       TION REVIEW 32 (September-October 1972): 495-501. Figures.

      This article attempts to consider organizational conflicts
      from the administrator's point of view. It outlines some
      methods that an administrator may use to develop a strategy
      for conflict resolution. It identifies the most common
      kinds of organizational conflicts, underscores the impor-
      tance of differentiating between conflicts (e.g., between
      those that foster creative tension and those that are po-
      tentially destructive to the organization), and presents
      a model for determining the degree to which they are
      important and should be resolved. The article concludes
      with some specific proposals for resolving organizational
      conflicts.

683   Dunsire, Andrew. CONTROL IN A BUREAUCRACY. New York:
       St. Martin's Press, 1978. xii, 263 p.

      Dunsire elaborates on a theory about control in a bu-
      reaucracy and attempts to understand the dynamics of
      control. Chapters include discussions of implementation
      in a bureaucracy, the superior-subordinate relationship,
      planning and monitoring, achieving compliance, coordi-
      nation, managing equilibrium, and the nature of control
      in a bureaucracy. This book is a useful resource for com-
      prehending these phenomena.

684   Etzioni, Amitai. "Authority Structure and Organizational Effective-
       ness." ADMINISTRATIVE SCIENCE QUARTERLY 4 (June 1959): 43-
       67.

      Etzioni believes that an important factor in the ability of
      an organization to achieve its goals is its authority struc-
      ture. If goals and authority structure are incompatible,
      goals may be modified to the extent that means become
      parts of the goals themselves. The author analyzes several
      organizational assumptions to show that, in practice, the
      assumptions must be modified according to the major goals
      of the organization.

685   Fletcher, T.W. "The Nature of Administrative Loyalty." PUBLIC AD-
       MINISTRATION REVIEW 18 (Winter 1958): 37-42.

      The author discusses the importance of loyalties in an in-
      dividual's life, the role of administrative loyalty, blind
      loyalty and disloyalty, loyalty conflicts, loyalty and
      ethics, and the components in human relationships that
      inspire loyalty. Fletcher concludes that loyalty is a
      prime factor in enhancing the effectiveness of any orga-

nization and that loyalty insures productivity and work
satisfaction, which are legitimate goals in maintaining
the effectiveness of any governmental agency.

686   Golembiewski, Robert T. "Authority as a Problem in Overlays: A
        Concept for Action and Analysis." ADMINISTRATIVE SCIENCE QUAR-
        TERLY 9 (June 1964): 23-49.

        The purpose of this article is to build a conceptual ap-
        proach to authority relationships in organizations which
        facilitates interpretation of existing research and encourages
        significant future research. Golembiewski focuses upon
        several concepts common in the study of authority. Au-
        thoritative relations are conceived as "integrative," or
        having "traditional," "functional," and "behavioral" com-
        ponent overlays. The crucial issue in Golembiewski's
        application of the integrative conceptual approach illus-
        trated in this essay is increasing the congruence of the
        several overlays so that they substantially reinforce one
        another.

687   Janowitz, Morris. "Changing Patterns of Organizational Authority:
        The Military Establishment." ADMINISTRATIVE SCIENCE QUARTERLY
        3 (March 1959): 473-93.

        The author maintains that bureaucratic authority has be-
        come generally less direct, arbitrary, and authoritarian
        as social demands and organizational forms have grown
        more complex. He analyzes the bases and manifestations
        of this change in the military establishment, often regarded
        as the prototype of bureaucracy. The essential change,
        brought about by new weapons, the automation of warfare,
        the demands of technical expertise, and the emphasis
        upon individual initiative, is from an authority system based
        upon domination to one based upon the techniques of manipu-
        lation.

688   Meyer, Marshall W. "Two Authority Structures of Bureaucratic Orga-
        nization." ADMINISTRATIVE SCIENCE QUARTERLY 13 (September
        1968): 211-28. Tables.

        The authors attempt to link the formal structure of bureau-
        cratic organizations to decision-making processes, and in
        particular, to centralization and decentralization of au-
        thority. They collect interview data from 254 city, county,
        and state departments of finance. These data show that,
        controlling for an organization's size, decision-making
        authority is more highly centralized as the number of sub-
        units in an organization increases. However, the data
        also indicate that as the number of levels of supervision
        grows, there is greater decentralization and at the same

time proliferation of rules that specify criteria to guide decisions.

689   Payne, Roy L., and Mansfield, Roger. "Relationships of Perceptions of Organizational Climate to Organizational Structure, Context, and Hierarchical Position." ADMINISTRATIVE SCIENCE QUARTERLY 18 (December 1973): 515-26.

The authors explore the relationships among contextual, structural, and climate variables at the organizational level of analysis as well as the influence of the position of individuals in the organizational hierarchy on perceptions of climate. They indicate that persons higher in the hierarchy seem to perceive their organization as less authoritarian, and that organizational climate was found to be greatly influenced by organizational size and dependence.

690   Peabody, Robert L. "Authority Relations in Three Organizations." PUBLIC ADMINISTRATION REVIEW 23 (June 1963): 87-92. Tables.

This essay constitutes the results of an exploratory study of superior-subordinate relationships in three local public service organizations--a police station, a welfare agency, and an elementary school--and suggests some modifications in the use of the concept of authority. The author finds that perceptions of authority differ, not only from organization to organization, but also from the point of view of the superior, subordinate, and the neutral observer.

691   _____. "Perceptions of Organizational Authority." ADMINISTRATIVE SCIENCE QUARTERLY 6 (March 1962): 463-82.

This essay argues that the bases of formal authority (legitimacy and position) need to be distinguished from sources of functional authority (technical competence and human relations skills) which support and often compete with formal authority. Peabody develops four analytical types of authority relations from both the literature and his examination of superior-subordinate relationships among members of three public service organizations.

692   Pondy, Louis R. "Organizational Conflict: Concepts and Models." ADMINISTRATIVE SCIENCE QUARTERLY 12 (September 1967): 296-320.

Pondy identifies three types of conflict among the subunits of formal organizations: 1) bargaining conflict among the parties to an interest group relationship, 2) bureaucratic conflict between the parties to a superior-subordinate relationship, and 3) systems conflict among

parties to a lateral or working relationship. He analyzes
the organization's reaction to conflict in each case by
using the Barnard-Simon model of inducements-contributions
balance theory.

693   . "Varieties of Organizational Conflict." ADMINISTRATIVE
SCIENCE QUARTERLY 14 (December 1969): 499-505.

Pondy compares and contrasts the viewpoints and findings
of seven empirical studies of conflict within and between
organizations. He distinguishes between frictional conflict within a stable organization structure and strategic
conflict aimed at changing the organization structure.
He also discusses the importance of attitudes as causes
and effects of conflict.

694   Presthus, Robert V. "Authority in Organizations." PUBLIC ADMINI-
STRATION REVIEW 20 (Spring 1960): 86-91.

Authority seems to grow out of a dynamic, reciprocal
relationship between leader and led, in which the values,
perceptions, and skills of followers play a critical role in
defining and legitimating the authority of organizational
leaders. Presthus writes that four interlocking bases--the
technical expertise of the leader, his formal role or position in the organization's hierarchy, his rapport with
subordinates or his ability to mediate their individual
needs for security and recognition, and the subordinates'
generalized deference toward authority--constitute the
acceptance of authority in organizations.

695   Pugh, D.S.; Hickson, D.J.; Hinings, C.R.; and Turner, C. "The
Context of Organization Structures." ADMINISTRATIVE SCIENCE
QUARTERLY 14 (March 1969): 91-114. Tables.

The authors examine aspects of organizational context
considered relevant to organizational structure. They
analyze concepts of organizational context (origin and
history, ownership and control, size, charter, technology,
location and dependence on other organizations) and construct operationally defined scales.

696   . "Dimensions of Organization Structure." ADMINISTRATIVE
SCIENCE QUARTERLY 13 (June 1968): 65-105. Tables.

The authors define and operationalize five primary dimensions of organization structure: specialization, standardization, formalization, centralization, and configuration.
They suggest four basic dimensions of structure, conceptualized as structuring of activities, concentration of authority, line control of workflow, and size of supportive
component.

697   Reimann, Bernard C. "On the Dimensions of Bureaucratic Structure:
        An Empirical Reappraisal." ADMINISTRATIVE SCIENCE QUARTERLY
        18 (December 1973): 462-76.

        Reimann reveals that nineteen manufacturing firms in
        northeast Ohio were analyzed for lack of autonomy, func-
        tional specialization, delegation of authority, centraliza-
        tion index, functional dispersion, staff density, hierar-
        chical control, functional specificity, administrative den-
        sity, and vertical span. These measures were selected as
        representative of some chief components of organization
        structure, such as the authority hierarchy and configuration.
        The results, according to Reimann, reveal that the con-
        cept of a multidimensional structure space has considerable
        merit for organization research.

698   Rizzo, John R.; House, Robert J.; and Lirtzman, Sidney I. "Role
        Conflict and Ambiguity in Complex Organizations." ADMINISTRATIVE
        SCIENCE QUARTERLY 15 (June 1970): 150-63. Tables.

        This essay describes the development and testing of ques-
        tionnaire measures of role conflict and ambiguity. The
        authors analyze responses of managers and show these two
        constructs to be factorially identifiable and independent.
        The article indicates that derived measures of role con-
        flict and ambiguity tend to correlate in expected direc-
        tions with measures of organizational and managerial
        practices and leader behavior and with member satisfac-
        tion, anxiety, and propensity to leave the organization.

699   Rosengren, William R. "Structure, Policy, and Style: Strategies of
        Organizational Control." ADMINISTRATIVE SCIENCE QUARTERLY
        12 (June 1967): 140-64.

        Rosengren attempts to explain some relationships between
        structure and control achieved through supervisory style.
        He studies eighty large governmental psychiatric hospitals
        and fifty-two small private hospitals. With some excep-
        tions, he finds maximum structural control (approximating
        that of bureaucratic organizations) in association with
        limited employee control, while minimal structural control
        (resembling that of less bureaucratic organizations) is as-
        sociated with more pervasive employee control. He dis-
        cusses these patterns in their relation to classical Weberian
        conceptions of formal organizations and other theoretical
        foundations.

700   Rudolph, Lloyd I., and Rudolph, Susanne Hoeber. "Authority and
        Power in Bureaucratic and Patrimonial Administration: A Revisionist
        Interpretation of Weber on Bureaucracy." WORLD POLITICS 31
        (January 1979): 195-227.

The authors assert that Weber's ideas on bureaucracy, despite considerable qualification and alteration, remain the model for analysis of administration and formal organizations. They incorporate his ideal-type concepts of bureaucratic and patrimonial administration but revise them through theoretical and historical reinterpretation and application. The persistence of patrimonial components establishes administrative efficiency by lessening conflict and promotes organizational loyalty, discipline, and efficiency.

701   Scott, W. Richard; Dornbusch, Sanford M.; Busching, Bruce C.; and Laing, James D. "Organizational Evaluation and Authority." ADMINISTRATIVE SCIENCE QUARTERLY 12 (June 1967): 93-117.

The authors analyze authority systems in formal organizations in terms of the process by which the performance of organizational participants is evaluated. They view authority as an attempt to control the behavior of others and describe four different kinds of authority rights, each of which is a component of the evaluation process. They define authority systems in terms of distribution of these rights among participants.

702   Stahl, O. Glenn. "More on the Network of Authority." PUBLIC ADMINISTRATION REVIEW 20 (Winter 1960): 35-37.

In this article, the author expands on an earlier article (see next entry). Again Stahl's concern is the relationship of line and staff. He supplements his main point (that staff responsibility for sustaining the organization's operations necessarily involves authority, by emphasizing that the means may be important ends in themselves, especially in government) by pointing out that overspecialization of both staff and line is the real villain.

703   _____. "The Network of Authority." PUBLIC ADMINISTRATION REVIEW 18 (Winter 1958): ii-iv.

Stahl concludes "that 'line' and 'staff' are hardly distinguishable as indicators of power status; that the terms are merely convenient for identifying 1) those functions of an organization that are direct subdivisions of its programs purposes and 2) those that are oriented principally to its inner form, its sustenance, and its methods; that it is more useful to view these two types of specialization as intersecting lines of authority than as primary versus incidental functions, especially in the public service." The author's distinctions between line and staff provide for a most interesting and insightful analysis.

704   Thompson, James D. "Organizational Management of Conflict."
       ADMINISTRATIVE SCIENCE QUARTERLY 4 (March 1960): 389-409.

       This essay focuses on organization wide management of
       conflict as distinguished from local settlement of conflict.
       Thompson suggests that conflict generated by administrative
       allocations is rooted in technology and is controlled by
       organization structuring, that latent-role conflict, stem-
       ming from the labor force, is controlled by recruitment
       and selection procedures, and that conflict occasioned
       by competing pressures on members, based on the nature
       of the task environment, is controlled by organizational
       posture. He advances a number of propositions and draws
       on research findings to illustrate that various types of or-
       ganizations have different vulnerabilities and defenses
       against these sources of conflict.

705   Thompson, Victor A. "Hierarchy, Specialization, and Organizational
       Conflict." ADMINISTRATIVE SCIENCE QUARTERLY 5 (March 1961):
       485-521.

       The author asserts that intraorganizational conflict, to the
       extent that it is organizationally determined, is a function
       of 1) disagreement over the necessity of authoritatively
       created interdependence, 2) growing disparity between
       rights and abilities, 3) scalar status violations involved
       in technologically created interdependencies, and 4) dif-
       ferentiation of values and reality perceptions brought about
       by the controls over interpersonal communication exercised
       by the hierarchical system, the status system, and the
       specialization system.

706   Wise, Charles R. CLIENTS EVALUATE AUTHORITY: THE VIEW FROM
       THE OTHER SIDE. Beverly Hills, Calif.: Sage Publications, 1976.
       91 p.

       Recognizing that citizen participation is a central concern
       of management, Wise examines the interactions between
       public servants and clients. He points out that political
       authorities in the American system must constantly face
       challenges with regard to their legitimacy in the eyes of
       the public and implies that organizational authorities
       should be evaluated in a like manner.

D. ORGANIZATION DEVELOPMENT AND THE INDIVIDUAL

707   Argyris, Chris. "The Individual and Organization: Some Problems of
       Mutual Adjustment." ADMINISTRATIVE SCIENCE QUARTERLY 2
       (June 1957): 1-24.

"If formal organization is defined by the use of such principles as task specialization, unity of direction, chain of
command, and span of control, then employees work in
a situation in which they tend to be dependent, subordinate, and passive to a leader. This type of situation
may create frustration, conflict, and failure for the employee. He may react by regressing, decreasing his efficiency, and creating informal systems against management."

708   _____. INTEGRATING THE INDIVIDUAL AND THE ORGANIZA-
TION. New York: John Wiley and Sons, 1964. vii, 330 p.

The primary objective of this book is to present the author's preliminary thinking and theorizing about how organizations might be redesigned to take into account
human energies and competencies. Four chapters entail
a revised view of Argyris' book, PERSONALITY AND
ORGANIZATION (see no. 709). He examines the relation between the environment and the internal behavior
of the organization, discusses organizational effectiveness
and ineffectiveness, theorizes how organizations might be
redesigned, and offers a model for further studies. A
main theme is that the problem of integrating the individual and the organization is one in which both have
to give in order to profit from the other.

709   _____. PERSONALITY AND ORGANIZATION: THE CONFLICT
BETWEEN SYSTEM AND THE INDIVIDUAL. New York: Harper and
Brothers, 1957. xiii, 291 p.

This book helps the reader understand some of the basic
causes of human behavior in industrial plants, banks, insurance firms, trade unions, and government bureaus and
gives the reader a systematic and integrated picture of
some of the current research on human relations in on-
going organizations. Argyris notes that the realization
by practitioners of the importance of understanding the
causes of human behavior in organizations represents a
significant trend in the field of organization and administration. "Once they understand," the author writes, "it
is an easy matter to predict and control behavior."

710   _____. "Personality and Organization Theory Revisited." ADMINI-
STRATIVE SCIENCE QUARTERLY 18 (June 1973): 141-67.

Argyris reviews the post-1963 literature relevant to the
theoretical framework of personality and organization,
to ascertain the degree to which parts of the theory are
confirmed and disconfirmed. He suggests that organizational theory requires a model of man because without it
theory could become limited to the status quo.

711 _____. "Personality vs. Organization." ORGANIZATIONAL DY-
NAMICS 3 (Autumn 1974): 2-17.

Argyris states that behavioral science research should be
normative. It is the goal of the behavioral scientist to
intervene selectively in the organization whenever there
seems a reasonable chance of bettering the quality of life
without endangering organizational viability. The article
suggests that most organizations are limited in the opportunities that they afford most employees to meet their potential. Argyris concludes that employees perceive accurately that few people at the top want to increase
opportunities for self-actualization and that even fewer
people at the top are competent to do the job.

712 Bennis, Warren G. ORGANIZATION DEVELOPMENT: ITS NATURE,
ORIGINS, AND PROSPECTS. Reading, Mass.: Addison-Wesley Publishing Co., 1969. viii, 87 p.

This book is a primer on organization development written
for people in organizations who may be interested in
learning more about this educational strategy. The author
hypothesizes that every age develops an organizational
form most appropriate to the genius of that age and that
certain unparalleled changes are taking place which make
it necessary to revitalize and rebuild our organizations,
that the only viable way to change organizations is to
change the systems within which people work and live
(i.e., culture), and that a new social awareness is required by people in organizations. Chapters include discussions on what organization development is and is not,
the basic conditions for OD, questions and answers for
professionals and practitioners, the problem of sensitivity
training, and reconsiderations.

713 Bowers, David G. "Organizational Development: Promises, Performances, Possibilities." ORGANIZATIONAL DYNAMICS 4 (Spring
1976): 50-62.

Organizational development is a vague rubric that includes
process consultation, survey feedback, sensitivity training,
and job design. Bowers suggests that when OD is ex-
ecuted well, it is a complex venture requiring a substantial investment of resources, a careful and rigorous diagnosis of the situation, and a consulting style capable of
responding in a variety of ways to different conditions.

714 Connor, Patrick E. "A Critical Inquiry into Some Assumptions and
Values Characterizing OD." ACADEMY OF MANAGEMENT REVIEW
2 (October 1977): 635-43.

Connor reviews assumptions underlying values reflected in OD philosophy and practice. This essay is a critical perusal of OD values, assumptions, and their implications.

715   Culbert, Samuel A., and Reisel, Jerome. "Organization Development: An Applied Philosophy for Managers of Public Enterprise." PUBLIC ADMINISTRATION REVIEW 31 (March–April 1971): 159–69.

Organization development (OD) is an application of behavioral science knowledge that provides managers a technology for managing change in their organization. This article describes the identifying characteristics of OD and relates these characteristics to managerial problems.

716   Filley, Alan C. INTERPERSONAL CONFLICT RESOLUTION. Glenview, Ill.: Scott, Foresman and Co., 1975. 180 p.

Filley discusses types and sources of conflict, methods of conflict resolution and problem solving, the language of conflict and problem solving, personal styles of conflict resolution, attitudes and problem solving, organizing for conflict or cooperation, stages of integrative decision making, and changing conflict resolution skills and behavior.

717   Follett, Mary Parker. DYNAMIC ADMINISTRATION: THE COLLECTED PAPERS OF MARY PARKER FOLLETT. Edited by Henry C. Metclaf and L. Urwick. New York: Harper and Brothers, 1940. 320 p.

Follett was a major advocate of human interaction concepts. This book, written during the 1920s, sets forth the belief that the output of the industrial structure depends upon comprehension of individual and group incentives. She looks for valid components of organization which would tie together the essential forces of mankind's progress. Collectively the fourteen papers comprising the book consider participation, power, leadership, conciliation, the psychology of control, giving orders, management becoming a profession, individualism in a planned society, responsibility, and constructive conflict. She introduces numerous questions still a part of contemporary studies of organizational behavior and evolution.

718   Frye, Nelson; Seifert, George; and Yaney, Joseph P. "Organizational Change Through Feedback and Research (OD) Efforts." GROUP AND ORGANIZATION STUDIES 2 (September 1977): 296–309.

This article reports that action research was undertaken by a large midwestern utility company to learn what would happen to an organization that was undergoing severe reorganizational stresses while employing organization development techniques to minimize those stresses. The reader learns that OD work included consultation with the top executive, team-building activities, attitude surveys and survey feedback, and vertical communications. The authors conclude that additional research is needed to determine what impact the different OD programs have on an organization.

719   Gardner, John W. SELF-RENEWAL: THE INDIVIDUAL AND THE INNOVATIVE SOCIETY. New York: Harper and Row, 1963. xvi, 141 p.

Gardner writes: "If a society hopes to achieve renewal, it will have to be a hospitable environment for creative men and women. It will also have to produce men and women with the capacity for self-renewal. . . . (R)enewal—of societies or of individuals—depends in some measure on motivation, commitment, conviction, the values men live by, the things that give meaning to their lives. . . . The renewal of societies and organization can go forward only if someone cares. Apathy and lowered motivation are the most widely noted characteristics of a civilization on the downward path. Apathetic men accomplish nothing. Men who believe in nothing change nothing for the better. They renew nothing and heal no one." Chapters in this text include discussions on growth, decay, and renewal, self-renewal, versatility, innovation, obstacles to renewal, tyranny without a tyrant, conditions of renewal, organizing for renewal, individuality and its limits, commitment and meaning, attitudes toward the future, and moral decay and renewal.

720   Giblin, Edward J. "Organization Development: Public Sector and Practice." PUBLIC PERSONNEL MANAGEMENT 5 (March-April 1976): 108-19.

The article indicates that the crisis atmosphere of public agencies may facilitate organizational development programs, but it is questionable whether or not existing OD approaches are applicable to public-sector organizations. The reader learns that resistance against OD programs stems from such inherent problems as 1) yearly rather than long-range planning and 2) conflicts between legislators and high-level administrators that are greater than the management-union conflicts of private industry.

721   Golembiewski, Robert T. "Organization Development in Public Agencies: Perspectives on Theory and Practice." PUBLIC ADMINISTRATION REVIEW 29 (July-August 1969): 367-77. Figures.

This article provides a variety of perspectives on the

characteristics of OD programs and summarizes experience
from a number of OD efforts in public agencies at federal
and local levels. No attempt was made to evaluate the
effectiveness of any particular OD application. The author does note that applications of OD programs in government agencies face some unique problems and that these
unique problems tend to go unrecognized or underrecog-
nized by OD teams in part because students of public administration have been underrepresented on such teams.

722　Golembiewski, Robert T.; Hilles, Rick; and Kagno, Munro S. "A
Longitudinal Study of Flexi-time Effects: Some Consequences of an
OD Structural Intervention." In CURRENT ISSUES AND STRATEGIES
IN ORGANIZATION DEVELOPMENT, edited by W. Warner Burke,
pp. 384-425. New York: Human Sciences Press, 1977.

The authors set forth a flexible work-hours program and
explore some of its chief effects, employing both attitudinal and factual data. They report an unusual kind of
OD intervention, a structural one, and discuss specific
outcomes of a widely applied design on the basis of
anecdotal evidence and without the support of OD values
and methods.

723　Goodman, Roger J. "Public Personnel Administration Requires an OD
Effort." PUBLIC PERSONNEL MANAGEMENT 7 (May-June 1978):
192-97.

Goodman emphasizes the diagnosis and intervention phases
of organization development (OD) in public personnel administration and discusses open system theory, management
by objectives, team building, and intergroup conflict approaches for dealing with administrators and line managers.
The author admits that measuring changes in behavior and
attitudes in public sector organizations will prove difficult,
but suggests that OD will assist in institutionalizing necessary alterations.

724　Grodzins, Morton. "Public Administration and the Science of Human
Relations." PUBLIC ADMINISTRATION REVIEW 11 (Spring 1951):
88-102.

This article comprises 1) a description of some of the hypotheses and conclusions of the science of human relations
in terms of their usefulness to the practicing public administrator; 2) an analysis of the factors limiting the utility
of human relations in administrative practice; and 3) a
critique of the manipulative purposes to which a science
may be put when brought to bear upon problems of human
relations and human management.

725   Kahn, Robert L. "Organizational Development: Some Problems and Proposals." JOURNAL OF APPLIED BEHAVIORAL SCIENCE 10 (October-November-December 1974): 485-502.

> Kahn suggests that the weaknesses of organizational development consist of the repetition of a few unrefined theoretical propositions, an undefined and convenient label for many activities, the process emphasis in most research literature on OD, loss of sight of the structure as the principal target of change, and separation of structure and process. In order to render OD viable, the author proposes to converge the language of OD with the larger realm of organizational theory and practice.

726   Kirkhart, Larry, and White, Orion F., Jr. "The Future of Organization Development." PUBLIC ADMINISTRATION REVIEW 34 (March-April 1974): 129-40.

> The purpose of this article is to assess the future direction of organization development, against what the authors perceive to be the major issue of advanced industrial society—"technicism." Kirkhart and White show that grid OD and situational-emergent OD constitute two contrasting paradigms and that when the differences between them are distinguished, the meaning of and social implications that are inherent to the future evolution of OD are more clearly revealed.

727   Knowles, Malcolm S. "Human Resources Development in OD." PUBLIC ADMINISTRATION REVIEW 34 (March-April 1974): 115-23. Table.

> Knowles describes an andragogical model of human resources development and reviews components of pedagogical and andragogical methods of learning and teaching. He compares assumptions and process elements of pedagogy and andragogy with regard to self-concept, experience, readiness, time perspective, orientation to learning, climate, planning, diagnosis of needs, formulation of objectives, design, activities, and evaluation.

728   Likert, Rensis. THE HUMAN ORGANIZATION: ITS MANAGEMENT AND VALUE. New York: McGraw-Hill Book Co., 1967. ix, 258 p.

> Likert intends this volume for those interested in applying the results of quantitative research to improve the management of the human resources of their enterprises. He describes the nature of science-based management and presents evidence concerning the need for more adequate and accurate data. The author examines productivity and labor systems under different management systems (exploitative, authoritative, benevolent authoritative, consultative, and participative group).

729   McGill, Michael E. "The Evolution of Organization Development 1947-1960." PUBLIC ADMINISTRATION REVIEW 34 (March-April 1974): 98-105.

                McGill reviews the antecedents of organization development, provides both public and private perspectives on OD, discusses the integration of the individual and the organization of OD, and illustrates the first OD program at Esso-Standard Oil during 1957-58.

730   McGregor, Douglas. THE HUMAN SIDE OF ENTERPRISE. New York: McGraw-Hill Book Co., 1960. x, 246 p.

                In a public administration classic, McGregor reveals characteristics of Theory X and Theory Y. Theory X is the traditional view of direction and control while Theory Y includes the integration of individual and organizational goals. According to McGregor, Theory X states that the average human being has an inherent dislike of work and will avoid it if he/she can, that most people must be coerced, controlled, directed, threatened with punishment to get them to put forth adequate effort toward the achievement of organizational objectives, and that the average human being prefers to be directed, wishes to avoid responsibility, has relatively little ambition, and wants security above all. Theory Y assumes that the expenditure of physical and mental effort in work is as natural as play or rest, that external control and the threat of punishment are not the only means for bringing about effort toward organizational objectives, that commitment to objectives is a function of the rewards associated with their achievement, that the average human being learns, under proper conditions, not only to accept but to seek responsibility, that the capacity to exercise a relatively high degree of imagination, ingenuity, and creativity in the solution of organizational problems is widely, not narrowly, distributed in the population, and that under the conditions of modern industrial life, the intellectual potentialities of the average human being are only partially utilized. This text is highly recommended to both students and practitioners of public administration.

731   Marguilies, Newton; Wright, Penny L.; and Scholl, Richard W. "Organization Development Techniques: Their Impact on Change." GROUP AND ORGANIZATION STUDIES 2 (December 1977): 428-48.

                The authors review and evaluate the research on the impact of organizational development interventions. They note that OD facilitates organizational change in a variety of change interventions. OD advocates believe that OD concepts will improve problem solving ability, increase successful adaptation to rapid societal change, and give organization managers the most recent data on management concepts and methods. The authors indicate areas for improved research and offer directions for future research.

732   Maslow, Abraham H. EUPSYCHIAN MANAGEMENT: A JOURNAL. Homewood, Ill.: Richard D. Irwin and Dorsey Press, 1965. xii, 277 p.

The author explains that the word "eupsychia" means "moving toward psychological health." Maslow describes the interrelations between psychological theory and an enlightened, modern management.

733   _____. MOTIVATION AND PERSONALITY. New York: Harper and Brothers, 1954. xiv, 411 p.

Maslow brings together in this text many of his earlier essays in psychology. He discusses elements of a psychological approach to science; problem centering versus means centering in science; holistic-dynamic theory in the study of personality; motivation theory; human motivation; the role of basic need gratification in psychological theory; the instinctoid nature of basic needs; higher and lower needs; psychopathogenesis and the theory of threat; destructiveness instinctoid; the expressive component of behavior; self-actualizing people; cognition of the individual and of the generic; unmotivated and purposeless reactions; psychotherapy, health, and motivation; normality, health, and values; and positive psychology. He warns the reader that these discussions are only a portion of his systematic psychology and that this volume presents "too rosy and optimistic a picture of human nature."

734   _____. TOWARD A PSYCHOLOGY OF BEING. New York: Van Nostrand Reinhold Co., 1968. 240 p.

Maslow writes of a future based on the intrinsic values of humanity and states that "This inner nature, as much as we know of it so far, seems not to be intrinsically evil, but rather either neutral or positively 'good.' What we call evil behavior appears most often to be a secondary reaction to frustration of this intrinsic nature." He analyzes growth and motivation, growth and cognition, creativeness, and human values in developing a larger jurisdiction for psychology. He was one of the initial writers to think in terms of peak experiences and self-actualization. This is a most important book for both students and practitioners of public administration.

735   Morrison, David E. "Stress and the Public Administrator." PUBLIC
       ADMINISTRATION REVIEW 37 (July-August 1977): 407-14.

       The author, a medical doctor, emphasizes that stress is a
       legitimate concern of public administrators. Morrison
       describes stress, its hidden problems, and interpersonal
       pressures and offers some suggestions for dealing with it.

736   Peter, Laurence F., and Hull, Raymond. THE PETER PRINCIPLE.
       New York: William Morrow and Co., 1969. 179 p.

       The authors ask why the human race is floundering in a
       morass of occupational, academic, and administrative
       inefficiency? Peter and Hull, in a delightful, dead-pan,
       humorous manner, reveal why the world is so completely
       fouled up and provide proven techniques for creative
       control of personal, social, and business problems. They
       analyze the reasons for human failure and tell how to
       achieve a state of well-being by avoiding that unwanted,
       ultimate promotion. Students of Freud, Potter, and
       Parkinson will be fascinated by this satirical examination
       of man's tendency to escalate himself to oblivion at his
       level of incompetence.

737   Platt, C. Spencer. "Humanizing Public Administration." PUBLIC
       ADMINISTRATION REVIEW 7 (Summer 1947): 193-99.

       The author believes that better management of human re-
       lations leads to greater organizational productivity and to
       greater satisfaction for organization members. Although
       he maintains that much of the work on developing methods
       and skills for managing human relations is being done in
       private industry (ca. 1947), public agency managers can
       make their agencies more effective through the use of
       similar methods and skills. This essay is interesting for
       its early post-World War II thinking on this subject.

738   Rand, Neil E. "Organization Development: A New Modality for
       Community Mental Health." AMERICAN JOURNAL OF COMMUNITY
       PSYCHOLOGY 6 (April 1978): 157-70.

       This article reviews organization development as being a
       legitimate tool for advancing mental health programs and for
       setting forth objectives of community mental health centers.
       The author contends that organization development is a legiti-
       mate and efficient modality for the community mental health
       practitioner to utilize in reaching large numbers of people
       in establishing positive mental health, primary prevention,
       better interpersonal relations, and personal growth activities.

739   Schein, Edgar H. ORGANIZATIONAL PSYCHOLOGY. Englewood
        Cliffs, N.J.: Prentice-Hall, 1965. xi, 114 p.

        This text reflects the general historical trend from an
        individual-oriented industrial psychology toward a group-
        and-systems-oriented organizational psychology. Chapters
        include the field of organizational psychology; psycho-
        logical problems in organizations; recruitment, selection,
        training, and allocation; organizational man and the
        process of management; groups and intergroup relation-
        ships; the organization as a complex system; and organiza-
        tional effectiveness.

740   Scott, William G. "The Theory of Significant People." PUBLIC AD-
        MINISTRATION REVIEW 33 (July-August 1973): 308-13.

        The main elements in the Theory of Significant People are
        "1) The Significant People are the administrative elite
        who have used mind techniques. This elite is significant
        because (a) they do the significant jobs, and because (b)
        they are superior to everybody else. 2) Their justification
        is not the 'control' of the mass of the people, rather it
        is, to do their jobs better. 3) The moral grounds for using
        mind techniques stems from the significant job: more people
        benefit from more efficient performance of the significant
        job."

741   Simon, Herbert A. "Organizational Man: Rational or Self-Actualizing?"
        PUBLIC ADMINISTRATION REVIEW 33 (July-August 1973): 346-53.

        The author addresses rationality, the need for power,
        work motivation and the need for achievement, and self-
        actualization, or concepts that must be incorporated into
        the design of a human institution if that institution is to
        be viable. Simon concludes: "The society we live in
        maintains a delicate balance between human freedom and
        social constraint. From time to time, we may wish to
        shift that balance, but with due care that we not destroy
        it. We can point to no other society in human history
        that has come even close to ours in offering such a
        balance, not only to the few but to the many. We would
        do well to understand thoroughly how the system is con-
        structed. After we disassemble it, we might want very
        badly to put it together again."

742   Stahl, O. Glenn. "Loyalty, Dissent, and Organizational Health."
        BUREAUCRAT 3 (July 1974): 162-71.

        Stahl indicates that the literature on loyalty and con-
        formity in the organization is authored by professors or
        persons without experience in the domains of large bureau-

cracies. The author believes that loyalty and reasonable conformity are crucial to organized efforts, that "yes" persons and unquestioned conformity are not functional, that loyalty is benefitted by "open" communications, and that subordinates have no choice but to implement decisions once they have been made.

743 Thompson, Victor A. WITHOUT SYMPATHY OR ENTHUSIASM. University: University of Alabama Press, 1975. 137 p.

Thompson examines compassion in the context of the organizational and procedural structures of our modern, technologically oriented bureaucracies. He looks at organizational development, sensitivity training, decentralization, scientific advance, new products and industries, civil rights and liberties, means and ends, political machines and prefectural administration, the ombudsman, and the new developments in public administration.

744 Warrick, D.D. "Applying OD to the Public Sector." PUBLIC PERSONNEL MANAGEMENT 5 (May-June 1976): 186-90.

Warrick asserts that organizational development is likely to be productive in the public sector. He maintains that most obstacles can be resolved with careful planning and that OD has experienced rapid growth in the public sector.

E. MANAGEMENT

745 Barnard, Chester I. THE FUNCTIONS OF THE EXECUTIVE. Cambridge, Mass.: Harvard University Press, 1938. xxxvi, 334 p.

This public administration classic provides a comprehensive theory of cooperative behavior in formal organizations. Barnard elaborates on the concept of an organization as a social system, defines formal and informal organizations, distinguishes between effectiveness and efficiency, incorporates noneconomic motivation into a theory of incentives, states that the unifying principle of cooperative systems is purpose, and reveals that the efficiency of organization relates most directly to the sense that the organization's purpose is proper and important. The author offers a theory of cooperation and organization and studies the functions and methods of operation of executives in formal organizations. Sections include discussions on cooperative systems, the theory and structure of formal organizations, the elements of formal organizations, and the functions of organizations in cooperative systems.

746   Bozeman, Barry. PUBLIC MANAGEMENT AND POLICY ANALYSIS.
        New York: St. Martin's Press, 1979. x, 371 p.

> The author states that he has written this text primarily
> for students in masters in public administration (MPA)
> programs and for advanced undergraduates. He emphasizes
> that this is not a how-to book for he assumes that prac-
> titioners know or will learn "the specifics, the nuts and
> bolts, of their jobs." Bozeman's goal is "to enhance
> the ability of prospective public managers to think system-
> atically about the problems they encounter." Sections
> include public administration in perspective, the organi-
> zational context, public management routines, and policy
> analysis in public organizations.

747   Brown, David S., ed. FEDERAL CONTRIBUTIONS TO MANAGE-
        MENT: EFFECTS ON THE PUBLIC AND PRIVATE SECTORS. New
        York: Praeger Publishers, 1971. 409 p.

> Brown edits a series of papers presented at George Wash-
> ington University which emphasize the positive side of
> government. These studies focus on ways that government
> improves management. Topics include records management,
> management auditing, and advisory committees.

748   Cleveland, Harlan. "The American Public Executive: New Functions,
        New Style, New Purpose." In THEORY AND PRACTICE OF PUBLIC
        ADMINISTRATION: SCOPE, OBJECTIVES, AND METHODS, edited
        by James C. Charlesworth, pp. 165-78. Philadelphia: American
        Academy of Political and Social Science, 1968.

> Cleveland's thesis is that our growing cultural complexity
> is having a fundamental effect on the decision-making
> process, that it is creating the necessity for a wider
> sharing of responsibility in the typical administrative
> situation, and that the process is shifting from the ad-
> ministrative pole to the political pole.

749   Doig, Jameson W. "Managing Subordinates: Constraints and Oppor-
        tunities in Complex Organizations." In PUBLIC ADMINISTRATION
        AND PUBLIC POLICY, edited by H. George Frederickson and Charles
        R. Wise, pp. 161-73. Lexington, Mass.: D.C. Heath and Co., 1977.

> The specific task of this essay is to examine the tools
> available to an administrator for shaping subordinates'
> actions in order that the goals of the organization may
> be achieved. In encountering complex questions of ad-
> ministrative purpose and power, the author believes that
> the most important issue is that of accountability, or to
> whom and to what values are subordinates and their ad-
> ministrators accountable? Doig maintains that the pattern

of actual accountability and control is always a matter for
empirical study and is most usefully couched in terms of
degrees of control.

750   Drucker, Peter F. "Managing the Public Service Institution." PUBLIC
INTEREST 33 (Fall 1973): 43-60.

Drucker indicates that service institutions, such as schools
and universities, hospitals, and public utilities, are becoming an important component of our society. Businesses
are paid for satisfying the customer; service institutions are
usually compensated from a budget allocation. In a budget-
based institution, "results" suggest a larger budget while
"performance" is the capacity to hold or to increase one's
budget. The development of understandable objectives and
aims from the description of function and mission is required for success in a service institution.

751   _____. THE PRACTICE OF MANAGEMENT. New York: Harper and
Brothers, 1954. ix, 404 p.

The initial aim of this text is to narrow the gap between
what can be done and what is being done in the practice
of management. Drucker pens this book for the citizen
without direct management experience because he believes
that the citizen needs to know what management is, what
it does, and what he can rightfully expect from it. He
also aims this volume as a guide for people in major management positions, enabling them to examine their own
work and performance, to diagnose their weaknesses and
to improve their own effectiveness and the results of the
enterprise for which they are responsible. Sections include discussions of the nature of management, managing
a business, managing managers, the structure of management, the management of worker and work, and the responsibilities of management.

752   Fayol, Henri. GENERAL AND INDUSTRIAL MANAGEMENT. Translated from the French edition by Constance Storrs. London: Sir Isaac
Pitman and Sons, 1949. xxvii, 110 p.

In this administration classic, Fayol sets forth his ideas in
four parts, including conceptual analyses of the necessity
and possibility of teaching management, of principles and
elements of management, of personal observations and experience, and of lessons of the war. The author's general
principles of management include division of work, authority, discipline, unity of command, unity of direction,
subordination of individual interests to the general interest,
remuneration, centralization, scalar chain or line of authority, order, equity, stability of tenure of personnel,

initiative, and esprit de corps. This text is an original in administrative conceptualization.

753   Fox, Douglas M. MANAGING THE PUBLIC'S INTEREST: A RESULTS ORIENTED APPROACH. New York: Holt, Rinehart and Winston, 1979. xiv, 304 p. Paper.

This textbook includes actual examples from all levels of government, regions of the country, and types of agencies. The author hopes "that the approaches we discuss are not academic exercises, but managerial methods that have relevance to the real world of government." Chapter headings include program planning, reorganizing for re-sults, output-oriented supervision, management by objec-tives, program evaluation, budgeting for results, produc-tivity, personnel performance appraisal, and putting re-sults oriented approaches together.

754   Gates, Bruce L. "Better Policy Administration Through Management Science?" In PUBLIC ADMINISTRATION AND PUBLIC POLICY, edited by H. George Frederickson and Charles R. Wise, pp. 147-58. Lexington, Mass.: D.C. Heath and Co., 1977.

The purpose of this essay is to explore the past and future role of the management sciences in the administration of public policy. Gates discusses the theory and practice of management science, management science and administra-tion, the pragmatism of management science, knowledge, rationality, and organizational systems, and management science in the 1970s. He concludes that the utility of the management sciences in the public sector is increasingly seen as being dependent on factors outside the limited jurisdiction of management sciences.

755   Golembiewski, Robert T.; Gibson, Frank; and Miller, Gerald, eds. MANAGERIAL BEHAVIOR AND ORGANIZATION DEMANDS: MAN-AGEMENT AS A LINKING OF LEVELS OF INTERACTION. 2d ed. Itasca, Ill.: F.E. Peacock Publishers, 1978. viii, 482 p.

Selections in this book of readings are arranged according to the number of employees managed in organizations. The editors include essays based on managing by ones and twos, tens and twenties, hundreds, and thousands. This volume attempts to bring to students and to practitioners of administration a representative slice of the several relevant managerial literatures.

756   Golembiewski, Robert T., and White, Michael, eds. CASES IN PUBLIC MANAGEMENT. Chicago: Rand McNally College Publishing Co., 1976. xlv, 236 p.

The goal of this collection of readings is to provide cases from public agencies that will serve as catalysts for managerially relevant analysis and discussion. The editors indicate that all cases in this volume deal with a problem or situation that has existed or that now exists in some public organization. They provide a useful introductory guide to this series of case studies.

757   Gross, Bertram M. ORGANIZATIONS AND THEIR MANAGING. New York: Free Press, 1968. xxxix, 708 p.

This volume is a condensed, one-volume edition of Gross's THE MANAGING OF ORGANIZATIONS (1964). This treatment views any organization as a "dynamic people-resource system operating at specific locations in space and time." A major purpose is to provide a "general systems language" to help students and practitioners learn more about the guidance of real-life organizations. Gross discusses the inevitability of conflict, the imperatives of power, and the persistence of many time-honored administrative fallacies. He presents a dynamic view of system structure with internal conflict, tension, and change. The author analyzes five guidance processes (decision making, communicating, planning, activating, and evaluating). Seven dimensions of performance include satisfying interests, producing outputs, using resources efficiently or profitably, investing in the system, mobilizing resources, observing codes, and behaving rationally. This is a comprehensive guide to the management of organizations.

758   Helco, Hugh. A GOVERNMENT OF STRANGERS: EXECUTIVE POLITICS IN WASHINGTON. Washington, D.C.: Brookings Institution, 1977. 272 p.

Helco explores the important but obscure process by which high-ranking political appointees and bureaucrats interact with each other. The author concentrates on the people themselves rather than on particular institutions of formal divisions of power. He interviews some 200 present and former government executives, from the Hoover administration to the Carter administration. Helco seeks to know who these political appointees and bureaucrats are and how they came to positions of power. He explores why some people in government do better than others in getting what they want. And finally, he probes the extent to which any political leader can hope to guide what government does by controlling the people (i.e., bureaucrats) who do it.

759   Likert, Rensis. NEW PATTERNS OF MANAGEMENT. New York:
       McGraw-Hill Book Co., 1961. vii, 279 p.

       The author intends this volume for persons concerned with
       the problems of organizing human resources and activity,
       including those who are actively engaged in management
       and supervision and students of administration and organi-
       zation. Likert presents a theory of organization based
       on the management principles and practices of managers
       who are achieving the best results in American business
       and government.

760   McGregor, Douglas. THE PROFESSIONAL MANAGER. Edited by
       Caroline McGregor and Warren G. Bennis. New York: McGraw-
       Hill Book Co., 1967. xvi, 202 p.

       Four themes dominate this book, edited by McGregor's
       widow and a colleague. The importance of theory, vul-
       nerability of practitioners to emotional reactions which
       are never adequately dealt with and which interfere with
       perceptions of reality, the transactional nature of influence
       and that "win-lose" conflicts need not be sum-zero situa-
       tions, and organizational efforts allowing diversity and in-
       congruities and collaboration and teamwork are themes of
       this work. Chapters include discussions of the manager
       and the human sciences, managerial behavior, improving
       organizational effectiveness, power and control, and
       teamwork and tension.

761   McTighe, John J. "Management Strategies to Deal with Shrinking
       Resources." PUBLIC ADMINISTRATION REVIEW 39 (January-February
       1979): 86-90.

       McTighe describes factors affecting strategy development
       (political attitudes, organizational mission, cause of re-
       source decline, personnel system, centralization, clientele,
       and past stability) and offers a prescription for scaling
       down the organization (examine organization mission, ex-
       amine marginal investments, install rational choice mecha-
       nisms, encourage employee participation, and retain open-
       ness of the organization). The author concludes that this
       article "provides no easy solutions to the problems facing
       government managers throughout the country in this era
       of limits."

762   Murphy, Thomas P., and Pak, Chong M. "Management Training for
       Executives: The Federal Executive Institute Experience." SOUTHERN
       REVIEW OF PUBLIC ADMINISTRATION 2 (March 1979): 436-47.

       Murphy and Pak state that the most important ingredient
       for a successful management development program for

executives is the environment of the executive's organization. They observe that President Carter's proposal for a
Senior Executive Service (SES) calls for a review of the
basic components of an effective executive development
program for top federal managers. The authors emphasize
that "governmental training or educational delivery systems
for senior executives should not be centralized in such a
way that all executives must take a specific curriculum
from a specific institution."

763   Nigro, Felix A. "Managers in Government and Labor Relations."
        PUBLIC ADMINISTRATION REVIEW 38 (March–April 1978): 180-84.

        Nigro states that "perhaps the most harmful current illusion
        about public employee unions is that they are the primary
        cause of the financial difficulties of many cities." He
        concludes that "the principal reasons for the financial
        difficulties of the cities, however, are their greatly
        diminished tax base and the straitjacket of constitutional
        and statutory limitations on their taxing power."

764   Scanlan, Burt K. PRINCIPLES OF MANAGEMENT AND ORGANIZA-
        TIONAL BEHAVIOR. New York: John Wiley and Sons, 1973. vi,
        512 p.

        This book is devoted to the study of management thought.
        Chapters include historical development of management
        thought, planning, management by objectives, problem
        analysis and decision making, quantitative tools for de-
        cision making, organization through departmentation, de-
        centralization, delegation, organizational climate and
        philosophy, human motivation, and management philosophy.

765   Starling, Grover. MANAGING THE PUBLIC SECTOR. Homewood,
        Ill.: Dorsey Press, 1977. xvii, 473 p.

        Starling's textbook emphasizes a practitioner's approach to
        the study of public administration. He prefaces the text
        by stressing that "the main body of this book differs from
        most of the literature in that it provides how-to-do-it
        techniques that can be applied immediately in any organi-
        zation at any level." Parts include the environment of
        public administration, the management of government pro-
        grams, financial management, and the management of
        people.

766   Stover, Carl F. "Changing Patterns in the Philosophy of Management."
        PUBLIC ADMINISTRATION REVIEW 18 (Winter 1958): 21-27.

        Stover addresses the meanings of philosophy, philosophies
        in practice, and the relationship between good management
        and sound philosophical views.

767   Taylor, Frederick Winslow. THE PRINCIPLES OF SCIENTIFIC MAN-
      AGEMENT. New York: Frederick Taylor, 1911. Reprint. New
      York: W.W. Norton and Co., 1967. 144 p.

      This brief essay by the founder of scientific management
      has served for over fifty years as a primer for admini-
      strators and for students of managerial techniques. Although
      scientific management was developed primarily as a system
      for increasing productivity in industry, its principles have
      been applied to all kinds of large-scale enterprises, in-
      cluding operations within departments and agencies of the
      federal government.

F. FUTURE ORGANIZATION CHANGES

768   Aldrich, Howard E. ORGANIZATIONS AND ENVIRONMENTS.
      Englewood Cliffs, N.J.: Prentice-Hall, 1979. 384 p.

      This work deals with organizational change. Each chapter
      covers a different aspect of the conditions under which
      organizations change. One highlight is that politically
      sensitive items, often not treated, are presented throughout
      this work. The author attempts to "give students an ap-
      preciation of the conceptual and methodological issues
      facing organizational sociology."

769   Argyris, Chris. ON ORGANIZATIONS OF THE FUTURE. Beverly
      Hills, Calif.: Sage Publications, 1973. 48 p.

      In this short manuscript, Argyris discusses organizational
      deterioration as a major force for change, organizational
      research and interpersonal competence, organizational
      change in the executive system, and guideposts for or-
      ganizational structures. He concludes: "The medium is
      the message of lasting change; and in organizations, the
      medium is human behavior." Argyris offers insightful hints
      for "tinkering with the system."

770   Biggart, Nicole Woolsey. "The Creative-Destructive Process of Or-
      ganizational Change: The Case of the Post Office." ADMINISTRA-
      TIVE SCIENCE QUARTERLY 22 (September 1977): 410-26.

      Biggart asserts that studies of organizational change tend
      to center on identifying the reasons for change while ig-
      noring the process of change. This article deals with the
      destructive aspects of reorganization that must take place
      if change is to be successful.

771   Caldwell, Lynton K. "Managing the Transition to Post-Modern Society."
      PUBLIC ADMINISTRATION REVIEW 35 (November-December 1975):
      567-72.

The author maintains that U.S. society is entering a period of major historical transition. He describes these transitions as periods of intellectual transformation, of changes in concepts, images, and values. Caldwell characterizes "modern" concepts in the following terms: popular rights, autonomous egoism, progressive expansion, economic primacy, technological imperative, and permanent revolution. He characterizes "post-modern" concepts in the following terms: social responsibilities, organic interdependence, controlled growth, ecological necessity, selective innovation, and dynamic equilibrium. This is a most interesting look into America's administrative future.

772   Carroll, James D. "Service, Knowledge, and Choice: The Future as Post-Industrial Administration." PUBLIC ADMINISTRATION REVIEW 35 (November-December 1975): 578-81.

Carroll believes that the future of public administration is post-industrial administration. He characterizes post-industrial administration in terms of service, knowledge, and choice. He writes: "Administration is knowledge. Knowledge is power. Administration is power." According to the author, the ideology of "redistribution" of income and the ideology of economic growth contribute to the welfare state as it has developed in the United States.

773   Chapman, Richard L., and Cleaveland, Frederic N. "The Changing Character of the Public Service and the Administrator of the 1980s." PUBLIC ADMINISTRATION REVIEW 33 (July-August 1973): 358-66.

Four major trends are seen as challenges to the public service today, and as important determinants of the public service in the next decade: 1) pressures for centralization and for decentralization; 2) unionization of the public service; 3) increased citizen involvement; and 4) the impact of technological change.

774   Cleveland, Harlan. THE FUTURE EXECUTIVE: A GUIDE FOR TO-MORROW'S MANAGERS. New York: Harper and Row, 1972. 144 p.

Cleveland's point is that the future is horizontal and that there is a bright future for complexity in bureaucratic environments. He concludes that there is a blurring of public and private responsibilities in the United States and that a style of complexity is emerging. This is a very useful volume for understanding the dynamics of leadership potentials and problems in the 1980s.

775   Drucker, Peter F. THE AGE OF DISCONTINUITY: GUIDELINES TO
       OUR CHANGING SOCIETY. New York: Harper and Row, 1968.
       xiii, 402 p.

            Drucker maintains that major discontinuities exist in four
            areas. He believes that genuinely new technologies are
            upon us, that we face major changes in the world's
            economy, that the political matrix of social and economic
            life is changing quickly, and that knowledge during the
            past few decades has become the central capital, the
            cost center, and the crucial resource of the economy.
            Sections include discussions of knowledge technologies,
            the international economy, a society of organizations,
            and the knowledge society. The author does not project
            trends; he examines discontinuities. He does not forecast
            tomorrow; he looks at today. Drucker concludes: "No
            one needs to be told that the central question we face
            with respect to man's future is not what it shall be, but
            whether it shall be. If we do not survive, the concerns
            of this book will, of course, perish with us. But if we
            do survive, its concerns will become our tasks."

776   Dunsire, A. "Administrative Doctrine and Administrative Change."
       PUBLIC ADMINISTRATION BULLETIN 15 (December 1973): 39-56.

            Dunsire notes that "overall comprehensive strategy plan-
            ning" is an important element in research on administrative
            change. He posits that commitment to specialization is
            enhanced when there is philosophical or doctrinal change.
            Dunsire indicates that longer chains of political control,
            less unresponsiveness, less adaptability, decreased coordi-
            nation, and more administrative fragmentation may result
            from an increase in size and specialization.

777   Elazar, Daniel J. "Toward Federal-State Partnerships in Science and
       Technology." STATE GOVERNMENT 48 (Spring 1975): 131-35.

            Elazar writes that states should develop new roles in tech-
            nology and science and cooperate with federal units in
            policy making and implementation. The article discusses
            dissemination of information, innovation, control of activi-
            ties, and mutual distribution of resources in federal-state
            arrangements. Prototypes for sharing in distribution are
            income-sharing, grants-in-aid, and councils of government
            such as the Appalachian Regional Commission. The four-
            state and federal Delaware River Basin Commission is an
            example of cooperation in control and improvement.

778   Frederickson, H. George. "Public Administration in the 1970s: De-
       velopments and Directions." PUBLIC ADMINISTRATION REVIEW 36
       (September-October 1976): 564-76. Tables.

In an excellent overview of the history of public administration, the author examines change and responsiveness, rationality, management-worker and management-citizen relations, and the structure of administration.

779   Gates, Bruce L. "Knowledge Management in the Technological Society: Government by Indicator." PUBLIC ADMINISTRATION REVIEW 35 (November-December 1975): 589-93.

Gates cites knowledge management techniques as a means of improving organizational responsiveness to societal demands or needs. He sees such techniques as altering the nature and locus of political dialogue within and between societal institutions. Gates maintains that "government by indicator" is the result. He concludes that the values inherent in the indicator's perspective on reality are subject to political modification.

780   Goerl, George Frederick. "Cybernetics, Professionalization, and Knowledge Management: An Exercise in Assumptive Theory." PUBLIC ADMINISTRATION REVIEW 35 (November-December 1975): 581-88.

This article examines facets of the cybernetic or "self-guiding" society. According to the author, a self-guiding society possesses the ability to determine and change its course of action. Goerl believes that societal guidance is fundamental to society's effort to acquire the capability to "realize itself" through setting and achieving goals. He concludes that "professionalization symbolizes the importance of non-hierarchial authority needed for full and free communication while it also legitimates the authority of the knowledge expert." Goerl emphasizes that the legislator or politician has become dependent upon the expert's information.

781   Gordon, Joel. "Operating Statistics as a Tool of Management." PUBLIC ADMINISTRATION REVIEW 4 (Summer 1944): 189-96.

The author discussses the formulation of the operating research program (including progress reporting and progress analysis, statistical measurement and analysis of administrative performance, and statistical measurement and analysis of program results), and techniques of handling operating data (including problems in collection of data, and problems in compiling, analyzing, and presenting data).

782   Gulick, Luther. "Democracy and Administration Face the Future." PUBLIC ADMINISTRATION REVIEW 37 (November-December 1977): 706-11.

"As we face the future, we in public administration face a fundamental need to restructure our analysis not only of our political responsibilities, but also our understanding of man as a social animal in a changing world. . . . Democracy will survive, though to do so it must be greatly modified in concept and in execution."

783   Hafstad, Lawrence R. "Science and Administration." PUBLIC AD-MINISTRATION REVIEW 11 (Winter 1951): 10-16.

The author suggests that the effectiveness of government in the sponsorship of scientific research and development will be enhanced if people concerned with research administration would 1) provide incentives to persons entering the scientific field and create opportunities for the best of them to emerge as project leaders, 2) encourage the establishment of budget and accounting procedures uniquely adapted to scientific research and development which will make possible both stability and flexibility, and 3) recognize that pure research can be coordinated only by the scientists themselves, but that applied research can be coordinated by experts who are in a position to evaluate the relative worth of particular projects.

784   Henry, Nicholas L. "Bureaucracy, Technology, and Knowledge Management." PUBLIC ADMINISTRATION REVIEW 35 (November-December 1975): 572-78.

Henry focuses on public policies for knowledge management and higher education for public administration. He believes that public administrators should have a greater voice in prescribing policy for knowledge management. He insists that a facet of knowledge management even more germane to public administrators than policy prescription is the education of public administrators. Henry emphasizes that education represents an area in which the efforts of scholars can be felt with greater immediacy. Public administration is a unique field and "a key to its uniqueness lies in its conception of the role knowledge plays in the bureaucratic policy-making process in technological societies."

785   _____. "Knowledge Management: A New Concern for Public Administration." PUBLIC ADMINISTRATION REVIEW 34 (May-June 1974): 189-96.

Henry contends that knowledge is assuming a new importance in public policy making in the United States and that there is a need for new policies to deal with the management of knowledge. He maintains that new technological and decision-making uses of information affect not only public policy outcomes, but also the public policy process itself. He concludes that current knowledge management policies are inadequate.

786   Heydebrand, Wolf. "Administration of Social Change." PUBLIC ADMINISTRATION REVIEW 24 (September 1964): 163-65.

Heydebrand writes that Charles Lindblom's "The Science of 'Muddling Through'" thesis (PUBLIC ADMINISTRATION REVIEW, 1959) and Yehezkel Dror's criticisms of the Lindblom piece (which adjoins this article) are inadequate: "In general, it can be said that 'muddling through' and gradualism are clearly less authoritarian forms of problem-solving than the insistence on achieving specific objectives by specific means. Yet the question remains whether gradual, incremental change is only a form of adaptation which leaves basically intact what ought to be changed. Though the politics of 'freedom now' possesses unrealistic overtones, it nevertheless exposes the failure of incremental change to represent satisfactory change. In other words, neither Lindblom nor Dror deal adequately with the problem of levels on which change may be conceptualized."

787   Kaufman, Herbert. "The Direction of Organizational Evolution." PUBLIC ADMINISTRATION REVIEW 33 (July-August 1973): 300-307.

The author recognizes that there will be a broadening of the number of groups and values that are accommodated in large organizations, that there will be increased inclusiveness and interdependence, and that a great many of the complaints about large organizations will continue into the next century and probably well beyond. Kaufman writes: "We need to know not merely what will happen in the immediate future, but why it happens, or we can never improve our understanding."

788   _____. THE LIMITS OF ORGANIZATIONAL CHANGE. University: University of Alabama Press, 1971. 124 p.

Kaufman discusses why organizations tend not to change, involuntary and voluntary factors causing organizations to change, and reasons why organizational change is dampened and concludes that the line separating the advocates of total changes from those who favor piecemeal, gradual change may, in practice, be rather thin. Proponents of large-scale change usually find that they have to settle for more continuity than they bargained for, that the older the organization, the more flexible it typically is, that the larger the organization, the more flexible it is likely to be, and that larger organizations are likely to provide more scope for individual preferences and unconventional ideas.

789   Keating, William Thomas. "On Managing Ignorance." PUBLIC AD-
       MINISTRATION REVIEW 35 (November-December 1975): 593-97.

       Keating writes that the most recent and significant illus-
       tration of the trend of extending governmental authority
       into new areas of human activity is the emerging accep-
       tance of public responsibility for protecting and enhancing
       the quality of the natural environment. He states that it
       will be difficult to identify and to evaluate the environ-
       mental side effects of a technology prior to its implemen-
       tation. The author notes that nuclear energy has been
       developed despite the absence of complete knowledge of
       its full environmental costs and risks. This article is
       especially interesting in light of events at the Three Mile
       Island nuclear facility in 1979.

790   Krislov, Joseph. "The Supply of Arbitrators: Prospects for the 1980's."
       MONTHLY LABOR REVIEW 99 (October 1976): 27-30.

       This article relates that the American Arbitration Associa-
       tion (AAA) and the Federal Mediation and Conciliation
       Service (FMCS) are the two major agencies supplying
       lists of arbitrators. An attempt is made to develop a
       reasonable estimate of the number of arbitration awards
       now and the number expected by 1980. Krislov believes
       that there will be over 40,000 awards in the early 1980s.
       He indicates that the actual pattern in 1980 will probably
       include both increases in the number of arbitrators and
       more intensified use of a small number of arbitrators.

791   Lambright, W. Henry, and Flynn, Paul J. "Bureaucratic Politics and
       Technological Change in Local Government." JOURNAL OF URBAN
       ANALYSIS 4 (1977): 93-118.

       In order for innovation in local public service to occur,
       bureaucrats must be motivated by an external threat or
       opportunity from other government levels. The authors
       maintain that the solution to a problem must enhance
       bureaucratic self-interest. To use innovations, agencies
       assure employees that jobs will not be endangered; they
       seek outside pressures to keep local forces aligned; and
       they deliberately dampen the innovation to assure accep-
       tance by the coalition.

792   Lindblom, Charles E. "Contexts for Change and Strategy: A Reply."
       PUBLIC ADMINISTRATION REVIEW 24 (September 1964): 157-58.

       The author responds to the major objections that Yehezkel
       Dror brings against Lindblom's model of decision making
       via 'muddling through' ("The Science of 'Muddling Through'"
       PUBLIC ADMINISTRATION REVIEW, 1959). Lindblom

notes that his 1959 version of the 'muddling through' was further refined and detailed as the strategy of disjointed incrementalism in his later work, A STRATEGY OF DECISION (Free Press of Glencoe, 1963).

793   McCaffery, Jerry. "Knowledge Management in Fiscal Policy Formation." PUBLIC ADMINISTRATION REVIEW 35 (November–December 1975): 598-602.

McCaffery examines policy making in fiscal management in order to see how the theme of knowledge as power occurs in budgeting, taxing, and managing aggregate demand. He notes that fiscal policy making is characterized by the presence of ambiguity, policy making by experts, and the dominance of expertise. The author emphasizes that the role of expertise is crucial, that the problem in taxation is complexity, and that Congress acts as a broker for competing tax experts and tax interests.

794   Patti, Rino. "The New Scientific Management: Systems Management for Social Welfare." PUBLIC WELFARE 33 (Spring 1975): 23-31.

Patti emphasizes that administrators in the social welfare field should design and implement management training programs according to organizational and political conditions. The author recognizes the importance of systems management perspectives and technology in the administration of social welfare programs. Social welfare administrators need specialized training in theoretical, empirical, and practical skills.

795   Price, Don K. GOVERNMENT AND SCIENCE: THEIR DYNAMIC RELATION IN AMERICAN DEMOCRACY. New York: New York University Press, 1954. ix, 203 p.

Price posits that "American science in relation to government is in an uncomfortable pair of dilemmas. The main article of its faith is academic freedom, which would clearly be extinguished by a Communist triumph. . . . Yet it is now obvious to everyone that the structure of scientific research in American universities and industry has come to depend heavily on federal grants and federal contracts." Chapters include discussions of the republican revolution, freedom or responsibility, federalism by contract, security and publicity risks, the machinery of advice, and the structure of policy.

796   _____. "1984 and Beyond: Social Engineering or Political Values?" In AMERICAN PUBLIC ADMINISTRATION: PAST, PRESENT, FUTURE, edited by Frederick C. Mosher, pp. 233-52. University: University of Alabama Press, 1975.

The author summarizes the prospects for social engineering or political values in 1984 and beyond in the following manner: "A scientific era breeds its own types of superstition. In our contemporary Orwellian mythology, 1984 is the year of the Apocalypse, when political freedom and humane values are to be destroyed by the dark angels of technology. So you may suppose the title of this essay is to suggest a deadline for doomsday. Nothing could be further from my mind."

797   _____. THE SCIENTIFIC ESTATE. Cambridge, Mass.: Harvard University Press, 1965. xi, 323 p.

Price is concerned about the problem of the relation of science and scientists to the political ideas and the constitutional system of the United States, not as Jefferson or Franklin thought it would turn out to be, but as it has developed since 1787. The author believes that the scientific revolution is moving the public and private sectors closer together, is bringing a new order of complexity into the administration of public affairs, and is upsetting our system of checks and balances.

798   Ream, Norman J. "The Computer and Its Impact on Public Organization." PUBLIC ADMINISTRATION REVIEW 28 (November-December 1968): 494-503.

Ream concludes: "A failure by public administrators to react affirmatively in using computers more effectively could result in the strangulation of government through the information 'weight' resulting from rapid population growth, the increasing character of the scientific social economic climate, and the need for government to lead and not just to react to resulting demand."

799   Riggs, Fred W. "Administration and a Changing World Environment." PUBLIC ADMINISTRATION REVIEW 28 (July-August 1968): 348-61.

The purpose of this article is to call attention to the extraordinarily difficult dilemmas in which thoughtful military and civilian public officials find themselves today. Riggs argues that our changing world environment compels us to raise questions about governmental legitimacy, but that we are handicapped in doing so by some fundamental conceptual ambiguities. These include: the term public administration itself, the relation between a bureaucracy and its political context, the concept and organization of legitimacy, the American tradition of constitutionalism, responsiveness and responsibility in government, bureaucratic power and performance, and the revolutionary principle.

800   Simon, Herbert A. "Applying Information Technology to Organization
        Design." PUBLIC ADMINISTRATION REVIEW 33 (May-June 1973):
        268-78.

> Simon writes that the major problems of governmental or-
> ganization today are not problems of departmentalization
> and coordination of operating units, but ones of organizing
> information storage and information processing--not problems
> of the division of labor, but problems of the factorization
> of decision making. He concludes that these organizational
> problems are best attacked by examining the information
> system in abstraction from agency and department structure.

801   Veillette, Paul T. "The Impact of Mechanization on Administration."
        PUBLIC ADMINISTRATION REVIEW 17 (Autumn 1957): 231-37.

> This article represents an attempt to place the relationship
> of mechanization to administration in a perspective that
> will be meaningful to both practitioner and academician.
> The problem is approached from three standpoints: 1) the
> general evolution of data processing; 2) the direction of
> its future development in state government; and 3) the
> impact of this development on organization and administration.

802   Whisler, Thomas L. THE IMPACT OF COMPUTERS ON ORGANIZA-
        TIONS. New York: Frederick A. Praeger, 1970. 188 p.

> Whisler focuses on the organizational impact of the computer
> emphasizing that it is in organizations that the confrontations
> between man and computer occur and that computer perfor-
> mance can be measured in its usefulness to organizations.

803   White, Orion F., Jr. "Social Change and Administrative Adaptation."
        In TOWARD A NEW PUBLIC ADMINISTRATION: THE MINNOWBROOK
        PERSPECTIVE, edited by Frank Marini, pp. 59-83. Scranton, Pa.:
        Chandler Publishing Co., 1971.

> White analyzes and illustrates some important ways in
> which our society is changing, indicates how these changes
> are affecting political and administrative reality, and
> urges the development of a cluster of adaptations through
> confrontation instead of the politics of contract and bar-
> gain. He suggests the "politics of love" and "adaptation
> by confrontation" as alternatives to "politics by contract"
> and "adaptation as conflict."

Chapter 6

PUBLIC PERSONNEL ADMINISTRATION

A. GENERAL SELECTIONS

804   Baker, Bruce R., and Danielson, William F. "Recruitment." In
       POLICE PERSONNEL ADMINISTRATION, edited by O. Glenn Stahl
       and Richard A. Staufenberger, pp. 59-68. Washington, D.C.: Police
       Foundation, 1974.

       The authors discuss the labor market, salaries and benefits,
       the numbers of police positions for which to recruit, re-
       cruitment of minority persons, separation rates, impact of
       standards, job attractions, agency reputation, selection
       procedure, and recruitment planning techniques in exami-
       ning conditions affecting police personnel recruitment and
       the elements of effective recruitment.

805   Benveniste, Guy. THE POLITICS OF EXPERTISE. San Francisco:
       Boyd and Fraser Publishing Co., 1977. 276 p.

       Benveniste provides an integrated overview of bureau-
       cratic phenomena, illustrating that bureaucracies are in
       a state of crisis, that people and organizations operate
       in fear and seek protection through rules and regulation,
       that red tape is inevitable in these circumstances, that
       spread-organizations control other organizations as a de-
       fensive strategy, that corruption weakens organizations,
       and that clients suffer as a result of corruption. The em-
       phasis is on why people behave the way that they do,
       what has been done about it, and what might be done.

806   Bower, Joseph L. "Effective Public Management." HARVARD BUSI-
       NESS REVIEW 55 (March-April 1977): 131-40.

       This article suggests that to be efficient in the public
       sector, a manager must be a politician. The public sector
       manager influences the purpose, structure, and people of
       organizations; but he must not bid for political power.

Because time is short, the tools limited, and the political context consuming, good public managers are in short supply.

807   Brown, David S. "The Staff Man Looks in the Mirror." PUBLIC AD-
        MINISTRATION REVIEW 23 (June 1963): 67-73.

        This article reports what staff persons say are their chief
        satisfactions and dissatisfactions, how they feel their work
        is seen by others, measured, and evaluated, how they
        evaluate the importance of their work, and how they try
        to solve the problems they encounter.

808   Campbell, Alan K. "Revitalizing the Civil Service." NATIONAL
        CIVIC REVIEW 67 (February 1978): 76-79.

        The author maintains that federal employees are more
        educated, experienced, and capable than ever before
        while competition for federal jobs is becoming increasingly
        keen. This article notes that civil service does not rely
        simply on competition to employ the best person for a
        particular job. Civil service personnel are seeking top
        candidates and encouraging them to enter federal service.
        The reader learns that means of discovering qualified
        candidates are the Presidential Management Intern Program
        and the Cooperative Education Program.

809   Cayer, N. Joseph. PUBLIC PERSONNEL ADMINISTRATION IN THE
        UNITED STATES. New York: St. Martin's Press, 1975. 178 p.

        Cayer describes the political environment of public per-
        sonnel administration, the evolution of the personnel
        system, the operation of the merit system, the processes
        and human aspects of public personnel administration,
        rights and duties of public employees, the role of public
        personnel administration in a democracy, and cross-national
        variations in personnel administration.

810   Cornog, Geoffrey Y. "The Personnel Turnover Concept: A Reappraisal."
        PUBLIC ADMINISTRATION REVIEW 17 (Autumn 1957): 247-56.
        Table.

        Cornog defines the concept of turnover, evaluates the
        concept as an aid to understanding the turnover process
        and as a concept in the study of organization, probes the
        causes of difficulties with the turnover concept, and con-
        cludes that while the traditional definition of turnover is
        structural and procedural, it obviously relates to a funda-
        mental process of organization--maintaining the indispen-
        sable services of organization members.

811   Coven, Mark. "Public Employees." HARVARD CIVIL RIGHTS--CIVIL
        LIBERTIES REVIEW 12 (Summer 1977): 559-84.

        Coven's analysis states that the judicial distinction be-
        tween policymaking and nonpolicymaking employees is an
        unreasonably narrow view of the constitutional importance
        of the words and deeds of high-level officials, disregarding
        a historical function of the first amendment. He suggests
        that there be greater judicial sensitivity of the inherent
        values of the first amendment if the public official's detri-
        mental comments on job performance assume more impor-
        tance than the public and political processes. The author
        points out that the first amendment's right to know is
        supportive of public accountability and representative
        democracy.

812   Cummings, Milton C., Jr.; Jennings, M. Kent; and Kilpatrick, Franklin P.
        "Federal and Nonfederal Employees: A Comparative Social-Occupational
        Analysis." PUBLIC ADMINISTRATION REVIEW 27 (December 1967):
        393-402. Tables.

        In this article, comparisons are made between national
        samples of federal civilian employees and nonfederal em-
        ployees in key social and occupational characteristics.

813   Dodson, Charles, and Haskew, Barbara. "Why Public Workers Stay."
        PUBLIC PERSONNEL MANAGEMENT 5 (March-April 1976): 132-38.

        Dodson and Haskew discovered that the percentage of
        state employees with high job satisfaction was small. The
        job turnover rate was approximately 30 percent as public
        employees are not sufficiently reinforced by pay benefits,
        personal friendships, company loyalty, and other job oppor-
        tunities. About 33 percent of the state employees ex-
        perienced a high degree of job satisfaction and motivation
        while 57 percent found little reason for remaining on the
        state payroll.

814   Dotson, Arch. "The Emerging Doctrine of Privilege in Public Employ-
        ment." PUBLIC ADMINISTRATION REVIEW 15 (Spring 1955): 77-88.

        The main elements of this doctrine are the law of office,
        the rule of tenure, the rule of political neutrality, the
        rule of association and collective bargaining, and the
        rule of loyalty. Dotson examines the present context of
        the doctrine as public law and public policy. He notes
        that the function of the doctrine is to define the relation-
        ship between the state and the citizen when the latter is
        employed by the former. By terms of "the doctrine of
        privilege," public employment has been converted into a
        legal privilege. This is a very insightful essay on the future
        of public employment as seen in the mid-1950s.

815   _____. "A General Theory of Public Employment." PUBLIC AD-
MINISTRATION REVIEW 16 (Summer 1956): 197-211.

> Three principles embody the essential standards of the
> author's proposed theory of public agency. He designates
> "democratic effectiveness," "compensatory right," and
> "equitable advantage" as principles. Dotson maintains
> that public employment is a public relationship, indicating
> that it is and must be a relation between the state and
> segment of the body politic. The author claims "that the
> public employee has no 'privilege' in his job, and if he
> strikes, this action cannot automatically be regarded as
> refusal 'to serve the people.' Strikes are caused by a
> breakdown in the normal means of adjustment of labor
> disputes, and there is no reason why such failures should
> not occur in the public service."

816   Entwisle, Doris R., and Walton, John. "Observations on the Span of
Control." ADMINISTRATIVE SCIENCE QUARTERLY 5 (March 1961):
522-33. Tables.

> The authors present data on spans of control in colleges
> and small companies, review classical explanations of
> limits on span of control, suggest an explanation based
> on clique behavior, and conclude that sizes of spans are
> very similar and also that there is a small positive cor-
> relation between the size of organization and the size of
> span.

817   Frederickson, H. George. "Understanding Attitudes Toward Public
Employment." PUBLIC ADMINISTRATION REVIEW 27 (December
1967): 411-20. Tables.

> This article considers factors which influence competitive
> abilities of our governments in the manpower market.
> Frederickson, a former president of the American Society
> for Public Administration, explains the sources of varying
> attitudes toward public employment at different levels of
> the government.

818   Gardner, Neely. "Power Diffusion in the Public Sector: Collaboration
for Democracy." JOURNAL OF APPLIED BEHAVIORAL SCIENCE 10
(1974): 367-72.

> Gardner states that change agents will need to make value
> judgments about the propriety of initiating actions that
> influence the balance between the survival and well-being
> of the government employee, the organization, and the
> private citizen. The author examines the power force-
> field of public sector officials and agencies in order that
> we understand basic difficulties and contradictions in the

task of social power diffusion. In stating that the bureaucracy of government is both ally and enemy of the
chief executive and the legislative body, Gardner reveals
that if power to induce implementation is difficult to
achieve, the power to inhibit implementation is not.

819   Gibson, Frank K., and James, George A. "Student Attitudes Toward
Government Employees and Employment." PUBLIC ADMINISTRATION
REVIEW 27 (December 1967): 429-35. Tables.

This essay presents a survey of high school and college
student attitudes toward local, state, and federal government in one Georgia college community. The findings
indicate that attitudes change abruptly between the ages
of 18 and 21, that women had generally more positive
attitudes than did men toward the public service, that
rural students had a poorer attitude toward all government,
particularly local, than did their city-raised student colleagues, that black respondents had a better attitude
toward all levels of government than did whites, that
local government consistently received the poorest attitude
responses, and that state government consistently received
the most favorable responses.

820   Golembiewski, Robert T. "Specialist or Generalist? Structure as a
Crucial Factor." PUBLIC ADMINISTRATION REVIEW 25 (June 1965):
135-41. Figures.

Using the performance of nursing services as a basis for
analysis, the author contrasts traditional and unorthodox
patterns of organization and shows that "even simple variations in ways of organizing work can significantly affect
the relative merits of generalist and specialist roles."
He concludes that the adoption of a specific organizational structure strongly influences total performance and
the development of supervisory capacity, and he also finds
significant managerial advantage in the unorthodox pattern
and its generalist bias.

821   _____, ed. PERSPECTIVES ON PUBLIC MANAGEMENT: CASES
AND LEARNING DESIGNS. Itasca, Ill.: F.E. Peacock Publishers,
1976. xii, 279 p.

In this book of readings, the editor includes selections on
managing organizational adaptation, need fulfillment, multiple loyalties, everyday cases, balance of forces, knowledge of self and others, the difficult cases, interpersonal
conflict, variations in role content, the subtleties of delegation, the demands of hierarchy and specialty, office
dynamics and headquarters-field relations, effectiveness
within law and tradition, and managing the whole ball

of wax. He discusses public management as applied
social science; public management as value-laden (personal and institutional orientations); and perspectives on
public management.

822   Golembiewski, Robert T., and Cohen, Michael, eds. PEOPLE IN
PUBLIC SERVICE: A READER IN PUBLIC PERSONNEL ADMINISTRA-
TION. Itasca, Ill.: F.E. Peacock Publishers, 1976. xv, 609 p.

In a most comprehensive coverage of the literature of
public personnel administration, the editors include readings
on the major influences on the development, practice,
and monitors of performance of public personnel administration.

823   Guyot, James F. "Government Bureaucrats Are Different." PUBLIC
ADMINISTRATION REVIEW 22 (December 1962): 195-202. Tables.

Guyot compares middle managers in business and in the
federal government on measures of their motivation to
achieve, to affiliate with others, and to seek power.
He concludes that government bureaucrats show a higher
level of achievement motivation while businessmen are
higher in affiliation and that the government bureaucrat
emerges as more energetic, less dependent, and no more
power-hungry than his opposite in business.

824   Harvey, Donald R. THE CIVIL SERVICE COMMISSION. New York:
Frederick A. Praeger, 1969. 233 p.

Harvey discusses the history of the commission, examines
its organization and specific functions, analyzes the commission's relations with other agencies of the government,
with Congress, and with various interest groups, relates
the problems with enforcement of regulations, and denotes
the effects on and response to broad changes in policy.

825   Howell, Paul L. "Needed: A Dynamic Civil Service Pension Program."
PUBLIC ADMINISTRATION REVIEW 22 (December 1962): 182-87.
Tables.

The author examines policies used in the investment of
most civil service retirement funds and identifies some of
the problems causing restrictive investment practices and
some of the changes that must be made to increase the
productivity of invested assets.

826   Hunt, Thelma. "Critical Issues Facing Personnel Administrators Today."
PUBLIC PERSONNEL MANAGEMENT 3 (November-December 1974):
464-72.

Hunt concludes that mandated governmental regulations, unionism, employee expectations, broad social problems, increased citizen involvement, and pressure to assume an attitude of change are critical issues that confront and require action by personnel administrators.

827   Indik, Bernard P. "The Relationship between Organization Size and Supervision Ratio." ADMINISTRATIVE SCIENCE QUARTERLY 9 (December 1964): 301-12. Table.

The author finds in the five sets of organizations studied in this research that the relationship between the organization unit size and supervision ratio is logarithmic in form and negative in scope. Indik concludes that Parkinson's observation of the disproportionate increase in "chiefs" to "Indians" as organizations increase in size is not supported by the data presented in this article.

828   Janowitz, Morris, and Wright, Deil. "The Prestige of Public Employment: 1929 and 1954." PUBLIC ADMINISTRATION REVIEW 16 (Winter 1956): 15-21. Tables.

The research of the authors indicates that since 1930 the prestige value of public employment has undergone a marked shift in the favorable direction. According to Janowitz and Wright, the groups that express highest evaluation of public employment continue to be the lower class, the lower status, and the lesser educated.

829   Johnson, Gary R. "The Image of the Administrator." PUBLIC PERSONNEL MANAGEMENT 2 (November-December 1973): 418-23.

The day-by-day influence of decisions on his image cannot be an administrator's concern. A person needing constant self-image feedback should not be an administrator. Since job performance will determine his image, the administrator must be adaptable enough to always stay ahead of problem situations, think ahead, and anticipate problems.

830   Jones, Charles O. "Reevaluating the Hatch Act: A Report on the Commission on Political Activity of Governmental Personnel." PUBLIC ADMINISTRATION REVIEW 29 (May-June 1969): 249-54.

The Commission of Political Activity of Government Personnel was created in October 1966 for the purpose of reviewing the Hatch Act and making recommendations for change. This article discusses the principal issues before the commission, analyzes the criteria utilized in making judgments, and denotes the conclusions reached. Jones believes that political activity of government personnel is an issue which will persist until changes are made in existing policy.

831   Jones, Roger W. "Developments in Government Manpower: A Federal Perspective." PUBLIC ADMINISTRATION REVIEW 27 (June 1967): 134-41.

Jones describes some of the important and interesting developments in executive training since the passage of the 1958 Government Employees Training Act. He concludes that manpower planning and career development became respectable concerns with the passage of this legislation. This is an insightful commentary on employee mobility and analysis of losses and turnover, pay and fringe benefits, labor-management relations, the use of technology in personnel administration, and intragovernmental personnel matters in the United States during the mid-1960s.

832   Jones, William A., Jr. "Occupational Perceptions of Federal Personnel Administrators in a Regional City." PUBLIC PERSONNEL MANAGEMENT 5 (January-February 1976): 52-59.

Jones summarizes a study of the occupational perceptions of federal personnel administrators in a regional headquarters city. The article includes data gathered from 90 percent of the GS-9 through GS-13 personnel administrators in the city through the use of a questionnaire. In addition to reporting occupational perception data, the article presents demographic data and an analysis of interrelationships between various types of data.

833   Klinger, Donald E., and Nalbandian, John. "Personnel Management by Whose Objectives?" PUBLIC ADMINISTRATION REVIEW 38 (July-August 1978): 366-72.

The authors state that the academician's development of a theoretical framework, the practitioner's concern for selecting appropriate personnel management techniques, and the employee's concern with interpreting how the organization will affect his or her future are important for determining what objectives will be applied in personnel management. This essay calls for a new approach to public personnel management.

834   Larson, Arthur D. "Representative Bureaucracy and Administrative Responsibility: A Reassessment." MIDWEST REVIEW OF PUBLIC ADMINISTRATION 7 (April 1973): 79-90.

This article reviews the theory behind the concept of representative bureaucracy, that is, that the composition of

the bureaucracy reflect the socioeconomic, geographic,
and other groupings of American society. Larson summarizes the arguments of the proponents of representative
bureaucracy and also notes the deficiencies of this concept.

835   Lee, Robert D., Jr. PUBLIC PERSONNEL SYSTEMS. Baltimore:
University Park Press, 1979. 456 p.

Lee examines personnel administration within a systems
context and considers the individual components of the
system in relationship with other components. He surveys
the current status and likely future directions of public
personnel systems. He considers the traditional topics of
recruiting, testing, and selecting and the emerging forces
of public sector collective bargaining and equal employment opportunity for minorities and women. Lee includes
coverage of the Civil Service Reform Act of 1978 and
reviews federal, state, and local public personnel systems.

836   Lee, Robert D., Jr., and Lucianovic, William M. "Personnel Management Information Systems for State and Local Governments." PUBLIC
PERSONNEL MANAGEMENT 4 (March-April 1975): 84-89.

The authors relate that personnel management serves to
bring new employees into the organization, to administer
day-to-day operations involving current employees, to
assess the capabilities of existing personnel and plan for
future requirements, to link personnel with the budgetary
system so as to control public programs, to provide information essential in labor-management relations and negotiations, and to support other related functions such as payroll and employee benefits.

837   Leich, Harold H. "Rank in Man or Job? Both!" PUBLIC ADMINI-
STRATION REVIEW 20 (Spring 1960): 92-99.

Leich demonstrates that job-oriented personnel systems pay
substantial attention to the personnel rank of their members,
and that, conversely, personnel-oriented systems pay substantial attention to the level and requirements of the job.
All viable personnel systems have paid attention both to
the person and his/her job, although some systems occa-
sionally emphasize one aspect at the expense of the other
(but both have always been present). This article presents
a good analysis of the two personnel systems.

838   Loehr, Virginia M.; Arellano, Esther; Levine, Edward M.; Porter,
Wayne; and Posegate, John. "Personnel Selection Methods Used in
Arizona Local Government." PUBLIC PERSONNEL MANAGEMENT
2 (September-October 1973): 327-31.

> The authors state that a chief aim of the Selection Re-
> source Center, an intergovernmental personnel program,
> is to promote cooperative personnel programs and to pro-
> mote technical aid in selection problems to local public
> jurisdictions in Arizona. The reader is informed that
> smaller jurisdictions are more likely to consider education
> and state police files of their applicants than larger juris-
> dictions but that both large and small jursidictions tend
> to look at local police files and licenses or credentials
> of applicants.

839   Lutz, Carl F., and Morgan, James P. "Jobs and Rank." In POLICE
       PERSONNEL ADMINISTRATION, edited by O. Glenn Stahl and
       Richard A. Staufenberger, pp. 17-44. Washington, D.C.: Police
       Foundation, 1974.

> The authors emphasize that the distinction between a
> position, representing an impersonal collection of work,
> and an incumbent, who happens to occupy the position
> and is charged with carrying out its duties and responsi-
> bilities, is fundamental. They describe the classification
> process and probe the traditional classification structure
> in the police service. In conclusion, they outline modern
> concepts of position management, classification, and com-
> pensation for the police service.

840   McGregor, Eugene B., Jr. "Future Challenges for Public Personnel
       Administration." In PUBLIC ADMINISTRATION AND PUBLIC POLICY,
       edited by H. George Frederickson and Charles R. Wise, pp. 29-42.
       Lexington, Mass.: D.C. Heath and Co., 1977.

> The assumption that the boundaries of personnel admini-
> stration are determined by standard practices in a per-
> sonnel office or by the chapter headings of a single,
> standard personnel textbook is misleading. The author
> states that management analyses of public personnel should
> include an examination of major functional requirements
> of human resources administration and the policy dilemmas.

841   Morgan, David R., and Regens, James L. "Political Participation
       Among Federal Employees: The Hatch Act and Political Equality."
       MIDWEST REVIEW OF PUBLIC ADMINISTRATION 10 (December 1976):
       193-200. Tables.

> Morgan and Regens conclude that the Hatch Act imposes
> rather severe limits on the political activity of federal
> employees and in part, the demand for repeal or modifi-
> cation of the Hatch Act is based on this sentiment. This
> research suggests that changes in the legislation would
> make very little difference in the political behavior of
> most federal bureaucrats, who currently participate at only
> slightly higher rates than other U.S. citizens.

842   Newland, Chester A. "Public Personnel Administration: Legalistic Reforms vs. Effectiveness, Efficiency, and Economy." PUBLIC ADMINISTRATION REVIEW 36 (September-October 1976): 529-37. Tables.

> Newland states that public personnel administration in the United States has been the focus of political conflicts and doctrinaire reform movements throughout the nation's history. He examines the enormous growth of governments since the 1940s, the rapid growth of unions and of collective bargaining since the 1950s, and the widespread growth of litigious, public service-rights populism since the 1960s. This essay constitutes an excellent summary analysis of American public personnel administration.

843   Nigro, Felix A. "Public Personnel: Agenda for the Sixties." PUBLIC ADMINISTRATION REVIEW 21 (Autumn 1961): 191-97.

> Nigro puts developments in public personnel administration into perspective with a brief review of the failures and achievements of the last thirty years (ca. 1961) and presents a challenging agenda for public personnel in the 1960s. This review is especially valuable for its analysis of the state of public personnel administration in the early 1960s.

844   Nigro, Felix A., and Nigro, Lloyd G. THE NEW PUBLIC PERSONNEL ADMINISTRATION. Itasca, Ill.: F.E. Peacock Publishers, 1976. xi, 337 p.

> This text on public personnel administration is an analytical, problem-centered book. The authors focus on historical background and examine personnel challenges, organizations of personnel careers and the structure of the service, classification and pay, recruitment, selection, career management, training, grievances and appeals, constitutional rights of the public employee, and the future of public personnel administration. This volume is useful resource material for both student and practitioner.

845   Parsons, William W. "The Personnel Function in Public Management." PUBLIC ADMINISTRATION REVIEW 17 (Summer 1957): 149-55.

> Parsons discusses the roles of responsibility, decentralization, overspecialization, coordination, training, interdepartmental personnel councils, and the appraisal system in emphasizing that personnel management is not an end in itself. "We must have faith in human potentials. The isolation, centralization, overspecialization of the personnel function all imply a lack of trust. We must be willing to take a chance."

846   Patten, Thomas H., Jr., ed. CLASSICS OF PERSONNEL MANAGE-
        MENT. Oak Park, Ill.: Moore Publishing Co., 1979. xii, 625 p.

        In this comprehensive collection of essays, the editor in-
        cludes articles on the roots of modern personnel work, the
        role of personnel, the dynamics of selection, staffing, and
        employee mobility, individual and organizational develop-
        ment, job enrichment and quality of life, performance
        review and management by objectives, pay planning and
        administration, safety and health, work group behavior,
        collective bargaining and labor relations, and a future
        perspective on personnel.

847   Pincus, Ann. "How to Get a Government Job." WASHINGTON
        MONTHLY 8 (May-June 1976): 22-27.

        This article relates that congressmen can request specific
        individuals for jobs but that the best way to get hired is
        to have contacts inside the agency. Richard Nixon was
        the first president to challenge the control of the civil
        service of Roosevelt-Truman appointees. Pincus states
        that the Ford administration has not attempted to meddle
        with the civil service.

848   Reeves, Floyd W. "Civil Service as Usual." PUBLIC ADMINISTRA-
        TION REVIEW 4 (Autumn 1944): 327-41.

        The author explores the potential gains of civil service
        after the end of World War II denoting some principles of
        personnel administration and analyzing findings of presi-
        dential reports concerning improvements in the civil service.
        He discusses the implications of present practices (ca.
        1940s) and attitudes in the civil service profession.

849   Ripley, Randall B., and Baumer, Donald C. "National Politics and
        Public Service Employment." In MANAGING HUMAN RESOURCES,
        edited by Charles H. Levine, pp. 271-93. Sage Urban Affairs Annual
        Reviews, no. 13. Beverly Hills, Calif.: Sage Publications, 1977.

        The authors contend that support for and opposition to federal
        creation of job opportunities are economic in origin. The
        article mentions that the programs of the Comprehensive
        Employment and Training Act concern finding jobs for dis-
        advantaged minorities, are in response to rapidly spiraling
        unemployment, and are a countercyclical program for the
        most severely disadvantaged. The emphasis has changed
        from spending and hiring to maintaining existing levels of
        employment. At some point, those participating in CETA
        programs should move out into unsubsidized jobs.

850   Rosenbloom, David H.   FEDERAL SERVICE AND THE CONSTITUTION:
      THE DEVELOPMENT OF THE PUBLIC EMPLOYMENT RELATIONSHIP.
      Ithaca, N.Y.: Cornell University Press, 1971. 267 p.

      > Rosenbloom discusses the position of civil servants in the
      > executive branch, reviews the changing concepts of the
      > role of the civil servant and his political rights, and
      > concludes that the current tendency to give government
      > employees more of the ordinary rights of citizenship is
      > significant and appropriate.

851   _____. "Forms of Bureaucratic Representation in the Federal Service."
      MIDWEST REVIEW OF PUBLIC ADMINISTRATION 8 (July 1974): 159-
      77.

      > This essay seeks to develop the concept of representative
      > bureaucracy by analyzing the major forms of bureaucratic
      > representation found in the federal service. Rosenbloom
      > notes that the most important recent development con-
      > cerning this concept is the differentiation of passive and
      > active representation. He concludes that the earlier as-
      > sumption that passive representation automatically and
      > consistently yields active representation is unsupportable.

852   _____. "Public Personnel Administration and the Constitution: An
      Emergent Approach." PUBLIC ADMINISTRATION REVIEW 35 (January-
      February 1975): 52-59.

      > The author analyzes recent judicial decisions concerning
      > the procedural and substantive constitutional rights of public
      > employees. His research indicates that the courts have
      > adopted an idiographic approach to many of the issues
      > involved; this approach is of greatest importance with re-
      > gard to procedural due process, freedom of speech, asso-
      > ciation, and thought, and equal protection.

853   Rosow, Jerome M.   "Public Sector Pay and Benefits." PUBLIC AD-
      MINISTRATION REVIEW 36 (September-October 1976): 538-43.

      > Rosow discusses three systems for fixing government pay,
      > including legislative, executive, and collective bargaining.
      > He states that employee benefit plans in the public service
      > have been assumed to be one of the advantages over pri-
      > vate employment. Finally, he notes that pensions stand
      > out above all other benefits, concluding that pension
      > issues include integration with social security, pension
      > benefit formulae, escalation with prices, contributory pay-
      > ments, comparison of benefits to take home pay, and costs.

854   Rubin, Richard S.   "Flexitime: Its Implementation in the Public Sector."
      PUBLIC ADMINISTRATION REVIEW 39 (May-June 1979): 277-82.

Rubin believes that "in most situations, experience with the flexitime system indicates that the greater the degree of flexibility, the greater the benefits ." This article discusses the benefits, problems, and main issues that are involved in the use of flexitime by government agencies and its implications for labor relations.

855   Saltstein, Alan, ed. PUBLIC EMPLOYEES AND POLICYMAKING. Pacific Palisades, Calif.: Palisades Publishers, 1979. ix, 289 p. Paper.

Saltstein states that these readings were written and selected to give the background needed to cope with current personnel problems. Too often public administration instructors have confused applied education with learning the minutae of administrative life in particular agencies. He maintains that such data are of little value unless placed within a broader background which emphasizes the role of administrator within the American federal system and the importance of personnel decisions to the problems of the larger society.

856   Scism, Thomas E. "Employee Mobility in the Federal Service: A Description of Some Recent Data." PUBLIC ADMINISTRATION REVIEW 34 (May-June 1974): 247-54.

Data from the U.S. Civil Service Commission's 10 percent statistical sample were inspected in 1970 for a study on mobility. For each individual, comparisons of 1964 and 1969 data were made for agency, occupation, geographical location, and salary. Scism states that those labeled as nonmobile comprised two-thirds of the sample while the next largest group changed occupation but not agency or geographical location. Within grade groups, geographical mobility was greatest for the upper grades while occupational mobility declined sharply as grade level increased.

857   Shafritz, Jay M. POSITION CLASSIFICATION: A BEHAVIORAL ANALYSIS FOR THE PUBLIC SERVICE. New York: Praeger, 1973. 146 p.

Shafritz compares the negative role of the public personnel agency in protecting the merit system with its positive role in assisting management in the maintenance of a viable personnel system. The author holds that the negative role is dominant and produces contradictory behavior. The purpose of his study is to resolve this conflict.

858   Shimberg, Benjamin, and di Grazia, Robert J. "Promotion." In
       POLICE PERSONNEL ADMINISTRATION, edited by O. Glenn Stahl
       and Richard A. Staufenberger, pp. 101-24. Washington, D.C.:
       Police Foundation, 1974.

            The authors describe the significance of promotional
            policies and practices for police personnel, denote pres-
            ent procedures and what's wrong with them, and discuss
            procedures that some jurisdictions are using to improve or
            to strengthen police promotional policies.

859   Stahl, O. Glenn. "Of Jobs and Men." PUBLIC ADMINISTRATION
       REVIEW 29 (July-August 1969): 379-84.

            This essay is an adaptation of an address which the author
            delivered at the Conference on Personnel Administration
            of the Indian Institute of Public Administration, New
            Delhi, on March 7, 1968, and which was previously
            published in the INDIAN JOURNAL OF PUBLIC ADMINI-
            STRATION, April-June 1968. Stahl, director of the
            Bureau of Policies and Standards of the U.S. Civil Service
            Commission at the time of this article, writes a concise
            review of the common features in all progressive admini-
            strative systems, including the idea of work-centered
            motivation, specialization, and characteristics of tasks
            in career systems.

860   _____. PUBLIC PERSONNEL ADMINISTRATION. 7th ed. New
       York: Harper and Row, 1976. viii, 575 p.

            Stahl is the authority in public personnel administration
            in the United States, and this text is the best source to
            consult on this subject. He stresses that the major purpose
            of this volume is "to bring together in one place the
            principal doctrine and ideas gleaned from both experience
            and research in the field." Chapter topics cover modern
            public service, structure of a personnel system, staffing,
            motivation and effectiveness, conduct, employee organi-
            zation and collective relations with management, separa-
            tion, personnel organization, and developmental areas.

861   Stanley, David T. CHANGING ADMINISTRATIONS: THE 1961 AND
       1964 TRANSITIONS IN SIX DEPARTMENTS. Washington, D.C.:
       Brookings Institution, 1965. x, 147 p.

            Stanley concentrates on the more detailed problems of the
            transfer of responsibility in the early 1960s in six federal
            organizations: the Departments of State, Defense, Interior,
            Agriculture, Health, Education, and Welfare, and the
            Federal Aviation Agency. He concludes that "the task
            of preparing for a new administration can be reduced and

shortened if the President-elect will fill more of his ap-
pointive jobs from inside government. Normal political
pressures and his own inclinations will tend to keep him
from doing so."

862   Teasley, C.E. "A Systems Approach to Public Personnel Administration:
Some Implications for Research and Practice." MIDWEST REVIEW OF
PUBLIC ADMINISTRATION 10 (March 1976): 3-13.

Teasley reviews the components of the traditional framework of general personnel administration and outlines the
expectancy model of public personnel administration, based
on the inputs of job behavior, role perceptions, reinforce-
ments, traits and abilities, and motivation. This essay
constitutes a useful review of the literature.

863   Thompson, Frank J., ed. CLASSICS OF PUBLIC PERSONNEL POLICY.
Oak Park, Ill.: Moore Publishing Co., 1979. x, 401 p.

Thompson provides essays giving a historical overview of
the field, institutions, personnel management processes,
labor relations, and equal employment opportunity and
employee rights. This is a useful volume for both the
student and practitioner of public personnel administration.

B. PROFESSIONALISM IN PUBLIC SERVICE

864   Beaumont, Enid F. "A Pivotal Point for the Merit Concept." PUBLIC
ADMINISTRATION REVIEW 34 (September-October 1974): 426-30.

This article reviews the arguments that the civil service
has moved too far in the direction of employee protec-
tionism, which conflicts with demands for better management and higher productivity, and that traditional methods
no longer permit adequate response to changing manpower
requirements. Beaumont looks at the value assumptions
behind the above arguments and relates these arguments
to social science findings about the human side of organizations. He states that merit has not been clearly defined; it could mean merit system, merit principle, merit
concept, civil service, or public personnel administration.

865   Blume, Stuart S., and Chennells, Elizabeth. "Professional Civil Servants: A Study in the Sociology of Public Administration." PUBLIC
ADMINISTRATION 53 (Summer 1975): 111-31.

Blume and Chennells emphasize that the ethos of the work
environment ranks with individual character traits when

examining work involvement of professional civil servants. Task-oriented participants in this survey experience little conflict or dissatisfaction with work environments. Some 40 percent of participants seek advancement in their professions while approximately 25 percent do not desire promotion.

866   Camp, Paul M., and Lomax, W. Richard. "Bilateralism and the Merit Principle." PUBLIC ADMINISTRATION REVIEW 28 (March-April 1968): 132-37.

The authors begin their essay in the following manner: "In the public service, we have seen the unilateral development of merit systems to guard against improper influence in the filling of career positions." They examine bilateral negotiations in light of merit systems and union contracts, union testimony and proposals, bilateralism and promotion policy in the career service and conclude that progress has been made in personnel administration because of the activities of unions.

867   Campbell, Alan K. "Civil Service Reform: A New Commitment." PUBLIC ADMINISTRATION REVIEW 38 (March-April 1978): 99-103.

Campbell reviews prospects for the Merit Systems Protection Board, Office of Personnel Management, the 1978 Civil Service Reform Act, and the Senior Executive Service, obstacles to affirmative action, the impact of veterans' preference, and the climate for change.

868   DeLong, Earl H. "Who Are the Career Executives?" PUBLIC ADMINISTRATION REVIEW 19 (Spring 1959): 108-13.

The author suggests the type of career executive program that the federal government needs: "a system for discovering those relatively rare persons who have both thorough knowledge of the career civil service and the 'sparkle, breadth, agility, and articulateness' of the political leader, who can bring to the political executive the resources of the career staff and bring to his subordinates an understanding of the political executives' goals." DeLong describes the managerial requirements for senior personnel, the kind of person required for these positions, the scope and administration of the career executive service, and the alternatives in federal public personnel administration.

869   Egger, Rowland. "Civil Servants at Mid-Career: Management Training in American Universities." PUBLIC ADMINISTRATION 54 (Spring 1976): 83-98.

Egger suggests that most mid-careerists' work experience promotes a parochial point of view. The principle of functional specialization practically guarantees a limited and self-centered outlook. The fundamental question is whether it is possible to superimpose the knowledge that lies at the heart of administrative vision on a foundation of technical education and specialized work experience.

870   Emmerich, Herbert, and Belsley, G. Lyle. "The Federal Career Service--What Next?" PUBLIC ADMINISTRATION REVIEW 14 (Winter 1954): 1-12.

The authors believe that there are signs and portents that the American federal career service is in danger and that this danger has become acute at a time of change in political administrations. They describe the danger and what can be done to avoid it. The dual reward of the American public service, is to increase its flexibility and responsiveness to political change at the same time that its compentence and stability are enhanced. This article reflects the perspectives of administrative change immediately following the inauguration of the Eisenhower administration in 1953.

871   Fisher, John E. "Do Federal Managers Manage?" PUBLIC ADMINISTRATION REVIEW 22 (Spring 1962): 59-64.

The author writes that the basic problem of federal government management is not that administrators are not being affected by the revolutionary advancements in management tools and techniques; but is the broad deficiency of management sophistication and knowledge which impedes government administration at all levels of management. He offers several suggestions for increasing management sophistication.

872   Foster, Gregory D. "The 1978 Civil Service Reform Act: Post-Mortem or Rebirth?" PUBLIC ADMINISTRATION REVIEW 39 (January-February 1979): 78-86.

This article reviews key aspects of the enacted reforms (merit principles, the Senior Executive Service, and veterans' preference) and assesses each of the above reforms with respect to its impact on equal employment opportunity and labor-management relations. Foster states that "pluralistic obstructionism, political in-fighting and compromise, and out right pettifogging manifested in this latest effort at civil service reform leave no doubt as to why the batting average for such endeavors over the past four decades stands at a paltry .050 (one hit in 20 at-bats)."

873   Grusky, Oscar. "Career Mobility and Organizational Commitment."
       ADMINISTRATIVE SCIENCE QUARTERLY 10 (March 1966): 488-503.
       Tables.

          The author posits that the strength of a person's commit-
          ment to an organization is influenced by the rewards that
          he or she has received from the system and the kinds of
          experiences that he or she has had to undergo in order
          to receive the rewards. Grusky hypothesizes that 1) the
          greater the rewards received, the greater the degree of
          the person's commitment; and 2) the greater the obstacles
          the person has overcome in order to obtain the organiza-
          tion's rewards, the greater his or her commitment.

874   Harvey, Donald R. THE CIVIL SERVICE COMMISSION. New York:
       Praeger Publishers, 1970. xiii, 233 p.

          Harvey reviews the historical development of the Civil
          Service Commission from 1883 to modern times. He offers
          a nonevaluative, objective interpretation of public per-
          sonnel developments of the commission prior to the im-
          pacts of affirmative action plans and equal opportunity
          programs. Harvey includes appendixes which list career
          opportunities, regions, laws, and commissioners of the
          civil service in the United States.

875   Kaufman, Gary G. "Managerial Mobility: A Cost-Benefit Analysis
       of Job Rotation." BUREAUCRAT 3 (January 1975): 462-85.

          Kaufman states that following World War II, job rotation
          became a way of American life, produced by a need for
          managerial generalists and following the growth of multi-
          functional technological organizations. He suggests that
          job rotation improves flexibility and adaptability, de-
          veloping "whole organization" perspectives and exposing
          the executive to increasing job challenges. A study of
          job rotation in the Internal Revenue Service indicates that
          job rotation benefits both managers and organizations,
          providing a variety of experiences for executives and
          lessening executive stagnation.

876   Kranz, Harry. "Are Merit and Equity Compatible?" PUBLIC AD-
       MINISTRATION REVIEW 34 (September-October 1974): 434-40.

          Kranz contends that a "representative bureaucracy" is de-
          sirable for political, economic, and social reasons. He
          believes such a system would have beneficial effects on
          minorities, on consumers and clients, on bureaucratic or-
          ganizations, and on the American governmental system.
          He defines the concept of a "representative bureaucracy"
          and offers suggestions for changes needed in the present
          bureaucratic system.

877   McClung, Glenn G. "'Qualified' vs. 'Most Qualified': A Review
       of the Issues of Competitive Merit Selection." PUBLIC PERSONNEL
       MANAGEMENT 2 (September–October 1973): 366–69.

           McClung believes that any capable personnel manager
           acknowledges the necessity for some discretion on the part
           of the appointing authority. Examination results, however
           inadequate, should ordinarily set forth the best order in
           which to consider candidates for appointment. The author
           alludes that insistence on the merit system of selection,
           through competitive examination, is a portion of the de-
           licate check and balance system of responsible government.
           Merit systems are rather conservative and slow to move,
           but, once moving, their inertia is a potent force with
           a lasting influence on the entire society.

878   McGregor, Eugene B. "Politics and the Career Mobility of Bureau-
       crats." AMERICAN POLITICAL SCIENCE REVIEW 68 (March 1974):
       18–26.

           McGregor discusses the role of federal career civil ser-
           vants in the initiation, defense, and execution of public
           policy. He notes that political executives have difficulty
           in controlling the career civil service's impacts upon the
           president's policies. He reveals the impermeability of
           organizational boundaries within the American civil service
           system and concludes that the careers of most federal
           service employees end at the bureau level of administration.

879   Morstein Marx, Fritz. "The Mind of the Career Man." PUBLIC AD-
       MINISTRATION REVIEW 20 (Summer 1960): 133–38.

           Noting that the career man holds a particularly important
           place in the management of public affairs, the author
           probes both strengths and weaknesses (including inflexi-
           bility, narrowness, specialization, integrity, breadth, and
           spirit) of the person whose primary task is to provide the
           needed technical competence in administration.

880   Musolf, Lloyd D. "Separate Career Executive Systems: Egalitarianism
       and Neutrality." PUBLIC ADMINISTRATION REVIEW 31 (July–August
       1971): 409–19.

           Separate personnel systems for the higher civil service re-
           flect the range and variety of modern government. But
           their adoption must take account of values applicable to
           American personnel systems. This article presents rationales
           for egalitarianism and neutrality.

881   Nigro, Felix A. "The Politics of Civil Service Reform." SOUTHERN
       REVIEW OF PUBLIC ADMINISTRATION 3 (September 1979): 196–239.

Nigro reviews President Carter's proposals for the Civil
Service Reform Act of 1978, discusses their political context, notes administration strategy in this regard, and
examines actions by the U.S. Senate and House of
Representatives on this legislation.

882   Nigro, Lloyd G., and Meier, Kenneth J.   "Bureaucracy and the
People: Is the Higher Federal Service Representative?"   BUREAUCRAT
4 (October 1975): 300-308.

Nigro and Meier report a demographic analysis undertaken
to determine whether the civil service mirrors the community it serves and if it will be alert to the desires and
needs of that population. The bureaucratic group studied
was the higher federal bosses, those executives most likely
to have a considerable impact on national policies affecting large portions of the population. The authors conclude that federal supervisors are usually representative
of the public at large.

883   Nottage, Raymond. "The Potential for Professionalism in the Public
Service."   PUBLIC ADMINISTRATION 33 (June 1974): 167-74.

Nottage reveals that professional categories include person-
based, with emphasis on knowledge and an apprenticeship,
and employer-based, with emphasis on employer-supplied
knowledge and skills and on results for the employer.
Both categories are widely used in the public service,
but in the future, the needs of society will be in the
arrangement of human affairs and social organization.
With emphases on community and national interests, government programs must be designed to accomplish complex
tasks. This design will require much from a cluster of
government professionals.

884   Paget, Richard M. "Strengthening the Federal Career Executive."
PUBLIC ADMINISTRATION REVIEW 17 (Spring 1957): 91-96.

In defining the problem of strengthening the federal career
executive, the author calls for the selection process to
be improved, notes that compensation scales must be kept
realistic and competitive, suggests that executive training
and development must be stimulated, believes opportunities
for broader experience must be presented to federal administrators, indicates that career opportunities to carry
top level responsibilities must not be limited arbitrarily
by an effort to keep the civil servant out of politics,
and recognizes that pride in the federal service and con-
comitant recognition of status must be developed as a
foundation for a program to strengthen career top management in our government.

885   Perkins, John A. "Higher Education and Training for Administrative
       Careers." PUBLIC ADMINISTRATION REVIEW 18 (Winter 1958):
       14-20.

              Perkins is concerned about securing qualified personnel
              for government and its administration. He addresses the
              issue of graduate programs in public administration, and
              implies that education for public administration has not
              measured up to the needs of our time.

886   Pincus, William. "The Opposition to the Senior Civil Service."
       PUBLIC ADMINISTRATION REVIEW 18 (Autumn 1958): 324-31.

              The author, a proponent of the Senior Civil Service, ex-
              amines the arguments of the opposition, and suggests that
              they might mask personal considerations: concern of career
              administrators over being left out or, if included, at being
              transferred against their wishes; concern of former admini-
              strators that their opportunity for lateral entry to high-
              level positions would be diminished and that the positions
              would be drained of opportunity for policy leadership.
              Pincus concludes that a Senior Civil Service, such as that
              proposed by the Hoover Commission, is a necessity for
              better government and a logical culmination of American
              experience.

887   Pomerlau, Raymond. "The State of Management Development in the
       Federal Service." PUBLIC PERSONNEL MANAGEMENT 3 (January-
       February 1974): 23-28.

              Pomerlau reveals that the explicit purpose of management
              development programs is to extend the span of utility for
              those managers who may be confronted with premature
              obsolescence and to prepare high-potential mid-managers
              for assuming higher managerial functions. He indicates
              that the Federal Executive Institute attempts to heighten
              responsiveness to national needs and goals, to increase
              appreciation of the totality of the governmental system,
              and to improve knowledge of managerial processes.

888   Reining, Henry, Jr. "The FSEE: The University Point of View."
       PUBLIC ADMINISTRATION REVIEW 16 (Winter 1956): 11-14.

              The author writes: "There can be no doubt of the effi-
              cacy of the FSEE [Federal Service Entrance Examination]
              as a recruiting device. It not only can be predicted that
              it will work out well, but it can be demonstrated on the
              basis of the first filings that it already has been sucessful
              in this respect." Reining believes that simplification,
              foolproof nature of the method, reserve register, coordi-
              nation of recruitment, and personnel planning are advan-
              tages for the university graduate who is interested in a
              career with the federal service.

889 Rinehart, Jeffrey C., and Bernick, E. Lee. "Political Attitudes and Behavior Patterns of Federal Civil Servants." PUBLIC ADMINISTRA-TION REVIEW 35 (November-December 1975): 603-11. Tables.

This article focuses on whether restrictions are necessary to produce an impartial, effective, and efficient public service and to prevent the development of a spoils bu-reaucracy. Rinehart and Bernick conclude that the Hatch Act restrictions on voluntary political activity do not appear to be useful tools for providing efficient and im-partial administration.

890 Rosen, Bernard. "Merit and the President's Plan for Changing the Civil Service System." PUBLIC ADMINISTRATION REVIEW 38 (July-August 1978): 301-4.

This article concerns the Carter administration's proposals for changing the federal personnel system. Rosen's major concern is Carter's proposal for a Senior Executive Service with its grant of sweeping authority for presidential ap-pointees to reassign and demote almost all top career executives and replace them with political or other career appointees. The author believes that it is important for the public interest that political appointees not have "suffocating power" over career executives.

891 Rosenbloom, David H., and Obuchowski, Carole Cassler. "Public Personnel Examinations and the Constitution: Emergent Trends." PUBLIC ADMINISTRATION REVIEW 37 (January-February 1977): 9-18.

The authors examine recent judicial decisions concerning the constitutionality of public personnel examinations. They argue that these decisions are challenging the tra-ditional political paradigm of public personnel administra-tion by stressing the value of representation.

892 Schott, Richard L. "Professionals and the Public Service: Time for Some Second Thoughts." MIDWEST REVIEW OF PUBLIC ADMINISTRA-TION 12 (March 1978): 12-18.

Schott notes that those persons educated in the professions rather than in administration or management figure promi-nently in the higher echelons of the federal executive branch. He argues that it is time to examine carefully the prevailing view of the implications of professionaliza-tion for the public service.

893 Sherwood, Frank P. "The Federal Executive Institute--Academy for the Bureaucracy." In GOVERNMENT MANAGEMENT INTERNSHIPS AND EXECUTIVE DEVELOPMENT: EDUCATION FOR CHANGE, edited by Thomas P. Murphy, pp. 233-43. Lexington, Mass.: D.C. Heath and Co., 1973.

Sherwood relates the role and purposes of the Federal
Executive Institute in the bureaucracy of the federal government, stating that one reason for FEI's creation was
the insularity of the federal system and parochialism of
the average executive.

894   Smith, Darrell Hevenor. THE UNITED STATES CIVIL SERVICE COM-
       MISSION: ITS HISTORY, ACTIVITIES, AND ORGANIZATION.
       Baltimore, Md.: Johns Hopkins Press, 1928. xii, 153 p.

       Smith discusses the history of civil service in the United
       States and traces developments from the early years until
       1927. He examines the spoils system, movement for re-
       form, and the 1883 Pendleton Act in this process. He
       also reviews the activities and organization of the Civil
       Service Commission.

895   Sorensen, James E., and Sorensen, Thomas L. "The Conflict of Pro-
       fessionals in Bureaucratic Organizations." ADMINISTRATIVE SCIENCE
       QUARTERLY 19 (March 1974): 98-106.

       The Sorensens relate that the complexity of modern weapon
       systems has generated a number of approaches to weapons
       development, including use of interlocking networks of
       contractor organizations; government-owned, contractor-
       managed laboratories; and the government-owned, govern-
       ment-managed, or in-house laboratory. Incompatibilities
       between technical needs and navy regulations cause the
       personnel of the supply, purchasing, and construction
       departments at navy laboratories to frustrate the genuine
       needs of the technical managers.

896   Staats, Elmer. "Career Planning and Development: Which Way Is
       Up?" PUBLIC ADMINISTRATION REVIEW 37 (January-February 1977):
       73-76.

       The author offers four myths and four truths with regard to
       career planning and development for young professionals in
       government. Myths include: there is room at the top;
       the key to success is to be in the right place at the right
       time; good salesmen make good managers; and career plan-
       ning and development is a function of the personnel de-
       partment. Truths include: The best opportunity is the one
       you have; all development is self-development; all de-
       velopment is individual; and opportunity for development
       should be universal.

897   Stanley, David T. "Excellence in Public Service--How Do You Really
       Know?" PUBLIC ADMINISTRATION REVIEW 24 (September 1964):
       170-74.

       Stanley identifies three levels of measurement of excellence

in the public service: first, one the author calls im-
pressionistic; second, one that might be called presumptive; and the third, proven. He dismisses the impression-
istic and presumptive levels as having less validity than
the proven level. He includes program evaluation and
evaluation of people in the proven category.

898   _____. THE HIGHER CIVIL SERVICE: AN EVALUATION OF FEDERAL
PERSONNEL PRACTICES. Washington, D.C.: Brookings Institution,
1964. x, 145 p.

This text is a brief study of the higher civil service--some
16,000 executives and professionals (General Schedule
grades 15-18) whose performance is critical in determining
the effectiveness and efficiency of the entire government.
The author analyzes the operation of the higher federal
civil service with reference to criteria for an effective
personnel system.

899   _____. "Merit: The Now and Future Thing." PUBLIC ADMINI-
STRATION REVIEW 34 (September-October 1974): 451-52.

Stanley states: "The pressure to apply merit principles,
in this politico-economic-cultural-administrative setting,
is just one of many pressures. In any given situation
(or class of situations) forces of law, political strength,
power of personality, inertia, expediency, and group
action will resolve the pressures." He describes the
minimum necessities for the application of merit in the
public service and asks what level of quality there is in
government.

900   Stanley, David T.; Mann, Dean E.; and Doig, Jameson W.   MEN
WHO GOVERN: A BIOGRAPHICAL PROFILE OF FEDERAL POLITICAL
EXECUTIVES. Washington, D.C.: Brookings Institution, 1967. xiv,
169 p.

The authors examine federal political executives, beginning
with the Franklin Roosevelt administration and continuing
through the early appointments of Lyndon Johnson, from
the mid-1930s until the mid-1960s. They sketch profiles
of these men--where they come from, their age, religion,
politics, where they went to college, what they did before they were appointed, how long they held federal
office, and what they did afterward. They study the
careers of leaders in the civil service, the foreign service,
and the military services.

901   Stockard, James G.   "The FSEE and the Staffing of Federal Agencies."
PUBLIC ADMINISTRATION REVIEW 16 (Winter 1956): 6-10.

"No one can predict with certainty the success or failure of FSEE (Federal Service Entrance Examination) as government's bid for its fair share of college caliber manpower. To the writer, FSEE is the most positive recruitment step ever taken to strengthen the career service. To be successful, FSEE must have the unwavering support of educators, federal officials, and all personnel specialists, especially those concerned with placement and training activities."

902   U.S. General Accounting Office. ANNUAL ADJUSTMENTS--THE KEY TO FEDERAL EXECUTIVE PAY. FPCD-79-31. Washington, D.C.: Government Printing Office, 17 May 1979. 36 p.

Salary increases for federal executives have been limited or denied by statutes which allow for annual and quadrennial adjustments. This has resulted in problems of executive recruitment and retention for federal agencies. About 12,400 top managers at other levels of responsibility are also being denied annual pay adjustments to which they are entitled because their salaries are limited by executive salaries. Without monetary adjustments problems of recruitment and retention will continue.

903   _____. FEDERAL EMPLOYMENT EXAMINATIONS: DO THEY ACHIEVE EQUAL OPPORTUNITY AND MERIT PRINCIPLE GOALS? Washington, D.C.: Government Printing Office, 15 May 1979. 128 p.

This study focuses on the Professional and Administrative Career Examination (PACE) and the Junior Federal Assistant, Accountant-Auditor, and Social Worker examinations. GAO found that PACE and the Junior Federal Assistant examination screen out black applicants at a much higher rate than whites and that few blacks who pass the tests score high enough for a realistic job opportunity. The Office of Personnel Management believes that there is a clear relationship between performance on PACE and job performance. Critics of the test say that this relationship has not been adequately proven.

904   Van Riper, Paul P. "The Senior Civil Service and the Career System." PUBLIC ADMINISTRATION REVIEW 18 (Summer 1958): 189-200.

The author discusses the pros and cons of the Senior Civil Service proposal and concludes that arguments, pro and con, are difficult to prove in a scientific sense. He offers the need for a representative bureaucracy, the wisdom of free occupational choice, avoiding over-institutionalization, attacking the executive shortage at the proper point, placing politics in its proper role, clarifying traditional analogies, and the limitations of administrative reform as standards of judgment underlying the career system.

905   Warner, W. Lloyd; Van Riper, Paul P.; Martin, Norman H.; and
       Collins, Orvis F. THE AMERICAN FEDERAL EXECUTIVE: A STUDY
       OF THE SOCIAL AND PERSONAL CHARACTERISTICS OF THE CIVILIAN
       AND MILITARY LEADERS OF THE UNITED STATES FEDERAL GOVERN-
       MENT. New Haven, Conn.: Yale University Press, 1963. xvii,
       405 p.

           The purposes of this text include finding out what kinds
           of persons are in the highest civilian and military positions
           of the federal government, who they and their families
           are, what they are like as individuals, where they come
           from, whether they are representative of the kinds of
           citizens ordinarily found in the United States; discovering
           how government leaders reached their positions, what
           routes they took, and what career lines were formed by
           their movement to the top; learning how the leaders of
           the federal government compare in these respects with
           American big business leaders; and drawing broad general-
           izations about the representative character of the American
           federal bureaucracy and, in turn, about the nature of
           occupational mobility and succession in American society.
           Sections cover the image of the bureaucrat, social origins,
           family influence, education, the careers of federal execu-
           tives, and the private and public worlds of federal execu-
           tives.

906   _____. "A New Look at the Career Civil Service Executive."
       PUBLIC ADMINISTRATION REVIEW 22 (December 1962): 188-94.
       Tables.

           The authors report research on backgrounds of 7,640 federal
           career civil servant executives at the GS-14 level and
           above and compare them with other types of federal ex-
           ecutives and with big business leaders. They discuss levels
           of entry, career lines, and representative bureaucracy in
           the federal service.

907   White, Leonard D. "The Senior Civil Service." PUBLIC ADMINI-
       STRATION REVIEW 15 (Autumn 1955): 237-43.

           The author discusses the plan of the senior civil service
           (membership, functions, status), analyzes the role of
           Schedule C appointments of political executives vis-à-vis
           the senior civil service, posits two corollaries promoting
           the combination of the two concepts (one, that attention
           was needed to build up a more effective political top
           command; and two, that executive training programs on
           a much larger scale and at a higher level were urgently
           required), and predicts the prospects for the senior civil
           service (drawn from General Schedule grades 15-18) to
           become a viable reality.

908   Willbern, York. "Professionalization in the Public Service: Too Little
        or Too Much?" PUBLIC ADMINISTRATION REVIEW 14 (Winter 1954):
        13-21.

        Willbern discusses the rise of professionalism in the public
        service, the advantages and disadvantages of the process
        of professionalization in the public service, and appro-
        priate lines of development with regard to the public
        service professions and professionalization. This essay is
        an excellent review of civil service professionalism in the
        mid-1950s.

909   Wurf, Jerry. "Merit: A Union View." PUBLIC ADMINISTRATION
        REVIEW 34 (September-October 1974): 431-34.

        Wurf states: "Merit means different things to different
        people. What I mean by merit is a set of standards set
        up by management which permit a reasonable and objec-
        tive judgment of an applicant's ability to perform a job.
        The criteria may include education standards, tests, or
        experience requirements. The criteria must vary to fit
        the job, must reasonably relate to the work to be per-
        formed, and must be insulated from politics, favoritism,
        and caprice on the part of management. Those who meet
        the criteria should qualify, but from among those who
        qualify, the senior employee should be chosen."

910   Wynia, Bob L. "Executive Development in the Federal Government."
        PUBLIC ADMINISTRATION REVIEW 32 (July-August 1972): 311-17.

        Executive development never has been a priority within
        our governmental structure. Wynia attempts to point out
        some of the flaws in the present system of training federal
        executives and looks to the development of a new and
        improved education and training system.

911   Young, Philip. "The Federal Service Entrance Examination." PUBLIC
        ADMINISTRATION REVIEW 16 (Winter 1956): 1-5.

        Young, a former chairman of the U.S. Civil Service Com-
        mission, points out that the Federal Service Entrance Ex-
        amination was conceived and developed for the purpose
        of bringing into the career civil service a sufficient number
        of highly qualified young men and women who can grow
        with the service and become the career executive, scien-
        tific, and professional leaders of the future. In this in-
        formative essay, the author spells out the requirements of
        the FSEE.

C. LABOR-MANAGEMENT RELATIONS

912   Atwood, Jay F. "Collective Bargaining's Challenge: Five Imperatives for Public Managers." PUBLIC PERSONNEL MANAGEMENT 5 (January-February 1976): 24-32.

> Atwood suggests that, during the last ten years, the most noteworthy development in the area of public personnel management is the emergence of collective bargaining in the public service. The public manager deals with the rising employee expectations to participate in decision making, confronting public expectations for economical and responsible management. One conclusion is that the future will bring conflict as public employees participate in decisions that formerly were the responsibility of the manager.

913   Durante, John A. "The Effect of Collective Bargaining on the Productivity of the Employees of Suffolk County, New York." In PRODUCTIVITY BARGAINING IN THE PUBLIC SECTOR, edited by Josef P. Sirefman, pp. 363-403. Hofstra University Yearbook of Business, Series 12, vol. 3. Hempstead, N.Y.: Hofstra University, 1977.

> Durante asserts that granting of collective bargaining rights to public employees at federal, state, and local levels of government is the most important development in industrial relations in the 1960s. He examines the hypothesis that collective bargaining makes possible new approaches in relating remuneration to productivity in public employment.

914   Feigenbaum, Charles. "Civil Service and Collective Bargaining: Conflict or Compatibility." PUBLIC PERSONNEL REVIEW 3 (May-June 1974): 244-52.

> Feigenbaum maintains that public sector collective bargaining is a power process and power rests with political officials. Where an effective merit system exists, the self-interests of public employees make them hostile to patronage. He suggests that the subject of compulsory union membership or support illustrates the three-way tension between the labor organization's need for institutional security, the individual's desire to protect his right of nonassociation, and the merit system's insistence that employment be based on merit.

915   Feuille, Peter, and Long, Gary. "The Public Administrator and Final Offer Arbitration." PUBLIC ADMINISTRATION REVIEW 34 (November-December 1974): 575-83. Table.

> The purpose of this article is to use the Eugene, Oregon, experience as a base to discuss the variety of final offer

arbitration procedures which can be constructed. The authors hope that this information will result not only in an increased appreciation that there is no such thing as the final offer procedure, but also in an increased awareness that the various kinds of final offer payments will have differing impacts upon the parties' incentives to bargain and incentives to arbitrate.

916   Fogel, Walter, and Lewin, David. "Wage Determination in the Public Sector." INDUSTRIAL AND LABOR RELATIONS REVIEW 27 (April 1974): 410-31.

The authors indicate that two different salaries exist among municipal employees. Most blue-collar and lower level white-collar municipal employees receive higher wages than their counterparts in the private sector; wages are lower for managerial and professional persons in public sector occupations; fringe benefits and job security provisions are more evident in public sector employment opportunities; and state and local governments provide static employment opportunities. The article points out that market forces are not significant in determining salaries of state and local government employees.

917   Fowler, Robert Booth. "Normative Aspects of Public Employee Strikes." PUBLIC PERSONNEL MANAGEMENT 3 (March-April 1974): 129-37.

Fowler relates that public employee strikes are a growing part of political reality in America. The demands of government employees and citizens lead toward legalization of the right to strike for public employees. He concludes that use of Taft-Hartley-style schemes to minimize the danger is a palliative which sounds attractive but remains untested and speculative.

918   Frederickson, H. George. "Role Occupancy and Attitudes Toward Labor Relations in Government." ADMINISTRATIVE SCIENCE QUARTERLY 14 (December 1969): 595-606. Tables.

Frederickson questions occupants of five local government roles--legislators, elected executives, appointed executives, labor representatives, and arbitrators--on their attitudes toward labor-management conflict in government. He examines the relation between different role occupants and attitudes toward conflict, bargaining, authoritarianism, delegation, strikes, forms of conflict resolution, and critical services. Occupants of elected roles were less prepared than appointed role occupants to negotiate productively with labor.

919   Grodin, Joseph R. "Arbitration of Public Sector Labor Disputes: The
        Nevada Experiment." INDUSTRIAL AND LABOR RELATIONS REVIEW
        28 (October 1974): 89-102.

        Grodin explains that the Governor of Nevada has the
        authority to order compulsory arbitration for disputes be-
        tween local governments and their employees. At the
        request of either party, a factfinder is required to make
        a preliminary determination of the ability of the local
        government to meet additional financial demands. The
        reader is informed that Nevada is unique in vesting the
        screening authority in an elected official, in setting up
        criteria that go beyond the simple determination of whether
        bargaining impasses exist or whether further mediation
        would be futile, and in elevating the ability-to-pay
        criterion into an undue precondition.

920   Hananel, Eric. "The Collective Bargaining Process and Its Effect on
        Productivity in the Transportation Administration." In PRODUCTIVITY
        BARGAINING IN THE PUBLIC SECTOR, edited by Joseph P. Sirefman,
        pp. 112-40. Hofstra University Yearbook of Business, Series 12, vol.
        3. Hempstead, N.Y.: Hofstra University, 1977.

        This essay discusses collective bargaining and novel methods
        relating remuneration to productivity in public employment.
        New York City is considered the leader in utilizing this
        concept.

921   Hartman, James B. "Collective Bargaining in the University." IN-
        TERCHANGE 6 (1975): 32-43.

        Hartman maintains that an important factor in explaining
        the generation of conflict in the modern university is its
        complex bureaucratic structure. He contends that the
        conflict between the individual and needs for organiza-
        tional efficiency and control is directly related to the
        increasing professionalism of the disciplines. The political
        model is a more suitable conceptual device for describing
        university organization than are the bureaucratic or col-
        legiate prototypes.

922   Hopkins, Anne H.; Rawson, George E.; and Smith, Russell L. "Public
        Employee Unionism in the States: A Comparative Analysis." ADMINI-
        STRATION AND SOCIETY 8 (November 1976): 319-41.

        The authors examine data collected from a five-state
        random sample of state public employees: Tennessee,
        Nebraska, New York, Wisconsin, and Oregon. They
        maintain that employees in the most unionized states tend
        to believe that unions affect the work situation in a posi-
        tive manner. The authors discuss attitudes of union mem-
        bers and nonmembers in terms of a particular state's stage of
        union development.

923   Ingrassia, Anthony F.   "Bilateralism: The Government's Form of Collective Bargaining."   BUREAUCRAT   2 (Spring 1973):   8-16.

Ingrassia defines bilateralism as a type of personnel management under which employees, through their chosen
union representatives, participate in the implementation
and formulation of personnel policies and practices influencing their working conditions.   He concludes that
there is a necessity for gradual expansion of shared decision making and evolutionary changes in the system
employed to promote bilateralism.

924   Jones, William A., Jr.   "Collective Bargaining in the Federal Service."
SOUTHERN REVIEW OF PUBLIC ADMINISTRATION   1 (September
1977):   192-202.

This article provides an overview of the development of
the Executive Order program in labor relations, to offer
comments and generalizations on the present status of the
program, and to include selected references providing the
reader with quick access to additional information.

925   Juris, Harvey A., and Feuille, Peter.   POLICE UNIONISM: POWER
AND IMPACT IN PUBLIC SECTOR BARGAINING.   Lexington, Mass.:
D.C. Heath and Co., 1973.   228 p.

The authors examine the nature of police employee organizations, nature of the collective bargaining process in
police services, impact of police unions on policy formulation, unions and professionalization, unions and the
power to manage, and the relations between unions and
black officer organizations.   This work is based on field
experiences in twenty-two urban areas.

926   Kleingartner, Archie.   "Collective Bargaining Between Salaried Professionals and Public Sector Management."   PUBLIC ADMINISTRATION
REVIEW   33 (March-April 1973):   165-72.

The author analyzes the problem of defining the appropriate
scope of negotiations among professionals in the public
sector.   Employee organizations seek to expand the scope
of negotiations; management seeks to retain as many issues
as possible for purely managerial decisions.

927   Levine, Charles H.; Perry, James L.; and DeMarco, John J.   "Collective Bargaining in Municipal Governments: An Interorganizational
Perspective."   In MANAGING HUMAN RESOURCES: A CHALLENGE
TO URBAN GOVERNMENTS, edited by Charles H. Levine, pp. 159-
99.   Beverly Hills, Calif.:   Sage Publications, 1977.

The authors emphasize the complexity of municipal collective bargaining. They design a theoretical framework based on interorganizational theory for examining collective bargaining in public employment. They claim that the collective bargaining field is dominated by crises, passion, and moral polarization.

928   Levinson, Marc. "AFSCME: Public Employees in Trouble." NATION 225 (September 10, 1977): 208-10.

The reader learns that the American Federation of State, County, and Municipal Employees is on the defensive. Strikes have caused former allies, such as the press and the black community, to denounce the union and have made for a divided membership. The vigorous leftist movement within the union contradicts leadership policy and jeopardizes negotiations. Competition in organizing public employees is increasing.

929   Lewin, David. "The Prevailing-Wage Principle and Public Wage Decisions." PUBLIC PERSONNEL MANAGEMENT 3 (November-December 1974): 473-85.

Lewin suggests that wage rate range serves as a convenient device reflecting prevailing private-market rates for a bench mark position. The fixed nature of public-wage schedules may not facilitate close matching with the private rates found in dynamic labor markets. He concludes that no operational definition of prevailing wages is uniformly applicable to government's occupational structure and that external market data must be combined with internal wage-setting criteria.

930   McGriff, John H. "The States and Public Sector Labor Relations." PUBLIC ADMINISTRATION SURVEY 24 (May 1977): 1-5.

McGriff asserts that there is no federal law covering state and local government labor relations although about forty states do regulate some aspects of state and local labor-management relations. Several recent task forces have recommended that their state legislature create independent public employee labor relations boards or agencies to enforce state laws regarding public labor relations and that these relations agencies maintain impartiality.

931   Mankin, Lawrence D. "Public Employee Organizations: The Quest for Legitimacy." PUBLIC PERSONNEL MANAGEMENT 6 (September-October 1977): 334-40.

Mankin examines in detail two strategies employed to force a recognition of legitimacy: strikes and productivity bargaining. The success of productivity bargaining within the public sector is still unpredictable. He alleges that there are indications that as legitimacy of public employee associations is increasingly accepted, management will reevaluate its philosophy and its operating procedures.

932   Marshall, James F. "Public-Employee Associations--Roles and Programs." PUBLIC PERSONNEL MANAGEMENT 3 (September-October 1974): 415-24.

Marshall asserts that the most underrated element in public-sector labor relations is the role of public-employee associations. Independent associations represent over one million public employees in state and local government. He states that structural differences of independent associations allow talent, programming, and funding to remain at the local level. This assures maximum effort for individual employee and organization.

933   Meyer, Herbert H. "The Pay-for-Performance Dilemma." ORGANIZATIONAL DYNAMICS 3 (Winter 1975): 39-50.

Meyer suggests that a merit pay plan is very difficult to administer. Since managers are usually inclined to make relatively small salary discriminations between individuals in the same job, discriminations are likely to be based on factors other than performance. He provides several illustrations showing that people tend to rate themselves much higher than do their superiors and that abandonment of pay as a motivator is desirable.

934   Miller, Glenn W. "Impact of Early Collective Negotiations by Public Employees." PUBLIC PERSONNEL MANAGEMENT 6 (March-April 1977): 106-15.

The author reports that legislation controlling public employee relations is expected to be less restrictive in the future. Since the experience and capacities of union personnel and of organized workers will grow, Miller indicates that employee representation in Kansas' public sector will improve.

935   Newland, Chester A. "Collective Bargaining Concepts: Applications in Governments." PUBLIC ADMINISTRATION REVIEW 28 (March-April 1968): 117-26.

Newland examines the conceptual framework of collective bargaining, legal requirements and adaptations to government, special problems of collective bargaining in government, various bargaining approaches, and the requirements of Taft-Hartley Act for bargaining with respect to wages, hours, and other terms and conditions of employment.

Newland surmises: "As governments adopt collective bargaining, some choice of emphasis between conflict and
cooperation may be possible (since conflict is an available
choice), but experience in private industry indicates that
conflict persists even where cooperative efforts prevail."

936   Nigro, Felix A. "The Implications for Public Administration." PUBLIC
        ADMINISTRATION REVIEW 28 (March-April 1968): 137-47.

The author offers a redefinition of "sovereignty" as the
legal basis for requiring and justifying unilateralism in
the public service, denotes changes occurring in Illinois
and Michigan with regard to collective bargaining, and
concludes that the collective negotiations movement suggests that government is moving into a third stage of the
administration-policy relationship, with the initial stage
the separation of administration from policy and the
second stage the essential and increasing policy-formulating
role of the administrator in modern society. This article
is an excellent review of the literature.

937   _____. "The Implications for Public Administration." PUBLIC AD-
        MINISTRATION REVIEW 32 (March-April 1972): 120-26. Table.

The author presents in detail eight specific ways in which
public administration has been affected by collective negotiations in the public service, considers the resulting
changes in the relative influence of different participants
in the public policy-making process, discusses the concern
about the public interest, and concludes with an evaluative
balance sheet on the changed roles of collective bargaining and public administration. This is an excellent essay
for denoting these developments into the early 1970s.

938   Nigro, Felix A., and Nigro, Lloyd G. "Public Sector Unionism."
        In MANAGING HUMAN RESOURCES, edited by Charles H. Levine,
        pp. 141-57. Beverly Hills, Calif.: Sage Publications, 1977.

The authors maintain that public officials have difficulty
understanding and accepting collective bargaining and
that they believe unions wish to displace management.
They assert that collective bargaining does contribute to
the strain on local government budgets and promotes closer
scrutiny of expenditures. Unions abuse their power; but
important benefits are gained in terms of employee morale
and valuable worker input.

939   Northrup, David E. "Management's Cost in Public Sector Collective
        Bargaining." PUBLIC PERSONNEL MANAGEMENT 5 (September-
        October 1976): 328-34.

Northrup states that negotiators should analyze a number of direct, indirect, and measurable costs attributed to collective bargaining in the public sector. Direct costs comprise compensation, measurable costs comprise duration of agreement, impasse procedures, and negotiation and consultation, and indirect costs include the effects on morale and motivation, future management implications, and accomplishment of objectives. Northrup indicates that management will improve its capacity to bargain if it can analyze its costs more accurately.

940   Overton, C.E. "Compulsory Arbitration: A Strike Alternative for Police." ARBITRATION JOURNAL 29 (March 1974): 33-42.

Overton states that compulsory arbitration has a major impact on collective bargaining with the police. He asserts that management believes that the role of collective bargaining is diminishing, and the overwhelming majority of persons interviewed in a Rhode Island study agreed, that compulsory arbitration is superior to a strike for settling disputes.

941   Perry, James L., and Hunt, Carder W. "Evaluating the Union-Management Relationship in Government." PUBLIC ADMINISTRATION REVIEW 38 (September-October 1978): 431-36. Tables.

Perry and Hunt state that absenteeism and turnover, labor productivity, adaptability-flexibility, job satisfaction, commitment, and user satisfaction constitute evaluative criteria for determining organizational effectiveness in government. The authors emphasize that an explicit evaluative framework is required for judging the quality of the union-management relationship.

942   Perry, James L., and Levine, Charles H. "An Interorganizational Analysis of Power, Conflict, and Settlements in Public Sector Collective Bargaining." THE AMERICAN POLITICAL SCIENCE REVIEW 70 (December 1976): 1185-1201.

Perry and Levine state that collective bargaining negotiates the balance of organizational inducements and member contributions, that bargaining conflicts result in divergent goals for the union and government organizations, and that reconciliation of such goals depends on the joint decision-making process in collective bargaining. The tasks of the collective bargaining system are to insure municipal employees' rights and to satisfy the community's pluralistic interests.

943   Posey, Rollin B. "The New Militancy of Public Employees." PUBLIC ADMINISTRATION REVIEW 28 (March-April 1968): 111-17.

Posey probes the growth of unionization of governmental employees, denotes militant activity and attitude and reasons for militancy, and explores the role of the National Education Association (NEA) in the organization of the nation's public school teachers.

944   Post, Russell Lee, Jr. "Collective Bargaining by Teachers--Long-Range Implications." PUBLIC PERSONNEL MANAGEMENT 3 (September-October 1974): 431-34.

Recognizing that the collective bargaining process ideally promotes stability in labor-management situations, Post emphasizes that the teaching goal is still education. He suggests that the role, power, and prestige of the teacher will be in danger if teacher organizations continue to emphasize monetary rewards. Racial and economic problems must get primary consideration by teachers if collective bargaining is to remain a useful method, and not a negative one, in labor-management relations.

945   Public Affairs Research Council of Louisiana. COLLECTIVE BARGAINING IN THE PUBLIC SECTOR. Baton Rouge, La.: 1975. 32 p.

This book observes that the right of public employees to join unions has been protected by the courts and that there are ten states with no legislation authorizing governmental employees to negotiate with employers and to enter binding contracts. Where negotiations are carried out, the following areas are accepted as negotiable: wages and salaries, fringe benefits, retirement plans, union security clauses, working conditions, grievance procedures, and seniority.

946   Redburn, Thomas. "Government Unions: The New Bullies on the Block." WASHINGTON MONTHLY 6 (December 1974): 19-27.

Redburn maintains that government unionization is necessary to increase wages, but he reveals that collective bargaining has resulted in resistance to outside efforts to examine government performance. The author suggests that strong unions are removing the entire question of better quality service from the bargaining process, while managers are joining with them to insulate the public bureaucracy from any realistic analysis of incompetence and performance.

947   Rice, William V., Jr. "A Systems Model for Labor-Management Negotiations in the Federal Sector." PERSONNEL JOURNAL 53 (May 1974): 331-37.

Rice compares paternalistic management practices of the

past with the new participative system of collective bargaining. The author emphasizes that presidential Executive
Orders 10988 (1962), 11491 (1969), and 11616 (1971)
introduce collective bargaining methods in the public
sector which parallel procedures employed in private enterprise. He illustrates the labor management system of
the Air Force as a model of labor negotiations.

948   Schlessberg, Norman. "The Impact of Collective Bargaining on Pro-
       ductivity in the Public Services." In PRODUCTIVITY BARGAINING
       IN THE PUBLIC SECTOR, edited by Josef P. Sirefman, pp. 141-211.
       Hofstra University Yearbook of Business, Series 12, vol. 3. Hempstead,
       N.Y.: Hofstra University, 1977.

       Schlessberg analyzes productivity measurement, the appli-
       cation of general principles of productivity and measure-
       ment, the impact of unionization upon productivity, ap-
       proaches enhancing productivity and its measurement, and
       the impact of productivity issues upon collective bargain-
       ing in the public services. He discusses these considera-
       tions and their impacts upon New York City public em-
       ployees.

949   Sharpe, Carleton F., and Freedman, Elisha C. "Collective Bargain-
       ing in a Nonpartisan, Council-Manager City." PUBLIC ADMINISTRA-
       TION REVIEW 22 (Winter 1962): 13-18.

       The authors discuss the basic problems of collective bar-
       gaining and its impacts upon the Hartford, Connecticut,
       system of government. This article is useful for gaining
       an understanding of collective bargaining in municipal
       government in the early 1960s.

950   Silbiger, Sara. "The Missing Public--Collective Bargaining in Public
       Employment." PUBLIC PERSONNEL MANAGEMENT 4 (September-
       October 1975): 290-99.

       Silbiger believes that other municipalities and cities can
       learn from the institutional structure of municipal labor
       relations in New York City. Union influence for muni-
       cipal employees in New York has risen steadily in the
       1970s, but there is little linkage between this development
       and the city's general public interest. She concludes
       that bilateralism will fade slowly, if at all, in the Big
       Apple.

951   Spero, Sterling D. "Collective Bargaining in Public Employment:
       Form and Scope." PUBLIC ADMINISTRATION REVIEW 22 (Winter
       1962): 1-5.

       Spero describes the form and scope of collective bargaining

in government. He denotes that the opponents of collective bargaining regard it as a process presupposing
equality between the parties to the employment relationship, an assumption which conflicts with the claims of
the sovereign employer and runs counter to the "nature
of the state."

952   Stanley, David T. MANAGING LOCAL GOVERNMENT UNDER
UNION PRESSURE. Washington, D.C.: Brookings Institution, 1972.
177 p.

Stanley interviews union leaders and government officials,
inspecting the influence that unions of local government
employees had on the administration of nine urban areas.
Major areas of change include employment relationship;
hiring, promotion, and grievances; classification, pay,
and benefits; work management and working conditions;
budget and finance; and general impacts.

953   Stanley, Preston O. "Cost Determination in Federal Collective Bargaining." PUBLIC PERSONNEL MANAGEMENT 5 (September-October
1976): 335-42

The author states that costs of federal collective bargaining originate from responsibilities of the collective bargaining process, procedures and processes unique to collective bargaining, productivity, requirements, efficiency,
morale of employees, and certain overhead costs.

954   Stenberg, Carl W. "Labor Management Relations in State and Local
Government: Progress and Prospects." PUBLIC ADMINISTRATION
REVIEW 32 (March-April 1972): 102-7.

State and local governments have only recently awakened
to the implications of the unionization of their labor force.
The author predicts that during the 1970s more and more
state and local jurisdictions would adopt comprehensive
and special legislation and formal policies for dealing
with their organized employees. Stenberg posits that
unionization, bargaining, and strikes in the public service
indicate that state and local governments are under mounting pressure to achieve a workable balance between the
rights of their employees and the service responsibilities
and accountability of the public employer.

955   Stieber, Jack. "The Future of Public Employee Unionism in the United
States." INDUSTRIAL RELATIONS 28 (December 1974): 825-37.

Stieber states that organization of public employees in
the United States dates back to the 1830s, but that such
organization was not an important feature of the American

labor movement until the 1960s. Unions active in government include public unions, mixed unions, employee associations which concentrate on public grievances and lobbying, uniformed protective organizations representing police and fire fighters, and professional organizations whose primary function is to serve those concerns but which have become active in collective bargaining.

956   Terry, Newell B. "Collective Bargaining in the U.S. Department of the Interior." PUBLIC ADMINISTRATION REVIEW 22 (Winter 1962): 19-23.

The author describes the extent of collective bargaining, the limitations on collective bargaining, the selection of the bargaining agent, and limitation on workers' activities in the Department of the Interior. This brief essay is useful for gaining information on early collective bargaining in the federal government.

957   Tyler, Gus. "Why They Organize." PUBLIC ADMINISTRATION REVIEW 32 (March-April 1972): 97-101.

This article describes the stages of labor history in the United States, notes the rise in demand for services, and cites the forces influencing public employee unionization. Why, in summary, do they organize? The author says "for the same reason that boys and girls become men and women. They grow up and demand adult status. The grievances that employees raise, the hopes they voice, the recognition they demand, the influence they seek in the larger society--all these are part of growing up. It's as natural as life itself."

958   Valdes, William C. "The Trend of Negotiations in the Federal Service." BUREAUCRAT 2 (Spring 1973): 47-53.

Valdes states that a broad range of subjects have been quietly negotiated by management and labor. These include hazard pay, environmental pay, hours and schedules of work, promotion procedures, assignment of overtime and vacations, discipline, dues allotments, union steward rights and responsibilities, union representation on committees, safety conditions and practices, wash-up time, and tools.

959   Van Asselt, Karl A. "Impasse Resolution." PUBLIC ADMINISTRATION REVIEW 32 (March-April 1972): 114-19.

The author elaborates on four basic methods of resolving impasses without resorting to the strike. These include direct negotiations, mediation, fact-finding, and arbitration.

960   Weber, Arnold R.   "Federal Labor Relations: Problems and Prospects."
       BUREAUCRAT 2 (Spring 1973):   69-78.

           Weber maintains that the federal personnel administration
           system has four distinct components: 1) basic conditions of
           employment are essentially established by law, which
           diminishes the scope of collective bargaining; 2) basic
           levels of compensation are not subject to managerial dis-
           cretion or the exercise of economic sanctions by employee
           organizations; 3) elements of wage structure are determined
           by law and by Congress; and 4) the size and complexity
           of the federal personnel system must be seen as a force
           in its own right.

961   Zander, Arnold S.   "A Union View of Collective Bargaining in the
       Public Service." PUBLIC ADMINISTRATION REVIEW 22 (Winter
       1962):   5-13.

           "Why does the union in the public service want collec-
           tive bargaining?   The union wants collective bargaining
           because it is concerned with the general welfare of the
           public employee, raising wage levels in public employ-
           ment, improving working conditions, and providing job
           security, and because it is equally concerned with im-
           proving the public service.   The one is dependent upon
           the other."   Zander defines the meaning of collective
           bargaining, notes obstacles to the concept, and describes
           the mechanics of collective bargaining.

Chapter 7

GOVERNMENTAL DISCRIMINATION

AND EQUAL EMPLOYMENT

A. GENERAL SELECTIONS

962   Anderson, Bernard E. "Full Employment and Economic Equality."
CIVIL RIGHTS DIGEST 8 (Winter-Spring 1976): 18-25.

Anderson asserts that an effective full employment policy
is necessary to insure the future economic gains of women
and minorities. The goal should be not only to reduce
joblessness, but also to equalize occupational status, which
often is characterized by discriminatory hiring standards,
racial exclusion in promotions, sexism in job assignments,
and inequality in fringe benefit coverage.

963   Benokraitis, Nijole V., and Feagin, Joe R. AFFIRMATIVE ACTION
AND EQUAL OPPORTUNITY: ACTION, INACTION, REACTION.
Boulder, Colo.: Westview Press, 1978. xix, 255 p.

The authors of this text examine employment in government, industry, and higher education and enrollment in
colleges and universities in order to determine the status
of women and minorities as employees and students. They
describe the machinery of affirmative action, its budget
and staff problems, the compliance and enforcement processes, and the results of the program. In the final chapter,
they include a theoretical explanation for the resistance
to affirmative action and express their pessimism about
the program's ability to accomplish its goals. This text
is an excellent review of the problems and prospects of
affirmative action concepts and programs.

964   Boyd, Rose Williams, and Schick, Richard P. MODELS FOR AFFIRMA-
TIVE ACTION.   Washington, D.C.: National Civil Service League,
1977. 90 p.

The authors define affirmative action and describe the basic components of an affirmative action plan and a compliance evaluation checklist for an affirmative action program. The models for affirmative action programs, as examined in this brief manuscript, include the legal basis and dissemination of affirmative action policy statement, grievance process, utilization analysis, labor market analysis, identification of problem areas, implementation strategies, numerical goals and timetables, and monitoring and reporting procedures. Boyd and Schick offer a very informative guide to affirmative action procedures and concepts.

965   Browning, Edgar K. "Inequality, Income and Opportunity: I. How Much More Equality Can We Afford?" PUBLIC INTEREST 43 (Spring 1976): 90-110.

Browning maintains that in spite of misleading government statistics, the distribution of income in the United States has become dramatically more equal in recent years due to egalitarian government policies. He examines economic and ethical implications of additional redistribution of wealth to indicate that massive redistribution would be unwise.

966   Campbell, Alan K. "Approaches to Defining, Measuring, and Achieving Equity in the Public Sector." PUBLIC ADMINISTRATION REVIEW 36 (September-October 1976): 556-62.

Campbell states that the issue of equity and what it means is hardly new; the current effort to give it operational meaning in concrete policy areas is new. He examines equity in terms of school finance, noneducation municipal services, and the reorganization of local government.

967   Chitwood, Stephen R. "Social Equity and Social Service Productivity." PUBLIC ADMINISTRATION REVIEW 34 (January-February 1974): 29-35.

This essay examines the emphasis on increasing the productivity of government activities and assesses its historical relation to earlier government management movements. Chitwood illustrates how productivity measures have traditionally neglected social equity in the distribution of public services. He identifies the important relationships between productivity measures and social equity in supplying government services. Chitwood categorizes the distribution patterns and standards which may be used in measuring the social equity with which public services are provided.

968   Finkle, Arthur L. "Avoiding the High Costs of Job Discrimination
       Remedies." PUBLIC PERSONNEL MANAGEMENT 5 (March–April
       1976): 139–42.

       Finkle asserts that the cost of settling a job discrimination
       issue in court is high. Public employers may prefer to
       settle disputes through affirmative action programs or by
       accepting a program imposed by an administrative agency.
       The author maintains that while it is good practice to
       resolve conflicts before facing court action, the time and
       money spent by government and private nonprofit agencies
       on cases of little financial merit is staggering.

969   _____. "The Pragmatic Philosophy of Affirmative Action." BUREAU-
       CRAT 3 (July 1974): 130–39.

       Finkle states that affirmative action plans are becoming
       the explosive social issue of the 1970s. He maintains
       that, confusion aside, affirmative action can be accom-
       modated into a merit system without changing its sub-
       stance. He believes that the introduction of remedial
       action on job discrimination by the federal government
       has enormous implications for state merit system agencies.

970   Flanagan, Robert J. "Actual Versus Potential Impact of Government
       Antidiscrimination Programs." INDUSTRIAL AND LABOR RELATIONS
       REVIEW 29 (July 1976): 486–507.

       Flanagan states that racial inequality has narrowed most
       rapidly among females, in newer labor-force cohorts, and
       in the South. He maintains that it is hard to measure
       the effects of government activity intended to advance
       the economic status of minorities and projects that time-
       series and cross-section approaches have had modest im-
       pacts upon the relative economic gains of blacks in the
       1960s.

971   Gusfield, Joseph R. "Equalitarianism and Bureaucratic Recruitment."
       ADMINISTRATIVE SCIENCE QUARTERLY 2 (March 1958): 521–41.
       Tables.

       Bureaucratization and equalitarianism are major trends in
       Western society and the use of objective criteria in re-
       cruitment for bureaucratic positions is a reflection of these
       trends. The author examines recent analyses of social
       mobility and organizations in this context and finds that
       bureaucratic norms have nonbureaucratic consequences.
       Gusfield reveals that occupational mobility in professions
       often regarded as open is limited and is apparently a
       function of their expanding size rather than an increase
       in competitive equality associated with bureaucratic norms.

972   Harmon, Michael M. "Social Equity and Organizational Man: Mo-
        tivation and Organizational Democracy." PUBLIC ADMINISTRATION
        REVIEW 34 (January-February 1974): 11-18.

        Harmon concludes that "the concept of social equity simply
        does not square with the dominant utilitarian premises on
        which the study and practice of public administration have
        for so many years been based. . . . If social equity is
        to be elevated to a central position among the values of
        the discipline, a serious rethinking is required about the
        manner in which 'responsible' choices of administrators
        are defined and about the appropriate structure of and
        distribution of power within public organizations."

973   Hart, David K. "Social Equity, Justice, and the Equitable Admini-
        strator." PUBLIC ADMINISTRATION REVIEW 34 (January-February
        1974): 3-11.

        Hart suggests that this is the time of social equity. He
        points out that social equity needs a fuller substantive
        ethical content; that the advocates of this concept base
        their justifications and prescriptions on the "extant American
        ethical paradigm"; that this paradigm denies legitimacy to
        social equity and is suffering from declining public con-
        fidence; that John Rawls's A THEORY OF JUSTICE is a
        most promising alternative ethical paradigm; and that Rawls's
        theory of justice can provide an ethical foundation for a
        substantive theory of social equity and for a professional
        code for "equitable public administrators."

974   Hellriegel, Don, and Short, Larry. "Equal Employment Opportunity:
        In the Federal Government: A Comparative Analysis." PUBLIC AD-
        MINISTRATION REVIEW 32 (November-December 1972): 851-58.
        Tables.

        This article identifies and discusses three distinct stages in
        the development of equal employment opportunity in the
        federal government. The stages are labeled the period of
        inaction, period of reaction, and period of proaction.
        The policies and procedures with respect to equal oppor-
        tunity of employment are briefly explained for each stage.
        A comparative analysis of the stages is undertaken with
        respect to the levels of employment and advancement of
        racial minorities in the federal government.

975   Higgins, James M. "The Complicated Process of Establishing Goals for
        Equal Employment." PERSONNEL JOURNAL 5 (December 1975):
        631-37.

        Higgins relates that the Equal Employment Opportunity
        Commission and the Office of Federal Contract Compliance

have been tardy and indefinite in establishing equal employment opportunity program requirements and in enforcing affirmative action program compliance.

976   Hill, Herbert. "Affirmative Action and the Quest for Job Equality." REVIEW OF BLACK POLITICAL ECONOMY 6 (Spring 1976): 263-78.

Hill maintains that affirmative action programs will be necessary if the goal of Title VII of the Civil Rights Act of 1964 is to be realized. He points out that affirmative action is a redistribution and reallocation of jobs and income within the political and economic structure. He believes that voluntary compliance and good faith efforts do not eliminate job discrimination.

977   Johnson, George E., and Welch, Finis. "The Labor Market Implications of an Economywide Affirmative Action Program." INDUSTRIAL AND LABOR RELATIONS REVIEW 29 (July 1976): 508-22.

The number of skilled minority workers in the economy, the extent of minority discrimination in society, and the response of organizations to proposed changes in the employment environment determine the quota of minority hiring in an economywide affirmative action program. Johnson and Welch discuss probabilities in the transfer of income from skilled workers to unskilled workers.

978   Kranz, Harry. THE PARTICIPATION BUREAUCRACY. Lexington, Mass.: D.C. Heath and Co., 1976. 244 p.

Kranz maintains that increased minority employment by the nation's bureaucracy is a positive force in American society. Increased minority employment benefits minorities as citizens and as public employees, consumers and potential recipients benefit from minority hiring, and the entire American system benefits. He claims that an unrepresentative elite has dominated the executive, legislative, and judicial branches of government and that a participatory bureaucracy has helped alleviate this imbalance.

979   Long, James E. "Employment Discrimination in the Federal Sector." JOURNAL OF HUMAN RESOURCES 11 (Winter 1976): 86-97.

A count of the number of blacks and females in pay grades and job classes suggests that federal hiring and promotion procedures are biased in favor of white and male workers. The article shows that even after making adjustments for productivity differences according to race and sex, it is estimated that blacks and females earn considerably less than white males in federal employment. The author im-

plies that barriers to equal opportunity in federal employment are lower for blacks than for females.

980   Lovell, Catherine. "Three Key Issues in Affirmative Action." PUBLIC
ADMINISTRATION REVIEW 34 (May-June 1974): 235-37.

The author contends that the distinction between affirmative action and "non-descrimination," the necessity of
preferential hiring and the setting of target quotas in the
affirmative action process, and the reexamination of traditional standards of "quality" constitute the three key
issues in affirmative action.

981   McGregor, Eugene B., Jr. "Social Equity and the Public Service."
PUBLIC ADMINISTRATION REVIEW 34 (January-February 1974): 18-
29.

McGregor discusses the implications of the clash between
"social equity" and "merit" for civil service employment
in the United States. His sole concern is with the politics of the struggle to define social equity in the public
services in the United States. He concludes: "The advocate of excellence and the proponent of social equity
appear to be allies. Both find it essential to discover
what public servants actually do for work and how people
come to be educated, recruited, selected, and promoted
in the work they do. Rarely have two so disparate concerns found such common ground."

982   McNamara, Donna B.; Scherer, Joseph J.; and Safferstone, Mark J.
PREPARING FOR AFFIRMATIVE ACTION: A MANUAL FOR PRACTICAL
TRAINING. Garrett Park, Md.: Garrett Park Press, 1978. 142 p.

The authors offer a very informative manual for implementing an affirmative action program. Chapter discussions
include establishment of workshop objectives, sex bias in
the 1970s, the legal basis for affirmative action, various
myths of American society and factual information in regard to minorities and protected classes (women), legal
knowledge questionnaire concerning federal equal employment regulations and affirmative action guidelines, and
traditional characteristics of masculinity and femininity.
This is recommended to practitioners who want to know
how affirmative action can work.

983   Okun, Arthur M. EQUALITY AND EFFICIENCY: THE BIG TRADEOFF.
Washington, D.C.: Brookings Institution, 1975. 124 p.

In this analysis, the American system emerges as a viable,
if uneasy, compromise in which the market has its place
and democratic institutions keep it in check. Okun

posits that America's political and social institutions distribute rights and privileges universally and proclaim the equality of all citizens while its economic institutions, with efficiency as their guiding principle, create disparities among citizens in living standards and material welfare. Society's concern for human dignity can be directed at reducing the economic deprivation that stains the record of American democracy--through progressive taxation, transfer payments, job programs, broadening equality of opportunity, eliminating racial and sexual discrimination, and lowering barriers to capital. This is a most important book for students and practitioners of public administration.

984   Porter, David O., and Porter, Teddie Wood. "Social Equity and Fiscal Federalism." PUBLIC ADMINISTRATION REVIEW 34 (January-February 1974): 36-43.

The Porters emphasize that there is no single or simple definition of social equity. Recognizing that tax competition, uneven distributions of income and wealth among jurisdictions, pervasive spillovers of benefits and costs among state and local governments, and more productive federal income taxes are factors which affect fiscal balance among local, state, and federal levels of government, the authors conclude that the net impact of these factors is a growing fiscal imbalance. Despite these failings, there are few incentives in general revenue sharing legislation that will stimulate "any serious reforms." They state that national policy is needed to guide in reforming local governments because the locals are the "least rational, least ordered, and least able to operate as full partners in federalism."

985   Reeves, Earl J. "Equal Employment and the Concept of the Bureaucracy as a Representative Institution." MIDWEST REVIEW OF PUBLIC ADMINISTRATION 6 (February 1972): 3-13.

This article focuses primarily on the attempts to gain equal employment opportunities for blacks. Reeves believes that "a genuinely representative bureaucracy must be representative of its own internal composition and that this representativeness must extend through all levels of the hierarchy. This requires an opportunity for blacks and other minorities to pursue a career with real opportunities for advancement to positions of decision making, even if this requires the use of quotas and compensatory hiring, training and promotion programs."

986 _____. "Making Equality of Employment Opportunity a Reality in the Federal Service." PUBLIC ADMINISTRATION REVIEW 30 (January-February 1970): 43-49.

> "If everyone competing under the merit system started from an equal beginning there would be no problem. But everyone does not start equally and there is a need for a more flexible approach to the merit system which will place more emphasis on potential and less on formal measures of educational achievement and experience."

987 Rosen, Bernard. "Affirmative Action Produces Equal Employment Opportunity for All." PUBLIC ADMINISTRATION REVIEW 34 (May-June 1974): 237-41.

> Rosen, executive director of the U.S. Civil Service Commission, writes that "affirmative action is the logical extension of a nondiscrimination policy in employment. The United States Civil Service Commission does not think of equal employment opportunity as a separate program outside the mainstream of personnel management, nor does it administer it that way. Equal employment opportunity and employment based on merit principles are truly synonymous concepts."

988 Rosenbloom, David H. FEDERAL EQUAL EMPLOYMENT OPPORTUNITY: POLITICS AND PUBLIC PERSONNEL ADMINISTRATION. New York: Praeger Publishers, 1977. xiii, 184 p.

> The author concentrates on the politics of the Federal Equal Employment Opportunity Program, describing the nature of bureaucratic politics in the federal government and how administration may be infused with politics. Rosenbloom illustrates the extent to which organizational and administrative choices may be political choices and how agencies use their control over the implementation of policies in order to protect their "cultures" and values. The author suggests that the equal employment opportunity policy arena is dominated by those persons seeking to maintain the merit system and those seeking a far more representative federal service.

989 Saltzstein, Grace Hall. "Representative Bureaucracy and Bureaucratic Responsibility: Problems and Prospects." ADMINISTRATION AND SOCIETY 10 (February 1979): 465-75.

> Saltzstein relates that students, in examining representative bureaucracy, express considerable interest in linkage between active and passive representation. Representative bureaucracy, as a method of promoting administrative responsibility, remains misunderstood and poorly operationalized. The purpose of this article is to provide an

explanation of the theory, to evaluate existing operation-
alization concepts, and to formulate conclusions regarding
the utility of representative bureaucracy theory as legitimation of bureaucratic policy making.

990   Schiller, Bradley R. "Inequality, Income, and Opportunity: II:
       Equality, Opportunity, and the 'Good Job.'" PUBLIC INTEREST 43
       (Spring 1976): 111-20.

       Schiller states that evidence suggests that distribution of
       income in the United States is immune to major economic and
       public policy changes. He indicates that such rigidity
       of income distribution presents a serious challenge to
       equality and opportunity concepts. The author conveys
       that his evidence implies that aggregate income distribu-
       tion is a misleading index of opportunity stratification.
       Black workers are less likely to advance in the area of
       earnings distribution and are more likely to fall back
       when they reach the top of the distribution.

991   Segers, Mary C. "Equality in Contemporary Political Thought: An
       Examination and An Assessment." ADMINISTRATION AND SOCIETY
       10 (February 1979): 409-36.

       Segers considers ideas of contemporary Anglo-American
       political thought on equality. The thrust of this essay
       considers the discussion in the United States between neo-
       conservatives and egalitarians concerning definition of basic
       equality, meaning of equality of opportunity, and proper
       policies essential to guarantee to all citizens equal oppor-
       tunity for occupational achievement. The author declares
       that a crucial idea emerging from this analysis is that equal
       provision is not identical provision and that to treat people
       as equals may at times require that we handle them dif-
       ferently.

992   Sowell, Thomas. "'Affirmative Action' Reconsidered." PUBLIC IN-
       TEREST 42 (Winter 1976): 47-65.

       Sowell asserts that affirmative action programs have done
       nothing to improve the employment circumstances of mi-
       norities and females. He concludes that the results of
       many affirmative action initiatives are undeserved accom-
       plishments by minority and female persons. Sowell states
       that persons from these groups in society were already
       making progress without government programs of this type
       and that affirmative action concepts have caused many
       Americans to question the legitimacy of such advancements.

993 White, Orion, Jr., and Gates, Bruce L. "Statistical Theory and
     Equity in the Delivery of Social Services." PUBLIC ADMINISTRATION
     REVIEW 34 (January-February 1974): 43-51.

     White and Gates argue "that American society is moving
     toward a post-industrial condition and that public orga-
     nizations must change both their concept of social equity
     as well as their structure and processes if inequities are
     to be reduced or prevented from growing worse in the
     future." The authors suggest "a picture of a society
     which is no longer centered around the processes of pro-
     duction and consumption. . . . The key to the image
     of post industrialism is that symbols will replace goods
     as the substance of the economic exchange process."
     They call for openness and participation in the admini-
     strative processes by which social services are distributed.

B. MINORITIES

994 Barnett, Marguerite Ross, and Hefner, James A., eds. PUBLIC POLICY
     FOR THE BLACK COMMUNITY: STRATEGIES AND PERSPECTIVES.
     Port Washington, N.Y.: Alfred Publishing Co., 1976. xii, 270 p.
     Paper.

     Selections include discussions on American racial public
     policy from a theoretical perspective, the ghetto, black
     politics in the South, legal strategy for blacks, a com-
     parative analysis of black and white wealth, problems,
     policies, and prospects for blacks in the American economy,
     and public policy and some political consequences. All
     of the authors caution against the confusion of symbolic
     and real power and emphasize that blacks in America
     must confront the "illusion of inclusion."

995 Berman, William C. THE POLITICS OF CIVIL RIGHTS IN THE TRUMAN
     ADMINISTRATION. Columbus: Ohio State University Press, 1970.
     xi, 261 p.

     Among the most significant domestic developments during
     the Truman presidency was the emergence of the civil
     rights movement. Berman suggests that Truman's sponsor-
     ship and endorsement of a civil rights program beginning
     in 1948 was not synonymous with active support for its
     passage. He concludes that Truman's greatest civil rights
     achievement, illustrating the intelligent use of executive
     power to change, within narrow limits, a racist social
     structure, was the desegregation of an authoritarian mili-
     tary establishment.

996   Cousens, Frances Reissman. PUBLIC CIVIL RIGHTS AGENCIES AND
       FAIR EMPLOYMENT: PROMISE VS. PERFORMANCE. New York:
       Frederick A. Praeger, 1969. xviii, 162 p.

       This book is based on evaluation of employment patterns
       and opportunities for blacks and other nonwhites in a
       number of selected industries and in areas served by public
       fair employment or civil rights agencies. The findings
       generate some serious reservations about the relevance
       and viability of civil rights programs in the present con-
       text of race relations. Chapters include discussions of
       the Equal Employment Opportunity Commission (EEOC),
       an analysis of employment patterns by industry, geographic
       comparisons of employment patterns, and recommendations
       for additional research. This volume concludes that public
       agencies should be persuaded to depart from their tradi-
       tional reliance on complaints and to move in the direction
       of developing methods and conducting pattern surveys.

997   Diaz de Krofcheck, Maria Delores, and Jackson, Carlos. "The Chicano
       Experience with Nativism in Public Administration." PUBLIC ADMINI-
       STRATION REVIEW 34 (November-December 1974): 534-39. Tables.

       This article identifies certain underlying mechanisms exist-
       ing in public institutions which selectively exclude Chi-
       canos from participating in policy making and in rendering
       services to the public. The authors explore underlying
       philosophic values and assumptions which are held by the
       majority culture and which perpetuate the exclusionary
       mechanism directed at Chicanos.

998   Dobbins, Cheryl, and Walker, Dollie R. "The Role of Black Colleges
       in Public Affairs Education." PUBLIC ADMINISTRATION REVIEW 34
       (November-December 1974): 540-52. Charts.

       The authors discuss the organizational structure, or the
       explicit role, of black colleges in public affairs education
       present and future, how the role can be implemented, the
       obstacles to fulfilling this role and responsibility, and
       recommendations for the expansion of this role in the future.
       Dobbins and Walker state that black colleges and univer-
       sities are intent on becoming forums which bring together
       people who are both fearful and distrustful of local gov-
       ernment administrators and planners.

999   Gibson, Frank K., and Yeager, Samuel. "Trends in the Federal Em-
       ployment of Blacks." PUBLIC PERSONNEL MANAGEMENT 4 (May-
       June 1975): 189-95.

       The authors relate that for the period 1962-70, black rep-
       resentation slowly improved in all civil service regions.

When compared to the black percentage of the population, blacks were overrepresented in most regions in general
schedule positions. When compared to nonblacks, blacks
were overrepresented in the lower grade levels and underrepresented in upper grade levels.

1000   Glazer, Nathan. AFFIRMATIVE DISCRIMINATION: ETHNIC IN-
        EQUALITY AND PUBLIC POLICY. New York: Basic Books, 1975.
        248 p.

        In examining government policies in employment, school
        desegregation, and residential location, Glazer discusses
        the emergence of an American ethnic pattern, analyzes
        affirmative action in employment, education, and housing,
        examines the white ethnic political reaction, and probes
        issues of morality, politics, and the future of affirmative
        action. This text is an excellent primer for examining
        the affirmative action executive orders and related legis-
        lation of the 1970s.

1001   Goldstein, Morris, and Smith, Robert S. "The Estimated Impact of
        the Antidiscrimination Program Aimed at Federal Contractors." IN-
        DUSTRIAL AND LABOR RELATIONS REVIEW 29 (July 1976): 523-43.

        The authors state that for black males, changes in relative
        employment and relative wage share were greater in con-
        tractor than in noncontractor firms and still greater in
        firms subjected to compliance review. The reader learns
        that the changes for black females were not significantly
        different among the three groups. White females and
        other minorities declined in relative employment and
        relative wage share in contractor firms.

1002   Hall, Grace, and Saltzstein, Alan. "Equal Employment for Minorities
        in Municipal Government." SOCIAL SCIENCE QUARTERLY 57
        (March 1977): 864-72.

        In a survey of twenty-six Texas cities, the authors found
        that public employment reflects substantial variations in
        hiring patterns of blacks and Spanish-surnamed minorities.
        Spanish-surnamed employment is more directly related to
        characteristics of that minority than is the case for blacks.
        The authors conclude that employment opportunity for
        blacks seems to be greater in rapidly growing central
        cities and that Mexican-Americans are more likely to be
        employed in environments having a stable population and
        less employment in manufacturing concerns.

1003   Hamilton, Charles V. "Racial, Ethnic, and Social Class Politics and
        Administration." PUBLIC ADMINISTRATION REVIEW 32 (October
        1972): 638-48.

Hamilton discusses the politics of protest, participation, and governance of newly politicized groups and presents implications for public administration.

1004   Harper, Robert. "Black Administrators and Administrative Law." JOURNAL OF AFRO-AMERICAN ISSUES 3 (Spring 1975): 197-206.

Harper states that nearly 20 percent of the administrators employed in the federal civil service are black, that black administrators have numerous opportunities to exercise and implement power, and that black bureaucrats act within lawful limits to insure that black communities receive public goods and services. It is uncertain if black bureaucrats' power will be used to enhance the power of the government agency or to exercise more complete accountability to the black community.

1005   Harvey, James C. BLACK CIVIL RIGHTS DURING THE JOHNSON ADMINISTRATION. Jackson: University and College Press of Mississippi, 1973. xiv, 245 p.

The author analyzes all facets of civil rights activities during the Johnson administration, including the Civil Rights Act of 1964 and the presidential election, the Voting Rights Act of 1965 and the Civil Rights Act of 1968, coordination of federal civil rights activities, black public civilian employment and blacks in the armed forces, housing and private employment, voting and education, and health and welfare services. This text is an excellent primer for understanding the origins of affirmative action and equal opportunity efforts on behalf of black Americans during the 1970s.

1006   _____. CIVIL RIGHTS DURING THE KENNEDY ADMINISTRATION. Hattiesburg: University and College Press of Mississippi, 1971. 87 p.

The purpose of this brief text is to analyze and evaluate the actions of the Kennedy administration (1961-63) in civil rights. Harvey emphasizes Kennedy's use of the different levers available to the chief executive in dealing with the problem of racial discrimination. He suggests that the image of the presidency under Kennedy changed from a position of neutrality on civil rights under Dwight D. Eisenhower to one of positive action on behalf of black Americans.

1007   Herbert, Adam W. "The Evolving Challenges of Black Urban Administration." JOURNAL OF AFRO-AMERICAN ISSUES 3 (Spring 1975): 173-79.

Herbert states that challenges for black urban administrators will include greater emphasis on local service productivity, program competition for government funds in an era of resource scarcity, continued expectations for benefits received from public programs, and declining hiring and promotion of minority professionals.

1008 _____. "The Minority Administrator: Problems, Prospects, and Challenges." PUBLIC ADMINISTRATION REVIEW 34 (November-December 1974): 556-63. Tables.

The author observes that the role demands on minority administrators include system demands, "traditional" role expectations, colleague pressures, community accountability, personal commitment to community, and personal ambition.

1009 Howard, Lawrence C. "Black Praxis of Governance: Toward an Alternative Paradigm for Public Administration." JOURNAL OF AFRO-AMERICAN ISSUES 3 (Spring 1975): 143-59.

This article shows how the word "praxis" encompasses the method by which blacks are moving to collapse theory into practice to attain liberation. A move away from both the theory and practice of administration and toward establishment of a black praxis of governance is needed. The author describes how black demands for change articulate, in large measure, the position of the oppressed in America and clarify the ideal for white Americans. He believes that the crisis, in which the black community encounters difficulties in confrontation with public officials or in negotiation with bureaucracies, is an administrative paradigm problem.

1010 Hunt, Deryl G. "The Black Perspective on Public Management." PUBLIC ADMINISTRATION REVIEW 34 (November-December 1974): 520-25.

This article suggests the urgent need for changes in public management as government must be made more responsive to the aspirations of blacks as a collective group. Hunt offers specific suggestions as to the role that universities, government agencies, professional organizations, and foundations might have in realizing the black perspective on public management.

1011 Levine, Charles H. "Beyond the Sound and Fury of Quotas and Targets." PUBLIC ADMINISTRATION REVIEW 34 (May-June 1974): 240-41.

In examining the utilization of numerical quotas and target figures to increase minority group representation in public organizations, Levine denotes impacts of mobility, leverage for investment in personal development, human resources investment, authority and responsibility, organizational experience, and policy influence upon the concepts of quotas and targets.

1012   Levy, Burton. "Effects of 'Racism' on the Racial Bureaucracy." PUBLIC ADMINISTRATION REVIEW 32 (September-October 1972): 479-86.

This article deals with the post-1965 emergence of black power, civil disorder, and racism as the American problem, as differentiated from previous notions of prejudice or discrimination. The author examines the effect of these phenomena on the policies, politics, and techniques of bureaucracy. Ways in which organizational policies were modified, the relationships of government agencies to the general community and to the black community, and the effect of racial conflict upon black-white relations are probed in this essay.

1013   Nelson, William E., Jr. "Black Elected Administrators: The Trials of Office." PUBLIC ADMINISTRATION REVIEW 34 (November-December 1974): 526-33.

This article analyzes a variety of problems faced by black elected administrators as they attempt to fulfill the black community's urgent desire for institutional reform and a radical shift in governmental priorities. Nelson makes an inventory of the number of blacks elected to public office in recent years and the kind of positions they have held, analyzes the significant problems common to black elected administrators, considers the strategies adopted by black elected administrators to overcome these problems, and comments on the lessons that can be learned from the experiences of black elected officials.

1014   Rich, Wilbur C. "Future Manpower in Urban Management: A Black Perspective." JOURNAL OF AFRO-AMERICAN ISSUES 3 (Spring 1975): 160-72.

Rich suggests that the black perspective on urban management is that blacks will be more aggressive in assuming government roles in society. This perspective is that changes in the manner and attitudes of how things are done is not sufficient for American blacks. Action, participants gaining "know how" on the job, technical skills for the unskilled, and the acquisition of jobs are the future resources of blacks and the road to exercising real political power.

1015   Robinson, Rose M. "Conference on Minority Public Administrators."
        PUBLIC ADMINISTRATION REVIEW 34 (November-December 1974):
        552-56.

        The Conference of Minority Public Administrators (COMPA),
        is an affiliate of the American Society for Public Admini-
        stration (ASPA). Established in 1970, the author states
        that COMPA is concerned with the improvement of the
        quality of public services affecting the lives and well-
        being of minority citizens and the expansion of oppor-
        tunities for members of minority groups to assume leader-
        ship in the public service.

1016   Rose, Winfield H., and Chia, Tiang Ping. "The Impact of the Equal
        Employment Opportunity Act of 1972 on Black Employment in the
        Federal Service: A Preliminary Analysis." PUBLIC ADMINISTRATION
        REVIEW 38 (May-June 1978): 245-51. Tables.

        This article sketches the historical development of equal
        employment opportunity and affirmative action, analyzes
        what these terms mean, and examines the statistical record
        to assess the effectiveness of these programs in enhancing
        the number and status of black employees in the U.S.
        civil service.

1017   Rosenbloom, David H., and Grabosky, Peter N. "Racial and Ethnic
        Competition for Federal Service Positions." MIDWEST REVIEW OF
        PUBLIC ADMINISTRATION 11 (December 1977): 281-90. Tables.

        The authors believe that an examination of interminority
        group competition for bureaucratic positions is theoretically
        important because it focuses attention on different racial
        and ethnic employment patterns, attendant patterns of
        discrimination, and subcultural congruence with dominant
        social values. They conclude that greater knowledge
        concerning subcultural congruence with bureaucratic needs
        and dominant societal values would enable us not only to
        design equal employment opportunity programs but also to
        understand more fully some of the constraints on the
        further development of passive bureaucratic representation.

1018   Thompson, Frank J. "Bureaucratic Responsiveness in the Cities: The
        Problem of Minority Hiring." URBAN AFFAIRS QUARTERLY 10
        (September 1974): 40-68.

        Thompson maintains that responsiveness to low-resource
        groups is in short supply. He asserts that sympathetic
        officials and responsiveness scorecards tend to precipitate
        concessions even when low-resource challengers cannot
        convince officials that they deserve more. Uncertainty
        can spur concessions, impede them, or thwart challengers.

1019 _____. "Minority Groups in Public Bureaucracies: Are Passive and Active Representation Linked?" ADMINISTRATION AND SOCIETY 8 (August 1976): 201-26.

> Thompson asserts that despite the doubts of some observers, existing evidence suggests that nonwhite civil servants actively represent the minority community more than white officials do, particularly under certain circumstances. This article suggests that at least in part, linkage is a function of conditions in the organization's environment, the mobilization of employees into organized groups, and the physical and positional location of minority civil servants within the agency.

1020 Williams, Cortez H. "Employing the Black Administrator." PUBLIC PERSONNEL MANAGEMENT 4 (March-April 1975): 76-83.

> Williams states that black administrators in white corporate and governmental structures are in a relatively new situation. Because of cultural diversity, black administrators encounter a wide spectrum of sociopolitical administrative problems. The author reveals that black administrators have few opportunities to comprehend bureaucratic relevance which, in the long run, weakens their abilities to understand technical and administrative problems.

C. SEXUAL DISCRIMINATION

1021 Abramson, Joan. OLD BOYS--NEW WOMEN: THE POLITICS OF SEX DISCRIMINATION. New York: Praeger Publishers, 1979. 300 p.

> Using six case studies to illustrate the human dimension of sex discrimination, Abramson explores the politics of government antidiscrimination enforcement. The case histories discuss women who filed sex discrimination complaints and were met with harrassment from employers and neglect from agencies. The author describes the history and current status of enforcement and analyzes possible new strategies.

1022 Acker, Joan, and Van Houten, Donald R. "Differential Recruitment and Control: The Sex Structuring of Organizations." ADMINISTRATIVE SCIENCE QUARTERLY 19 (June 1974): 152-63.

> The author suggests that men generally have more power in organizations than women; this is labelled the sex power differential. This sex structuring of organizations may be as important as social-psychological factors in understanding sex differences in organizational behavior. They conclude that sex differences in organizational participation

are related to differential recruitment of women into jobs
requiring dependence and passivity, to selective recruitment of particularly compliant women into these jobs,
and to control mechanisms used in organizations for women.

1023   Bishop, Joan Fiss. "The Women's Movement in ASPA." PUBLIC AD-
MINISTRATION REVIEW 36 (July-August 1976): 349-54.

Bishop outlines legal precursors to women's activities in
public administration, reviews the rise of the women's
liberation movement, notes the birth of the American
Society for Public Administration in 1971, and relates
the contributions of various task forces and committees
within ASPA toward the progress of women in public administration.

1024   Chapman, J. Brad, and Luthan, Fred. "The Female Leadership Dilemma." PUBLIC PERSONNEL MANAGEMENT 4 (May-June 1975):
173-79.

This article suggests that the female leader is caught in
a dual-conflict concerning the organization and herself.
Chapman and Luthan reveal that the female leader will
be criticized as being too intuitive and passive. The
eventual solution lies in new thinking in recruitment,
selection, placement, training, and organizational
development.

1025   Denhardt, Robert B., and Perkins, Jan. "The Coming of Death of
Administrative Man." PUBLIC ADMINISTRATION REVIEW 36 (July-
August 1976): 379-84.

Noting that administrative man provides not only a starting
point from which all major components of the rational
model of organization flow, but also a model for the
culturally dominant version of how people in organizations
should act, the authors focus on alternative theories of
organization developed in the women's movement. They
consider the possible implications of the new patterns upon
the ways individuals think about and behave in complex
organizations.

1026   Fox, Elliot M. "Mary Parker Follett: The Enduring Tradition."
PUBLIC ADMINISTRATION REVIEW 28 (November-December 1968):
520-29.

The author distinguishes this pioneer of modern management in the following manner: "She was a woman who
achieved a place in what was then largely a man's world.
She was one of the first to see that the handling of people
constituted a major problem of modern management. She

was quite unique in recognizing that the concepts that
had mainly concerned political philosophers were relevant
also to the process of management, administration, and
leadership in almost any field of human endeavor."

1027   Foxley, Cecelia H. LOCATING, RECRUITING AND EMPLOYING
        WOMEN: AN EQUAL OPPORTUNITY APPROACH. Garrett Park,
        Md.: Garrett Park Press, 1976. 357 p.

        This volume is directed at employers in order to help them
        provide equal opportunity for women workers. The author
        describes today's women workers, their education and
        training, the laws, regulations and programs which give
        them employment protection, and ways of recruiting,
        employing, and working with women. Foxley, director
        of affirmative action at the University of Iowa, offers
        students and practitioners of public administration the in-
        formation they will need to know about affirmative action.

1028   Friedan, Betty. THE FEMININE MYSTIQUE. New York: W.W. Norton
        and Co., 1963. 410 p.

        Friedan's book does not concern government or affirmative
        action for women, but it is a classic in the American
        woman's crisis and search for her identity in society. The
        insights and interpretations both of theory and fact are
        recommended to male bureaucrats, in general, and male
        political and administrative leaders, in particular. This
        is an excellent primer for understanding the role of
        American women in the workplace and in the home.

1029   Fulenwider, Claire Knoche. FEMINISM IN AMERICAN POLITICS:
        A STUDY OF IDEOLOGICAL INFLUENCE. New York: Praeger Pub-
        lishers, 1979. 220 p.

        Investigating the influence of feminism on political atti-
        tudes and behavior, Fulenwider discusses ideas of the
        women's movement, the impact of feminism on the po-
        litical attitudes of behavior of American women, and
        feminism as a political ideology and social movement.
        He examines the relationship of feminism to a wide range
        of political attitudes, including support for protest or sense
        of citizen duty and trust in government. He covers the
        effects of feminism on political participation in campaign
        work, protest activity, and conventional partisan activity.

1030   Galloway, Judith M. "The Impact of the Admission of Women to the
        Service Academies on the Role of the Woman Line Officer." AMERICAN
        BEHAVIORAL SCIENTIST 19 (May-June 1976): 647-64.

        Galloway examines the performance of women at civilian

colleges with regard to academics, athletics, and extra-
curricular activities. She concludes that women have not
only excelled but have performed in excess of expectations
at such formerly all-male schools as Amherst and Yale.
She notes that background information on the experiences
of women in high stress situations comes from Outward
Bound schools, astronaut and aquanaut testing programs,
and military training programs. Her results imply that
women were more radiation resistant, less prone to heart
attacks, and more durable in the face of loneliness,
cold, pain, and noise.

1031   Hall, Douglas T. "A Model of Coping with Role Conflict: The Role
Behavior of College Educated Women." ADMINISTRATIVE SCIENCE
QUARTERLY 17 (December 1972): 471-86. Tables.

Hall presents a model of role conflict coping behavior
based upon three levels in the role process. Type I
coping, structured role redefinition, involves altering
external, structurally imposed expectations relative to a
person's position. Type II coping is personal role redefinition, changing one's expectations and perception of
one's own behavior in a given position. Type III coping,
reactive role behavior, entails attempting to find ways to
meet all role expectations, assuming that demands are un-
changeable and must be met. Hall indicates that the
simple act of coping (as opposed to noncoping) may be
more strongly related to satisfaction in women than the
particular type of coping strategy employed.

1032   Harrison, Evelyn. "The Working Woman: Barriers in Employment."
PUBLIC ADMINISTRATION REVIEW 24 (June 1964): 78-85. Tables.

The author identifies and debunks some of the conventional
assumptions concerning comparative employment characteristics of men and women workers. Harrison writes that
the personal insistence of former President Lyndon B.
Johnson that women play a larger role in government
provided a significant impetus to advancing their employment status in the federal service. This article is useful
for understanding progress made by American women in the
early and mid-1960s and their problems.

1033   Hooyman, Nancy R., and Kaplan, Judith S. "New Roles for Professional Women: Skills for Change." PUBLIC ADMINISTRATION
REVIEW 36 (July-August 1976): 374-78.

Hooyman and Kaplan implement a training program for
removing barriers to women's participation in upper-echelon
decision-making processes. The training model deals with
values, skills, and knowledge within internal, interpersonal,

and organizational contexts. While it focuses upon women
in the human services, the model is relevant to women
attempting to increase their power in a variety of professions.

1034   Howard, Lawrence C. "Civil Service Reform: A Minority and Woman's
        Perspective." PUBLIC ADMINISTRATION REVIEW 38 (July–August
        1978): 305-9.

        The author is concerned about the lack of emphasis on
        the behalf of minorities, women, and the handicapped
        in the proposed Civil Service Reform Act of 1978. He
        states that minorities and women should closely examine
        proposed reform in the public service because they de-
        pend so heavily upon government for employment.

1035   Jongeward, Dorothy, and Scott, Dru, eds. AFFIRMATIVE ACTION
        FOR WOMEN: A PRACTICAL GUIDE. Reading, Mass.: Addison-
        Wesley Publishing Co., 1973. xvi, 334 p.

        The term affirmative action is used in this book in both
        a specific and general sense. It refers to progress re-
        lated to an equal employment opportunity program and
        similar programs which assist women to move toward
        equality of opportunity. The editors include essays on
        the organization woman, women's lack of achievement,
        the impact of legislation and litigation on working women,
        women in government and affirmative action, women in
        organized religion, working black women, and a strategy
        for change.

1036   Koch, James V., and Chizmar, John F. THE ECONOMICS OF
        AFFIRMATIVE ACTION. Lexington, Mass.: D.C. Heath and Co.,
        1976. xiii, 158 p.

        The purpose of this book is to determine how affirmative
        action salary programs actually operate and what their
        actual economic effects are. Koch and Chizmar consider
        the impact of the affirmative action program for women
        faculty at Illinois State University upon resource allocation
        and evaluate this program in terms of economic efficiency.
        They place emphasis on the relationship of the factual-
        counterfactual methodology to the legal requirements for
        affirmative action and to the equal-pay-for-equal-work
        criterion. They include a useful bibliography.

1037   Markoff, Helene S. "The Federal Women's Program." PUBLIC AD-
        MINISTRATION REVIEW 32 (March–April 1972): 144-51. Tables.

        The primary efforts of the Federal Women's Program have
        been directed toward three main objectives: 1) creating

the legal, regulatory, and administrative framework for
achieving equality of opportunity without regard to sex;
2) bringing practice in closer accord with merit principles
through the elimination of attitudes, customs, and habits
which have previously denied women entry into certain
occupations, as well as high level positions through the
career service; and 3) encouraging qualified women to
compete in examinations for federal employment and to
participate in training programs leading to advancement.
Equal opportunity for women is public policy. The Federal
Women's Program is designed to insure that this policy
becomes practice.

1038   Murphy, Irene L. PUBLIC POLICY ON THE STATUS OF WOMEN:
AGENDA AND STRATEGY FOR THE 70S. Lexington, Mass.: D.C.
Heath and Co., 1973. xi, 129 p.

This book is for those practitioners and students of public
administration who want to know more about the formation
of national policy on equality for women and the factors
that are most likely to influence its future course. It is
recommended for the in-depth analysis of the political
aspect of the feminist issue. Chapters include discussions
of the gap between rhetoric and reality, the Nixon administration and the status of women, the response of
Congress to the women's movement, the resources and
constituents of the women's rights lobby, an agenda for
the 1970s, and strategy and tactics for the 1970s.

1039   Neuse, Steven M. "Professionalism and Authority: Women in Public
Service." PUBLIC ADMINISTRATION REVIEW 38 (September–October
1978): 436-41. Tables.

This essay finds that women rank higher on measures of
professionalism and are less committed to hierarchical
authority than are men. The author maintains that there
has been a significant change in female attitudes toward
professionalism and authority in recent years and that
continued sexual stereotyping will lead to higher levels
of frustration among female public employees.

1040   Newgarden, Peggy. "Establishing Affirmative Action Goals for Women."
PUBLIC ADMINISTRATION REVIEW 36 (July–August 1976): 369-74.

This article examines the federally recommended process
for determining affirmative action goals and suggests a
more workable set of criteria for arriving at measurable
affirmative action goals for women. Newgarden provides
a history of affirmative action goals, compares the criteria for establishing affirmative action objectives for
women with the criteria used to develop objectives for

other labor force minorities, and presents a set of common denominators which can be used for developing reasonable affirmative action goals for women.

1041   Rizzo, Ann-Marie. "Perceptions of Membership and Women in Administration: Implications for Public Organizations." ADMINISTRATION AND SOCIETY 10 (May 1978): 33-48.

This essay discusses the unique situation of the female administrator, her perceptions of membership in the organization, and how these understandings reflect her efficacy and impact on the organization. Rizzo considers how the psychology of membership affects effective participation of female managers in public organizations.

1042   Sigelman, Lee. "The Curious Case of Women in State and Local Government." SOCIAL SCIENCE QUARTERLY 56 (March 1976): 591-604.

This article reveals that research on the occupational status of women tends to concentrate on positions in the private sector. On the basis of data from the U.S. Civil Service Commission's Bureau of Intergovernmental Personnel Programs, it is evident that women are employed equally in terms of numbers but not in terms of positions of responsibility.

1043   Stewart, Debra W. "Women in Top Jobs: An Opportunity for Federal Leadership." PUBLIC ADMINISTRATION REVIEW 36 (July-August 1976): 357-64.

This article is grounded in the assumption that expansion of employment opportunity for women in American society calls for a focus, not on jobs per se, but rather on job stratification. Stewart spells out obstacles to change for women in American society and public administration, denoting that blockage of female entry into high-level decision-making positions is rooted in the political, biological, and sociological factors.

1044   Van Wagner, Karen, and Swanson, Cheryl. "From Machiavelli to Ms.: Differences in Male-Female Power Styles." PUBLIC ADMINISTRATION REVIEW 39 (January-February 1979): 66-72.

This article develops a conceptual framework for analyzing power-related behavior in an organizational setting. The authors apply the framework to the question of whether women managers can be expected to behave differently from their male counterparts because of possible differences in their orientations toward power. Van Wagner and Swanson state: "men, in general, tend to be more assertive and

other-directed. . . . In contrast, women . . . see themselves as the object of assertive behavior. Thus, while
men find strength and power in external action, women
perceive themselves as finding power from internal resources."

1045   Wallace, Phyllis A., and LaMond, Annette M., eds. WOMEN,
MINORITIES, AND EMPLOYMENT DISCRIMINATION. Lexington,
Mass.: D.C. Heath and Co., 1977. xiv, 203 p.

The editors include a series of essays which examine economic
theories of employment discrimination, the role of worker
experiences in the study of employment discrimination,
psychological aspects of female participation in the labor
force, modes of research on discrimination in employment
and pay, black employment in the South, a model of a
segmented labor market, and a dynamic theory of racial
income differences. They provide an overview of the
status of research on employment discrimination and a
prospectus which defines common dimensions for future
research.

Chapter 8

PRODUCTIVITY

A. GENERAL SELECTIONS

1046   Adams, Harold W. "Solutions as Problems: The Case of Productivity."
PUBLIC PRODUCTIVITY REVIEW 1 (September 1975): 36-43.

Adams surmises that any meaningful increase in productivity in state government will present problems of adaptation. He emphasizes that the choices are few and
clear: fewer people, fewer hours, or greater product.
Adams concludes that reducing the public workforce faces
severe political and organizational problems. He maintains
that fewer people runs counter to the need of the economy
at large to maintain consumer demand, that fewer hours
is a more desirable alternative, and that increasing the
product seems, on the balance, the most feasible approach
although it is not without its problems.

1047   Multi-Municipal Productivity Project of Nassau County. AN APPROACH
TO PRODUCTIVITY IN THE PUBLIC SECTOR: A PROCEDURAL MAN-
UAL. Mineola, N.Y.: 1975. 102 p.

The major premise of this approach to productivity improvement is that municipal services can best be improved
through systems analysis and not through individual performance evaluation.

1048   Balk, Walter L. IMPROVING GOVERNMENT PRODUCTIVITY: SOME
POLICY PERSPECTIVES. Beverly Hills, Calif.: Sage Publications,
1975. 70 p.

In this very useful book on productivity in the public
sector, the author provides an overview of productivity
programs in the public sector, describes motivation within
public agencies for productivity, discusses measurement
and information systems, examines agency environments
and processes of influence, and states some basic assumptions concerning program implementation.

1049 _____. "Toward a Government Productivity Ethic." PUBLIC AD-
MINISTRATION REVIEW 38 (January-February 1978): 46-50.

Balk believes that "narrowing the definition of productivity to that of agency performance gives the term operational and control stability. . . . If agency public administrators can articulate how they associate improvement
means with results (or ends) within their particular organizations, then we have an extremely valuable insight."
He posits that the central thrust of productivity improvement is clarification of long-term goals and specification
of performance and believes that it is "critical for managers and employees in government to develop a solid
productivity ethic."

1050 _____. "Why Don't Public Administrators Take Productivity More
Seriously?" PUBLIC PERSONNEL MANAGEMENT 3 (July-August
1974): 318-24.

The author believes that government workers and private
employees are not enthusiastic about the idea of productivity because bosses usually attempt to engineer productivity without involving employees. Balk states that extensive layoffs have occurred in government and that employees may consider the concept of productivity as a
threat to their jobs. He believes that special rewards
should be granted to those who are more productive, yet
management is usually vague about the material consequences to employees. Government administrators lack
control and authority of most of their counterparts in
business.

1051 Bridges, Edwin M.; Doyle, Wayne J.; and Mahan, David J. "Effects
of Hierarchical Differentiation on Group Productivity, Efficiency, and
Risk Taking." ADMINISTRATIVE SCIENCE QUARTERLY 13 (September
1968): 305-19. Tables.

The authors hypothesize that hierarchically differentiated
groups will 1) exhibit less risk-taking behavior, 2) be
less efficient, and 3) be less productive than hierarchically
differentiated groups. Organizational theorists point out
that the superiority of groups over individuals are found
only in undifferentiated groups, such as peer groups.
They indicate that stimulation of social interaction is restricted in hierarchically differentiated groups and attempt to determine whether hierarchically differentiated
groups would be as productive on a problem-solving task
as hierarchically undifferentiated groups. They examine
the effects of formally based status differences on group
efficiency and risk taking.

1052   Burkhead, Jesse, and Hennigan, Patrick J. "Productivity Analysis:
        A Search for Definition and Order." PUBLIC ADMINISTRATION
        REVIEW 38 (January-February 1978): 34-40.

>   The authors describe public sector characteristics, the
>   consumption process of public goods, reciprocal exter-
>   nalities, system-analysis approaches to productivity, and
>   a taxonomy of productivity research (activity-output
>   measurement, employee incentives, organizational be-
>   havior, productivity bargaining, and technology transfer).
>   They conclude that "the difficulties that emerge from
>   productivity analysis in the public sector are, at basis,
>   rooted in the absence of discrete units of government
>   output."

1053   Burnham, Donald C. PRODUCTIVITY IMPROVEMENT. New York:
        Columbia University Press, 1973. 73 p.

>   The author, chairman of the Westinghouse Electric Company,
>   examines the history of productivity improvement and its
>   effect on civilization, methods of improving productivity,
>   and the need for productivity improvement in the future.

1054   Capozzola, John M. "Productivity Bargaining: Problems and Prospects."
        NATIONAL CIVIC REVIEW 65 (April 1976): 176-86.

>   The author relates that the fiscal crisis affecting many
>   American cities highlight the need for productivity bar-
>   gaining and that the process involves a change in the
>   ratio of input to output between a base period and a
>   reference period. The reader is informed that productivity
>   bargaining involves technical, legal, managerial, social,
>   and political issues. He concludes that the development
>   of meaningful standards is the major technical and legal
>   problem.

1055   Cummings, Thomas G., and Molloy, Edmond S. IMPROVING PRODUC-
        TIVITY AND THE QUALITY OF WORK LIFE. New York: Praeger
        Publishers, 1977. 328 p.

>   The authors discuss autonomous groups, job restructuring,
>   participative management and structural change (i.e.,
>   organization-wide change, behavior modification, flexi-
>   time, and reward systems), which represent the major work
>   innovations being tested in organizations in the late 1970s.
>   Cummings and Molloy evaluate the efficacy of the strate-
>   gies and provides researchers, managers, and consultants
>   with sound advice on choosing, implementing, and evalua-
>   ting a program relevant to their organizations.

1056   Cummings, Thomas G.; Molloy, Edmond S.; and Glen, Roy H.   "In-
        tervention Strategies for Improving Productivity and the Quality of
        Work Life."   ORGANIZATIONAL DYNAMICS   4 (Summer 1975):
        52-68.

> The authors review the empirical literature on job satis-
> faction, industrial organization, and productivity. Only
> 57 of the 550 studies examined dealt with organizational
> experiments in which actual changes were carried out
> under relatively controlled conditions. Cummings, Molloy,
> and Glen find that knowledge of "action levers," knowl-
> edge of contingencies, and knowledge of change strate-
> gies are needed to formulate an effective strategy for im-
> proving productivity and satisfaction.

1057   Denison, Edward F. "The Puzzling Drop in Productivity." BROOK-
        INGS BULLETIN 15 (Fall 1978): 10-12.

> Denison asserts that American productivity grew rapidly
> by historical norms during most of the postwar era and
> that approximately ten years ago the rate began to de-
> cline. The author alleges that until 1974, the slowdown
> was not particularly disturbing from the standpoint of long-
> term growth. This article discusses the factors that made
> the national-income-per-person-employed rate increase
> during the 1948-69 period, as well as those factors that
> made it turn downward after that.

1058   Farris, George F. "Chickens, Eggs, and Productivity in Organiza-
        tions." ORGANIZATIONAL DYNAMICS 3 (Spring 1975): 2-15.

> Farris suggests that productivity in organizations is not
> solely the end product of individual and organizational
> characteristics but is also an important cause of such
> characteristics. There are multiple causal relationships
> among productivity, individual characteristics, and ex-
> ternal factors.

1059   Gannon, Martin J., and Paine, Frank T. "Factors Affecting Produc-
        tivity in the Public Service: A Managerial Viewpoint." PUBLIC
        PRODUCTIVITY REVIEW 1 (September 1975): 44-50.

> Gannon and Paine report a study in which managers were
> interviewed about their areas of concern. The authors
> found the areas of greatest concern were organization and
> staffing, control over hiring and firing, work-planning
> factors, management policy and judgment, and manage-
> ment response to lower levels. The article suggests that
> there was relatively little concern about rewards and pro-
> motions and about measurement of employee performance.

1060   Gardner, John W. EXCELLENCE: CAN WE BE EQUAL AND EX-
        CELLENT TOO? New York: Harper and Brothers, 1961. xiv, 171 p.

> Gardner provides a discussion on conditions under which
> excellence is possible in American society. He also
> covers the kinds of equality that can and must be recog-
> nized, and the kinds that cannot be forced. He feels:
> "if a society holds conflicting views about excellence--
> or cannot rouse itself to the pursuit of excellence--the
> consequences will be felt in everything that it under-
> takes." This book is an excellent primer for facing prob-
> lems in the public sector during the 1980s.

1061   Gilder, George. "Public Sector Productivity." PUBLIC PRODUC-
        TIVITY REVIEW 1 (September 1975): 4-8.

> Gilder defines productivity as a combination of effective-
> ness and efficiency and denotes concern in government
> with productivity analysis (i.e., ratio between resources
> and results). Government productivity is viewed as a
> managerial problem which escapes the economic discipline
> imposed on the private sector. The public sector has now
> absorbed so much of the economy that attention to pro-
> ductivity analysis is required if public administrators are
> to meet the contradictory public demands for lighter tax-
> ation and more services.

1062   Glaser, Edward M. PRODUCTIVITY GAINS THROUGH WORKLIFE
        IMPROVEMENT. New York: The Psychological Corp., 1976. 352 p.

> This volume is a state of the art report on programs for
> increasing job satisfaction and productivity through the
> redesign of work systems. The author describes, in detail,
> more than thirty cases and includes guidelines for intro-
> ducing a systematic redesign of work systems.

1063   Goldoff, Anna C., with Tatage, David C. "Joint Productivity Com-
        mittees: Lessons of Recent Initiatives." PUBLIC ADMINISTRATION
        REVIEW 38 (March-April 1978): 184-86.

> The authors discuss the attitudes of labor and management
> with regard to planning a joint productivity program.
> They believe that "the biggest obstacle to joint coopera-
> tion is union mistrust of productivity efforts. . . . Joint
> productivity programs are fragile institutions. Poor orga-
> nizational planning, union mistrust, the overlap of col-
> lective bargaining issues, and inattention to program
> evaluation are common problems encountered by them."

1064   Harrison, Jared F. IMPROVING PERFORMANCE AND PRODUCTIVITY:
        (WHY WON'T THEY DO WHAT I WANT THEM TO DO?). Reading,
        Mass.: Addison-Wesley, 1978. 163 p.

The aim of this text is to change employees' work habits. Harrison identifies people problems, suggests corrections for deficiencies, and examines an effective system in work-related and social situations. In order to accomplish the goal of redirecting people's efforts, the author states that the manager must find out what's going on, discover who is involved and what their impacts are, and determine how to apply the system of making necessary corrections. The manager's task is to influence people to cease poor work habits and redirect their energies toward more functional routines.

1065   Hayward, Nancy S. "The Productivity Challenge." PUBLIC ADMINISTRATION REVIEW 36 (September–October 1976): 544–50.

Hayward defines public sector productivity, relates Washington State's experience in this area, describes a productivity improvement strategy, denotes sources of productivity gains (technology, human resources, financial resources, and alternative delivery options), and gives a national perspective on the productivity challenge in the United States. She concludes that the era of productivity improvement has arrived.

1066   Hayward, Nancy [S.], and Kuper, George. "The National Economy and Productivity in Government." PUBLIC ADMINISTRATION REVIEW 38 (January–February 1978): 2–5.

The authors examine the plight of productivity growth, the government role in national productivity improvement, government's impact on other sectors of the economy, government productivity in expanding its own resources, and implications of the intergovernmental system. This article is a brief but informative review of the national economy and governmental productivity.

1067   Holzer, Mark, ed. PRODUCTIVITY IN PUBLIC ORGANIZATIONS. Port Washington, N.Y.: Dunellen, 1975. 328 p.

This unique approach to public sector productivity offers a systematic perspective on recent demands for enhanced output-input ratios in government organizations. Holzer is editor-in-chief of the PUBLIC PRODUCTIVITY REVIEW. The contributions to this book represent much of the most recently published work on productivity in public sector organizations.

1068   Hornbruch, Frederick W., Jr. RAISING PRODUCTIVITY: TEN CASE HISTORIES AND THEIR LESSONS. New York: McGraw-Hill, 1977. 339 p.

This authoritative reference draws from a wide variety of
industries and points out productivity case studies in real-
life situations. This text covers such fundamental problems as controlling inflationary forces, measuring employee
contributions, stimulating and rewarding employees, and
utilizing a computer effectively and economically.

1069   Horton, Raymond D. "Productivity and Productivity Bargaining in
        Government: A Critical Analysis." PUBLIC ADMINISTRATION RE-
        VIEW 36 (July–August 1976): 407–14.

        Several considerations are suggested by this article. At
        the conceptual level, it is important for public managers
        to recognize the difference between increased production
        and increased productivity. With respect to implementa-
        tion, productivity bargaining appears to have some in-
        herent limitations as a managerial tool. A final con-
        sideration concerns neither productivity nor productivity
        bargaining but rather their relative importance compared
        to collective bargaining and other governmental functions.
        This article suggests that productivity bargaining is likely
        to yield only minimal impacts on government services,
        some of these negative, until practitioners and academics
        better understand the nature of productivity and productivity
        bargaining in government.

1070   IMPLEMENTING A PRODUCTIVITY PROGRAM: POINTS TO CON-
        SIDER. Washington, D.C.: Joint Financial Management Improvement
        Program, 1977. 68 p.

        While the focus of much of the productivity literature has
        been on productivity in the federal government, this work
        is based on observations of productivity programs in state
        and local governments and various private business firms.
        This is an up-to-date publication that provides step-by-
        step directions on how to implement a productivity program.

1071   IMPROVING FEDERAL PROGRAM PERFORMANCE. New York: Com-
        mittee for Economic Development, 1971. 86 p.

        The Research and Policy Committee of the Committee for
        Economic Development focuses attention on the develop-
        ment, execution, and evaluation of federal programs.
        CED underscores the need to examine the choice of policy
        goals and program objectives, the selection of programs
        that will achieve those objectives, and the execution and
        evaluation of program performance.

1072   Kendrick, John W. "Public Capital Expenditures and Budgeting for
        Productivity Advance." PUBLIC ADMINISTRATION REVIEW 32
        (November–December 1972): 804–7.

Kendrick recommends a systematic procedure for developing cost-reducing innovations and related investment projects, for reviewing the economic rationality of such related projects, proposes that agencies and existing revolving funds should have separate capital budgets for both internal investments and investments designed to increase the capacity and/or productivity of the outside economy, concludes that the interest and depreciation (or amortization) charges on agency investments would bring government cost accounting more closely in line with private practice and permit better estimates of total productivity and cost-saving estimates of total productivity, and suggests that post investment audits should be made by all government organizations and spot checked by the General Accounting Office to determine whether the anticipated cost-savings were in fact realized.

1073 _____. UNDERSTANDING PRODUCTIVITY: AN INTRODUCTION TO THE DYNAMICS OF PRODUCTIVITY CHANGE. Baltimore: Johns Hopkins University Press, 1977. 141 p.

Kendrick summarizes the current state of knowledge concerning productivity in the United States. Chapters include discussions of productivity concepts, productivity measurement, meaning of productivity, comparisons of productivity change, causes of productivity advance, economic impacts of productivity change, and various policy options for promoting productivity.

1074 Kull, Donald C. "Productivity Programs in the Federal Government." PUBLIC ADMINISTRATION REVIEW 38 (January-February 1978): 5-9. Table.

Kull reviews programs offered by the General Accounting Office, Office of Management and Budget, Civil Service Commission, Joint Financial Management Improvement Program, and National Center for Productivity and Quality of Working Life. He concludes that "substantial progress has been made in the development of workable productivity measurement systems for major portions of the federal civilian workforce."

1075 League of Women Voters of Los Angeles. DOES CIVIL SERVICE ENHANCE OR INHIBIT PRODUCTIVITY? Los Angeles: 1977. 53 p.

This report mentions that there are several difficulties to overcome if the consideration of increased productivity in Los Angeles is to become a reality. The continued presence of local government revenue does not depend on how well government performs, nor is there a penalty for local governments which fail to install new operating methods or to exploit opportunities. This report alludes that there are few rewards for improving, and no generally accepted measures of, local government productivity. The report suggests that management can ponder several options for challenging productivity problems, including establishing performance standards and adopting flexible working hours.

1076   Lucey, Patrick J. "Productivity: An Essential Strategy for Survival." PUBLIC PRODUCTIVITY REVIEW 1 (September 1975): 30-35.

Lucey believes that America can no longer depend upon scientific superiority and an unlimited supply of raw materials. He insists that there must be more concern for improved productivity and that the public sector should take the lead in this movement. The chief goals are the establishment of a general productivity ethic and the employment of creative managerial techniques. The productivity improvement program carried out in Wisconsin has included efforts to improve motivation; new methods of recruitment and promotion; interchange programs with the private sector and with other levels of government; and intensive reevaluation and retrenchment aimed at the elimination of useless programs.

1077   Mali, Paul. IMPROVING TOTAL PRODUCTIVITY: MBO STRATEGIES FOR BUSINESS, GOVERNMENT, AND NOT-FOR-PROFIT ORGANIZATIONS. New York: John Wiley, 1978. 409 p.

Mali asserts that this book broadens awareness and comprehension of the notion of managerial productivity, what it is and how it's measured, and defines the trends and barriers that deny its improvement. He describes strategies and new skills that can be employed for productivity improvement.

1078   Newland, Chester A. "Personnel Concerns in Government Productivity Improvement." PUBLIC ADMINISTRATION REVIEW 32 (November-December 1972): 807-15.

Three topics have been dominant among concerns with personnel productivity measurement in governments: 1) productivity bargaining, 2) formal production incentive systems, and 3) manpower planning. This article examines the first of these topics in some detail and briefly discusses the other two.

1079   Orzechowski, William Paul. "Labor Intensity, Productivity, and the Growth of the Federal Sector." PUBLIC CHOICE 19 (Fall 1974): 123-26.

The author shows that the benefits provided by the public

sector are similar to the output of the service sector and
that both sectors could be expected to be relatively labor-
intensive. He suggests that the rapid rise in the cost of
government services could be due to a low rate of productivity in the public sector.

1080   Peterson, Peter G. "Productivity in Government and the American
Economy." PUBLIC ADMINISTRATION REVIEW 32 (November-
December 1972): 740-47. Tables.

Peterson, a former Secretary of Commerce and former
chairman of the National Commission on Productivity,
maintains that improving productivity in the public sector
of the U.S. economy is fundamental to the success of the
current federal effort to create, through a variety of
policy initiatives, an environment that will spur a higher
rate of long-term productivity growth in the economy as
a whole. This article lists comparisons of world gross
national products, an index of real GNP growth, and
average annual percent changes in compensation, productivity, and unit labor costs in manufacturing during
the 1960s.

1081   Proctor, John R. "Productivity and Effectiveness of Inspection Services."
PUBLIC PRODUCTIVITY REVIEW 1 (September 1975): 22-29.

Proctor relates that Fairfax County, Virginia, has developed a simple techniques program to measure and increase productivity and effectiveness of inspection services.
Productivity can be increased by expediting service delivery if inspectors are relieved of certain clerical functions and travel time is reduced. Proctor concludes that
effectiveness can be increased by concentrating on chief
responsibilities and by introducing a quality control system
in which inspections are periodically checked by the inspectors' supervisors.

1082   PRODUCTIVITY: THE PERSONNEL CHALLENGE. Englewood Cliffs,
N.J.: Prentice-Hall, 1973. 209 p.

The editorial staff of Prentice-Hall surveys members of the
American Society for Personnel Administration and reports
how personnel executives have helped their companies
achieve higher productivity.

1083   Quinn, Robert E. "Productivity and the Process of Organizational
Improvement: Why We Cannot Talk to Each Other." PUBLIC AD-
MINISTRATION REVIEW 38 (January-February 1978): 41-45. Tables.

Quinn's article is concerned with three themes, including
the meaning of productivity terms, public sector executives'

feelings of frustration and relief, and guidelines for productivity success and principles for implementing change.

1084   Rosenbloom, Richard S. "Thinking Ahead: The Real Productivity
        Crisis Is in Government." HARVARD BUSINESS REVIEW 51 (September-
        October 1973): 156-58, 160-62.

> In the 1960s government was the fastest growing segment
> of employment, with most growth taking place in state
> and local government. The author suggests that there is
> no input concerning productivity in state and local gov-
> ernment and that none of the chief trends operating in
> the private arena, such as rewards for creativity or sanc-
> tions for failures, applies in government. He perceives
> four elements which are necessary for continued progress:
> 1) governments must learn to better utilize contemporary
> methods of management; 2) larger numbers of skilled and
> scientifically instructed people must be hired in state and
> local government; 3) the businesses which provide goods
> and services to government must initiate the employment
> of more utilitarian technology and systems; and 4) the
> system of compensation for government executives must
> be changed to make for greater productivity.

1085   Rosener, Judy B. "Improving Productivity in the Public Sector: An
        Analysis of Two Tools--Marketing and Citizen Involvement." PUBLIC
        PRODUCTIVITY REVIEW 2 (Spring-Summer 1977): 3-11.

> Rosener sets forth that, in terms of public sector produc-
> tivity, efficiency and effectiveness must be evaluated and
> that two management tools, marketing and citizen partici-
> pation, can enhance the productivity of government. The
> reader is informed that when citizens are involved in
> policy making, productivity is enhanced.

1086   Sibson, Robert E. INCREASING EMPLOYEE PRODUCTIVITY. New
        York: American Management Association, 1976. 210 p.

> This authoritative guide is packed with the most effective
> practices, suggestions, ideas, and examples on how to in-
> crease employee productivity. The author provides suc-
> cessful plans of action for immediate results.

1087   Siegfried, John J. "Public Sector Productivity." ATLANTA ECO-
        NOMIC REVIEW 27 (September-October 1977): 29-34.

> Siegfried implies that government is an inappropriate
> location for cost effective activities. The incapability
> to measure public sector output directly is a hindrance
> in estimating changes in government productivity. One

way of approaching the problem would be to measure the consequences of government services, such as crime rate or achievement test scores.

1088   Silverman, Eli B. "Productivity in Government: A Note of Caution." MIDWEST REVIEW OF PUBLIC ADMINISTRATION 7 (July 1973): 143-53.

The author states: "Productivity, like patriotism, is in vogue today. And just as the American flag is symbolic of a range of patriotic values, productivity is a codeword for a wide spectrum of values which needs to be explored." He attempts to underscore the similarities in objectives and implementation obstacles between productivity and other management efforts reflecting the Comprehensiveness, Efficiency, Rationality, and Technology (CERT) value system.

1089   Spizman, Lawrence M. "Productivity and Public Employment Programs." PUBLIC PRODUCTIVITY REVIEW 3 (Spring 1978): 44-64. Tables.

The central focus of this article is an examination of some of the policy considerations that administrators should address when evaluating the productivity of Public Employment Programs (PEP) for the optimal allocation of public service jobs. Spizman concludes that the hiring of low-income family heads for PEP positions appears to be most beneficial to society, especially when secondary labor force members are hired. These conclusions are based on cost-benefit ratio technique which allows the reader flexibility in choosing among alternative groups, discount rates, time periods, and productivity levels.

1090   Staudohar, Paul D. "An Experiment in Increasing Productivity of Police Service Employees." PUBLIC ADMINISTRATION REVIEW 35 (September-October 1975): 518-22.

This article focuses on increasing employee motivation, for example, creating psychological incentives, through financial reward or job enrichment, which can increase individual or group output. Staudohar maintains that the Orange County, California, plan is an innovative experiment which will stimulate similar schemes in other cities.

1091   Thayer, Frederick C. "Productivity: Taylorism Revisited (Round Three)." PUBLIC ADMINISTRATION REVIEW 32 (November-December 1972): 833-40.

"The thrust of the argument is that we are being asked to return all the way to Taylorism as it first was used by that gentleman himself and that, if we succumb to the pied

pipers of Taylorism, we will realize only a quantum jump
in repression and alienation among all those employed in
organizations which glorify 'productivity,' and at a time
when the survival of the planet is likely to require limits
on production instead of constant increases in it."

1092   Thomas, John S.   "Demand Analysis: A Powerful Productivity Improve-
        ment Technique."   PUBLIC PRODUCTIVITY REVIEW   3 (Spring 1978):
        32-43.

        In this article, Thomas cites various examples of demand
        analysis, such as allocating a larger percentage of a
        police work force to the greatest crime period in any
        given day. He gives several cases of demand measures
        that have proven useful and discusses, as considerations
        for conducting a demand analysis, response requirements,
        variations over time, geographic factors, and administra-
        tive flexibility.

1093   Toombs, William.   PRODUCTIVITY: BURDEN OF SUCCESS. Wash-
        ington, D.C.: American Association for Higher Education, 1973. 55 p.

        Toombs examines the meaning of productivity within the
        academic setting and relates findings to current manage-
        ment and planning approaches used by higher education
        administrators. This informative pamphlet is an excellent
        introduction for those interested in the application of man-
        agement techniques to higher education.

1094   Turner, Wayne E., and Craig, R.J.   "Productivity Improvement Pro-
        grams in the Public Sector."   PUBLIC PRODUCTIVITY REVIEW   3
        (Spring 1978):   3-22.

        This article observes that a reason for failure in produc-
        tivity improvement efforts is that many organizations are
        not ready for sophisticated techniques. Turner and Craig
        indicate that public organizations need to adopt the prin-
        ciple of utilizing the simplest technique to effectively
        solve the problem.

1095   U.S. General Accounting Office.   FEDERAL PRODUCTIVITY SUFFERS
        BECAUSE WORD PROCESSING IS NOT WELL MANAGED. Washington,
        D.C.: Government Printing Office, 6 April 1979. 46 p. FGMSD-
        79-17.

        This report concludes that word processing systems can in-
        crease government office productivity. Technological ad-
        vances in office machines and new approaches to the sec-
        retarial function--word processing systems--offer potential
        for a more efficient and economical output of written
        communication. If people, equipment, and procedures

are used and managed properly, the new technology could result in a significant breakthrough in government office productivity.

1096   W.E. Upjohn Institute for Employment Research. WORK IN AMERICA. Cambridge: MIT Press, 1973. 262 p.

Chapters include functions of work, effects of work problems on various segments of society, the health costs of jobs, redesign of work, and federal policy with regard to jobs. This report was the result of a special task force appointed by the Secretary of Health, Education, and Welfare to explore the role of work in American society with special reference to the consequences and opportunities of government activities.

1097   Wise, Charles R. "Productivity in Public Administration and Public Policy." In PUBLIC ADMINISTRATION AND PUBLIC POLICY, edited by H. George Frederickson and Charles R. Wise, pp. 175-95. Lexington, Mass.: D.C. Heath and Co., 1977.

The purpose of this essay is to delineate the meaning of productivity for public policy processes and to raise some of the policy questions that are implied by this thrust in public administration. Wise defines productivity concepts involved, discusses efforts to conceptualize productivity ideas, outlines the expected roles for productivity analysis in policy formation, and raises questions posed by the productivity movement for prospective public policies.

1098   Wofford, J.C. "Managerial Behavior, Situational Factors, and Productivity and Morale." ADMINISTRATIVE SCIENCE QUARTERLY 16 (March 1971): 10-17. Tables.

Wofford establishes a comprehensive framework for the problem of managerial behavior and investigates some of the critical components of the framework. He defines distinctive dimensions of managerial behavior and of situational variables by factor analysis and correlates these dimensions with effectiveness criteria to identify significant situational influences. The results of this study show the importance of situational variables in influencing the effectiveness of managerial behavior.

1099   Wolfe, Joan L., and Heaphy, John F., eds. READINGS ON PRODUCTIVITY IN POLICING. Washington, D.C.: Police Foundation, 1976. 160 p.

The editors offer essays which examine productivity concepts from different perspectives and suggest types of measurement which may be applied to gauge police pro-

ductivity. These essays explore the accuracy and usefulness of traditional measurements of police productivity,
the development of new measurements for police activities,
and the customary methods of providing police service.

B. PRODUCTIVITY MEASUREMENT

1100   Balk, Walter L. "Technological Trends in Productivity Measurement."
        PUBLIC PERSONNEL MANAGEMENT 4 (March-April 1975): 128-33.

> Balk relates that there is no real technological difficulty
> in measuring many government tasks because they are
> relatively routine. Well-established techniques can be
> applied to understand the nature of the work. New mea-
> surement technologies must be devised to measure produc-
> tivity in more ambiguous task areas.

1101   Davies, Celia, and Francis, Arthur. "The Many Dimensions of Per-
        formance Measurement." ORGANIZATIONAL DYNAMICS 3 (Winter
        1975): 51-65.

> The authors relate the effects of organization structure
> upon performance outcomes in three medium-sized English
> hospitals, examining utilization, innovation, morale, and
> goal achievement. They conclude that there is no one
> best way to maintain high performance.

1102   Fisk, Donald M. "Issues in Local Government Productivity Measurement."
        PUBLIC MANAGEMENT 56 (June 1974): 6-8.

> Fisk states that some municipal employees now are being
> paid according to their productivity. The most trouble-
> some problems in measuring productivity are in assessing
> outputs by quantity and quality, in deciding whose efforts
> should be measured, and in utilizing resulting information.
> The author concludes that in order to establish a produc-
> tivity reporting system, personnel must have an under-
> standing of analysis, management information, and the
> existing accounting system.

1103   Fisk, Donald M., and Winnie, Richard E. "Output Measurement in
        Urban Government: Current Status and Likely Prospects." SOCIAL
        SCIENCE QUARTERLY 54 (March 1974): 725-40.

> The authors report that urban government output measure-
> ment has progressed rapidly within the past decade. They
> discuss budget documents from thirty cities, nine counties,
> and two consolidated cities and conclude that most gov-
> ernments collect some data on quantitative outputs, that
> some collect data on qualitative aspects of outputs, and
> that measurement techniques vary by service or program area.

1104   Hatry, Harry P. "Issues in Productivity Measurement for Local Gov-
        ernments." PUBLIC ADMINISTRATION REVIEW 32 (November-
        December 1972): 776-84. Tables.

        Hatry believes that productivity measurements are important
        devices for letting a local government know its current
        status. "Measurements help identify procedures or ap-
        proaches that are worth pursuing, and those that are not.
        Used in dealings with employees, they can provide a
        basis for incentive plans and the sharing of benefits of
        increased productivity." Productivity measurement can
        help governments to identify priority areas needing atten-
        tion and the degree to which specific actions have helped.
        This is an excellent essay for exploring conceptual problems
        of productivity on the local scene.

1105   _____. "Problems in Performance Auditing of Local Services."
        PUBLIC MANAGEMENT 56 (February 1974): 20-23.

        Hatry suggests that auditors need to review what is ac-
        complished under the title of program assessment at the
        local level. Lack of guidelines, scarcity of lucidly de-
        lineated program objectives, and a general lack of stan-
        dards are chief obstacles, along with the general unavail-
        ability of performance information connected to program
        goals. The author projects a long delay before performance
        auditing can be implemented on a wide scale.

1106   _____. "The Status of Productivity Measurement in the Public Sector."
        PUBLIC ADMINISTRATION REVIEW 38 (January-February 1978): 28-
        33. Tables.

        Hatry discusses productivity measurement and its current
        status, emerging measurement methods, effectiveness-
        measurement procedures, measuring output-input ratios,
        and comprehensive measurement systems and states that
        "an underlying issue at all levels of government is the
        problem of setting up regular uses for performance measures
        that are sufficiently attractive to make agency people wish
        to cooperate in the measurement effort and use."

1107   International City Management Association. WORK MEASUREMENTS
        IN LOCAL GOVERNMENTS. Washington, D.C.: October 1974.
        21 p.

        This report notes that work measurement provides local
        governments with techniques necessary to evaluate their
        operations in terms of costs required to provide services.
        A work measurement study is conducted by reviewing
        assignments and work movement via the use of work dis-

tribution charts and process flow charts. Governments
conducting work measurement studies are advised to hold
orientation sessions for employees and supervisors, to establish study plans and project completion dates, to conduct
the study, to report results to management, and to provide
for continuing program review.

1108   Kendrick, John W. "Exploring Productivity Measurement in Govern-
        ment." PUBLIC ADMINISTRATION REVIEW 23 (June 1963): 59-66.

        The author reviews the development of productivity mea-
        sures, explains the concept and meaning of productivity,
        defines the measuring of output, addresses the problem of
        weighting certain productivity factors, discusses input mea-
        surement, mentions the uses of productivity ratios, and
        offers suggestions for future work examining productivity
        measurement in government.

1109   Landy, Frank J., and Goodin, Carl V. "Performance Appraisal."
        In POLICE PERSONNEL ADMINISTRATION, edited by O. Glenn Stahl
        and Richard A. Staufenberger, pp. 165-84. Washington, D.C.: Police
        Administration, 1974.

        Landy and Goodin describe the state of the art of police
        performance appraisal, review the more common philosophies
        of performance evaluation, probe the relationship between
        performance appraisal and specific personnel decisions,
        state some problems in gathering performance information,
        and cite recent developments in performance appraisal.
        They propose procedures for developing a performance
        appraisal system.

1110   Mark, Jerome A. "Meanings and Measures of Productivity." PUBLIC
        ADMINISTRATION REVIEW 32 (November-December 1972): 747-53.

        The author describes concepts of productivity and their
        interpretation, available measures of productivity (including
        labor and capital), limitations of available measures, the
        usefulness of productivity data, and the relationships be-
        tween productivity and unemployment. He concludes:
        "Measures of productivity have improved substantially in
        sophistication and accuracy in recent years. While they
        are still inadequate to answer all the questions that might
        be asked of them, they do provide insights into many of
        the economic problems of the day."

1111   Morris, Thomas D.; Corbett, William H.; and Usilaner, Brian L.
        "Productivity Measures in the Federal Government." PUBLIC ADMINI-
        STRATION REVIEW 32 (November-December 1972): 753-63. Charts.

        This article examines productivity measures in terms of

work measurement, unit costs, productivity, and manpower
planning. The authors construct productivity indices and
denote the uses and misuses of such indices. This is an
excellent primer on productivity in government in the
early 1970s.

1112   Mundell, Marvin. MEASURING AND ENHANCING THE PRODUC-
       TIVITY OF SERVICE AND GOVERNMENT ORGANIZATIONS. Tokyo:
       Asian Productivity Organization, 1975. iv, 296 p.

       Mundell provides a logical framework for answering im-
       portant questions about government service activities and
       for assisting in the integration of productivity techniques.

1113   O'Neill, Michael E., and Unwin, Ernest A. "Productivity Measure-
       ment: A Challenge for Implementation." PUBLIC PRODUCTIVITY
       REVIEW 2 (Fall 1977): 27-37.

       This article probes the concept of productivity measure-
       ment, with emphasis on a criminal justice environment.
       O'Neill and Unwin indicate that various notions exist at
       the agency level regarding the definition of productivity
       and the potential consequences of implementing a produc-
       tivity measurement system. They point toward a common
       understanding of productivity from an agency standpoint
       and a prototype for possible implementation by operational
       agencies. One of the main thrusts of this essay is to
       develop a tool for assessing the agency's organizational
       receptivity to productivity implementation via a training
       and development model.

1114   Ostrom, Elinor. "The Need for Multiple Indicators in Measuring the
       Output of Public Agencies." POLICY STUDIES JOURNAL 2 (Winter
       1973): 85-92.

       The major focus of this essay is the development of multi-
       mode measurements of three municipal services: street
       light, street repair, and urban recreation facilities. The
       author suggests that those areas were chosen since a phys-
       ical measure can be developed or has been developed
       for each of them. For each of these areas, Ostrom probes
       the types of relationships which exist between the physical
       measures of service output and relationships between in-
       ternal records and public officials' estimates of services,
       physical measures, citizens' perceptions and evaluations
       of service levels.

1115   Rifkind, Bernard D.; Conner, Raymond A.; and Chad, Seymour W.
       "Applying Work Measurement to Personnel Administration." PUBLIC
       ADMINISTRATION REVIEW 17 (Winter 1957): 14-19. Tables.

The authors describe major factors affecting manpower requirements, including the mission of the agency, the scope of field activities, and the stability of agency programs. The work measurement package used in this study was reviewed in 1953 by a work group consisting of representatives of the Civil Service Commission and other federal agencies. The authors describe functions, operations, and work units in their measurement of employee work efforts. This research was conducted for the United States Air Force.

1116   Scheppach, Raymond C., Jr., and Woehicke, L. Carl. TRANSPORTATION PRODUCTIVITY: MEASUREMENT AND POLICY APPLICATIONS. Lexington, Mass.: Lexington Books, 1975. 124 p. Tables.

Scheppach and Woehicke focus on productivity measurement for applications in rail, air, and motor freight transportation. They offer recommendations for policy uses of productivity measures along with a discussion of various conceptual and measurement problems.

1117   U.S. Comptroller General. THE WORK MEASUREMENT SYSTEM OF THE DEPARTMENT OF HOUSING AND URBAN DEVELOPMENT HAS POTENTIAL BUT NEEDS FURTHER WORK TO INCREASE ITS RELIABILITY. FPCD-77-53. Washington, D.C.: U.S. General Accounting Office, 15 June 1977. 37 p.

The budget staffing requests of HUD should be based on techniques which are reliable and useful. The concept of work measurement offers the potential to do this. This GAO review states that the department has made progress in developing work measurement standards and recommends that HUD be encouraged to continue developing its work measurement system and increase the reliability of its work standards.

1118   Wagman, Barry L. "An Approach to Measuring the Productivity of Staff Functions." PUBLIC PERSONNEL MANAGEMENT 3 (September-October 1974): 425-30.

In order to determine the attainment of objectives, it is necessary to translate them into output measures. Wagman suggests that output measures should reflect the values set forth by the objectives and should define specific things to be examined in describing and evaluating achievement. Input measures show the resources consumed in the production of output. For both measures, quality as well as quantity should be reflected.

1119   Wallace, Robert J. "Productivity Measurement in the Fire Service." PUBLIC PRODUCTIVITY REVIEW 2 (Spring-Summer 1977): 12-36. Tables.

> This article explores the problems encountered in measuring the productivity of the fire service. After reviewing previous attempts at productivity measurement and the associated problems of input-output definition, Wallace offers an alternative approach to productivity measurement. The author concludes that one can only speculate about future changes in fire service productivity.

C. EFFECTIVENESS AND EFFICIENCY

1120   Becker, Selwyn W., and Neuhauser, Duncan. THE EFFICIENT ORGANIZATION. New York: Elsevier, 1975. 237 p.

> The authors present a theory of formal organizations, ranging from voluntary organizations to hierarchical systems and discuss how to define and measure organizational efficiency.

1121   Blair, Louis H., and Schwartz, Alfred I. HOW CLEAN IS OUR CITY? A GUIDE FOR MEASURING THE EFFECTIVENESS OF SOLID WASTE COLLECTION ACTIVITIES. Washington, D.C.: Urban Institute, 1972. 67 p.

> The Urban Institute, in cooperation with the District of Columbia, developed and tested a system for measuring the effectiveness of solid waste collection and street cleaning operations. The authors describe the procedures used and emphasize the training of inspectors, the inspection operations, and offer an analysis of citizen complaints.

1122   Brody, Ralph, and Krailo, Holly. "An Approach to Reviewing the Effectiveness of Programs." SOCIAL WORK 23 (May 1978): 226-32.

> The authors recommend the Results-Oriented Social Services Evaluation (ROSSE) paradigm in order to review and evaluate effective funding of programs for voluntary agencies. Brody and Krailo examine the delivery of human service programs which are based on the relationships of planning, organizing, and evaluating. They define objectives commonly used by voluntary agencies as operations, production, and impacts.

1123   Campbell, John P. "On the Nature of Organizational Effectiveness." In NEW PERSPECTIVES ON ORGANIZATIONAL EFFECTIVENESS, edited by Paul S. Goodman et al., pp. 13-55. San Francisco: Jossey-Bass, 1977.

Campbell calls for the development of organizational
effectiveness criteria which can be employed to compare
organizations and to evaluate organizational development
efforts. Organizational effectiveness is regarded as a
model with interrelated variables. The reader learns that
the goal-centered prototype and the systems model assess
organizational effectiveness. Simulation studies, or intensive case studies, offer the best approaches to analyze
organizational effectiveness.

1124   Cohen, Michael, and Collins, John N. "Some Correlates of Organization Effectiveness." PUBLIC PERSONNEL MANAGEMENT 3
(November-December 1974): 493-99.

The Social and Rehabilitation Service administers a group
of federal programs delivering grant-in-aid funds primarily
to the states. Cohen and Collins measure field office
effectiveness by evaluating the quality and effectiveness
of contacts between field office personnel and state agency
personnel. They find that widespread participation and
adaptiveness are characteristic of the more effective offices
and organizations. These findings suggest that internal
organizational characteristics are more important causes
of effectiveness than environmental characteristics.

1125   Hatry, Harry P., et al. HOW EFFECTIVE ARE YOUR COMMUNITY
SERVICES? PROCEDURES FOR MONITORING THE EFFECTIVENESS
OF MUNICIPAL SERVICES. Washington, D.C.: Urban Institute,
1977. 318 p.

This joint Urban Institute-International City Management
Association publication raises issues in nine functional
areas that should make department heads and other local
officials sensitive to the needs of citizens they serve.
It gives officials some new ways to think about their role
in the delivery of essential services.

1126   Kotter, John P. "Power, Success, and Organizational Effectiveness."
ORGANIZATIONAL DYNAMICS 6 (Winter 1978): 27-40.

Kotter contends that importance of power-centered behavior
to managerial career success depends upon factors that
delineate managerial jobs. The author defines when and
why power-oriented behavior promotes organizational
health and effectiveness and when and why it does not.

1127   Kuper, George H. "Productivity Improvement: The Route to More
Effective Public Management." PUBLIC MANAGEMENT 56 (June
1974): 2-5.

Kuper believes that increased productivity is one way the

public administrator can deal with increased demands for more, different, and better services; demands for increased compensation to the labor force in terms of dollars and fringe benefits; and the growing reluctance of taxpayers to pay additional taxes. He states that productivity growth can come from the introduction of technology such as labor-saving devices for workers, better-educated workers, personnel placed in proper positions, and appropriate economy measures.

1128   McArthur, Robert E. "Bureaucracy and Administrative Responsibility." PUBLIC ADMINISTRATION SURVEY 24 (March 1977): 1-4.

McArthur asserts that the most encouraging device for increased productivity is more efficient management. He discusses periodic reexamination of governmental organization, legislative oversight and evaluation of administrative operations, long-term recruitment strategies and in-service educational programs, a meaningful system of managerial incentives, and the enhancement of the career civil service in the public mind. He concludes that these options should be employed for improving bureaucratic productivity.

1129   Makielski, S.J., Jr. "The Preconditions to Effective Public Administration." PUBLIC ADMINISTRATION REVIEW 27 (June 1967): 148-53.

Makielski believes that four major preconditions--the existence of a skill pool, the existence of organizational experience, the existence of an organizational language, and an established set of administrative norms--determine the success of public policy and administration. He concludes that the absence of the necessary preconditions has serious implications for developing areas and for nations attempting to aid these areas.

1130   Mishan, E.J. COST-BENEFIT ANALYSIS. New York: Praeger Publishers, 1976. 478 p.

This volume is a balanced presentation of all aspects of cost benefit analysis which describes the crucial economic concepts and procedures that underlie the technique used in cost benefit studies. Mishan uses case studies to explain economic concepts which are relevant to cost-benefit analysis and their uses and limitations. The book includes a section on program evaluation that confronts some of the issues which frequently arise in estimating the benefits of public projects.

1131   Morris, John A., Jr., and Ozawa, Martha N. "Benefit-Cost Analysis and the Social Service Agency: A Model for Decision-Making." ADMINISTRATION IN SOCIAL WORK 2 (Fall 1978): 271-82.

The authors note the increasing prevalence of the sophisticated input analysis of the Planning, Programming, and Budget System. They review the methodology of cost-benefit analysis in detail and offer a decision-making paradigm for using it.

1132   Newland, Chester A. "Policy/Program Objectives and Federal Management: The Search for Government Effectiveness." PUBLIC ADMINISTRATION REVIEW 36 (January-February 1976): 20-27. Table.

The purpose of this article is to examine management by objectives (MBO), in the context of dominant federal management and budgeting trends since the 1940s, of which MBO is one of the more important developments. Newland's thesis is that performance budgeting, productivity measurement, planning, programming, and budgeting systems (PPBS), the social indicators movement, MBO, and program evaluation are intimately related management approaches in an increasingly difficult search for government effectiveness.

1133   Scott, W. Richard. "Effectiveness of Organizational Effectiveness Studies." In NEW PERSPECTIVES ON ORGANIZATIONAL EFFECTIVENESS, edited by Paul S. Goodman et al., pp. 63-95. San Francisco: Jossey-Bass, 1977.

Scott relates that development of universal criteria for assessing effectiveness is difficult because different parties use varying and potentially conflicting criteria generated from different theoretical models. The reader learns that criteria cannot be objective; therefore, the concept of general organizational effectiveness is unclear. The author calls for the development and examination of more precise criteria which relate particular measures of effectiveness to certain organizational features.

1134   Tomzinis, Anthony R. PRODUCTIVITY, EFFICIENCY, AND QUALITY IN URBAN TRANSPORTATION SYSTEMS. Lexington, Mass.: Lexington Books, 1975. 237 p. Tables.

Tomzinis offers a comprehensive framework for studies on productivity, efficiency, and quality of services in urban transportation systems, a productivity matrix for urban transportation systems, and an efficiency analysis of urban transportation networks, among other measures, in one of the first published studies emphasizing productivity measurement of various transport systems. This volume is an important

reference work for transportation planners and management
specialists in transportation and urban systems.

1135   Ulberg, Cy, and Cizanckas, Victor I. "Motivation, Effectiveness,
        and Satisfaction." In POLICE PERSONNEL ADMINISTRATION, edited
        by O. Glenn Stahl and Richard A. Staufenberger, pp. 152-64. Wash-
        ington, D.C.: Police Foundation, 1974.

        The authors review both positive and negative motivators,
        describe the elements of officer effectiveness, and em-
        phasize the importance of employee satisfaction in an
        effort to secure good performances by increasing officers'
        ability to perform well and by providing opportunities for
        officers to perform activities in which they are interested.

1136   Ward, James H. "An Approach to Measuring Effectiveness of Social
        Services: Problems and Resolutions." ADMINISTRATION IN SOCIAL
        WORK 1 (Winter 1977): 409-19.

        The author discusses the intensified demand for measuring
        the effectiveness of social service programs. This essay cov-
        ers an evaluation of salient organizational and admini-
        strative problems, the importance of well qualified per-
        sonnel, and a well-formulated plan for confronting and
        solving the problems of measuring the effectiveness of
        social services.

1137   Wildavsky, Aaron. "The Political Economy of Efficiency: Cost-Benefit
        Analysis, Systems Analysis, and Program Budgeting." PUBLIC ADMINI-
        STRATION REVIEW 26 (December 1966): 292-310.

        "The encroachment of economics upon politics is not dif-
        ficult to understand. Being political in perspective is
        viewed as bad; having the perspective of the economist
        is acclaimed as good. As a discipline, economics had
        done more with its theory, however inadequate, than has
        political science. Under some conditions economists can
        give you some idea of what efficiency requires. It is a
        rare political scientist who would even concern himself
        with political rationality. Economists claim to know and
        work to defend their interests in efficiency; political
        scientists do not even define their sphere of competence.
        Thus the market place of ideas is rigged at the start."

1138   Winnie, Richard E., and Hatry, Harry P. MEASURING THE EFFECTIVE-
        NESS OF LOCAL GOVERNMENT SERVICES: TRANSPORTATION.
        Washington, D.C.: Urban Institute, 1972. 84 p.

        This publication is a consumer oriented approach to as-
        sessing the quality of local transportation. The authors

propose a system to estimate effectiveness of transportation-related services. They provide twelve specific measures, keyed to such goals as accessibility, convenience, travel time, safety, and maintenance of environmental quality. They also provide summary recommendations and cost estimates.

1139   Yamada, Gordon T.   "Improving Management Effectiveness in the Federal Government." PUBLIC ADMINISTRATION REVIEW 32 (November-December 1972): 764-70. Charts.

Distinguishing efficiency from effectiveness, the author examines the impacts of OMB Circular No. A-44 in terms of cost reduction, management improvement, and management review. Yamada concludes that Circular A-44 is an "umbrella" under which overall agency management review and improvement actions could be administered and reported and which could provide a more responsive and effective government.

D. MOTIVATION

1140   Bingham, Richard D.   "Innovation, Bureaucracy, and Public Policy: A Study of Innovation Adoption by Local Government." WESTERN POLITICAL QUARTERLY 31 (June 1978): 178-205.

Bingham declares that affluence, social problems, and other factors dramatically influence responsibility and size of local government. This analysis reviews innovativeness in housing, school districts, public libraries, and municipal governments in American cities with 50,000 or more population in 1960. The author employs the innovation-decision prototype in his analysis; and, for each component of analysis, he explores two innovations.

1141   Downey, Edward H., and Balk, Walter L.   EMPLOYEE INNOVATION AND GOVERNMENT PRODUCTIVITY: A STUDY OF SUGGESTION SYSTEMS IN THE PUBLIC SECTOR. Personnel Report No. 763. Chicago: International Personnel Management Association, 1976. v, 90 p.

This study is useful to those interested in improving government productivity. The authors use specific examples in analyzing the suggestion system in the public sector. They review in depth a formal statewide suggestion system, including step-by-step instructions.

1142   Downs, George W., and Mohr, Lawrence B.   "Toward a Theory of Innovation." ADMINISTRATION AND SOCIETY 10 (February 1979): 379-408.

This essay strives to eliminate further conceptual barriers
to the development of a workable theory of innovation.
The author suggests that the chief tasks in overcoming
conceptual problems are building a theory of the "innovation decision" as the unit of analysis, lifting the level
of generality of independent variables, splitting innovation
into diffusion and adoption, and promoting the conceptualization of innovation.

1143   Eyestone, Robert. "Confusion, Diffusion, and Innovation." AMERICAN
        POLITICAL SCIENCE REVIEW 71 (June 1977): 441-47.

Eyestone indicates that interactive effects are more common
in policy innovations requiring a long time to diffuse among
the states. He notes the existence of diffusion mechanisms,
as some policies diffuse directly from a federal prototype
while others diffuse among states via a segmented pattern
of emulations. State minimum wage legislation as a case
of federal influence in the diffusion process is discussed.
Eyestone suggests that several models of policy diffusion
seem to be operating and that there is more than one
possible pattern of emulation of policy innovations, comments on the problems inferring anything useful about
state politics from the study of policy innovations among
the states, presents a technique for identifying clusters
of similar policies on the basis of their diffusion patterns
and illustrates its use with fair employment practices,
civil rights, and labor legislation, and examines the
history of state minimum wage legislation, indicating the
importance of repeals, amendments, and reinstatements
in addition to initial adoptions.

1144   Friedlander, Frank, and Walton, Eugene. "Positive and Negative
        Motivations Toward Work." ADMINISTRATIVE SCIENCE QUARTERLY
        9 (September 1964): 194-207. Tables.

Much of the confusion concerning job motivation results
from a failure to distinguish between positive and negative
motivations. Friedlander and Walton interview eighty-two
scientists and engineers who indicate that their reasons
for remaining with the organization are quite different
from (and not merely opposite to) those that might cause
one to leave.

1145   Gellerman, Saul W. MOTIVATION AND PRODUCTIVITY. New York:
        American Management Association, 1963. 304 p.

The author, a nationally renowned authority on motivation,
summarizes and evaluates the best studies in the field.
He details how these studies can be used to solve problems
of leadership, recruitment, morale, organization change,

and labor relations through changes in work environment
and the individual.

1146   Jain, Tej K. "Bureaucracy and Work Motivation: An Empirical As-
        sessment of the Conceptualizations of Max Weber and Warren Bennis."
        ADMINISTRATIVE CHANGE 4 (January-June 1977): 191-212.

        Jain asserts that the theoretical position of Warren G.
        Bennis is that bureaucracy is negatively related to work
        motivation. This theory contrasts Max Weber's position
        that bureaucracy is positively related to work motivation.
        The author finds that a high level of bureaucracy relates
        in a positive way to intrinsic motivation. Demographic
        data, levels of bureaucracy, or subscale of bureaucracy
        cannot significantly explain the extrinsic motivation level
        of superintendents.

1147   Katzell, Raymond A., et al. "Improving Productivity and Job Satis-
        faction." ORGANIZATIONAL DYNAMICS 4 (Summer 1975): 69-80.

        The author maintains that large-scale and enduring im-
        provements in both performance and job satisfaction appear
        to depend on developing methods to relate human concerns
        to economic concerns. There are several ways to improve
        both productivity and job satisfaction; but there is no
        single-target program or standard formula for uniform ap-
        plication to all situations. This article asserts that the
        difficulty for the policy maker is that far reaching changes
        must be made to effect large-scale improvements in the
        production of human resources before the desired effects
        become visible.

1148   Katzell, Raymond A.; Yankelovich, Daniel, et al. WORK, PRODUC-
        TIVITY, AND JOB SATISFACTION: AN EVALUATION OF POLICY-
        RELATED RESEARCH. New York: The Psychological Foundation,
        1975. 432 p.

        This book is a multidisciplinary evaluation of research
        dealing with features of work which affect both the pro-
        ductivity and job satisfaction of employees. This is a
        valuable contribution to our understanding of job satis-
        faction and productivity, the "critical mass" principle,
        the "motivation" principle, shared benefits of a produc-
        tivity program, job design, patterns of control, patterns
        of compensation, and system-wide changes with regard to
        productivity and job satisfaction.

1149   Marz, Roger H. "Myth, Magic, and Administrative Innovations."
        ADMINISTRATION AND SOCIETY 10 (August 1978): 131-38.

Marz examines the spread of administrative innovation
through state and local governments. He attributes the
propensity to innovate to the unrequited search for certainty. This article explains why governments adopt new
procedures like benefit cost analysis and zero base budgeting and what the latent and manifest functions of such
innovations are.

1150   Newstrom, John W.; Reif, William E.; and Monczka, Robert M.
"Motivating the Public Employee: Fact vs. Fiction." PUBLIC PER-
SONNEL MANAGEMENT 5 (January-February 1976): 67-72.

This study dispells the stereotype of public employees as
security-oriented. The data show that security is felt to
be less important by public employees than by those in
the private sector. Personnel directors become diagnos-
ticians and situational analysts. They examine environmental impacts and organizational characteristics; they
must be sensitive to employees' changing needs. The
result is the development of effective reward systems for
satisfying employees and the creation of a productive environment.

1151   Pajer, Robert G. "The Relationship of Morale to Productivity: What
It Means Today." PUBLIC PERSONNEL REVIEW 31 (October 1970):
273-78.

Pajer's research presents a positive relationship between
morale and productivity. He investigates why some
analyses indicate no relationship between morale and
productivity and why other research efforts show positive
associations in this regard. Motivation toward task performance at high levels seems to fulfill certain human
needs. Such performances tend to occur in organizations
where intrinsic and extrinsic rewards are associated with
performance.

1152   Scanlan, Burt K. "Determinants of Job Satisfaction and Productivity."
PERSONNEL JOURNAL 55 (January 1976): 12-14.

Scanlan maintains that the first determinant of job satisfaction is the nature of supervision. He emphasizes the
degree to which the supervisor is considerate and the
degree to which the employees can influence decisions.
Other determinants include the location of the work group,
wages, promotion opportunities, and hours of work.

1153   Sharkansky, Ira. "Constraints on Innovation in Policy Making: Economic Development and Political Routines." In TOWARD A NEW
PUBLIC ADMINISTRATION: THE MINNOWBROOK PERSPECTIVE,

edited by Frank Marini, pp. 262-79. Scranton, Pa.: Chandler Publishing Co., 1971.

> The author seeks "an understanding of which limitations may come to the policy maker from economics and which from his own decision routines, and under what conditions these limitations are likely to inhibit innovation." With a review of pertinent literature, Sharkansky examines both economic constraints and the constraints of routine decision processes which limit the administrator's capacity for innovation.

1154   Thompson, Victor A. "Bureaucracy and Innovation." ADMINISTRATIVE SCIENCE QUARTERLY 10 (June 1965): 1-20.

> Thompson examines the relationship between bureaucratic structure and innovative behavior by comparing conditions within the bureaucratic structure with conditions found by psychologists to be most conducive to individual creativity. Conditions within bureaucracy are determined by a drive for productivity and control, and a situation inappropriate for creativity. He offers alterations in bureaucratic structure to increase innovativeness, including increased professionalism, a looser and more untidy structure, decentralization, freer communications, rotation of assignments, greater reliance on group processes, and changes in many management practices.

1155   _____. BUREAUCRACY AND INNOVATION. University: University of Alabama Press, 1969. 167 p.

> The author states that "the subject of this book is the relation between bureaucratic structures and innovativeness. . . . In the past, innovation in society took place largely through the birth of new (innovative) organizations and the death of old (traditional) ones. Given the capital requirements of today's technology, this method seems too wasteful. We must hope that existing organizations can learn to innovate." Thompson offers a provocative analysis of a wide variety of approaches to the problem of improving organizational responses to rapid technological and social change.

E. STATE AND LOCAL GOVERNMENT PRODUCTIVITY

1156   Ballantyne, Duncan. IMPROVING LOCAL GOVERNMENT PRODUCTIVITY. New York: Center for Productive Public Management, 1977. 123 p.

> The author discusses local government productivity improve-

ment efforts through an analysis of the current literature
and surveys seventeen cities and counties involved in productivity improvement programs.

1157   Brostz, Allyn, and Morgan, David R. IMPROVING MUNICIPAL PRO-
         DUCTIVITY. Norman: University of Oklahoma, Bureau of Government
         Research, 1977. 58 p.

         This self-service guide consists of overview chapters which
         define the productivity process, as well as sections on
         data collection and measurement, implementation, and the
         employment of productivity information in municipal de-
         cision making. The study's input originates from a mailed
         questionnaire to Oklahoma cities of over 10,000 persons.

1158   Crane, Edgar; Lentz, Bernard F.; and Shafritz, Jay M. STATE GOV-
         ERNMENT PRODUCTIVITY: THE ENVIRONMENT FOR IMPROVEMENT.
         New York: Praeger Publishers, 1976. 284 p.

         The authors present a technical analysis of the environ-
         ment necessary for the adoption of productivity improve-
         ment programs. They base their analysis on a model de-
         veloped with the assistance of officials of several states
         and feature inputs, actors inside and outside state gov-
         ernment, throughputs, outputs, and outcomes.

1159   Foster, R. Scott. "State and Local Government Productivity and the
         Private Sector." PUBLIC ADMINISTRATION REVIEW 38 (January-
         February 1978): 22-27.

         This analysis works from three perceptions of economic
         activity in a state or local jurisdiction--a market economy,
         a pluralistic economy, and a holistic economy. This ar-
         ticle presents an interesting and insightful way of examin-
         ing productivity.

1160   Greytak, David; Phares, Donald; and Morley, Elaine. MUNICIPAL
         OUTPUT AND PERFORMANCE IN NEW YORK CITY. Lexington,
         Mass.: Lexington Books, 1976. 206 p.

         This detailed and intensive study has important implications
         for local governments and their functions. Using primary
         source data to examine operational changes in New York
         City agencies from 1960 to 1973, the authors analyze
         output and performance in sanitation, health and hospitals,
         human resource services, police, and fire.

1161   Hamilton, Edward K. "Productivity: The New York City Approach."
         PUBLIC ADMINISTRATION REVIEW 32 (November-December 1972):
         784-95. Tables.

The author, the former Deputy Mayor of the City of New York, denotes that the NYC Productivity Program of former Mayor John V. Lindsay was designed to maintain and improve the quality of service provided to New Yorkers despite the shrinkage in the city work force. Lindsay's program was a response to repeated city budget crises and called for improvements in productivity that could be measurable in hard, quantitative terms wherever possible. The New York program was publicized in August 1972 through a 225-page statement of work objectives and measurement units keyed to a specific timetable with quarterly subtargets.

1162   Hatry, Harry [P.], and Dunn, Diana R. MEASURING THE EFFECTIVE-NESS OF LOCAL GOVERNMENT SERVICES: RECREATION. Washington, D.C.: Urban Institute, 1971. 49 p.

The authors propose measures that will supplement the type of data usually collected for local recreational facilities and activities, including accessibility, crowdedness, participation roles, safety, and overall perceptions of citizen satisfaction with recreation opportunities.

1163   Hatry, Harry [P.], et al. MEASURING THE EFFECTIVENESS OF BASIC MUNICIPAL SERVICES: INITIAL REPORT. Washington, D.C.: Urban Institute, 1974. 116 p.

The authors present the results of a joint Urban Institute–International City Management Association effort in St. Petersburg, Florida, and Nashville, Tennessee. Procedures are developed by which local government can obtain regular feedback on how well it is providing basic services to citizens. Tentative effectiveness indicators have been designed to monitor: 1) solid waste collection and disposal; 2) recreation, 3) library services, 4) police services, with emphasis on crime control, 5) fire protection, 6) local transportation services, 7) water supply, 8) waste water treatment, and 9) the handling of complaints and service requests.

1164   Hayes, Frederick O'R. "City and County Productivity Programs." PUBLIC ADMINISTRATION REVIEW 38 (January-February 1978): 15-18.

Hayes, past director of the budget for the City of New York, examines local productivity programs in eight cities and reveals that "there is no widespread demand for productivity programs. I found no instance of significant citizen pressure for the introduction of a productivity program." He concludes that "the potential for productivity improvement in local government in America is enormous, but there is little likelihood that realization will be very rapid."

1165   _____. PRODUCTIVITY IN LOCAL GOVERNMENT. Lexington, Mass.: Lexington Books, 1977. 295 p.

> This discussion of productivity program results provides a basis for developing a better understanding of managerial change and innovation in local government. This text serves as an excellent introduction to government productivity programs. The author includes detailed reports from Dallas, Detroit, Milwaukee, New York's Nassau County, Palo Alto, Phoenix, and Tacoma productivity projects.

1166   IMPROVING PRODUCTIVITY IN STATE AND LOCAL GOVERNMENT. New York: Committee on Economic Development, 1976. 92 p.

> The Research and Policy Committee of the Committee for Economic Development report calls on financially hard-pressed cities and states to improve their effectiveness and efficiency. CED urges public officials, politicians, and citizen groups to make productivity a major national issue. This volume identifies four areas of opportunity for improving productivity: strengthening management; motivating the work force; improving technology and increasing capital investment; and measuring results and the full impact of government programs.

1167   Lovell, Catherine. "Training for Productivity Improvement: Long Beach, California." SOUTHERN REVIEW OF PUBLIC ADMINISTRATION 2 (March 1979): 458-74.

> Lovell emphasizes that productivity improvement requires a total system commitment institutionalized as a fundamental part of ongoing organizational processes. She recognizes that "productivity, from the systemic viewpoint, is not a special set of activities or techniques 'added on' to the central purpose of the organization but is an integral part of the jobs of everyone in the organization."

1168   Lucey, Patrick J. "Wisconsin's Productivity Policy." PUBLIC ADMINISTRATION REVIEW 32 (November-December 1972): 795-99.

> The author, a former governor of Wisconsin, developed a productivity policy for his state which began in the following manner: "As a matter of policy, all state agencies will be required to improve their management efficiency in the 1973-75 budget years, maintaining essential public services but cutting service delivery costs by at least 2.5 per cent annually." This article includes a nine point program with specific instructions for implementing the above policy directive.

1169   _____. "Wisconsin's Progress with Productivity Improvements."
PUBLIC ADMINISTRATION REVIEW 38 (January–February 1978): 9–12.

> Lucey, former governor of Wisconsin, writes that two major
> trends characterize agency productivity innovations from
> 1973 to 1976. One trend is toward agency centralization
> of management support services such as typing, payroll,
> and personnel administration. A second trend is the con-
> tinued substitution of sophisticated technology for human
> operations to achieve greater speed, accuracy, and ca-
> pacity to handle complex tasks.

1170   Ross, John, and Burkhead, Jesse. PRODUCTIVITY IN THE LOCAL
GOVERNMENT SECTOR. Lexington, Mass.: Lexington Books, 1974.
192 p.

> The authors answer some persistent taxpayer questions about
> the impact of productivity programs on the efficiency and
> effectiveness of local government services. The text is
> complete with notes, tables, figures, appendix, and bib-
> liography on the literature of productivity in government.

1171   Tannian, Francis X. PRODUCTIVITY OF CITY SERVICES. Newark,
Del.: College of Urban Affairs and Public Policy, University of
Delaware, 1977. 96 p.

> This report focuses on city service performance as viewed
> by urban residents, suburban commuters, and two business
> groups in an East Coast central city. The author notes
> differences in satisfaction for twelve municipal services
> between residents and nonresidents of the city.

Chapter 9

POLITICAL ECONOMY AND FINANCE

A. BUDGETING

1172   Amacher, Ryan; Tollison, Robert D.; and Willet, Thomas D. "Budget
        Size in a Democracy: A Review of the Arguments." PUBLIC FINANCE
        QUARTERLY 3 (April 1975): 99-121.

> The authors discuss the contributions of the private and
> public sectors in a mixed economy. They argue that, if
> the American voters and political parties were able to
> enact a public budget with perfect information, a better
> budgetary product would be the result. They emphasize
> that the American federal system is complex and that the
> interdependent democratic parties seek voters with imper-
> fect information. They point out that drawing conclusions
> about budget size is a judgmental problem.

1173   Appleby, Paul H. "The Role of the Budget Division." PUBLIC AD-
        MINISTRATION REVIEW 17 (Summer 1957): 156-58.

> Appleby, then director of the budget of New York, de-
> scribes the budget function. He believes that the primary
> responsibility and the primary capacity of budgeteers is
> to develop a rational budget philosophy.

1174   Bailey, John J., and O'Connor, Robert J. "Operationalizing Incre-
        mentalism: Measuring the Middles." PUBLIC ADMINISTRATION
        REVIEW 35 (January-February 1975): 60-66. Tables.

> In a useful review of the literature, the authors examine
> the works of Dahl, Lindblom, Wildavsky, Fenno, Sharkansky,
> and Dye. Bailey and O'Connor illustrate the logical and
> analytical problems encountered when the distinction be-
> tween process and output are not observed.

1175   Berman, Jules. "The Budget Process: New Rules for an Old Game."
        PUBLIC WELFARE 33 (Fall 1975): 24-29.

> The author reports that a more conservative political

milieu, increasing concern about the economy and the
federal deficit, and the less trusting relationship between
the administration and Congress have led to sweeping alterations in the federal budgeting procedure. The reader
is told that the budgeting system before the Congressional
Budget and Impoundment Control Act of 1974 laid the
chief burden of setting priorities and developing an over-
all fiscal program on the administration. Members of
Congress will now have to be persuaded that proposed
programs are more beneficial than alternatives and the
competition for funding will be greater.

1176   Burkhead, Jesse. GOVERNMENT BUDGETING. New York: John
        Wiley and Sons, 1956. xi, 498 p.

        The study of government budgeting is a study in applied
        economics, in the allocation of public resources. Burkhead
        looks at operations, reviews budgetary organization and
        procedure, probes decision-making routines in government,
        examines governmental and nongovernmental influences
        that affect the decision-making process, and emphasizes
        budgeting in the national government.

1177   Caiden, Naomi. "Patterns of Budgeting." PUBLIC ADMINISTRATION
        REVIEW 38 (November-December 1978): 539-44.

        The major assumption of this article is that discussions of
        the management of public financial resources are concen-
        trating upon a single pattern, either ignoring the possi-
        bility that other patterns may exist or treating them as a
        residual category relatively devoid of interest. Caiden
        illustrates patterns of budgeting according to resource
        mobilization, accountability, and administrative control.

1178   Clark, Terry Nichols. "Can You Cut a Budget Pie?" POLICY AND
        POLITICS 3 (December 1974): 3-31.

        Clark assumes that voting is a leading behavioral measure
        of values. In contrast to referenda and simple pools, the
        budget pie idea presents the respondent with a circle and
        has him divide it into sections corresponding to the pro-
        portion of the total budget that he would allocate to
        each. He asserts that the budget pie generates more in-
        formation about values.

1179   Denzau, Arthur T., and Mackay, Robert J. "Bureaucratic Discretion
        and Public Sector Budgets." ARIZONA REVIEW 25 (May 1976): 1-9.

        The authors maintain that a new prototype of public sector
        budgeting is analogous to the standard economic theory of
        monopolistic price discrimination. The discretionary budget

is the difference between the bureau's budget and the
minimum total cost of producing the bureau's output.
A bureau can segment voters into those closely tied to
its product and those who have good alternatives to its
output. The voter will try to choose in accordance with
his most preferred budget level.

1180   Dunbar, Roger L.M. "Budgeting for Control." ADMINISTRATIVE
SCIENCE QUARTERLY 16 (March 1971): 88-96. Tables.

Dunbar defines a budgetary control system as a hierarchically linked combination of a goal-setting and a goal-
achieving machine. He discusses the effects of four inputs to the goal-setting machine: 1) setting difficult as
opposed to easy goals; 2) allowing the budgeted individual
to participate in setting the goal; 3) providing financial
reward for goal achievement; and 4) providing inadequate
extrinsic reward for goal achievement.

1181   Eghtedari, Ali, and Sherwood, Frank. "Performance Budgeting in
Los Angeles." PUBLIC ADMINISTRATION REVIEW 20 (Spring 1960):
63-69.

This article compares elements of performance budgeting
theory with the practice in Los Angeles. The authors
conclude that the performance approach can result in a
strengthening of the executive budget and can have an
effect on program planning and the central control of
decisions going into the executive budget, that the measurement of work in a governmental jurisdiction is practical
and feasible, that there are positive benefits to be gained
from such measurement, and finally, that the performance
budget need not be based on the accounting system. They
offer questions or observations for additional research in
this area.

1182   Executive Office of the President. Office of Management and Budget.
THE UNITED STATES BUDGET IN BRIEF. Washington, D.C.: Government Printing Office, 1971-- . Annual.

This is a very useful document, published on an annual
basis, for both students and practitioners of public administration. It was originally published in 1950 by the
Bureau of the Budget as THE FEDERAL BUDGET IN BRIEF
and in 1962 as THE BUDGET IN BRIEF. It includes facts
and figures on current budget estimates and describes
federal programs by functions, including national defense,
international affairs, general science, space and technology, energy, natural resources and environment, agriculture, commerce and housing credit, transportation,

community and regional development, education, training,
employment, and social services, health, income security,
veterans benefits and services, administration of justice,
general government, general purpose fiscal assistance
(revenue sharing), and net interest on the public debt.
It includes the president's budget message, describes the
budget process, lists budget tables, defines budget terms,
and provides a concise , nontechnical overview of the
annual budget of the federal government.

1183   Finley, James J. "The 1974 Congressional Initiative in Budget Making."
        PUBLIC ADMINISTRATION REVIEW 35 (May-June 1975): 270-78.

        Finley describes the legislative climate for the 1974
        Congressional Budget and Impoundment Control Act, the
        principal provisions of the law, the congressional time-
        table for action required, and antiimpoundment laws.
        This is a useful review of this important legislation which
        changed the way that Congress conducted the business of
        the federal budget.

1184   Fisher, Virginia L. "Conference Training in Federal Budgeting."
        PUBLIC ADMINISTRATION REVIEW 9 (Autumn 1949): 265-71.

        According to the author, the evidence from her research
        suggests 1) that a strong training program in any of the
        management specializations, like budgeting, calls for
        an active role for the central agency most closely asso-
        ciated with the specialization; 2) that the success of such
        a program depends in very large part on acceptance
        among its principal beneficiaries, the line agencies; 3)
        that the essential working knowledge about administering
        the program can be communicated without great effort;
        4) that it is more productive to share in an exchange of
        ideas and experiences within a relatively small group
        than to be pinned down to a lecture course; 5) that a
        training program built on group discussion puts large re-
        sponsibility on those who function as the leaders; and
        6) that training in any specialized work may be expected
        to be practically useful in proportion to its broadening
        influence, or a broadly conceived training program which
        frees the specialist from undue narrowness and provides
        adjacent fields of specialization.

1185   Frazer, William J., Jr. "The Government Budget Constraint." PUBLIC
        FINANCE QUARTERLY 6 (July 1978): 381-87.

        This article discusses the government budget constraint and
        examines the issue of symmetry between the definitions of
        monetary and fiscal policy. The author describes arbitrary
        monetary policy, reviews several operational, definitional,

and analytical problems, and defends the monetarist position on the government budget constraint.

1186   Friedman, Lewis B. BUDGETING MUNICIPAL EXPENDITURES: A STUDY IN COMPARATIVE POLICY MAKING. New York: Praeger Publishers, 1975. vii, 249 p.

Friedman seeks to advance previous research on budgeting by directing the study of government budgeting toward a policy-analysis framework. He extends the contemporary emphasis on empirical investigation of the budgetary process to a concern with specific expenditure outputs. Through a comparative analysis of fourteen cities, the connection between how decisions are made and what spending choices are made is examined. Chapters include discussions of a model of municipal budgeting, a research design, expenditure outputs, budget roles, informal influence, formal authority, and cognitive and evaluative mechanisms of choice.

1187   Gerwin, Donald. "Towards a Theory of Public Budgetary Decision Making." ADMINISTRATIVE SCIENCE QUARTERLY 14 (March 1969): 33-46. Tables.

This article examines the process by which public administrators allocate financial resources. From the assumption that the administrator seeks to reduce conflict over the allocation of the budget, the author presents propositions about revenue forecasts, appropriations for subunits, increases in compensation, and debt service. The propositions are compared to results of related research.

1188   Golembiewski, Robert T., and Rabin, Jack, eds. PUBLIC BUDGETING AND FINANCE: READINGS IN THEORY AND PRACTICE. Itasca, Ill.: F.E. Peacock Publishers, 1975. xi, 513 p.

The editors offer a comprehensive volume of readings on public budgeting and finance. Selections include conceptual, institutional, economic, strategic, administrative, behavioral, organizational, and technical contexts of public budgeting and finance. This text is an excellent resource guide to budgeting.

1189   Hale, George E. "State Budget Execution: The Legislature's Role." NATIONAL CIVIC REVIEW 66 (June 1977): 284-90.

This article discusses decision-making aspects of budget execution and reveals that state legislatures express increased concern with controls over such execution. Some legislatures are adopting novel procedures for analyzing administrative regulations, supervising state auditors, and utilizing additional audits.

1190   Hale, George E., and Douglas, Scott R. "The Politics of Budget
        Execution: Financial Manipulation in State and Local Government."
        ADMINISTRATION AND SOCIETY 9 (November 1977): 367-78.

        The authors point out that political scientists examine the
        approval of budget requests rather than budget execution.
        This article reviews existing studies which relate to budget
        execution in state and local governments.

1191   Harris, Joseph P. "Needed Reforms in the Federal Budget System."
        PUBLIC ADMINISTRATION REVIEW 12 (Autumn 1952): 242-50.

        Continued deficit financing, which has caused many
        persons to ask whether the government has not lost its
        ability to manage its finances soundly, and the immense
        size of the present federal budget ($80 billion, or 28
        percent of the national income) constitute the author's
        reasons for calling for proposals for reforming the bud-
        getary system. Harris believes that Congress needs to
        consider broad changes which will permit the government
        to better manage its finances.

1192   Harvey, George Y. "Contract Authorization in Federal Budget Pro-
        cedure." PUBLIC ADMINISTRATION REVIEW 17 (Spring 1957):
        117-24. Table.

        The author defines contract authorization as establishing
        an account against which obligations may be incurred.
        He explains this process in light of the performance budget
        effort of 1950.

1193   Hirsch, Werner Z. "Toward Federal Program Budgeting." PUBLIC
        ADMINISTRATION REVIEW 26 (December 1966): 259-69. Table.

        Program budgeting in the federal government will allow
        key management functions to be carried out which are
        not now (ca. 1966) under administrative budgeting. Pro-
        gram budgeting will provide formal ways of regularly
        evaluating alternatives, of stimulating marginal tradeoffs
        among resources, of identifying problem areas, of gener-
        ating improved management and investment strategies and
        procedures, of formulating planning and operating theories,
        and of defining information requirements. Hirsch con-
        cludes that program budgeting attempts to make explicit
        the relationships between direct outputs and programs and
        the nation's objectives and purposes. This is an excellent
        essay for understanding program budgeting in the mid-1960s.

1194   Hirsch, Werner Z.; Sonenblum, Sidney; and Teeples, Ronald K.
        LOCAL GOVERNMENT PROGRAM BUDGETING: THEORY AND
        PRACTICE. New York: Praeger Publishers, 1974. 216 p.

The authors note that program evaluation and tradeoff analysis constitute a set of activities producing decision-relevant information. They imply that the implementation of program budgeting analysis must be pragmatic and suggest that good analysis rarely leads to implementation in the face of opposition from interest groups. There is a need for analytic studies that can improve specific, often relatively low-level decisions.

1195   Howard, S. Kenneth. "Budget Execution: Control vs. Flexibility." MIDWEST REVIEW OF PUBLIC ADMINISTRATION 2 (February 1968): 20-27.

After briefly discussing the purposes of control, the author considers the tension that exists between the need for various types of control and the desirability of granting management flexibility in execution. He reviews the types of control (legality, policy conformance, program accomplishment) and maintains that flexibility is necessary when economic conditions change.

1196   Hyde, Albert C., and Shafritz, Jay M., eds. GOVERNMENT BUDGETING: THEORY, PROCESS, POLITICS. Oak Park, Ill.: Moore Publishing Co., 1978. viii, 548 p.

In a most comprehensive treatment of government budgeting, the editors include selections on developing budgetary theory and process, performance budgeting and work management, PPBS and the systems approach, zero-base budgeting, and legislative, comparative, and management dimensions of budgeting. The book is organized around the notion that old budget systems never die but simply change names, undergo cosmetic surgery, or move on to other places. This text is an excellent resource guide to budgeting.

1197   Ippolito, Dennis S. THE BUDGET AND NATIONAL POLITICS. San Francisco: W.H. Freeman and Co., 1978. x, 217 p. Paper.

The purpose of this textbook is to introduce the student to the political relevance of the budget by examining the institutional responsibilities and conflicts, decision-making factors, and policy implications that characterize the budgetary process. The author's scope extends primarily to presidential and congressional influences on budgetary policy. Ippolito maintains that the political processes surrounding the budget are little understood, that the federal budget is a direct reflection of American politics, and that the budget defines the range of programs in education, defense, welfare, and health. Chapters include an overview of the federal budget, executive planning

and formulation, the power of the purse, budget implementation, and budgets and politics.

1198   Jasper, Herbert N. "A Congressional Budget: Will It Work This
        Time?" BUREAUCRAT 3 (January 1975): 429–43.

        Jasper relates that the Congressional Budget and Impound-
        ment Control Act of 1974 was an action by Congress de-
        signed to implement the new congressional budget system.
        The political climate included President Nixon's veto of
        inflationary spending programs. The Act sets up a Con-
        gressional Budget Office, adopts a current service budget,
        shifts the fiscal year to October 1–September 30, and
        suggests a timetable for existing programs.

1199   Kramer, Fred A., ed. CONTEMPORARY APPROACHES TO PUBLIC
        BUDGETING. Cambridge, Mass.: Winthrop Publishers, 1979. ix,
        239 p.

        This book of readings includes thirteen essays on govern-
        mental budgeting. Kramer introduces the text with a
        section on the political nature of public budgeting which
        is followed by selections that discuss the possibilities and
        difficulties of program budgeting, management by objec-
        tives, and zero–base budgeting. He includes examples
        of how the techniques are applied at state, federal, and
        local levels of government administration.

1200   Lee, Robert D., Jr., and Johnson, Ronald W. PUBLIC BUDGETING
        SYSTEMS. 2d ed. Baltimore: University Park Press, 1977. 369 p.

        This textbook provides a comprehensive, systematic pre-
        sentation of all aspects of budgeting at federal, state,
        and local levels. Lee and Johnson discuss both political
        and technical problems of budgeting and examine personnel
        and intergovernmental relations in the budgetary process.
        Chapter discussions include the public sector in perspective,
        program information and budgetary reform, PPBS, budget
        execution, accounting, and information systems, budget
        preparation, role of the legislature, and program analysis.

1201   Lee, Robert D., Jr., and Staffeldt, Raymond J. "Executive and
        Legislative Use of Policy Analysis in the State Budgetary Process:
        Survey Results." POLICY ANALYSIS 3 (Summer 1977): 395–405.

        This research includes a survey that shows that the conduct
        of policy analysis has increased considerably in state bud-
        getary systems since 1970. The authors indicate that a
        majority of budget offices and many major operating agen-
        cies and legislatures now conduct both "effectiveness
        analysis" and "productivity–analysis." The major gap

between the existence of analysis and its use in policy
deliberations is discussed.

1202   LeLoup, Lance T. BUDGETARY POLITICS: DOLLARS, DEFICITS,
DECISIONS. Brunswick, Ohio: King's Court Communications, 1977.
261 p.

LeLoup begins with a discussion of the context of budgeting, including a framework for budget analysis, fiscal
policy and the economy, and budget composition and
control. He describes agency budgetary strategies, the
role of the Office of Management and Budget, presidential and congressional priorities, the process of congressional authorization and appropriations, and budget execution and agency operations in the context of decisions
and processes of budgeting. His final emphasis is on the
results of budgeting, examining who pays the taxes, who
benefits from government spending, and what reforms are
needed in the budgeting process.

1203   _____. "The Myth of Incrementalism: Analytical Choices in Budgetary Theory." POLITY 10 (Summer 1978): 488-509.

LeLoup integrates isolated challenges germane to inter-
pretive and analytical choices in the development of budgetary theory. New trends refocusing budgetary theory
on annual budgeting and multiyear budgetary decisions
are a promising theoretical development.

1204   LeLoup, Lance T., and Moreland, William B. "Agency Strategies and
Executive Review: The Hidden Politics of Budgeting." PUBLIC AD-
MINISTRATION REVIEW 38 (May-June 1978): 232-39. Tables.

The authors explore various budgetary roles and strategies
(agencies, departments, Office of Management and Budget,
Congress) and examine the feasibility of agency assertive-
ness (public support, presidential support, congressional
support, values, attitudes, and orientation of administrators, and constraints), and conclude that "the hidden
politics of national budgeting, expressed in agency and
department estimates, reveal much more variation than
we have been led to believe."

1205   Lewis, Verne B. "Toward a Theory of Budgeting." PUBLIC ADMINI-
STRATION REVIEW 12 (Winter 1952): 42-54.

This article analyzes three propositions derived from economic theory which appear to be applicable to public
budgeting and to be appropriate building blocks for an
economic theory of budgeting. The three theories include
relative value (budget decisions must be made on the basis

of relative values), incremental analysis (budget analysis must include a comparison of relative values, an operation accomplished by dividing available resources into increments and considering which of the alternative uses of each increment would yield the greatest return), and practical limitations (a formula for budget analysis which appears to be theoretically sound is not always easy to apply).

1206   Lyden, Fremont J., and Miller, Ernest G., eds. PUBLIC BUDGETING: PROGRAM PLANNING AND EVALUATION. Rev. ed. Chicago: Rand McNally, 1978. ix, 460 p.

This is a revision of the second edition of PLANNING PROGRAMMING BUDGETING: A SYSTEMS APPROACH TO MANAGEMENT (1972). Included are essays on the historical evolution of budgeting in the United States up to and including the advent of PPBS, the role and potential of budgeting in the political process, the program planning and evaluation base of budgeting, program structure and information requirements, the problem of relating goals to systems, problems and experiences faced in the implementation of program budgeting and program evaluation, and future potentialities of PPBS and other operations research-management science technologies.

1207   Meier, Kenneth John, and Van Lohuizen, J.R. "Bureaus, Clients, and Congress: The Impact of Interest Group Support on Budgeting." ADMINISTRATION AND SOCIETY 9 (February 1978): 447-66.

This article examines the hypothesis that the budget process responds to interest group pressures, for twenty bureaus in the Department of Agriculture for the fiscal years 1971-76. Meier and Van Lohuizen indicate that cultivating clientele support among interest groups and members of Congress appears to aid a bureau's budget position. The authors state that bureaus with strong support not only avoid budget cuts but grow rapidly from year to year.

1208   Miles, Jerome A. "The Congressional Budget and Impoundment Control Act: A Departmental Budget Officer's View." BUREAUCRAT 5 (January 1977): 391-404.

Miles relates that the purpose of this legislation was not to curtail government expenditures but to permit Congress to establish levels of expenditure, to develop a system for controlling impoundments, to establish national priorities, and to give Congress the authority to carry out its new responsibilities.

1209   Millett, John D. "Governmental Budgets and Economic Analysis."
        PUBLIC ADMINISTRATION REVIEW 23 (September 1963): 125-31.
        Tables.

> Governmental budgets at all levels have a new dimension
> in their significance to the economic objectives of the
> American society. Millett believes that we must examine
> governmental budgets more closely in terms of their eco-
> nomic role and their economic impact and that we must
> inquire into the relative merits of government expenditures
> in contributing to the realization of economic goals.

1210   Ott, David J., and Ott, Attiat F. FEDERAL BUDGET POLICY.
        Washington, D.C.: Brookings Institution, 1977. 178 p. Tables.

> The purpose of this book is to help the nontechnical
> reader understand the budget and how budget decisions
> are made. The Otts trace the history of federal expendi-
> tures, taxes, and the national debt, describe the budget
> process and explain the concepts used in the budget, ana-
> lyze the effect of fiscal policy on economic activity, and
> discuss methods of determining the appropriate level of
> federal expenditures.

1211   Ripley, Randall B., et al. "Explaining Changes in Budgetary Policy
        Actions." ADMINISTRATION AND SOCIETY 6 (May 1974): 22-47.

> Ripley delineates the impact of external environment and
> bureaucratic structure on the policy responses of govern-
> mental agencies. The linear additive model developed
> for the study was modified to account for interactive effects
> from personnel change, age of department or agency, its
> growth, mission or goals, and external historical relevance.

1212   Schick, Allen. "Contemporary Problems in Financial Control." PUBLIC
        ADMINISTRATION REVIEW 38 (November-December 1978): 513-19.

> Schick emphasizes that control is the first requisite of
> budgeting. He examines the internalization of control,
> the problems of intergovernmental money, the difficulties
> of multipocket budgeting, the conflicts in government
> by contract, entitlements and third party payments, and
> new methods of control.

1213   _____. "Control Patterns in State Budget Execution." PUBLIC AD-
        MINISTRATION REVIEW 24 (June 1964): 97-106.

> The author examines some of the major factors accounting
> for the persistence of control patterns in state budget
> execution. Among the factors related to rigidity in bud-
> get execution are the budget officer's conception of his

responsibilities, mistrust of line departments, the political environment of budgeting, the informational needs and resources of the budget office, the uncontrollability of the budget, the precarious balance of revenues and expenditures, and lack of performance standards.

1214   Shadoan, Arlene Theuer. "Development in State Budget Administration." PUBLIC ADMINISTRATION REVIEW 23 (December 1963): 227-31.

Shadoan believes that the budgeting function in the states is in a period of transition. After conducting interviews in fourteen states, she found changes occurring in the concept of the budget process, in the roles of the participants in the budget process, and in the type of staff performing the budget functions.

1215   Smith, Harold D. "The Budget as an Instrument of Legislative Control and Executive Management." PUBLIC ADMINISTRATION REVIEW 4 (Summer 1944): 181-88.

The former director of the U.S. Bureau of the Budget (Office of Management and Budget) lists historical budget principles, including publicity, clarity, comprehensiveness, budget unity, detailed specification, prior authorization, periodicity, and accuracy, in this analysis of the budget and executive management. He discusses new principles of executive management, including executive programming, executive responsibility, reporting, adequate tools, multiple procedures, executive discretion, flexibility in timing, and two way budget organization. This essay is an interesting discussion of managing the U.S. budget in the mid-1940s.

1216   Smithies, Arthur. "Government Budgeting." In INTERNATIONAL ENCYCLOPEDIA OF THE SOCIAL SCIENCES, edited by David L. Sills, pp. 184-92. New York: Macmillan Co., and Free Press, 1968.

Smithies states that "the process of decision making that results in a budget, whatever its complexities, contains three necessary ingredients: 1) determination of the variety of policy objectives the government intends to pursue, such as defense, education, or law enforcement; 2) estimation of the cost of pursuing each of these objectives in varying degrees; and 3) an assessment of the willingness and ability of the public to pay for the government's program as a whole." He discusses program budgeting and the economic impact of the budget and concludes that "modern governments . . . are coming to recognize that budgeting and policy making are part of the same process." This essay is an excellent review of the literature.

1217   Stallings, Wayne. "Improving Budget Communications in Smaller Local
        Governments." GOVERNMENTAL FINANCE 7 (August 1978): 18-25.

> With support from the National Science Foundation and
> the Municipal Finance Officers Association, Stallings
> documents budgetary and financial management practices
> which can be employed by smaller units of local govern-
> ments in order to strengthen financial policy making.
> This essay centers on the results of that project.

1218   "Symposium on Budget Theory." PUBLIC ADMINISTRATION REVIEW
        10 (Winter 1950): 20-31.

> The concepts of state and local budgeting in a federal
> system, federal grant policies, budgetary time cycles,
> capital budgeting, the performance budget, units of work
> data, executive-legislative relations, and comparative
> studies of budget practices constitute the emphasis of this
> budget analysis. The conference for this symposium was
> held at the Public Administration Clearing House at Princeton,
> New Jersey, July 7-9, 1949.

1219   Thurber, James A. "Congressional Budget Reform and New Demands
        for Policy Analysis." POLICY ANALYSIS 2 (Spring 1976): 197-214.

> Thurber relates that the Budget and Impoundment Control
> Act of 1974 provides for a systematic examination of
> priorities, expenditures, revenues, and debt. The Con-
> gressional Budget Office (CBO) currently has the best
> position, structure, legal authority, and leadership to
> generate useful policy analysis. However, there is no
> guarantee that appropriate information will be collected.
> The article notes that CBO is developing five-year pro-
> jections of budgetary authority and outlays, revenues,
> tax expenditures, deficits, and surpluses.

1220   U.S. General Accounting Office. FEDERAL BUDGET OUTLAY ESTI-
        MATES: A GROWING PROBLEM. PAD-79-20. Washington, D.C.:
        Government Printing Office, 9 February 1979. 50 p.

> The chairman, Budget Process Task Force, House Committee
> on the Budget, requested GAO to undertake several re-
> lated studies on federal budget estimates, focusing first
> on accuracy with regard to outlays. GAO found that
> variances between estimates and actuals are increasing.
> First estimates generally are less than actuals; second
> estimates have been greater than actuals. In 1977, for
> example, there was a $17 billion swing from an $8.6
> billion longfall to an $8.4 billion shortfall. The budget
> year estimates reflect the administration's concern about
> the growing deficit and the need to hold down spending.

1221   Walker, Robert A. "The Relation of Budgeting to Program Planning."
        PUBLIC ADMINISTRATION REVIEW 4 (Spring 1944): 97-107.

> "The problem of giving intelligent direction to the ad-
> ministration of public programs through adequate planning
> cannot be divorced from the budgeting function. The
> linking of the two in practice has proved the sterility of
> the theory, widely held among the professional planners,
> that planning must be divorced from administration and
> 'political' influence in order to preserve its purity."
> Walker discusses the contribution of planning to budget
> preparation, the contribution of budgeting to program
> planning, and the programming of public works projects.

1222   Wanat, John. "Bureaucratic Politics in the Budget Formulation Arena."
        ADMINISTRATION AND SOCIETY 7 (August 1975): 191-212.

> Wanat analyzes 142 line-items in the Department of Labor
> for the 1959-68 period; and, for each case, he includes
> data for the previous year's appropriation by Congress,
> Labor's allowance and recommendations to the Budget
> Bureau, and the latter's approved request. The author
> concludes that agencies counteract hindrances to expansion
> by renewing and enlarging their plans for expansion in the
> following year.

1223   Warren, Ronald S., Jr. "Bureaucratic Performance and Budgetary
        Reward." PUBLIC CHOICE 24 (Winter 1975): 51-58.

> Warren develops a simple model of budgeting behavior
> in order to determine whether a bureau that performs
> better than expected is likely to be rewarded by higher
> future budgets. Data for the model were derived from
> productivity measures developed by the Advisory Council
> on Executive Organization and were applied to the Se-
> curities and Exchange Commission for the period 1945-69.
> The findings suggest that unexpected success in meeting
> program objectives might result in a reduction in future
> budget allocations.

1224   White, Michael J. "Budget Policy: Where Does It Begin and End?"
        GOVERNMENTAL FINANCE 7 (August 1978): 2-9.

> White indicates that budget policy originates in the funda-
> mental political forces of public choices and of institutions.
> Without continual vigilance to a wide range of budget
> policy issues, budgeters risk developing an ideological
> system of budgeting which is not in touch with everyday
> needs.

1225 Wildavsky, Aaron [B.]. "A Budget for All Seasons? Why the Tra-
      ditional Budget Lasts." PUBLIC ADMINISTRATION REVIEW 38
      (November-December 1978): 501-9.

      Why has traditional budgeting lasted so long? According
      to Wildavsky, traditional budgeting has the "virtue of its
      defects. . . .Traditional budgeting makes calculations
      easy precisely because it is not comprehensive. History
      provides a strong base on which to rest a case. The
      present is appropriated to the past which may be known,
      instead of the future, which cannot be comprehended."
      This essay is an excellent introduction to an era of resource
      scarcity for the 1980s.

1226 _____. BUDGETING: A COMPARATIVE THEORY OF BUDGETARY
      PROCESSES. Boston: Little, Brown and Co., 1975. xvi, 432 p.

      The author's purpose is to collect in one place existing
      knowledge on budgeting. The focus is explicitly com-
      parative. Wildavsky classifies the processes of budgeting
      studied in this book according to the ways that they ex-
      emplify the dominant variables at work in producing
      characteristic forms of budgetary behavior. He examines
      budgets from American cities, American states, and deviant
      cases from a variety of American public organizations.

1227 _____. "Budgeting as a Political Process." In INTERNATIONAL
      ENCYCLOPEDIA OF THE SOCIAL SCIENCES, edited by David L.
      Sills, pp. 192-99. New York: Macmillan Co. and Free Press, 1968.

      The author conceives "of budgets as attempts to allocate
      financial resources through political processes" and states
      that "the study of budgeting offers a useful perspective
      from which to analyze the making of policy." He dis-
      cusses budgetary calculations, coordination and supervision,
      budgetary goals, budgetary strategies, and budgets of
      firms. "Budgeting," writes Wildavsky, "is concerned with
      the translation of financial resources into human purposes.
      Since funds are limited, a budget may become a mecha-
      nism for allocating resources." This essay is an excellent
      review of the literature.

1228 _____. "Political Implications of Budgetary Reform." PUBLIC AD-
      MINISTRATION REVIEW 21 (Autumn 1961): 183-90.

      Wildavsky argues that few, if any, budget reformers
      realize that any effective change in the budgetary process
      inevitably results in changes in the "who gets what" of
      government decisions. He identifies some of the major
      political implications of budgetary reform. This article

is valuable for its pre-planning, programming, budgeting systems and pre-zero-based budgeting conceptual commentary.

1229 _____. THE POLITICS OF THE BUDGETARY PROCESS. 3d ed. Boston: Little, Brown and Co., 1979. xxxvi, 311 p. Paper.

This text is considered the definitive work on the politics of the budgetary process. Previous editions were published in 1964 and 1974. Reference to the various editions will tell the reader what has happened to the federal budgetary process in the intervening years. This last edition is complete with charts describing a chronological and graphic representation of the budgetary cycle. Chapters include discussions on budgets, calculations, strategies, reforms, appraisals, planning, programming, budgeting systems and zero base budgeting, and Congress. Also included is a very useful guide to budget terms and concepts and a bibliography. This book is the best source to consult for understanding the budgetary process.

1230 Yeager, James H., Jr. "Budgetary Cutbacks, Political Promises, and the Unemployment Problem." PUBLIC CHOICE 23 (Fall 1975): 115-20.

When politicians strive to set aside government financial reductions that increase unemployment in certain areas, they may promote negative aspirations on the part of temporarily unemployed workers. The politicians interfere, in this manner, with laid-off employees' search for jobs. In projecting length of unemployment, the worker's age, previous employer, educational attainment, and occupation become statistically pertinent.

B. ORGANIZATIONAL DECISION MAKING

1231 Alutto, Joseph A., and Belasco, James A. "A Typology for Participation in Organizational Decision Making." ADMINISTRATIVE SCIENCE QUARTERLY 17 (March 1972): 117-25. Tables.

The authors conceptualize the variable "decisional participation" as the difference between the number of decisions in which an individual desires to participate and the number of decisions in which he or she actually participates. After identifying subjects characterized by conditions of decisional deprivation, equilibrium, and saturation, Alutto and Belasco show that individuals in each of these groups differ by age, sex, teaching level, employing organization, seniority, perceptions of administrative influence, perceptions of role conflict, and attitudinal militancy.

1232   Argyris, Chris. "Organizational Man: Rational and Self-Actualizing."
        PUBLIC ADMINISTRATION REVIEW 33 (July-August 1973): 354-57.

        Argyris calls for more research to integrate the concepts
        of rationality and self-actualization. The author dis-
        courages polarizing the usage of the terms rationality and
        self-actualization.

1233   _____. "Some Limits of Rational Man Organizational Theory." PUBLIC
        ADMINISTRATION REVIEW 33 (May-June 1973): 253-67. Charts.

        The author points out that rational man organizational
        theories (e.g., Simon, March, Allison) exclude important
        variables, do not permit prediction of events, and are
        supportive of the status quo. Argyris examines the role
        of descriptive and normative theories. If the explanatory
        power of organizational theory and its relevancy are to
        be increased, a more complex and humanistic model of
        man and more normative research are required.

1234   Cherniss, Cary, and Egnatios, Edward. "Participation in Decision-
        Making by Staff in Community Mental Health Programs." AMERICAN
        JOURNAL OF COMMUNITY PSYCHOLOGY 6 (April 1978): 171-90.

        Staff participation in decision making was examined in
        twenty-two community mental health programs in Michigan.
        For every work-connected decision, the practitioners place
        emphasis on greater participation in decision making. The
        study indicates that those working in high participation
        programs enjoy greater job satisfaction, less role ambiguity,
        greater use of their skills, better communication among
        staff, and greater goal perception and attainability.

1235   Dror, Yehezkel. "Muddling Through--'Science' or Inertia?" PUBLIC
        ADMINISTRATION REVIEW 24 (September 1964): 153-57.

        The author reexamines the decision-making theory of
        Charles Lindblom's "The Science of 'Muddling Through'"
        (see 1247), finds it wanting where rapid social change
        is occurring, and presents a new "normative" model for
        policy makers. "The limited validity of the 'muddling
        through' thesis and its inertia-reinforcing implications con-
        stitute a very serious weakness. This criterion in no way
        diminishes Lindblom's pioneering role in pointing out the
        shortcomings of the 'rational-comprehensive' policy making
        model."

1236   Etzioni, Amitai. "Mixed-Scanning: A 'Third' Approach to Decision-
        Making." PUBLIC ADMINISTRATION REVIEW 27 (December 1967):
        385-92.

Etzioni claims that mixed scanning reduces the unrealistic aspects of rationalism by limiting the details required in fundamental decisions and helps to overcome the conservative slant of incrementalism by exploring longer-run alternatives. The mixed scanning model accomplishes this by combining 1) high-order, fundamental policy-making processes which set basic directions and 2) incremental ones which prepare for fundamental decisions and work them out after they have been reached.

1237   Gore, William J. ADMINISTRATIVE DECISION MAKING: A HEURISTIC MODEL. New York: John Wiley and Sons, 1964. viii, 191 p.

Gore offers a general model of the decision-making process. Phases of this model include perception, evaluative set, estimation of consequences, and maneuver for position. In delineating the scope and focus of this model, Gore gives both a conceptual orientation and theoretical perspective. He discusses functions of the decision-making process, organization theory underlying the decision concept, and the fragmented nature of decision theory. The general model of the decision-making process is useful for ascertaining a practical interpretation of decision theory. This text also includes a useful glossary.

1238   _____. "Administrative Decision-Making in Federal Field Offices." PUBLIC ADMINISTRATION REVIEW 16 (Autumn 1956): 281-91.

The objective of this study was the development of a model which would explain the varying decision-making processes of a sample of federal field offices in the state of Washington. Eighteen field offices, embracing several cabinet departments and federal agencies, were included in this research. Four phases of decision-making activities identified in the field offices were perception of the need for a change in policy, the interpretation determining the initial objectives behind which the field office's power and influence were mobilized, the initiation of negotiations (struggle for power) with power centers outside the office to procure enough support to sustain the chosen course of action, and formalization of a policy statement consistent with regulations.

1239   Gore, William J., and Silander, Fred S. "A Bibliographical Essay on Decision Making." ADMINISTRATIVE SCIENCE QUARTERLY 4 (June 1959): 97-121.

The authors conclude that a formerly emergent and often consistent body of administrative theory has become fractured by new approaches such as human relations, operations

research, and democratic management, that there is a
large body of literature dealing more or less directly with
some facet of decision making, and that most organizational systems imply an ideology a half century out of
date, denying the very existence of modern social science.

1240   Holland, Thomas P. "Information and Decision-Making in Human
        Services." ADMINISTRATION IN MENTAL HEALTH 4 (Fall 1976):
        26-35.

        Holland observes that the acceptance of past operating
        procedures is declining in public and private institutions.
        Organizations are required to review their programs against
        specific performance measures while planners are developing
        extensive procedures for obtaining and using information
        about human needs. The author believes that collecting,
        assessing, and using such information is crucial to the
        design and management of more effective services. He
        states that technology seems to have advanced more
        rapidly than the ability to use it effectively.

1241   Howard, S. Kenneth. "Analysis, Rationality, and Administrative
        Decision Making." In TOWARD A NEW PUBLIC ADMINISTRATION:
        THE MINNOWBROOK PERSPECTIVE, edited by Frank Marini, pp.
        285-301. Scranton, Pa.: Chandler Publishing Co., 1971.

        This essay suggests that economic rationality can make a
        definite contribution to public decision making, but the
        public administrator must practice a kind of rationality
        that encompasses much more than economics. Howard
        discusses the complex world of the administrator and takes
        a critical look at planning, programming, budgeting systems,
        and asks what kind of rationality is envisioned by those
        who would rationalize public-expenditure decisions.

1242   Hy, Ronald J., and Mathews, Walter M. "Decision Making Practices
        of Public Service Administrators." PUBLIC PERSONNEL MANAGE-
        MENT 7 (May-June 1978): 148-54.

        This article considers how administrators cope with routine,
        daily problems. A questionnaire was mailed to one hundred
        administrators and the feedback indicated that administra-
        tors do not incorporate systematic decision-making tech-
        niques.

1243   Inbar, Michael. ROUTINE DECISION-MAKING: THE FUTURE OF
        BUREAUCRACY. Beverly Hills, Calif.: Sage Publications, 1979.
        239 p.

        This work discusses bureaucracy as a decision-making system.

Inbar stresses routine organizational decision making as an important topic of investigation. He proposes a rationale for modeling and computerizing certain processes of repetitive bureaucratic decision making. His model is interdisciplinary and brings to bear on the discussion findings from psychology and sociology as well as methods and perspectives from systems analysis and computer simulation.

1244   Jennings, M. Kent. "Public Administrators and Community Decision Making." ADMINISTRATIVE SCIENCE QUARTERLY 8 (June 1963): 18-43.

This article focuses on the community decision-making roles of administrators and of influentials. Jennings draws comparisons between the administrative elites of two southern communities and between the administrators and the influentials within each community. In both communities, he finds that administrators were moderately to highly involved in, and influential over, community decision making.

1245   Jones, Roger W. "The Model as a Decision Maker's Dilemma." PUBLIC ADMINISTRATION REVIEW 24 (September 1964): 158-60.

The author identifies three kinds of reactions to Charles Lindblom's "The Science of 'Muddling Through'" (see 1247). According to Jones, many readers believed that Lindblom's piece was interesting reading, but that both the phrase and thesis did not apply to them. Other readers were confused by Lindblom's emphasis on value-seeking as the initial step to decision making. They also dismissed the article as not applying to them. A third response found people impatient, if not annoyed, with the abstractions of some of Lindblom's language. For example, terms like "branch" and "root" gave some practitioners a feeling of academic remoteness from the day-to-day necessities of getting things done and decisions made.

1246   Landau, Martin. "Redundancy, Rationality, and the Problem of Duplication and Overlap." PUBLIC ADMINISTRATION REVIEW 29 (July-August 1969): 346-58.

The author contends that the appearance of duplication and overlap in administrative agencies is not necessarily a sign of waste and inefficiency. It is becoming increasingly evident that large-scale organizations function as self-organizing systems and tend to develop their own parallel circuits, transforming such "residual" parts as "informal groups" into constructive redundancies. He notes that redundancy provides safety factors, permits flexible responses to anomalous situations and provides a creative potential for those who are able to see it.

1247   Lindblom, Charles E. "The Science of 'Muddling Through.'" PUBLIC
ADMINISTRATION REVIEW 19 (Spring 1959): 79-88.

>In one of the most important essays written on the concept
and process of decision making in organizations, Lindblom
posits characteristics of the rational-comprehensive (root)
and successive limited comparisons (branch) methods.
Lindblom discusses intertwining evaluation and empirical
analysis, relations between means and ends, the test of
"good" policy, noncomprehensive analysis, and succession
of comparisons. He points out that the decisions of individual administrators must be integrated with decisions
of others to form the mosaic of public policy.

1248   Long, Norton E. "Public Policy and Administration: The Goals of
Rationality and Responsibility." PUBLIC ADMINISTRATION REVIEW
14 (Winter 1954): 22-31.

>The author believes that no problem is more momentous
for the modern democratic state than its capacity to develop rational, responsible, goal-oriented policy. Long
writes: "A major task of administration is the formulation
of policy proposals for consideration by the political executive and the legislature. The capacity of our administrative organizations to perform rationally and re-
sponsibly the task of formulating the policy alternatives
for politically responsible superiors is the major criterion
of organization efficiency." This essay is an excellent
discussion of the difficulties of the policy-administration
dichotomy and the interaction of rationality and responsibility upon that dichotomy.

1249   McCamy, James L. "Analysis of the Process of Decision-Making."
PUBLIC ADMINISTRATION REVIEW 7 (Winter 1947): 41-48.

>The author discusses the process of decision making with
regard to both personal application and ex-personal application (those which are more the concern of the agency
than of the person involved in decision making). McCamy
provides both an interesting and insightful way of viewing
the needs of the individual and the bureaucratic agency.

1250   McCleery, Mickey. "On Remarks Taken Out of Context." PUBLIC
ADMINISTRATION REVIEW 24 (September 1964): 160-62.

>"The point is . . . that what Lindblom ["The Science of
'Muddling Through,'" see 1247], and others see as a
radically rationalist theory of autonomous bureaucracy is
nothing more than the traditional theory of responsible
bureaucracy, refined and removed from its political context. It is a theory originally designed to apply to

situations of limited discretion where the relevant values
were ranked and ordered by the political system just as
prices were ordered by the market. It was . . . a
normative theory of how decisions should be made rather
than an empirical theory of how they were made."

1251   Maslove, Allan M.   "Public Sector Decision-Making and the Technology
        of Consumption." PUBLIC CHOICE 27 (Fall 1976): 59-70.

        Maslove presents a public sector decision-making model.
        The basic unit of identification in the model is the in-
        dividual or family. The article infers that the members
        of the community derive utility from a series of com-
        modity attributes; that is, utility is not taken from goods
        themselves but rather from service characteristics that
        flow from these goods. This article concludes that this
        approach establishes a convenient method of handling
        interdependencies which are pervasive in these prototypes.

1252   Milburn, Thomas W., and Billings, Robert S. "Decision-Making Per-
        spectives from Psychology: Dealing with Risk and Uncertainty."
        AMERICAN BEHAVIORAL SCIENTIST 20 (September-October 1976):
        111-26.

        The authors point out that decision making is more com-
        plicated than the classical model of rational decision
        making assumes. Recognizing that the classical model
        posits that the only uncertainty concerns the probabilities
        of alternatives leading to consequences, Milburn and
        Billings state that uncertainty includes the definition of
        the problem, the place of the problem on the agenda, the
        alternatives, consequences, probabilities, and values in-
        volved, implementation concerns, and the political, eco-
        nomic, and social environments. They examine the process
        by which individuals subjectively determine the level of
        risk of an alternative action.

1253   Pettigrew, Andrew. THE POLITICS OF ORGANIZATIONAL DECISION-
        MAKING. New York: Barnes and Noble Books, 1974. 302 p.

        Pettigrew examines competition for power and status among
        a group of individuals in a single organization over time.
        Such political behavior in organizations is best understood
        in light of the organization's history and future aspirations.

1254   Pfiffner, John M. "Administrative Rationality." PUBLIC ADMINI-
        STRATION REVIEW 20 (Summer 1960): 125-32.

        This article uncovers the bases of information and ration-
        ality used in administrative policy making. Pfiffner re-
        veals that policy, or a rule of action intended to provide

relative stability, consistency, uniformity, and continuity,
is, in the administrative situation, the product of three
bodies of thought and knowledge, including 1) means-end
rationality concerned primarily with physical phenomena,
2) behavioral rationality concerned primarily with human
behavior, and 3) normative rationality concerned primarily
with what ought to be. The author notes that the good
administrator uses all of these models of rationality in
making a decision.

1255   Simon, Herbert A. ADMINISTRATIVE BEHAVIOR: A STUDY OF
DECISION-MAKING PROCESSES IN ADMINISTRATIVE ORGANIZA-
TION. New York: Macmillan, 1957. 3d ed. New York: Free
Press, 1976. I, 364 p.

Previous editions of this public administration classic were
published in 1945 and 1947. Simon states that this book
is for organization watchers and for organization designers.
He proposes "a theory of human choice or decision-
making that aims to accommodate both those rational aspects of choice that have been the principal concern of
the economists and those properties and limitations of the
human decision-making mechanisms that have attracted the
attention of psychologists and practical decion-makers."
Chapters 4 and 5 represent the core of this book. In
earlier chapters, Simon deals with certain methodological
issues. In later chapters, he examines the influence
processes in detail in order to discuss the effects of organization on the decision-making process and illustrates
how the analysis can be used to deal with questions of
organization structure.

1256   _____. "Administrative Decision Making." PUBLIC ADMINISTRATION
REVIEW 25 (March 1965): 31-37.

Writing on the twenty-fifth anniversary of the establishment
of the American Society for Public Administration, the
author surveys operations research and management science,
experiments in decision making, the structure of decisions,
and prominent landmarks along the road of decision-making
research over the twenty-five-year period.

1257   _____. "Decision-Making and Administrative Organization." PUBLIC
ADMINISTRATION REVIEW 4 (Winter 1944): 16-30.

Simon discusses the necessity for "vertical" specialization
(coordination, expertise, and responsibility), the range of
discretion (influence over value and fact and implications
for unity of command), organizational influences on the
subordinate (authority, organizational loyalties, the criterion

of efficiency, advice and information, and training), the
communication of influence, and administrative processes
for insuring correct decisions. He concludes that "organization involves a 'horizontal' specialization of work
and a 'vertical' specialization in decision making--the
function of the latter being to secure coordination of the
operative employees, expertness in decision making, and
responsibility to policy-making agencies."

1258 _____. MODELS OF MAN: SOCIAL AND RATIONAL. New York:
John Wiley and Sons, 1957. xiv, 287 p.

Simon sets forth a consistent body of theory of the rational
and nonrational aspects of human behavior in a social
setting. The essays appeared in thirteen journals. Simon
arranges them into four categories: 1) those concerned
with interpersonal influence and the underlying concept
of causation required for the operational definition of
influence, 2) those concerned with interaction processes
in social groups, 3) those concerned with "the decision
to belong, or the inducements-contributions theory of
motivation for group membership, and 4) those concerned
with the nature of human rationality and the interaction
of rational and nonrational in human decision making.
The author believes "when these essays are viewed in
juxtaposition, it can be seen that all of them are concerned with laying foundations for a science of man that
will accommodate comfortably his dual nature as a social
and as a rational animal."

1259 _____. THE NEW SCIENCE OF MANAGEMENT DECISION. New
York: Harper and Brothers, 1960. xii, 50 p.

This short text is a compilation of three lectures by the
author during 1960. Lecture one outlines new techniques
for programmed decision making, lecture two discusses
heuristic problem solving, and lecture three probes organizational design, or man-machine systems for decision
making. Simon examines the executive as decision maker
and reviews traditional decision-making methods.

1260 Skok, James E. "Participation in Decision Making: The Bureaucracy
and the Community." WESTERN POLITICAL QUARTERLY 27 (March
1974): 60-79.

Skok states that reform is generally associated with centralized, professionalized community decision making. The
socioeconomic status hypothesis states that there is a relationship between the socioeconomic status of the community's
residents and the level of organization and participation
in that community. He analyzes two counties in suburban

Maryland: Montgomery County, a professional, upper-
class, white-collar county and Prince George's County,
a middle-class, blue-collar county.

C. PLANNING, PROGRAMMING, AND BUDGETING SYSTEMS (PPBS)

1261   Behan, R.W. "The PPBS Controversy: A Conflict of Ideologies."
MIDWEST REVIEW OF PUBLIC ADMINISTRATION 4 (February 1970):
3-16.

Ideological disputes examined in this article are 1) economics vs. politics, 2) quantitative vs. qualitative, 3)
planning vs. laissez-faire, 4) monistic vs. plural public
interest, and 5) centralization vs. decentralization.
Behan writes: "Budgeting will continue to be incremental,
and the governmental process will continue to be characterized by partisan mutual adjustment. But the consideration of alternatives and cost minimization are performance
principles of great merit."

1262   Black, Guy. "Externalities and Structure in PPB." PUBLIC ADMINI-
STRATION REVIEW 31 (November-December 1971): 637-43.

This article recommends a dual system of budgeting. The
author claims that introducing externalities explicitly into
the formal structure of the PPBS concept would be a new,
difficult step. He concludes: "If organization followed
output structure, it would not be necessary, but so long
as it does not, it is essential if a program budget is to
achieve output orientation."

1263   Botner, Stanley B. "Four Years of PPBS: An Appraisal." PUBLIC
ADMINISTRATION REVIEW 30 (July-August 1970): 423-31.

The author surveys the experience of federal agencies
with the PPBS concept and concludes that, while progress
has been made, on the whole, the results are disappointing.
He assesses the impact and effectiveness of PPBS, suggests
factors which have hindered more fruitful implementation,
and describes recent actions to correct some of the deficiencies.

1264   Capron, William M. "PPB and State Budgeting." PUBLIC ADMINI-
STRATION REVIEW 29 (March-April 1969): 155-59.

Capron asks if PPBS is directly relevant for, and applicable to, state government. He believes "PPBS can be
viewed as an information system designed particularly to
improve the quality and organization of information for
executive decisions." In this regard, he states that PPBS

can reduce certain operational weaknesses in budget systems, including defacto abdication by the chief executive of his proper functions, or improper centralization of detailed decisions at the chief executive level.

1265   Churchman, C.W., and Schainblatt, A.H. "PPB: How Can It Be Implemented?" PUBLIC ADMINISTRATION REVIEW 29 (March–April 1969): 178–89. Tables.

Using the program structure for management of statewide alcohol related problems, the authors illustrate the implementation of a PPB system. They conclude: "It is our contention in this paper that neither existing technology nor management know-how based on 'experience and judgment' is capable of producing sound policies and plans with small risk of error. All the decisions that are being made today to implement various programs may be seriously wrong, no matter who makes them or what claims are made of expertise. Consequently, if a 'contest' between PPB experts and politicians does develop, there may be no winners."

1266   Frank, James E. "A Framework for Analysis of PPB Success and Causality." ADMINISTRATIVE SCIENCE QUARTERLY 18 (December 1973): 527–43.

Frank maintains that a PPBS generally involves consideration of full-system costs, focus on government objectives, measurement of benefits or efficiency of alternate schemes to attain goals, identification of options for achieving goals, and presentation of information for inclusion in budgetary decision methods.

1267   Gorham, William. "Sharpening the Knife That Cuts the Public Pie." PUBLIC ADMINISTRATION REVIEW 28 (May–June 1968): 236–41.

The author describes the Department of Health, Education, and Welfare's planning-programming-budgeting system. He discusses the development of the department's five-year plan, the plan format, and prospects for improvement. He points out difficulties and choices and stresses the important but limited contribution of PPBS to HEW's programs and claims that PPBS will not replace but will aid the traditional political and budgeting processes.

1268   Greenhouse, Samuel M. "The Planning-Programming-Budgeting System: Rationale, Language, and Idea-Relationships." PUBLIC ADMINISTRATION REVIEW 26 (December 1966): 271–77.

Greenhouse writes that accountability, objectives, programs, program alternatives, output, progress management (evaluation), input, alternative ways to do a given job, and systems analysis constitute the rationale, language, and ideas for the PPBS concept. This article is quite useful to the layperson in understanding PPBS.

1269   Gross, Bertram M. "The New Systems Budgeting." PUBLIC ADMINI-
STRATION REVIEW 29 (March-April 1969): 113-37.

Gross describes the planning, programming, budgeting "breakthrough," the basic concepts of PPBS, traditional budgeting, Hoover-style performance budgeting, systems analysis, the Keynesian revolution and the effects of total public spending, the new microeconomics and the effects of specific programs, and some implications of future diffusion in a comprehensive review of PPBS. Gross admits: "The spread of the new budgeting system in the United States has been accompanied by mounting confusion. As with any significant innovation, it has been met by both inertia and hard fought resistance--particularly among old time budget personnel. This has led to ritualization, overformalization, and overdocumentation, Indeed, the flood of PPB paperwork, clogging the channels of gov-ernment communication, has in some cases threatened the very capability for rational action that it was supposed to enhance."

1270   Harper, Edwin L.; Kramer, Fred A.; and Rouse, Andrew M. "Imple-mentation and Use of PPB in Sixteen Federal Agencies." PUBLIC ADMINISTRATION REVIEW 29 (November-December 1969): 623-31. Tables.

The authors discovered that policy analysis in most agencies is not performed much differently than it was before the advent of the PPBS concept, that agencies varied widely in the rate at which they elected to emphasize the pro-cess for integrating analytic output with decision making, that the most important factor determining the relative effectiveness of an agency's PPBS efforts was the active support and use of PPB by the agency head, and that there was uncertainty within the agencies as to whether PPB was primarily intended to be an agency management tool or to fulfill the requirements of the Bureau of the Budget (now Office of Management and Budget).

1271   Hatley, Richard V., and Jain, Tej Kumar. "Implementing PPBS for Governmental Decision Making." ADMINISTRATIVE CHANGE 3 (July-December 1975): 1-15.

The authors suggest that once an organization decides to consider adoption of PPBS, it is essential that the orga-nization accept the cyclical process of the system as well as the basic concepts. An important purpose of PPBS is to draw a complete picture of an organization's efforts to meet its internal and environmental obligations in order that the validity of each program can be assessed in terms of goals and costs relative to other programs.

1272   Markham, Emerson, and McConkey, William C. "PPBS as Aid to Decision-Making." MIDWEST REVIEW OF PUBLIC ADMINISTRATION 3 (February 1969): 65-69.

The authors, employees of the U.S. Post Office Department (now U.S. Postal Service) and Bureau of the Budget (now Office of Management and Budget), comment on an article by Robert Wessel (see 1282) in this journal expressing reservations to the use of PPBS procedures. They believe "that the planning-programming-budgeting system can make a vast improvement in the management of scarce resources as our leaders attempt to govern and direct our country."

1273   Mosher, Frederick C. "Limitations and Problems of PPBS in the States." PUBLIC ADMINISTRATION REVIEW 29 (March-April 1969): 160-67.

Mosher stresses that PPBS has been and is being oversold and, in some ways, misrepresented by its own advocates; that much of the literature and some of the behavior relating to PPBS is premised on an oversimplified view of the world, of the society, and of government; that there are certain intrinsic difficulties of PPBS which its advocates have not acknowledged or dealt with effectively; that the states present certain special problems for PPB systems; and that federalism itself presents particularly difficult problems for PPBS at all levels of government.

1274   Mushkin, Selma J. "PPB in Cities." PUBLIC ADMINISTRATION REVIEW 29 (March-April 1969): 167-77. Table.

This article concerns itself with the practices in implementing planning, programming, budgeting systems in city and county governments and the challenge to research and education offered by these practices.

1275   Schick, Allen. "A Death in the Bureaucracy: The Demise of Federal PBB." PUBLIC ADMINISTRATION REVIEW 33 (March-April 1973): 146-56.

The author writes that budget routine concerns means of standardized procedures, timetables, classifications, and rules. He believes that PPBS failed because it did not penetrate the vital routines of putting together and justifying a budget. Schick concludes that the analysts had little influence over the form or content of the budget and were "always separate but never equal."

1276 _____. "The Road to PPB: The Stages of Budget Reform." PUBLIC
ADMINISTRATION REVIEW 26 (December 1966): 243-58. Table.

The author describes three stages of budget reform in the
United States: central control of spending and the budget,
efficient performance of work and prescribed activities,
and the planning orientation of PPB. He also stresses
the functions of budgeting, stages of budget reform as
well as the control, management, and planning orientations of PPB. This is an excellent essay for understanding
the premises of PPBS in the mid-1960s.

1277 _____. "Systems Politics and Systems Budgeting." PUBLIC ADMINI-
STRATION REVIEW 29 (March-April 1969): 137-51.

The author begins this article by noting that change in
budgeting means change in politics. Schick states: "The
politico-budgetary world is much different from what it
was in 1965 when PPB was launched, and it probably will
not be the same again. While PPB cannot claim parentage
for many of the changes, neither can it be divorced from
the ferments now sweeping the domestic political scene."
The author identifies the distinctive and contrasting elements of the old and new politics and budgeting concepts,
analyzes the persistence of process politics and the challenge of systems politics, assesses the preparedness of
politics and budgeting for the systems view, and develops
a taxonomy of political process deficiencies.

1278 Silverman, Eli B., and Gatti, Francis C., Jr. "PPB on the State
Level." BUREAUCRAT 4 (July 1975): 117-46.

Pennsylvania adopted a total systems approach to PPB in
1968. The authors emphasize that program subcategories
are an important part of the hierarchical arrangement,
with eight general interdepartmental programs. Program
categories center on general goal-oriented statements; and
the program subcategory constitutes the crucial link in the
structure by making objectives quantifiable. In a discussion
of the Department of Education's consumption of approximately half the state's budget, the author analyzes twenty-
six subcategories of the department and finds them to be
adequate in terms of specific and quantifiable objectives,
homogeneous target populations, and time.

1279 Skok, James E. "Sustaining PPBS in State Government: Pennsylvania's
Second Generation Adaptions." BUREAUCRAT 6 (Fall 1977): 50-63.

Skok provides a systematic, historical study of how PPBS
is employed in Pennsylvania. He concludes that Pennsylvania functions under a series of revised procedures

which can be labeled a second generation PPBS. The effects of these changes link planning and budgeting, but not at the broad supradepartmental level.

1280   Stein, Harry A. "Limitations of PPB Systems at the State and Local Levels." MIDWEST REVIEW OF PUBLIC ADMINISTRATION 5 (February 1971): 27-34.

The purpose of this article is to analyze PPB systems and to point out some of the factors that limit its success, drawing upon the author's experience with program-budgeting in Wisconsin. Stein cites a lack of standardization in program structure between governments and an inability to analyze completely alternative means to accomplish an objective as major limitations of PPB systems.

1281   Sudama, Trevor. "PPBS and Theories of Decision-Making, Bureaucracy and Politics." POLITICAL SCIENCE 29 (July 1977): 39-56.

The author mentions that PPBS is an effort to combine the three basic functions of budgeting into a complete system. He considers the history of PPBS, emphasizes the conceptual differences between PPBS and traditional budgeting, reviews the relationship of PPBS to decision-making theory, and indicates the implication of PPBS for theories of bureaucracy and democratic politics. He observes the prospects for the successful operation of PPBS in the U.S. and Canadian government machinery.

1282   Wessel, Robert J. "Reservations to PPBS Use." MIDWEST REVIEW OF PUBLIC ADMINISTRATION 2 (August 1968): 88-94.

Wessel's reservations fall into five categories, including lack of understanding by decision makers, faulty or erroneous data, potential misuse for purposes of administrative self-protection or expansion, the risk of deletion of public services or the failure to add certain services in the future due to a failure to show proper cost-benefit relations, and misuses of PPB to the disadvantage of unorganized groups affected by it.

1283   Wildavsky, Aaron. "Rescuing Policy Analysis from PPBS." PUBLIC ADMINISTRATION REVIEW 29 (March-April 1969): 189-202.

Wildavsky explains why the model of PPBS at the Department of Defense was a poor one. He recalls the origins of PPBS in the Rand Corporation where, after the Second World War, a talented group of analysts devoted years of effort to understanding defense policy problems. The author continues: "The fixation on program structure is the most pernicious aspect of PPBS. Once PPBS is adopted,

it becomes necessary to have a program structure that
provides a complete list of organization objectives and
supplies information on the attainment of each one. In
the absence of analytic studies for all or even a large
part of an agency's operations, the structure turns out to
be a sham that piles up meaningless data under vague
categories." Wildavsky claims that PPBS discredits policy
analysis, and that to collect vast amounts of random data
is hardly a serious analysis of public policy. He says
the conclusion is obvious: "The shotgun marriage between
policy analysis and budgeting should be annulled. Attempts
to describe the total agency program in program memoranda should be abandoned."

D. MANAGEMENT BY OBJECTIVES (MBO)

1284   Aplin, John C., Jr., and Schoderbek, Peter P. "How to Measure
MBO." PUBLIC PERSONNEL MANAGEMENT 5 (March-April 1976):
88-95.

> The authors relate that public agencies have not ex-
> perienced as much success with management-by-objectives
> programs as have private organizations. Public expecta-
> tions for responsive, flexible, and innovative programs
> by government agencies contribute to the failure of possible
> MBO programs. Aplin and Schoderbek reveal that the
> criteria for public agency program delivery should include
> definition of the type and quality of service, estimates
> of the target group and number of persons, an estimation
> of costs and results, and a point in time for evaluation.

1285   Badway, M.K. "Applying MBO to the Public Sector." BUREAUCRAT
6 (Fall 1977): 3-18.

> This article explores MBO implementation in service or-
> ganizations and reports evidence showing that these prob-
> lems are not insurmountable, citing actual experiences
> and practices of MBO applications in such organizations.
> Badway sets forth a set of conditions for efficient imple-
> mentation of MBO in service organizations. Failure of
> MBO in many cases is due to its poor implementation.

1286   Brown, David S. "Management by Objectives: Promise and Problems."
BUREAUCRAT 2 (Winter 1974): 411-20.

> Brown relates that most MBO or related systems include
> a specification of objectives, compliance standards,
> quantifiable goals, and provision for revising goals and
> goal standards. MBO forces managers to think seriously
> about their objectives and to shape them into meaningful

and measurable terms. The disadvantage is that the MBO
system is new to those systems which have developed in
both industry and government.

1287   Carroll, Stephen J., Jr., and Tosi, Henry L. "Goal Characteristics
        and Personality Factors in a Management by Objectives Program."
        ADMINISTRATIVE SCIENCE QUARTERLY 15 (September 1970): 295-
        305. Tables.

        The authors correlate different characteristics of goals
        established in a management by objectives program to
        criteria hypothesized to represent success of the program.
        They calculate correlations after personality and job
        factors were held constant. The results indicate that
        establishing clear and important goals produced favorable
        results, especially for certain personality types.

1288   DeWoolfson, Bruce H., Jr. "Public Sector MBO and PPB: Cross
        Fertilization in Management Systems." PUBLIC ADMINISTRATION
        REVIEW 35 (July-August 1975): 387-95. Table.

        This article argues that MBO and PPBS are not mutually
        exclusive or contradictory approaches to complex manage-
        ment situations in the public sector, but are in fact com-
        plimentary types of management systems. DeWoolfson
        compares and contrasts the key features of MBO and PPB
        to identify possible ways of improving upon present and
        future management systems efforts.

1289   Drucker, Peter F. "What Results Should You Expect? A Users' Guide
        to MBO." PUBLIC ADMINISTRATION REVIEW 36 (January-February
        1976): 12-19.

        Drucker believes that "MBO is both management by
        objectives and management by objectives. What is needed,"
        he says, "are two sets of specifications—one spelling out
        the results in terms of objectives and one spelling out the
        results in terms of management."

1290   Havens, Harry S. "MBO and Program Evaluation, or Whatever Hap-
        pened to PPBS?" PUBLIC ADMINISTRATION REVIEW 36 (January-
        February 1976): 40-45.

        Havens indicates that many who lived through the ex-
        perience of PPBS find similarities in MBO and expect the
        latter to survive, as a system, about as long as PPBS
        survived. The author states that one fundamental similarity
        in PPBS and MBO is that both concepts are sound ideas
        that were carried to absurd extremes. He concludes "that
        MBO, the process of setting objectives and managing
        toward their achievement, is but one element in a complex
        analytical/political/managerial decision-making process."

1291   Jun, Jong S. "Management by Objectives in the Public Sector."
        PUBLIC ADMINISTRATION REVIEW 36 (January-February 1976): 1-5.

>   Jun examines the rationale for employing MBO in govern-
>   ment and describes the elements for an effective MBO,
>   including the concepts of self-management and decentral-
>   ization, an integrated approach to management, communi-
>   cation and feedback process, and organizational develop-
>   ment and change.

1292   McConkey, Dale D. MBO FOR NONPROFIT ORGANIZATIONS.
        New York: American Management Association, 1975. 240 p.

>   The author describes how MBO can help supervisors and
>   subordinates delegate, eliminate problems of growing
>   workloads, appraise objectives and provide total organi-
>   zation control. McConkey's employment of hard facts
>   and actual case studies make this an invaluable guide to
>   MBO.

1293   Mehta, C.S. "Management by Objectives." ADMINISTRATIVE
        CHANGE 3 (July-December 1975): 92-96.

>   Mehta observes that management by objectives has come
>   to be accepted as an empirical style of management.
>   MBO is highly participative, places emphasis on results,
>   and leaves freedom of judgment and power of discretion
>   to the individual manager. The reader is told that each
>   manager should indicate the results which (s)he expects to
>   achieve and such forecasts should be in line with the
>   objectives of the organization.

1294   Murray, Stuart, and Kuffel, Tom. "MBO and Performance Linked
        Compensation in the Public Sector." PUBLIC PERSONNEL MANAGE-
        MENT 7 (May-June 1978): 171-76.

>   Murray and Kuffel probe the relationship between MBO
>   performance and compensation in the public sector. Research
>   on MBO in the private sector supports its value as an effective
>   motivational technique when compensation is connected
>   to performance. The article suggests that government
>   agencies receive increasing pressure to be more account-
>   able and to improve managerial effectiveness.

1295   Newland, Chester A. "MBO Concepts in the Federal Government."
        BUREAUCRAT 2 (Winter 1974): 354-61.

>   Newland suggests that management by objectives is an
>   approach which stresses setting goals, objectives, and
>   priorities and then manages to achieve defined results.
>   Although MBO's key elements are understandable to most

managers and employees, the underlying concepts and
their application require sustained, deliberate effort. The
key objectives include the setting of goals in terms of
results to be accomplished in a given time, developing
plans, allocating resources, involving people in implementation of plans, and monitoring progress with specific
milestones. He notes that common obstacles include
dilution of efforts, crisis management, employer-employee
goal divergence, organizational structure, cost inflation,
and macro-manpower problems.

1296   Newland, Chester A., et al. MBO AND PRODUCTIVITY BARGAIN-
ING IN THE PUBLIC SECTOR. Chicago: International Personnel
Management Association, 1974. 80 p.

This collection of papers provides perspective on MBO
and productivity bargaining. There is special emphasis
on the labor-management dimensions of MBO and productivity for personnel administrators.

1297   Odiorne, George S. "MBO in State Government." PUBLIC ADMINI-
STRATION REVIEW 36 (January-February 1976): 28-33.

This article constitutes a composite of experience with
MBO in three different states compiled into a single
illustrative case example. Odiorne states that the basic
MBO pattern consists of a five part program, including
concepts of goal setting, budgeting, autonomy, feedback,
and payoffs. He reviews the system, problems, and lessons
of MBO in state government.

1298   Rose, Richard. "Implementation and Evaporation: The Record of MBO."
PUBLIC ADMINISTRATION REVIEW 37 (January-February 1977): 64-
71.

Rose maintains that introducing a management technique
to "solve" a problem of government does not dispose of
problems, but simply substitutes the implementation of the
solution for the problem defined. He believes that analyzing the brief history of MBO in the federal government
in the 1970s can help public administrators understand the
indeterminate nature of success and failure in the implementation of new ideas. The author concludes that the
difficulty of deciding whether MBO has become accepted,
disappeared, or simply "evaporated" illustrates how difficult it is to evaluate a program in terms of its immediate
consequences.

1299   Schoderbek, Peter P., and Plambeck, Donald L. "The Missing Link
in Management by Objectives--Continuing Responsibilities." PUBLIC
PERSONNEL MANAGEMENT 7 (January-February 1978): 19-25.

The authors identify and clarify many of the problems
discovered in the public sector when applying MBO principles including continuing responsibilities, the job description, performance standards, continuing functions,
distribution of responsibility, responsibility by position,
and impact of changes in boss-subordinate relationships.

1300   Sherwood, Frank P., and Page, William J., Jr. "MBO and Public
Management." PUBLIC ADMINISTRATION REVIEW 36 (January-
February 1976): 5-12. Table.

Sherwood and Page review the background of MBO, its
introduction into the federal government by the Nixon
administration, the role of leadership in MBO, and the
future of this management concept in government.

1301   Skok, James E. "Planning Programming-Budgeting Systems and the
State Legislative Process." In MAKING GOVERNMENT WORK:
ESSAYS IN HONOR OF CONLEY H. DILLON, edited by Richard P.
Claude and James C. Strouse, pp. 98-107. College Park: University
of Maryland, 1977.

Skok believes that the most significant finding of this essay
is that "program measures and other PPB-generated data
are actually used in the budget analysis and appropriation
processes." He presents empirical evidence that, in some
states during one budget cycle, PPB-generated data and
information were used in ways intended by PPB reformers
and finds that appropriations for a small number of programs actually were determined on the basis of programmatic analysis throughout the decision-making process.

1302   Stillman, Richard J. II. "MBO Comes to the Department of Justice."
MIDWEST REVIEW OF PUBLIC ADMINISTRATION 10 (June 1976):
87-94.

Stillman concludes that MBO can strengthen the policy
direction of the Department of Justice through requiring
explicit statements of program goals, of interrelations
between goals and resources, and of formal tracking of
progress toward the goals over time. He denotes that
MBO is handicapped by decentralized managerial controls
in the Justice Department and by incremental budgeting
traditions which are favored by Congress and by professional program managers. This article includes the advantages and disadvantages of MBO in the Department of
Justice.

1303   Tosi, Henry; Hunter, John; Chesser, Rod; Tarter, Jim R.; and Carroll,
Stephen. "How Real are Changes Induced by Management by Objec-

tives?" ADMINISTRATIVE SCIENCE QUARTERLY 21 (June 1976): 276-306.

> The authors report longitudinal studies undertaken in two companies to examine the effects of certain aspects of MBO. They employ cross-lag correlational techniques to draw causal inferences. This essay probes contradictory results and derives several mathematical models to explain the pattern of the correlations. The authors conclude that the subjects' perceptions of MBO changed over time.

1304   Wallace, Robert T. "A New Test for Management by Objectives." BUREAUCRAT 2 (Winter 1974): 362-67.

> President Nixon distributed a memorandum to heads of twenty-one departments and agencies accounting for 95 percent of the budget and more than 90 percent of the total civilian work force in April 1972. The department and agency heads were prompted to focus on results within the coming fiscal year. This memorandum was a catalyst for a result-oriented environment, creating a situation in which line management would think through necessary action, and helping set a pattern of active participation.

E. ZERO-BASE BUDGETING (ZBB)

1305   Adams, Bruce, and Sherman, Betsy. "Sunset Implementation: A Positive Partnership to Make Government Work." PUBLIC ADMINI- STRATION REVIEW 38 (January-February 1979): 78-81.

> The authors discuss the sunset concept, sunset principles, and state and federal action and present a workable ap- proach for state sunset laws, including evaluation work plans, preparation of evaluation reports, and evaluation criteria.

1306   Blodgett, Terrell. "Zero-Base Budgeting Systems: Seventeen Steps to Success." NATIONAL CIVIC REVIEW 67 (March 1978): 123-29.

> Blodgett declares that zero-base budgeting requires justifi- cation of all activities with each new budget year and that managers may not simply alter the previous year's budget or justify only the increases they are requesting. ZBB is not an involved procedure; it is a logical approach for arriving at a budget which maintains necessary services. The budgeting plan should consist of concisely stated ob- jectives, criteria for accurate workload measurement, an accounting system which promotes budgetary input for the program efforts, and a professional budget staff.

1307   Buttrick, Shirley M., and Miller, Vernon. "An Approach to Zero-Base
        Budgeting." ADMINISTRATION IN SOCIAL WORK 2 (Spring 1978):
        45-58.

> This article describes the model of ZBB developed by one
> school of social work as part of its annual budget request.
> The model represents an innovation in the more usual zero-
> base approaches and is designed to meet the needs of the
> nonprofit enterprise--education and other human services
> activities. The paradigm is defined within the theoretical
> framework of political scientist Aaron Wildavsky.

1308   Charnovitz, Steve. "Evaluating Sunset: What Will It Mean?" BU-
        REAUCRAT 6 (Fall 1977): 64-79.

> The central idea of this concept is that all federal pro-
> grams should be reviewed. Charnovitz believes that ap-
> plying the sunset process to the entire federal government
> is not workable and is most likely to do serious damage
> to both the substance of controversial programs and the
> process of policy making. This article discusses what
> sunset is and how it differs from present budgeting systems,
> the experience with sunset in the states, the operation
> of the federal sunset process, purposes of sunset in the
> federal government, and improvements in sunset legislation.

1309   Cheek, Logan M. ZERO BASED BUDGETING COMES OF AGE.
        New York: American Management Association, 1977. 303 p.

> The author denotes that ZBB differs from all other systems
> in that it requires an annual budgeting procedure which
> makes no assumptions about carrying over previous revenue
> commitments without close scrutiny. This volume offers
> a balanced appraisal of ZBB, points out the strengths and
> weaknesses of the concept, stresses the motivational as-
> pects necessary before it is accepted by the staff, and
> discusses steps to set up the system in any business.

1310   Cowen, Scott S., et al. "Zero-Base Budgeting as a Management
        Tool." MSU BUSINESS TOPICS 26 (Spring 1978): 29-40.

> The authors suggest that zero-base budgeting has become
> popular in the public and private sectors within the last
> ten years and conclude that ZBB is an efficient technique
> for controlling support areas. ZBB requires each manager
> to justify budget requests, to identify activities as decision
> units, and to rank these entities according to their impor-
> tance.

1311   Draper, Frank D., and Pitsvada, Bernard T. ZERO-BASE BUDGETING
        FOR PUBLIC PROGRAMS. Washington, D.C.: University Press of
        America, 1978. 148 p.

The authors declare that this text is styled as a handbook
for people practicing ZBB. This text was written by people
who make government budgets for instruction in public
administration. Chapters are devoted to the mechanics,
benefits, costs, problems, and prospects of ZBB.

1312   Dworak, Robert J. "Zero-Base Budgeting and Sunset Laws: Do They
        Go Together?" NATIONAL CIVIC REVIEW 67 (March 1978): 118-22.

        Dworak declares that zero-base budgeting is a management
        process concerned with budget preparation and that sunset
        legislation is a process of policy review dealing with the
        termination of the statutory authorization of programs.
        ZBB is an appropriation process while sunset legislation
        is an authorization process which functions in relation
        to, but independent of, the budgetary process.

1313   Gordon, L.A., and Heivilin, D.M. "Zero-Base Budgeting in the
        Federal Government: An Historical Perspective." GAO REVIEW 13
        (Fall 1978): 57-64.

        In this article, the authors offer a historical analysis of
        ZBB in the federal government. They define budgeting
        concepts and reveal that the elimination of some pro-
        grams, identification of program trade-offs, greater in-
        volvement by top officials in the budget process, im-
        proved communications among top, middle, and lower
        levels of management, and greater comprehension of pro-
        gram goals are benefits of ZBB.

1314   Hartman, Robert W. "Next Steps in Budget Reform: Zero-Base Review
        and the Budgetary Process." POLICY ANALYSIS 3 (Summer 1977):
        387-94.

        Hartman states that Jimmy Carter advocates ZBB and multi-
        year appropriations as elements in his reorganization plans
        to eliminate unneeded, redundant, or wasteful federal
        programs. The author concludes that the answer to a
        workable zero-base review is a budgetary process which
        is selective and evolutionary.

1315   Hebert, F. Ted. "Zero-Base Budgeting in Historical and Political
        Context: Institutionalizing an Old Proposal." MIDWEST REVIEW OF
        PUBLIC ADMINISTRATION 11 (September 1977): 163-81.

        The author examines the concept of zero-base budgeting
        in the state of Georgia and compares ZBB to earlier re-
        form attempts, including PPBS. He concludes: "Zero-
        base budgeting, then, is something other than what the
        name implies, and probably less than what the name im-
        plies if the Georgia system is taken as the archetype.

ZBB is an attempt to institutionalize a combination of older proposals for budget reform." This essay is an excellent review of this budgeting concept.

1316   Herzlinger, Regina E. "Zero-Base Budgeting in the Federal Government: A Case Study." SLOAN MANAGEMENT REVIEW 20 (Winter 1979): 3-14.

Herzlinger relates that the implementation of a zero-base budgeting system in federal government agencies, established by President Carter in 1977, produced a wide variety of results within specific departments. The author describes the ZBB process of the Public Health Service.

1317   Lauth, Thomas P. "Zero-Base Budgeting in Georgia State Government: Myth and Reality." PUBLIC ADMINISTRATION REVIEW 38 (September-October 1978): 420-30. Tables.

The author states that zero-base budgeting and incrementalism co-exist in Georgia. Despite incrementalism, ZBB functions as a management approach to budgeting requiring more extensive program information and greater justification for funding requests. This essay reviews the operational definition of ZBB in Georgia, the persistence of incrementalism, and the achievements of ZBB in that state.

1318   McCaffery, Jerry. "Budgeting: Problems, Perspectives and the Promise of Zero-Based Budgeting." In PUBLIC ADMINISTRATION AND PUBLIC POLICY, edited by H. George Frederickson and Charles R. Wise, pp. 121-33. Table. Lexington, Mass.: D.C. Heath and Co., 1977.

McCaffery states that the framework of zero-base budgeting is reminiscent of management by objectives but without the emphasis on the mutuality of goal setting and trust. He says that budget technology will continue to be based on expenditure development, but these routines will be supplemented with various analytic tools as program size and complexity demand better analysis. He concludes that last year's budget will still be the best predictor of next year's--despite ZBB.

1319   _____. "MBO and the Federal Budgetary Process." PUBLIC ADMINISTRATION REVIEW 36 (January-February 1976): 33-39. Table.

McCaffery compares MBO with PPBS and relates the importance of both concepts in the federal budgetary process. He concludes: "Where MBO has made progress in the federal establishment, it tends to be used as a tool for resource allocation within the fiscal year and depends on reshuffling of funds within the budget base. It is then mainly a manpower management tool."

1320   Ogden, Daniel M., Jr. "Beyond Zero Based Budgeting." PUBLIC
        ADMINISTRATION REVIEW 38 (November–December 1978): 528–29.

        Ogden concludes that zero-base budgeting, in practice,
        is expensive and time consuming, that a good manager
        uses it when he or she expects that the gains will out-
        weigh the costs, that few managers would deny that ana-
        lyzing and defending the entire budget is a useful tool
        in selected circumstances, and that little can be learned
        about most programs from an annual zero-based budget.

1321   Otten, Gerald L. "Zero-Base Budgeting: Implications for Social
        Services?" ADMINISTRATION IN SOCIAL WORK 1 (Winter 1977):
        369–78.

        This essay delves into the forces supporting budgetary re-
        vamping, with primary emphasis on the contemporary
        appeal of zero-base budgeting. Otten declares that there
        are likenesses between PPBS and ZBB concepts. The ar-
        ticle projects that ZBB will lead social workers to revise
        their approaches to budgeting for social service admini-
        stration.

1322   Pyhrr, Peter A. "The Zero-Base Approach to Government Budgeting."
        PUBLIC ADMINISTRATION REVIEW 37 (January–February 1977): 1–8.

        Pyhrr writes an authoritative discussion of the zero-base
        approach, procedures of ZBB, the decision package con-
        cept, the ranking process, and practices and problems.
        His essay should be consulted by both academics and
        practitioners interested in learning the basics of zero-base
        budgeting.

1323   _____. ZERO BASE BUDGETING: A PRACTICAL MANAGEMENT
        TOOL FOR EVALUATING EXPENSES. New York: John Wiley and
        Sons, 1973. xv, 231 p.

        Because the need for an effective budget procedure is in-
        creasingly apparent in both industry and government, this
        book is a classic in the field of budgeting. Pyhrr is the
        recognized authority on zero-base budgeting, and this
        volume sets the standard for applying this budgeting con-
        cept in government. Chapters include the zero-base bud-
        geting process, implementation problems and benefits of
        ZBB, decision packages, procedures for an effective rank-
        ing process, ZBB and PPBS computer applications, and
        ZBB and the management process.

1324   Rehfuss, John. "Zero-Base Budgeting: The Experience to Date."
        PUBLIC PERSONNEL MANAGEMENT 6 (May–June 1977): 181–87.

Rehfuss posits that zero-base budgeting is not the ultimate answer to financial and budgetary problems but that it has a good chance of surviving in some viable form. He alludes that ZBB must be applied more extensively before an accurate appraisal can be made.

1325   Schick, Allen. "The Road from ZBB." PUBLIC ADMINISTRATION REVIEW 38 (March-April 1978): 177-80.

Schick discusses ZBB, denoting its successes, its managerial purposes, and its limits. He states: "ZBB could be speedily installed because it did not really change the rules by which budgetary decisions are made. It changed the terminology of budgeting, but little more."

1326   Suver, James D., and Brown, Ray L. "Where Does Zero-Base Budgeting Work?" HARVARD BUSINESS REVIEW 55 (November-December 1977): 76-84.

The authors conclude that zero-base budgeting works in reevaluating objectives in the corporate planning process but requires increased time and effort in preparation. ZBB enhances the quality of management information but does not seem to affect significantly the allocation of funds. They assert that ZBB provides a systematic method for addressing problems.

1327   Tyer, Charles B. "Zero-Base Budgeting: A Critical Analysis." SOUTHERN REVIEW OF PUBLIC ADMINISTRATION 1 (June 1977): 85-107.

Tyer provides an overview of zero-base budgeting, analyzes issues in ZBB, and describes the experience of ZBB in the state of Georgia. He concludes that ZBB is a reform effort in a long list of reform proposals which attempt to "rationalize" decision making and budgeting.

1328   U.S. Congress. Senate. Committee on Government Operations. Subcommittee on Intergovernmental Relations. COMPENDIUM OF MATERIALS ON ZERO-BASE BUDGETING IN THE UNITED STATES. Washington, D.C.: Government Printing Office, 1977. 384 p.

This analysis asserts that ZBB is an effort to cope with limitations on state resources. ZBB methods and applications vary among the states and thus identification of a common core of practices in participating ZBB states is improbable. Approximately twelve states employ features of ZBB and their experiences should be evaluated to help Congress fashion a version that is appropriate to the scale and functions of the federal government.

1329   Versel, Mark J. "Zero-Base Budgeting: Setting Priorities Through
        the Ranking Process." PUBLIC ADMINISTRATION REVIEW 38
        (November-December 1978): 524-27.

        Versel writes that managers at each level of the organi-
        zation must decide who should participate in ranking,
        what procedures should be adopted for conducting ranking,
        and what must be done to meld the chosen procedures
        with the budget process and timetable. The author de-
        fines ranking as "the process through which managers are
        asked to array their priorities by choosing among all the
        decision packages presented to them."

1330   Wholey, Joseph S. ZERO BASE BUDGETING AND PROGRAM
        EVALUATION. Lexington, Mass.: D.C. Heath and Co., 1978.
        xiii, 157 p.

        Wholey illustrates how simplified zero-base budgeting
        and program evaluation processes can be used by policy
        makers to control government costs and achieve policy
        objectives without creating a massive flow of irrelevant
        paperwork. The author's principal points originate from
        case studies of zero-base budgeting and program evaluation
        efforts in local government and in regional and federal
        agencies. Wholey concludes that the key to efficient,
        effective government is the personal involvement of top
        policy makers in setting realistic objectives and then
        mobilizing needed support. This text is an excellent
        resource guide to budgeting and evaluation concepts.

1331   Wildavsky, Aaron [B.], and Hammond, Arthur. "Comprehensive Versus
        Incremental Budgeting in the Department of Agriculture." ADMINI-
        STRATIVE SCIENCE QUARTERLY 10 (December 1965): 321-46.

        The authors interview Department of Agriculture personnel
        to determine the impacts of incremental versus compre-
        hensive modes of decision making. They find that a zero-
        base budget could be described but not practiced. They
        conclude that comprehensive, zero-base budgeting vastly
        overestimates one's limited ability to calculate and grossly
        underestimates the importance of political and techno-
        logical constraints. They also maintain that the required
        calculations could not be made and would not lead to
        substantial changes.

1332   Worthley, John A., and Ludwin, William G. ZERO BASE BUDGET-
        ING IN STATE AND LOCAL GOVERNMENT. New York: Praeger
        Publishers, 1979. 140 p.

Based on practical experience with ZBB at the state and local government level, this volume details the successes and failures of ZBB, its history, and the literature and controversies surrounding it. Case studies ranging from New Jersey and Georgia to Wilmington, Delaware, and the Illinois Department of Corrections illustrate that ZBB can provide a workable, replicable budgeting system for state and local government.

F. POLITICAL ECONOMY AND FINANCE

1333   Dahl, Robert A., and Lindblom, Charles E. POLITICS, ECONOMICS AND WELFARE: PLANNING AND POLITICO-ECONOMIC SYSTEMS RESOLVED INTO BASIC SOCIAL PROCESSES. Rev. ed. Chicago: University of Chicago Press, 1976. 1,577 p.

This is an effort "to incorporate certain aspects of politics and economics into a single consistent body of theory. Behind much political and economic theory lies the implicit, sometimes explicit, question: What are the conditions under which numerous individuals can maximize the attainment of their goals through the use of social mechanisms? That question, specifically directed to politico-economic processes, is the focus of this study." In this revision of their 1953 edition, the authors explore the impacts of social techniques and rational social action, ends and means, some social processes for rational calculation, some social processes for control, social processes for economizing, the price system, hierarchy, polyarchy, bargaining, and bargaining as a politico-economic technique.

1334   Feldstein, Martin. "Unemployment Compensation: Its Effect on Unemployment." MONTHLY LABOR REVIEW 99 (March 1976): 39-41.

The article relates that the majority of recipients collect benefits that are at least 50 percent of their previous gross wage. The reader learns that temporary layoffs are an important part of unemployment in the economy. Temporary unemployment is almost costless to workers and to their companies, as many firms with high layoff rates have paid less in taxes than their employees have received in benefits.

1335   Flanders, Ralph E. "Administering the Employment Act--The First Year." PUBLIC ADMINISTRATION REVIEW 7 (Autumn 1947): 221-27.

The former senator from Vermont writes an informative
and interesting essay on the administrative implementation
of the Employment Act of 1946 during its initial year of
operation. He describes the functions of the Council of
Economic Advisors and the Congressional Joint Committee
on the Economic Report. This article is an insightful
analysis of the president's most influential economic advisory group's original purposes and problems.

1336   Furstenberg, Frank, Jr., and Thrall, Charles A. "Counting the Jobless:
        The Impact of Job Rationing on the Measurement of Unemployment."
        ANNALS OF THE AMERICAN ACADEMY OF POLITICAL AND SOCIAL
        SCIENCE 418 (March 1975): 45-59.

        The authors observe that the official definition of un-
        employment is poorly designed to reflect the size of the
        population available for work. One of the most important
        considerations affecting labor market behavior is how
        strongly an individual feels he or she has the right to a
        job and an obligation to work. Noting that job rationing
        conceals the level of joblessness in the society, the au-
        thors believe that it works to the advantage of employers
        who want a flexible labor pool, eliminating large numbers
        of people who might be employed.

1337   Hawkins, Augustus F. "Planning for Personal Choice: The Equal
        Opportunity and Full Employment Act." ANNALS OF THE AMERICAN
        ACADEMY OF POLITICAL AND SOCIAL SCIENCE 418 (March 1975):
        13-16.

        This article contends that the Equal Opportunity and Full
        Employment Act is a critical piece of legislation. This
        legislation expands and implements the Employment Act
        of 1946 and requires the president to develop a full em-
        ployment and national purposes budget. Hawkins main-
        tains that there is an urgent need for passage of this
        legislation in order that full employment and the right
        to a job will exist for each individual who wants to work.

1338   Heller, Walter W. NEW DIMENSIONS OF POLITICAL ECONOMY.
        Cambridge, Mass.: Harvard University Press, 1966. viii, 203 p.

        Heller, chairman of the Council of Economic Advisors
        under Presidents Kennedy and Johnson, reviews presidential
        reliance on economists, discusses the role of the Council
        of Economic Advisors, probes the promise of modern eco-
        nomic policy, examines fiscal policy, and offers perspec-
        tives on strengthening the fiscal base of American feder-
        alism. The author was the first advocate of per capita
        revenue sharing and offers the reader approximately 30
        pages of detail on the particulars of his revenue sharing
        concept.

1339   Hoselitz, Bert F. "Levels of Economic Performance and Bureaucratic
       Structures." In BUREAUCRACY AND POLITICAL DEVELOPMENT,
       edited by Joseph LaPalombara, pp. 168-98. Princeton, N.J.: Princeton
       University Press, 1963.

           The purpose of this essay is to examine whether concepts
           of political modernization can be meaningfully applied
           to a concrete problem, the analysis of the interrelations
           between levels of economic performance of different so-
           cieties and the bureaucratic structures which they create
           for themselves.

1340   Lekachman, Robert. "Managing Inflation in a Full Employment Society."
       ANNALS OF THE AMERICAN ACADEMY OF POLITICAL AND SOCIAL
       SCIENCE 418 (March 1975): 85-93.

           Lekachman maintains that rearrangements of power, privi-
           lege, income, and wealth would attain price stability
           with full employment. The reader is informed that the
           Equal Opportunity and Full Employment Act of 1976 is a
           step toward achieving full employment.

1341   Lindblom, Charles E. "Economics and the Administration of National
       Planning." PUBLIC ADMINISTRATION REVIEW 25 (December 1965):
       274-83.

           The author discusses historical and contemporary contri-
           butions of economics to public administration, the market
           mechanism as an administrative device, planning vs. the market,
           market socialism, and planning via the market mechanism.

1342   Musgrave, Richard A., and Musgrave, Peggy B. PUBLIC FINANCE
       IN THEORY AND PRACTICE. New York: McGraw-Hill Book Co.,
       1976. xvi, 778 p.

           This text combines a thorough understanding of fiscal in-
           stitutions with a careful analysis of the economic issues
           which underlie budget policy. It deals with many of the
           central economic and social issues of the 1970s. Sections
           include an introduction to fiscal functions and institutions
           and the theory of social goods, expenditure structure,
           revenue structure, effects on efficiency and capacity out-
           put, fiscal stabilization, and fiscal federalism.

1343   Nourse, Edwin G. "Public Administration and Economic Stabilization."
       PUBLIC ADMINISTRATION REVIEW 7 (Spring 1947): 85-92.

           The author, chairman of the original Council of Economic
           Advisors when this article was published, writes about the
           application of the Employment Act of 1946, under which
           the council was created, and concludes that the 1946

legislation is "strictly in line with the spirit of 1776."
Concerning the establishment of the CEA, Nourse states
"we are possessed of no administrative authority or power
to issue directives. Ours is a purely consultative and
advisory role not merely as to the President, individually but
also, as a staff arm of the President, to a considerable number
of administrative offices in the federal government." This article presents interesting insights into the original purposes of
this important economic legislation.

1344   Olson, Mancur, Jr. THE LOGIC OF COLLECTIVE ACTION: PUBLIC
        GOODS AND THE THEORY OF GROUPS. Cambridge, Mass.: Harvard
        University Press, 1965. x, 176 p.

        "The view that groups act to serve their interests presum-
        ably is based upon the assumption that the individuals in
        groups act out of self-interest. . . . But it is not in
        fact true that the idea that groups will act in their self-
        interest follows logically from the premise of rational and
        self-interested behavior. It does not follow, because the
        individuals in a group would gain if they achieved their
        group objective, that they would act to achieve that ob-
        jective, even if they were all rational and self-interested.
        Indeed, unless the number of individuals in a group is
        quite small, or unless there is coercion or some other
        special device to make individuals act in their common
        interest, rational, self-interested individuals will not act
        to achieve their common or group interests. . . . The
        widespread view, common throughout the social sciences,
        that groups tend to further their interests, is accordingly
        unjustified, at least when it is based, as it usually is,
        on the (sometimes implicit) assumption that groups act in
        their self-interest because individuals do." The conclusions
        of this text are as relevant to the sociologist and the po-
        litical scientist as they are to the economist.

1345   Ostrom, Vincent, and Ostrom, Elinor. "Public Choice: A Different
        Approach to the Study of Public Administration." PUBLIC ADMINI-
        STRATION REVIEW 31 (March-April 1971): 203-16.

        The authors examine the traditional theory of public ad-
        ministration, review Herbert Simon's challenge to public
        administration and the works of political economists, de-
        note the nature of public goods and services and the
        effect of decision structures upon collective action, and
        call for new perspectives in the study of public admini-
        stration. This article is quite pertinent to the dilemmas
        of the field, and the references provide an excellent
        review of the literature of the public choice field.

1346   Pechman, Joseph A. FEDERAL TAX POLICY. New York: W.W.
        Norton and Co., 1971. 344 p.

> This comprehensive volume explains in nontechnical terms
> the nature of the U.S. tax system and the effects of
> taxation on the economy. Pechman's coverage ranges
> from a step-by-step description of the passage of a tax
> bill in Congress to a systematic review of virtually the
> entire tax spectrum: personal and corporate income taxes,
> general and selective consumption taxes, payroll taxes,
> estate and gift taxes, and property taxes. He analyzes
> conflicting views on controversial issues of fiscal policy.

1347   Petersen, J.E.; Spain, C.L.; and Laffey, M.F., eds. STATE AND
        LOCAL GOVERNMENT FINANCE AND FINANCIAL MANAGEMENT:
        A COMPENDIUM OF CURRENT RESEARCH. Washington, D.C.:
        Government Finance Research Center, 1978. 690 p.

> This resource text for practitioners and professionals is di-
> vided into three parts. The initial part contains sixteen
> essays which consider research activities and indicate
> topics that require additional study. The second section
> describes more than nine hundred research projects in
> finance. The final part concludes with a guide of the
> seven hundred chief investigators whose research is reported
> in this volume.

1348   Pierce, Lawrence C. THE POLITICS OF FISCAL POLICY FORMA-
        TION. Pacific Palisades, Calif.: Goodyear Publishing Co., 1971.
        1971. xii, 225 p.

> This book describes the entire fiscal policy-making pro-
> cess, discusses the federal government's forecasts of eco-
> nomic activity, looks at the impact of economic tech-
> nology, organizational procedures, and political possibili-
> ties at each stage of the decision-making process, attempts
> to account for as many of the determinants as possible
> which affect each of a sequence of decisions leading to
> a fiscal policy choice, and summarizes the major features
> of fiscal policy formation by presenting an inventory of
> propositions which may be tested against other kinds of
> governmental decisions.

1349   Schultze, Charles L. THE POLITICS AND ECONOMICS OF PUBLIC
        SPENDING. Washington, D.C.: Brookings Institution, 1968. viii,
        143 p.

> Schultze, director of the Budget Bureau under President
> Johnson and chairman of the Council of Economic Advisors
> under President Carter, discusses the evolution of bud-
> getary techniques, describes Planning, Programming, Bud-

geting Systems (PPBS) in brief, examines "muddling
through" as an alternative view of the decision process,
recognizes the role of analysis in political decisions,
places PPBS in a political context, and notes future
directions for analysis. He states that "the complexity
of the social problems with which the nation is now
grappling and their variety from community to community
call for both a national commitment of resources and
strong local participation in the use of those resources."
This text provides excellent insights into the budgeting
and decision-making processes.

1350   Sharkansky, Ira. THE POLITICS OF TAXING AND SPENDING.
Indianapolis: Bobbs-Merrill Co., 1969. 210 p. Tables.

Sharkansky deals comprehensively with 1) the underlying
social and economic forces affecting tax and spending
policy, 2) the issues and controversies surrounding the
collection and distribution of monies, 3) the institutions
and processes of taxation and appropriations, and 4) the
behavior of decision makers who must write tax laws and
formulate budgets. The author uses comparative analysis
throughout this volume in an effort not only to describe
but also to explain taxing and spending decisions.

1351   Shearer, Derek, and Webb, Lee. "How to Plan in a Mixed Economy."
NATION 221 (October 11, 1975): 336-40.

The authors suggest that the nation's large private corporations can predetermine desired rates of return and create
demands for products. They maintain that economic planning should begin by setting publicly debated socioeconomic goals, followed by devising a combination of micro-
and macroeconomic mechanisms. They suggest that real
full employment should be achieved by passing the Equal
Opportunity and Full Employment Act of 1976 and that
this legislation would require the president to follow
economic policies and programs that would guarantee jobs
for all.

1352   Stack, Steven. "Direct Government Involvement in the Economy."
AMERICAN SOCIOLOGICAL REVIEW 43 (December 1978): 880-88.

Stack evaluates the Keynesian concept that the degree of
direct government involvement in the economy should reduce income inequality via economic growth and full employment. A regression analysis of data from thirty-two
nations suggests that the degree of direct government involvement in the economy is the single most important
factor connected with income inequality.

1353   Wamsley, Gary L., and Zald, Mayer N. THE POLITICAL ECONOMY
       OF PUBLIC ORGANIZATIONS: A CRITIQUE AND APPROACH TO
       THE STUDY OF PUBLIC ADMINISTRATION. Lexington, Mass.:
       D.C. Heath and Co., 1973. x, 110 p.

           This text grew out of the authors' discontent with the
           current state of public administration theory; also their
           belief that the recent development of the political
           economy approach to organizations by Zald might solve
           some of the major conceptual problems of the field of
           public administration. Chapter 1 states the authors'
           discontent with the current state of public administration
           theory, reviews alternative approaches, and outlines the
           political economy approach. Subsequent chapters detail
           the major dimensions and concepts of the framework,
           focus upon the environment of external political-economic
           relations, structures, and processes of public agencies,
           and address some of the traditional and modern concerns
           of public administration.

1354   Weber, Arnold R. IN PURSUIT OF PRICE STABILITY: THE WAGE-
       PRICE FREEZE OF 1971. Washington, D.C.: Brookings Institution,
       1973. 137 p.

           Weber believes the unique aspect of these direct controls
           lies in the fact that they were begun in a peacetime
           situation. The reader is told that a wage-price freeze
           reflects short-term tactical and political necessities and
           functions as a prelude to more refined policies. The
           government hoped to preserve the effectiveness of the
           freeze through the ninety-day period by combining the
           presumption of compliance with the capacity for inflicting
           public retribution. In conclusion, the reader is informed
           that the freeze worked with a considerable degree of
           effectiveness, was remarkably free from political influences
           in its execution, and demonstrated that governmental
           controls can be sufficient with minimal preparation.

1355   Weber, Max. THE PROTESTANT ETHIC AND THE SPIRIT OF CAPI-
       TALISM. Translated by Talcott Parsons. New York: Charles Scrib-
       ner's Sons, 1958. xvii, 292 p.

           Weber, in this historical essay, attributes the development
           of free enterprise mostly to psychological principles de-
           veloping from the Protestant Reformation. Spiritual moti-
           vations such as diligence and worldly self-denial are un-
           derstood as the foundation of capitalism and its require-
           ments for rational planning, individual regimentation,
           bureaucratic structure, and science. Weber opens with
           a discourse on social stratification and the essence of
           capitalism, looks at particular religious creeds, and ends

with a premonition that the United States will participate in a debauchery of materialism when the free enterprise system is divorced from its religious origins.

1356 _____. THE THEORY OF SOCIAL AND ECONOMIC ORGANIZA-
TION. Translated by A.M. Henderson and Talcott Parsons. New
York: Oxford University Press, 1947. x, 436 p.

Weber's productive life is examined in a thorough preface
by Talcott Parsons. Weber's concept of social structure
and social involvement in contemporary Western civilization has profoundly affected organizational theory in
American sociology. Contained in the work is Weber's
typology of authority: legal-rational, the foundation of
bureaucratic structure; customary, allied with older types
of organization based on morals; and charismatic, an
unsettled revolutionary power which if acceptable under-
goes an alteration to become routine administration.

1357 Weidenbaum, Murray L. "The Second Managerial Revolution: The
Shift of Economic Decision-Making from Business to Government."
In PLANNING, POLITICS, AND THE PUBLIC INTEREST, edited by
Walter Goldstein, pp. 45-76. New York: Columbia University Press,
1978.

Weidenbaum maintains that our industrial economy is undergoing a bureaucratic phenomenon. He delves into the
new wave of government regulation, the changing locus
of economic decision making, the costs of government involvement in business decisions, feedback effects on business decisions, the chances for additional government
regulations, and reforms in the regulatory process.

Chapter 10

CENTRALIZATION AND DECENTRALIZATION

A. CITIZEN PARTICIPATION

1358   Aberbach, Joel D., and Rockman, Bert A. "Administrators' Beliefs
        About the Role of the Public: The Case of American Federal Exec-
        utives." WESTERN POLITICAL QUARTERLY 31 (December 1978):
        502-22.

> Aberbach and Rockman assert that reconciliation of
> professional bureaucracy and democratic institutions is one
> of the major perplexities of the future. They declare
> that a small percentage of administrators are ready for
> citizen participation. They value participation in ad-
> ministration of poverty and welfare programs.

1359   Aleshire, Robert A. "Power to the People: An Assessment of the
        Community Action and Model Cities Experience." PUBLIC ADMINI-
        STRATION REVIEW 32 (September 1972): 428-43.

> The author states that any attempt to discuss the costs,
> benefits, and limitations of citizen participation should
> recognize and deal with the essential question--power.
> The basic tenet of a democratic form of government is
> that power flows from the free will of each individual
> and is joined through a compact to create the will of
> the community. Aleshire considers Great Society pro-
> grams which purport to give power to the people in a
> participatory sense.

1360   Austin, David M. "Resident Participation: Political Mobilization or
        Organizational Co-optation?" PUBLIC ADMINISTRATION REVIEW
        32 (September 1972): 409-20. Table.

> The emphasis of this article is on the relation of the
> citizen participation experience to the continuing issues
> of citizen involvement and citizen action in a society

that is both democratic and contentious. The findings
point to general conclusions in three areas. "First, the
relation of the official federal policy on resident participation to the patterns of participation actually found
in local CAAs (Community Action Agencies). Second,
the impact of resident participation within the local
community. Third, the relation of resident participation
under OEO (Office of Economic Opportunity) to the
general issue of citizen participation in a democratic
society."

1361   Barber, Daniel M. "Citizen Participation and the Planning Process."
        MUNICIPAL MANAGEMENT 1 (Summer 1978): 37-42.

This essay discusses workable strategies and tactics that
can be utilized in attaining effective citizen input in the
municipal planning process. Barber reviews the numerous
programmatic and philosophical decisions that should be
made prior to citizen participation. He recommends approaches that are within the often modest budget requests
of smaller cities. He examines tensions confronting
municipal personnel in the citizen participation process.

1362   Bjur, Wesley E., and Siegel, Gilbert B. "Voluntary Citizen Partici-
        pation in Local Government: Quality, Cost, and Commitment."
        MIDWEST REVIEW OF PUBLIC ADMINISTRATION 11 (June 1977):
        135-49. Table.

According to the authors, citizen apathy and insufficient
municipal income in the face of skyrocketing service costs
are fairly common problems associated with the functioning
of contemporary local government units. They propose a
manner in which both complaints can be addressed and
resolved through different models of voluntary citizen
participation. They discuss the tradeoffs between the
different models, all of which are aimed at increased
citizen participation and improved quality of municipal
services.

1363   Boone, Richard W. "Reflections on Citizen Participation and the
        Economic Opportunity Act." PUBLIC ADMINISTRATION REVIEW 32
        (September 1972): 444-56.

The author concludes that the origin of the maximum
feasible participation idea cannot be understood apart
from the community action concept and its genesis. The
Community Action Program of the Economic Opportunity
Act of 1964 was an important opportunity for local community groups to obtain and administer federal resources.
This was neither a mandate for new federally-administered
programs nor ones administered by the states. It was an

attempt to move administrative authority closer to people
directly affected by federal legislation.

1364   Brophy, Michael C., et al. "Evaluation of Community Action Programs: Issues and Alternatives." In PROGRAM EVALUATION FOR
MENTAL HEALTH: METHODS, STRATEGIES, PARTICIPANTS, edited
by Robert D. Coursey et al., pp. 205-24. New York: Grune and
Stratton, 1977.

> This essay copes with the predicaments and potentials in
> evaluating the work of community action programs. The
> authors do not concentrate on a particular technique of
> data collection but rather on the general strategies and
> issues germane to evaluation of community action programs.

1365   Caputo, David A. "The Citizen Component of Policy Evaluation."
POLICY STUDIES JOURNAL 2 (Winter 1973): 92-97.

> Caputo maintains that if policy evaluation is to become
> more sophisticated and applicable to more policy areas,
> the citizen component must be fully developed. The
> perception and ultimate evaluation of policy by the
> citizen directly affected must be taken into account.
> He suggests that the optimum strategy is to develop a
> methodology broad enough to incorporate citizen evaluation
> of widely different policies and to permit individual
> methodological adaptations to meet the specific needs of
> the policy or program.

1366   Carrell, Jeptha J. "Citizen Participation and Decentralization."
MIDWEST REVIEW OF PUBLIC ADMINISTRATION 3 (February 1969):
3-12.

> Carrell defines the concept of decentralization, illustrates
> kinds of decentralization, indicates standards for citizen
> participation and decentralization, denotes that the utili-
> zation of PPBS is a desirable prerequisite to citizen par-
> ticipation or decentralization, examines why decentraliza-
> tion of federal agency decisions was needed, and provides
> several reasons why decentralization and better citizen
> participation have not been very successful.

1367   Chatman, Linwood, and Jackson, David M. "Citizen Participation--
An Exercise in Futility: An Action Program for ASPA." PUBLIC AD-
MINISTRATION REVIEW 32 (May-June 1972): 199-201.

> Assuming that the white man's system does not apply to
> nonwhite minorities and that the white man's system is
> unwilling to share any significant part of its power, the
> authors provide specific steps for ASPA (American Society for
> Public Administration) to follow including the following recom-

mendations: 1) recruit minority group people for ASPA membership, 2) create strong ASPA community outreach, and 3) use
minority-owned businesses.

1368   "Citizen Participation Recommendations." PUBLIC ADMINISTRATION
        REVIEW 32 (May-June 1972): 222-23.

        The purpose of this short article is to foster a more
        realistic and constructive debate in public administration
        on the topic of citizen participation. This essay includes
        discussions of federal legislation and agency guidelines of
        participatory efforts, resources available in colleges and
        universities, and the role of ASPA in promoting more
        effective citizen participation efforts.

1369   Cole, Richard L. CITIZEN PARTICIPATION AND THE URBAN POLICY
        PROCESS. Lexington, Mass.: D.C. Heath and Co., 1974. 192 p.

        Cole examines a variety of citizen participation programs
        which have been initiated by municipalities and the federal
        government in the late 1960s and early 1970s. He probes
        the impact of these programs on individual participants and
        on the American political system as a whole.

1370   Cook, James B., and Frederickson, H. George. "Citizen Participation
        and the Administration of Public Policy." In PUBLIC ADMINISTRATION
        AND PUBLIC POLICY, edited by H. George Frederickson and Charles
        R. Wise, pp. 99-108. Lexington, Mass.: D.C. Heath and Co., 1977.

        The authors reveal that pressure is on American public ad-
        ministrators, at most every level, to deal directly with
        the question of citizen participation. Theorists, scientists,
        and practicing politicians do not agree about the proper
        place for citizen participation, the democratic option is
        one that provides citizens with the chance to determine
        the role of their participation, and public administrators
        are in a position either to help or to hinder citizens'
        opportunities to become involved.

1371   Cunningham, James V. "Citizen Participation in Public Affairs."
        PUBLIC ADMINISTRATION REVIEW 32 (October 1972): 589-602.

        This essay seeks to summarize the nature and impact of
        the participative phenomenon, to consider possible expla-
        nations for its existence, and to seek some understanding
        of its extraordinary growth since the end of World War II.
        The author looks at citizen participation within a broad
        context of human history, examines the main elements of
        the U.S. experience, offers a definition of the phenom-
        enon, tests the genuineness of the contemporary phenom-
        enon, and attempts to analyze the contemporary situation
        with some projection into the future.

1372   Cupps, D. Stephen. "Emerging Problems of Citizen Participation."
        PUBLIC ADMINISTRATION REVIEW 37 (September–October 1977):
        478-87.

> Cupps analyzes the problems which have accompanied the
> growth of the citizen participation and public interest
> movements. The author identifies the potential short-
> sightedness of administrative response to citizen demands,
> problems of representation and legitimacy, the style and
> tactics of citizen groups, and the absence of sophisticated
> cost-benefit analysis of public interest policies and pro-
> grams as primary concerns confronting citizen participation.

1373   Fauri, David P. "Citizen Participation and the Rationale for Program
        Participation in Social Service Organizations." MIDWEST REVIEW OF
        PUBLIC ADMINISTRATION 8 (January 1974): 42-51.

> The author examines citizen participation from four per-
> spectives, including traditional "democratic participation,"
> participation through "social protest" outside the traditional
> political process, "community development," or efforts of
> citizens and governmental authorities united to improve
> economic, social, and cultural conditions of communities,
> and "program participation," operating with participation
> beginning at the community level and seeking assistance
> from specific government programs. Fauri suggests that
> program participation can help social service organizations
> more effectively meet the needs of those served and that
> it offers a potentially useful modification to the govern-
> mental administrative processes by increasing citizen in-
> volvement in public programs.

1374   Fraenkel, Richard M. "Community Development Goals and Citizen
        Participation." COMMUNITY DEVELOPMENT JOURNAL 12 (October
        1977): 177-85.

> Fraenkel believes the main disadvantage of public policy
> education is that implementation at the local level could
> undermine community consensus and established patterns
> of political participation at the local level.

1375   Fritz, D. "The Advocacy Agency and Citizen Participation: The Case
        of the Administration on Aging and the Elderly." JOURNAL OF
        HEALTH AND HUMAN RESOURCES ADMINISTRATION 1 (August
        1978): 79-108.

> This article contends that the advocacy agency concept
> asserts an alternative mode of citizen participation. The
> concept is debated on the basis that citizen participation
> diminishes alienation, improves program effectiveness,
> secures feedback, mobilizes resources, and enhances re-
> sponsiveness.

1376   Gittell, Marilyn. "Decentralization and Citizen Participation in
        Education." PUBLIC ADMINISTRATION REVIEW 32 (October 1972):
        670-86. Tables.

> Gittell notes the expansion of professionalization and
> school bureaucracies in recent decades, the failure of
> integrated schools, the emergence of community control,
> the recommendations of the Bundy Plan for education,
> the dilemmas of the Ocean Hill-Brownsville experiment
> (i.e., anti-Semitism and racism), the problems of evalu-
> ating decentralization and community control, and urban
> school reform of the 1970s. She concludes: "Quality
> public education without the involvement and participa-
> tion of the consumers is a contradiction in terms." This
> essay presents an excellent review of the literature.

1377   Hallman, Howard W. "Federally Financed Citizen Participation."
        PUBLIC ADMINISTRATION REVIEW 32 (September 1972): 421-27.

> Should federal funds be used to support citizen participa-
> tion? If so, how should this be accomplished? The au-
> thor explores answers to these queries by reviewing four
> programs: urban renewal, the juvenile delinquency-gray
> area projects, community action, and model cities. This
> essay shows that there has been an evolving and steadily
> broadening concept of what is proper and of how federal
> and local agencies should proceed.

1378   Hamilton, Randy H. "Bridging the Gap Between Citizens and City
        Government." In EMERGING PATTERNS IN URBAN ADMINISTRA-
        TION, edited by F. Gerald Brown and Thomas P. Murphy, pp. 64-
        79. Lexington, Mass.: Heath Lexington Books, 1970.

> Hamilton views the city from the perspective of the con-
> sumers of the outputs of urban administration, the citizens.
> He adds a note of urban optimism as he reviews the sub-
> stantial success that has been achieved in many aspects
> of city improvement, both in terms of quality and quantity
> of output services and in terms of reformed governmental
> institutions. He examines the problems that are with us
> today and tries to anticipate some of those that will beset
> urban areas in the next thirty years.

1379   Kloman, Erasmus. "Citizen Participation in the Philadelphia Model
        Cities Program: Retrospect and Prospect." PUBLIC ADMINISTRATION
        REVIEW 32 (September 1972): 402-8.

> Kloman presents a retrospective evaluation of the issues
> and an appraisal of the future prospects for citizen par-
> ticipation in the Philadelphia Model Cities Program. He

concludes: "Overshadowing the entire issue of the future of the Philadelphia program is a cloud of uncertainty about the future of the national Model Cities Program. Unless the national program receives vigorous leadership and real commitment from both federal and city governments, it has little chance of realizing the potential for which it was once heralded."

1380   McCaffery, Jerry, and Bowman, John H. "Participatory Democracy and Budgeting: The Effects of Proposition 13." PUBLIC ADMINISTRATION REVIEW 38 (November-December 1978): 530-38. Table.

This article explores the complexities of Proposition 13 in the context of fiscal policy making. McCaffery and Bowman express serious reservations about the feasibility of participatory democracy in determining priorities of budgeting expertise. They denote that Proposition 13 brought extensive changes in California intergovernmental relations.

1381   Miller, S.M., and Rein, Martin. "Participation, Poverty, and Administration." PUBLIC ADMINISTRATION REVIEW 29 (January-February 1969): 15-25.

The authors focus on the evolving purposes to which the phrase "maximum feasible participation" was applied under the Economic Opportunity Act of 1964. They note that maximum feasible participation emerged unclear, unexamined, and misunderstood. Too many agendas permitted this concept to mature in uncertain terrain. They conclude: "It may not always be possible to bring together without conflict ideals of efficiency, humanity, and democracy. But we cannot surrender to efficiency as the highest social value."

1382   Paulson, Darryl. "Citizen Participation in Local Budgeting." SOUTHERN REVIEW OF PUBLIC ADMINISTRATION 1 (December 1977): 293-302.

This article examines the operation of the St. Petersburg, Florida, Budget Review Committee from 1972 through 1977 and describes the committee's achievements and shortcomings. Paulson believes that citizen budget review committees can make important contributions if they have a clear perception of their responsibilities and limitations. According to the author, the major service that the committee can provide is in the areas of representation, budget clarity, and priority setting.

1383   Riedel, James A. "Citizen Participation: Myths and Realities."
        PUBLIC ADMINISTRATION REVIEW 32 (May-June 1972): 211-20.

        Riedel discusses the realities of and offers postulates on
        citizen participation. Voting, single issue interest, less
        participation at the local level than at the national level,
        the lack of responsiveness among government officials, and
        group participation are themes addressed in five postulates.

1384   Rosenbaum, Walter A. "The Paradoxes of Public Participation." AD-
        MINISTRATION AND SOCIETY 8 (November 1976): 355-83.

        Rosenbaum believes that greater participation within gov-
        ernment bureaucracy has meant that agencies are more
        sensitive to the interests of citizens, that the interests
        participating are more diversified, and that citizens are
        influencing the making of public policies. He states
        that there are problems in the enforcement of more par-
        ticipatory government and with narrow issue groups domi-
        nating politics and policy making for certain specific
        concerns. He believes that the intervention of the courts
        and revision of certain legislation are possible ways to
        correct this lack of enforcement.

1385   Rosener, Judy B. "Citizen Participation: Can We Measure Its Ef-
        fectiveness?" PUBLIC ADMINISTRATION REVIEW 38 (September-
        October 1978): 457-63. Table.

        Rosener states that there is little agreement among and
        between citizens and administrators concerning their goals
        and objectives. She suggests that the use of evaluation
        research methodology could produce an acceptable frame-
        work for the conceptualization and measurement of citizen
        participation effectiveness.

1386   Schumaker, Paul D., and Billeaux, David M. "Group Representation
        in Local Bureaucracies." ADMINISTRATION AND SOCIETY 10
        (November 1978): 285-316.

        Schumaker explores a number of reasons why some active
        groups are better represented in local bureaucracies than
        other active groups. The authors analyze 1,397 group-
        agency relationships in fifty-five cities and offer some
        tentative propositions.

1387   Strange, John H. "Citizen Participation in Community Action and
        Model Cities Programs." PUBLIC ADMINISTRATION REVIEW 32
        (October 1972): 655-69.

        The author examines the meanings, implementation, re-

strictions, attitudes, objectives, conditions, and techniques of citizen participation. This essay presents an
excellent review of the literature.

1388 _____. "The Impact of Citizen Participation on Public Administration."
PUBLIC ADMINISTRATION REVIEW 32 (September 1972): 457-70.

The author discusses the tradition of citizen participation
in the United States, the meaning of citizen participation,
the extent of participation, restrictions on participation,
the impact of participation upon participants, the impact
of participation upon Model Cities and Community Action
Programs, and the impact of participation upon the community. This is a very useful essay for understanding the
roles of citizen participation in government programs in
the early 1970s.

1389 Terrell, Paul. "Citizen Participation and General Revenue Sharing."
SOCIAL WORK 20 (November 1975): 429-34.

Terrell maintains that numerous community programs have
received public funds for the first time through revenue
sharing. He explains the use of special community meetings and newspaper questionnaires by county officials to
publicize the available funds and to solicit ideas and
support. Citizens respond with great interest in local
arrangements for planning and budgeting. Most local
governments combine their revenue funds with general
funds and ask public and private agencies to submit requests and proposals.

1390 Van Meter, Elena C. "Citizen Participation in the Policy Management
Process." PUBLIC ADMINISTRATION REVIEW 35 (December 1975):
804-12.

The author examines citizen participation as a policy
management tool, discusses the management of citizen
participation, reviews institutional constraints on citizen
participation, stresses the need to balance small group
needs against the general good, and relates technical
assistance needs. Van Meter, associated with the League
of Women Voters, denotes that the League believes that
the involvement of citizens in the policy management
process can help restore citizen confidence in government
by 1) providing the governmental manager information on
perceived performance of the operating departments and
2) the citizen the information needed to make realistic
demands upon the government.

1391   Wolman, Harold. "Organization Theory and Community Action
        Agencies." PUBLIC ADMINISTRATION REVIEW 32 (January-February
        1972): 33-42.

> This article is an attempt to understand and analyze the
> politics of community action agencies. Community action
> agencies are agencies set up to administer community
> action programs of individual cities under the Economic
> Development Act. The author emphasizes the imperative
> of survival for an organization and the necessity of ob-
> taining sufficient environmental support in order to assure
> survival. The displacement of goals caused by survival
> needs, the effort to coopt the environment, and the in-
> ternal conflict caused by this process are analyzed in
> this case study.

1392   Zimmerman, Joseph F. "Neighborhoods and Citizen Involvement."
        PUBLIC ADMINISTRATION REVIEW 32 (May-June 1972): 201-10.

> The author discusses the new reform movement, the idea
> of the federated city, the principal financial obstacles
> in the path of creating neighborhood governments, and
> the role of community schools as these issues impact the
> involvement of citizens in the process. Zimmerman con-
> cludes that "so long as quality services in adequate amounts
> are delivered on the neighborhood level, the average citizen
> will be little interested in community control of governmental
> institutions and functions. He will confine his civic activities
> to voting and an occasional protest against the inadequate
> delivery of a service or a major proposed project which poses
> a threat of disrupting his neighborhood."

1393   Zuzak, Charles A. "Participatory Democracy and the Public Admini-
        strator." In MAKING GOVERNMENT WORK: ESSAYS IN HONOR
        OF CONLEY H. DILLON, edited by Richard P. Claude and James C.
        Strouse, pp. 1-7. College Park: University of Maryland, 1977.

> Zuzak maintains that the nature of the citizen-government
> relationship is changing with the rise of the administrative
> state and massive governmental bureaucracy. The new
> citizen politics has shifted from a legislative and an
> electoral context to an arena of nonelectoral politics.
> He concludes: "People, through governmental structures,
> may at times share the decision-making on the larger
> issues, but they do not share in decisions about the more
> trivial ones."

B. ETHICS AND POWER

1394   Appleby, Paul H. MORALITY AND ADMINISTRATION IN DEMO-
        CRATIC GOVERNMENT. Baton Rouge: Louisiana State University
        Press, 1952. xiii, 261 p.

> Appleby states: "Morality is a conception deriving from,
> and developed in, associations with human beings. . . .
> Morality begins in arrangements between human beings,
> ordering relationships to mutual advantage but with mutual
> discipline. Even in the simplest of human associations
> these arrangements involve the reconciliation of differing
> values. Negotiation is minimized by establishing these
> arrangements as habits, customs, taboos, freeing those
> concerned to come to terms about new problems in new
> understandings or in amendments to old ones." The au-
> thor addresses the problems in morality to a variety of
> situations in government administration, including executive
> responsibility, pressure groups, administrative loyalty, and
> political responsibility.

1395   Armstrong, DeWitt C. III, and Graham, George A. "Ethical Prepa-
        ration for the Public Service." BUREAUCRAT 4 (April 1975): 5-23.

> This article maintains that professional education has an
> important contribution to make in preparing public officials
> and public administrators to be faithful to the public
> interest and worthy of the public trust. Scandals within
> the federal government usually involve political executives.
> The authors believe that the professional school is the
> place to identify ethical issues and to develop values.

1396   Bailey, Stephen K. "Ethics and the Public Service." PUBLIC AD-
        MINISTRATION REVIEW 24 (December 1964): 234-43.

> The author reviews Paul H. Appleby's MORALITY AND
> ADMINISTRATION (see 1394) and uses Appleby's norma-
> tive model for personal ethics, such as, "politics and
> hierarchy force public servants to refer private and special
> interests to higher and broader public interests," as a
> beginning point for examining the mental attitudes and
> moral qualities necessary to an explicit theory of personal
> ethics in the public service.

1397   Boulding, Kenneth E. THE ORGANIZATIONAL REVOLUTION: A
        STUDY IN THE ETHICS OF ECONOMIC ORGANIZATION. New
        York: Harper and Brothers, 1953. xxxiv, 286 p.

> The subject of this book is a striking movement in modern
> life which the author describes as the "organizational

revolution." Boulding points out the great rise in the
number, size, and power of organizations of many diverse
kinds, including the rise of the labor movement, the
farm organization movement, the great corporation, the
trust and the cartel, and other economic organizations.
An examination of the effects of this revolution upon
ethics and human values is essential.

1398   Bowman, James E. "Ethics in the Federal Service: A Post Watergate
View." MIDWEST REVIEW OF PUBLIC ADMINISTRATION 11 (March
1977): 3-20. Tables.

The evidence presented in this article permits several
conclusions, including the points that public administrators
demonstrate a high degree of concern about the ethical
dimensions of American government and public policy
issues despite the current decline of public service prestige,
that the respondents in this survey profess a fairly high
set of ethical practices in everyday management operations,
and that a renewed institutional emphasis on professional
conduct does offer the opportunity for conscientious public
servants to act ethically. However, acts of leadership,
codes of ethics, and ethics legislation are not foolproof.

1399   Brown, Peter G. "Ethics and Policy Research." POLICY ANALYSIS
2 (Spring 1976): 325-40.

Brown asserts that the influence of values on policy-
relevant research is more pervasive than is commonly
acknowledged. The analyst should recognize that the
research effort is permeated with questions of descriptive
and normative ethics. This article suggests that values
under scrutiny should be identified and selected in the
definition of the problem.

1400   Cleveland, Harlan. "Systems, Purposes, and the Watergate." OPER-
ATIONS RESEARCH 21 (September-October 1973): 1019-23.

Cleveland believes that systems built through management
science are not complete enough and tend to be much
too exact. He suggests that the absence of personal responsibility would make a systems analyst conclude that
any benefits from bugging the Democratic headquarters
in the Watergate complex could not be justified by the risk.
Some men of sophistication seem not to have figured the
risks of keeping their involvement secret and keeping the
White House in the clear.

1401   "A Code of Public Ethics." PUBLIC ADMINISTRATION REVIEW 13
(Spring 1953): 120-22.

This essay includes exerpts from a code prepared by the Citizens Commission on Ethics in Government, Arlington County, Virginia, and includes twenty-six areas of interest in public ethics. Areas of controversy include self-interest, private gain and public office, conflicts of loyalty, rule of disclosure, importance of personal example, meeting specific suspicions, use of public information, avoiding obligations to grant favors, and avoiding wrong appearances.

1402   Cohen, Michael. "Religious Revivalism and the Administrative Centralization Movement." ADMINISTRATION AND SOCIETY 9 (August 1977): 219-32.

Cohen contends that the administrative centralization movement has greatly influenced government since the late nineteenth century. The era was one in which religious revivalism (Calvinism) stimulated a number of social and political reform movements, including an effort to bring about proper conduct of government administrative personnel. Cohen suggests the achievement of this goal by centralizing executive branch activities according to classic principles of organization.

1403   Dvorin, Eugene P., and Simmons, Robert H. FROM AMORAL TO HUMANE BUREAUCRACY. San Francisco: Canfield Press, 1972. 88 p.

Written as a response to the growing dissatisfaction with present administrative structures, the authors offer a critical analysis of the uses of executive power and bureaucratic institutions, and stress the need for evaluating · our institutions in terms that reflect human values as opposed to the single value of efficiency.

1404   Golembiewski, Robert T. MEN, MANAGEMENT, AND MORALITY: TOWARD A NEW ORGANIZATIONAL ETHIC. New York: McGraw-Hill Book Co., 1965. xiv, 320 p.

This text treats problems of ethical consequence in organizations, problems that are restricted enough to permit remedial action based upon relatively firm findings from the developing behavioral sciences. The focus is upon organizing work, and the aim is to use the author's knowledge of behavior in organizations to approach a set of moral values accepted in the Western tradition and to approach those values without sacrificing either efficiency or economy.

1405   _____. "Organization as a Moral Problem." PUBLIC ADMINISTRATION REVIEW 22 (Spring 1962): 51-58. Table.

According to the author, conflict between elements of

the traditional theory of organization and values derived from America's Judaeo-Christian tradition raises moral problems in organizing. Recognizing that hierarchical conformation is never neutral, Golembiewski believes that the neglect of organization as a moral problem cannot be condoned.

1406   Goodin, Robert E. "Ethical Perspectives on Political Excuses." POLICY AND POLITICS 5 (June 1977): 71-78.

Under certain conditions, there are good reasons for excusing individuals from moral responsibilities. Goodin reveals that policy evaluation should consider the "plea of impossibility" and excuses. He maintains that the ethical evaluation of entire polities is not merely accomplished with the appraisal of actions and policies.

1407   Humes, Samuel. "The New Manager Wants to Shoot Santa Claus: A Case Study of Ethics and Morality." BUREAUCRAT 4 (April 1975): 56-63.

This article concerns conflicts of interest. Humes reveals that a county manager sought to restrict Christmas presents and Christmas parties by businesses under contract with the county. He examines the relationships of ethics, county government, and politics and points out that certain county officials eventually received sentences for criminal conduct.

1408   Long, Norton E. "Power and Administration." PUBLIC ADMINISTRATION REVIEW 9 (Autumn 1949): 257-64.

"The lifeblood of administration is power. Its attainment, maintenance, increase, dissipation, and loss are subjects the practitioner and student can ill afford to neglect. Loss of realism and failure are almost certain consequences. . . . Attempts to solve administrative problems in isolation from the structure of power and purpose of the polity are bound to prove illusory." This essay remains one of the classics in the literature of public administration.

1409   McKinney, Jerome B., and Howard, Lawrence C. PUBLIC ADMINISTRATION: BALANCING POWER AND ACCOUNTABILITY. Oak Park, Ill.: Moore Publishing Co., 1979. xii, 436 p. Paper.

This textbook presents public administration as a "tension between the necessary exercise of power and the search for accountability by public servants. Growing disillusionment about the behavior of some public administrators makes a new approach to the teaching of public manage-

ment essential." McKinney and Howard focus on middle-
and lower-level managers as they believe that these are
the positions most students of public administration will
occupy for most of their professional careers. Chapters
include the lessons of Watergate, the environment and
setting of public administration, public policy, organization theory and management practice, planning, decision
making and communication, leadership, human resources,
financial management, productivity and evaluation, intergovernmental relations, and balancing power with accountability.

1410   Mosher, Frederick, et al. WATERGATE: IMPLICATIONS FOR RE-
        SPONSIBLE GOVERNMENT. New York: Basic Books, 1974. 137 p.

        This report attempts to assess the impact of Watergate on
        the future of American government. Commissioned by
        the Select Committee on Presidential Campaign Activities
        and prepared by a panel of the National Academy of
        Public Administration, the report examines the weak points
        that Watergate has revealed in American governmental
        institutions. The report analyzes the presidency, the
        White House staff, the Congress, the Department of
        Justice, and the civil service. Recommendations for
        government reform are offered.

1411   Newstrom, John W., and Ruch, William A. "The Ethics of Manage-
        ment and the Management of Ethics." MSU BUSINESS TOPICS 23
        (Winter 1975): 29-37.

        Newstrom and Ruch examine managerial ethics in a survey
        of 121 managers participating in executive development
        programs in southwestern United States. They find that
        all respondents have an individualized set of ethical stan-
        dards and that ethical beliefs of employees are similar to
        perceptions of top management ethics. Managers capitalize
        on opportunities to be unethical and believe that their
        colleagues are far more unethical than they.

1412   Palumbo, Dennis J. "Power and Role Specificity in Organization
        Theory." PUBLIC ADMINISTRATION REVIEW 29 (May-June 1969):
        237-48. Tables.

        The author uses data from a national sample of fourteen
        local public health departments to explore whether a
        single continuum underlies several different organizational
        variables relating to the way control is achieved in an
        organization. The underlying dimension of the continuum
        is seen as the distribution of power and could be charac-
        terized as the degree of specificity of role prescription
        in the organization. Palumbo concludes that centralization,

formalization, specialization, and span of control, or
structural variables, might be used as measures of the
degree of role specificity in an organization.

1413   Partridge, P.H. "An Evaluation of Bureaucratic Power." PUBLIC
        ADMINISTRATION 33 (June 1974): 99-115.

        The author maintains that an evaluation of bureaucratic
        power must address the location of power and influence
        in public bureaucracies, the quality of bureaucratic power
        vis-a-vis the quality of power possessed by other persons,
        and the roles of government and society. Partridge sug-
        gests that bureaucratic influence and power resist assimi-
        lating the principles and values of democratic politics.

1414   Pope, Carl E. "Defining Morality: A Note on the Regulation and
        Control of Nude Dancing in California Bars." CRIMINAL JUSTICE
        AND BEHAVIOR 2 (September 1975): 276-96.

        Pope reveals that the California Department of Alcoholic
        Beverage Control has been granted chief responsibility
        for controlling public licensing and other activities as-
        sociated with the sale of alcoholic beverages. Through
        a systematic study of case records and participant obser-
        vation, Pope examines the agency policies, its connection
        to local law enforcement, the conduct (bottomless dancing),
        and the procedures employed by the agency to eliminate
        this behavior.

1415   Rich, Robert F. "Systems of Analysis, Technology Assessment, and
        Bureaucratic Power." AMERICAN BEHAVIORAL SCIENTIST 22
        (January-February 1979): 393-416.

        Rich probes the attractiveness of technology assessment
        for government officials, the translation of technology
        assessment into governmental practice, the bureaucratization
        of this movement, the impact of technology assessment
        upon policy makers, and critical problems confronting
        technology assessment.

1416   Rohr, John A. "The Study of Ethics in the P.A. Curriculum."
        PUBLIC ADMINISTRATION REVIEW 36 (July-August 1976): 398-406.

        The author outlines a method for integrating the study of
        ethics into a public administration curriculum. Rohr ex-
        amines the relationship between administrative discretion
        and the political role of the bureaucrat. In studying
        Supreme Court opinions, Rohr believes that the bureaucrat
        will be exposed to many conflicting interpretations of
        American values. He states that there are four charac-
        teristics of Supreme Court decisions that are suitable for

ethical reflection on the values of the American people, including the institutional, dialectic, concrete, and pertinent.

1417 Rourke, Francis E., ed. BUREAUCRATIC POWER IN NATIONAL POLITICS. Boston: Little, Brown and Co., 1978. xii, 478 p.

The selections of this book focus on the role of executive organizations in the policy process and illuminate how bureaucratic organizations influence public policy. Chapter topics cover administrative agencies and their constituencies, the power of bureaucratic expertise, the struggle for power in bureaucratic politics, bureaucratic and other elites, bureaucratic politics and administrative reform, and public control over bureaucratic power.

1418 Salancik, Gerald R., and Pfeffer, Jeffrey. "The Bases and Uses of Power in Organizational Decision Making: The Case of a University." ADMINISTRATIVE SCIENCE QUARTERLY 19 (December 1974): 453–73.

The authors examine sources and uses of subunit power in organizational decision making. The article suggests that department chairpersons favor graduate students and national prestige as important resources. Statistical analysis of resource allocation indicates that power is more highly correlated with critical and scarce resources, allocation of graduate fellowships, grants for faculty research, and allocation of summer faculty fellowships.

1419 Samuels, Warren J. "Grants and the Theory of Power." PUBLIC FINANCE QUARTERLY 3 (October 1975): 320–45.

Samuels points out that the basic predicaments facing theoretical and empirical exploration in grants economics are the identification, comparison, and measurement problems. The author emphasizes that power is a common characteristic in exchange and grants economies. He discusses interdependence of utility functions, rights and grants, and the role of power in comprehending grants economics.

1420 Sayre, Wallace S. "Trends of a Decade in Administrative Values." PUBLIC ADMINISTRATION REVIEW 11 (Winter 1951): 1–9.

Sayre says that the dominant administrative values with which the decade (1940-50) began were those concepts embodied in two profoundly influential documents: the RE-PORT of the President's Committee on Administrative Management, and the PAPERS ON THE SCIENCE OF AD-MINISTRATION by Luther Gulick et al. He concludes

that the decade closed with a more complex set of administrative values than that with which it began. The
trend in administrative values is nowhere more sharply
illuminated than in the changing interpretations placed
upon the concept of the role of science in administration.
This essay is an interesting review of the literature of
this ten-year period.

1421   Simmons, Robert H., and Dvorin, Eugene P.   PUBLIC ADMINISTRA-
        TION: VALUES, POLICY, AND CHANGE.   Port Washington, N.Y.:
        Alfred Publishing Co., 1977.   xv, 687 p.

        The authors believe that this textbook will "meet the
        needs of those who are discontent with the value-free
        neutrality approach so long and so assiduously cultivated
        within public administration."   They feel that "public
        administration is not value-free, but, to the contrary,
        'value-full.'"   They "choose not to hide behind the guises
        of 'scientific objectivity' or scholarly remoteness tradi-
        tionally associated with the scientific management move-
        ment or the early behavioral approaches."   Also included
        are discussions of lost horizons, conflicting values, new
        horizons, and the administered world.

1422   Stenberg, Carl W.   "Citizens and the Administrative State: From
        Participation to Power."   PUBLIC ADMINISTRATION REVIEW   32
        (May-June 1972):   190-98.

        The author describes citizen participation in the United
        States during three periods of post-World War II history.
        He examines the concept of citizen participation and
        analyzes some of the answers that the literature of public
        administration and political science gives to such questions
        as: 1) Who are the citizens?   2) How do they get to
        participate?   3) What forms does this involvement take?
        4) What is the purpose of citizen participation?   and
        5) What has been its impact?

1423   Studer, Kenneth E., and Chubin, Daryl E.   "Ethics and the Unintended
        Consequences of Social Research: A Perspective from the Sociology
        of Science."   POLICY SCIENCES   8 (June 1977):   111-24.

        The authors express concern for the credibility of sociology,
        probe the definition of a social ethic, and seek a sense
        of research responsibility.   They indicate that an "in-
        discriminate advocacy of knowledge" creates implications
        for the power of scientific knowledge, client-professional
        relationships, and data collection.

1424   Sundquist, James L.   "Reflections on Watergate: Lesson for Public
        Administration." PUBLIC ADMINISTRATION REVIEW 34 (September-
        October 1974): 453-61.

> Sundquist, in an excellent inquiry into the impacts of
> Watergate on public administration, believes that public
> administration and political science have glorified the
> presidency and overlooked the potential for abuses. He
> wonders if "checks and balances" are not there after all
> and emphasizes that internal checks, the Cabinet and
> bureaucracy, become the safeguard of plural decision
> making. He ends this essay with his own approach to
> the problem: "Empower Congress to act by a simple
> majority to remove the President and call a new election.
> But, to deter the Congress from acting from trivial or
> fractious causes, require that the Congress upon removing
> the President itself be dissolved and all its members forced
> to face a new election. They would have to take their
> decision, if effect, to a referendum."

1425   Tideman, T. Nicolaus. "Ethical Foundations of the Demand-Revealing
        Process." PUBLIC CHOICE 29, special supplement (Spring 1977):
        71-76.

> Tideman states that the demand-revealing process is based
> upon utilitarian ethics. He presents four utilitarian cri-
> teria for evaluation (i.e., decision making cost, wealth
> certainty, efficiency, and equality). The reader is in-
> formed that the demand-revealing process is superior in
> utilitarian terms to alternatives.

1426   Wakefield, Susan. "Ethics and the Public Service: A Case for In-
        dividual Responsibility." PUBLIC ADMINISTRATION REVIEW 36
        (November-December 1976): 661-66.

> The author reviews the unique requirements for ethics in
> the public service and provides a good overview of recent
> literature in this area. She concludes that the "develop-
> ment of the attitudes and qualities of character incident
> to individual responsibility cannot be left to chance. In
> order for individual values to be a viable force for an
> ethical public service, rigorous efforts must be made to
> build and strengthen internal commitments to moral gov-
> ernment."

1427   Waldo, Dwight. "Reflections on Public Morality." ADMINISTRATION
        AND SOCIETY 6 (November 1974): 267-82.

> Waldo states that public administration, in its early years,
> avoided problems of morality, stating that problems were
> technical. As public administration reflected business

administration concepts, this perspective found reinforce-
ment. Legal questions came about by administrative de-
fault or political necessity. The courts cannot continue
to define and to preserve public morality.

1428 Windle, Charles, and Neigher, William. "Ethical Problems in Program
Evaluation: Advice for Trapped Evaluators." EVALUATION AND
PROGRAM PLANNING 1 (1978): 97-108.

Windle and Neigher assert that the concurrent use of
conflicting and incompatible evaluation models enhances
the chances of ethical predicaments in program evaluations. They discuss an Amelioration Model, an Accountability Model, and an Advocacy Model. The initial prototype provides better information for program decision
makers, the second centers on public data disclosure and
evaluates citizen participation, and the third advances
program interests in the competition for resources.

1429 Wolfson, Robert J. "The U.S. Think Tank and Morality: A Personal
Memoir." MAXWELL REVIEW 11 (Spring 1975): 9-19.

The author notes that the Rand Corporation was the initial
"think tank" to become active in the systems analysis
movement. Wolfson relates problems of the early years
of Rand's operations and concludes that the separation of
policy analysis from responsibility contributes to the amoral
reputations of "think tanks" in U.S. society. He cites
the use of Rand analyses by the Department of Defense,
Department of State, and the White House.

1430 Wood, Robert C. "Ethics in Government as a Problem in Executive
Management." PUBLIC ADMINISTRATION REVIEW 15 (Winter 1955):
1-7.

The author discusses the impacts of corruption in government administration upon departments and agencies in the
bureaucracy. He points out the difficulties and inadequacies of developing investigatory facilities in the bureaucracy and congressional committees.

1431 Zald, Mayer N., ed. POWER IN ORGANIZATIONS. Nashville:
Vanderbilt University Press, 1970. xii, 336 p.

The editor states that the theme of this volume is central
to the study of organizations, no matter what the discipline.
The essays represent a variety of methodological and theoretical approaches, as the topics of this text encourage
academics and practitioners of public administration to
examine the creative processes by which organizations
generate power. Included are essays on social process

and power, division of labor, decentralization, organizational adaptation, political economy, and internal resource allocation.

C. ADMINISTRATIVE CENTRALIZATION AND DECENTRALIZATION

1432   Aiken, Michael. "Relationship of Centralization to Other Structural Properties." ADMINISTRATIVE SCIENCE QUARTERLY 12 (June 1967): 72-92. Tables.

> This essay examines two different ways of measuring the distribution of power in sixteen health and welfare organizations. Aiken relates participation in decision making concerning allocation of organizational resources to the degree of complexity by measuring 1) the number of occupational specialties, 2) the amount of professional training, and 3) the amount of professional activity. He also relates participation in decision making concerning allocation of organizational resources to the degree of formalization by measuring the degree of job codification and the amount of rule observation.

1433   Barnett, Richard R., and Topham, Neville. "Evaluating the Distribution of Local Outputs in a Decentralized Structure of Government." POLICY AND POLITICS 6 (September 1977): 51-70.

> Barnett and Topham review arguments for assigning various economic roles to the differing levels of government, consider why, from society's standpoint, the localities fail to carry out efficiently the functions assigned to them, suggest a system of intergovernmental grants for resolving the difficulty, and emphasize the distribution impacts of federal grants-in-aid, local outputs, local tax bases, and public goods in general.

1434   Benson, George C.S. "A Plea for Administrative Decentralization." PUBLIC ADMINISTRATION REVIEW 7 (Summer 1947): 170-78.

> The author discusses arguments for and against decentralization. Arguments for include: speed and efficiency, internal coordination and responsibility, administrative experimentation and adaptation, external coordination, development of line executives, economy of operations, reduction of administrative detail at headquarters, and improvement of public relations. Arguments against include: political responsibility, weakened lines of technical control, lack of qualified personnel, and lack of uniform policy. Benson concludes that "increased administrative decentralization in the federal government and the larger state governments is a most desirable step." This

article is valuable for a practical understanding of administrative decentralization.

1435   Carey, William D. "Control and Supervision of Field Offices."
PUBLIC ADMINISTRATION REVIEW 6 (Winter 1946): 20-24.

Carey examines the headquarters function in the control
and supervision of field offices, concludes that the management audit is no easy exercise in control and supervision, reveals that seldom does an agency spell out the
duties and responsibilities of the itinerant supervisor, and
indicates that a serious intention to control and supervise
field operations necessitates the formulation of useful work
measurements for program appraisal and budget planning.

1436   Fesler, James W. "Approaches to the Understanding of Decentralization." JOURNAL OF POLITICS 27 (August 1965): 536-66.

The author discusses methodological problems and several
approaches to understanding decentralization. Methodological problems include polarization of centralization
and decentralization, weaknesses of indices of these concepts, and differentiating degrees of decentralization
within a nation. Fesler describes doctrinal, political,
administrative, and dual approaches.

1437   _____. AREA AND ADMINISTRATION. University: University of
Alabama Press, 1949. 158 p.

Fesler addresses the problem of administrative areas and
notes that, by the distribution of governmental authority,
nations decide whether government will be a dictatorship,
a government by and for the few, or a government by
and for the many. He describes the role of governmental
areas and indicates that intergovernmental relations are
central to understanding the areal aspects of administration. The basic distribution of administrative authority
within governments is functional and explains the role of
field service areas. Fesler states that basic structural
reform and perfection of cooperative techniques are ways
for reconciling function and area. This book is a public
administration classic and should be consulted for probing
problems of centralization and decentralization.

1438   _____. "The Basic Theoretical Question: How to Relate Area and
Function." In THE ADMINISTRATION OF THE NEW FEDERALISM:
OBJECTIVES AND ISSUES, edited by Leigh E. Grosenick, pp. 4-14.
Washington, D.C.: American Society for Public Administration, 1973.

"The conflict between area and function has manifested
itself in so many countries, at so many levels of govern-

ment, and over so many centuries, that this problem may
be one that we simply must live with rather than go
around desperately wondering why we cannot solve it.
To recognize this is no minor achievement."

1439   _____. "Centralization and Decentralization." In INTERNATIONAL
ENCYCLOPEDIA OF THE SOCIAL SCIENCES, edited by David L.
Sills, pp. 370-79. New York: Macmillan Co. and Free Press, 1968.

Fesler states that "administrative centralization and decentralization describe a condition or a trend in an areal
hierarchy of power." This condition or trend contrasts
"the powers of administrators whose formal authority extends over a large geographic area (for example, a nation) with the powers of administrators whose formal authority is confined to particular segments or subsegments
of that area (for example, regions, states, or provinces,
districts, local communities)." In an excellent review of
the literature, Fesler reviews the history of these phenomena and analyzes delegation of power, the roles of
local and intermediate governments, intragovernmental
decentralization, extranational experience, and research
trends and needs.

1440   _____. "Criteria for Administrative Regions." SOCIAL FORCES 22
(October 1943): 26-32.

The author states that criteria to guide the development
of regional patterns for federal field administration relate
to whether the adoption of a formal regional pattern is
desirable, how many regions there should be, where regional boundaries should be placed, and where regional
headquarters should be located.

1441   _____. "Federal Administrative Regions." AMERICAN POLITICAL
SCIENCE REVIEW 30 (February 1936): 257-68.

The author states that the central problem of the administrative structure of government is that of defining administrative jurisdictions. The value of this article is that
the reader gains an appreciation for the rudimentary organization of the federal government in the 1930s. Fesler
discusses the prospects for federal administrative regions,
a concept that did not materialize until 1969.

1442   _____. "Field Organization." In ELEMENTS OF PUBLIC ADMINI-
STRATION, edited by Fritz Morstein Marx, pp. 264-93. New York:
Prentice-Hall, 1946.

Fesler discusses the growth of field organization, centralization and decentralization, field-headquarters relations,

interagency coordination in the field, and the prospects
of joint field planning. Factors that usually control the
degree to which an agency centralizes or decentralizes
its authority include the factor of responsibility, administrative factors, functional factors, and external factors.

1443   Goodrick, M. George. "Integration vs. Decentralization in the
        Federal Field Service." PUBLIC ADMINISTRATION REVIEW 9
        (Autumn 1949): 272-77.

        Pointing out that some 90 percent of the employees of
        the federal government work outside Washington, D.C.,
        the author posits reasons for integrating field functions,
        lists reasons for decentralizing functions to the field,
        analyzes the problems concerning integration versus de-
        centralization, and emphasizes the need for achieving an
        effective balance between integration and decentralization.

1444   Green, Gerson. "Administrative Decentralization: A Premature Step
        Beyond Community Control." PUBLIUS 6 (Fall 1976): 141-43.

        In this article, Green explicates John Mudd's "Beyond
        Community Control" (see 109). The author insists that Mudd
        mistakenly maintains that improved municipal service is more
        important to the working class and poverty populations
        than the redistribution of political power. He concludes
        that most neighborhood leaders are primarily concerned
        with questions of urban planning and investment.

1445   Hart, David K. "Theories of Government Related to Decentralization
        and Citizen Participation." PUBLIC ADMINISTRATION REVIEW 32
        (October 1972): 603-21.

        This essay concentrates upon the arguments surrounding the
        vital question: why should people participate? Hart ex-
        plores the issue of decentralization, the arguments sup-
        porting participatory democracy, and the arguments against
        participatory democracy. He presents an excellent review
        of the literature on this subject.

1446   Herbert, Adam W. "Does Decentralization Mean a Change in Mana-
        gerial Philosophy?" In THE ADMINISTRATION OF THE NEW FEDER-
        ALISM: OBJECTIVES AND ISSUES, edited by Leigh E. Grosenick,
        pp. 85-90. Washington, D.C.: American Society for Public Admini-
        stration, 1973.

        The argument of this author is that the success or failure
        of federal decentralization efforts will be as much a func-
        tion of the attitudes and values of administrators as of the
        financial, political, and administrative support the move-
        ment receives. Herbert answers these questions in this

essay: What is decentralization? Why should the federal government decentralize? What are the administrative challenges of decentralization? What changes are occuring in managerial philosophy?

1447   . "Management Under Conditions of Decentralization and Citizen Participation." PUBLIC ADMINISTRATION REVIEW 32 (October 1972): 622-37.

Herbert discusses perspectives on American society and bureaucracy, assesses the ideology and direction of public administration, describes the new public administration, analyzes the managerial implications of decentralization-citizen participation, names essential managerial skills for this process, and suggests the implications of citizen participation for schools of public administration, This essay is an excellent review of the above concerns.

1448   Howard, Lawrence C. "Decentralization and Citizen Participation in Health Services." PUBLIC ADMINISTRATION REVIEW 32 (October 1972): 701-17.

This essay is organized around two themes: increasing consumer participation in medical services; and its consequence, the resultant expansion of citizenship through healthier communities. The author focuses on how consumer participation adds the care of people for each other to professionally offered medical services, describes the Comprehensive Neighborhood Health Center, a new medical-health institution in which consumer and community participation is a central concern, introduces the idea of a health-base for health care, and examines the role of the public affairs profession in an emerging medical-health service field in which political concerns have become prominent. Howard presents an excellent review of the literature.

1449   Ink, Dwight, and Dean, Alan L. "A Concept of Decentralization." PUBLIC ADMINISTRATION REVIEW 30 (January-February 1970): 60-63.

This article sets forth the conceptual framework implied by the term "decentralization." The authors denote that decentralization is an important aspect of the overall effort to streamline federal programs and to reduce program management costs to a minimum, posit some general principles for decentralization, discuss the major issues in decentralization, and point out the constraints on decentralization.

1450   Kaufman, Herbert. "Administrative Decentralization and Political
        Power." PUBLIC ADMINISTRATION REVIEW 29 (January-February
        1969): 3-15.

>   The author probes dissatisfaction with the American system,
>   noting that the existing representative organs are capable
>   of giving only quite general mandates to administrative
>   agencies (yet it is the day-to-day decisions and actions
>   of officials and employees in the lower levels which
>   affect individual citizens), that the pluralistic nature of
>   the political system provides abundant opportunities for
>   vetoes by opponents of change, and that the scale of
>   organization in our society has grown so large that only
>   through large-scale organization does it seem possible to
>   have a significant impact. With these factors in mind,
>   Kaufman discusses the sources of conflict and coalition
>   in an era of alienation, decentralization, and participation.

1451   _____. THE FOREST RANGER: A STUDY IN ADMINISTRATIVE BE-
        HAVIOR. Baltimore: Johns Hopkins Press, 1960. xv, 259 p.

>   Kaufman offers a composite picture of the Forest Service.
>   Part 1 describes the tendencies toward fragmentation of
>   the Forest Service, the factors that operate to divide it
>   into its component units and render each unit an inde-
>   pendent miniature of the agency as a whole. Part 2
>   lists the factors that tend to hold the Forest Service to-
>   gether, to integrate the activities of personnel, and to
>   forge a national policy in the face of circumstances con-
>   ducive to many local, unrelated policies. The author
>   states that the Forest Service has enjoyed a substantial
>   degree of success in producing field behavior consistent
>   with headquarters directives and suggestions. He reviews
>   how this has been accomplished and what practices and
>   procedures achieved such results.

1452   Macy, John W., Jr. "To Decentralize and to Delegate." PUBLIC
        ADMINISTRATION REVIEW 30 (July-August 1970): 438-44.

>   The observations of the author, a former chairman of the
>   Civil Service Commission, provide interesting insights
>   into the programmatic problems of the federal bureaucracy
>   during the 1970s. Macy offers recommendations for suc-
>   cessful coordination, decentralization, and delegation of
>   department and agency programs.

1453   Mansfield, Roger. "Bureaucracy and Centralization: An Examination
        of Organizational Structure." ADMINISTRATIVE SCIENCE QUARTERLY
        18 (December 1973): 466-88.

>   The author discusses Weber's definition of bureaucracy (see 198),

which projects a system of administrative structure that could be applied in any work organization irrespective of organizational aims. Social scientists argue for an approach to the study of organizations based on the discovery of scalable dimensions of organizational structure.

1454   Myren, Richard A. "Decentralization and Citizen Participation in Criminal Justice Systems." PUBLIC ADMINISTRATION REVIEW 32 (October 1972): 718-38.

This essay examines decentralization and citizen participation in police agencies, in prosecution and adjudication, and in corrections, describes the elements of team policing and the democratic team model, notes the roles of civilian review boards and ombudsmen, and concludes that the criminal justice systems of the United States are in trouble. Myren presents an excellent review of the literature.

1455   Ostrom, Vincent. "The Contemporary Debate over Centralization and Decentralization." PUBLIUS 6 (Fall 1976): 21-32.

Ostrom posits that the contemporary argument over centralization and decentralization is indicative of the end of federalism and the beginning of a new era in American political experience in which the Imperial Presidency beckons. The article relates that the main preoccupation has been with strengthening the authority of governmental officials' authority. The author's focus is upon governmental reorganization and not on the constitutional balance between national and local interests.

1456   Porter, David O., and Olsen, Eugene A. "Some Critical Issues in Government Centralization and Decentralization." PUBLIC ADMINISTRATION REVIEW 36 (January-February 1976): 72-84.

This article examines the critical issues involved in government centralization and decentralization. The analysis is based upon the premise that values, tasks, and organizational structure should be interrelated in an effective organization. Porter and Olsen maintain that decisions affecting centralization or decentralization should be based upon and made only after a thorough study of the economic, political, and administrative characteristics unique to the organization.

1457   Redford, Emmette S. "Problems of Mobilization Agencies in Establishing Field Organizations." PUBLIC ADMINISTRATION REVIEW 12 (Summer 1952): 166-72.

Redford states that public convenience, avoidance of the administrative and political evils of centralized decisions

on particular applications of law and policy, and program
effectiveness are three reasons for an adequate field
structure. He calls for standardization for the regional
structures, information on field personnel in existing
agencies who could be used in emergency installation of
new field organizations, appointment of top executives
and safeguards against outright political appointments,
integration of control for field operations, and attention
by top administrators to field operations soon after the
establishment of new departments or agencies.

1458   Rein, Martin. "Decentralization and Citizen Participation in Social
        Services." PUBLIC ADMINISTRATION REVIEW 32 (October 1972):
        687-700.

        Martin reviews competing philosophical traditions (universalist-
        formalist versus selectivist-discretionary approach), offers
        a definition of social services, and denotes the difficulties
        in examining the relationship between performance stan-
        dards and behavior outcomes among different social service
        programs. "American social service policies seem to
        emerge without full agreement on the primary aims they
        should serve."

1459   Rouse, John E., Jr., and Huss, John D. "Modernizing the Federal
        Field Structure." MIDWEST REVIEW OF PUBLIC ADMINISTRATION
        6 (August 1972): 87-97.

        This article deals with the reorganization and decentraliza-
        tion of the social agencies of the federal government
        (Departments of Housing and Urban Development, Health,
        Education, and Welfare, Labor, Office of Economic Op-
        portunity, and Small Business Administration) into ten
        coterminous regions throughout the nation. This analysis
        takes into account factors of geographical distribution of
        workloads, geographical centrality, transportation accessi-
        bility, costs of relocations, and political criteria. Rouse
        and Huss define modernizing the federal field structure
        as "increasing logistically and politically the Federal
        Government's responsiveness to the problems and needs of
        post-industrial America."

1460   Schmandt, Henry J. "Municipal Decentralization: An Overview."
        PUBLIC ADMINISTRATION REVIEW 32 (October 1972): 571-88.

        "The decentralization literature clearly indicates that the
        priorities assigned to administrative values are undergoing
        change. Instead of the traditional stress on economy,
        efficiency, and centralization as guides for institutional
        reform, consumer control and client-oriented services have
        assumed a far more important place in the discourse."

This essay is an excellent review of the theoretical perspectives, the decentralization rationale, organizational
issues, powers and functions, finance, and future prospects
for municipal decentralization.

1461   Shalala, Donna E., and Merget Astrid E.   "The Decentralization
       Option."   In ORGANIZING PUBLIC SERVICES IN METROPOLITAN
       AMERICA, edited by Thomas P. Murphy and Charles R. Warren, pp.
       141-51. Lexington, Mass.:   Lexington Books, 1974.

       The authors offer views of political decentralization,
       justification for decentralization, decentralization versus
       centralization, and an operational definition of decen-
       tralization. There are four critical indicators of decen-
       tralization, including 1) the size or scale of the unit,
       2) functional responsibility, 3) policy making authority,
       and 4) expenditure and revenue-raising authority.

1462   _____. "Decentralization Plans." In ORGANIZING PUBLIC SERVICES
       IN METROPOLITAN AMERICA, edited by Thomas P. Murphy and
       Charles R. Warren, pp. 153-77. Lexington, Mass.: Lexington Books,
       1974. Table.

       The authors review an assortment of plans prescribing
       various degrees of decentralization, including New York's
       command decentralization, or decentralization through
       coordination, Dayton's decentralization through planned
       variation, New York City school "single-function" de-
       centralization, Advisory Commission on Intergovernmental
       Relations and Committee for Economic Development plans,
       or models of two-tier government, Indianapolis' minigov-
       ernments, and the London plan, or total reorganization.

1463   Vosburgh, William W., and Hyman, Drew.   "Advocacy and Bureau-
       cracy: The Life and Times of a Decentralized Advocacy Program."
       ADMINISTRATIVE SCIENCE QUARTERLY 18 (December 1973): 433-48.

       The authors examine the Governor's Branch Offices, a
       citizen advocacy program in the ghetto areas of Penn-
       sylvania, during its four-year development. The philosophy
       of this advocacy program, based on views of bureaucratic,
       access, response time, responsiveness and citizen advocacy,
       led to unusual organizational structure and procedures.
       The authors believe that the program raises issues about
       the feasibility and chances for success of an advocacy
       program in a bureaucratic setting.

1464   Weed, Frank J.   "Centralized and Pluralistic Organizational Structures
       in Public Welfare."   ADMINISTRATION AND SOCIETY 9 (May 1977):
       111-36.

Weed reports that two types of organizational structure--
centralized and pluralistic--found in forty-eight states'
public assistance organizations are partly accounted for
by the administrative ideology dominant at the formative
stage. Pluralistic and centralized structures tend to have
long-lasting effects on some of the internal components
of public assistance organizations.

1465   Whelan, Noel. "Administrative Structures for Regional Development:
        Considerations Relevant to Central Government." ADMINISTRATION
        24 (Autumn 1976): 283-301.

Whelan asserts that there are a number of fundamental
issues which underlie any organizational or structural
change for regional development. These issues include
devolution of the functions of central government, geographical administering of various public services, and
functions for each level of administration.

1466   Wilken, William H. "The Impact of Centralization on Access and
        Equity." In ORGANIZING PUBLIC SERVICES IN METROPOLITAN
        AMERICA, edited by Thomas P. Murphy and Charles R. Warren, pp.
        127-37. Lexington, Mass.: Lexington Books, 1974. Table.

Wilken reviews the literature of centralization and access,
centralization and the number of governments, centralization and the type of government, centralization and the
number and selection of officials, centralization and
method of official selection, centralization and the access
of minorities, and centralization and equity. He spells
out the limitations of service centralization and lists conditions for success.

1467   _____. "The Impact of Centralization on Effectiveness, Economy,
        and Efficiency." In ORGANIZING PUBLIC SERVICES IN METRO-
        POLITAN AMERICA, edited by Thomas P. Murphy and Charles R.
        Warren, pp. 107-25. Lexington, Mass.: Lexington Books, 1974.

The author concludes that centralization of service performance seems to make metropolitan government more
effective, efficient, and economical, but unquestionably
more effective than either efficient or economical; that
gains in effectiveness resulting from centralization seem
to be greatest in the area of personnel quality and utilization; that gains in effectiveness are also substantial
when measured in terms of the ability of the reorganized
governments to cope with problems pertaining to public
works and metropolitan physical development; and that
gains in effectiveness are much less impressive when measured in terms of the capacity of the reformed governments
to deal with problems related to "software" services and
problems of human development.

1468 _____. "Successful Centralizing Reorganizations." In ORGANIZING PUBLIC SERVICES IN METROPOLITAN AMERICA, edited by Thomas P. Murphy and Charles R. Warren, pp. 53-69. Lexington, Mass.: Lexington Books, 1974. Tables.

> The author reviews case histories of successful centralizing reorganizations in Toronto, Canada; Nashville, Tennessee; Jacksonville, Florida; Indianapolis-Marion County, Indiana; and Minneapolis-St. Paul, Minnesota. He concludes that important steps toward the centralization of metropolitan services have been made in a wide-range of socioeconomic and political environments.

1469 Yin, Robert K. DECENTRALIZATION OF GOVERNMENT AGENCIES: WHAT DOES IT ACCOMPLISH? Santa Monica, Calif.: Rand Corp., 1978. 16 p.

> This brief report evaluates the advantages and disadvantages of decentralized units. The author notes the commonly known tradeoffs of centralization and decentralization with concern for efficiency, equity, and responsiveness to residents' needs. He looks at public services which are functionally organized, including transportation, public safety, education, health, and housing.

D. ADMINISTRATIVE LEADERSHIP AND COMMUNICATION

1470 Aplin, John C., Jr., and Thompson, Duane E. "Feedback: Key to Survey-Based Change." PUBLIC PERSONNEL MANAGEMENT 3 (November-December 1974): 524-30.

> The authors relate that survey feedback systems are gaining in usage because decisions improve, employee satisfaction increases, and employees become more involved in resolving problems confronting the organization. Aplin and Thompson point out that the minimal expense of the system permits even small agencies to use feedback systems.

1471 Argyris, Chris. "Leadership, Learning, and Changing the Status Quo." ORGANIZATIONAL DYNAMICS 4 (Winter 1976): 29-43.

> Argyris indicates that American society programs individuals with action theories that are counterproductive to individual growth and organizational effectiveness. In noting the use of such theories to design organizations, the author posits two models. Model I emphasizes that individuals articulate purposes and control others for the purpose of achieving goals in an organizational environment. Model II emphasizes articulateness and advocacy in order to secure the most valid information.

1472   Bavelas, Alex. "Leadership: Man and Function." ADMINISTRATIVE
        SCIENCE QUARTERLY 4 (March 1960): 491-98.

        The author makes the distinction between the idea of
        leadership as a personal quality and the idea of leadership
        as an organizational function. The first leads us to look
        at the qualities and abilities of individuals and the second
        leads us to look at the patterns of power and authority
        in organizations. He concludes that it is no accident
        that daring and innovation wane as an organization grows
        large and successful.

1473   Bednarek, Frank; Benson, Louis; and Mustafa, Husain. "Identifying
        Peer Leadership in Small Work Groups." SMALL GROUP BEHAVIOR
        7 (August 1976): 307-16.

        The authors analyze and explain the selection of particular
        individuals for leadership roles by members of their work
        group, utilizing factor analysis to reduce the number of
        variables describing leadership traits. They describe four
        leadership attributes (i.e., task leadership, maturity,
        social influence, and flexibility) which apply to the small
        work groups.

1474   Bennis, Warren [G.]. "Leadership: A Beleaguered Species?" OR-
        GANIZATIONAL DYNAMICS 5 (Summer 1976): 2-16.

        Bennis suggests that the steady erosion of institutional
        autonomy is the cause of a decline in able leadership.
        Government requirements, union rules, and pressures of
        organized consumers and environmentalists are basic rea-
        sons for the loss of institutional self-determination. He
        illustrates that administrators are increasingly restricted
        by potential or real legal issues. He emphasizes that
        institutions must realize that they need leadership and
        that organizational leadership requires its distinctive
        language and conceptual framework.

1475   _____. "Leadership Theory and Administrative Behavior: The Problem
        of Authority." ADMINISTRATIVE SCIENCE QUARTERLY 4 (December
        1959): 259-301.

        The author selects the problem of authority as the critical
        dimension through which various theories and practices of
        organizational behavior are expressed. He identifies two
        major moevments, the traditional theorists and the human
        relations proponents, in a review of philosophies, ide-
        ologies, and practices. He gives attention to contem-
        porary revisions and models that endeavor to ameliorate
        tensions between the two movements. He also presents
        an explication of leadership that attempts to account for

the efficacy of certain leadership propositions with respect
to a priori criteria of organizational effectiveness.

1476   Bons, Paul M., and Fiedler, Fred E.   "Changes in Organizational
Leadership and the Behavior of Relationship- and Task-Motivated
Leaders." ADMINISTRATIVE SCIENCE QUARTERLY 21 (September
1976):   453-73.

The authors examine the Contingency Model of Leadership
Effectiveness, which postulates that the leaders' motivational structure and situational favorableness will determine
the performance of leaders. The model provides a basis
for probing the impacts of job rotation, succession, and
reassignment of superiors on the leaders' behaviors and
performances. Bons and Fiedler conclude that changes
in job relationships primarily affect task-related behaviors
whereas leadership style affects person-related behaviors.

1477   Bowers, David G., and Seashore, Stanley E.   "Predicting Organiza-
tional Effectiveness with a Four-Factor Theory of Leadership." AD-
MINISTRATIVE SCIENCE QUARTERLY 11 (September 1966):   238-63.
Tables.

The authors suggest that this conceptual model (four basic
dimensions of leadership: support, interaction facilitation,
goal emphasis, and work facilitation) is useful and that
leadership's relation to organizational outcomes may best
be studied when both leadership and effectiveness are
multidimensional. They evaluate the impact of both
supervisory and peer leadership upon outcomes of satisfaction and factorial performance measures.

1478   Browning, Larry; Hopper, Robert; and Whitehead, Jack.   "Influence:
The Organizer in Communication Systems." GROUP AND ORGANI-
ZATION STUDIES 1 (September 1976):   355-69.

The authors assert that influence processes are important
keys to understanding the essence of organizational communication. A buffer area surrounds the individual in
which influences operating as external constraints interact
with internal characteristics. The entire boundary of influence which frames individual behavior varies in its
permeability under different conditions.

1479   Corson, John J.   "The Role of Communication in the Process of Administration." PUBLIC ADMINISTRATION REVIEW 4 (Winter 1944):
7-15.

The author discusses three principal purposes for which the
administrator formulates and uses means of communication,
including the conveyance of instructions and policy de-

cisions down the line of authority, transmittal to the administrator of the reports, suggestions, and experiences of employees at each vantage point of operating experience, and creation of a common understanding of the group purpose. The difficulty of conveying instructions or decisions to decentralized field operations is perhaps the most common illustration of communication problems.

1480   Desmond, Richard E., and Seligman, Milton. "A Review of Research on Leaderless Groups." SMALL GROUP BEHAVIOR 8 (February 1977): 3-24.

The article relates that some leaderless groups work productively while some do not. The authors suggest that leaderless groups are not a unitary occurrence. Leaderless techniques include alternate sessions, completely leaderless sessions, instrumented feedback, and self-directed groups.

1481   Dorsey, John T., Jr. "A Communication Model for Administration." ADMINISTRATIVE SCIENCE QUARTERLY 2 (September 1957): 307-24.

Dorsey indicates that decision may be conceived as a communication process or a series of interrelated communication events. Organization is an elaborate communication system, which suggests the possibility of a "learning net" type of model for studying organizations. The author suggests some possibilities for adapting communication theory and states that the concepts of feedback and homeostasis give such a model a dynamic quality.

1482   Doyle, Wayne J. "Effects of Achieved Status of Leader on Productivity of Groups." ADMINISTRATIVE SCIENCE QUARTERLY 16 (March 1971): 40-50. Tables.

The author examines the relationship between the achieved status of the leader and productivity in group problem solving of twenty-seven experimental groups. The findings demonstrate that high achieved status of leaders has both functional and dysfunctional consequences.

1483   Fiedler, Fred E. "The Effects of Leadership Training and Experience: A Contingency Model Interpretation." ADMINISTRATIVE SCIENCE QUARTERLY 17 (December 1972): 453-70. Tables.

This article summarizes recent studies based on the contingency model of leadership effectiveness which suggest why research typically has failed to show that leadership training and experience increase organizational performance. The contingency model postulates that group performance depends on the match between situational favorableness, or the leader's control and influence, and leadership motivation. Based on the contingency model, Fiedler suggests new strategies of leadership training and job rotation.

1484   _____. "The Leadership Game: Matching the Man to the Situation." ORGANIZATIONAL DYNAMICS 4 (Winter 1976): 6-16.

Empirical studies of leadership training generally show that people with little or no training perform about as well as people with much training. The author concludes that there is no evidence that any particular leadership training method consistently improves organizational performance.

1485   Foster, Robert N. "Bridging the Communications Gap to Assess Social Services." SOCIAL AND REHABILITATION RECORD 3 (June 1976): 8-11.

Foster assesses the impact of a system for delivering social services. Over half of all clients reported their problems completely solved, two-thirds reported receiving and completing services, and a majority were unable to distinguish between services provided and the goals toward which those services were directed.

1486   Hale, George H. "Executive Leadership versus Budgetary Behavior." ADMINISTRATION AND SOCIETY 9 (August 1977): 169-90.

Hale relates that studies underestimate the barriers to using the budgetary process as a mechanism for guiding public organizations. The infinite adaptability of public administrators to alterations in executive priorities is described by examining budgeting under two successive, sharply contrasting chief executives in Delaware.

1487   Hill, Norman C., and Ritchie, J.B. "The Effects of Self-Esteem on Leadership and Achievement: A Paradigm and a Review." GROUP AND ORGANIZATION STUDIES 2 (December 1977): 491-503.

Hill and Ritchie declare that the literature focuses on superior-subordinate interactions. They discuss the importance of self-esteem, impacts of self-esteem upon organizational contexts, and the implications of these impacts for researchers, managers, and consultants.

1488   Hills, R. Jean. "The Representative Function: Neglected Dimension of Leadership Behavior." ADMINISTRATIVE SCIENCE QUARTERLY 8 (June 1963): 83-101.

This article reports the results of an empirical test of the
thesis that an adequate concept of leadership must include
the performance of the leader in representing the interests
of the group to higher organizational levels and to the
organization's clientele. Hills develops two indexes and
incorporates them into a Leader Behavior Description
Questionnaire.

1489   House, Robert J. "Leadership Training: Some Dysfunctional Conse-
       quences." ADMINISTRATIVE SCIENCE QUARTERLY 12 (March 1968):
       556-71.

       House describes three specific sources of social influences
       and advances three dimensions of social influence. He
       reviews earlier studies to illustrate how social influence
       variables account for the dysfunctions of leadership train-
       ing. He hypothesizes relationships between various types
       of leadership training and the social influences. House
       advances a proposition to explain and permit prediction
       of the consequences of leadership training in varying
       situations.

1490   _____. "A Path Goal Theory of Leader Effectiveness." ADMINI-
       STRATIVE SCIENCE QUARTERLY 16 (September 1971): 321-38. Tables.

       House presents an explanation of the effects of leader
       behavior on subordinate satisfaction, motivation, and per-
       formance. He analyzes dimensions of leader behavior
       such as leader initiating structure, consideration, authori-
       tarianism, hierarchical influence, and closeness of super-
       vision in terms of path-goal variables such as valence and
       instrumentality. The theory specifies some of the situa-
       tional elements upon which the effects of specific leader
       behaviors are contingent. The usefulness of the theory
       is domonstrated by showing how several seemingly unre-
       lated prior research findings could have been deduced
       from its general propositions and by applying it to recon-
       cile apparently contradictory findings from other studies.

1491   Kaufman, Herbert, with Couzens, Michael. ADMINISTRATIVE FEED-
       BACK: MONITORING SUBORDINATES' BEHAVIOR. Washington, D.C.:
       Brookings Institution, 1973. 83 p.

       This book reports on a study of administrative feedback
       from subordinates to leaders in nine federal bureaus. Kaufman
       describes the processes by which information about sub-
       ordinates flows back to headquarters and assesses that in-
       formation in an effort to find out whether leaders could,
       if they wanted to, learn what happens below.

1492 Kavanagh, Michael J. "Leadership Behavior as a Function of Subordinate Competence and Task Complexity." ADMINISTRATIVE SCI-
ENCE QUARTERLY 17 (December 1972): 591-600. Tables.

Kavanagh uses a modified role projection technique to
determine the effects of subordinate competence (low and
high) and task complexity (simple and complex) on perceptions of leadership behavior. He views this behavior
in terms of consideration (C) and initiating structure (IS).
With leadership treated as a dyadic infleunce process,
Kavanagh hypothesizes that subordinates hold expectations
of the proper level of structuring that their supervisor
should provide. He hypothesizes that two variables--
subordinate competence and task complexity--directly
affect the subordinate's expectation of the proper level
of structuring.

1493 Levine, Charles H. "Leadership: Problems, Prospects, and Implications of Research Programs Aimed at Linking Empirical and Normative
Modeling." In PUBLIC ADMINISTRATION AND PUBLIC POLICY,
edited by H. George Frederickson and Charles R. Wise, pp. 53-60.
Lexington, Mass.: D.C. Heath and Co., 1977.

Levine examines the leadership theories of Fred E. Fiedler,
Robert J. House, and Victor H. Vroom in order to assist
the reader in understanding leadership theory and the
levels of analysis problem and in building the conceptual
bridge from empirical to normative theory. After integrating contingency, goal, and decision-process theories,
the author concludes that some changes must take place
in the way that researchers "normally" conduct leadership
research before any real progress can be made toward developing a theory of policy leadership in government or a
theory for designing leadership roles in policy implementing
systems.

1494 Lord, Robert G. "Functional Leadership Behavior: Measurement and
Relation to Social Power and Leadership Perceptions." ADMINISTRA-
TIVE SCIENCE QUARTERLY 22 (March 1977): 114-33.

Lord considers a conceptual definition and measurement of
functional leadership behavior and relates this definition
and measurement concept to other processes. He develops a concept of leadership functions, based on theoretical and empirical considerations and defines the opera-
tionalization of this concept by an interaction coding
procedure. He emphasizes conceptual distinctions among
leadership processes.

1495 Luecke, David S. "The Professional as Organizational Leader." AD-
MINISTRATIVE SCIENCE QUARTERLY 18 (March 1973): 86-94.

The author finds that professionals serving in top level positions of organizational leadership can have differing emphases on orientation to their profession and to the organization. Luecke analyzes two perspectives and the ways of combining them in relation to leadership effectiveness and work satisfaction. He concludes that the organizational perspective was more important for determining effectiveness than the professional perspective, but that both perspectives contribute to satisfaction.

1496   Lundstedt, Sven. "Administrative Leadership and Use of Social Power." PUBLIC ADMINISTRATION REVIEW 25 (June 1965): 156-60.

Contrasting styles of leadership--the authoritarian and the democratic, the permissive and the coercive--the author brings to bear contemporary research in social psychology and conceptions of the exercise of social power. "Clarity of thought in decision making and strength of character are a necessary ingredient in democratic leadership because the decisions about the correct use of social power are far more complex and difficult. It is far easier to be autocratically simple minded than to make the necessary refined and complex distinctions about the use of social power within organizations and in all human affairs."

1497   McGregor, Douglas. LEADERSHIP AND MOTIVATION: ESSAYS OF DOUGLAS McGREGOR. Edited by Warren G. Bennis and Edgar H. Schein. Cambridge: MIT Press, 1966. xxiii, 286 p.

This volume includes a valuable collection of essays by Douglas McGregor. Parts of this text include McGregor's managerial philosophy, leadership concepts, ideas on union-management relations, growth and development of individuals and groups, and literature on the manager and the human sciences. The editors believe that the essays illustrate the continuities and growth in McGregor's thoughts on organizational life.

1498   Meadows, Mark E. "Personal Communication and Organizational Effectiveness." PUBLIC SECTOR 1 (January 1978): 1-16.

Meadows sets forth the essence of communication problems, identifies barriers to effective communication, explores elements of the communication process, and presents useful communication methods. He believes that determined effort to apply sound communication practices will enhance the communication process in public organizations.

1499   Mehta, B. "Communication in Administration: Some Ideas and Issues." ADMINISTRATIVE CHANGE 3 (January-June 1976): 68-73.

Centralization and Decentralization

Mehta states that communication among the agencies within a bureaucracy is particularly important in matters of economic development. The three essential steps in the communication process are the transmittal, reception, and comprehension of a communicated message.

1500   Miles, Robert H., and Petty, M.M. "Leader Effectiveness in Small Bureaucracies." ACADEMY OF MANAGEMENT JOURNAL 20 (June 1977): 238-50.

Miles tests the conditioning effects of organizational size by examining the relationships between leader initiating structure and consideration and organizational outcomes. The reader is told that a leader initiating structure is more effective in smaller agencies.

1501   Nadler, David A. "The Use of Feedback for Organizational Change: Promises and Pitfalls." GROUP AND ORGANIZATION STUDIES 1 (June 1976): 177-86.

Nadler suggests that organizational change includes the organized collection of data and the process of feeding those data back to organization members. This process, recognized as survey feedback, serves as a means of diagnosing the organization and initiating intervention activities. Survey research feedback has good effects and the process of collecting, analyzing, and using the data is an important determinant of the nature and extent of the effects.

1502   Reddin, W.J. "An Integration of Leader-Behavior Typologies." GROUP AND ORGANIZATION STUDIES 2 (September 1977): 282-95.

Reddin denotes the conflicting nature of many leader-behavior studies. He calls for an effectiveness dimension for the purpose of teaching leadership concepts and examines several typologies which entail a wide variety of leadership behaviors.

1503   Rossel, Robert D. "Instrumental and Expressive Leadership in Complex Organizations." ADMINISTRATIVE SCIENCE QUARTERLY 15 (September 1970): 306-16. Tables.

Rossel investigates instrumental and expressive leadership orientations among managers and supervisors in eight production organizations that varied in required labor commitment. Managers and supervisors respond differently to situations necessitating high required labor commitment. He concludes that leadership should be seen in the context of the organization and its adjustment to the demands of its environment.

1504   Schaefer, Roberta Rubel. "Democracy and Leadership: Some Reflections on the Political Education of Civil Servants." SOUTHERN RE-
VIEW OF PUBLIC ADMINISTRATION 2 (December 1978): 345-74.

>   Schaefer concludes that "an education which emphasizes
>   the distinctive contribution of the bureaucracy to the
>   governing of the nation conveys the idea that civil ser-
>   vants are and ought to be engaged in the serious delibera-
>   tion of important substantive issues of public policy."
>   She believes that a political education could bring public
>   servants popular respect and encourage civil servants to
>   gain a more general appreciation of American institutions
>   and values.

1505   Selznick, Philip. LEADERSHIP IN ADMINISTRATION: A SOCIO-
LOGICAL INTERPRETATION. New York: Harper and Row, 1957.
xii, 162 p.

>   Selznick outlines a perspective for the study of leadership
>   in administrative organizations. He states that the in-
>   stitutional leader "is primarily an expert in the promotion
>   and protection of values." He reviews some premises
>   about leadership, examines the default of leadership,
>   probes critical and routine decisions, defines the mission
>   and role of leadership, explains the institutional embodi-
>   ment of purpose, and offers a basic, useful, and sophisti-
>   cated analysis of leadership.

1506   Simpson, Richard L. "Vertical and Horizontal Communication in Formal
Organizations." ADMINISTRATIVE SCIENCE QUARTERLY 4 (September
1959): 188-96.

>   Simpson notes that traditional theory holds that communi-
>   cation in organizations should, and does, move vertically
>   throughout the hierarchy, rather than cutting across the
>   lines of authority. He interviews supervisors in a textile
>   mill and concludes with the hypothesis that mechanization
>   reduces the need for close supervision and vertical com-
>   munication since the machines, instead of the foreman,
>   set the work pace of subordinates.

1507   Tannenbaum, Robert; Weschler, Irving R.; and Massarik, Fred. LEADER-
SHIP AND ORGANIZATION: A BEHAVIORAL SCIENCE APPROACH.
New York: McGraw-Hill Book Co., 1961. xiv, 456 p.

>   This book presents a selected collection of writings in the
>   areas of leadership, training, and organization from 1950
>   to 1960. Parts of this volume include discussions of lead-
>   ership and the influence process, sensitivity training,
>   studies in organization, commentaries, and bibliographies.
>   The organization of this book does not follow a chrono-

logical pattern but seeks to present various concepts and methods within a logical framework. This is a valuable contribution to the literature of organizational leadership.

1508   Thayer, Lee O. ADMINISTRATIVE COMMUNICATION. Homewood, Ill.: Richard D. Irwin, 1961. xiv, 344 p.

The purpose of this book is to offer to the reader a number of basic concepts by which the nature and dynamics of communication in organizations may be studied and understood. The author's objective is not to theorize about communication and administration, but to describe what the thoughtful administrator needs to know about communication as he or she uses it. Sections include the dynamics, qualities, functions, methods, problems, and organizational behavior of administrative communication. Thayer presents a functional approach to the nature and dynamics of communication and provides the reader with usable new insights into the communication process.

1509   Van Fleet, David D. "Toward Identifying Critical Elements in a Behavioral Description of Leadership." PUBLIC PERSONNEL MANAGEMENT 3 (January-February 1974): 70-82.

Van Fleet posits that the critical incident technique is quite valuable in examining leadership behavior. He develops a behavioral description of leadership in research that includes nearly fifty topics from many different organizations. He collects incidents describing leadership behavior and condenses them into behavior groups and classes.

1510   Vroom, Victor H., and Yetton, Philip W. LEADERSHIP AND DECISION-MAKING. Pittsburgh: University of Pittsburgh Press, 1973. viii, 233 p.

Vroom and Yetton offer a normative model of managerial styles which favors participation where possible. This model differentiates four elemental leadership processes used to solve organizational problems: autocratic, consultative, group, and delegated. The authors focus on the "particular problem to be solved and the context in which the problem occurs." They posit a leader-centered model which relies heavily on the leader's judgment of the situation, presuming the accuracy of the leader's perceptions.

1511   Walker, Thomas G. "Leader Selection and Behavior in Small Political Groups." SMALL GROUP BEHAVIOR 7 (August 1976): 363-68.

The purpose of this essay is to examine the impact of varying leader selection systems on the performance of political decision-making groups. The results support the hypothesized linkage between leader selection systems and group performance. The author claims that this relationship has been demonstrated previously in the experimental laboratory, but this association has never been verified in a real world decision-making setting. This analysis corroborates the experimental findings and demonstrates the differential impact of leader selection procedures in small political groups.

1512   Whitcomb, G. Robert, and Williams, Eleanor Golar. "Leadership and Productivity in Planning Organizations: A Case Study." ADMINISTRATION IN SOCIAL WORK 2 (Spring 1978): 85-94.

This essay discusses the effects of two divergent leadership styles on the productivity of a planning organization. The reader learns that, under different leadership styles, a private welfare and health council in a medium-sized American city varied remarkably in its output of planning activities and decision formulation.

1513   Yetton, Philip W., and Vroom, Victor H. "The Vroom-Yetton Model of Leadership: An Overview." In MANAGERIAL CONTROL AND ORGANIZATIONAL DEMOCRACY, edited by Bert King, Siegfried Streufert, and Fred E. Fiedler, pp. 133-49. Washington, D.C.: V.H. Winston and Sons, 1978.

The authors present their theory of leadership. They distinguish five management styles and seven situational variables and present data to illustrate that managers change their styles according to the seven situational variables. Yetton and Vroom discuss plans for future research within their paradigm.

1514   Zaleznik, Abraham. "Managers and Leaders: Are They Different?" HARVARD BUSINESS REVIEW 55 (May-June 1977): 67-78.

Zaleznik declares that managers and leaders are different types of people. He suggests that the development of managerial skill occurs via socialization and that the development of leadership occurs via personal mastery. The author warns against stifling of young leaders in organizations and advocates organizational mentors who allow young leaders psychological space for feedback and emotional growth.

Chapter 11

COMPARATIVE AND DEVELOPMENTAL

ADMINISTRATION

1515   Arora, Ramesh K. COMPARATIVE PUBLIC ADMINISTRATION. New
Delhi, India: Associated Publishing House, 1973. 192 p.

> Arora probes the intellectual environment from which the
> central concepts of comparative public administration have
> developed. The works of Max Weber and Fred Riggs re-
> ceive prominent emphasis in this ecological-development
> approach.

1516   Barker, Ernest. THE DEVELOPMENT OF PUBLIC SERVICES IN WEST-
ERN EUROPE, 1660–1930. London: Oxford University Press, 1964.
Reprint. Hamden, Conn.: Archon Books, 1966. viii, 93 p.

> This comparative analysis evaluates public services in
> Great Britain, France, and Prussia, or Germany. Barker
> states: "When we consider the history of the Modern
> State, not only in education, but in all its services and
> activities, we cannot but recognize the debt which all
> States owe to one another. . . . There has been a
> rivalry of methods, but it has not been unfriendly; one
> country has studied, adopted, or tried to improve the
> methods of another; and all have combined, however un-
> consciously, to promote the growth of a common European
> standard of administration and public service."

1517   Bayley, David H. "The Effects of Corruption in a Developing Nation."
WESTERN POLITICAL QUARTERLY 19 (December 1966): 719–32.

> Bayley examines the impacts of corruption with a devel-
> oping nation. He points out that corruption in a de-
> veloping polity does not necessarily inhibit modern eco-
> nomic and social development, that is, become dysfunc-
> tional. In fact, the author indicates that corruption,
> in part, can function beneficially.

1518   Bendor, Jonathan. "A Theoretical Problem in Comparative Administration." PUBLIC ADMINISTRATION REVIEW 36 (November-December
1976): 626-31.

              Bendor suggests that if there is a central theme in the
field of comparative administration, it is the idea of development. He supplements the "development cluster"
theme with a modified Darwinian evolutionary model.

1519   Berger, Monroe. "Bureaucracy East and West." ADMINISTRATIVE
SCIENCE QUARTERLY 1 (March 1957): 518-29.

              Berger analyzes the Egyptian higher civil service and
concludes that Western bureaucratic theory, with its Max
Weberian influence, is unsuitable for comprehending non-
Western bureaucracies. He calls for the development of
new theories.

1520   Braibanti, Ralph. "Public Bureaucracy and Judiciary in Pakistan."
In BUREAUCRACY AND POLITICAL DEVELOPMENT, edited by Joseph
LaPalombara, pp. 360-440. Princeton, N.J.: Princeton University
Press, 1963. Tables.

              This essay attempts to analyze one instance in which two
institutions, largely of British importation--public bureaucracy and the writ jurisdiction--have been confronted by
a variety of social, economic, and historical forces and
have been changed thereby, but in a somewhat different
manner than in Western countries. This research has
obvious limitations, the first of which is the omission of
any extended consideration of the influence of inadequate
structure and procedure as a factor contributing to the rise
of grievances within the bureaucracy.

1521   Chapman, Brian. THE PROFESSION OF GOVERNMENT. London:
Unwin University Books, 1959. 352 p.

              The author analyzes the most important questions facing
modern public administration in a genuine comparative
study of public administration. He describes each country
separately and offers a discussion of politics and administration which is provocative and stimulating and in places
profound. Chapman writes: "This book is a contribution
to the study of comparative government; it is an attempt
to write a text book for a subject which does not yet
exist."

1522   Chaturvedi, U.R. "The Problem of Leadership in an Underdeveloped
Country." INDIAN JOURNAL OF POLITICAL SCIENCE 25 (April-
June 1964): 1-4.

Chaturvedi stresses the symbolism of the leader of an underdeveloped country as he should exert influence over
the nation's population, the representativeness of the
leader for the people's wishes and aspirations, creativeness
of the leader, and the people's problem-solving capacity.

1523   Crozier, Michael. THE BUREAUCRATIC PHENOMENON. Chicago:
University of Chicago Press, 1964. 320 p.

Crozier focuses on the behavior of human beings who are
members of an organization, examines the basic personality
traits and social values that help to account for this behavior, and traces the sources of these traits and values
in the general culture or in the particular classes and
occupations with which the organizations' members are
identified. He relates bureaucracy to its external environment, with French bureaucracy and the French social
system. The theory and realities of bureaucratic patterns
as they relate to power, uncertainty, the functional
characteristics of Weberian bureaucracy, and dysfunctional
traits of the bureaucratic behavior of employees is examined.

1524   Danforth, Devaratnam. "Citizen Participation in Community Development." PLANNING AND ADMINISTRATION 5 (Spring 1978): 41-
52.

Danforth asserts that local government must be able to
elicit spontaneous participation of the people in their own
development. He states that the government of Sri Lanka
assumed such an approach to community development.
The village council, town council, urban council, and
municipal council are four varieties of local democracy,
that each council possesses independent power and geographical boundaries. The author reveals that these local
authorities function as a stimulant for incorporating communities in development programs.

1525   Diamant, Alfred. "European Models of Bureaucracy and Development."
INTERNATIONAL REVIEW OF ADMINISTRATIVE SCIENCES 32
(1966): 309-20.

Diamant examines European patterns of modernization and
bureaucratic institutions. Emphasis is placed upon the
maintenance of equilibrium, problems of status quo, and
concerns of rationalization and maximization.

1526   _____. "The Relevance of Comparative Politics to the Study of Comparative Administration." ADMINISTRATIVE SCIENCE QUARTERLY 5
(June 1960): 87-112.

Diamant believes that students of comparative administration can find useful research tools in the growing methodological literature of comparative politics. This essay examines two main types of conceptual models: "general system" models, which attempt conceptualization for all societies, and "political culture" schemes, which assume that a classification of political systems must precede the development of dimensions for comparison.

1527   Dillon, Conley H. THE AREA REDEVELOPMENT ADMINISTRATION: NEW PATTERNS IN DEVELOPMENTAL ADMINISTRATION. College Park: Bureau of Governmental Research, University of Maryland, 1964.

The Area Redevelopment Administration, established by the Area Redevelopment Act in 1961, focused almost exclusively upon single purpose programs, such as those for agriculture, urban renewal, health, and water resources. Dillon describes the administration's organization and administrative procedures, progress and problems with program administration, and prospects for cooperative developmental administration.

1528   Dimock, Marshall E. "Management in the USSR--Comparisons to the United States." PUBLIC ADMINISTRATION REVIEW 20 (Summer 1960): 139-47.

"Forces inherent in both centralization and bureaucracy tend to transcend the political differences of the USSR and the United States. The Russians rely on planning to secure greater areas of freedom of action than operating officials have had; we are trying to decide whether additional planning would limit our greater operating freedom; if so how much and is it worth the cost. Their system of planning and control facilitates coordination; we still have trouble in these areas. They have borrowed our economic incentive system; we seem to be dropping it--perhaps more than we should. Their educational system encourages thoroughness and mental discipline, ours originality and resourcefulness."

1529   Dorsey, John T., Jr. "The Bureaucracy and Political Development in Viet Nam." In BUREAUCRACY AND POLITICAL DEVELOPMENT, edited by Joseph LaPalombara, pp. 318-59. Princeton, N.J.: Princeton University Press, 1963.

The author formulates the central idea of a developmental theory based on changes in energy conversion levels as follows: "as levels of energy conversion in a society rise, political, social, and economic structures and processes undergo transformations." Dorsey emphasizes that the role

of bureaucracies in political development is manifold and
little understood. However, when measured by any of
the currently available indices, Vietnam was one of those
nations which derived relatively little energy from its
environment.

1530   Dunsire, A. ADMINISTRATION: THE WORD AND THE SCIENCE.
Bristol, Engl.: Martin Robertson, 1973. x, 262 p.

The author discusses administration in the British context.
He reviews the development of the term, tracing its origins
to Cicero, Chaucer, Bentham, and Taylor and explains
the application of the term in the civil service. He
discusses the study of bureaucracy, according to Von Stein,
Le Play, Saint-Simon, Spence, Schmoller, and Weber.
Dunsire evaluates European administrative science and the
American science of administration and traces the rise of
comparative administration and explains elements of the "new
administrative science." The author distinguishes between
theory and practice in public administration, centralization
and specialization, and public administration and private
management. This is highly recommended for an overview of
public administration with its comparative and European components.

1531   Eisenstadt, S.N. "Bureaucracy and Political Development." In BU-
REAUCRACY AND POLITICAL DEVELOPMENT, edited by Joseph
LaPalombara, pp. 96-119. Princeton, N.J.: Princeton University
Press, 1963.

"Within the political sphere, the equivalent of such self-
sustained growth is the ability to absorb varieties and
changing types of political demands and organization.
It also includes the skill to deal with new and changing
types of problems which the system produces or which it
must absorb from outside sources. . . . In later stages
of modernization, when more specialized types of bureaucracy develop, the stage shifts to the stability of the
general framework of political struggle. Emphasis is also
upon the continuity of political symbols, the extent of
political articulation, and the cohesion within and between major social groups. At this stage the very availability of ruling elites with their political and organizational ability depends on the stability of such framework
as well as on the availability of cohesive articulated
strata."

1532   Fainsod, Merle. "Bureaucracy and Modernization: The Russian and
Soviet Case." In BUREAUCRACY AND POLITICAL DEVELOPMENT,
edited by Joseph LaPalombara, pp. 233-67. Princeton, N.J.: Princeton
University Press, 1963.

The concern of this essay is with the potentialities and limits of bureaucracies as modernizing instruments. Primary attention is devoted to Russian and Soviet experience insofar as it purports to serve as a model for the less-developed nations. Fainsod states: "If Soviet experience has proved nothing else, it has demonstrated that rapid industrialization can be achieved by dictatorial methods, and that democratizing and industrializing tendencies do not necessarily go hand in hand. In other words, the process of modernization need not be a seamless web in the Anglo-American, West European sense."

1533 _____. "The Structure of Development Administration." In DEVELOPMENT ADMINISTRATION: CONCEPTS AND PROBLEMS, edited by Irving Swerdlow, pp. 1-24. Syracuse, N.Y.: Syracuse University Press, 1963.

Using illustrations in India, Pakistan, and Burma, Fainsod examines structural and procedural problems of development administration in underdeveloped nations. He notes the lack of trained administrators and the problems of adaptation from colonial administration to independence. He indicates that new administrative structures must develop new administrative roles and that lines of authority have become unclear. He concludes that development policies are often incompatible with administrative realities.

1534 Fox, Guy H., and Joiner, Charles A. "Perceptions of the Vietnamese Public Administration System." ADMINISTRATIVE SCIENCE QUARTERLY 8 (March 1964): 443-81.

The authors' interviews with top-level Vietnamese civil servants reveal a pattern of disillusionment with the mandarinic philosophy permeating much of Vietnam's public administration system. Fox and Joiner indicate that respondents accepted administrative centralization of a large public sector as vital in developmental administration. This essay was completed prior to the November 1963 coup.

1535 Gittell, Marilyn. "A Typology of Power for Measuring Social Change." AMERICAN BEHAVIORAL SCIENTIST 9 (April 1966): 23-28.

The author posits four possible combinations of elites, that is, single elite, undifferentiated mass; primary elite challenged by the lesser elite; power diffused among many competing, relatively equal elites; and a vertical elite structure with two or more strata of competing elites. In this typology, Gittell offers an evaluation of the relationship between power distribution and social change.

1536   Heady, Ferrel. "Bureaucratic Theory and Comparative Administration."
        ADMINISTRATIVE SCIENCE QUARTERLY 3 (March 1959): 509-25.

> Recognizing that theories of bureaucracy developed in the
> West have serious shortcomings for the analysis of bureau-
> cratic behavior in both Western and non-Western settings,
> Heady posits that bureaucratic theory should stress essential
> structural features and should not include a specific pat-
> tern of behavior, thus permitting research into various
> patterns of bureaucratic behavior in both Western and
> non-Western societies.

1537   _____. "Comparative Administration: A Sojourner's Outlook."
        PUBLIC ADMINISTRATION REVIEW 38 (July-August 1978): 358-65.

> The author concludes that "comparative public admini-
> stration . . . has failed to establish itself as a field of
> study with a generally accepted restricted range of topics
> to be addressed." This essay is an excellent review of
> comparative administration's relevance and focus at the
> start of the 1980s.

1538   _____. PUBLIC ADMINISTRATION: A COMPARATIVE PERSPECTIVE.
        Englewood Cliffs, N.J.: Prentice-Hall, 1966. xii, 115 p. Paper.

> This is the first comprehensive effort to assess the present
> state of the comparative study of public administration and
> to characterize the administrative systems in a wide range
> of modern nation-states. This text is a starting point for
> the student of public administration who is interested in
> extending his or her interest beyond a single country or
> group of countries closely related historically and po-
> litically. Heady reviews administrative systems that have
> wide variations among them, focuses on public bureau-
> cracies as common governmental institutions, and places
> special emphasis on relationships between bureaucracies
> and political regime types. The author provides an ex-
> cellent overview of comparative bureaucracies and po-
> litical systems.

1539   _____. "Recent Literature on Comparative Public Administration."
        ADMINISTRATIVE SCIENCE QUARTERLY 5 (June 1960): 134-54.

> Heady surveys recent comparative administration literature
> under four broad categories: 1) materials on theory, ap-
> proach, methodology, and model building, 2) comparative
> studies of Western societies, 3) comparative studies of non-
> Western societies, and 4) materials on individual countries
> of interest for comparative purposes. He notes that the
> output of materials on comparative administration has in-
> creased significantly and that several bibliographies on the
> subject are now available.

1540 Heady, Ferrel, and Stokes, Sybil L., eds. PAPERS IN COMPARATIVE PUBLIC ADMINISTRATION. Ann Arbor: University of Michigan Press, 1962. vii, 243 p.

> This is a composite of ten papers penned during the developing years of comparative public administration. The history and status of this area, some conceptual prototypes for understanding comparative information, and substantive problems of administration in developing nations are examined.

1541 Heaphey, James. "Comparative Public Administration: Comments on Current Characteristics." PUBLIC ADMINISTRATION REVIEW 28 (May–June 1968): 242–49.

> The author discusses "academic analysis," the quest for quantifiable data, "creative juxtaposition" of theory and data, topical country-by-country description, and problems of administrative action as "prevailing visions" of comparative administration. He suggests the physics "principle of complementarity" as a useful metaphor for the study of comparative administration.

1542 Henderson, Keith M. "A New Comparative Public Administration?" In TOWARD A NEW PUBLIC ADMINISTRATION: THE MINNOW-BROOK PERSPECTIVE, edited by Frank Marini, pp. 234–50. Scranton, Pa.: Chandler Publishing Co., 1971.

> The author grapples with the past, present, and alternative futures of comparative public administration as a field of study. He attempts to assess the merits of international comparative study, or the transference of the comparative perspective to the study of public administration within the United States, with special attention to current American problems and relevance to practicing public administrators.

1543 Hirsch, Werner Z. "Program Budgeting in the United Kingdom." PUBLIC ADMINISTRATION REVIEW 33 (March–April 1973): 120–28.

> The author notes that program budgeting in the United Kingdom must be examined in light of the particular political and constitutional environment in which the government operates. There are only two tiers of government, the national government and the local authorities. A three-part system of Public Expenditure Survey, the Programme Analysis and Review, and the Central Policy Review constitutes the fulcrum on which budget decision making rests. The writer believes that the need to tailor new procedures to the existing incentive structure is a most important lesson to be learned from the British process.

1544   Johnson, Harry G. "A Theoretical Model of Economic Nationalism in New and Developing States." POLITICAL SCIENCE QUARTERLY 80 (June 1965): 169–85.

   Johnson posits a model of economic nationalism for developing countries. He places importance on the establishment of a middle class as a condition essential to the viability of a national state.

1545   Jun, Jong A. "Renewing the Study of Comparative Administration: Some Reflections on the Current Possibilities." PUBLIC ADMINISTRATION REVIEW 36 (November–December 1976): 641–47.

   This brief essay emphasizes the need for the renewal of the study of comparative administration and suggests new directions. Jun discusses the scope of comparative administration, cites theoretical models for comparison, recognizes the need for a new perspective in theoretical knowledge and methodology, calls for expanding areas of comparative study, and concludes that "comparative administration during the '60s was in an initiating and theorizing period; so far, the '70s have been a reflecting period."

1546   Kassem, M. Sami. "Organization Theory: American and European Styles." INTERNATIONAL STUDIES OF MANAGEMENT AND ORGANIZATION 6 (Fall 1976): 46–59.

   Kassem describes the classical model of organization (principles taken from practical experiences) and the human relations model (emphasis on people instead of structures). Europeans (e.g., Marx, Freud, and Weber) pioneered various concepts and theories with regard to bureaucracies and the United States has been the recipient of these ideas, providing a pragmatic society where practical application could test modern management methods and techniques.

1547   Kee, Woo Sik. "Fiscal Decentralization and Economic Development." PUBLIC FINANCE QUARTERLY 5 (January 1977): 79–97.

   Empirical tests of several hypotheses are performed for sixty-four selected countries. Kee indicates that the degree of fiscal decentralization in both developed and developing countries is greatly dependent on the ratio of intergovernmental transfer payments, form of government (federal versus nonfederal), level of per capita income, and the degree of urbanization. However, government form loses its statistical significance as an explanatory variable when developing countries alone are examined, and the degree of openness of the economy emerges as an important explanatory variable.

1548   Kingsley, J. Donald. "Bureaucracy and Political Development, with
        Particular Reference to Nigeria." In BUREAUCRACY AND POLITICAL
        DEVELOPMENT, edited by Joseph LaPalombara, pp. 301-17. Princeton,
        N.J.: Princeton University Press, 1963.

>   The author confines his observations largely to four gov-
        emments of the Federation of Nigeria, with only occa-
        sional glances elsewhere in sub-Saharan Africa. Kingsley
        claims that Nigeria is a large and complex country and
        the problems of bureaucracy and political development it
        presents are representative in degree of all the former
        British areas in Africa, east or west. He believes that
        Nigeria presents fascinating opportunities to the student
        of politics because of its size, its diversity, its federal
        structure, and its varying rates of development.

1549   Krishna, Daya. "Shall We be 'Diffracted'? A Critical Comment on
        Fred Riggs' 'Prismatic' Societies and Public Administration." ADMINI-
        STRATIVE CHANGE 2 (June 1974): 48-55.

>   Krishna believes the clarification of societies offered by
        Fred Riggs (see 1576) introduces confusion by combining
        the technological, political, and social perspectives with-
        out clearly separating one perspective from another.

1550   Landau, Martin. "Development Administration and Decision Theory."
        In DEVELOPMENT ADMINISTRATION IN ASIA, edited by Edward W.
        Weidner, pp. 73-103. Durham, N.C.: Duke University Press, 1970.

>   Landau posits that there are modes of conduct which are
        conducive to development and modes which are not. He
        suggests that this difference may be treated in terms of
        the ground upon which a decision is justified. The author
        emphasizes that "what distinguishes one society from the
        other is the ground upon which a decision is validated,
        the rules by which it is assigned legitimacy."

1551   LaPalombara, Joseph. "Bureaucracy and Political Development: Notes,
        Queries, and Dilemmas." In his BUREAUCRACY AND POLITICAL DE-
        VELOPMENT, pp. 34-61. Princeton, N.J.: Princeton University
        Press, 1963.

>   The author is concerned with the use of the concept
        "modernity" as applied to political systems in that there
        exists considerable confusion and disagreement regarding
        its meaning. He offers some characteristics of political
        change (degree of structural differentiation, magnitude,
        degree of achievement orientation, and degree of secu-
        larization) and concludes that these characteristics have
        implications for the public sector as well.

1552   _____ . "An Overview of Bureaucracy and Political Development."
In his BUREAUCRACY AND POLITICAL DEVELOPMENT, pp. 3-33.
Princeton, N.J.: Princeton University Press, 1963.

> LaPalombara writes: "The implied proposition here is
> that, particularly in the new states where the need for
> national integration is paramount, the proliferation of
> functional specialists in administration will add to the
> many centrifugal forces that already exist. When a
> society is run by all sorts of social and political forces
> pulling in conflicting, disintegrative directions, the ad-
> ministrative generalist may be a vital cement, holding
> the system together." In this introduction to a series of
> articles by the same title, LaPalombara addresses problems
> regarding the exercise of effective political control over
> the bureaucracy.

1553   Lee, Hahn-Been. "The Role of the Higher Civil Service Under Rapid
Social and Political Change." In DEVELOPMENT ADMINISTRATION
IN ASIA, edited by Edward W. Weidner, pp. 107-31. Durham, N.C.:
Duke University Press, 1970.

> This essay is an attempt to analyze the place of the higher
> civil service in a setting of rapid social and political
> change and to ascertain those conditions under which it
> can play a role contributing to administrative development.
> Lee attempts to build a limited theoretical framework
> around a typology of bureaucratic roles and a model of
> political elite structure and bureaucratic roles and to
> apply this theoretical framework to administrative develop-
> ment in Korea during the 1960s.

1554   Loveman, Brian. "The Comparative Administration Group, Development
Administration and Antidevelopment." PUBLIC ADMINISTRATION RE-
VIEW 36 (November-December 1976): 616-21.

> This article calls into question the results that can be
> expected from development administration. Loveman
> recognizes that administration is a necessary condition
> for development but suggests that development cannot be
> administered. He states: "Human beings must be able
> to rethink and redefine their own values and the conditions
> of their daily lives. Human choice must be expanded.
> This cannot take place to great extent when government
> administrators continually increase their capabilities to
> 'reshape' the physical, human, and cultural environment--
> at their discretion."

1555   Matsuo, Takayoshi. "The Development of Democracy in Japan." DE-
VELOPING ECONOMIES 4 (October 1966): 612-37.

Matsuo reviews democratic growth in Japan and emphasizes conditions pertinent for political modernization. He recaps the history of the Taisho period in Japan and illustrates the difficulties in achieving political modernization in a backward capitalist nation during a time of imperialism. He suggests certain political developments which must be realized before democracy can be achieved.

1556   Milne, R.S. "Bureaucracy and Development Administration." PUBLIC ADMINISTRATION 51 (Winter 1973): 411-25.

Milne states that particular features of bureaucracy need modifying in developing countries and that bureaucracy, in some form, is inevitable. He posits that there are unlikely to be any easily identifiable structural remedies for administrative defects in countries where the level of resources and the cultural conditions are so unpromising. He suggests that improvement is not impossible.

1557   _____. "Mechanistic and Organic Models of Public Administration in Developing Countries." ADMINISTRATIVE SCIENCE QUARTERLY 15 (March 1970): 57-67.

Milne discusses the analyses by Fred Riggs and Victor Thompson (see 1569 and 1593, respectively) of the shortcomings of public administration in developing countries. Thompson advocates some kind of organic model for these countries as opposed to the varieties of the mechanistic model which developing countries usually attempt to follow. The author maintains that the cultures in developing countries do not permit either mechanistic or organic organizations to work effectively. He advances hypotheses on the differences in organizational loyalty and on the effects of formal and informal organization between developing and developed countries.

1558   Morelos, P.C. "Practical Concepts of Development Programming for Underdeveloped Economies." QUARTERLY JOURNAL OF ADMINISTRATION 13 (October 1978): 17-37.

Morelos provides an orientation to the nature, workings, and uses of government programming. He mentions that a large barrier exists between plan formulation and plan implementation in the majority of underdeveloped nations. The author believes that programming is the answer to this barrier.

1559   Morstein Marx, Fritz. "The Higher Civil Service as an Action Group in Western Political Development." In BUREAUCRACY AND POLITICAL DEVELOPMENT, edited by Joseph LaPalombara, pp. 62-95. Princeton, N.J.: Princeton University Press, 1963.

The author's concerns in discussing the higher civil service's sense of engagement, action patterns, defense of the status quo, and support for reform of bureaucracy include: quest of administrative strength, bureaucracy and constitution- alism, responsibility and self-interest, status officialdom, functional expertise, umbrella of duty, formal legitimacy, policy counsel, program formulation, public management, administration and stability, entrenchment of tradition, divisionist tendencies, source of ideas, participation in strategy councils, language of achievement, the virtue of noncommitment, and motivational factors.

1560 _____. "Inventory of Administrative Study in Europe: The Speyer Conference." PUBLIC ADMINISTRATION REVIEW 29 (July-August 1969): 359-66.

This article is a report on the conference of the Speyer Academy of Administrative Sciences in Germany where administrative scientists from throughout Europe met in 1968 to consider the state and tendencies of administrative sciences in European countries. Participants concluded that administrative study had gained a firmer institutional hold in Europe, resulting in new centers of teaching, training, or research, in new periodicals, and in the availability of new literature.

1561 Pai Panandiker, V.A. "Developmental Administration: An Approach." INDIAN JOURNAL OF PUBLIC ADMINISTRATION 10 (January-March 1964): 34-44.

This article is intended to provide a conceptual framework for operationalizing the end-goals of a national develop- mental system.

1562 Pelt, Adrian. "Peculiar Characteristics of an International Admini- stration." PUBLIC ADMINISTRATION REVIEW 6 (Spring 1946): 108- 14.

Pelt notes the similarities between the organization of the United Nations and the League of Nations, describes the UN Secretariat, and probes the financial procedures of the international organization.

1563 Peters, B. Guy. THE POLITICS OF BUREAUCRACY: A COMPARATIVE PERSPECTIVE. New York: Longmans, 1978. ix, 246 p. Paper.

"If our knowledge of administration in any one country is inadequate, then our lack of knowledge of the comparative dimensions of administration is appalling." This textbook examines comparative administration and comparative politics. Chapter discussions include the growth of government and

administration, political culture and public administration,
the recruitment of public administrators, problems of administrative structures, and the politics of administrative
accountability.

1564   Pye, Lucian W. "Democracy, Modernization, and Nation Building."
In SELF-GOVERNMENT IN MODERNIZING NATIONS, edited by
Roland J. Pennock, pp. 6-25. Englewood Cliffs, N.J.: Prentice
Hall, 1964.

Pye analyzes the impacts of modernization upon traditional
cultures. He emphasizes that the capacity to reconcile
universal and parochial values is crucial in nation-building
efforts. Authoritarianism may be appropriate for the early
stages of development, but later periods will demand more
representation of the masses in governmental institutions.

1565   _____. "Mao Tse-Tung's Leadership Style." POLITICAL SCIENCE
QUARTERLY 91 (Summer 1976): 219-35.

Pye reveals that Mao's true secret was his propensity to
evoke and to manipulate human emotions, to sustain the
interplay between narcissism and worship that is necessary
for charismatic leadership. Mao's leadership style was a
conscious acceptance of contradictions in policy, a feature
Mao absorbed into the Marxist idea of dialectic. Pye
indicates that Mao vacillated between deliberate risk-
taking and cautious rationalism. Mao never committed
himself to any objective or person, playing out his am-
bivalences in public and keeping hold on the emotions
of the masses.

1566   Quah, Jon S.T. "Comparative Public Administration: What and Why?"
ADMINISTRATIVE CHANGE 4 (January-June 1977): 175-90.

Quah asserts that comparative public administration is one
of the most recent areas of specialization in the study of
administration. He notes the emphasis of comparative
public administration on theory-building and development
administration and that American scholars dominate this
field of study. The article suggests that the study of
comparative public administration serves both theoretical
and practical concerns.

1567   Raphaeli, Nimrod. "Comparative Public Administration: An Overview."
In his READINGS IN COMPARATIVE PUBLIC ADMINISTRATION, pp.
1-25. Boston: Allyn and Bacon, 1967.

This is a very useful introduction to the study of comparative public administration, its major trends and emphases.
The author offers interdependent definitions, abstract con-

cepts, and hypotheses in this opening chapter of his book
of readings.

1568   _____, ed. READINGS IN COMPARATIVE PUBLIC ADMINISTRA-
TION. Boston: Allyn and Bacon, 1967. xii, 490 p.

This book of readings is a very valuable contribution to
the literature of comparative public administration. Raphaeli
includes an introduction to comparative public administration and sections on the "idiographic" approach, development administration, and a conceptual approach in
comparative administration. He states that "the purposes
of comparative public administration are twofold--to compare and contrast, in analytical and conceptual frameworks, varying administrative systems; and, more recently,
to enrich and enlarge the literature and knowledge about
development administration."

1569   Riggs, Fred W. ADMINISTRATION IN DEVELOPING COUNTRIES:
THE THEORY OF PRISMATIC SOCIETY. Boston: Houghton-Mifflin,
1964. xvi, 477 p.

Talking about the prismatic prototype, Riggs uses structural-
functional analysis in projecting two perfect societies at
opposite poles on a scale of development which he defines
as "fused" and "diffracted." Intermingled with social,
economic, political and cultural subsystems is the administrative subsystem in a prismatic society. The author de-
picts conduct in these subsystems, utilizing ideas like
formalism, price indeterminacy, overlapping and hetero-
geneity, bazaar-canteen economics, kaleidoscopic stratification of elites, poly-communalism, poly-normativism,
elects, the status-contract nexus, blocked throughputs,
double talk, the dependency syndrome, and the interference
complex. One can understand the contradictory property
of administrative arrangements in evolving societies through
an exacting sala prototype of bureaucratic conduct.

1570   _____. "Bureaucrats and Political Development: A Paradoxical
View." In BUREAUCRACY AND POLITICAL DEVELOPMENT, edited
by Joseph LaPalombara, pp. 120-67. Princeton, N.J.: Princeton
University Press, 1963.

"A phenomenon of the utmost significance in transitional
societies is the lack of balance between policy making
institutions and bureaucratic policy implementing structures.
The relative weakness of political organs means that the
political function tends to be appropriated, in considerable
measure, by bureaucrats. Intra-bureaucratic struggles become a primary form of politics." Riggs deals with the
way in which bureaucratic interests affect political develop-

ment, not how the declared political aims of officials impinge on politics, but how the existence and self-interest of bureaucratic institutions affect, directly or indirectly, the growth of political institutions.

1571 _____. THE ECOLOGY OF PUBLIC ADMINISTRATION. New York: Asia Publishing House, 1961. viii, 152 p.

The author includes in his prismatic concept of society an ecological consideration of administration in the United States. The prismatic prototype of administration in Third World nations has been typified by the view that things are not as expected. The prismatic scenario is formed in a Third World nation when Western power and foundations are fused with traditional societies and mores. A new jargon is established to define the resulting inconsistencies of administration.

1572 _____. "The Group and the Movement: Notes on Comparative and Development Administration." PUBLIC ADMINISTRATION REVIEW 36 (November-December 1976): 648-54.

Riggs states that the florescence of the comparative administration movement in the 1960s rested upon the excited interest of American public administration scholars who had returned from their overseas experiences in a shaken but hopeful mood, upon the availability of modest but strategically essential foundation funding, and upon the existence of an institutional base, albeit an ephemeral one, in the form of an associational committee. The author believes that all three of these resource bases have now substantially vanished. He concludes that American scholarship in public administration has become increasingly parochial as it ignores what is happening in the rest of the world.

1573 _____. "The Idea of Development Administration." In DEVELOP-MENT ADMINISTRATION IN ASIA, edited by Edward W. Weidner, pp. 25-72. Durham, N.C.: Duke University Press, 1970.

The author provides an ecological definition of development, reviews fundamental concepts of administrative behavior, probes determinants and dilemmas of development administration, and concludes with comments on the idea of development and on the meaning of administration. He points out that the most popular idea of development is increasing outputs.

1574 _____. "Notes on Literature Available for the Study of Comparative Public Administration." AMERICAN POLITICAL SCIENCE REVIEW 47 (June 1954): 515-37.

The author reviews the literature of the early 1950s and
questions whether "principles" of administration developed
in the American context have general validity or whether
they merely describe administrative institutions and practices in the United States. In examining this literature,
Riggs maintains that the interdependence of administrative
institutions and behavior with other nations' cultural, economic, and political contexts has become apparent and
has necessitated a revision of old working assumptions.

1575 _____. "Prismatic Financial Administration." PHILIPPINE JOURNAL
OF PUBLIC ADMINISTRATION 4 (April 1960): 132-50.

Riggs distinguishes between traditional (fused), inter-
mediately developed (prismatic), and highly industrialized
(refracted) societies and reveals that government costs and
needs outdistance government revenues. He applies this
model to actual conditions.

1576 _____. "Prismatic Societies and Public Administration: Towards an
Ecological-Developmental Orientation." ADMINISTRATIVE CHANGE
1 (December 1973): 91-95.

Riggs defines a prismatic society as one that is differentiated but poorly integrated. He suggests that dissemination of specialized technologies necessitates organization
and bureaucracy, and differentiation is the key element
in the process of development. The reader is told that
political leaders integrate the performance of the many
specialized roles mandated by modern government. It is
much easier to train people to perform specialized roles
than to integrate these roles.

1577 _____. "Prismatic Society and Financial Administration." ADMINI-
STRATIVE SCIENCE QUARTERLY 5 (June 1960): 1-46.

Riggs states that the failure of national income and government revenue to keep pace with growing demands for
government expenditures creates an acute crisis in the
administrative system of every underdeveloped country.
He says that the nature of this crisis can be more clearly
understood if a theoretical model, entitled the "exopris-
matic society," is used for analysis. He notes that the
term "prismatic" is used for types of social systems based
on "functional-structural" analysis and that the prefix
"exo-" designates a predominance of external as contrasted
with internal dynamics or pressures in the processes of
change. Riggs reveals that a characteristic combination of
symptoms or stresses, called the "dependency syndrome,"
occurs in the model and that this syndrome prevents efficient
tax collection, budgeting, and expenditures control

and is in turn reinforced by the dilemmas of financial administration.

1578 _____. "Relearning An Old Lesson: The Political Context of Development Administration." PUBLIC ADMINISTRATION REVIEW 25 (March 1965): 70-79.

With millions of dollars being spent for technical assistance programs and research, the author finds the premises and assumptions underlying the assistance to be faulty. Riggs calls for research funds supportive of empirical field work on the basic characteristics of sociopolitical systems. He is concerned with the weaknesses of administrative performance in underdeveloped countries vis-a-vis the cultivation of democratic politics in these nations.

1579 _____. "The 'Sala' Model: An Ecological Approach to the Study of Comparative Administration." PHILIPPINE JOURNAL OF PUBLIC ADMINISTRATION 6 (January 1962): 3-16.

The author states that a model, like that of the sala, is not intended to serve as a description of any particular society or system of government but serves an heuristic purpose, giving us a tool by which we can better describe and understand situations in real life and relate administrative behavior to ecological factors typical of transitional societies. Riggs suggests that we need to construct alternative, ecologically based models to help us in the study of administration abroad.

1580 _____, ed. FRONTIERS OF DEVELOPMENT ADMINISTRATION. Durham, N.C.: Duke University Press, 1971. 605 p.

The essays in this volume are theoretical for the most part as this text is largely based on papers presented at the 1966 Comparative Administration Group of the American Society for Public Administration. Chapter topics include the context and study approaches in development administration, policy and reform strategies, functional approaches, structural approaches, and the broad frameworks for administrative reform.

1581 Sadek, S.E.M. THE BALANCE POINT BETWEEN LOCAL AUTONOMY AND NATIONAL CONTROL. Brussels: Mouton and Co., 1972. xii, 336 p.

This book is a comparative study of the relations between central and local government in Britain, France, Yugoslavia, and the Arab Republic of Egypt. The author reveals that there are varying degrees of decline in local autonomy, an increase in the power, influence or domination of the central governments, an ever increasing

dependence by municipalities on central grants or subsidies, and the by-passing of local authorities in planning and regional development. Sadek offers useful
analyses for insights into centralization aspects of European, Communist, and Middle Eastern systems of government.

1582   Savage, Peter. "Optimism and Pessimism in Comparative Administration." PUBLIC ADMINISTRATION REVIEW 36 (July-August 1976):
415-23.

This article examines some of the failings and achievements of the comparative administration movement, the
assumptions and purposes it began with, the fads and
fancies it embraced, and the mixed legacy it has left
for school and practitioners. Savage points out that
surface indications for the future of comparative administration are bleak.

1583   Sayre, Wallace S. "Bureaucracies: Some Contrasts in Systems." IN-
DIAN JOURNAL OF PUBLIC ADMINISTRATION 10 (April-June 1964):
219-29.

This essay is concerned with choices about the forms and
methods of bureaucracy and not with the "probably un-
answerable and somewhat metaphysical question of whether
bureaucracy is villain or hero." The author assumes that
it may, in some periods and some places, be either or a
mixture of both. The discussion focuses upon how bureaucrats are chosen, the role of bureaucrats in decision
making, and the control of bureaucrats.

1584   Sharkansky, Ira. "Structural Correlates of Least Developed Economies:
Parallels in Governmental Forms, Politics, and Public Policies Among
the Least Developed Countries and the Least Developed American
States." PUBLIUS 5 (Spring 1975): 171-94.

The author reveals that the least developed states and
countries have traits in common which are related to
processes of economic development. Policy makers in the
developing countries should look to the least developed
American states for patterns to imitate instead of to the
wealthier states or to the U.S. government. He concludes
that the states at the lower end of the political economy
spectrum approach the developing countries most closely
in their scale of economic and political activities.

1585   Sharp, Walter R. "International Bureaucracies and Political Development." In BUREAUCRACY AND POLITICAL DEVELOPMENT, edited
by Joseph LaPalombara, pp. 441-74. Princeton, N.J.: Princeton
University Press, 1963. Tables.

This essay attempts to examine the role of international staff groups, part of the operational structure of the United Nations family of agencies, in political development. The author concludes that this role appears to be appreciable and growing but thus far quite subsidiary to other forces, sporadic and uneven, and primarily indirect. Sharp suggests that these limitations could be tested by attitude surveys which would almost certainly reveal how little actual knowledge of local UN operations has reached elite groups, let alone the masses.

1586   Siffin, William J. "Two Decades of Public Administration in Developing Countries." PUBLIC ADMINISTRATION REVIEW 36 (January-February 1976): 61-71.

Siffin examines the state of the art of American public administration during the past twenty years and assesses the effects of efforts to apply derivations of that art in developing countries. He concludes that chief successes have been in transferring administrative technologies, that there have been significant failures and inadequacies, particularly in public administration education in developing countries, and that a root problem of promoting development through improved public administration has been one of seeking developmental outcomes from system-maintenance oriented tools and concepts.

1587   Sigelman, Lee. "In Search of Comparative Administration." PUBLIC ADMINISTRATION REVIEW 36 (November-December 1976): 621-25.

This article focuses on methodological problems facing comparative public administration. Sigelman examines problems of theory and research in comparative public administration and points out some methodological perspectives for the future. He concludes that "comparative public administration is floundering at a time when other social scientists have finally come to appreciate the centrality of bureaucracy and bureaucrats in the political process."

1588   Smith, Brian. "The Substance and Boundaries of Development Administration." PUBLIC ADMINISTRATION BULLETIN 22 (December 1976): 25-40.

Smith writes that the science of development administration concerns the efficiency of governmental organizations in performing developmental tasks. He emphasizes the cultural environment of administration at the expense of contextual factors which might be more relevant to the structural problems that face societies seeking to contemporize their economies. This article alludes that there

are recognizable differences between bureaucracies in
poor, agricultural, neocolonized countries and those in
Western countries. The author concludes that development administration has not done enough to reveal these
differences.

1589   Spengler, Joseph J. "Bureaucracy and Economic Development." In
BUREAUCRACY AND POLITICAL DEVELOPMENT, edited by Joseph
LaPalombara, pp. 199-232. Princeton, N.J.: Princeton University
Press, 1963.

This essay studies the role of the public bureaucracy in
economic development to ascertain what may be done to
increase the effectiveness of this role. It relates only
to the role of bureaucracy in a mixed economy, that is,
one in which the public sector is of significant size and
yet not almost coterminous with the economy, as in the
Soviet Union. Spengler defines the concept of economic
development, describes developmental processes, probes
determinants of economic development, explains inter-
sectoral relations, and explores bureaucracy's role in economic development.

1590   Springer, J. Fred. "Empirical Theory and Development Administration:
Prologues and Promise." PUBLIC ADMINISTRATION REVIEW 36
(November-December 1976): 636-41.

Springer argues that the empirical study of public bureaucracies must recognize their hierarchical complexity. He
points out that development administration is starved for
theories which will guide the pooling of empirical knowledge, orient new research, and recommend administrative
policy.

1591   _____. "Observation and Theory in Development Administration."
ADMINISTRATION AND SOCIETY 9 (May 1977): 13-44.

Springer suggests that the development of sound empirical
theory is a major, and elusive, objective for students of
comparative administration. He suggests that the lack of
progress toward this goal is partly attributed to the "complexity" of the empirical phenomena, or the "operational
space," encompassed by the field. He points out that a
review of the literature reveals that most existing studies
are limited in their coverage of this "space."

1592   Stone, Donald C. "Organizing the United Nations." PUBLIC AD-
MINISTRATION REVIEW 6 (Spring 1946): 115-29.

The author discusses the work of the preparatory commission,

analyzes the method of resolving administrative issues,
describes the role and functions of the Secretary-General,
notes the General Assembly control over the Secretary-
General, examines the organization of the general staff
and service functions, delineates the role of the Assistant
Secretaries-General, and reveals some problems in staffing
the organization. This article is an excellent conceptualization of the United Nations in its initial stages of
development.

1593   Thompson, Victor A. "Administrative Objectives for Development
        Administration." ADMINISTRATIVE SCIENCE QUARTERLY 9 (June
        1964): 91-108.

        Thompson surmises that administrative practices and prin-
        ciples of the West derive from a preoccupation with con-
        trol and therefore have little value for development ad-
        ministration in underdeveloped countries, where the need
        is for an adaptive administration, or one that can incor-
        porate constant change. He does suggest that adaptive
        administrative principles can be derived from the research
        and theories of the behavioral sciences and that these
        should become the administrative objectives of development
        administrators. These objectives include an innovative
        atmosphere, the operationalizing and sharing of goals,
        the combining of planning, or thinking, and acting, or
        doing, the minimization of parochialism, the diffusion
        of influence, the increasing of toleration of interdepen-
        dence, and the avoidance of bureaupathology.

1594   Tilman, Robert O. "Emergence of Black-Market Bureaucracy: Ad-
        ministration, Development, and Corruption in the New States." PUBLIC
        ADMINISTRATION REVIEW 28 (September-October 1968): 437-44.

        This article utilizes a simple dichotomous market model
        drawn from economic theory to analyze the emergence of
        administrative corruption. The author argues that the
        ideal type of modern bureaucracy posits a system analogous
        to the mandatory pricing system of market economics,
        while corrupt bureaucratic systems more resemble the free
        market. Tilman concludes with observations about the
        control of bureaucratic black marketing, its utility in
        economic and political development, and its future in
        the underdeveloped world.

1595   United Nations Technical Assistance Programme. A HANDBOOK OF
        PUBLIC ADMINISTRATION: CURRENT CONCEPTS AND PRACTICE
        WITH SPECIAL REFERENCE TO DEVELOPING COUNTRIES. New
        York: 1961. vii, 126 p.

        This handbook states the basic elements for public ad-

ministration improvement in developing countries. The
purpose of this text is to evaluate, summarize, and present in nontechnical language the general consensus of
many observers concerning current concepts and practice
of public administration with regard to developing countries.
It is addressed primarily to government officials who are
concerned with promoting the economic, social, and administrative development of their countries. The book's
aim is to help administrators of developing countries to
overcome obstacles to improved administrative management and to formulate programs and priorities.

1596   Weidner, Edward W. "Development and Innovational Roles." In DE-
VELOPMENT ADMINISTRATION IN ASIA, edited by Edward W.
Weidner, pp. 399-421. Durham, N.C.: Duke University Press, 1970.

Weidner states that development means change and that
innovation is not all of one piece. The author concludes
that "the problem of how to maximize the effectiveness
of a bureaucracy so that it contributes to growth in the
direction of modernity or nation-building and socioeconomic progress is a problem of how to strengthen innovational forces in the bureaucracy." He analyzes the
process for strengthening innovational roles for development.

1597   _____. "The Elements of Development Administration." In DEVELOP-
MENT ADMINISTRATION IN ASIA, edited by Edward W. Weidner,
pp. 3-24. Durham, N.C.: Duke University Press, 1970.

The author discusses conditions of development, planned
directional growth with system change, planned directional
growth with no system change, planned system change with
no directional growth, planning with no growth or system
change, unplanned directional growth with system change,
unplanned directional growth with no system change, unplanned system change with no directional growth, and
no plans, no change in static society.

1598   _____. TECHNICAL ASSISTANCE IN PUBLIC ADMINISTRATION
OVERSEAS: THE CASE FOR DEVELOPMENT ADMINISTRATION.
Chicago: Public Administration Service, 1964. xi, 247 p.

The objective of this research is to describe major programs of technical assistance in public administration, to
examine broadly their impact, and to reach some conclusions as to their significance. Included in this volume
are programs of technical assistance in public administration of the United Nations, the Ford Foundation, consulting firms, and American universities. Research for
this text stems primarily from field work accomplished in
twenty-three countries during the 1957-61 period.

1599   _____, ed. DEVELOPMENT ADMINISTRATION IN ASIA. Durham, N.C.: Duke University Press, 1970. xxiii, 431 p.

This volume contains essays that were presented at the Seminar on Development Administration, held at the East-West Center, University of Hawaii, in 1966. Parts of this text include chapters concerning theory, practice, and technical assistance in development administration. Authors include prominent scholars from the United States and Asia.

1600   Welch, Claude E., Jr. "The Comparative Study of Political Modernization." In POLITICAL MODERNIZATION, edited by Claude E. Welch, Jr., pp. 1-17. Belmont, Calif.: Wadsworth Publishing Co., 1967.

The author concludes that modernization is a complex process and brings a fundamental transformation of society, economy, and polity, that modernization is no certainty and that disruption is likely, and that should not be assumed that drastic change will be peaceful. Welch's essay serves as an introduction to a book of readings in political modernization.

1601   Williams, Robert. "The Problem of Corruption: A Conceptual and Comparative Analysis." PUBLIC ADMINISTRATION BULLETIN 22 (December 1976): 41-53.

Williams believes that a chief foible of comparative analysis is that too little empirical analysis has been done on corruption's consequences. He points out that the most obvious gap in the literature is the little attention paid to political systems where corruption has been effectively curtailed. The article suggests that researchers fail to place corruption in a wide social, political, and economic context.

ADDENDUM

Adams, Bruce. "The Limitations of Muddling Through: Does Anyone in Washington Really Think Anymore?" PUBLIC ADMINISTRATION REVIEW 39 (November-December 1979): 545-52.

Adams considers the nature of the political decision-making process in Washington in 1979 more than twenty years after the publication of Charles Lindblom's classic article "The Science of Muddling Through" (PUBLIC ADMINISTRATION REVIEW, 1959). He addresses the limitations of muddling through in an increasingly complex political environment and emphasizes that "a system that runs people ragged for 12 to 18 hours a day, shortens their perspectives and squeezes out their creativity and imagination. They reach the point of diminishing returns." This is an insightful adaptation of Lindblom's thinking.

Altschuler, Alan A., and Thomas, Norman C., eds. THE POLITICS OF THE FEDERAL BUREAUCRACY. New York: Harper and Row, 1977. 379 p.

The editors include material on citizen participation in bureaucracy, administrative decision making, the role of minorities in public administration, the Planning, Programming, Budgeting Systems experience, and the lessons of Watergate. They examine how American society reconciles its dependence on large scale public bureaucracy with the ideals and processes of mass democracy. This is an excellent anthology on the federal government and its bureaucracy.

Barton, Rayburn. "Role Advocated for Administrators by the New Public Administration." SOUTHERN REVIEW OF PUBLIC ADMINISTRATION 3 (March 1980): 463-86.

Barton attempts to delineate the roles advocated by the "new public administration." Major roles advocated include the social equity advocate, the change agent, the representative bureaucrat, the advocacy administrator, and the nonconsolidating bureaucrat. This essay provides an excellent discussion of the roles of public administrators in the 1980s.

Addendum

Berman, Larry. THE OFFICE OF MANAGEMENT AND BUDGET AND THE PRESIDENCY, 1921-1979. Princeton, N.J.: Princeton University Press, 1979. 180 p.

> The author maintains that the effectiveness of the Office of Management and Budget depends upon its responsiveness to presidential needs. However, Berman contends that presidential "needs must be for a neutral institutional conscience within the Executive Office and not for a partisan instrument for managing executive branch policies." This brief book is the first comprehensive study of OMB. Berman draws on a wide range of material including unpublished documents from the Records Division of the OMB, Presidential Libraries, interviews with former directors and senior employees of OMB, and results of a questionnaire that he administered to all OMB employees. Berman concludes "that the OMB's recent problems stemmed not from arbitrary usurpation of power or loss of credibility, but from the misuse of the OMB for purposes for which it was not intended."

Bernstein, Samuel J., and O'Hara, Patrick G. PUBLIC ADMINISTRATION: ORGANIZATIONS, PEOPLE, AND PUBLIC POLICY. New York: Harper and Row, 1979. 510 p.

> Bernstein and O'Hara provide a provocative text which is a comprehensive, concept-oriented introduction to public administration. This volume is organized around three focal points--organizations, people, and public policy. The authors synthesize theory and analytical tools from law, political science, sociology, psychology, management science, economics, and policy sciences. They include new approaches to the analysis of public policy that includes chapters on systems concepts, program evaluation, and computer applications. Also included are analytical tools and techniques necessary for effective and creative management of modern public organizations.

Boyle, John M. "Reorganization Reconsidered: An Empirical Approach to the Departmentalization Problem." PUBLIC ADMINISTRATION REVIEW 39 (September-October 1979): 458-65. Tables.

> Boyle asks if measurable, objective criteria for governmental reorganization can be developed? He believes that objective criteria can be developed, operationalized, and tested if the purpose of the reorganization is specified. This article focuses upon an empirical investigation into a particular organization, a study of New York City administration. A fundamental purpose of this essay is to demonstrate how a basic assumption of the classical school may be operationalized.

Bozeman, Barry. PUBLIC MANAGEMENT AND POLICY ANALYSIS. New York: St. Martin's Press, 1979. 384 p.

> Bozeman offers a comprehensive introduction to the field of public administration. With emphasis upon management science and policy

analysis, he provides an interdisciplinary approach which enhances the prospective public manager's ability to think systematically about problem solving. Major sections include public administration in perspective, the organizational context, public management routines, and policy analysis in public organizations.

Bozeman, Barry, and Slusher, E. Allen. "Scarcity and Environmental Stress in Public Organizations." ADMINISTRATION AND SOCIETY 11 (November 1979): 335-55.

The authors considers some of the possible effects of sustained scarcity, particularly sharp declines in public spending and public employment, on public organization behavior. The focus is on the effects of scarcity on four types of strategic choices in public organizations: domain selection, development and deployment of technology, organization structure, and organization process. Bozeman and Slusher argue that narrow efficiency criteria will become paramount and will give rise to more formal, centralized, and rigid organization structures and a habituation of organizational responses to environmental change.

Brickman, Ronald. "Patterns of Administrative Decentralization in France: An Analysis of University Reform." ADMINISTRATION AND SOCIETY 11 (November 1979): 283-305.

Brickman analyzes the extent, nature, and processes of change in the distribution of authority between the national administration and the local academic institutions. He examines the French university system after reforms in the aftermath of the 1968 demonstrations. He points out several consistencies which help explain why decentralization proceded as far as it did.

Briscoe, Dennis R., and Leonardson, Gene S. EXPERIENCES IN PUBLIC ADMINISTRATION. Belmont, Calif.: Duxbury Press, 1980. 304 p.

The authors emphasize experiential teaching and learning for teachers and students in a text in which all material has been successfully class-tested. Each exercise has precise learning objectives, time stipulations, and suggestions for working with large or small groups. The exercises require students to actively use tools of management in the simulation of actual policy formation and implementation. Sections include discussions of public administration, organization behavior and theory, management of public agencies, and careers in public administration.

Caiden, Naomi. "Budgeting in Poor Countries: Ten Assumptions Reexamined." PUBLIC ADMINISTRATION REVIEW 40 (January-February 1980): 40-46.

Ten common assumptions include 1) a common pattern of budgeting that will fit all circumstances; 2) budgeting aim of national economic planning; 3) budget improvement based on adequate resources;

4) budget decisions that can be separated from policy decisions;
5) whatever coordinated best is best; 6) comprehensive decisions
are superior to partial decisions and complex solutions are better
than simple solutions; 7) prerequisites of budgeting are a matter
of technique and will rather than the product of environmental
conditions; 8) politics are less important than economics; 9) good
budgeting is a matter or regulation; and 10) budgeting is relevant
to development.

Caldwell, Lynton K. "Biology and Bureaucracy: The Coming Confrontation."
PUBLIC ADMINISTRATION REVIEW 40 (January-February 1980): 1-12.

Caldwell states that the impact of bioscience and the new science
of sociobiology is beginning to be felt in those public services most
directly concerned with human behavior (i.e., mental health, medicine, domestic relations, housing, urban planning, criminal justice,
education, and welfare). He points out that the growing knowledge
of the biology of human behavior threatens the assumptions upon
which modern government and bureaucracy have been based. Caldwell emphasizes that "biological findings continue to undermine assumptions long accepted in public law and policy. Even the necessity and durability of bureaucratic government are being ques-
tioned as possibly contrary to human nature as revealed by sociobiology." This is a provocative look into the future of public
administration.

Cates, Camille. "Beyond Muddling: Creativity." PUBLIC ADMINISTRATION
REVIEW 39 (November-December 1979): 527-32.

Cates states that what Lindblom is to incrementalism, Weber is to
bureaucracy. She points out the differences in muddling and creativity. The approach of muddling is rational, while the approach
of creativity is nonrational. The basic strategy of muddling is
security in change maximizing whereas in creativity, advancement
is significant as a basic strategy. The focus of muddling is marginal and incremental but the focus of creativity is new. The
organizational structure of muddling is bureaucracy while the organizational structure of creativity is open, temporary, and organic. The values of muddling include logic, predictability, stability, order, and security. The values of creativity are intuition,
innovation, change, ambiguity, and risk. Cates's essay is a de-
lightful, yet bright, commentary on Lindblom's creativeness (Charles
E. Lindblom, "The Science of Muddling Through," PUBLIC ADMINI-
STRATION REVIEW, 1959).

Cayer, N. Joseph. MANAGING HUMAN RESOURCES: AN INTRODUCTION
TO PUBLIC PERSONNEL ADMINISTRATION. New York: St. Martin's Press,
1980. 260 p.

The author explores personnel administration as a product of its
political environment and evaluates the consequences upon personnel of equal opportunity-affirmative action, labor relations, pro-

ductivity improvement, public criticism, and tax revolt. Cayer is particularly attentive to intergovernmental relations, labor relations, and personnel systems management.

Christenson, James A., and Sachs, Carolyn E. "The Impact of Government Size and Number of Administrative Units on the Quality of Public Services." ADMINISTRATIVE SCIENCE QUARTERLY 25 (March 1980): 89-101. Tables.

The authors maintain that the nature of the relationship of organizational size and structure to organizational performance is a major question in macro-organizational theory. This essay tests the hypothesized relationships of various measures of government size and number of administrative units to citizens' perceptions of the quality of common public services for one hundred different localities in North Carolina. The method includes the construction of a scale of public services that provides a new mode of investigating and evaluating the quality of public services. The findings reveal that size of government is positively related to the perceived quality of public services.

Clynch, Edward J. "Zero Base Budgeting: A Strategy for Institutionalization." MIDWEST REVIEW OF PUBLIC ADMINISTRATION 13 (September 1979): 157-61. Table.

Clynch concludes that the presence of adequate data and personnel with needed analytical skills is not sufficient to assure the institutionalization of zero-base budgeting. He points out that ZBB must also contend with the potential apposition of political forces who believe that budgetary changes result in detrimental outcomes. A political climate conducive for budget reforms intended to raise questions about current expenditures is a crucial part of an implementation strategy. This strategy recognizes that meaningful budget reform is not instantaneous.

Cooper, Terry L. "Bureaucracy and Community Organization: The Metamorphosis of a Relationship." ADMINISTRATION AND SOCIETY 11 (February 1980): 411-44.

Cooper analyzes the relationship between the Pico-Union Neighborhood Council (PUNC) and the Community Redevelopment Agency of Los Angeles. He reveals that the pressure of bureaucratic perspectives and role demands is a significant factor in the interaction of public agencies and community organizations and that the neighborhood council, in spite of independent funding, has moved from militant advocacy, with broad community participation, to community development directed largely by professionals, with substantially reduced involvement from community residents.

Dillman, David L. "Budgeting for Uncertainty: An Application of the Delphi Technique." SOUTHERN REVIEW OF PUBLIC ADMINISTRATION 3 (March 1980): 444-62.

The Delphi method is an analytic tool that is designed for anonymously securing the opinions of a group of experts via a series of questionnaires. According to Dillman, it is intended to complement the budgetary concepts such as Planning, Programming, Budgeting Systems, Zero Base Budgeting, and traditional methods of budgeting. Delphi systematically considers previously neglected dimensions of cost-benefit problems. The author concludes that the Delphi budgeting model requires revision before it can be practical.

Dodd, Lawrence C., and Schott, Richard L. CONGRESS AND THE ADMINI-STRATIVE STATE. New York: John Wiley and Sons, 1979. 364 p.

Dodd and Schott examine historical development (revealing each institution's impact on the other rather than analyzing congressional "control" of administration), congressional oversight (not only studies the work of committees and subcommittees but looks at the total range of congressional activities affecting the bureaucracy), and policymaking and policy implementation in the administrative state (pointing out recent developments which may encourage greater subsystem complexity, increased autonomy at the bureau level, and a more insulated and less responsive policy process within the executive branch). This broad, integrated treatment of congressional-bureaucratic relations is based on current literature and the authors' experience in Washington.

Drucker, Peter F. "The Deadly Sins in Public Administration." PUBLIC AD-MINISTRATION REVIEW 40 (March-April 1980): 103-6.

Drucker's "deadly sins" include 1) making sure that a program will not have results is to have a lostly objective (i.e., health care, aid to the disadvantaged); 2) trying several things at once is guaranteed to produce nonperformance; 3) believing that "fat is beautiful" despite the obvious fact that mass does not do work, but that brains and muscle do; 4) doing something on a grand scale at the first attempt will bring disaster; 5) making sure that you cannot learn from experience is a prescription for nonperformance; 6) and the daming and most common ailment of the inability to abandon when an administrative program is failing. The author maintains that "a public service program that does not conduct itself in contemplation of its own mortality will very soon become incapable of performance."

Eichner, Alfred S., and Brecher, Charles M. CONTROLLING SOCIAL EXPEN-DITURES: THE SEARCH FOR OUTPUT MEASURES. New York: Universe Books, 1979. 224 p.

The authors address how domestic programs in education, health, mental health, child welfare, social service, and public assistance can be administered more effectively. They explain how measuring the output of such programs can be overcome by the creation of an information analog utilizing particular kinds of data about individuals being served by the programs. They use New York City as a laboratory and report on the success in actually deriving measures for the employment training programs operated by NYC. This book should be of interest to officials with responsibility for human resources programs.

Fesler, James. PUBLIC ADMINISTRATION. Englewood Cliffs, N.J.: Prentice-Hall, 1980. 384 p.

Felser describes, critically analyzes, and interrelates administrative theories and practices in an attempt to improve understanding of the administration of governmental affairs. Focusing primarily on the American national government, his problem-oriented approach emphasizes those problems which are persistent or recurrent, the solutions attempted, and the causes of policy successes and failures. He believes that the most effective approach to public administration is a sustained descriptive and analytical thrust toward understanding one complete politico-administrative system. A comprehensive review of rational, programmed, adjudicative, incremental, and participative decision-making models is included.

Florestano, Patricia S., and Gordon, Stephen B. "Public vs. Private: Small Government Contracting with the Private Sector." PUBLIC ADMINISTRATION REVIEW 40 (January-February 1980): 29-34. Tables.

The authors state that administrators agree strongly that contracting out provides a better quality service and, somewhat less strongly, agree that the service costs less. They conclude that the potential for public-private contracting is yet untapped. This essay is based upon a four-page questionnaire to 803 state and local government member agencies of the National Institute of Governmental Purchasing.

Foster, John L. "Role Orientation in Bureaucracy." SOUTHERN REVIEW OF PUBLIC ADMINISTRATION 3 (March ·1980): 487-513.

This essay reviews the literature of bureaucratic roles and suggests an alternative form of role concept. The author examines the usefulness of the alternative form with data drawn from officials in the Atlanta, Georgia, Model Cities experiment. Foster presents two general hypotheses: 1) Both bureaucratic orientation and ambition should be associated with variations in several forms of bureaucratic attitudes; 2) The effects of orientation and ambition should be relatively independent of each other. He concludes that there is support for the two general hypotheses.

Fritschler, A. Lee, and Ross, Bernard H. BUSINESS REGULATION AND GOVERNMENT DECISION MAKING. Cambridge, Mass.: Winthrop Publishers, 1980. 256 p.

Fritschler and Ross examine the issues and procedures of government decisionmaking, specifically from the standpoint of the business executive. They assist executives knowledgeable about management of their own corporations but who need to know how their corporations affect and are affected by government. The authors note that government spending decisions and regulations shape and change executive decisions of what is produced, how it is produced and distributed, and who is involved in the production process. Governments have become central to the environment in which executives operate.

Gilbert, G. Ronald, and Sauter, John V. "The Federal Executive Institute's Executive Development Programs." PUBLIC PERSONNEL MANAGEMENT 8 (November-December 1979): 407-15.

This article reviews some of the practices of executive development in the federal government. The authors identify some of the discrepancies existing between espoused policy in federal executive development and that which is actually practiced. They note that executive development (XD) is undergoing some changes as a result of the Civil Service Reform Act of 1978 and that the Senior Executive Service (SES) represents a substantial change in the way executives will be selected, evaluated, and paid.

Golembiewski, Robert T., and Proehl, Carl W., Jr. "Public Sector Applications of Flexible Workhours: A Review of Available Experience." PUBLIC ADMINISTRATION REVIEW 40 (January-February 1980): 72-85. Tables.

The authors analyze major characteristics of public sector flex-time (F-T) applications, reveal major behavioral effects, examine major employee attitudinal effects, and explain the importance of supervisory attitudes regarding flexible workhours. "Many see F-T as a low cost fringe benefit--as improving the quality of work and as impacting on employee attitudes and turnover--but not especially relevant to productivity." This essay presents an excellent overview of public sector implementation of flexible workhours.

Hale, George E. "Federal Courts and the State Budgetary Process." ADMINISTRATION AND SOCIETY 11 (November 1979): 357-68.

The author stresses that judicial activism already is an important influence on the state budgetary process. He maintains that the rise of an activist judiciary transfers power from elected executives and legislators, frustrates retrenchment, opens up new opportunities for budgetary games, and both demands creative public management and narrows the range of administrative discretion. It is somewhat surprising that so little thinking about public budgeting reflects the new role of the courts.

Hargrove, Erwin C. "The Bureaucratic Politics of Evaluation: A Case Study of the Department of Labor." PUBLIC ADMINISTRATION REVIEW 40 (March-April 1980): 150-59.

Hargrove proposes that attitudes toward knowledge influence bureaucratic behavior and that these attitudes are derived in part
from bureaucratic positions and in part from the professional modes
of thought which reside in different governmental roles. He notes
that the federal role under CETA was loosely supervisory and evaluative rather than tightly administrative. He concludes that the
structure of the CETA programs provides possible remedies for de-
ficiences of method and of organization.

Hargrove, Erwin C., and Dean, Gillian. "Federal Authority and Grassroots
Accountability: The Case of CETA." POLICY ANALYSIS 6 (Spring 1980):
127-49.

After noting that the Comprehensive Employment and Training Act
of 1973 (CETA) assumed that prime sponsors would join local political accountability and planning for local labor market needs, the
authors examine the federal role and assumptions guiding other block
grant programs. They compare these programs and conclude that
the bureaucratic political incentives of implementors were initially
ignored, but that program failings can be improved by appealing
to political incentives. They point out that "capable institutions
develop slowly and are subtly molded by political and organization
contexts. We see the nurturing of such institutions as the primary
federal task."

Hopkins, Anne H. "Perceptions of Employment Discrimination in the Public
Sector." PUBLIC ADMINISTRATION REVIEW 40 (March-April 1980): 131-37.
Tables.

Based on a mail questionnaire sent to public employees in five states,
the author examines the scope and correlates of employee perceptions
of discrimination based on age, sex, and race. She concludes that
almost one in five state employees perceive some form of job discrimination. Although nonwhites are proportionately more likely to
feel racial discrimination, large proportions of women perceive sex
discrimination, and large proportions of older workers perceive age
discrimination.

Karl, Barry D. "Louis Brownlow." PUBLIC ADMINISTRATION REVIEW 39
(November-December 1979): 511-16.

The author celebrates the one hundredth birthday of Brownlow en-
thusiastically and without reservation. Noting that Brownlow's contributions to the field of public administration were largely in the
creation of professional organizations, Karl recognizes that it is
difficult to memorialize men like Brownlow in a genuinely appropriate form. Karl comments: "He understood something historians often have to struggle to understand: that the organization of memory
is the halfway house between truth and reality that makes history an
art, not a science." When Karl recalls the life and times of Louis

Brownlow, he returns to the very basics of American public administration, the discipline and the challenge.

Klingner, Donald E. PUBLIC PERSONNEL MANAGEMENT: CONCEPTS AND STRATEGIES. Englewood Cliffs, N.J.: Prentice-Hall, 1980. 384 p.

Klingner emphasizes the importance of law, the perspective of the individual employee, and the close relationship between public personnel management and public policy. He evaluates the effectiveness of different techniques, includes laws, objectives, and techniques related to a range of public agencies, ties personnel managment to behavioral science research and public administration, probes often-neglected subjects such as personnel management information systems, occupational safety and health, and career-life planning, and includes extensive analysis of recent changes in federal civil service, labor relations, and affirmative action programs.

Kovach, Kenneth A. "The F.L.R.A. and Federal Employee Unionism." PUBLIC PERSONNEL MANAGEMENT 9 (January-February 1980): 7-10.

The author examines federal sector labor relations from the original executive orders of the early 1960s through the 1979 Civil Service Reform Act and Reorganization Plan No. 2. He devotes special attention to the Federal Labor Relations Authority and its roles as overseer of federal labor policy.

Lane, Frederick S., ed. MANAGING STATE AND LOCAL GOVERNMENT: CASES AND READINGS. New York: St. Martin's Press, 1980. 509 p.

This text deals exclusively with state and local issues and covers organizational behavior and structure, employee relations, budgeting, planning, policy implementation and analysis, program evaluation, productivity improvement, and cutback management topics. Lane spans the entire field of public services and policy and includes essays on human services, criminal justice, health care, transportation, recreation, education, environmental protection, and sanitation. This book is comprehensive and carefully designed for teaching the concepts and skills of public management in the 1980s.

Langbein, Laura Irwin. DISCOVERING WHETHER PROGRAMS WORK: A GUIDE TO STATISTICAL METHODS FOR PROGRAM EVALUATION. Santa Monica, Calif.: Goodyear Publishing Co., 1980. 225 p.

Langbein offers a practical guide to the statistical methods used to determine whether public policies are achieving their intended goals. She provides a complete overview of the process and principles of evaluation research and the advantages and disadvantages of each method are discussed with specific examples from the arenas of deadlines, budgets, and self-interest. Langbein stresses the effect of the

political environment on evaluations as well as the statistical problems of causal inference. She encourages evaluators to select the
combination of methods most appropriate for the specific situation
which they confront.

Levine, Charles H., ed. MANAGING FISCAL STRESS: THE CRISIS IN THE
PUBLIC SECTOR. Chatham, N.J.: Chatham House Publishers, 1980. 344 p.

Levine explores the political and economic problems, constraints,
alternatives, and choices available to public managers concerned
with fiscal stress. He probes a new field of inquiry and suggests
that the readings in this volume are intended to be both exploratory and suggestive--to explore the causes, constraints, and consequences of fiscal stress and to suggest alternatives for balancing
fiscal solvency with adequate, equitable, and stable levels of public
services and benefits. Sections include discussions of the causes
of fiscal stress, decision making, resources, productivity, and
cutbacks.

Lewin, David; Horton, Raymond D.; and Kuhn, James W. COLLECTIVE BAR-
GAINING AND MANPOWER UTILIZATION IN BIG CITY GOVERNMENTS.
New York: Universe Books, 1979. 158 p.

The authors examine collective bargaining impacts in contrasting
labor relations, political, and public employment patterns of Los
Angeles, Chicago, and New York City. They analyze specific impacts which affect manpower utilization and productivity, the effectiveness of management officials, the effect of unions on public
employee wages, and the effect of collective bargaining on personnel administration.

Lindblom, Charles E. "Still Muddling, Not Yet Through." PUBLIC ADMINI-
STRATION REVIEW 39 (November-December 1979): 517-26.

The author gives a 1980 edition of his public administration classic
("The Science of Muddling Through," PUBLIC ADMINISTRATION
REVIEW, 1959). For Lindblom, "muddling through" is incrementalism. "Many critics of incrementalism believe that doing better
usually means turning away from incrementalism. Incrementalists
believe that for complex problem solving it usually means practicing incrementalism more skillfully and turning away from it only
rarely." Lindblom's current commentary is just as provocative
as was his thinking more than twenty years earlier.

Lynn, Laurence E., Jr. DESIGNING PUBLIC POLICY: A CASEBOOK ON THE
ROLE OF POLICY ANALYSIS. Santa Monica, Calif.: Goodyear Publishing Co.,
1980. 500 p.

This text includes an anthology of cases which are designed to improve the policymaker's ability to deal with complex policy issues
in actual practice. Because policy problems are often ill defined
and resistant to formal analytic techniques, the cases emphasize
that the policy analyst must be creative with respect to the unique

problems and needs of the decision maker. Every case illustrates advantages and disadvantages of specific analytic concepts and techniques.

Lynn, Naomi B., and Vaden, Richard E. "Federal Executives: Initial Reactions to Change." ADMINISTRATION AND SOCIETY 12 (May 1980): 101-20. Table.

The authors mailed a questionnaire to federal executives to determine their attitudes toward proposed reforms to be included in the 1978 Civil Service Reform Act. This article examines their apprehensions toward the proposed legislation. The most frequently expressed theme was the fear that the new legislation would lead to politicization of the civil service. Other themes were: affirmative action, bureaucratic image, bonuses, cronyism, managerial power, pay, performance evaluations, and unions. These themes offer insights into political and internal dynamics of instituting bureaucratic change.

Matlack, William F. STATISTICS FOR PUBLIC POLICY AND MANAGEMENT. Belmont, Calif.: Duxbury Press, 1980. 480 p.

This is a statistics text specifically written for students whose careers will be in the public sector. Matlack attempts to provide all the elements needed to give public administration students a clear and understandable look at statistics, in a nonthreatening style with numerous learning aids and a wide range of applications and examples from the public sector. Examples are drawn from such areas as health care, education, the environment, psychology, race and sex discrimination, and the administration of justice.

Mowitz, Robert J. THE DESIGN OF PUBLIC DECISION SYSTEMS. Baltimore: University Park Press, 1980. 168 p.

Mowitz describes the concepts and technologies for designing comprehensive governmental decision systems that are politically responsive, research-oriented, and information-sensitive. His basic hypothesis is that the capacity to govern, or to deal with uncertainty and complexity, is dependent upon the redesign of existing systems and that such redesign is possible. Mowitz describes recent experience with program budgeting decision systems and discusses methods for dealing with issues related to establishing a comprehensive program decision structure.

Murphy, Jerome T. GETTING THE FACTS: A FIELDWORK GUIDE FOR EVALUATORS AND POLICY ANALYSTS. Santa Monica, Calif.: Goodyear Publishing Co., 1980. 261 p.

Murphy provides a working guide to public program evaluation using nonquantitative methods, including interviewing, transient observa-

tion, and document analysis. He covers major problems in gathering facts, including distinguishing fact from rumor, coping with
officials who are reluctant to describe the workings of their programs, dealing with one's own biases, and deciding when enough
data has been collected to begin a report. Murphy offers detailed
advice on interviewing procedures and outlines the standards and
techniques of writing a good report.

Musolf, Lloyd D., and Seidman, Harold. "The Blurred Boundaries of Public
Administration." PUBLIC ADMINISTRATION REVIEW 40 (March-April 1980):
124-30.

Using government sponsored enterprises as an illustration, Musolf and
Seidman call attention to the blurred boundaries of public administration and stress the desirability of establishing clear lines of
accountability in a constitutional democracy. They conclude that
"frequent resort to twilight zone organizations derives not so much
from their intrinsic qualities as from an unfortunate rigidity and
unimaginativeness in government regulations." The authors point
out that the alternative of employing government-sponsored enterprises and other extra-governmental institutions should not be ex-
cluded when their superiority to other institutions can be demonstrated.

Nachmias, David, ed. THE PRACTICE OF POLICY EVALUATION. New York:
St. Martin's Press, 1980. 478 p.

This is a collection of twenty-one evaluation studies. Controversial policy issues include income maintenance, human resources
development, equality of educational opportunity, equal employment and economic opportunity, housing and community development, law enforcement and criminal justice, health care, and
energy and transportation. Nachmias illustrates both quantitative
and qualitative methodologies and impact, process, and cost-
effectiveness evaluations. This text is both timely and comprehensive.

Nakamura, Robert T., and Smallwood, Frank. THE POLITICS OF POLICY
IMPLEMENTATION. New York: St. Martin's Press, 1980. 203 p.

The authors offer an innovative and integrated approach to policy
studies literature providing a conceptual overview of the policy
process by analyzing different environments which determine how
policy is made, implemented, and evaluated. They illustrate how
a program can be guided from formulation through implementation
and includes illustrations from employment programs, urban programs,
education, transportation, immigration, science and technology,
civil rights, and medical services. This text was designed for
courses in policy implementation or public policy courses.

Addendum

Osborn, Richard N.; Hunt, James G.; and Jauch, Lawrence R. ORGANIZA-
TION THEORY: AN INTEGRATED APPROACH. New York: John Wiley
and Sons, 1980. 611 p.

> This text includes a systematic top-down organization of chapters
> in order that one moves from the environment and total organiza-
> tion down into the organization, ending at the work unit level.
> The authors consistently use variables to predict and explain vari-
> ous aspects of organization and subunit "success." Sections of
> this textbook include discussions of the criteria for evaluating or-
> ganizational success, the environment of organizations, organiza-
> tional characteristics, and subsystems, groups, and leadership. Ex-
> amples from many different kinds of organizations and many differ-
> ent organizational environments are used. The text includes a
> mix of public and private, large and small organizations.

Pattenaude, Richard L., and Landis, Larry M. "Consultants and Technology
Transfer in the Public Sector." PUBLIC ADMINISTRATION REVIEW 39
(September-October 1979): 414-20.

> The author points out that consultant activity is potential technol-
> ogy transfer. They believe that consultants can be a rich and
> valuable source of technology-information transfer for public or-
> ganizations. They address the technology transfer capacity of
> leadership (transfer potential "medium"), of management (transfer
> potential "low"), of analysis (transfer potential "high"), and of
> augmentation (transfer potential "low"). This is a very useful ana-
> lysis of the role of consultants in the public service.

Pursely, Robert D., and Snortland, Neil. MANAGING GOVERNMENT OR-
GANIZATION: AN INTRODUCTION TO PUBLIC ADMINISTRATION. Belmont, Calif.: Duxbury Press, 1980. 640 p.

> The authors emphasize the managerial, on-the-job usefulness of
> the subject matter, whether the topic be budgeting systems or
> scientific management. They prepare readers for entering the
> public sector by showing how things get done at the policy-making
> level as well as at entry level and at middle management. Case
> studies are integrated throughout each chapter to illustrate real-
> world issues and to induce students to think about the types of
> situations which they will encounter later. Pursley and Snortland
> include full chapters on administrative ethics, intergovernmental
> relations, collective bargaining, affirmative action and equal em-
> ployment, government revenues and expenditures, finance, and
> budgeting.

Radin, Beryl A. "Leadership Training for Women in State and Local Government." PUBLIC PERSONNEL MANAGEMENT 9 (March-April 1980): 52-60.
Table.

Radin presents some of the problems and suggests some solutions for the woman employed at the state-local level of government. This essay is based on a survey of one hundred women in three levels of state-local government.

Ranson, Stewart; Hinings, Bob; and Greenwood, Royston. "The Structure of Organizational Structures." ADMINISTRATIVE SCIENCE QUARTERLY 25 (March 1980): 1-17.

This article examines the problem of explaining how organizational structures change over time. Its focus is both specific and traditional. The authors argue for a more unified theoretical and methodological analysis that is adequate at the levels of meaning and causality. They disagree with the typical connection of structures as a formal framework counterposed to the interactive patterns of organizational members. They stress the way structures are continually produced and recreated by members so that the structures embody and become constitutive of their provinces of meaning.

Riggs, Fred W. "The Ecology and Context of Public Administration: A Comparative Perspective." PUBLIC ADMINISTRATION REVIEW 40 (March-April 1980): 107-15.

Riggs believes that we need "to view our administrative problems in both an ecological framework--related to the increasingly acute environmental problems not only of the United States but of the whole world--and also in a context of interdependency, taking into account the relations of bureaucratic to extra-bureaucratic institutions and those of central to peripheral countries in our growingly interdependent world system." The author maintains that public administration's perspective should be "an environed and contextualized open system--rather than a closed and self-sufficient system." Riggs emphasizes that an "open system" is even more significant at a time when the international climate of an increasingly tumultous world is fraught with growing tensions.

Roos, Leslie L., Jr., and Hall, Roger I. "Influence Diagrams and Organizational Power." ADMINISTRATIVE SCIENCE QUARTERLY 25 (March 1980): 57-71.

Roos and Hall examine the use of influence diagrams to help understand political processes within organizations. This technique is illustrated through a case study of a new extended care facility connected to a hospital. The authors discuss the improvement in performance that may be derived from the use of influence diagrams and the implications of the case for important issues in organization theory, particularly those dealing with internal politics and conflict.

Addendum

Rosenbloom, David H. "Kaiser vs. Weber: Perspective From the Public Sector." PUBLIC PERSONNEL MANAGEMENT 8 (November-December 1979): 393-96.

> Brian Weber is a white male who was hired at Kaiser's Gramercy plant in 1969. In 1974 Kaiser announced that it was offering a total of nine positions in three on-the-job training programs for skilled craft jobs. Weber applied for all three programs but was not selected. The successful candidates--five black and four white-- were chosen in accordance with 50 percent minority admission quota mandated under the 1974 collective bargaining agreement. Two of the successful black applicants had less seniority than Weber, and Weber brought class action. The author states that the justices' support for Kaiser in this case makes it evident that a majority of the Supreme Court is sympathetic to affirmative action.

Sauser, William I., Jr. "Evaluating Employee Performance: Needs, Problems and Possible Solutions." PUBLIC PERSONNEL MANAGEMENT 9 (January-February 1980): 11-18.

> Sauser considers some of the benefits of a well constructed evaluation system, examines the merits and drawbacks of two sources of performance information, and discusses four possible solutions in the performance rating process. He claims that unfair decisions are frequently made about employees based upon such biased sources as hearsay and reputation. He emphasizes that a fair employee performance evaluation system enhances organizational effectiveness.

Shapek, Raymond A. "The Intergovernmental Personnel Act Program and Management Capacity Development." PUBLIC PERSONNEL MANAGEMENT 9 (March-April 1980): 75-85. Tables.

> Shapek discusses the evolution and successes of the Intergovernmental Personnel Act in its capacity-building role. He believes that the Act represents one of the rare success stories in federal program development. He notes that while IPA is highly successful and well regarded, this legislation continues to remain a comparatively small grant-in-aid program.

Skok, James E. "Budgetary Politics and Decision-Making: Development of an Alternative Hypothesis for State Government." ADMINISTRATION AND SOCIETY 11 (February 1980): 445-60.

> Based on fiscal years 1975-76 and 1976-77 in Pennsylvania state government, the author develops a hypothesis which accurately reflects the empirical events of the actual budgeting process during these periods and which takes into account other recent empirical research findings. Skok concludes that there are two distinct styles

of budgetary decision making--distributive and redistributive--in state government budgeting. Rational-comprehensive approaches and techniques have some success in influencing the final outcome in a distributive mode whereas rational comprehensive analysis is replaced by partisan-mutual-adjustment techniques when the process turns from distributive to redistributive.

Al-Teraifi, Al-Agab A. "Promotion in the Sudanese Civil Service." PUBLIC PERSONNEL MANAGEMENT 9 (January-February 1980): 19-23.

The author examines promotion and advancement policies and practices in the Sudanese civil service. He finds weaknesses to be greater emphasis on seniority (regardless of the employee's performance) rather than merit, absence of uniform standards of promotion, automatic grants of annual increments, and the predominance of ascriptive rather than achievement criteria in personnel promotion and advancement.

Thomas, John Clayton. "Governmental Overload in the United States: A Problem of Distributive Policies?" ADMINISTRATION AND SOCIETY 11 (February 1980): 371-391.

Thomas explains that American government has become "overloaded" in recent years, that it is costing too much while achieving too little. Government excesses and overload as a function of distributive policies and politics are considered as well as the merits of various technical and political approaches, including the mid-1970s "tax revolt." The author argues that government overload is based in large part on an excess of distributive policies, policies which give benefits to one or more groups, without much of a redistributive impact.

_____. "The Growth of American Public Expenditure: Recent Trends and Their Implications." PUBLIC ADMINISTRATION REVIEW 40 (March-April 1980): 160-65.

Thomas' findings suggest that public expenditures have been growing as a share of the total American economy at least since World War II, that the responsibility for that growth must be shared at least equally by the federal government and state-local governments rather than being laid primarily on the federal government, and that the growth may mean the evolution of a kind of a peculiarly American welfare state without a pronounced redistributive impact. Despite growing concern over the growth of American public expenditures, there is no consensus on the nature of that growth.

Thompson, Frank J. "Professionalism, Mistrust of Politicians and the Receptivity of Civil Servants to Procedural Buffers: The Case of Personnel Officers." MIDWEST REVIEW OF PUBLIC ADMINISTRATION 13 (September 1979): 143-56. Tables.

This essay examines two sets of related hypotheses: 1) that certain work-related characteristics (especially professionalism) precipitate greater political mistrust among administrators; 2) that, in turn, this mistrust generates greater receptivity to procedural buffers. The author emphasizes the need for caution in considering the sources and implications of political mistrust among public administrators and indicates that contrary to some speculation, no simple relationship exists between greater political mistrust and professionalism.

Urban, Michael E. "Theory and Ideology in Soviet Administration: A Rejoinder to Vidmer." ADMINISTRATION AND SOCIETY 12 (May 1980): 93-99.

Urban criticizes the idea of a "Soviet administrative paradigm" as advocated in Richard Vidmer's essay (see next entry). Urban maintains that Vidmer's paradigm is found wanting on a number of conceptual grounds, in particular, how do we select and deploy the concepts which we use to explain the social world?, and what is socialism? Urban points out that Vidmer's "Soviet administrative paradigm" is replaced by the concept of ideology which is to account for observable patterns in the Soviet literature on administration and to explain the form taken by these patterns.

Vidmer, Richard F. "Administrative Science in the USSR: Doctrinal Constraints on Inquiry." ADMINISTRATION AND SOCIETY 12 (May 1980): 69-92.

Despite great diversity and apparent confusion in the field, Vidmer concludes that there is an identifiable paradigm which units theorists of otherwise highly divergent perspectives. He believes that the Soviet paradigm in administrative science "modernizes" the traditional categories of political economy into systems or cybernetic terminology and focuses on the rational aspects of organizational activity. He states that the Soviet paradigm conspicuously avoids concepts that could undermine the imagery of "optimal" performance. While the general Soviet paradigm itself is unlikely to break down, there are prospects for change within various sub-categories.

Walker, David B. "Constitutional Revision, Incremental Retrenchment, or Real Reform: An Analysis of Current Efforts to Curb Federal Growth." BUREAUCRAT 9 (Spring 1980): 35-47.

Walker addresses the issues of how government can be made representative and responsive as well as responsible and restrained. He describes three schools of reform which include ways and means of curbing federal government growth in the spending and/or revenue areas. He explains the popularity of "Pinwheel Federalism" which

emerges from direct federal links to practically all subnational
governments and the tendency to accord equal treatment to all
public interest groups, regardless of their functional and jurisdictional positions within the fifty state-local fiscal-servicing systems.
Walker's essay is an excellent commentary on American federalism
and intergovernmental relations in the 1980s.

Welborn, David M., and Brown, Anthony E. "Power and Politics in Federal
Regulatory Commissions." ADMINISTRATION AND SOCIETY 12 (May 1980):
37-68.

> The authors state that patterns of power and political processes
> within public agencies are poorly understood. They examine seven
> federal regulatory commissions to ascertain the structure and founda-
> tions of power in them and salient characteristics of their mobiliza-
> tion and utilization. Viewed from a political-economy perspective
> and based upon interview data, this analysis shows that contrary
> to common perceptions, the structure of power in the commissions
> is marked by substantial stability and integration in the position
> of chairmen.

White, Michael J., et al. MANAGING PUBLIC SYSTEMS: ANALYTIC TECH-
NIQUES FOR PUBLIC ADMINISTRATION. Belmont, Calif.: Duxbury Press,
1980. 416 p.

> This volume is an outgrowth of a management analysis course taught
> by the authors at the University of Southern California. Important
> features are the authors' sensitivity to students' backgrounds (i.e.,
> lack of mathematical training), managerial approach, a wide range
> of examples, and topic flexibility. Chapter discussions include
> classical and systems theories, flowcharting concepts, network ana-
> lysis, forecasting for planning, rational and incremental decision
> making, probability theory, payoff matrix, service access, deci-
> sion trees, goal programming, queueing theory, operations research,
> simulation, marginal analysis, cost-benefit analysis, tradeoff analyses,
> program evaluation, and organizational accounting systems.

Wildavsky, Aaron. "Why Amending the Constitution is Essential to Achieving
Self-Control Through Self-Limitation of Expenditure." BUREAUCRAT 9 (Spring
1980): 48-53.

> Wildavsky deals with the difficult questions of whether there are
> statutory alternatives, whether the expenditure limitation is fit
> to discuss in a constitution, and whether it embodies fundamental
> and lasting considerations. He concludes that he "can think of no
> reason why Americans should not limit their government to spend-
> ing a fixed portion of national product." He discusses the criteria
> for a constitutional amendment and its rationale.

Williams, J.D. PUBLIC ADMINISTRATION: THE PEOPLE'S BUSINESS.
Boston: Little, Brown and Co., 1980. 576 p.

> Williams emphasizes the idea that managing the people's business
> is just that--the business of the people. He shows that both
> public servants and the public itself bear responsibility for public
> administration and stand to benefit from what it can offer. He
> demonstrates whether an agency succeeds or fails. Williams' hu-
> manistic emphasis does not preclude extensive treatment of standard
> public administration topics as administrative structures and politics,
> decision-making, budgeting, bureaucracy, and ethics. He offers
> an innovative and refreshing perspective on public sector management.

Wright, Deil S. "Intergovernmental Games: An Approach to Understanding
Intergovernmental Relations." SOUTHERN REVIEW OF PUBLIC ADMINISTRA-
TION 3 (March 1980): 383-403.

> Wright identifies intergovernmental relations games and offers ex-
> planations of each. The games are grouped in two categories of
> IGR participants: state-local officials and officials of the national
> government. He shows that "significant power remains broadly dis-
> persed throughout the system despite strong pressures to pyramid it
> in a few places," that "'green power' or money remains the major
> stake sought by IGR players in spite of a notable 'regulatory' shift
> in recent years," and that human relations and human behavior con-
> tinue to have a significant contribution in understanding intergovern-
> mental relations.

Wriston, Michael J. "In Defense of Bureaucracy." PUBLIC ADMINISTRATION
REVIEW 40 (March-April 1980): 179-83.

> Wriston surmises that the major problem with bureaucracy is not
> whether it is necessary, but what we can do to control it and to
> optimize its use. He concludes that the emergence of bureaucracy
> has been central to achieving and securing a democratic organiza-
> tion has contributed to our present levels of affluence and develop-
> ment. "As a protection against corruption and the willful misuse of
> power, the impersonal and 'inflexible' rules and regulations of bu-
> reaucracy have been a relief and an advance."

Appendix A

ASPA—AMERICAN SOCIETY
FOR PUBLIC ADMINISTRATION

To advance the Science, Process,
and Art of Public Administration

The American Society for Public Administration is a nationwide nonprofit, educational and professional organization dedicated to improved management in the public service through exchange, development, and dissemination of information about public administration.

ASPA has over 20,500 members and subscribers representative of all governmental levels, program responsibilities, and administrative interest. Its membership includes government administrators, teachers, researchers, consultants, students, and civic leaders. In addition, government agencies, universities, and other organizations are affiliated with the Society on an institutional basis.

Since its inception in 1939, ASPA has provided national leadership in advancing the "science, processes, and art" of public administration. It is the only organization of its kind in the United States aiming broadly to improve administration of the public service at all levels of government and in all functional and program fields. In an age of specialization, the Society provides a complementing force for interchange and identification of common public administration goals and objectives.

Society members are located in every state as well as overseas. Many activities are carried out through more than ninety chapters in major governmental and educational centers. The ASPA program includes publications, meetings, education, research, and various special services, all aimed at improved understanding and strengthened administration of the public service.

Appendix A

MEMBERSHIP BENEFITS

Chapter Affiliation

ASPA membership automatically opens the door for participation in a chapter. Affiliating with a local ASPA chapter, an important dimension of Society membership, affords the opportunity to build a strong professional network with other administrators. Chapters provide a local forum for the exchange of public administration experiences, and for involvement in a variety of professional activities.

Section Membership

ASPA members with an interest in specialized areas of public administration are eligible to join one or more sections. Section membership provides opportunities to address specific concerns as part of the nationwide professional network. Areas such as budget and finance, international and comparative administration, minorities in public administration, criminal justice, human resources, science and technology, professional development, and education are the current topics of ASPA sections.

PUBLIC ADMINISTRATION REVIEW (PAR)

Professionals rely on this bimonthly journal as their leading source of information and comment on public administration. PAR presents authoritative research, articles on today's issues, and reviews of publications--all by recognized experts in public administration.

PUBLIC ADMINISTRATION TIMES (PAT)

The Society's newspaper, published twice monthly, reports on timely developments, innovative programs, and prevalent issues in the field of public service. The special RECRUITER section presents a nationwide listing of career opportunities available at all professional levels.

National Conference

More than 2,500 participants attend ASPA's annual national conference. Over 160 program sessions, exhibits, nationally known speakers, and an extensive career placement service highlight conference activities. The conference program examines major issues, current trends in the profession, and areas of special interest.

Regional Conferences

In addition to the national conference, a series of regional conferences is presented. Each conference addresses regional public administration issues through a program including workshops, panels, and guest speakers.

Special Publications

A varied publications series featuring special studies, research findings, and topical symposium reports is available through ASPA.

Professional Study Tours

This special program gives members an exclusive opportunity to participate in educational tours. The Society has recently sponsored tours of the People's Republic of China and the Soviet Union.

Workshops

Workshops are offered to provide training opportunities and to improve professional skills and competence. Program evaluation, budgeting techniques, and productivity improvement are some of the topics presented at ASPA workshops.

Group Insurance

Four comprehensive, low cost group insurance plans are available to members. The plans include Group Term Life Insurance, In-Hospital Indemnity Insurance, Accidental Death and Dismemberment Protection, and Disability Income.

MEMBERSHIP CATEGORIES

Individual--open to any one with an interest in the goals of the society.

Foreign--open to interested persons living abroad, but not receiving mail at an APO or FPO address.

Life--receive all benefits of individual membership plus free basic registration for national conferences, national recognition, and complimentary copies of all special ASPA publications.

Agency Affiliates--agencies, institutions, or organizations are eligible. Special benefits include subscriptions to PAR and PAT, special publications, complimentary basic registrations at the national conference, and a limited number of free advertisements in the RECRUITER.

Appendix B

ASPA NATIONWIDE CHAPTER DIRECTORY
AND 1980 CHAPTER PRESIDENTS

REGION I

CONNECTICUT

Donald W. Goodrich
Director, Municipal Consulting
Connecticut Public Expenditure
  Council
470 Main Street
Portland 06480
(203) 527-8187

MAINE

Barbara Cottrell
Deputy Director State
  Development Office
State Office Building
Augusta 04333
(207) 289-2656

MASSACHUSETTS

James A. Medeiros
U.S. Public Health Service
63 Bridle Path
North Andover 01845
(617) 223-7833

NEW HAMPSHIRE - no chapter

RHODE ISLAND

John W. Stout
Coordinator
Operations Division
Roger Williams College
Bristol 02809
(401) 255-2371

VERMONT

Henry O. Marcy
Director of Operations
State Dept. of Budget and Management
14 Summer Street
St. Johnsbury 05819
(802) 829-2376

REGION II

NEW JERSEY

Thomas H. Bush
Deputy Director
Division of Purchase and Property
State House, Room 305
Trenton 08625
(609) 292-4724

NEW YORK

Capital District (Albany)

William T. Tyrrell
Assistant Director
Division of Alcoholism and
   Alcohol Abuse
44 Holland Avenue
Albany 12229
(518) 474-5121

Central New York (Syracuse)

Steve Kulick
Assistant Crime Control
   Coordinator
123 Ruskin Avenue
Syracuse 13207
(315) 473-5690

Long Island

Frank R. Jones
Deputy Suffolk County Executive
65 Jetson Lane
Hauppauge 11787
(516) 234-2622·

Lower Hudson Valley

Andrew C. Siess
Personnel Technician
Westchester County
148 Martine Avenue, Room 100
White Plains 10601
(914) 682-3176

New York Metropolitan

Marc Holzer
Associate Professor
Government and Public Administration
John Jay College of Criminal Justice
445 West 59th Street
New York 10019
(212) 489-5030

Niagara Frontier

Glenn R. Nellis
Executive Assistant to the President
State University College
1300 Elmwood Avenue
Buffalo 14222
(716) 878-4101

Rochester–Monroe County

Linda M. Bretz
Director, Rochester Public Library
115 South Avenue
Rochester 14604
(716) 428-7345

Southern Tier

Theodore Bassano
Business Manager
Owego Apalachin C.S.C.
36 Talcott Street
Owego 13827
(607) 754-2620

REGION III

National Capital Area

Bradley H. Patterson, Jr.
Senior Staff Member
The Brookings Institution
1775 Massachusetts Avenue, N.W.
Suite 401
Washington, D.C. 20036
(202) 797-6273

REGION IV

DELAWARE

Paul A. Ferguson
Assistant Director
University Health Service
Laurel Hall

DELAWARE Cont.

University of Delaware
Newark 19711
(302) 738-2871

MARYLAND

Iris Gelberg
Assistant Director
Intergovernmental Affairs
Office of Program Development
National Institute of Mental Health
4400 Hornbeam Drive
Rockville 20853
(301) 443-3175

PENNSYLVANIA

Central Pennsylvania

Michael A. Sand
Executive Director
Pennsylvania-Delaware Association
for Community Action
P.O. Box 865
Harrisburg 17108
(717) 238-5558

Northeast Pennsylvania

Dr. Andrew Shaw, Jr.
Institute of Regional Affairs
165 South Franklin
Wilkes College
Wilkes-Barre 18703
(717) 824-4651 ext. 227

Philadelphia

Anthony M. Corbisiero
Deputy Regional Director
Heritage Conservation & Recreation
Service
U.S. Department of Interior
600 Arch Street
Philadelphia 19106
(215) 597-4743

Pittsburgh Area

Joseph Pois
Emeritus Professor of Public
Administration
University of Pittsburgh
GSPIA - 3 GO7
Forbes Quadrangle
230 South Bouquet Street.
Pittsburgh 15260
(412) 624-3627

VIRGINIA

Northern Virginia

Ray Lora
U.S. Marshall Service
1028 North Montana Street
Arlington 22205
(703) 285-1260

Tidewater Area

Marvin W. Lee
Deputy Executive Director
Norfolk Redevelopment & Housing
Authority
6906 Pallster Road
Norfolk 23518
(804) 623-1111

Virginia

Mary Saunders Hale
Director Regional Office
Department of Welfare
5021 Brook Road
Richmond 23227
(804) 264-3050

WEST VIRGINIA

David Williams
West Virginia University
Department of Public Administration
Morgantown 26506
(304) 293-2614

Appendix B

REGION V

ALABAMA

Central Alabama

Ellen C. Austin
Governmental Aids Coordinator
East Alabama Regional Planning
   & Development Commission
P.O. Box 2186
Anniston 36202
(205) 237-6741

Montgomery

Robert Jackson
Planner, Commission on Aging
4426 Plummer Drive
Montgomery 36106
(205) 832-6640

Northern Alabama

Delia W. Black
Career Program Coordinator
U.S. Army
1206 Chandler Road, S.E.
Huntsville 35801
(205) 876-5814

ARKANSAS

Robert Pursley
University of Arkansas
S-106C S. Administration
33rd & University
Little Rock 72204
(501) 569-3195

FLORIDA

Central Florida

Tom Kelly
Volusia County Manager
P.O. Box 429

Central Florida Cont.

Deland 32720
(904) 736-2700

Gold Coast

Phyllis A. Ward
Director Student Services
College of Business & Public Adm.
Florida Atlantic University
Boca Raton 33431
(305) 395-5100

Gulf Coast

James L. Mason
Assistant City Clerk
P.O. Box 1827
Mobile 36601
(205) 438-7411

North Florida

John Thomas
Executive Director
State Association of County
   Commissioners
P.O. Box 549
Tallahassee 32302
(904) 224-3148

Northeast Florida

Frank Reneke
Information Systems Officer
City Hall, Room 200
220 East Bay Street
Jacksonville 32202
(904) 633-3951

South Florida

Walter C. Anders
Administrator
Lutheran Medical Center
2001 East Ridge Village Drive
Miami 33147
(305) 233-8931

Suncoast

Angie G. Mason
Administrative Services Officer
Budget & Management Dept.
P.O. Box 2842
St. Petersburg 33731
(813) 893-7436

Treasure Coast

John Sullivan
Professor, Public Administration
Florida Atlantic University
4706 Australian Avenue
West Palm Beach 33407
(305) 848-1429

GEORGIA

Brad Doss
Institute of Governmental
    Administration
Georgia State University
University Plaza, Box 451
Atlanta 30303
(404) 658-3353

KENTUCKY

Jack Lesley
Administrative Supervisor
Division of Highway Enforcement
State Office Building, Room 212
Frankfort 40622

LOUISIANA - no chapter

MISSISSIPPI

Thommie Stingley, Jr.
City of Jackson
P.O. Box 17
Jackson 39205
(601) 960-1670

NORTH CAROLINA

Central Piedmont

Daniel S. Hoyle, Jr.
Manpower Project Administrator
Mecklenburg County Personnel
    Department
316-E. Morehead Street, #307
Charlotte 28202
(704) 374-3248

Piedmont Triad

John H. Bain
Town Manager
Town of Gibsonville
129 West Main Street
Gibsonville 27249
(919) 449-7035

Research Triangle

Robert W. Morgan
Administrative Assistant
Department of General Services
101 City Hall Plaza
Durham 27702
(919) 683-4100

SOUTH CAROLINA

Lowcountry

Joyce Shillabeer
103 Heritage Street
Summerville 29403
(803) 873-6953

South Carolina

G. Robert Cook
2812 Bratton Street
Columbia 29205
(803) 254-4055

Appendix B

TENNESSEE

East Tennessee

Sandy Kelley
East Tennessee Development
    District
4149 Jomandowa Lane
Knoxville 37919
(615) 584-8553

Memphis-Mid-South

Vicki Reitano
Assistant Manager
Shelby County Government
1309 Glen Oaks
Memphis 38117
(901) 528-3409

Tennessee (Nashville)

Bruce D. Rogers
University of Tennessee
10th and Charlotte
Nashville 37203
(615) 251-1731

REGION VI

ILLINOIS

Central Illinois

Phillip M. Gonet
House Minority Appropriations
    Staff
220 State House
Springfield 62706
(217) 782-5632

Greater Chicago

Dean Eitel
Chief
Environmental Resources Branch

U.S. Army Corps of Engineers
North Central Division
536 South Clark
Chicago 60605
(312) 353-6320

Heart of Illinois

Alexander Crosman
Director
Peoria County Library System
107 Northeast Monroe
Peoria 61602
(309) 679-0778

INDIANA

Roger G. Hollands
Associate Professor
Ball State University
Political Science Department
Muncie 47306
(317) 285-1607

MICHIGAN

Detroit Metropolitan

Mary L. Williams
Ombudsman
20192 Renfrew
Detroit 48221
(313) 224-6243

Huron Valley

Byron Marshal
Administrative Assistant
City Manager Office
Ann Arbor Municipal Bldg.
100 N. 5th Ave., P.O. Box 647
Ann Arbor 48107
(313) 994-2700

Michigan Capital Area

Ilze V. Koch
House Fiscal Agency
3rd Floor -- Roosevelt Bldg.
222 Seymour Street
Lansing 48901
(517) 353-8080

OHIO

Central Ohio

Dr. Frederick Stocker
The Academy for Contemporary
    Problems
1501 Neil Avenue
Columbus 43201
(614) 421-7700

Metropolitan Toledo

Harold White
Health Plus, Executive Director
P.O. Box 8806
Toledo 43623
(419) 473-0500

Miami Valley

James F. Suddath, Jr.
Montgomery County Fiscal
    Administrator
451 W. 3rd Street
P.O. Box 972
Dayton 45422
(513) 225-4735

Northeast Ohio

Mark M. Levin
Assistant to City Manager
2953 Mayfield
Cleveland Heights 44118
(216) 321-0100

WISCONSIN

Milwaukee

Shirl Curtis Abbey
Village Manager Shorewood
3930 North Murray Avenue
Shorewood 53211
(414) 332-4200

Wisconsin Capital

Richard Stauber
Professor
University of Wisconsin
626 Lowell Hall
Department of Governmental Affairs
University Extension
Madison 53706
(608) 262-5951

REGION VII

IOWA

Iowa Capital

Richard Pattenaude
Associate Dean
College of Liberal Arts
Drake University
Des Moines 50311
(515) 271-2011

KANSAS

Kansas (Topeka)

Richard Vaden
College of Business Administration
Kansas State University
Manhattan 66506
(913) 532-6180

Appendix B

Wichita

Marjorie Lee Taylor
Director of Public Affairs
  Education
Wichita State University
  Box 111
Wichita 67208
(316) 689-3686

MINNESOTA

James Nobles
Deputy Legislative Auditor
122 Veterans Service Building
St. Paul 55155
(612) 296-4721

MISSOURI

Central Missouri

William Brown
Deputy Director
MO Dept. of Consumer Affairs
3242 S. Ten Mile Drive
Jefferson City 65101
(314) 751-4946

Greater Kansas City

Richard F. Davis
General Manager
Kansas City Area Transportation
  Authority
1350 East 17th Street
Kansas City 64108
(816) 471-6600

St. Louis Metropolitan

George Otte
Professor
St. Louis University
5214 Finkman
St. Louis 63109
(314) 658-3939

NEBRASKA

Hans Brisch
Assistant Vice President
  for Academic Affairs
University of Nebraska
3835 Holdrege
Lincoln 68583
(402) 472-2861

NORTH DAKOTA

Bismarck/Mandan

Robert J. Olheiser
Director
State Laboratories Department
1210 Albany Drive
Bismarck 58501
(701) 258-7832

OKLAHOMA

Dave Carmichael
Fed. Aviation Administration
8809 Shilling Shore Court
Oklahoma City 73132
(405) 686-4524

SOUTH DAKOTA

Siouxland

Dr. Michael J. Beville, Jr.
Director
Governmental Research Bureau
The University of South Dakota
Vermillion 57069
(605) 677-5242

REGION VIII

ARIZONA

Christine Gibbs
Legislative Analyst
Salt River Project
P.O. Box 1980
Phoenix 85001
(602) 273-2654

COLORADO

Colorado

Gordon Von Stroh
Director, School of Public
  Management
University of Denver
2881 South Sidney Court
Denver 80231
(303) 753-3435

Southern Colorado

Ms Jim Alice Scott
430 Westmark
Colorado Springs 80906
(303) 471-6868

NEVADA

Las Vegas

Robert E. Campbell
City of Henderson
243 Water Street
Henderson 89015
(702) 565-8921

Reno

John MacIntyre
Washoe County Manager
P.O. Box 11130
Reno 89520
(702) 785-4179

NEW MEXICO

Donald W. Smithburg
University of New Mexico
2413 Ada Place, N.E.
Albuquerque 87106
(505) 277-3560

TEXAS

Ark-La-Tex

Ned C. Muse
Assistant City Manager
P.O. Box 1967
Texarkana 75501
(214) 794-3434

Centex

Marvin S. Wheat
Office Manager
Texas Employment Commission
P.O. Box 2300
Waco 76703
(817) 754-5421

Houston Area

Paul I. Davis
Deputy General Manager
Gulf Coast Waste Disposal
  Authority
910 Bay Area Boulevard
Houston 77055
(713) 488-4115

North Texas

Ross Clinchy
North Texas State University
3837 Alta Vista Lane
Dallas 75229
(214) 358-0005

Sam Houston

Rhoda Philby

Sam Houston Cont.

President
Philby Business Mgmt. Servs
P.O. Box 2266
San Antonio 78298
(512) 224-6150

UTAH

Central Utah

Dee W. Henderson
Institute of Public Management
Brigham Young University
Provo 84602
(801) 374-1211 ext. 4221

Utah

R. Thayne Robson
Executive Director
Bureau of Economic and Business
  Research
University of Utah
Salt Lake City 84112
(801) 581-7274

REGION IX

ALASKA

Southcentral Alaska

Principal Administrative Officer
Department of Transportation
Municipality of Anchorage
Pouch 6-650
Anchorage 99502
(907) 264-4246

HAWAII (Honolulu)

Thomas W. Gilson
Professor
University of Hawaii
2404 Maile Way

HAWAII (Honolulu) Cont.

Honolulu 96822
(808) 948-8737

IDAHO - no chapter

MONTANA

Richard Haines
Professor
Department of Political Science
Montana State University
Bozeman 59717
(406) 994-4141

OREGON

Kenneth Maul
Deputy Director
Public Employment Retirement
  System
Box 73
Portland 97207
(503) 229-6027

WASHINGTON

Evergreen

James E. Todd
Consultant
4503 N.E. 93rd Street
Seattle 98115
(206) 524-7049

WYOMING - no chapter

REGION X

CALIFORNIA

Bakersfield

W.T. Wallace

Bakersfield Cont.

Assistant Auditor-Controller
3616 Elm Street
Bakersfield 93301
(805) 861-2331

Central California

Karl Svenson
Professor
California State University
North Maple & East Shaw Streets
Fresno 93744
(209) 487-1005

East Kern County

Linda Roush
Operations Research Analyst
China Lake Naval Weapons Center
537 South Allen
Ridgecrest 93555
(714) 939-3032

Inland Empire

Robert Tremont
Budget Officer
3900 Main Street
Riverside 92504
(714) 787-7608

Los Angeles Metropolitan

Lois Smith-Bupp
Director, Department of Humanities
   & Social Sciences
University Extension, UCLA
10995 Le Conte Avenue, #711
Los Angeles 90024
(213) 825-1545

Monterey Bay Area

Lydia Tolmacheff
Personnel Officer
200 Lincoln Avenue
Salinas 93901
(408) 758-7254

Orange County

Carol J. Gandy
Executive Assistant
Board of Supervisors
P.O. Box 687
Santa Ana 92701
(714) 834-3110

Sacramento

Cristy Jensen
Assistant Director
Public Affairs Center
University of So. California
1007 7th Street
Sacramento 95814
(916) 422-6911

San Diego

Madeline Marini
Planned Parenthood
2100 5th Avenue
San Diego 92101
(714) 231-1282

San Francisco Bay Area

Daniel M. Sprague
Program Coordinator & Lecturer
University Southern California
Claremont Hotel
Berkeley 94705
(415) 841-1316

San Joaquin Valley

C. Gregory Buntz
Associate Professor
University of the Pacific
School of Business & Public
   Administration

San Joaquin Valley Cont.

Stockton 95211
(209) 946-2476

Greater Santa Clara Valley

Sheila A. Stevens
5644 Orchard Park Drive
San Jose 95123
(408) 299-4311

Appendix C

NASPAA—NATIONAL ASSOCIATION OF SCHOOLS
OF PUBLIC AFFAIRS AND ADMINISTRATION

NASPAA OBJECTIVE AND 1980 COUNCIL MEMBERS

The National Association of Schools of Public Affairs and Public Administration (NASPAA) is an institutional membership organization of more than 225 programs of public affairs and public administration education, and associate members dedicated to the improvement of public service education.

The Association is chartered under the laws of the District of Columbia, and serves as a national center for information about programs and development in the field. NASPAA also strives to set goals and advance standards of educational excellence for the public service as well as represent the concerns and interest of member institutions in making national policy on public affairs and administration education and research matters.

The Association advances this purpose by:

      promoting cooperation among member institutions
      providing services to member institutions
      encouraging curriculum development and innovation in
            education and providing a forum for the discussion of education issues
            developing appropriate standards for educational programs and re-
            viewing the quality of those programs
            strengthening the research base of education for public affairs and
            administration, etc.

The organization of NASPAA consists of a president and president-elect, plus a 12 person executive council elected from the membership. Much of the work of the Association is done through a series of committees. There are standing committees on the constitution, standards and peer review.

NASPAA manages a number of programs of interest to public administration education programs and holds an annual conference on public service education.

Appendix D

NASPAA 1980 NATIONAL REPRESENTATIVES

ALABAMA

Gerald W. Johnson, Actg. Head
Dept. of Political Science
Auburn University
School of Arts & Sciences
Auburn, AL 36830

Edward B. Lewis, Chair
Dept. of Urban Studies
University of Alabama
University Station
Birmingham, AL 35294

Thomas Vocino, Chair
Dept. of Government
Auburn Univ. at Montgomery
Montgomery, AL 36100

Philip B. Coulter, Chair
Dept. of Political Science
University of Alabama, Drawer I
University, AL 35486

ALASKA

Garth N. Jones, Professor
School of Bus. & Public Adm.
University of Alaska
3221 Providence Drive
Anchorage, AK 99500

ARIZONA

Nicholas L. Henry, Director
Center for Public Affairs
Arizona State University
Tempe, AZ 85281

Don L. Bowen, Professor
Dept. of Public Administration
University of Arizona
4702 E. Burning Tree Place
Tucson, AZ 85718

CALIFORNIA

Jack Goldsmith, Professor
Public Policy & Adm. Dept.
California State College
9001 Stockdale Highway
Bakersfield, CA 93309

Steve Weiner, Assoc. Dean
Grad. School of Public Policy
University of California
2607 Hearst Avenue
Berkeley, CA 94720

T. Zane Reeves, Chair
Dept. of Public Adm.
California State Univ., Dom. Hills
1000 E. Victoria Street
Carson, CA 90747

Bryon M. Jackson, Prof.
Coordinator of Public Adm.
California State University
Chico, CA 95929

Alex McCalla, Acting Dean
Graduate School of Administration
University of California
Room 111, Voorhies Hall
Davis, CA 95616

Alan L. Saltzstein, Assoc. Prof.
Coordinator-MPA Program
California State University
800 N. State College Blvd.
Fullerton, CA 92634

Michael H. Smith, Director
Center for Public Policy & Adm.
California State University
25800 Hillary Street
Hayward, CA 94542

Lyman W. Porter, Dean
Graduate School of Adm.
University of California
Irvine, CA 92717

Mel D. Powell, Director
Center for Pub. Policy & Adm.
California State University
1250 Bellflower Boulevard
Long Beach, CA 90840

Barbara Bell, Chair
Dept. of Public Affairs
Pepperdine University
4631 S. Mullen Avenue
Los Angeles, CA 90043

Robert P. Biller, Dean
School of Public Adm.
University of Southern California
University Park
Los Angeles, CA 90007

Stanley Hopper, Chair
Dept. of Political Science
California State University
Los Angeles, CA 90032

Carl R. Jones, Chair
Administrative Sciences Dept.
Naval Postgraduate School
Monterey, CA 93940 (COD) 54J)

Bruce F. Grube, Asst. Prof.
Dept. of Political Science
California State Poly. University
3801 W. Temple Avenue
Pomona, CA 91768

Stahrl W. Edmunds, Dean
Graduate School of Adm.
University of California
Riverside, CA 92521

John A. Rehfuss, Chair
Dept. of Public Administration
California State University
6000 J Street
Sacramento, CA 95819

Margaret K. Gibbs, Chair
Dept. of Public Administration
California State College
5500 State College Parkway
San Bernadino, CA 92407

James D. Kitchen, Director
School of Pub. Adm. & Urban
   Studies, San Diego State University
San Diego, CA 92182

Biliana Cicin-Sain, Chair
Dept. of Political Science
University of California
Santa Barbara, CA 93106

Lawrence L. Giventer, Director
Graduate Studies in Public Adm.
Calif. State Coll.-Stanislaus
800 Monte Vista Avenue
Turlock, CA 95380

Dean Randy H. Hamilton
Graduate School of Public Adm.
Golden Gate University
536 Mission Street
San Francisco, CA 94105

Elliot H. Kline, Dean
School of Bus. & Public Adm.
University of the Pacific
3601 Pacific Avenue
Stockton, CA 95211

COLORADO

Philip O. Foss, Professor
Dept. of Political Science
Colorado State University
Ft. Collins, CO 80523

Robert F. Wilcox, Dean
Graduate School of Pub. Affrs.
University of Colorado
1100 14th Street
Denver, CO 80202

Gordon E. Von Stroh, Director
School of Public Management
University of Denver
Denver, CO 80208

Glenn B. Schroeder, Academic
   Coordinator, Dept. of Ed. Adm.
Public Administration Program
Univ. of Northern Colorado
Greeley, CO 80639

Kenneth Fox, Coordinator
Dept. of Public Adm. &
   Institutional Management
University of New Haven
West Haven, CO 06516

CONNECTICUT

Morton J. Tenzer, Director
MPA Program, U-106
University of Connecticut
Storrs, CT 06268

DELAWARE

Jerome R. Lewis, Asst. Dir., PA
College of Urban Affairs

DELAWARE Cont.

University of Delaware
Willard Hall
Newark, DE 19711

DISTRICT OF COLUMBIA

Robert E. Cleary, Interim Dean
College of Public Affairs
The American University
Room 101
Washington, D.C. 20016

Charlotte Gillespie
Director of Communications
American Society of Pub. Adm.
1225 Conn. Ave., NW. Ste 300
Washington, D.C. 20036

Charles W. Washington, Chair
Dept. of Public Administration
George Washington University
2129 G. Street, NW
Washington, D.C. 20037

Glenn A. Howard, Chair
School of Business & Public Adm.
Howard University
2345 Sherman Avenue, NW
Washington, D.C. 20059

Ken Nishimoto, Assoc. Prof.
School of Bus. & Public Mgmt.
University of D.C.
1331 H Street, NW
Washington, D.C. 20005

FLORIDA

John E. Miklos, Ph.D.
College of Business & Pub. Adm.
Florida Atlantic University
Boca Raton, Fl 33431

Joseph Penbera, Director
Dept. of Politics & Pub. Affrs.
University of Miami

FLORIDA Cont.

P.O. Box 248047
Coral Gables, FL 33124

Phyllis Brick, Director
MAPS Program
NOVA University
3301 College Avenue
Ft. Lauderdale, FL 33314

William Kelso, Director
Public Adm. Program
Dept. of Political Science
University of Florida
Gainesville, FL 32611

J. Arthur Heise, Ph.D., Chair
Dept. of Public Adm., SPAS
Florida International University
Tamiami Trail
Miami, FL 33199

James W. Witt, Coordinator
Graduate Studies Program
Faculty of Political Science
University of West Florida
Pensacola, FL 32504

Augustus B. Turnbull, III, Chair
Dept. of Public Adm.
Florida State University
Tallahassee, FL 32306

Jamil E. Jreisat, Chair
Dept. of Political Science
University of South Florida
Tampa, FL 33620

GEORGIA

James T. Jones, Chair
Public Administration Dept.
Atlanta University
223 Chestnut Street
Atlanta, GA 30314

William A. Jones, Director
Institute of Governmental Adm.
Georgia State University
University Plaza
Atlanta, GA 30303

Delmer D. Dunn, Director
Institute of Government
University of Georgia
Terrell Hall
Athens, GA 30602

J. Malcolm Moore, Prof.
Carl Vinson Prof. of Political
   Science/Public Adm.
Georgia College
Milledgeville, GA 31601

Robert Dick, Asst. Prof.
Dept. of Political Science
Georgia Southern College
Statesboro, GA 30458

IDAHO

Jerald A. Johnson, Director
MPA Program
Dept. of Government
Idaho State University
Pocatello, ID 83209

ILLINOIS

John L. Foster, Director
MPA Program
Dept. of Political Science
Southern Illinois University
Carbondale, IL 62901

Robert Aliber, Dean
Comm. on Pub. Policy Studies
University of Chicago
1050 E. 59th Street
Chicago, IL 60637

Melvin J. Dubnick, Asst. Prof.
Dept. of Political Science
Loyola University of Chicago

6525 N. Sheridan
Chicago, IL 60626

Robert J. McNeill, Director
Public Administration Program
Roosevelt University
430 E. Michigan Avenue
Chicago, IL 60605

Dominic G. Parisi, Director
Administrative Studies Center
DePaul University
25 E. Jackson Boulevard
Chicago, IL 60604

John Wanat, Director
Public Agency Adm. Program
Univ. of Illinois/Chicago Circle
Box 4348
Chicago, IL 60680

Robert Agranoff, Director
Center for Governmental Studies
Northern Illinois University
DeKalb, IL 60115

Michael A. Quinn, Director
Urban Studies Program
Southern Illinois University
Box 32-A
Edwardsville, IL 62026

Jean J. Couturier, Director
Pub. Mgmt. Program, Grad. Sch.
Northwestern University
2001 Sheridan Road, 4-083
Evanston, IL 60201

Irene F. Rothenberg, Director
P.A. Program., Dept. of Political
  Science, Barat College
Lake Forest, IL 60045

Tom Ticknor, Acting Director
Wood Inst. for Local & Regional
  Studies, Lake Forest College
Lake Forest, IL 60045

Richard W. Crockett, Director
Graduate Prog., Pub. Affrs./Adm.
Western Illinois University
422 Morgan Hall
Macomb, IL 61455

Michael Cohen, Coordinator
College of Bus. & Pub. Service
Governors State University
Park Forest South, IL 60466

John N. Collins, Director
Center for Policy Studies
Sangamon State University
Shepard Road
Springfield, IL 62708

Samuel K. Gove, Director
Inst. of Govt. & Public Affrs.
University of Illinois
1201 W. Nevada Street
Urbana, IL 61801

INDIANA

Charles F. Bonser, Dean
School of Pub. & Envir. Affairs
Indiana University
400 E. 7th Street, Room 333
Bloomington, IN 47405

Louis C. Gawthrop
Editor-in-Chief
Sch. of Pub. & Envir. Affairs
Indiana University
Bloomington, IN 47401

Joseph C. Ullman, Director
Center for Public Policy & Adm.
Purdue University, ENAD 323
Lafayette, IN 47907

Roger G. Hollands, Director
Bureau of Governmental Research
Dept. of Political Science
Ball State University
Muncie, IN 47306

James L. McDowell, Director
Ctr. for Governmental Services
Indiana State University
201 Holmstedt Hall
Terre Haute, IN 47809

IOWA

Victor A. Olorunsola, Chair
Dept. of Political Science
Iowa State University
503 Ross Hall
Ames, IO 50011

Mel Arslaner, Acting Director
Institute of Public Affairs
Drake University
Meredith Hall, Room 209A
Des Moines, IO 50311

KANSAS

Michael Fullington, Director
Dept. of Political Science
Emporia State University
1200 Commercial
Emporia, KS 66801

Raymond G. Davis, Director
Graduate Program in Pub. Adm.
Dept. of Political Science
Univ. of Kansas, Blake Hall
Lawrence, KS 66044

Naomi B. Lynn, Professor
Dept. of Political Science
Kansas State University
Manhattan, KS 66506

Glenn W. Fisher, Urban Studies
Wichita State University
Wichita, KS 67208

KENTUCKY

George Masannat, Head
Dept. of Government

KENTUCKY Cont.

Western Kentucky University
Room 300, Grise Hall
Bowling Green, KY 42101

Gary S. Cox, Ph.D., Dean
School of Public Affairs
Kentucky State University
Frankfort, KY 40601

Merlin M. Hackbart, Director
Graduate Studies
University of Kentucky
409 Commerce
Lexington, KY 40506

Dave Allen, Professor
Dept. of Political Science
University of Louisville
Louisville, KY 40208

Winfield H. Rose, Chair
Dept. of Political Science
Murray State University
College of Bus. & Pub. Affrs.
Murray, KY 42071

J. Allen Singleton, Chair
Dept. of Political Science
Eastern Kentucky University
Richmond, KY 40475

LOUISIANA

David B. Johnson, Director
MPA Program
Louisiana State University
Baton Rouge, LA 70803

MAINE

Kenneth T. Palmer, Coordinator
PA Prog. Dept. of Pol. Science
University of Maine
Orono, ME 04473

MARYLAND

Henry Bain, Director
Political Science Program
Univ. of Maryland, Balti. County
5401 Wilkens Avenue
Baltimore, MD 21228

Larry Downey, Director
MPA Program
University of Baltimore
Charles at Mt. Royal
Baltimore, MD 20201

Charles H. Levine, Director
Graduate Studies, Room 2113
Inst. of Urban Studies, Woods Hall
University of Maryland
College Park, MD 20742

MASSACHUSETTS

Jerome M. Mileur, Director
MPA Program, Dept. of Pol. Sci.
Univ. of Massachusetts
Amherst, MA 01003

Robert E. Gilbert, Prof.
Dept. of Political Science
Northeastern University
Boston, MA 02115

Richard L. McDowell, Dean
School of Management
Suffolk University
47 Mt. Vernon Street
Boston, MA 02108

Vincent Pivnicny, Mgmt. Faculty
College of Professional Studies
University of Massachusetts
Harbor Campus
Boston, MA 02125

Robert M. Weinberg, Director
Public Management Program
Boston University
212 Bay State Road
Boston, MA 02215

Graham T. Allison, Jr., Dean
JFK School of Government
Harvard University
Littauer Center
Cambridge, MA 02138

H. James Brown, Professor
Dept. of City & Regional Plng.
Harvard Univ., Grad. Sch. of Design
311 Gund Hall, 48 Quincy Street
Cambridge, MA 02138

William F. Lichliter, Coord.
Public Administration Program
Bentley College
Beaver & Forest Streets
Waltham, MA 02154

MICHIGAN

Edward M. Gramlich, Director
Institute of Pub. Pol. Studies
University of Michigan
1516 Rackham Building
Ann Arbor, MI 48104

Richard C. Elling, Director
Dept. of Political Science
Graduate Program in Pub. Adm.
Wayne State University
870 MacKenzie Hall
Detroit, MI 48202

Charles F. Cnudde, Chair
Dept. of Political Science
Michigan State University
303 S. Kedzie Hall
East Lansing, MI 48824

Peter Kobrak, Director
Center for Public Adm. Program
Western Michigan University
Kalamazoo, MI 49001

Delbert J. Ringquist, Chair
Dept. of Political Science
247 Anspach Hall
Central Michigan University
Mt. Pleasant, MI 48858

Appendix D

MINNESOTA

Robert A. Barrett, Director
Urban & Regional Studies Inst.
Mankato State University Box 7
Mankato, MN 56001

John S. Adams, Director
H.H.H. Institute of Public Affrs.
University of Minnesota
909 Social Studies Building
Minneapolis, MN 55455

MISSISSIPPI

Henry Hall, Director
Public Policy & Adm. Program
Jackson State Univ., Ayer Hall
Jackson, MS 39217

Howard Ball, Head
Dept. of Political Science
Mississippi State University
P.O. Box PC
Mississippi State, MS 39762

Donald S. Vaughn, Chair
Dept. of Political Science
University of Mississippi
University, MS 38677

MISSOURI

Robert B. Denhardt, Chair
Dept. of Public Adm.
University of Missouri
315 Middlebush Hall
Columbia, MO 65211

F. Gerald Brown, Director
Division of Public Adm.
University of Missouri
5100 Rockhill Road
Kansas City, MO 64110

John A. Eilers, Asst. Prof.
Dept. of Eng. Management
University of Missouri, Rolla
Harris Hall
Rolla, MO 65401

E. Terrence Jones, Director
Pub. Policy Adm. Masters Program
University of Missouri
8001 Natural Bridge
St. Louis, MO 63121

Kenneth F. Warren, MAPA Dir.
Dept. of Political Science
St. Louis University
St. Louis, MO 63103

MONTANA

Krishna K. Tummala, Director
MPA Program
Dept. of Political Science
Montana State University
Bozeman, MT 59715

NEBRASKA

John E. Kerrigan, Dean
College of Pub. Affrs. & Comm.
  Service
University of Nebraska, Omaha
Omaha, NE 68182

Clifton L. Ginn, Assoc. Prof.
Public Affairs Institute
Wayne State College
Wayne, NE 68787

NEW JERSEY

Eva Aronfreed, Coordinator
Public Administration
Glassboro State College
Glassboro, NJ 08028

Samuel Humes, Director
Graduate Program for Adm.
Rider College, P.O. Box 6400
Lawrenceville, NJ 08649

E. Drexel Godfrey, Jr., Director
MPA Program, Rutgers University
360 High Street
Newark, NJ 07102

Donald E. Stokes, Dean
W.W. School of Public & Intrnl.
Affairs, Princeton University
Princeton, NJ 08540

Anthony C. Neidhart, Director
Public Administration Inst.
Fairleigh Dickinson University
211 Montross Avenue
Rutherford, NJ 07070

Mary Boutilier, Chairperson
Dept. of Political Science
Seton Hall University
400 South Orange Avenue
South Orange, NJ 07079

Howard Rubin, Chair
Dept. of Political Science
Kean College of New Jersey
Union, NJ 07083

NEW MEXICO

Leonard Stitelman, Director
Division of Public Administration
University of New Mexico
Mesa Vista Hall
Albuquerque, NM 87131

NEW YORK

Richard H. Mattox, Director
Public Administration Program
Russell Sage College
140 N. Scotland Avenue
Albany, NY 12208

Orville F. Poland, Dean
Graduate School of Pub. Affrs.
SUNY, Albany, Mohawk Tower
1400 Washington Avenue
Albany, NY 12222

Thomas A. Dorsey, Coordinator
Prog. in Pub. Policy Analy, & Dept.
 of Political Science
SUNY/Binghamton
Binghamton, NY 13901

Dominic Nwasike, Chair
Social Science Division
Medgar Evers College, CUNY
1150 Carroll Street
Brooklyn, NY 11225

Richard Tobin, Asst. Prof.
Dept. of Political Science
SUNY/Buffalo, Amherst Campus
Spaulding Quad, Ellicott Complex
Buffalo, NY 14261

Carl L. Figliola, Chair
Dept. of Health Care & Pub. Adm.
C.W. Post Center, L.I. Univ.
Greenvale, NY 11548

Wendy B. Phoenix, Director
Public Management Program
Grad. School of Bus. & PA
Cornell University
Ithaca, NY 14853

David Bresnick, Chair
Dept. of Public Administration
Baruch College, CUNY
Box 336, 17 Lexington Avenue
New York, NY 10010

Demetrios Caraley, Director
Political Science-MPA
School of Intrnl. Affrs., Rm. 1427
Columbia University 420 W 118th
New York, NY 10027

Henry Cohen, Dean
Center for NY City Affairs
New School for Social Research
66 5th Avenue
New York, NY 10011

Dick Netzer, Dean
Graduate School of Public Adm.
New York University
4 Washington Square, North
New York, NY 10003

Peter D. Salins, Chair
Dept. of Urban Affairs
Hunter College
790 Madison Avenue
New York, NY 10021

Eli Silverman, Assoc. Dean
John Jay College, Crim. Justice
444 W. 56th Street - CUNY
New York, NY 10019

Harry Weiner, Dean
W.A. Harriman College of Urban
& Policy Sciences
SUNY/Stony Brook
Stony Brook, NY 11794

Guthrie S. Birkhead, Dean
Maxwell School, Syracuse Univ.
217 Maxwell Hall
Syracuse, NY 13210

NEVADA

James S. Roberts, Prof.
Dept. of Political Science
University of Nevada
Reno, NV 89557

NORTH CAROLINA

Deil S. Wright, Director
MPA Prog., 305 Hamilton Hall 070
Dept. of Political Science
University of N.C.
Chapel Hill, NC 27514

Schley Lyons, Chair
Dept. of Political Science
University of N.C.
Charlotte, NC 28223

Tyrone R. Baines, Director
Public Administration Program
N.C. Central University
Durham, NC 27707

Joel L. Fleishman, Director
Inst. of Political Science &
Public Affairs
Duke Univ., 4875 Duke Station
Durham, NC 27706

David M. Olson, Head
Dept. of Political Science
University of N.C.
237 Graham Building
Greensboro, NC 27412

Yong-dahl Song
Director of Graduate Studies
Dept. of Political Science
East Carolina University
Greenville, NC 27834

J. Oliver Williams, Director
Master of Public Affrs. Program
N.C. State University
P.O. Box 5305
Raleigh, NC 27650

Konrad M. Kressley, Director
Public Affairs Program
Catawba College
Salisbury, NC 28144

Richard S. Krajcik, Coordinator
Public Administration Curricula
Social Science Department
Winston-Salem State University
Winston-Salem, NC 27102

NORTH DAKOTA

Robert W. Kweit, Director
MPA Program
University of North Dakota
Dept. of Political Science
Grand Forks, ND 58202

OHIO

Yong H. Cho, Head
Department of Urban Studies
University of Akron
Akron, OH 44325

D.S. Chauhan, Director
Public Administration Program
Dept. of Political Science
Bowling Green State Univ.
Bowling Green, OH 43402

Edward R. Padgett, Director
MPA Prog., Dept. of Political
   Science
University of Cincinnati
1014 Crosley Tower
Cincinnati, OH 45221

Clinton V. Oster, Director
School of Public Administration
Ohio State University
1775 College Road, 302 Hagerty
Columbus, OH 43210

Frederick R. Inscho, Director
MPA Prog., Univ. of Dayton
300 College Park Avenue
Dayton, OH 45469

Marvin Meade, Professor
Dept. of Public Administration
Kent State University
Kent, OH 44242

OKLAHOMA

Walter F. Scheffer, Regent's Prof.
Graduate Prog. In Public Adm.
University of Oklahoma
455 W. Lindsey Street, # 305
Norman, OK 73069

Earl J. Reeves, Director
Urban Studies Program
University of Tulsa
600 S. College
Tulsa, OK 74104

ONTARIO

Joseph M. Galimberti, Exec.
Inst. of Pub. Adm. of Canada
897 Bay Street
Toronto, ON M5S 1Z7

OREGON

Bryan T. Downes, Assoc. Dean
School of Community Service & Public
   Affairs
University of Oregon
Eugene, OR 97403

Ronald C. Cease, Director
Masters Program in Public Adm.
Portland State University
P.O. Box 751
Portland, OR 97207

G.H. Mattersdorff, Co-Director
Public Administration Program
Lewis & Clark College
Campus Box 79
Portland, OR 97219

D. Jay Doubleday, Dean
Graduate School of Adm.
Willamette University
315 Winter Street
Salem, OR 97301

PENNSYLVANIA

Howard R. Whitcomb, Chair
Department of Government
Lehigh University
Maginnes Hall, # 9
Bethlehem, PA 18015

Gary L. Wamsley, Director
Ctr. for Pub. Adm. & Pub. Affrs.
Virginia Polytechnic Inst. & SU
Blacksburg, PA 24061

Miriam Ershkowitz, Director
Pub. Mgmt.-exec. Dev. Inst.
Temple Univ., 7308 Asbury Ave.
Melrose Park, PA   19126

Daniel M. Poore, Chair
Masters Prog. in Public Adm.
Penn State University
Capitol Campus
Middletown, PA   17057

Thomas Dunfee, Chair
Public Management, W283
Wharton School
University of Pennsylvania
Philadelphia, PA   19109

John Funari, Dean
Grad. School of Pub. & Intrnl. Affrs.
University of Pittsburgh
3G07 Forbes Quadrangle
Pittsburgh, PA   15260

Norman J. Johnson, Assoc.
Sch. of Urban & Public Affairs
Carnegie-Mellon University
Pittsburgh, PA   15213

Frank McGee, Chair
Dept. of Public Service
Marywood College
2300 Adams Avenue
Scranton, PA   28509

John G. Marrero, Chair
Department of Government
Shippensburg State College
Shippensburg, PA   17257

Robert J. Mowitz, Director
Institute of Public Adm.
Penn State University
211 Burrowes Building
University Park, PA   16802

RHODE ISLAND

Sol Lebovitz, Dean
The Graduate School
Bryant College
Smithfield, R.I.   02817

SOUTH CAROLINA

Roger R. Stough, Director
Ctr. for Metro. Aff. & Pub. Plcy.
The College of Charleston
Charleston, SC   29401

Steven W. Hays, Director
MPA Program, Dept. of Government
University of South Carolina
Columbia, SC   29208

SOUTH DAKOTA

Donald C. Dahlin, Chair
Dept. of Political Science
University of South Dakota
Vermillion, SD   57069

TENNESSEE

Thomas D. Ungs, Head
Dept. of Political Science
University of Tennessee
1005 McClung Tower
Knoxville, TN   37916

Helen M. Sawyer, Director
MPA Program
Dept. of Political Science
Memphis State University
Memphis, TN   38252

George Vernardakis, Director
MPA Program, Box 460
Middle Tennessee State Univ.
Murfreesboro, TN   37130

Charles Sampson, Head
Dept. of Government & Public Affairs
Tennessee State University
Nashville, TN   37203

TEXAS

Sherman M. Wyman, Prof.
Institute of Urban Studies
University of Texas
P.O. Box 19588
Arlington, TX 76019

Elspeth Rostow, Dean
LBJ Sch. of Public Affairs
University of Texas
Sid Richardson Hall, 3.100
Austin, TX 78712

Samuel A. Kirkpatrick, Head
Dept. of Political Science
Texas A & M University
130 Bolton Hall
College Station, TX 77843

Charles P. Elliott, Head
Dept. of Political Science
East Texas State University
Commerce, TX 75428

Jay D. Starling, Director
Grad. Program in Public Adm.
Southern Methodist University
Storey Hall
Dallas, TX 75275

Charldean Newell, Chair
Dept. of Political Science
North Texas State University
P.O. Box 5338, NT Station
Denton, TX 76203

Wendell G. Schaeffer, Professor
Grad. Prog. in Pub. Affrs. & Adm.
Texas Christian University
Ft. Worth, TX 76129

Donald F. Callaghan, Director
Program in Public Affairs
University of Houston, CLC
2700 Bay Area Boulevard
Houston, TX 77058

Wlater J. McCoy, Dean
School of Public Affairs
Texas Southern University
3201 Wheeler Avenue
Houston, TX 77004

Robert D. Thomas, Director
MPA Program
Dept. of Political Science
University of Houston
Houston, TX 77004

N. Joseph Cayer, Director
Center for Public Service
Texas Tech University
P.O. Box 4290
Lubbock, TX 79409

Bruce P. Ball, Coordinator
MPA Prog. Dept. of Government
Angelo State University
2601 West Avenue, North
San Angelo, TX 76901

Richard S. Howe, Jr., Director
Div. of Environmental Studies
University of Texas
San Antonio, TX 78285

Earl M. Lewis, Chair
Dept. of Urban Studies
Trinity University
P.O. Box 417
San Antonio, TX 78284

Thomas J. Williams, Ph.D.
Director MPA Program
Dept. of Political Science
Southwest Texas State Univ.
San Marcos, TX 78666

UTAH

Lennis Knighton, Director
Institute of Public Mgmt.
210 Jesse Knight Building
Brigham Young University
Provo, Utah 84602

Robert P. Huefner, Director
Institute of Government
University of Utah
214 Orson Spencer Hall
Salt Lake City, Utah 84112

VIRGINIA

Richard E. Zody, Chair
Grad. Program in Urban Affrs.
VPI & SU, EUS Building
Blacksburg, VA 24061

Patrick J. Conklin, Pres.
Am. Society for Public Adm.
Federal Executive Inst.
Route 29 North
Charlottesville, VA 22903

Steven E. Rhoads, Director
Public Administration Program
W.W. Dept. of Govt. & FA
Univ. of VA, 232 Cabell Hall
Charlottesville, VA 22901

Harold F. Gortner, Chair
George Mason University
Dept. of Public Affairs
4400 University Drive
Fairfax, VA 22030

Steve Mosher, Professor
Program Director for P.A.
Ferrum College
Ferrum, VA 24088

William R. Nelson, Head
Dept. of Political Science &
   Georgraphy
James Madison University
Harrisonburg, VA 22801

Leonard Ruchelman, Director
Inst. of Urban Studies & PA
Old Dominion University
Norfolk, VA 23508

Leigh Grosenick, Chair
Dept. of Public Adm.

VIRGINIA Cont.

Virginia Commonwealth Univ.
816 Franklin Street
Richmond, VA 23284

William L. Morrow, Professor
Dept. of Government
College of William & Mary
Williamsburg, VA 23185

WASHINGTON

Ralph Miner, Chair
Dept. of Political Science
Grad. Prog. in Pub. Policy Adm.
Western Washington State College
Bellingham, WA 98225

Robert Herold, Director
Graduate Prog. in Public Adm.
Eastern Washington University
Cheney, WA 99004

Willard Humphreys
Acting Dean for Grad. Studies
The Evergreen State College
Olympia, WA 98505

Brewster C. Denny, Dean
Graduate School of Public Affrs.
University of Washington, DP-30
Seattle, WA 98195

William H. Baarsma, Assoc. Prof.
School of Bus. & Public Adm.
University of Puget Sound
1500 North Warner
Tacoma, WA 90416

WEST VIRGINIA

Herman Mertins, Jr., Chair
Dept. of Public Administration
West Virginia University
302-B Woodburn Hall
Morgantown, WV 26506

WISCONSIN

William J. Murin, Director
MPSA Prog. & Inst. of Local Govt.
Univ. of Wisconsin-Parkside
Kenosha, WI 53141

Carlisle P. Runge, Director
Ctr. for Public Policy & Adm.
University of Wisconsin
322 North Hall
Madison, WI 53706

Richard D. Bingham, Chair
Dept. of Urban Affairs
University of Wisconsin
P.O. Box 413
Milwaukee, WI 53201

Stephen Hintz, Director
MPSA Program
University of Wisconsin

109 N/E Building
Oshkosh, WI 54901

VIRGIN ISLAND

Peter Pflaum, Professor
MPA/MBA Program
College of the Virgin Island
St. Thomas, VI 00801

CANADA

George S. Lane, Dean
Faculty of Business
University of Calgary
2920 24th Avenue, NW
Calgary, AB, Canada T2N 1N4

Appendix E

ASSOCIATE MEMBERS

Ralph Widner, President
Academy for Contemporary Prob.
1501 Neil Avenue
Columbus, Ohio 43201

Wayne Anderson, Executive Dir.
Advisory Commission on Intergovernmental Relations
1111 20th St., NW, Suite 2000
Washington, D.C. 20575

Robert Bugher, Exec. Director
American Public Works Assn.
Education Foundation
1313 E. 60th Street
Chicago, Ill. 60637

William J. Page, Jr., Exec. Dir.
Council of State Government
Iron Works Pike
P.O. Box 11910
Lexington, KY 40578

Thomas W. Carr, Acting Dir.
Federal Acquisition Institute
5001 Eisenhower Avenue
Room 7N08
Alexandria, VA 22333

Pat Conklin, Assoc. Director
Federal Executive Institute
Route 29 North
Charlottesville, VA 22903

Dr. Malcolm McCormick, Exec. Sec.
Harry S. Truman Scholarship
   Foundation
712 Jackson Place, NW
Washington, D.C. 20006

John C. Houlihan, Exec. Dir.
Institute for Local Self-Government
Hotel Claremont Building
Berkeley, CA 94705

Mark E. Keane, Exec. Director
International City Mgmt. Assn.
1140 Conn. Avenue, NW, 2nd Fl.
Washington, D.C. 20036

Francis H. Duehay, Director
Lincoln Filene Center for Citizenship
   & Public Affairs
Tufts University
Medford, Mass. 02155

Philip H. Whitbeck
Director of Adm. & Prog. Support
NASA/Johnson Space Ctr., Code BA
NASA Road #1
Houston, TX 77058

George H. Esser, Jr.
Executive Director & President
National Academy of Pub. Adm.
1225 Conn. Ave., NW, Suite 300
Washington, D.C. 20036

Bruce Talley, Associate Dir.
National Association of Counties
1735 New York Avenue, NW
Washington, D.C. 20006

Philip J. Rutledge, President
National Institute of Pub. Mgmt.
1625 Eye Street, NW, Suite 515
Washington, D.C. 20006

Alan Beals, Executive Vice-President
National League of Cities
1620 Eye St., NW, 4th Fl.
Washington, D.C. 20006

Norman Beckman, Director, BIPP
Office of Personnel Mgmt.
1900 E Street, NW, Room 2305
Washington, D.C. 20415

Cheryl J. Dobbins, Exec. Dir.
Positive Futures, Inc.
1522 K Street, NW, Ste. 910
Washington, D.C. 20005

T.J. Plunkett, Director
School of Public Administration
Queen's University
Kingston, Canada K7L3N6

John S. Bottum, Asst. Deputy
   Director, SEA-Extension
U.S. Dept. of Agriculture
Room 6408
Washington, D.C. 20250

The Honorable Elsa Porter
Asst. Secretary for Adm.
U.S. Dept. of Commerce
14th & Const. Ave., NW, Rm. 5
Washington, D.C. 20230

Helene S. Markoff, Director
Employee Development & Train
U.S. Dept. of Energy
100 Indiana Ave., NW, Rm. A5
Washington, D.C. 20545

The Hon. William A. Medina
Asst. Sec. for Administration
U.S. Dept. of HUD
451 7th St., SW, Room 10110
Washington, D.C. 20410

Jack Rottman, Chief
Career Management Group
U.S. Dept. of Justice
521 12th Street, NW
Washington, D.C. 20530

Bernard D. Jankowski, Chief
Training & Career Dev. Div.
   TAD/14, Dept. of Transportation
400 7th Street, SW, Rm. 9109
Washington, D.C. 20590

J. Elton Greenlee, Director
Office of Mgmt. & Organization
U.S. Dept. of Treasury
Main Treasury Bldg., Rm. 4406
Washington, D.C. 20220

The Hon. Elmer B. Staats
Comptroller General of the U.S.
U.S. General Accounting Office
441 G Street, NW
Washington, D.C. 20548

The Hon. A. Lee Fritschler,
U.S. Postal Rate Commission
Rm. 500, 2000 L St., NW
Washington, D.C. 20268

AUTHOR INDEX

This index includes all authors, editors, compilers, translators, and other contributors to works cited in the text. It is alphabetized letter by letter and numbers refer to entry numbers.

A

Aberbach, Joel D. 203, 1358
Abramson, Joan 1021
Acker, Joan 1022
Adams, Bruce 1305
Adams, Harold W. 1046
Adams, Thomas W. 486
Agranoff, Robert 606
Aiken, Michael 1432
Aldrich, Howard E. 768
Aleshire, Robert A. 1359
Altshuler, Alan A. 415
Alutto, Joseph A. 1231
Alwin, Duane F. 510
Amacher, Ryan 1172
Anderson, Bernard E. 962
Anderson, James E. 558
Anderson, Scarvia B. 511
Anderson, Wayne F. 532
Anderson, William 52, 445
Andrieu, M. 512
Aplin, John C., Jr. 1284, 1470
Appleby, Paul H. 129, 345, 559, 1173, 1394
Arellano, Esther 838
Argyris, Chris 641, 707-11, 769, 1232-33, 1471
Armstrong, DeWitt C. III 1395
Arnold, Peri E. 274
Arora, Ramesh K. 1515

Ascher, Charles S. 275
Aspin, Les 240
Attkisson, C. Clifford 514
Atwood, Jay F. 912
Auerbach, Arnold J. 678
Austin, David M. 1360

B

Baaklini, Abdo I. 241, 247
Backoff, Robert 607
Badway, M.K. 1285
Bahl, Roy W. 1
Bailey, John J. 1174
Bailey, Stephen K. 346, 1396
Baker, Bruce R. 804
Baldwin, Sidney 437
Balk, Walter L. 1048-50, 1100, 1141
Ball, Samuel 511
Ballantyne, Duncan 1156
Balutis, Alan P. 242
Banner, David K. 513
Banovetz, James 487
Barber, Daniel M. 1361
Barber, James David 204
Barclay, Warren M. 490
Barker, Ernest 1516
Barnard, Chester I. 745
Barnett, Marguerite Ross 994
Barnett, Richard R. 1433

Author Index

Barth, James R. 53
Baumer, Donald C. 849
Bavelas, Alex 1472
Bayley, David H. 1517
Beam, David R. 205
Beaumont, Enid 446, 864
Becharek, Frank 1473
Becker, Selwyn W. 642, 1120
Beckman, Norman 243-44
Behan, R.W. 1261
Beigel, Allan 514
Belasco, James A. 1231
Bell, Michael 2
Belsley, G. Lyle 870
Bendix, Reinhard 166
Bendor, Jonathan 1518
Bennett, George 130
Bennett, James T. 53
Bennis, Warren G. 643, 712, 760,
    1474-75, 1497
Benokraitis, Nijole V. 963
Benson, George C.S. 1434
Benson, J. Kenneth 644
Benson, Louis 1473
Benveniste, Guy 167, 805
Berger, Monroe 1519
Berkley, George E. 3, 416, 608
Berman, Jules 1175
Berman, Larry 206
Berman, William C. 995
Bernick, E. Lee 889
Biggart, Nicole Woolsey 770
Billeaux, David M. 1386
Biller, Robert P. 347
Billings, Robert S. 1252
Bingham, Richard D. 1140
Birch, Frank 590
Bish, Robert L. 87, 560
Bishop, Joan Fiss 1023
Bjur, Wesley E. 1362
Black, Guy 88, 1262
Blackwell, Barbara L. 515
Blair, Louis H. 1121
Blau, Peter M. 168-69, 645, 679
Blaustein, Eric 459
Blodgett, Terrell 1306
Blume, Stuart S. 865
Bolling, Richard 245
Bolman, William M. 515
Bons, Paul M. 1476

Boone, Richard W. 1363
Borst, Diane 301
Botner, Stanley B. 1263
Boulding, Kenneth E. 1397
Bower, Joseph L. 806
Bowers, David G. 713, 1477
Bowman, James E. 1398
Bowman, James S. 447
Bowman, John H. 1380
Boyd, Rose Williams 964
Bozeman, Barry 746
Brandl, John E. 448
Breyer, Stephen G. 302
Brademas, John 276
Bradford, James C. 4
Braibanti, Ralph 1520
Bridges, Edwin M. 1051
Brigham, John 561
Brody, Ralph 1122
Brophy, Michael C. 1364
Brostz, Allyn 1157
Brown, David S. 207, 277, 747,
    807, 1286
Brown, F. Gerald 5, 26, 88, 90,
    93, 95, 102, 111, 114, 119,
    125, 127, 1378
Brown, M. Craig 187
Brown, Peter G. 1399
Brown, Ray L. 1326
Browne, Edmond, Jr. 54
Browne, William P. 131
Browning, Edgar K. 965
Browning, Larry 1478
Brownlow, Louis 6, 348
Brozen, Richard 459
Bunkder, Douglas R. 516
Burke, W. Warner 722
Burkhead, Jesse 1052, 1170, 1176
Burnham, Donald C. 1053
Busching, Bruce C. 701
Buttrick, Shirley M. 1307
Byrd, Jack, Jr. 449

C

Cafagna, Dora 625
Caiden, Gerald E. 417, 609
Caiden, Naomi 1177
Caldwell, Lynton K. 208, 349-51,
    450, 771

Camp, Paul M. 866
Campbell, Alan K. 1, 352, 488, 808, 867, 966
Campbell, Donald T. 517
Campbell, Jack M. 7
Campbell, John P. 1123
Capron, William M. 1264
Caputo, David A. 55-56, 209, 518, 562, 1365
Carey, William D. 1435
Carlson, William A. 57
Caro, Robert 99
Carrell, Jeptha J. 1366
Carroll, James D. 451, 772
Carroll, Michael A. 58
Carroll, Stephen 1303
Carroll, Stephen J., Jr. 1287
Carron, Andrew S. 246
Carson, John J. 1479
Cary, Charles D. 519
Carzo, Rocco, Jr. 680
Cayer, N. Joseph 809
Chad, Seymour W. 1115
Chapman, Brian 1521
Chapman, J. Brad 1024
Chapman, Richard L. 773
Charlesworth, James C. 346, 350, 353, 360, 387, 406, 748
Charnovitz, Steve 1308
Chatman, Linwood 1367
Chaturvedi, U.R. 1522
Chauhan, D.S. 59
Cheek, Logan M. 1309
Chennells, Elizabeth 865
Cherniss, Cary 1234
Chesser, Rod 1303
Chia, Tiang Ping 1016
Chitwood, Stephen R. 967
Chizmar, John F. 1036
Chubin, Daryl E. 1423
Churchman, C.W. 1265
Cikins, Warren I. 452
Cizanckas, Victor I. 1135
Clark, Terry Nichols 1178
Claude, Richard P. 80, 596, 1301, 1393
Cleaveland, Frederic N. 773
Cleveland, Harlan 748, 774, 1400
Cohen, Michael 822, 1124, 1402
Cole, Richard L. 209, 1369

Collins, John N. 1124
Collins, Morris W.H., Jr. 453
Committee for Economic Development 89
Conner, Raymond A. 1115
Connor, Patrick E. 714
Cook, James B. 1370
Corbett, William H. 1111
Cornog, Geoffrey Y. 419, 810
Corwin, Ronald C. 681
Costello, Timothy 90
Cousens, Frances Reissman 996
Cotton, John F. 74
Coursey, Robert D. 1364
Couzens, Michael 1491
Coven, Mark 811
Cowen, Scott S. 1310
Cox, Gary B. 520
Cramton, Roger C. 303
Crane, Edgar G. 273
Craver, Gary 521
Critchfield, Brevard 8
Cole, Richard L. 56
Craig, R.J. 1094
Crane, Edgar G. 247, 1158
Crozier, Michael 1523
Culbert, Samuel A. 715
Cummings, Milton C., Jr. 812
Cummings, Thomas G. 1055-56
Cunningham, James V. 1371
Cupps, D. Stephen 1372

D

Dahl, Robert A. 354, 1333
Daneke, Gregory A. 563
Danforth, Devaratnam 1524
Danielson, William F. 804
Davidson, Roger H. 248
Davies, Celia 1101
Davis, Charles 126
Davis, David W. 40
Day, H. Talmage 494
Desmond, Richard E. 1480
Dean, Alan L. 278, 1449
deGrazia, Alfred 355-56
DeLong, Earl H. 868
DeMarco, John J. 115, 927
Dempsey, John R. 279
Denhardt, Kathryn G. 357

Denhardt, Robert B. 357, 610, 1025
Denison, Edward F. 1057
Denzau, Arthur T. 1179
Derr, C. Brooklyn 682
Deutsch, Karl 132
DeWoolfson, Bruce H., Jr. 1288
Diamant, Alfred 1525-26
Diaz de Krofcheck, Maria Delores 997
Diegelman, Robert F. 308
di Grazia, Robert J. 858
Dillon, Conley H. 358, 1527
Dimock, Gladys Ogden 418
Dimock, Marshall E. 170, 280, 367, 418, 1528
Divine, William R. 281
Dobbins, Cheryl 998
Dodson, Charles 813
Doig, Jameson W. 749, 900
Donaldson, William V. 454
Donovan, John C. 564
Dornbusch, Sanford M. 701
Dorsey, John T., Jr. 1481, 1529
Dotson, Arch 814-15
Douglas, Scott R. 1190
Dowling, John 646
Downey, Edward H. 1141
Downs, Anthony 133, 171
Downs, George W. 1142
Doyle, Wayne J. 1051, 1482
Draper, Frank D. 1311
Dreyfus, Daniel A. 249
Dror, Yehezkel 522, 1235
Drucker, Peter F. 750-51, 775, 1289
Dunbar, Roger L.M. 1180
Dunn, Diana R. 1162
Dunn, James A., Jr. 304
Dunn, William N. 647
Dunsire, Andrew 683, 776, 1530
Durante, John A. 913
Dvorin, Eugene P. 1403, 1421
Dwight, James S. 60
Dworak, Robert J. 1312
Dworkis, Martin B. 489
Dye, Thomas R. 565

E

Edmonds, Thom 455
Egger, Rowland 359, 869

Eghtedari, Ali 1181
Egnatios, Edward 1234
Eisenstadt, S.N. 172, 1531
Eimicke, William B. 134
Elazar, Daniel J. 17, 61, 777
Emmerich, Herbert 282, 360, 870
Engelbert, Ernest A. 456-57
Engman, Lewis A. 305
Entwisle, Doris R. 816
Ermer, Virginia B. 173
Etheredge, Lloyd S. 9
Etzioni, Amitai 135, 306, 611, 648, 684, 1236
Eulau, Heinz 250
Executive Office of the President 1182
Eyestone, Robert 1143

F

Fain, Tyrus G. 283
Fainsod, Merle 1532-33
Farris, George F. 1058
Fauri, David P. 1373
Fayol, Henri 752
Feagin, Joe R. 963
Feigenbaum, Charles 914
Feld, Richard D. 10
Feldstein, Martin 1334
Fesler, James W. 361, 1436-42
Feuille, Peter 915, 925
Fielder, Fred E. 1476, 1483-84, 1513
Filley, Alan C. 716
Finer, Herbert 591
Finkle, Arthur L. 490, 968-69
Finley, James J. 1183
Finney, David R. 11
Fish, Donald M. 525
Fisher, Frederick E. 458, 491
Fisher, John E. 871
Fisher, Louis 210
Fisher, Virginia L. 1184
Fisk, Donald M. 1102-3
Fitzgerald, Martin J. 251
Flanagan, Robert J. 970
Flanders, Ralph E. 1335
Flash, Edward S., Jr. 211
Fletcher, T.W. 685
Floden, Robert E. 523

Florestano, Patricia S. 91, 112, 293
Flynn, Paul J. 791
Fogel, Walter 916
Follett, Mary Parker 717
Foster, Gregory D. 872
Foster, R. Scott 1159
Foster, Robert N. 1485
Fowler, Robert Booth 917
Fox, Douglas M. 3, 284-85, 753
Fox, Eliot M. 1026
Fox, Guy 1534
Foxley, Cecelia H. 1027
Fozouni, Bahman 647
Fraenkel, Richard M. 1374
Francis, Arthur 1101
Frank, James E. 1266
Franklin, Grace A. 262
Franklin, Jack L. 524
Frazer, William J., Jr. 1185
Frederickson, H. George 13, 46, 202, 271, 362-63, 414, 593, 606, 674, 749, 754, 778, 817, 840, 918, 1097, 1318, 1370, 1493
Freedman, Elisha C. 949
Freeman, Sidney C. 12
Friedan, Betty 1028
Frieden, Bernard J. 532
Friedlander, Frank 1144
Friedman, Lewis B. 1186
Friedman, Nathalie 118
Friedrich, Carl J. 592
Fritschler, A. Lee 459, 469
Fritz, D. 1375
Frohock, Fred M. 566
Froomkin, Joseph 567
Frye, Alton 252
Frye, Nelson 718
Fulenwider, Claire Knoche 1029
Furstenberg, Frank, Jr. 1336

G

Gabler, L. Richard 2
Gabris, Gerald T. 92
Galloway, Judith M. 1030
Gamm, Larry 13
Gannon, Martin J. 1059
Gardner, John W. 719, 1060

Gardner, Neely 818
Gates, Bruce L. 754, 779, 993
Gatti, Francis C., Jr. 1278
Gaus, John M. 364-67
Gawthrop, Louis C. 136, 212, 593
Gellerman, Saul W. 1145
Gerth, H.H. 198
Gerwin, Donald 1187
Giblin, Edward J. 720
Gibson, Frank 419, 460, 755, 819, 999
Gibson, Kenneth 14
Gilder, George 1061
Gilmer, Jay 15
Gittell, Marilyn 1376, 1535
Gladden, E.N. 368
Glaser, Edward M. 1062
Glazer, Nathan 1000
Glen, Roy H. 1056
Glendening, Parris N. 16
Goerl, George Frederick 780
Goetz, Charles J. 63
Goldoff, Anna C. 1063
Goldstein, Morris 1001
Goldstein, Walter 1357
Golembiewski, Robert T. 419, 612, 649, 686, 721-22, 755, 820-22, 1188, 1404-5
Goodin, Carl V. 1109
Goodin, Robert E. 1406
Goodman, Paul S. 1123, 1133
Goodman, Roger J. 723
Goodnow, Frank J. 137
Goodrick, M. George 1443
Gordon, George J. 213, 420
Gordon, Gerald 642
Gordon, Joel 781
Gordon, L.A. 1313
Gore, William J. 1237-39
Gortner, Harold F. 421
Gouldner, Helen P. 613
Grabosky, Peter N. 1017
Grafton, Carl 10, 286, 307
Graham, George A. 461, 1395
Graham, William 1267
Grant, Daniel R. 93
Green, Gerson 1444
Greenhouse, Samuel M. 1268
Gregg, James M.H. 308

Author Index

Gregg, Roy G. 462
Greytak, David 1, 1160
Grodin, Joseph R. 919
Grodzins, Morton 17, 724
Grosenick, Leigh E. 4, 18, 25, 57, 60, 64, 66-67, 1438, 1446
Gross, Bertram M. 138, 757, 1269
Grubb, W. Norton 94
Grundstein, Nathan D. 95
Grupp, Fred W. 19
Grusky, Oscar 873
Guest, James W. 15
Gulick, Luther 174, 369-70, 400, 463, 782, 1420
Gulick, Peter R. 139
Gusfield, Joseph R. 971
Gustely, Richard D. 79
Guyot, James F. 823

H

Haas, J. Eugene 651
Hafstad, Lawrence R. 783
Hage, Jerald 650
Haider, Donald 214
Hale, George E. 1189-90, 1486
Hall, Douglas T. 1031
Hall, Grace 1002
Hall, Richard H. 651
Hallman, Howard W. 1377
Hamilton, Charles V. 1003
Hamilton, Edward K. 1161
Hamilton, Randy H. 309, 1378
Hammer, W. Clay 652
Hammond, Arthur 1331
Hananel, Eric 920
Harmon, Michael Mont 568, 594, 972
Harper, Edwin L. 1270
Harper, Robert 1004
Harris, Joseph P. 253, 1191
Harrison, Evelyn 1032
Harrison, Jared F. 1064
Hart, David K. 614, 973, 1445
Hart, John 215
Hatley, Richard V. 1271
Hartman, James B. 921
Hartman, Robert W. 1314
Harvey, Donald R. 824, 874

Harvey, George Y. 1192
Harvey, James C. 1005-6
Haskew, Barbara 813
Hatry, Harry P. 525-26, 1104-6, 1125, 1138, 1162-63
Havens, Harry S. 527, 1290
Haverman, Robert H. 254, 569
Hawkins, Augustus F. 1337
Hawkins, J. David 528
Hawkins, Robert B., Jr. 96, 287-88
Hawley, Claude E. 371
Hayes, Frederick O'R. 1164-65
Hayward, Nancy S. 1065-66
Heady, Ferrel 289, 1536-40
Heald, Karen A. 589
Heaphey, James J. 242, 247, 1099, 1541
Hebert, F. Ted 1315
Heclo, Hugh 175, 216, 758
Hedrick, James L. 536
Hefner, James A. 994
Heimovics, Richard D. 492
Heiss, F. William 529
Heivilin, D.M. 1313
Heller, Walter W. 1338
Hellriegel, Don 974
Henderson, A.M. 1356
Henderson, Keith M. 1542
Hennigan, Patrick J. 1052
Henry, Laurin L. 217
Henry, Nicholas L. 372, 422, 493, 784-85
Herbert, Adam W. 1007-8, 1446-47
Herring, E. Pendleton 140
Hershey, Cary 310
Herzlinger, Regina E. 1316
Hess, Stephen 218
Heydebrand, Wolf 786
Hickson, D.J. 653, 695-96
Higgins, James M. 975
Hildreth, William Bartley 460
Hill, Herbert 976
Hill, Norman C. 1487
Hilles, Rick 722
Hills, R. Jean 1488
Hills, William G. 423
Hinings, C.R. 695-96

Hirsch, Werner Z. 1193–94, 1543
Holland, Thomas P. 1240
Holzer, Mark 1067
Hombruch, Frederick W., Jr. 1068
Honan, Joseph C. 494
Honey, John C. 464
Hooyman, Nancy R. 1033
Hopkins, Anne H. 922
Hopper, Robert 1478
Horst, Pamela 530
Horton, Frank 311
Horton, Raymond D. 1069
Hoselitz, Bert F. 1339
House, Robert J. 698, 1489–90
Howard, Kenneth I. 533
Howard, Lawrence C. 1009, 1034, 1409, 1448
Howard, S. Kenneth 1195, 1241
Howell, Paul L. 825
Howitt, Arnold M. 97
Hughes, Larry 495
Hull, Raymond 736
Humes, Samuel 1407
Hummel, Ralph P. 176
Hunt, Carder W. 941
Hunt, Deryl G. 1010
Hunt, Thelma 826
Hunter, John 1303
Huntington, Samuel P. 312
Hy, Ronald J. 1242
Hyde, Albert C. 438, 531, 1196
Hyman, Drew 1463
Hyneman, Charles S. 141, 177

I

Inbar, Michael 1243
Indik, Bernard P. 827
Ingram, Helen 65
Ingrassia, Anthony F. 923
Ink, Dwight A. 66, 219–20, 313, 1449
International City Management Association 1107
Ippolito, Dennis S. 1197

J

Jackson, Carlos 997
Jackson, David M. 1367

Jackson, Henry M. 255
Jacobs, David 640
Jacoby, Henry 178
Jadlos, James P. 496
Jain, Tej Kumar 1146, 1271
James, George A. 819
Janowitz, Morris 687, 828
Jasper, Herbert N. 1198
Jenkins, John A. 314
Jennings, M. Kent 812, 1244
Johnson, Gary R. 829
Johnson, George E. 977
Johnson, Harry G. 1544
Johnson, Nevil 595
Johnson, Norman J. 651
Johnson, Ronald W. 1200
Joiner, Charles A. 1534
Jones, Bryan D. 98
Jones, Charles O. 20, 256, 315, 830
Jones, Roger W. 831, 1245
Jones, William A., Jr. 832, 924
Jongeward, Dorothy 1035
Jreisat, Jamil 373
Jun, Jong S. 1291, 1545
Juris, Harvey A. 925

K

Kagno, Munro S. 722
Kahn, Robert L. 179, 615, 725
Kammerer, Gladys M. 257
Kanes, Eveline 178
Kaplan, Judith S. 1033
Karl, Barry D. 375
Karnig, Albert K. 36
Kassem, M. Sami 1546
Katz, Daniel 615
Katzell, Raymond A. 1147–48
Kaufman, Gary G. 875
Kaufman, Herbert 99, 142, 180, 374, 616, 787–88, 1450–51, 1491
Kavanagh, Michael J. 1492
Kayali, Kaled M. 596
Keating, William Thomas 789
Kee, Woo Sik 1547
Keller, Lawrence F. 100
Kelly, Thomas C. 119
Kelsey, Judy 309

Author Index

Kendrick, John W. 1072-73, 1108
Kennedy, David J. 21
Kernaghan, Kenneth 597
Khandwalla, Pradip N. 617
Kharasch, Robert N. 316
Kilpatrick, Franklin P. 812
King, Bert 1513
Kingsley, J. Donald 1548
Kinnard, Douglas 189
Kirchner, Charles 15
Kiresuk, Thomas J. 532
Kirkhart, Larry 376, 726
Kirlin, John J. 465
Klay, William Earle 258
Kleingartner, Archie 926
Klinger, Donald E. 833
Kloman, Erasmus 1379
Knowles, Malcolm S. 727
Koch, James V. 1036
Koehler, Cortus T. 497
Kolberg, William H. 67
Kotter, John P. 1126
Kraft, John 53
Krailo, Holly 1122
Kramer, Fred A. 424, 570, 598, 1199, 1270
Kranz, Harry 876, 978
Krasnow, Erwin G. 317
Krause, Merton S. 533
Krishna, Daya 1549
Krislov, Joseph 790
Krislov, Samuel 181
Kroeger, Naomi 182
Kronenberg, Philip S. 377
Kuffel, Tom 1294
Kull, Donald C. 1074
Kuper, George H. 1066, 1127
Kurzman, Paul A. 378, 654

L

Labovitz, I.M. 101
Laffey, M.F. 1347
Laing, James D. 701
Lakshmanan, T.R. 102
Lambright, W. Henry 571, 791
LaMond, Annette M. 1045
Landau, Martin 618, 1246, 1550
Landy, Frank J. 1109
Lane, Frederick S. 425

Lang, James E. 979
LaPalombara, Joseph 1520, 1529, 1531-32, 1551-52, 1559, 1570, 1585, 1589
La Porte, Todd 466
Larson, Arthur D. 834
Laski, Harold J. 221
Laurance, Edward J. 259
Lauth, Thomas P. 1317
League of Women Voters of Los Angeles 1075
Leavitt, Harold J. 619
Lee, Hahn-Been 1553
Lee, Robert D., Jr. 835-36, 1200-1201
Lehne, Richard P. 68-69
Leich, Harold H. 837
Lekachman, Robert 1340
LeLoup, Lance T. 1202-4
Lentz, Bernard F. 1158
Leone, Robert A. 318
Lerner, Allan W. 620
Levenson, Alan I. 514
Levine, Charles H. 183, 621-22, 655, 849, 927, 942, 1011, 1493
Levine, Edward M. 838
Levinson, Harry 534
Levinson, Marc 928
Levitan, Sar A. 22, 143
Levy, Burton 1012
Levy, Sidney J. 319
Lewin, David 916, 929
Lewis, Eugene 144
Lewis, Frank L. 535
Lewis, Verne B. 1205
Liebert, Roland J. 103
Light, Alfred R. 23
Likert, Rensis 728, 759
Lindblom, Charles E. 145, 572, 786, 792, 1247, 1333, 1341
Lirtzman, Sidney I. 698
Litchfield, Edward H. 656
Loehr, Virginia M. 838
Lomax, W. Richard 866
Long, Gary 915
Long, Norton E. 104-5, 146, 1248, 1408

Longley, Lawrence D. 317
Lorch, Robert S. 426
Lord, Robert G. 1494
Loveland, John 467
Lovell, Catherine 24, 980, 1167
Loveman, Brian 1554
Lowi, Theodore J. 147
Lucey, Patrick J. 70, 1076, 1168-69
Lucianovic, William M. 836
Ludwin, William G. 1332
Luecke, David S. 1495
Lund, Sander H. 532
Lundberg, Craig C. 320
Lundstedt, Sven 1496
Luthan, Fred 1024
Lutrin, Carl E. 427
Lutz, Carl F. 839
Lyden, Fremont J. 1206

M

Maass, Arthur A. 599
McArthur, Robert E. 468, 1128
MacAvoy, Paul 302
McCaffery, Jerry L. 498, 793, 1318-19, 1380
McCamy, James L. 1249
McCleery, Mickey 1250
McClung, Glenn G. 877
McConkey, Dale D. 1292
McConkey, William C. 1272
McCurdy, Howard E. 428
MacDougall, William 25
McGill, Michael E. 321, 499, 729
McGregor, Caroline 760
McGregor, Douglas 730, 760, 1497
McGregor, Eugene B., Jr. 840, 878, 981
McGriff, John H. 930
Mackay, Robert J. 1179
Mackelprang, A.J. 459, 469
McKinney, Jerome B. 1409
McNamara, Donna B. 982
McTighe, John J. 761
Macy, John W., Jr. 1452
Mahan, David J. 1051
Mainzer, Lewis C. 184
Majone, Giandomenico 573
Makielski, S.J., Jr. 1129

Mali, Paul 1077
Mankin, Lawrence D. 931
Mann, Dean E. 900
Mansfield, Harvey C. 290
Mansfield, Roger 689, 1453
Marando, Vincent L. 291
March, James G. 623-24
Marcus, Philip M. 625
Margolis, Larry 71
Marguilies, Newton 731
Marini, Frank 347, 363, 376-77, 379, 466, 470, 571, 594, 803, 1153, 1241, 1542
Mark, Jerome A. 1110
Markham, Emerson 1272
Markoff, Helene S. 1037
Marshall, James F. 932
Martin, Norman H. 905-6
Martin, Roscoe C. 148
Marvin, Keith E. 536
Marx, Fritz Morstein 1442
Marz, Roger H. 1149
Maslove, Allan M. 1251
Maslow, Abraham H. 732-34
Massarik, Fred 1507
Mathews, David 185
Mathews, Walter M. 1242
Mathewson, Kent 26
Matsuo, Takayoshi 1555
Meadows, Mark E. 1498
Medeiros, James A. 471
Mehta, B. 1499
Mehta, C.S. 1293
Meier, Kenneth John 322, 429, 882, 1207
Melcher, Arlyn J. 537
Meltsner, Arnold J. 574-75
Meltzer, Alan H. 149
Merget, Astrid E. 1461-62
Merton, Robert K. 186
Metcalf, Henry C. 717
Meyer, Herbert H. 933
Meyer, Marshall W. 169, 187, 688
Meyer, Marshall W., and Associates 187
Miewald, Robert D. 430
Milburn, Thomas W. 537
Miles, Jerome A. 1208
Miles, Robert H. 1500

Miles, Rufus E., Jr. 292, 323-24
Millburn, Thomas W. 1252
Miller, Ernest G. 1206
Miller, Gerald 755
Miller, Glenn W. 934
Miller, S.M. 1381
Miller, Vernon 1307
Millett, John D. 380, 1209
Mills, C. Wright 198
Milne, R.S. 1556-57
Mishan, E.J. 1130
Mitchell, Terence R. 667
Mitnick, Barry M. 150, 325
Moe, Ronald C. 222
Mogulof, Melvin B. 106, 326
Mohr, Lawrence B. 1142
Molloy, Edmond S. 1055-56
Monczka, Robert M. 1150
Montana, Patrick J. 301
Montmollin, Maurice de 381
Moore, John E. 327
Morehouse, Thomas A. 538
Moreland, William B. 1204
Morelos, P.C. 1558
Morgan, David R. 107, 841, 1157
Morgan, Glenn G. 500
Morgan, James P. 839
Morley, Elaine 1160
Morrill, William A. 328
Morris, John A., Jr. 1131
Morris, Thomas D. 1111
Morrison, David E. 735
Morrow, William L. 260, 382
Morse, Ellsworth H. 539
Morstein, Marx Fritz 431-32, 879,
   1559-60
Mosher, Frederick C. 151, 359,
   361, 463, 472, 479, 482, 796,
   1273, 1410
Mouzelis, Nicos P. 657
Moynihan, Daniel P. 108
Mudd, John 109
Multi-Municipal Productivity Project
   of Nassau County 1047
Mundell, Marvin 1112
Murin, William J. 123
Murphy, Irene L. 1038
Murphy, John C. 72
Murphy, Michael J. 532
Murphy, Richard J. 329

Murphy, Thomas P. 26, 48, 88,
   90, 93, 95, 102, 110-14, 119,
   125, 127, 223, 291, 293, 330,
   486-87, 491-92, 495-96, 501-5,
   507-8, 762, 893, 1378, 1462,
   1467-68
Murray, Michael A. 152, 473-74
Murray, Stuart 1294
Musgrave, Peggy B. 1342
Musgrave, Richard A. 1342
Mushkin, Selma J. 73-74, 576,
   1274
Musicus, Milton 294
Muskie, Edmund S. 114
Musolf, Lloyd D. 880
Mustafa, Husain 1473
Myren, Richard A. 1454

N

Nachmias, David 577
Nadler, David A. 1501
Nagel, Stuart 475
Nalbandian, John 833
Nance, Kathy Newton 543
Nash, Christopher 540
Nathan, Richard P. 75-77, 224
Natemeyer, Walter E. 658
Nay, Joe N. 530
Neef, Marian 475
Negandhi, Anant R. 537
Neigher, William 1428
Neiman, Max 578
Nelson, William E., Jr. 1013
Neuhauser, Duncan 1120
Neuse, Steven M. 1039
Neustadt, Richard E. 225-26
Newgarden, Peggy 1040
Newland, Chester A. 842, 935,
   1078, 1132, 1295-96
Newstrom, John W. 1150, 1411
Newton, Robert D. 27
Nigro, Felix A. 433, 843-44,
   881, 936-38
Nigro, Lloyd G. 115, 433, 763,
   844, 882, 938
Nimmo, Dan D. 202, 484
Niskanen, William A., Jr. 188
Northrup, David E. 939
Nottage, Raymond 883

Nourse, Edwin G. 1343
Nuechterlein, Donald E. 223, 330
Nurick, Lloyd 153

O

Obuchowski, Carole Cassler 891
O'Connor, Robert J. 1174
Odiorne, George S. 1297
Ogden, Daniel M., Jr. 1320
Okun, Arthur M. 983
Olsen, Eugene A. 1456
Olson, Mancur, Jr. 1344
O'Neill, Michael E. 1113
Organ, Dennis W. 652
Orzechowski, William Paul 1079
Osman, Jack W. 94
Ostrom, Elinor 28, 1114, 1345
Ostrom, Vincent 29, 87, 383-84,
    396, 579, 1345, 1455
Ott, Attiat F. 1210
Ott, David J. 1210
Otten, Gerald L. 1321
Overton, C.E. 940
Owen, Henry 580
Ozawa, Martha N. 1131

P

Page, William J., Jr. 1300
Paget, Richard M. 884
Paine, Frank T. 1059
Pai Panandiker, V.A. 1561
Pajer, Robert G. 1151
Pak, Chong M. 762
Palumbo, Dennis J. 1412
Paper, Lewis J. 507
Parsons, Talcott 659-60, 1355-56
Parsons, William W. 845
Partridge, P.H. 1413
Passel, Peter 30
Patitucci, Frank 116
Patten, Thomas H., Jr. 846
Patterson, Kenneth D. 261
Patti, Rino 794
Patton, Michael Quinn 541
Paulson, Darryl 1382
Payne, Roy L. 689
Peabody, Robert L. 690-91
Pearce, David 540

Pearson, Norman M. 227
Pechman, Joseph A. 1346
Pedersen, Kjeld Moller 542
Pelt, Adrian 1562
Perkins, Jan 1025
Perkins, John A. 885
Perry, James L. 927, 941-42
Peter, Laurence F. 736
Peters, B. Guy 154, 1563
Petersen, J.E. 1347
Peterson, Peter G. 1080
Pettigrew, Andrew 1253
Pettigrew, Richard A. 295
Petty, M.M. 1500
Pfeffer, Jeffrey 646, 661, 1418
Pfiffner, John M. 626, 1254
Phares, Donald 1160
Pierce, Lawrence C. 1348
Pillsbury, Jolie Bain 543
Pincus, Ann 847
Pincus, William 886
Pitsvada, Bernard T. 1311
Pittsburgh. University. Administra-
    tive Science Center 627
Plambeck, Donald L. 1299
Plant, Katharine C. 283
Platt, C. Spencer 737
Plumlee, John 322
Poister, Theodore H. 581
Poland, Orville F. 544
Polsby, Nelson W. 228
Pomerlau, Raymond 887
Pondy, Louis R. 692-93
Pope, Carl E. 1414
Porter, David O. 31, 984, 1456
Porter, Teddie Wood 31, 984
Porter, Wayne 838
Posegate, John 838
Posey, Rollin B. 943
Post, Russell Lee, Jr. 944
Present, Philip E. 434
Press, Charles 146
Presthus, Robert V. 155, 435, 628,
    662-63, 694
Price, Don K. 795-97
Proctor, John R. 1081
Public Affairs Research Council of
    Louisiana 945
Pugh, D.S. 695-96
Pye, Lucian W. 1564-65
Pyhrr, Peter A. 1322-23

Q

Quah, Jon S.T. 1566
Quay, Herbert C. 545
Quinn, Robert E. 1083

R

Rabin, Jack 1188
Radnor, Michael 673
Radway, Laurence I. 599
Ramos, Alberto Guerreiro 664
Rand, Neil E. 738
Randall, Ronald 629
Raphaeli, Nimrod 1567-68
Rapp, Brian 116
Rawson, George E. 922
Ream, Norman J. 798
Reardon, Diane Frances 546
Redburn, Thomas 946
Reddin, W.J. 1502
Redford, Emmette S. 156, 385,
    1457
Reed, B.J. 92
Reeves, Earl J. 985-86
Reeves, Floyd W. 848
Reeves, H. Clyde 8
Reeves, Mavis Mann 16, 117
Regens, James L. 841
Rehfuss, John 54, 386, 1324
Reif, William E. 1150
Reimann, Bernard C. 697
Rein, Martin 1381, 1458
Reining, Henry, Jr. 888
Remy, Ray 32
Reynolds, Harry W., Jr. 436
Rice, William V., Jr. 947
Rich, Robert F. 1415
Rich, Wilbur C. 1014
Richard, Scott F. 149
Richards, Alan R. 19
Richardson, Ivan L. 437
Ricketts, Edmond F. 33
Ricks, Artel 157
Riedel, James A. 1383
Riesel, Jerome 715
Rifkind, Bernard D. 1115
Riggs, Fred W. 387, 799, 1569-80
Rinehart, Jeffrey C. 889
Ripley, Randall B. 262, 849, 1211

Ritchie, J.B. 1487
Rivlin, Alice M. 547
Rizzo, Ann-Marie 1041
Rizzo, John R. 698
Roback, Herbert 263-64
Robey, Daniel 537
Robinson, James A. 265
Robinson, Rose M. 1015
Rocheleau, Bruce 548
Rockman, Bert A. 203, 1358
Rogers, Theresa F. 118
Rohr, John A. 1416
Rondinelli, Dennis A. 78
Roos, Lawrence K. 119
Rose, Gale W. 476
Rose, Richard 229, 1298
Rose, Winfield H. 1016
Rosen, Bernard 890, 987
Rosenbaum, Walter A. 1384
Rosenbloom, David H. 189, 850-
    52, 891, 988, 1017
Rosenbloom, Richard S. 1084
Rosener, Judy B. 1085, 1385
Rosengren, William R. 699
Rosow, Jerome M. 853
Ross, Bernard H. 485
Ross, John P. 79, 1170
Ross, Leonard 30
Rossel, Robert D. 190, 1503
Rossi, Peter H. 549-50
Rourke, Francis E. 191, 1417
Rouse, Andrew M. 297, 1270
Rouse, John E., Jr. 80, 1459
Rowe, Lloyd A. 120
Rubin, Richard S. 854
Ruch, William A. 1411
Rudolph, Lloyd I. 700
Rudolph, Susanne Hoeber 700
Rushing, William A. 630
Rutman, Leonard 512, 551
Rycroft, Robert W. 331-32, 600

S

Sadek, S.E.M. 1581
Safferstone, Mark J. 982
Salanick, Gerald R. 661, 1418
Saltstein, Alan 855, 1002
Saltzstein, Grace Hall 989
Samuels, Warren J. 1419

Sapp, Carl 266
Saunders, Robert J. 5
Savage, Peter 388, 1582
Sayre, Wallace S. 1420, 1583
Scanlan, Burt K. 764, 1152
Scanlon, John W. 530
Schaefer, Roberta Rubel 1504
Schechter, Stephen L. 34
Schein, Edgar H. 665, 739, 1497
Scheppach, Raymond C., Jr. 1116
Scherer, Joseph J. 982
Schick, Allen 267-68, 389-90,
    1212-13, 1275-77, 1325
Schick, Richard P. 964
Schiller, Bradley R. 990
Schlessberg, Norman 948
Schmandt, Henry J. 1460
Schoderbek, Peter P. 1284, 1299
Schoenherr, Richard A. 679
Scholl, Richard W. 731
Schott, Richard L. 391, 892
Schubert, Glendon A. 158
Schultze, Charles L. 333, 580,
    1349
Schumaker, Paul D. 1386
Schwartz, Alfred I. 1121
Scism, Thomas E. 856
Scott, Dru 1035
Scott, W. Richard 645, 701, 1133
Scott, William G. 614, 666-67,
    740
Seashore, Stanley E. 1477
Segers, Mary C. 991
Seidman, Harold 35, 334
Seifert, George 718
Seitz, Steven Thomas 192
Seligman, Lee 36
Seligman, Milton 1480
Selznick, Philip 335, 1505
Settle, Allen K. 427
Shadoan, Arlene Theuer 1214
Shafritz, Jay M. 438, 531, 668,
    857, 1158, 1196
Shalala, Donna E. 1461-62
Shapek, Raymond A. 121
Shariff, Zahid 159
Sharkansky, Ira 582, 1153, 1350,
    1584
Sharp, Walter R. 1585
Sharpe, Carleton F. 949

Shearer, Derek 1351
Sherman, Betsy 1305
Sherman, Harvey 392, 631
Sherwood, Frank P. 626, 893,
    1181, 1300
Shimberg, Benjamin 858
Short, Larry 974
Sibson, Robert E. 1086
Siegel, Gilbert B. 1362
Siegfried, John J. 1087
Siffin, William J. 1586
Sigal, Leon V. 269
Sigelman, Lee 37, 1042, 1587
Silander, Fred S. 1239
Silbiger, Sara 950
Sills, David L. 166, 404, 1216,
    1227
Silver, Howard J. 230
Silverman, Eli B. 270, 1088,
    1278
Simmons, Robert H. 1403, 1421
Simon, Herbert A. 393-94, 439,
    624, 632, 741, 800, 1255-59
Simpson, Richard L. 1506
Singer, Neil M. 38
Sirefman, Josef P. 913, 920, 948
Skok, James E. 1260, 1279,
    1301
Sloan, Royal D., Jr. 477
Sloma, Donald 528
Smith, Brian 1588
Smith, Darrell Hevenor 894
Smith, Harold D. 1215
Smith, Michael P. 193, 669
Smith, Robert S. 1001
Smith, Russell L. 922
Smithburg, Donald W. 439
Smithies, Arthur 1216
Snyder, James C. 122
Somers, Herman M. 231
Somit, Albert 478
Sonenblum, Sidney 1194
Sorauf, Frank J. 160
Sorensen, James E. 895
Sorensen, Theodore C. 232
Sorensen, Thomas L. 895
Sowell, Thomas 992
Spain, C.L. 1347
Spengler, Joseph J. 1589

Spero, Sterling D. 951
Speth, Gus 336
Spiro, Herbert J. 601
Spizman, Lawrence M. 1089
Springer, J. Fred 1590-91
Staats, Elmer B. 552, 602-3, 896
Stack, Steven 1352
Staffeldt, Raymond J. 1201
Stahl, O. Glenn 702-3, 742, 804, 839, 859-60
Stallings, Wayne 1217
Stanley, David T. 861, 897-900, 952
Stanley, John 540
Stanley, Preston O. 953
Stanyer, Jeffrey 604
Starling, Grover 765
Starling, Jay D. 633
Staudohar, Paul D. 1090
Staufenberger, Richard A. 804, 839
Stein, Harold 583
Stein, Harry A. 1280
Stenberg, Carl W. 81-82, 954, 1422
Stene, Edwin O. 395, 670
Stevenson, Adlai E. 298
Stewart, Debra W. 1043
Stieber, Jack 955
Stillman, Richard J. II 396-97, 440, 1302
Stockard, James G. 901
Stokes, Sybil L. 1540
Stone, Alan 337
Stone, Alice B. 479, 671
Stone, Clarence N. 123
Stone, Donald C. 39, 479, 671, 1592
Storing, Herbert J. 398
Storrs, Constance 752
Stover, Carl F. 766
Strakosch, Lynn D. 488
Strange, John H. 1387-88
Strauch, Ralph E. 480
Stretch, John J. 605
Streufert, Siegfried 1513
Strouse, James C. 80, 596, 1301, 1393
Studer, Kenneth E. 1423
Stupak, Ronald J. 223, 330, 672
Sudama, Trevor 1281

Sullivan, Michael J. 510
Sundquist, James L. 40, 233-34, 1424
Suver, James D. 1326
Swanson, Cheryl 1044
Swerdlow, Irving 1533

T

Taggart, Robert 143
Tannenbaum, Robert 1507
Tannian, Francis X. 1171
Tansik, David A. 673
Tarter, Jim R. 1303
Taylor, Frederick Winslow 194, 767
Teasley, C.E. III 674, 862
Teeples, Ronald K. 1194
Terrell, Paul 83, 1389
Terry, Newell B. 956
Thayer, Frederick C. 634, 675, 1091
Thayer, Lee O. 1508
Thomas, John S. 1092
Thomas, Samuel F. 489
Thompson, Duane E. 1470
Thompson, Frank J. 863, 1018-19
Thompson, James D. 161-62, 635, 704
Thompson, Victor A. 195, 439, 636, 705, 743, 1154-55, 1593
Thrall, Charles A. 1336
Thrasher, Jean H. 524
Thurber, James A. 271, 1219
Tideman, T. Nicolaus 1425
Tilman, Robert O. 1594
Tollison, Robert D. 1172
Tomer, John F. 84
Tomzinis, Anthony R. 1134
Toombs, William 1093
Topham, Neville 1433
Tosi, Henry L. 1287, 1303
Trachtenberg, Stephen J. 507
Truman, David B. 163
Tullock, Gordon 196, 584
Turner, C. 695-96
Turner, Henry A. 399
Turner, Wayne E. 1094
Tyer, Charles B. 1327
Tyler, Gus 957

U

Ukeles, Jacob B. 585
Ulberg, Cy 1135
United Nations Technical Assistance
  Programme 1595
U.S. Advisory Commission on Inter-
  governmental Relations 41-43
U.S. Comptroller General 1117
U.S. Congress. Joint Economic
  Committee. Subcommittee on
  Economic Growth and Stabilization
  338
U.S. Congress. Senate. Committee
  on Governmental Affairs 553
U.S. Congress. Senate. Committee
  on Government Operations. Sub-
  committee on Intergovernmental
  Relations 1328
U.S. General Accounting Office
  44-45, 902-3, 1095, 1220
U.S. General Services Administration
  164
Unruh, Jesse M. 125
Unwin, Ernest A. 1113
Upjohn Institute for Employment
  Research, W.E. See W.E.
  Upjohn Institute for Employ-
  ment Research
Urwick, Lyndall 174, 400, 717
Useem, Michael 481
Usilaner, Brian L. 1111
Uveges, Joseph A., Jr. 441

V

Valdes, William C. 958
Vale, Vivian 235
Van Asselt, Karl A. 959
Van Fleet, David D. 1509
Van Horn, Carl E. 586
Van Houten, Donald R. 1022
Van Lohuizen, J.R. 1207
Van Maanen, John 462
Van Meter, Donald S. 586
Van Meter, Elena C. 1390
Van Riper, Paul P. 904-6
Van Wagner, Karen 1044
Veillette, Paul T. 801
Versel, Mark J. 1329
Vogel, Donald B. 676
Von Mises, Ludwig 197

Vosburgh, William W. 1463
Vroom, Victor H. 1510, 1513

W

Wagman, Barry L. 1118
Wagner, Richard E. 584
Wakefield, Susan 1426
Wald, Emanuel 401
Waldmann, Raymond J. 236
Waldo, Dwight A. 402-6, 442,
  482, 677, 1427
Walker, David B. 46-49, 82
Walker, Dollie R. 998
Walker, Robert A. 1221
Walker, Thomas G. 1511
Wallace, Phyllis A. 1045
Wallace, Robert J. 1119
Wallace, Robert T. 1303
Wallerstein, Louis S. 339
Walsh, Annmarie Hauck 340
Walton, Eugene 1144
Walton, John 816
Waltzer, Herbert 33
Wamsley, Gary L. 100, 407,
  1353
Wanat, John 1222
Wann, A.J. 237
Ward, James H. 1136
Warner, David C. 31
Warner, W. Lloyd 905-6
Warren, Charles R. 112, 291,
  293, 1462, 1467-68
Warren, Ronald S., Jr. 1223
Warrick, D.D. 744
Wasylenko, Michael J. 1
Weaver, Michael 508
Webb, Lee 1351
Weber, Arnold R. 960, 1354
Weber, Max 198, 1355-56
Weed, Frank J. 1464
Weidenbaum, Murray L. 341,
  1357
Weidman, Donald R. 554
Weidner, Edward W. 1550, 1553,
  1573, 1596-99
Weinberger, Casper W. 300, 342
Weiner, Stephen S. 523
Weinstein, Deena 199
Weintraub, Ruth G. 371, 489
Weisbrod, Burton A. 569

Weiss, Carol H. 483
Welch, Claude E., Jr. 1600
Welch, Finis 977
Weschler, Irving R. 1507
Wessel, Robert J. 1282
West, Jonathan P. 126
W.E. Upjohn Institute for Employ-
  ment Research 1096
Whately, Arthur 467
Whelan, Noel 1465
Whelan, Robert K. 123
Whisler, Thomas L. 802
Whitbeck, Philip H. 668
Whitcomb, G. Robert 1512
White, Leonard D. 367, 398,
  408-11, 443, 907
White, Michael 756, 1224
White, Orion F., Jr. 637, 726,
  803, 993
White, Richard W., Jr. 238
Whitehead, Jack 1478
Wholey, Joseph S. 530, 555-56,
  1330
Whyte, William H., Jr. 638
Wilcox, Herbert G. 639
Wildavsky, Aaron B. 239, 557,
  587, 1137, 1225-28, 1283, 1331
Wilken, William H. 1466-68
Willbern, York 412, 908
Willet, Thomas D. 1172
Williams, Cortez H. 1020
Williams, Eleanor Golar 1512
Williams, Robert J. 343, 1601
Williams, Robert L. 127
Willoughby, W.F. 444
Wilson, James Q. 200
Wilson, Woodrow 413
Windle, Charles 1428
Winnie, Richard E. 525, 1103,
  1138
Wise, Charles R. 13, 46, 202,
  271, 414, 593, 606, 674, 706,
  749, 754, 840, 1094, 1097,
  1318, 1370, 1493

Witte, Edwin E. 344
Woehicke, L. Carl 1116
Wofford, J.C. 1098
Wolf, James F. 509
Wolfe, Joan L. 1099
Wolfson, Robert J. 1429
Woll, Peter 201, 588
Wolman, Harold 1391
Wood, Robert C. 128, 1430
Wooten, Leland M. 321
Worthley, John A. 272-73, 1332
Wright, Deil S. 50-51, 85-86,
  828
Wright, Penny L. 731
Wright, Sonia R. 550
Wurf, Jerry 909
Wynia, Bob L. 165, 910

Y

Yamada, Gordon T. 1139
Yaney, Joseph P. 718
Yankelovich, Daniel 1148
Yanouzas, John N. 680
Yarwood, Dean 202, 484
Yeager, James H., Jr. 1230
Yeager, Samuel 999
Yetton, Philip W. 1510, 1513
Yin, Robert K. 589, 1469
Young, Philip 911

Z

Zald, Mayer N. 630, 640, 1353,
  1431
Zaleznik, Abraham 1514
Zander, Arnold S. 961
Zarb, Frank G. 535
Zarnowiecki, James 113
Zauderer, Donald G. 485
Zickler, Joyce K. 22
Zimmerman, Joseph F. 1392
Zuzak, Charles A. 1393

TITLE INDEX

This index includes all titles of books cited in the text. References are to entry numbers and alphabetization is letter by letter.

A

Active Society, The 135
Administration: The Word and the Science 1530
Administration in Developing Countries 1569
Administration in the Public Sector 421
Administrative Behavior 1255
Administrative Communication 1508
Administrative Decision Making 1237
Administrative Feedback 1491
Administrative Organization 626
Administrative Process and Democratic Theory 136
Administrative Questions and Political Answers 371
Administrative Reform 609
Administrative Revolution, The 608
Administrative State: An Introduction to Bureaucracy, The 431
Administrative State: A Study of the Political Theory of American Public Administration, The 402
Administrative Theories of Hamilton and Jefferson, The 349
Affirmative Action and Equal Opportunity 963
Affirmative Action for Women 1035
Affirmative Discrimination 1000
Age of Discontinuity, The 775

American Bureaucracy 201
American Federal Executive, The 905
American Federalism 41
American Politics in a Bureaucratic Age 144
American Public Administration 427
American System, The 17
Annual Adjustments--The Key to Federal Executive Pay 902
Approach to Productivity in the Public Sector 1047
Area and Administration 1437
Area Redevelopment Administration, The 1527
Are Government Organizations Immortal? 142
Assessment of Federal Regional Councils 44

B

Balance Point between Local Autonomy and National Control, The 1581
Behavioral Approaches to Public Administration 662
Behavior and Organization 649
Big Democracy 129
Black Civil Rights during the Johnson Administration 1005

Budget and National Politics, The 1197

Budget in Brief, The 1182

Budgetary Politics 1202

Budgeting: A Comparative Theory of Budgetary Processes 1226

Budgeting Municipal Expenditures 1186

Bureaucracy (Benveniste) 167

Bureaucracy (Von Mises) 197

Bureaucracy, Policy, and the Public 192

Bureaucracy, Politics, and Public Policy 191

Bureaucracy and Innovation 1155

Bureaucracy and Representative Government 188

Bureaucracy and the Modern World 195

Bureaucracy in a Democracy 141, 177

Bureaucracy in Modern Society 169

Bureaucratic Behavior in the Executive Branch 212

Bureaucratic Experience, The 176

Bureaucratic Opposition 199

Bureaucratic Phenomenon, The 1523

Bureaucratic Power in National Politics 1417

Bureaucratization of the World, The 178

C

Cases in Public Administration 441

Cases in Public Management 756

Changing Administrations 861

Changing Organizations 643

Citizen Participation and the Urban Policy Process 1369

Civil Rights during the Kennedy Administration 1006

Civil Service Commission, The 824, 874

Classics of Organizational Behavior 658

Classics of Organization Theory 668

Classics of Personnel Management 846

Classics of Public Administration 438

Classics of Public Personnel Policy 863

Clients Evaluate Authority 706

Collective Bargaining in the Public Sector 945

Comparative Analysis of Complex Organizations 611, 648

Comparative Public Administration 1515

Comparative Studies in Administration 627

Compendium of Materials on Zero-Base Budgeting in the United States 1328

Conducting the People's Business 423

Congress, the Bureaucracy, and Public Policy 262

Congressional Committees 260

Congressional Control of Administration 253

Contemporary Approaches to Public Budgeting 1199

Control in a Bureaucracy 683

Cost-Benefit Analysis 1130

Costs of Government Regulation of Business, The 338

Craft of Public Administration, The 416

Current Issues in Public Administration 425

D

Decentralization of Government Agencies 1469

Decision Making in the White House 232

Democracy and the Public Service 151

Democracy in the Administrative State 156

Design of Organizations, The 617

Development Administration in Asia 1599

Development of Public Services in Western Europe, 1660-1930, The 1516

Does Civil Service Enhance or Inhibit Productivity? 1075

Dynamic Administration 717

Dynamics of Bureaucracy, The 168
Dynamics of Public Administration, The 417
Dynamics of Public Bureaucracy 424

E

Ecology of Public Administration, The 1571
Economic Advice and Presidential Leadership 211
Economics of Affirmative Action 1036
Economic Theory of Democracy, An 133
Efficient Organization, The 1120
80,000 Governments 3
Elements of Public Administration 432
Employee Innovation and Government Productivity 1141
End of Liberalism, The 147
End to Hierarchy!, An 634
Energy Regulation by the Federal Power Commission 302
Equality and Efficiency 983
Eupsychian Management 732
Excellence 1060

F

Federal Budget in Brief, The 1182
Federal Budget Outlay Estimates 1220
Federal Budget Policy 1210
Federal Contributions to Management 747
Federal Employment Examinations 903
Federal Equal Employment Opportunity 988
Federal Evaluation Policy 556
Federal Grants-in-Aid 85
Federalists, The 408
Federal Organization and Administrative Management 282
Federal Productivity Suffers because Word Processing Is Not Well Managed 1095
Federal Reorganization 283
Federal Service and the Constitution 850
Federal Tax Policy 1346
Feminine Mystique, The 1028
Feminism in American Politics 1029

Forest Ranger, The 1451
Formal Organizations 645
From Amoral to Humane Bureaucracy 1403
From Max Weber 198
Frontiers of Development Administration 1580
Functional Federalism 74
Functions of the Executive, The 745
Future Executive, The 774

G

General and Industrial Management 752
General Revenue Sharing 62
Governmental Process, The 163
Government and Science 795
Government Budgeting 1176
Government Budgeting: Theory, Process, Politics 1196
Government of Strangers, A 758

H

Handbook of Organizations 623
Handbook of Public Administration, A 1595
Higher Civil Service, The 898
History of Public Administration, A 368
How Clean Is Our City? 1121
How Effective Are Your Community Services? 1125
Human Organization, The 728
Human Side of Enterprise, The 730

I

Ideal and Practice in Public Administration 385
Impacts of Computers on Organizations, The 802
Implementing a Productivity Program 1070
Improved Cooperation and Coordination Needed among All Levels of Government 45
Improving Federal Program Performance 1071

Improving Government Productivity 1048

Improving Local Government Productivity 1156

Improving Municipal Productivity 1157

Improving Performance and Productivity 1064

Improving Productivity and the Quality of Work Life 1055

Improving Productivity in State and Local Government 1166

Improving Total Productivity 1077

Increasing Employee Productivity 1086

In Pursuit of Price Stability 1354

Inside Bureaucracy 171

Inside the Bureaucracy 330

Institutional Imperative, The 316

Integrating the Individual and the Organization 708

Intellectual Crisis in American Public Administration, The 383, 396

Intelligence of Democracy, The 145

Inter-Governmental Grant System as Seen by Local, State, and Federal Officials, The 42

Interpersonal Conflict Resolution 716

Introduction to Program Evaluation, An 524

Introduction to the Study of Public Administration 443

It All Depends 631

J

Jacksonians, The 409

Jeffersonians, The 410

L

Leadership and Decision-Making 1510

Leadership and Motivation 1497

Leadership and Organization 1507

Leadership in Administration 1505

Limits of Organizational Change, The 788

Local Government Program Budgeting 1194

Locating, Recruiting and Employing Women 1027

Logic of Collective Action, The 1344

M

Making Federalism Work 40

Making Public Policy 561

Managerial Behavior and Organization Demands 755

Managing Local Government under Union Pressure 952

Managing Non-Profit Organizations 301

Managing Presidential Objectives 229

Managing the Public Sector 765

Managing the Public's Interest 753

Managing Urban America 107

Maximum Feasible Misunderstanding 108

MBO and Productivity Bargaining in the Public Sector 1296

MBO for Nonprofit Organizations 1292

Measuring and Enhancing the Productivity of Service and Government Organizations 1112

Measuring the Effectiveness of Basic Municipal Services 1163

Measuring the Effectiveness of Local Government Services: Recreation 1162

Measuring the Effectiveness of Local Government Services: Transportation 1138

Men, Management, and Morality 1404

Men Who Govern 900

Models for Affirmative Action 964

Models of Man 1258

Modern Organization 636

Modern Public Administration 433

Morality and Administration in Democratic Government 1394

Motivation and Personality 733

Motivation and Productivity 1145

Municipal Output and Performance in New York City 1160

N

Nerves of Government, The   132
New Dimensions of Political Economy   1338
New Patterns of Management   759
New Public Personnel Administration, The   844
New Science of Management Decision, The   1259

O

Old Boys--New Women   1021
On Organizations of the Future   769
Operations Research Models for Public Administration   449
Organisation and Bureaucracy   657
Organizational Behavior   652
Organizational Psychology   739
Organizational Revolution, The   1397
Organizational Society, The   628
Organizational Society: An Analysis and a Theory, The   155
Organization Development   712
Organization Man, The   638
Organizations   624
Organizations and Beyond   630
Organizations and Environments   768
Organizations and Their Managing   757
Organizations in Action   635
Organization Theory   667
Organizing the Presidency   218

P

Papers in Comparative Public Administration   1540
Papers on the Science of Administration   174, 400, 1420
Participation Bureaucracy, The   978
People and Public Administration   434
People in Public Service   822
Personality and Organization   709
Personnel Challenge, The   1082
Perspectives on Administration   442
Perspectives on Public Management   821
Peter Principle, The   736

Plot That Failed, The   224
Police Unionism   925
Policy and Administration   559
Policy Makers, The   564
Policy-Making Process, The   572
Political Bureaucracy   184
Political Economy of Public Organizations, The   1353
Politics, Economics and Welfare   1333
Politics, Position, and Power   35
Politics and Administration   137
Politics and Economics of Public Spending, The   1349
Politics and Public Policy in America   562
Politics and the Bureaucracy   429
Politics of Broadcast Regulation, The   317
Politics of Budgeting Federal Aid, The   31
Politics of Bureaucracy, The   196
Politics of Bureaucracy: A Comparative Perspective, The   1563
Politics of Civil Rights in the Truman Administration, The   995
Politics of Expertise, The   805
Politics of Fiscal Policy Information, The   1348
Politics of Organizational Decision-Making, The   1253
Politics of Taxing and Spending, The   1350
Politics of the Budgetary Process, The   1229
Politics of the Federal Bureaucracy, The   415
Polity, The   146
Position Classification   857
Power Broker, The   99
Power in Organizations   1431
Practical Program Evaluation for State and Local Government Officials   525
Practice of Management, The   751
Pragmatic Federalism   16
Preparing for Affirmative Action   982
President as Chief Administrator, The   237

Presidential Character, The 204
Presidential Power 225
President's Program Directors, The 223
Principles of Management and Organizational Behavior 764
Principles of Public Administration 444
Principles of Scientific Management 767
Productivity: Burden of Success 1093
Productivity, Efficiency, and Quality in Urban Transportation Systems 1134
Productivity Gains through Worklife Improvement 1062
Productivity Improvement 1053
Productivity in Local Government 1165
Productivity in Public Organizations 1067
Productivity in the Local Government Sector 1170
Productivity of City Services 1171
Professional Manager, The 760
Profession and Practice of Program Evaluation, The 511
Profession of Government, The 1521
Program Analysis for State and Local Governments 526
Program Evaluation in the Public Sector 531
Protestant Ethic and the Spirit of Capitalism, The 1355
Public Administration (Dimock and Dimock) 418
Public Administration (Lorch) 426
Public Administration (Presthus) 435
Public Administration: A Comparative Perspective 1538
Public Administration: A Critical Perspective 430
Public Administration: A Synthesis 428
Public Administration: Balancing Power and Accountability 1409
Public Administration: Concepts and Cases 440
Public Administration: Government in Action 437

Public Administration: Policy-Making in Government Agencies 582
Public Administration: Politics and the Political System 382
Public Administration: Readings in Institutions, Processes, Behavior, and Policy 419
Public Administration: Values, Policy, and Change 1421
Public Administration and Democracy 148
Public Administration and Policy Development 583
Public Administration and Public Affairs 422
Public Administration and the Legislative Process 242
Public Administration and the Public Interest 140
Public Administration as Political Process 386
Public Administration in a Democratic Context 134
Public Administration in America 420
Public Budgeting: Program Planning and Evaluation 1206
Public Budgeting and Finance 1188
Public Budgeting Systems 1200
Public Civil Rights Agencies and Fair Employment 996
Public Employees and Policymaking 855
Public Finance in Theory and Practice 1342
Public Interest, The 158
Public Management and Policy Analysis 746
Public Personnel Administration 860
Public Personnel Administration in the United States 809
Public Personnel Systems 835
Public Policy 588
Public Policy: Scope and Logic 566
Public Policy Evaluation 577
Public Policy for the Black Community 994
Public Policy Making 558

Public Policymaking Reexamined   522
Public Policy on the Status of
   Women   1038
Public Program Analysis   581
Public's Business, The   340
Public Use of Private Interest, The
   333

Q

Quest for a Federal Manpower
   Partnership, The   22

R

Raising Productivity   1068
Reader in Bureaucracy   186
Readings in Comparative Public
   Administration   1568
Readings on Productivity in Policing
   1099
Red Tape   180
Reflections on Public Administration
   365
Renewing Organizations   612
Representative Bureaucracy   181
Republican Era, 1869-1901, The   411
Research in Public Administration
   445
Reshaping Government in Metropolitan
   Areas   89
Responsibility in Government   601
Routine Decision-Making   1243

S

Scientific Estate, The   797
Scientific Management   194
Self-Renewal   719
Setting National Priorities   580
Social Psychology of Organizations,
   The   615
Social Science of Organizations, The
   619
Speaking Truth to Power   587
State and Local Government Finance
   and Financial Management   1347
State Government Productivity   1158
State Policies and Federal Programs
   30

States and Intergovernmental Aids,
   The   43
Structure of Organization, The   679
Systematic Thinking for Social
   Action   547

T

Technical Assistance in Public
   Administration Overseas   1598
Theory of Social and Economic
   Organization, The   1356
Toward a Critical Administrative
   Theory   647
Toward a New Public Administra-
   tion   379
Toward a Psychology of Being   734
Transportation Productivity   1116
TVA and the Grass Roots   335

U

Understanding Organizational
   Behavior   641
Understanding Productivity   1073
Understanding Public Policy   565
Understanding Urban Government
   87
Uneasy Partnership, The   10
United States Civil Service
   Commission, The   894
Urban Policy and Politics in a
   Bureaucratic Age   123
Utilization-Focused Evaluation   541

W

Watergate   1410
What Is Revenue Sharing?   63
Without Sympathy or Enthusiasm
   743
Work, Productivity, and Job
   Satisfaction   1148
Work in America   1096
Work Measurements in Local
   Governments   1107
Work Measurement System of the
   Department of Housing and Urban
   Development Has Potential but
   Needs Further Work to Increase
   Its Reliability   1117

Title Index

Z

Zero Base Budgeting 1323
Zero Base Budgeting and Program
  Evaluation 1330
Zero Based Budgeting Comes of Age
  1309

Zero-Base Budgeting for Public
  Programs 1311
Zero Base Budgeting in State and
  Local Government 1332

SUBJECT INDEX

This index is alphabetized letter by letter and numbers refer to entry numbers. Underlined numbers refer to major areas of emphasis within the topic.

A

Abortion, Supreme Court and 561
Academic freedom 795
Accountability and responsibility
    in government 24, 130, 152,
        166, 247, 414, 421, 424,
        430, 432, 435, 547-48,
        590-605, 811, 954, 989,
        1004, 1008, 1010-11, 1177,
        1248, 1268, 1409, 1426,
        1442
    in organizations 717, 749, 795
    in social science research 1423
Accountant-Auditor Examination 903
Administrative Conference of the
        United States 309
Advisory Commission on Intergovern-
        mental Relations 50
Affirmative action 183, 867, 874,
        963-64, 968-69, 976-77,
        980, 982, 987, 992, 1000,
        1005, 1016, 1027, 1035,
        1040
Airlines, regulation of 305
Air pollution and pollution control
        20, 315. See also Clean
        Air Act
Aliens, in the Southwest 11
Allied Services Act 15, 328
Allison, Graham T. 1233

American Arbitration Association
        790
American Federation of State, County,
        and Municipal Employees
        928
American Indians. See Indians
American Society for Public Ad-
        ministration 358, 370,
        472, 1082
    in promoting citizen participation
        1367-68
    women in 1023
American Society for Public Adminis-
        tration. Comparative Ad-
        ministration Group, papers
        of the 1966 meeting 1580
American Society for Public Adminis-
        tration. Conference of
        Minority Public Administra-
        tors 1015
American University 485. See also
        Urban Careers Program
Amherst College, women at 1030
Amtrack 306
Appalachian Regional Commission
        777
Appleby, Paul H. 148
Aquanauts, women as 1030
Arbitration and mediation, statistics
        on 790. See also Public
        employees, personnel ad-
        ministration for

Subject Index

Argyris, Chris 633
Arizona, personnel selection methods in 838. See also Tucson, Ariz.
Armed forces. See Military
Ash, Roy 206, 283
Ash Council Report 303
Asia, development administration in 1597, 1599
Association, right of. See Freedom of association
Astronauts, women as 1030
Atlanta, Ga., government reorganization in 293
Aurora, Ill., revenue sharing in 54
Authority 1472
    female attitudes toward 1039
    strengthening of public officials' 1455
    Weber on 1356
    See also Power

B

Balance theory 692
Barnard, Chester I., contribution to organizational theory 650
Barnard-Simon model 692
Beard, Charles 450
Behavior, human. See Organization (s), the individual and
Behaviorism, in public administration 353, 662. See also Organization(s), behavior and theory of
Behavior modification 1055
Bennis, Warren G. 1146
Bentham, Jeremy 1530
Better Communities Act (1973) 53
Black power 1012
Blacks
    attitudes toward government 819
    as elected officials 1013
    equality and discrimination for in government employment and administration 903, 928, 970, 979, 985, 994-95, 999, 1001-2, 1004-5, 1007, 1009-10, 1012-14, 1016, 1020, 1035, 1045

income distributions of 990
as police 925
public administration education and 452, 998
representation of in bureaucracies and legislatures 36
Block grants 46, 49, 82-83
    under the Rural Development Act 57
    utilization of in Missouri 92
Broadcasting industry, regulation of 317
Brownlow Committee 275, 282
Budget and finance 299, 416-17, 424, 430, 434-35, 438, 441, 547, 565, 580, 621-22, 1172-1230, 1342, 1409, 1435, 1486, 1575, 1577
    administrative agencies and 382
    in the Carter administration 205, 279, 283, 1314, 1316
    citizen participation in 62, 1380, 1382
    concern for in regulatory activities 338
    Congressional and legislative participation in 251-53, 258, 261, 270, 1175, 1183, 1189, 1196, 1198, 1200-1202, 1208, 1215, 1219, 1229
    Council of Governments programs and 32
    economics of 1209, 1216
    estimation processes in 1220
    executive branch and 1181, 1202, 1215
    General Accounting Office responsibilities for 603
    influence of public employment on 1
    interest groups and 1207
    knowledge management in creating 793
    local 62, 122, 580, 952, 1186, 1190, 1194, 1217, 1274, 1280, 1332, 1347, 1382, 1460
    organizational 621-22, 753

politics of 210, 564, 1197,
    1199-1200, 1204, 1213,
    1222, 1227-28, 1230, 1277,
    1281, 1349
productivity and 1065, 1072
in public service institutions 750
state 580, 1189-90, 1201, 1213-
    14, 1264-65, 1273, 1278-
    80, 1301, 1315, 1317,
    1327, 1332, 1347
training for 1184
See also Government spending;
    Performance budgeting; Plan-
    ning, Programming, and
    Budget System; Taxation;
    Zero base budgeting
Budget and Impoundment Control Act.
    See Congressional Budget
    and Impoundment Control
    Act (1974)
Bureaucracy 134, 161, 166-202,
    636, 805, 1424, 1531,
    1538, 1546, 1583, 1588,
    1590, 1596
attitudes of 165
attitudes toward 179, 484
autonomy in 190
blacks in 36
Carter's influence on 234
communication in 223, 1499
conflict in 421
Congress and 141, 200-201,
    253, 262, 269
criticism of and opposition to
    197, 199, 618
decision-making in 1243
defined 1453
in a democracy 141, 177
in developing countries 1556,
    1594
economic development and 1589
effect of on the budget 1211
in Europe 166, 1525, 1530
in France 197, 1523
innovation in 1154-55
interaction with clients 173, 182,
    637
interest groups and 131, 154
leadership in 1500
Marxian interpretation of 155

minorities in 189
motivation in 791
in Nigeria 1548
in Pakistan 1520
policy analysis and making in
    191, 386, 558-89, 592,
    606, 746, 754, 784-85
politics and 144, 173, 175,
    196, 203, 421, 430,
    799, 988, 1551-52,
    1563, 1570
power in 186, 427, 429, 574,
    799, 823, 1413, 1415,
    1417
psychology of 176, 197
as a representative body 181,
    183, 188-89, 834, 851,
    876, 904, 985, 989
sociology of 168, 186, 197
technology in creating 1576
textbooks and readings on 415
theory of 383, 657, 1536
the urban 123
in Vietnam 1529
See also Organization(s); Public
    administration; Public
    employees
Burma, public administration in
    1533
Business, regulation of. See Regu-
    lating agencies and regula-
    tion

C

Cabinet 228, 1424
under Nixon 215, 224
California
control of public morality in
    1414
Proposition 13 in 1380
school revenue in 94
See also Los Angeles; Orange
    County, Calif.; Palo Alto,
    Calif.; Sacramento, Calif.
Canada, Planning, Programming,
    and Budget System in 1281
Capitalism, the Protestant ethic and
    1355
Carter, James E. 14

administrative ability and theory
of 234, 675
budget under 1314, 1316
executive training under 762
federal-local relations under 14
government reorganization under
205, 277, 279, 283, 292,
295
power of 230
staffing under 226
Cabinet positions 228
Central city areas. See Urban areas
Centralization and decentralization
in government 2, 17, 24, 30,
60, 66-67, 75, 77, 80,
82, 88, 92, 96, 109, 118,
139, 219, 287, 416, 443,
547, 773, 1366, 1412,
1431, 1432-69
accountability and 604
budget and 1264
educational system 1376
fiscal areas 1547
management by objectives and
1291
personnel management 845
political power and 1450
productivity and 1169
quality of public administration
in 37
religious revivalism in 1402
under Nixon 12
organizational 606, 650, 688,
743, 752, 761, 764
Charlotte, N.C., government reorganization in 293
Chaucer, Geoffrey 1530
Checks and balances 1424
effect of the bureaucracy on 201
influence of science on 797
the merit system in 877
Chicanos. See Mexican-Americans
Cicero 1530
Cities. See Local government; Urban
areas
Citizen participation 88, 109, 118,
407, 435, 441, 592, 826,
1260, 1358-93, 1422,
1445, 1463
in the budgetary process 62,
1380, 1382

as a challenge to public service
773
in criminal justice agencies
1454
in democracy and federalism 17,
29
in education 1376, 1392
evaluation of the effectiveness
of 1385
in health care 1448
influence on government productivity 1085
in organizations 706
in policy making 559, 572,
1390
in revenue sharing 1389
in social service agencies 1373,
1458
in Sri Lanka 1524
Citizens Commission on Ethics in
Government (Arlington,
Va.) 1401
City managers 139
education for 454
public employee collective
bargaining in a government
using 949
Civil Rights Act (1964) 1005
Title VII 976
Civil Rights Act (1968) 1005
Civil rights and liberties 743,
1143
civil servant involvement in the
fight for 358
employment and 996
in the Johnson administration
1005
in the Kennedy administration
1006
public administration's concern
with 407
for public employees 844, 852
public policy and 565
in the Truman administration
995
See also Freedom
Civil service 439, 808, 847-48
as an action group 1559
as a career and profession 865,
868-70, 873, 875, 878-

80, 883-88, 892, 895-96, 898, 900-901, 904-8, 1128
control of by Nixon 209
in Egypt 1519
evolution of 151
pensions 825, 853
productivity and 1075
reform of 835, 867, 872
    in the Carter administration 205, 279, 881, 890
response to clients by 882
safeguards of 431
in social and political change 1553
training programs in 869, 884, 885, 907, 910
work environment of the 865
See also Bureaucracy; Merit system; Public employees; Senior Civil Service
Civil Service Reform Act (1978) 835, 867, 872, 881, 1034
Clean Air Act 114
Cleveland, government reorganization in 293
Cold war, taxation in 211
Collective bargaining. See Public employees
Colleges. See Education, higher
Columbia University. Gino Speranza Lectures 232
Commission on Organization of the Executive Branch 289
Committee for Economic Development. Research and Policy Committee 1071, 1166
Committee on Research in Public Administration (proposed) 358
Communication(s) 223, 416, 421, 426-27, 439, 555, 573, 579, 615, 645, 667, 676, 705, 718, 742, 757, 780, 1409, 1478-79, 1481, 1485, 1498-99, 1506, 1508
in Congressional-bureaucracy relations 269
in decision-making 546
feedback systems in 1470, 1491, 1501

theoretical analysis of 132
in urban political systems 578
See also Word processing
Communications Satellite Corp. 306
Communist countries, development of bureaucracies in 166.
    See also Russia; Yugoslavia
Community action programs and agencies 40, 108, 238
citizen participation in 1359-60, 1363-64, 1377, 1387-88, 1391
revenue sharing and 83
Community development programs
in federalism 75
in Sri Lanka 1524
See also Neighborhood and community government and control
Community mental health. See Mental health programs
Community Service Learning Program 502
Comprehensive Employment and Training Act (1973) 15, 22, 849
Comprehensive Neighborhood Health Center 1448
Comprehensiveness, Efficiency, Rationality and Technology (CERT) value system 1088
Computers 1068
impact on administration and organization 798, 800-802
Confidential communications. See Privacy, right of
Conflict
in American society 639
among professionals in a bureaucracy 895
in the executive branch 212
in labor relations 918, 921, 935, 942
organizational 606, 608, 615, 624, 636, 667, 670, 678, 681-83, 692-93, 698, 704-5, 716-17, 720, 723, 754, 757, 760, 803, 821
women and role 1031

Congressional Budget and Impoundment Control Act (1974)
   251, 1175, 1183, 1198,
   1208, 1219
Congressional Research Service 244,
   248, 252
Consolidation
   of governments 139, 293
   of police departments 28
Constitutional rights. See Civil
   rights and liberties
Consumerism, government regulation
   and 322
Consumers, public policy and 580
Conventional Public Administration
   (CPA) 647
Cooperative Education Program 808
Corruption (in politics) 805, 1601
   bureaucracies in increasing 200
   in developing nations 1517, 1594
   See also Ethics and morality
Cost-benefit analysis 512, 569,
   1130, 1137, 1149, 1372
   Planning, Programming and Budget
      System and 1282
   in social service agencies 1131
Council of Economic Advisers 211,
   226, 1335, 1338, 1343
Councils of Governments 26, 777
   ability to cope with regional
      problems 32
County government 89
   administration of 119
   myths concerning 25
   revenue sharing and 72
   See also Regionalism
Courts. See Judiciary
Creativity, the bureaucracy and
   1154
Credit, commercial, under the Rural
   Development Act 57
Criminal justice system 3
   allocation of functions in 112
   authority relations in 690
   citizen participation in 1454
   consolidation of metropolitan
      systems 28
   motivation, effectiveness, and
      satisfaction in 1135
   personnel management in 839

   labor relations 925, 940,
      955
   promotional procedures 858
   productivity of 1092, 1099,
      1109, 1113, 1160, 1163
   program evaluation in 545
   public policy and 565
   reform of 41
Culture
   as a creator of social conflict
      639
   federal government in the
      maintenance of 6
Cybernetics 132, 135, 780

D

Dade County, Fla., government of
   106
Dahl, Robert A. 1174
Dallas, government productivity in
   1165
Davenport, Frederick, contribution
   to public administration
   463
Dayton, Ohio, decentralization in
   1462
Debt, national 1210
Decision making 19, 151, 195,
   414, 420-22, 427, 434,
   551, 1231-60, 1409,
   1432, 1510-11
   bibliography on 1239
   in centralized and decentralized
      situations 12, 37, 1456
   in collective bargaining 942
   communication in 546
   community 1260
   congressional 249, 265
   by employees 608
   in the executive branch 212
   in government corporations 340
   group 124
   in human services 1240
   in mental health programs 1234
   metropolitan government and 88,
      106
   minorities in positions of 985
   mixed scanning in 1236
   models of 132, 449, 542,

566, 1237-38, 1243, 1245,
1251
organizational 619, 624, 632,
659, 676-77, 688, 716,
757, 764, 792, 800,
1231, 1253, 1255, 1257
Planning, Programming and Budget
System procedures in 1271-
72, 1281
presidential 214, 232
quantitative methodology in 480
theory of 1550
women and 1044
zero base budgeting and 1322
See also Citizen participation
Defense. See National defense
Delaware, government budgeting in
1486. See also Wilmington,
Del.
Delaware River Basin Commission
777
Democracy 29, 129, 145
bureaucracy in 141, 169, 177
criticism of pluralistic 407
economic theory of 133
federal executive attitudes toward
165
in Japan 1555
leadership in 1504
in modernization processes 1564
organizational 643
participatory 1445
the presidency and 218
public administration in a 134,
136, 156, 782
public service and its relation to
151
role of public personnel administration in 809, 811
Democratic socialism, success of
economic policy-making
under 337
Demonstration Cities and Metropolitan Development Act (1966).
Section 204 45
Denver, government reorganization
in 293
Desegregation in education 1000
Detroit, government productivity in
1165

Developing countries
assistance to 1578
bureaucracy in 1556
developmental programming for
1558, 1593
effect of corruption on 1517,
1594
government, politics, and public policies in 1584
leadership in 1522
model of economic nationalism
for 1544
public administration in 1533,
1540, 1557, 1569, 1571,
1586, 1595
See also Technical assistance;
names of developing
countries (e.g., Nigeria)
Dictatorships, success of industrialization in 1532
Discrimination in employment. See
Equality and discrimination
Domestic Council 222, 226, 236,
298
Due process of law, public employees and 852
Dye, Thomas R. 1174

E

Economic Development Act 1391
Economic growth and development
2, 1547
bureaucracies and 1589
government productivity and
1066
of the Southwestern states 11
Economic nationalism, model for
developing countries 1544
Economic Opportunity Act (1964)
1381
Community Action Program 1363
Economic policy and planning 580,
1338, 1351-52
determinants of 561
Economics
of affirmative action 1036
as a constraint on innovation
1153
democracy explained according
to 133

Subject Index

of Eisenhower 211
in employment theory 1045
of government budgets and fiscal
    policy 1209-10, 1216
influence of government on 151
politics of 3, 146
of public administration 140
in public administration education
    448
under democratic socialism 337
See also Keynesian economics;
    Microeconomics; Political
    economy
Education
    aid to in California 94
    authority relations in 690
    of blacks 1005
    budgeting for in Pennsylvania
        1278
    citizen participation in 109,
        1376, 1392
    decentralization of 1392, 1462,
        1469
    equality of 41
    finance of 966
        federal aid in 31
    idea of a cabinet department for
        323-24
    innovation in 1140
    management of 750
    program analysis in 512
    public policy and 565
    See also Desegregation in educa-
        tion; Public administration,
        study and teaching of
Education, higher 10
    affirmative action in 963
    blacks in 998
    collective bargaining in 921
    in creating a black perspective
        on public management
        1010
    management of 750
    productivity in 1093
    role of in American political
        economy 306
    scientific research in 795
    technical assistance programs of
        1598
    use of power in 1418
    women in 1030

Egypt
    central and local government
        relations in 1581
    civil service in 1519
Eisenhower, Dwight D.
    administrative changes upon the
        inauguration of 870
    civil rights under 1006
    Council of Economic Advisers
        and 211
    presidential powers under 225
Elections 133. See also Voting
Employees. See Public employees
Employment
    federal government in the
        maintenance of 6
    inflation and 1340
    urban 104
    See also Fair employment
        practices; Public employees;
        Unemployment
Employment Act (1946) 1335,
    1337, 1343
Energy 331-32
    Congress and 246
    public policy and 565, 580
    See also U.S. Federal Power
        Commission
England. See Great Britain
Environment
    as a determining component of
        bureaucratization 187
    effect of the social 174
    government agency 1048
    influence on budgeting 1211
        on policy making 558, 565,
            580
        on power and accountability
            1409
    organizational 615-16, 627,
        646, 651, 661, 708,
        762, 768
    technology and the 789
    in urban management and policy
        making 107, 578
    at work 865
    in a world of change 799
Environmental policy and issues
    336
    civil servant involvement in the
        fight for 358

Congress and 255
See also Air pollution and pollution control
Equal Employment Opportunity Act (1972) 1016
Equality and discrimination 165, 362-63, 407, 962-93, 1060
    for minorities 994-1020
    sexual aspects of 1021-45
    See also Affirmative action
Equal Opportunity and Full Employment Act (1976) 1337, 1340, 1351
Equal protection under the law, public employees and 852
Ethics and morality 110, 406, 433-34, 440-41, 448, 566, 1394, 1396-1407, 1410-11, 1420-21, 1423-30
    study of in public administration education 1395, 1416
Etzioni, Amitai 633
Eugene, Oreg., public employee collective bargaining in 915
Europe
    bureaucracies in 166, 1525
    public administration in 1530, 1560
Europe, Western
    bureaucracies in 186
    development of public services in 1516
    federal systems of 34
Executive branch
    budget and 1181, 1216, 1264
    business management techniques applied to 301
    civil servants in 850
    conflict, decision making, and loyalty in 212
    creation of the agencies of 307
    immortality of the departments of 142
    as a law maker 344
    public image of 319
    relationship to Congress 253, 266, 268, 271
        to other government branches 282

reporting procedures in 308
    roles of assistant secretaries and presidential appointees in 330
    supervision and control of bureaucracies by 166, 170, 177
    under Nixon 236
    under Roosevelt 237
    See also Presidency
Executives. See Public employees

F

Fair employment practices 1143
Fairfax County, Va., government productivity in 1081
Federal Assistance Review program 66
Federal Equal Employment Opportunity Program 988
Federal Executive Institute 223, 887, 893
Federal government. See Bureaucracy; Centralization and decentralization in government; Checks and balances; Local government, federal aid to; Politics; Presidency; State government, federal aid to; U.S. Congress; branches of the government (e.g., Executive branch); names of presidents (e.g., Nixon, Richard M.)
Federalism 10, 17, 29, 33, 41, 47, 60, 64, 66, 75, 287, 430, 795
    administration in 27, 40
    comparative study of 34
    the end of 1455
    fiscal aspects of 71, 984, 1338, 1342
    New Structuralism and 76
    Planning, Programming, and Budget System and 1273
    pragmatic nature of 16
    revenue sharing and 4, 55, 86
    subnational governments and 3
    under Nixon 213

under the Rural Development Act
57
urban administration and 114
Federalist Party, contribution to
public administration by
408
Federal Mediation and Conciliation
Services 790
Federal Records Act (1950) 157
Federal regional councils 64, 66-67,
238, 326
assessment of 44
Federal Service Entrance Examination
888, 901, 911
Federal Women's Program 1037
Feminist movement 1023, 1028,
1038
influence on political attitudes and
behavior 1029
Fenno, Richard F., Jr. 1174
Fiedler, Fred E. 1493
Finance, public. See Budget and
finance
Fire protection
allocation of functions in 112
labor relations in 955
productivity in 1119, 1160,
1163
Fiscal policy 275, 441, 984, 1185,
1202, 1210, 1338, 1342,
1346
decentralization of 1547
federalism in 10, 71
knowledge management in creating
793
politics of 61, 1348
state 73
under Nixon 235
See also Budget and finance;
Monetary policy
Flint, Charles, contribution to public
administration 463
Follett, Mary Parker 1026
Ford, Gerald R.
civil service 847
decision making under 214
power of 230
staffing under 226
Ford Foundation 619
technical assistance programs of
1598

Foreign policy and affairs 299,
580
Congress and 240
See also Technical assistance
Foundations, in creating a black
perspective on public
management 1010. See
also Ford Foundation
France
bureaucracy in 197, 1523
central and local government
relations in 1581
Freedom 159, 741, 796
bureaucracy as a limit on 197
See also Civil rights and liberties
Freedom of association, public
employees and 852
Freedom of Information Law (New
York, 1974) 153
Freedom of speech
federal executive attitudes toward
165
public employees and 811, 852
Free enterprise
defense of 197
federal government and 6
Protestant ethics and 1335
Freud, Sigmund, contribution to
organizational theory 1546
Fulton County, Ga., government
reorganization in 293

G

Georgia, government budgeting in
1315, 1317, 1327, 1332.
See also Atlanta, Ga.;
Fulton County, Ga.
Germany, bureaucracy in 197
Gerrymandering 134
Government
influence on society, economy,
and policy 151
planning in 167
psychology of dependence on 9
public images of 319
reform in 139, 607, 609
theoretical analysis of 132
See also Bureaucracy; County
government; Local govern-

ment; State government;
Public administration
Government agencies. See Executive
branch; Government Corporations; Regulatory agencies;
names of government agen-
cies under U.S. (e.g.,
U.S. Department of State)
Government corporations 334, 340
Government Employees Training Act
(1958) 831
Government purchasing, Councils of
Governments programs in 32
Government spending 2, 1202,
1269, 1577
politics of 1349-50
productivity and 1072
under Nixon 235
Grants 66, 71, 74, 114, 298,
360
by HEW 328
See also Block grants
Grants-in-aid 18, 41, 65, 74,
76, 85, 121, 360, 777,
1433
influence on local employment
68-69
survey of attitudes on 42
See also Block grants
Great Britain
administrative reform in 166
central and local government relations in 1581
policy-making in 572
program budgeting in 1543
Gross national product 1080
public expenditures as a percentage of 2
Groups 124, 441, 667
behavior in 658
interaction processes in 1258
leadership in 1473, 1480, 1482
organization of and values in
163, 439
psychology of 739
small 649
superiority over individuals 1051
theory of 1344
See also Interest groups; Organiza-
tion(s); Pressure groups

Gulick, Luther H., contribution to
public administration 383

H

Hamilton, Alexander 208
contribution to public administration 349
government reorganization and
288
Handicapped, civil service and the
1034
Harriman, Mary Averell, contribution to public administration 463
Hartford, Conn., public employee
collective bargaining in
948
Hatch Act 830, 841, 889
Health programs and agencies
analysis of 512
for blacks 1005
citizen participation in 1448
decentralization of 1469
leadership in 1512
power and control in public
1412, 1432
productivity in local 1160
public policy and 565
revenue sharing and 56
See also Industrial health and
safety; Mental health programs
Higher education. See Education,
higher
Hoover Commissions 275, 282,
289, 299, 886
the second 281
Hopkins, Harry, contribution to
public administration 378
Hospitals
allocation of functions in 112
management of 750
organizational structure of 699
productivity in 1101, 1160
role of in American political
economy 306
Hours of labor
flexible programs for 722, 854,
1053

relationship to productivity 1152
House, Robert J. 1493
Housing
    affirmative action in 1000
    for blacks 1005
    decentralization of services for
        1469
    federal role in 128
    innovation in local programs for
        1140
Housing, low-cost, intergovernmental
    relations in 117
Housing and Community Development
    Act (1974) 15
Human behavior. See Organiza-
    tion(s), the individual in
Humanism, organizational 598, 737
Human resource programs and services
    1409
    decision making in 1240
    in federalism 75
    productivity in 1065, 1122,
        1160

I

Ideology, impact on policy making
    559, 564
Illinois. Department of Corrections,
    budget of 1332
Illinois, public employee collective
    bargaining in 936. See
    also Aurora, Ill.
Illinois State University, affirmative
    action at 1036
Incentive systems. See Reward and
    incentive systems
Income
    distribution of 965, 990
    racial differences in 1045
Independent regulatory commissions.
    See Regulatory·agencies and
    regulation
India, public administration in 1533
Indianapolis, decentralization in
    1462
Indians, development of policies
    toward 561
Individuals
    behavior and motivations of 658

in groups 1344
in organizations 608, 610, 628,
    638, 707-11, 716-17,
    719, 724, 728-30, 732-
    37, 740-42
Industrial health and safety 846,
    958
    public policy and 580
Industrialization, success of in a
    dictatorship 1532
Industrialized areas, quality of
    public administration in
    37
Inflation
    full employment and 1340
    government productivity and
        1068
    influence on state fiscal policy
        73
Information technology 800
Integrated Grant Administration
    concept 67
Interest groups 131, 158, 424,
    432
    energy policy and 332
    function in the government
        process 163
    influence on bureaucracies 154
        on government agencies 147
    policy making and 588
    the public administrator and
        140, 382
    in the regulatory process 317
Intergovernmental Cooperation Act
    (1968). Title IV 45
Intergovernmental Personnel Act
    (1970) 48
Intergovernmental relations 1-51,
    275, 420, 1409, 1437
    in the budgetary process 1200
    in the Kansas City metropolitan
        area 111
    in low-cost housing projects 117
    planning and 13
    theory of 21
International City Management
    Association 1163
Interstate compacts and agreements
    8, 298
Iowa, University of 519

J

Jacksonian period, contribution to
public administration 409
Jacksonville, Fla.
centralization in 1468
government reorganization in 291
Japan, development of democracy in
1555
Jefferson, Thomas (Jeffersonians)
contribution to public administration 349, 410
federalism of 4
Job satisfaction 126, 381, 650,
669, 807, 941, 1056,
1062, 1147-48, 1150, 1152
feedback systems in 1470
loyalty and 685
morale and 1101
in police departments 1135
in state government 813
See also Motivation; Reward and
incentive systems
Johnson, Lyndon Baines
domestic policies of 40
presidential power under 225
women in government and 1032
Joint Financial Management Improvement Program 1074
Judiciary 158
control of the bureaucracy by 380
in Pakistan 1520
as a policy-maker 588
in the regulatory process 317
responsibility of 599
See also U.S. Supreme Court
Junior Federal Assistant Examination
903
Juvenile delinquency programs, citizen participation in 1377

K

Kansas, public employee union
representation in 934
Kansas City, intergovernmental
management in 111
Kennedy, John F. 225
acceptance of Keynesian
economics by 211
civil rights under 1006

Keynesian economics 211, 1269, 1352
Knowledge
management of 772, 775, 779-
80, 784-85, 793
similarity to power 211, 793
Korea, civil service in 1553
Korean War, Council of Economic
Advisers and 211

L

Laboring classes
concern for political power by
1444
history of 957
Labor laws and legislation 1143
Labor relations. See Public
employees
Laissez-faire. See Free enterprise
Language
of bureaucracies and organizations 176, 1129
use of in policy analysis 579
Law
administrative departments in
making of 344
of public administration 406,
416, 424
Leadership 119, 163, 352, 416,
420-21, 611, 615, 636,
643, 658, 667, 676,
694, 698, 717, 774,
1409, 1472-75, 1480,
1486, 1488, 1490, 1492-
97, 1500, 1502-5, 1507,
1509, 1511-12, 1514
in developing countries 1522
influence of self-esteem on
1487
influence on productivity 1482,
1512
in legislatures 250
of Mao Tse-Tung 1565
models of 1471, 1476-77,
1483, 1510, 1513
training and experience in
1483-84, 1489
women and 1024, 1026, 1043
League of Nations 1562
League of Women Voters 1390

Legislatures
    administration of 241-42, 272-
        73, 382, 432
    authority in 250
    blacks in 36
    budget and 270, 1189, 1196,
        1200-1201, 1215
    program review by 247
    responsibility of 599
    supervision of bureaucracies by
        166
    See also U.S. Congress
Le Play, . . . 1530
Liberalism 147
Library services
    allocation of functions in 112
    effectiveness of measurement of
        1163
    innovation in public 1140
Lindblom, Charles 1174, 1235,
        1245, 1247, 1250
Loans, low-interest to cities 105
Lobbyists
    Congress and 249
    in policy making 572
    the public administrator and 140
Local government 3, 100, 146
    accountability in 590
    administration of 18, 107, 114,
        116, 120
        team approaches to 124
        training in 115
    allocation of functions in 112
    budget in 62, 580, 952, 1186,
        1190, 1194, 1217, 1274,
        1280, 1332, 1382
    centralization and decentralization
        in 88, 118, 1460, 1462
    citizen participation in 1362,
        1378, 1382, 1386
    contracted services in 91
    cooperation with the federal
        government 14
    federal aid to 46, 49, 61, 92,
        105, 114, 360
    finance 122, 1347, 1460
    fiscal federalism and 984
    influence of federal decentraliza-
        tion on 30
        of grants-in-aid on employment
        68-69

    innovation in 1140
    internship programs of 491, 502
    labor relations in 927, 930,
        942, 949, 952, 954
    minority employment in 1002
    myths concerning 25
    personnel management in 121
    planning in 122
    policy making in 576
    political stability of 93
    productivity in 1047, 1070,
        1075, 1081, 1084, 1090,
        1102-5, 1107, 1114,
        1125, 1132, 1134, 1138,
        1156-57, 1159-67, 1170-
        71
    program evaluation in 525-26,
        529
    as providers of services to state
        governments 70
    reform and reorganization of 41,
        87, 89-90, 106, 291,
        293
    relations with state government
        15-16, 114
        with the central government
        1581
    revenue sharing and 59, 62,
        78, 84
    wage determination for employees
        of 916
    women in 1042
    See also County government;
        Suburbs; Urban areas
London, decentralization in 1462
Los Angeles
    government productivity in
        1075
performance budgeting in 1181
Loyalty
    conflicts of 1401
    in the executive branch 212
    organizational 685, 742,
        1257, 1557
    by public employees 813, 821

M

Management. See Public administra-
        tion; Public employees;
        Scientific management

Management by objectives 229, 846, 1077, 1132, 1199, 1284-1304, 1318-19
  labor-management relations and 1296
  in organizations 674, 723, 753, 764, 1292
Manpower and manpower planning 831, 1078, 1111
  in intergovernmental relations 48
  program analysis in 512
  in urban management 95
  See also Comprehensive Employment and Training Act (1973)
Mao Tse Tung, as a leader 1565
March, James G. 1233
Marx, Karl (Marxism)
  bureaucracy according to 155
  contribution to organizational theory 657, 1546
Mass transit 105
Maxwell, George, contribution to public administration 463
Meckleburg County, N.C., government reorganization in 293
Mediation. See Arbitration and mediation
Mental health programs 548
  decision making in 1234
  evaluation of 515
  organizational development in advancing 738
Merit system 151, 809, 857, 864, 866, 872, 876-77, 899, 909, 914, 933, 969, 981, 986-88, 1037
  examinations in 891, 903
Merit Systems Protection Board 867
Mexican-Americans
  discrimination against in public institutions 997, 1002
  social services for 11
Michels, Roberto, contribution to organizational theory 657
Michigan, public employee collective bargaining in 936. See also Detroit
Microeconomics 1269
Middle class
  importance to development of a national state 1544

taxation and the 2
  See also Laboring classes
Migrant laborers, social services for 11
Military
  authority structure of 687
  blacks in 1005
  characteristics of the leaders of 905
  Congress and 561, 564
  retention of personnel by 633
  women in 1030
Mills, C. Wright 155
Milwaukee, government productivity in 1165
Minimum wage 1143
Minneapolis, Minn., centralization in 1468
Minnowbrook Conference on New Public Administration 363, 379, 470, 571, 655
Minority groups
  in bureaucracies 189
  CETA programs for 849
  citizen participation by 1367
  federal aid to businessmen from 38
  equality and discrimination for in government employment and administration 835, 876, 963, 970, 977-98, 982, 992, 994-1020, 1034, 1040
  influence of centralization on 1466
  recruitment to public service 804
  See also Blacks; Mexican-Americans; Migrant laborers
Missouri, use of Community Development Block Grants in 92. See also St. Louis; St. Louis County
Model Cities Program 40
  citizen participation in 1359, 1377, 1379, 1387-88
  revenue sharing and 83
Modernization 1564, 1600
  European patterns of 1525
  political development and 1531
  in Russia 1532

Monetary policy 1185. See also
    Budget and finance; Fiscal
    policy
Montgomery County, Md., low-cost
    housing in 117
Morality. See Ethics and morality
Moses, Robert 99
Mosher, William E., contribution to
    public administration 463
Motivation 658, 719, 733-34,
    764, 823, 859, 862,
    1048, 1076, 1090, 1135,
    1144-46, 1166
  for group membership 1258
  leader influences on 1490, 1497
  management by objectives
    techniques in 1294
  noneconomic 745
  in state government 813
  See also Job satisfaction; Reward
    and incentive systems
Mudd, John 1444
Municipal government. See Local
    government

N

Nader, Ralph 283
Nashville, Tenn.
  centralization in 1468
  measurement of municipal service
    effectiveness in 1163
Nassau County, N.Y., government
    productivity in 1165
National Academy of Public
    Administration 113
National Association of Schools
    of Public Affairs and Ad-
    ministration 469, 474,
    502, 506
National Center for Productivity and
    Quality of Working Life
    1074
National Center for Public Service
    Internships 502
National defense 144
  Congress and 240
  in the Korean War 211
  public policy and 565, 580
  See also Military

National Education Association
    942
Nationalism. See Economic
    nationalism
Nationalization, of railroads 304
National security 299
National Urban Corps 502
National Urban Fellows program
    491, 502
Natural resources programs, in
    federalism 75
Nebraska, public employee
    unionism in 922
Neighborhood and community
    government and control
    87, 89, 103, 109, 392
  in New York City 96, 118
  in social programs 547
  See also Community development
    programs
Nevada, public employee collec-
    tive bargaining in 919
New Jersey, government budgeting
    in 1332
New Public Administration (NPA)
    647
New York, State University of,
    internship program at 508
New York City
  decentralization in 1462
  government productivity in
    1160-61
  neighborhood government in 96,
    109, 118
  public employee collective
    bargaining in 920, 948,
    950
New York City. Office of Neigh-
    borhood Government 109
New York State
  privacy law in 153
  public employee unionism in
    922
  See also Nassau County, N.Y.;
    Suffolk County, N.Y.
New York University. Graduate
    School of Public Administra-
    tion 446
New York University. Learning
    System for Administrators
    476

Nigeria, bureaucracy and political
    development in 1548
Nixon, Richard M.
    budget and 1198
    bureaucracy and 201, 203, 209
    civil service and 347
    the Domestic Council under 222,
        236
    federal regional councils and 67
    government reform under 12, 215,
        224, 263, 278, 283-85
    impoundment of funds by 235
    management by objectives and
        229, 1300, 1304
    "New Federalism" of 213
    staffing under 226
    status of women and the adminis-
        tration of 1038
Nuclear energy, environmental
    aspects of 789
Nudism, government control of in
    California 1414
Nursing, patterns of work organiza-
    tion in 820

O

Oklahoma, survey of local govern-
    ment productivity in 1157
Ombudsmen 743
Operations research 449
Orange County, Calif., government
    productivity in 1090
Oregon, public employee unionism
    in 922. See also Eugene,
    Oreg.
Organization(s) 138, 162, 606-40
    behavior and theory of 174, 195,
        367, 416, 420, 424, 435-
        36, 438, 615, 617, 623-
        24, 628, 635, 641-77,
        710, 725, 745, 1120,
        1233, 1409, 1546
    change and future outlook for
        768-803
    communication in 615, 645,
        667, 676, 705, 718, 757,
        780, 1478, 1498, 1501,
        1506, 1508
    comparative studies of 169, 627,
        648

conflict in 606, 608, 615,
    624, 636, 667, 670,
    678, 681-83, 692-93,
    698, 704-5, 716-17,
    720, 723, 754, 760,
    803, 821
decision making in 619, 624,
    632, 659, 676-77, 680,
    688, 716, 757, 764,
    792, 800, 1231, 1253,
    1257
development of 712-15, 718,
    720-23, 725-27, 729,
    731, 738, 743-45
efficiency and effectiveness of
    1120, 1123, 1126, 1133
ethics and 1397, 1404
the individual and 608, 610,
    628, 638, 654, 665,
    671, 689-90, 707-11,
    716-17, 719, 724, 728-
    30, 732-37, 740-42
loyalty in 685, 742, 1257,
    1557
management in 666, 669,
    745-67, 778
power and leadership in 611,
    615, 619, 636, 640,
    651, 658, 660, 667,
    676, 694, 698, 703,
    717, 741, 749, 760,
    1126, 1412, 1431, 1472,
    1475-77, 1483-84, 1488,
    1495, 1503, 1505, 1507,
    1510, 1514
psychology of 652, 739
research and the 623, 627, 641,
    667, 731, 781
sexual structuring of 1022,
    1025, 1041
social psychology of 615, 663,
    678
sociology of 645, 659-60
structure and authority in 679-
    81, 684-91, 694-97,
    703, 706, 752, 757
See also Bureaucracy; Public
    administration
Outward Bound Schools 1030

Subject Index

P

Pakistan, bureaucracy and the judiciary in 1520

Palo Alto, Calif., government productivity in 1165

Parliamentary government, compared to the presidential system 221

Participatory management. See Public administration, democratic and participatory approaches to; Organization(s), management in

Patronage, political 99, 160, 426, 894, 914

Payments for Municipal Services program (Wisconsin) 70

Peace, as a national goal 6

Peer groups 1051

Pendleton Act (1883) 329, 894

Pennsylvania
  decentralization in 1463
  Planning, Programming, and Budget System in 1278, 1280
  See also Philadelphia

Perfectionism, the public interest in 158

Performance appraisal. See Public administration, program evaluation in

Performance budgeting 275, 1132, 1181, 1192, 1196, 1218, 1269

Personnel management. See Public employees, personnel administration for

Philadelphia, Model Cities Program in 1379

Pittsburgh, University of. Graduate School of Business. Seminar in the Social Sciences of Organization 619

Planning, Programming, and Budget System 673, 1131-32, 1137, 1193-94, 1196, 1199-1200, 1206, 1216, 1228-29, 1241, 1261-83, 1288, 1290, 1301, 1315,

1321, 1323, 1349, 1366, 1543

Police. See Criminal justice system

Policy analysis. See Public administration, policy analysis and making in; U.S. Congress, policy analysis and making in

Political economy 100, 144, 1137, 1333-57, 1431

Political ethics. See Ethics and morality

Political parties 17, 133, 158, 233, 562
  bossism in 137
  control of presidents by 239
  effect of patronage on 160
  policy making and 572, 588
  public administrators and 382
  responsibility of 599

Political patronage. See Patronage, political

Political science 387
  in public administration education 474
  theory and models in 132, 202

Political science engineering 174

Politics 562
  of budgeting 210, 564, 1197, 1199-1200, 1213, 1222, 1227-28, 1230, 1277, 1281, 1349
  the bureaucracy in 144, 173, 175, 196, 203, 421, 430, 799, 822, 988, 1551-52, 1563, 1570
  comparative 1526
  economics of 3, 146
  effect of patronage on local 160
  federal executive attitudes toward 165
  of federal government organization 35
  of fiscal relations 61, 1348
  influence of the feminist movement on 1029
  of science on 797
  of metropolitan government 93, 123
  models of 565

of neighborhood government 96
of personnel administration 809
of policy-making 566, 573, 575,
    578, 582, 584
of program evaluation 529, 531
of public administration 136-37,
    140, 146, 380, 389-90,
    395, 402, 406, 416-18,
    426, 430, 436, 438-40,
    443, 447, 559, 582
role of interest groups in 163
study and teaching of 1504
of taxation 1350
theoretical analysis of 132
See also Corruption (in politics);
    Ethics and morality; Patron-
    age, political; Political
    economy
Pollution. See Air pollution and
    pollution control; Environ-
    mental policy and issues
Poor
concern for political power by
    1444
federal aid to 128
the New Structuralists and the
    76
public policy and 565
Poverty programs
citizen participation in 1358
criticism of 125
historical look at 108
Power 35, 135, 426, 451, 593,
    606, 818, 1408-9, 1419,
    1422, 1439, 1444, 1460
bureaucracies and 186, 427,
    429, 574, 799, 823,
    1413, 1415, 1417
collective bargaining as 914
congressional 564
decentralization and 1450
exercise of by leaders 1494,
    1496
in higher education 1418
influence of government reorgani-
    zation on 276
influence on social change 1535
institutionalization of 287
organizational 615, 619, 640,
    651, 658, 660, 667, 703,

717, 741, 749, 757,
    760, 1126, 1412, 1431,
    1472
presidential 225, 230
similarity to knowledge 211,
    793
trend in the theory of 8
women and 1044
Power resources. See Energy
Presidency 158, 203-39
administrative aspects of 219-
    20, 229, 231
budget and 1197, 1202, 1204
compared to parliamentary sys-
    tems 221
control of the bureaucracy by
    141, 177, 201
decision-making of 214, 232
Hamilton's theory of 208
the Office of Management and
    Budget and 216, 219
organization of 218
policy-making by 561, 588
power of 225, 230
prediction of performance of
    204
in the regulatory process 317
relationships with Congress 203,
    264, 266, 580, 1424
with government bureaus 207
reliance on economic advisers
    by 1338
responsibility of 599
staffing by 226-27, 861
cabinet positions 228
See also Executive branch; names
    of presidents (e.g., Nixon,
    Richard M.)
Presidential Management Intern
    program 488, 496, 808
President's Advisory Council on the
    Reorganization of the
    Executive Branch 215
President's Committee on Administra-
    tive Management. See
    Brownlow Committee
Press, Congress and the 249
Pressure groups, responsibility of
    599. See also Interest
    groups; Lobbying

Subject Index

Prince George's County, Md., urban
    management in 119
Privacy, right of 311
    in New York state 153
Privilege, doctrine of 814
Productivity. See Public employees,
    productivity of
Professional and Administrative Career
    Examination 903
Program analysis. See Public admin-
    istration, program evaluation
    in
Program budgeting. See Planning,
    Programming, and Budget
    System
Program Evaluation Act (1977) 553
Property tax 41, 70
    revenue sharing and 72
Protestantism, development of free
    enterprise and 1355
Psychology 732-34
    of bureaucracy 176, 197
    of dependence on government 9
    organizational 652, 739
    of structured society 155
    of women in the work force 1045
Public administration 18, 39, 149,
    151, 174, 184, 329, 345-
    414, 743, 1345, 1353
    behavioristic approaches to 353,
    662
    in the Carter administration 205,
    675
    comparative and developmental
    studies of 152, 1515-1601
    in the context of a democracy
    134, 136, 156
    in county government 119
    democratic and participatory
    approaches to 193, 345,
    432
    economics of 146
    in federalism 27
    history of 348, 351, 359, 361,
    364, 368, 374-75, 378,
    398-99, 908-11, 413, 778
    human relations in 724
    internships in 473, 486-509
    job placement in 473
    legislatures and 241-42

    in local government 18, 107,
    114, 116, 120
    training for 115
    policy analysis and making in
    191, 386, 558-89, 592,
    606, 746, 754, 989,
    1429
    politics of 136-37, 140, 146,
    382, 389-90, 395, 402,
    406, 416-18, 420, 430,
    436, 438-40, 443, 447,
    559, 582, 784-85
    professional nature of 391
    program evaluation in 510-57,
    567, 607, 753, 1130,
    1132, 1330, 1406, 1428,
    1435
    quality of 37
    research in 445, 449, 464,
    472, 480-81, 483-84
    role theory perspective for 202
    in small communities 97
    sociology of 865
    sources of innovation in 23
    stress in 735
    study and teaching of 353, 373,
    380, 419, 426, 446-48,
    450-51, 453, 457, 459-
    63, 465-66, 468-71, 474-
    78, 482, 484-85, 519,
    583, 784, 885, 998,
    1395, 1416, 1447
    in adult education 458
    blacks and 452
    city managers and 454
    in developing countries 1586
    evaluation in 467
    finance of 455
    history of 479
    standards 456
    survey of supervisors in 126
    textbooks and readings 382,
    415-44, 746, 765
    theory of 346, 349-50, 366,
    370, 373, 376-77, 382,
    394, 396, 402-3, 406,
    417, 428, 433, 447, 461,
    544, 583, 654-55
    See also Bureaucracy; Ethics and
    morality; Organization(s);

Public employment; headings that relate to public administration (e.g., Centralization and decentralization; Revenue sharing; Taxation)

PUBLIC ADMINISTRATION REVIEW 371

Public employees 1
  advocacy, protest, and political activity by 310, 358, 830, 841, 850, 852, 884, 889
  attitudes of 165
  attitudes toward 817-18
  blacks as 1013
  Councils of Governments in handling problems of 32
  discrimination and equality toward 835, 867, 874, 876, 962-93
    minorities 994-1020
    sexual aspects 1021-45
  influence of grants-in-aid on local 68-69
  management concerns relating to 745-67, 778, 871, 1128
    training programs in 762, 794, 869, 885
  manpower planning for 831
  personnel administration for 299, 421, 430, 433, 435, 438-39, 441, 443, 723, 804-961
    appraisal in 521, 753
    federal role in local and state 121
    history of 864
    labor relations 339, 416, 763, 773, 815, 826, 835-36, 842, 846, 854, 860, 866, 912-61, 1052, 1054, 1063, 1069, 1078, 1497
    politics of 809
    recruitment, promotions, and careers 439, 443, 473, 1076
  productivity of 381, 650, 669, 753, 941, 967, 1046-99, 1409
    black administrators and 1007
    case studies in 1068

demand analysis in 1092
effectiveness and efficiency in 152, 185, 700, 707-8, 745, 751, 757, 1120-39, 1162-63
in the federal government 1071-72, 1074, 1080, 1095, 1111, 1117, 1132, 1139
influence of leadership on 1482, 1512
innovation and motivation in 1101, 1140-55
labor-management relations and 920, 931, 941, 948, 1052, 1054, 1063, 1069, 1078
in local government 1047, 1070, 1075, 1081, 1084, 1090, 1102-5, 1107, 1114, 1125, 1134, 1138, 1156-57, 1159-67, 1170-71
loyalty in 685
measurement of 152, 1081, 1087, 1099, 1100-1119, 1162-63
merit concept and 864
morale and 1151
of pension assets 825
in state government 1046, 1065, 1070, 1084, 1158-59, 1166, 1168-69
statistics 2
See also Bureaucracy; Civil service; Job satisfaction; Merit system; Motivation; Reward and incentive systems

Public Employment Programs (PEP), productivity and 1089
Public finance. See Budget and finance; Government spending; Taxation
Public health agencies. See Health programs and agencies
Public Information Act 596
Public interest 140, 158
  policy making and 568
  typology of conceptions of 150

Public libraries. See Library services
Public officials. See Public employees
Public policy. See Public administration, policy analysis and making in; U.S. Congress, policy analysis and making in
Public safety, decentralization of services for 1469. See also Criminal justice system; Fire protection
Public services and goods 1345
  development of in Western Europe 1516
  distribution of in centralized and decentralized situations 1433, 1460, 1465, 1467-69
  of urban 98
  group theory and 1344
  relation to democracy 151
  See also Social services
Public utilities, management of 750
Public welfare. See Social welfare
Purchasing. See Government purchasing

R

Railroads 312
  nationalization of 304
Rand Corp. 1283, 1429
Rationalism; rationality 1232, 1235-36, 1246-48, 1250, 1252, 1254-55, 1258
  as an organizational imperative 614, 635, 667, 1233
  the public interest in 158
Realism, the public interest in 158
Reapportionment 134
Recession (1953-54), Council of Economic Advisers and 211
Records management 157, 400, 747
Recreation
  allocation of functions in 112
  measurement of effectiveness of 1162-63
Regionalism 7
  administrative structures for 1465
  Councils of Government in 32

local government and 106
See also Federal regional councils
Regulatory agencies and regulation 305, 322, 325, 327, 333, 337, 343, 357, 360, 420, 432, 441, 826, 1357
  costs of 318, 338, 341
  reform of 283
  See also names of regulatory agencies (e.g., U.S. Federal Power Commission)
Religion, influence on political ethics 1402. See also Protestantism
Reorganization Acts 289
  of 1949 290
Repression, public policy and 565
Research and development, government and 299, 481, 783, 795. See also Public administration, research in; Social science research
Resources, allocation of 1431
Results-Oriented Social Services Evaluation (ROSSE) 1122
Revenue sharing 42, 46, 49, 55, 59, 62, 64, 73, 75-78, 86, 984, 1338
  in administrative reform 18
  allocation in 53, 79, 84
  in Aurora, Ill. 54
  citizen participation in 1389
  county government and 72
  expenditure decisions in 56
  goals of 4
  human services agencies and 83
  myths of and opposition to 52, 63, 71
  social programs and 83
  state government and 59, 62, 78
  urban planning and 58
Reward and incentive systems 421, 1050, 1055, 1059, 1068, 1075, 1084, 1090, 1104, 1128, 1150-51. See also Motivation
Rhode Island, compulsory arbitration with police in 940

Riggs, Fred 1515, 1549, 1557
Rockefeller, Nelson, role in the
    Domestic Council 222
Roosevelt, Franklin D., administrative
    ability of 237, 282
Rural areas, programs of the Johnson
    administration in 40
Rural Development Act (1972) 57
Russia
    bureaucracy in 197, 1589
    compared to the U.S. 1528
    economic development in 1589
    modernization process in 1532
    policy making in 572

S

Sacramento, Calif., government
    reorganization in 293
Safe Streets Act 15
St. Louis
    government reorganization in 293
    police consolidation in 28
St. Louis County, urban management
    in 119
St. Paul, Minn., centralization in
    1468
St. Petersburg, Fla.
    budget process in 1382
    measurement of municipal service
        effectiveness in 1163
Saint Simon, . . . 1530
Sanitation services
    allocation of functions in 112
    productivity in 1160
    See also Sewerage; Solid waste dis-
        posal; Waste water treatment
Schmoller, . . . 1530
Schools. See Education; Education,
    higher
Science
    effect on political ideas 797
    federal government and 795
    federal-state partnership in 777
    role of in public administration
        1420
    See also Research and development;
        Technology
Scientific management 194, 643,
    657, 767, 794
    defense of 618

Scientific Public Administration
    (SPA) 647
Scientists, accountability of 596
Self-actualization 733-34, 1232
    concepts of 639
    in organizations 711, 741
Self-esteem, influence on leader-
    ship 1487
Self-interest 1344
Selznick, Philip 610
Senior Civil Service 886, 904,
    907
Senior Executive Service 867,
    872, 890
Sensitivity training 712-13, 743,
    1507
Serrano case 94
Services. See Public services and
    goods; Social services
Sewerage, allocation of functions
    in providing 112
Sexism. See Women
Sharkansky, Ira 1174
Simon, Herbert 383, 610, 1233,
    1345
Simulation methods, in decision-
    making 1243
Small businessmen, federal aid to
    minority 38
Social action, as a creator of
    social conflict 639
Social change 786, 803
    bureaucracy and 169
    civil service in 1553
    decision making during rapid
        1235
    organizational responses to 1155
    power distribution and 1535
Social control 174, 741
    through administration 388
Social engineering 796
Social indicators 1132
Socialism, versus free enterprise
    197. See also Democratic
        socialism
Social justice, in public policy
    566. See Equality and
        discrimination
Social planning 158
Social problems 826

Congressional committee roles in
    solving 260
identification of 547
Social psychology, of organizations
    615, 663, 678
Social reform, professionalization of
    564
Social science research
    applied to policy evaluation 538,
        550
    ethics of 1423
Social sciences
    in social policy 108
    use of in public administration
        275, 361, 376
Social security, federal government
    in maintenance of 6
Social services
    accountability in programs for
        605
    citizen participation in 1373,
        1458
    cost-benefit analysis in 1131
    equity in distribution of 993
    importance of communications to
        delivery of 1485
    measurement of effectiveness of
        1136
    for migrant workers 11
    program analysis in 512-13, 517,
        547, 552
    revenue sharing and 83, 256
    zero base budgeting in 1321
    See also Public services and goods
Social welfare 3, 10, 144
    allocation of functions in 112
    analysis of programs of for the
        1960s 143
    authority relationships in agencies
        for 690
    for blacks 1005
    bureaucracry in 182
    centralization of 1464
    citizen participation in programs
        for 1358
    federal take over of 73, 105
    leadership of programs for 1512
    power in agencies serving 1432
    program evaluation in 543
    public policy and 565
    reform of 41

Social Worker Examination 903
Society 138, 367
    bureaucracy based on the inter-
        dependence of 161
    influence of government on 151
    need of organizations in 162
    social-psychology of structured
        155
    theoretical analysis of 132, 135
Sociology
    of bureaucracies 168, 186, 197
    of organizations 645, 659-60
    of public administration 865
Solid waste disposal, efficiency
        measurement of activities
        in 1121, 1163
Southern California, University of.
        School of Public Administra-
        tion 465
Southern Regional Educational Board.
        Resource Development Pro-
        ject 491
Southern states, black employment
        in 1045
Southwestern states, economic
        development of 10
Spence, . . . 1530
Spending policy. See Government
        spending
Speyer Academy of Administrative
        Science (Germany) 1560
Spoils system. See Patronage,
        political
Sri Lanka, community development
        in 1524
State and Local Fiscal Assistance
        Act (1972) 59
State government 3, 7
    administration of 18
    blacks in 36
    budget in 1189-90, 1201, 1213-
        14, 1264-65, 1273, 1278-
        80, 1301, 1315, 1317,
        1327, 1332
    centralization and decentraliza-
        tion in 2, 1434
    cooperation among 8
    federal aid to 43, 46, 49, 65,
        73, 101, 360
    finance 1347
    fiscal outlook for 73

influence of federal decentralization on 30
innovation in 23, 1143
intern programs in 490, 495,
504-5
job satisfaction and motivation in
813
labor relations in 930, 954
management by objectives in 1297
as a mediator between local and
regional government 106
myths concerning 25
need to reform 41
payments to localities for services
70
personnel management in 121
policy making in 576
productivity in 1046, 1065,
1070, 1084, 1158-59, 1166,
1168-69
program evaluation in 525-26
relations with the federal government 11, 16, 777
role of in federalism 10
urban problems and 125
women in 1042
Stress. See Public administration,
stress in
Strikes and lockouts. See Public
employees, personnel
administration for
Suburban Intergovernmental Network
for Management Development
5
Suburbs, government in 103
Suffolk County, N.Y., public employee collective bargaining
in 912
Sunset laws 1305, 1308, 1312
Syracuse University. Maxwell
Schools of Citizenship and
Public Affairs 463
System analysis, management, and
theory 449, 537, 667-68,
723, 1137, 1268
in approaches to productivity
1047, 1052
in labor-management relations
947
in local government 1047

in personnel administration 835,
862
in social welfare 794

T

Tacoma, Washington, government
productivity in 1165
Taft-Hartley Act 917, 935
Tampa, Fla., government reorganization in 291
Taxation 984, 1202, 1210, 1346,
1577
during the cold war 211
effect of revenue sharing on 56
importance of productivity
analysis to 1061
knowledge management in 793
local 74
local bases for 1433
in metropolitan governance 106
the middle income family and 2
politics of 1350
progressive 983
public policy and 565
state 73-74
See also Property tax, Revenue
sharing
Taylor, Frederick W. (Taylorism)
381, 657, 1091, 1530
Teachers, labor relations of 943-
44
Technical assistance 1598-99
criticism of 1578
under the Rural Development Act
57
Technicians, role of in government
564
Technology 639, 775, 784
in administration of public
welfare programs 794
as a challenge to public service
773
in creating bureaucracies and
organizations 1576
federalism and 10
federal-state partnerships in 777
in government productivity 1065,
1084, 1100, 1127
influence on the environment
789

organizational responses to 1155
See also Word processing
Technology assessment 1415
Temple University, study of comparative federalism at 34
Tennessee, public employee unionism in 922
Texas. Department of Public Welfare, program evaluation in 543
Theory of Significant People 740
Theory X 675, 730
Theory Y 665, 730
Third sector organizations 306, 320-21, 342
Thompson, James D., contribution to organizational theory 630, 650
Thompson, Victor 1557
Toronto
centralization in 1468
government of 106
Trade-unions 826
need to be involved in the government's decisions 130
See also Public employees, personnel administration for
Transportation
allocation of functions in 112
decentralization of municipal services in 1469
General Accounting Office responsibility for 603
productivity and efficiency measurement in 1116, 1134, 1138, 1163
See also Mass transit
Trucking industry, regulation of 305
Truman, Harry S.
civil rights under 995
government reorganization under 289
presidential power under 225
Tucson, Ariz., survey of government administrators in 126

U

Under Secretaries Group 44
Unemployment
government budgeting and 1230

job rationing and 1336
relationship of productivity to 1110
Unemployment compensation 1334
United Kingdom. See Great Britain
United Nations 1585, 1592
organization of 1562
technical assistance programs of 1598
U.S. Administration on Aging and the Elderly 1375
U.S. Air Force 1115
labor-management system of 947
U.S. Area Redevelopment Administration 1527
U.S. Bureau of Indian Affairs 299
U.S. Bureau of the Budget 206
U.S. Civil Aeronautics Board 305
U.S. Civil Service Commission 824, 856, 874, 894, 987, 1074
U.S. Commission on Federal Paperwork 311
U.S. Commission on Political Activity of Government Personnel 830
U.S. Community Services Administration 238
U.S. Congress 158, 233, 245, 267
administrative structure of 257
budget and 251-53, 258, 261, 1175, 1183, 1204, 1208, 1219, 1229
the civil service system and 847
committees of 248, 260
decision making in 249
defense spending and 240, 259, 262, 561
energy policy and 246
environmental policy and 255
feminist movement and 1038
foreign policy and 240, 262
government reorganization and 263
Nixon reforms and 215
policy analysis and making in 243, 248, 252, 254 256, 268, 588
power in 564

in the regulatory process 317
relationship to other government
    branches 282
    to the bureaucracy 141, 200-
    201, 253, 262, 269, 380
    to the president and executive
    branch 235, 264, 266,
    268, 271, 580, 1424
seniority system in 134
taxation and 793
U.S. Congress. Budget Committees
    254
U.S. Congress. House. Rules Com-
    mittee, decision-making in
    265
U.S. Congress. Joint Committee on
    the Economic Report 1335
U.S. Congress. Senate. Armed
    Services Committee 259
U.S. Congressional Budget Office
    248, 254, 256, 1198,
    1219
U.S. Department of Agriculture 140,
    299, 861
    budget of 1207, 1331
U.S. Department of Defense 603,
    633, 861, 1429
    Planning, Programming, and
    Budget System in 1283
U.S. Department of Health, Educa-
    tion, and Welfare 328,
    861
    budget of 1267
    decentralization in 12, 80,
    1459
U.S. Department of Housing and
    Urban Development 313
    decentralization in 12, 1459
    internship programs of 487
    role in the urban environment
    128
    work measurement system of 1117
U.S. Department of Justice. Anti-
    trust Division 200
U.S. Department of Justice, manage-
    ment by objectives in 1302
U.S. Department of Labor 140
    budget of 1222
    decentralization in 1459
U.S. Department of State 140, 861,
    1429

U.S. Department of the Interior
    299, 861, 956
U.S. Department of the Treasury
    299
U.S. Equal Employment Opportunity
    Commission 975, 996
U.S. Federal Aviation Agency 861
U.S. Federal Communications Com-
    mission 200, 317
U.S. Federal Energy Administration
    331-32, 600
U.S. Federal Power Commission
    302
U.S. Federal Trade Commission
    140, 200, 314
U.S. Food and Drug Administration
    200
U.S. Forest Service 1451
U.S. General Accounting Office
    248, 251-52, 256, 536,
    539, 552, 602-3, 1072,
    1074
U.S. Internal Revenue Service 875
U.S. Interstate Commerce Commis-
    sion 140, 200, 305, 312
U.S. Law Enforcement Assistance
    Administration 308
U.S. Maritime Commission 200
U.S. National Aeronautics and
    Space Administration 486
U.S. National Air Pollution Control
    Administration 315
U.S. National Federal Mortgage
    Association 306
U.S. National Labor Relations
    Board 200
U.S. Navy, approaches to weapons
    development by 895
U.S. Office of Economic Opportunity
    238, 1360
    decentralization in 12, 1459
U.S. Office of Federal Contract
    Compliance 975
U.S. Office of Management and
    Budget 45, 206, 213,
    226, 235, 266, 296,
    535, 1074, 1139, 1202,
    1204, 1270
    the presidency and 216, 219
U.S. Office of Personnel Manage-
    ment 675, 867, 903

U.S. Office of Technology Assessment 248, 256
U.S. Postal Service 306, 770
U.S. Public Health Service, budget of 1316
U.S. Securities and Exchange Commission, budget of 1223
U.S. Small Business Administration
  decentralization in 12, 1459
  loan program of 38
U.S. Social and Rehabilitation Service 1124
U.S. Supreme Court
  abortion and 561
  political ethics and 1416
U.S. Tennessee Valley Authority 335
U.S. Veterans Administration 299
Universities. See Education, higher
Urban affairs
  education in 453
  public policy and 565
Urban areas 105
  administration of 95, 107, 114, 119-20
  allocation of government functions in 112
  federalism and 10
  federal role in 128
  impact of revenue sharing on 58
  need for full employment in 104
  the New Structuralists and 76
  planning in 102, 112, 127, 1444
  policies and politics in 123, 146, 578
  productivity measurement in government of 1103, 1134
  program analysis in 518
  quality of public administration in 1103, 1134
  state government and 425
  study of at Temple University 34
  transportation systems in 1134
Urban Careers Program 491
Urban Corps 491
Urban Institute 1163
Urban Observatory proposal 113
Urban renewal
  allocation of functions in 112
  citizen participation in 1377
U.S. See under United States

V
Values. See Ethics and morality
Veterans, preferences given to in public employment 867, 872
Vietnam
  bureaucracy and political development in 1529
  public administration in 1534
Vietnamese War, influence on defense policy 259
Voluntary agencies, effectiveness measurement in 1122
Von Stein, . . . 1530
Voting 1383
  by blacks 1005
  See also Elections
Voting Rights Act (1965) 1005
Vroom, Victor H. 1493

W
Wage-price controls 1354
Waste water treatment, effectiveness measurement of 1163
Watergate affair 441, 1400, 1409-10, 1424
  effect of 239
  presidential power and 230
Water Quality Act 114
Water supply services
  allocation of functions in 112
  effectiveness measurement of 1163
Weber, Max 1146, 1453
  contribution to organizational theory 648, 650, 657, 699-700, 1546
  contribution to public administration 383, 618, 1515, 1519, 1523, 1530
Weinberger, Casper 328
Wessel, Robert 1272
White, Leonard Dupee 364, 398
White House Fellows Program 507
Wildavsky, Aaron 1174, 1307
Wilmington, Del., government budgeting in 1332
Wilson, Woodrow
  contribution to public administration 348, 375, 383, 399, 413, 450

government reorganization by 288

Wisconsin
government productivity in 1076, 1168-69
Planning, Programming, and Budget System in 1280
public employee unionism in 922
See also Milwaukee

Women, in public employment 835, 962, 970, 979, 982, 992, 1001, 1021-45. See also Feminist movement

Word processing, government productivity and 1095

Working class. See Laboring classes

World War II, importance of science to 596

Y

Yale University, women at 1030

Yugoslavia, central and local government relations in 1581

Z

Zald, Mayer N. 1353

Zero base budgeting 1149, 1196, 1199, 1228-29, 1305-32